CORNERSTONE
BIBLICAL
COMMENTARY

General Editor
Philip W. Comfort
D. Litt. et Phil., University of South Africa;
Tyndale House Publishers;
Coastal Carolina University.

Consulting Editor, Old Testament
Tremper Longman III
PhD, Yale University;
Robert H. Gundry Professor of Biblical Studies, Westmont College.

Consulting Editor, New Testament
Grant Osborne
PhD, University of Aberdeen;
Professor of New Testament, Trinity Evangelical Divinity School.

Associate Editors
Jason Driesbach
MA, Biblical Exegesis and Linguistics, Dallas Theological Seminary;
Tyndale House Publishers.

Mark R. Norton
MA, Theological Studies, Wheaton Graduate School;
Tyndale House Publishers.

James A. Swanson
MSM, Multnomah Biblical Seminary;
MTh, University of South Africa;
Tyndale House Publishers.

CORNERSTONE BIBLICAL COMMENTARY

1-2 Chronicles

Mark J. Boda

GENERAL EDITOR

Philip W. Comfort

featuring the text of the

NEW LIVING TRANSLATION

TYNDALE HOUSE PUBLISHERS, INC. CAROL STREAM, ILLINOIS

Cornerstone Biblical Commentary, Volume 5a

Visit Tyndale's exciting Web site at www.tyndale.com

Designed by Luke Daab and Timothy R. Botts.

Library of Congress Cataloging-in-Publication Data

Cornerstone biblical commentary.
p. cm.
Includes bibliographical references and index.
ISBN 978-0-8423-3431-0 (hc : alk. paper)
1. Bible—Commentaries. I. Boda, Mark J.
BS491.3.C67 2006
220.7′7—dc22 2005026928

Printed in the United States of America

29 28 27 26 25 24 23
8 7 6 5 4 3 2

CONTENTS

VOLUME 5a: 1–2 Chronicles

Mark J. Boda
BTh, Ambrose University College;
MDiv, Westminster Theological Seminary;
PhD, University of Cambridge;
Professor of Old Testament, McMaster Divinity College.

GENERAL EDITOR'S PREFACE

The *Cornerstone Biblical Commentary* is based on the second edition of the New Living Translation (2007). Nearly 100 scholars from various church backgrounds and from several countries (United States, Canada, England, and Australia) participated in the creation of the NLT. Many of these same scholars are contributors to this commentary series. All the commentators, whether participants in the NLT or not, believe that the Bible is God's inspired word and have a desire to make God's word clear and accessible to his people.

This Bible commentary is the natural extension of our vision for the New Living Translation, which we believe is both exegetically accurate and idiomatically powerful. The NLT attempts to communicate God's inspired word in a lucid English translation of the original languages so that English readers can understand and appreciate the thought of the original writers. In the same way, the *Cornerstone Biblical Commentary* aims at helping teachers, pastors, students, and laypeople understand every thought contained in the Bible. As such, the commentary focuses first on the words of Scripture, then on the theological truths of Scripture—inasmuch as the words express the truths.

The commentary itself has been structured in such a way as to help readers get at the meaning of Scripture, passage by passage, through the entire Bible. Each Bible book is prefaced by a substantial book introduction that gives general historical background important for understanding. Then the reader is taken through the Bible text, passage by passage, starting with the New Living Translation text printed in full. This is followed by a section called "Notes," wherein the commentator helps the reader understand the Hebrew or Greek behind the English of the NLT, interacts with other scholars on important interpretive issues, and points the reader to significant textual and contextual matters. The "Notes" are followed by the "Commentary," wherein each scholar presents a lucid interpretation of the passage, giving special attention to context and major theological themes.

The commentators represent a wide spectrum of theological positions within the evangelical community. We believe this is good because it reflects the rich variety in Christ's church. All the commentators uphold the authority of God's word and believe it is essential to heed the old adage: "Wholly apply yourself to the Scriptures and apply them wholly to you." May this commentary help you know the truths of Scripture, and may this knowledge help you "grow in your knowledge of God and Jesus our Lord" (2 Pet 1:2, NLT).

PHILIP W. COMFORT
GENERAL EDITOR

ABBREVIATIONS

GENERAL ABBREVIATIONS

b.	Babylonian Gemara	Heb.	Hebrew	NT	New Testament
bar.	baraita	ibid.	*ibidem*, in the same place	OL	Old Latin
c.	*circa*, around, approximately	i.e.	*id est*, the same	OS	Old Syriac
cf.	*confer*, compare	in loc.	*in loco*, in the place cited	OT	Old Testament
ch, chs	chapter, chapters	lit.	literally	p., pp.	page, pages
contra	in contrast to	LXX	Septuagint	pl.	plural
DSS	Dead Sea Scrolls	M	Majority Text	Q	Quelle ("Sayings" as Gospel source)
ed.	edition, editor	*m.*	Mishnah	rev.	revision
e.g.	*exempli gratia*, for example	masc.	masculine	sg.	singular
et al.	*et alli*, and others	mg	margin	*t.*	Tosefta
fem.	feminine	ms	manuscript	TR	Textus Receptus
ff	following (verses, pages)	mss	manuscripts	v., vv.	verse, verses
fl.	flourished	MT	Masoretic Text	vid.	*videtur*, it seems
Gr.	Greek	n.d.	no date	viz.	*videlicet*, namely
		neut.	neuter	vol.	volume
		no.	number	*y.*	Jerusalem Gemara

ABBREVIATIONS FOR BIBLE TRANSLATIONS

ASV	American Standard Version	NCV	New Century Version	NKJV	New King James Version
CEV	Contemporary English Version	NEB	New English Bible	NRSV	New Revised Standard Version
ESV	English Standard Version	NET	The NET Bible	NLT	New Living Translation
GW	God's Word	NIV	New International Version	REB	Revised English Bible
HCSB	Holman Christian Standard Bible	NIrV	New International Reader's Version	RSV	Revised Standard Version
JB	Jerusalem Bible	NJB	New Jerusalem Bible	TEV	Today's English Version
KJV	King James Version	NJPS	The New Jewish Publication Society Translation (*Tanakh*)	TLB	The Living Bible
NAB	New American Bible				
NASB	New American Standard Bible				

ABBREVIATIONS FOR DICTIONARIES, LEXICONS, COLLECTIONS OF TEXTS, ORIGINAL LANGUAGE EDITIONS

ABD *Anchor Bible Dictionary* (6 vols., Freedman) [1992]

ANEP *The Ancient Near East in Pictures* (Pritchard) [1965]

ANET *Ancient Near Eastern Texts Relating to the Old Testament* (Pritchard) [1969]

BAGD *Greek-English Lexicon of the New Testament and Other Early Christian Literature*, 2nd ed. (Bauer, Arndt, Gingrich, Danker) [1979]

BDAG *Greek-English Lexicon of the New Testament and Other Early Christian Literature*, 3rd ed. (Bauer, Danker, Arndt, Gingrich) [2000]

BDB *A Hebrew and English Lexicon of the Old Testament* (Brown, Driver, Briggs) [1907]

BDF *A Greek Grammar of the New Testament and Other Early Christian Literature* (Blass, Debrunner, Funk) [1961]

BHS *Biblia Hebraica Stuttgartensia* (Elliger and Rudolph) [1983]

CAD *Assyrian Dictionary of the Oriental Institute of the University of Chicago* [1956]

COS *The Context of Scripture* (3 vols., Hallo and Younger) [1997–2002]

DBI *Dictionary of Biblical Imagery* (Ryken, Wilhoit, Longman) [1998]

DBT *Dictionary of Biblical Theology* (2nd ed., Leon-Dufour) [1972]

DCH *Dictionary of Classical Hebrew* (5 vols., D. Clines) [2000]

DLNTD *Dictionary of the Later New Testament and Its Development* (R. Martin, P. Davids) [1997]

DJD *Discoveries in the Judean Desert* [1955–]

DJG *Dictionary of Jesus and the Gospels* (Green, McKnight, Marshall) [1992]

DOTP *Dictionary of the Old Testament: Pentateuch* (T. Alexander, D.W. Baker) [2003]

DPL *Dictionary of Paul and His Letters* (Hawthorne, Martin, Reid) [1993]

DTIB *Dictionary of Theological Interpretation of the Bible* (Vanhoozer) [2005]

EDNT *Exegetical Dictionary of the New Testament* (3 vols., H. Balz, G. Schneider. ET) [1990–1993]

GKC *Gesenius' Hebrew Grammar* (Gesenius, Kautzsch, trans. Cowley) [1910]

HALOT *The Hebrew and Aramaic Lexicon of the Old Testament* (L. Koehler, W. Baumgartner, J. Stamm; trans. M. Richardson) [1994–1999]

IBD *Illustrated Bible Dictionary* (3 vols., Douglas, Wiseman) [1980]

IDB *The Interpreter's Dictionary of the Bible* (4 vols., Buttrick) [1962]

ISBE *International Standard Bible Encyclopedia* (4 vols., Bromiley) [1979–1988]

KBL *Lexicon in Veteris Testamenti libros* (Koehler, Baumgartner) [1958]

LCL Loeb Classical Library

L&N *Greek-English Lexicon of the New Testament: Based on Semantic Domains* (Louw and Nida) [1989]

LSJ *A Greek-English Lexicon* (9th ed., Liddell, Scott, Jones) [1996]

MM *The Vocabulary of the Greek New Testament* (Moulton and Milligan) [1930; 1997]

NA^{26} *Novum Testamentum Graece* (26th ed., Nestle-Aland) [1979]

NA^{27} *Novum Testamentum Graece* (27th ed., Nestle-Aland) [1993]

NBD *New Bible Dictionary* (2nd ed., Douglas, Hillyer) [1982]

NIDB *New International Dictionary of the Bible* (Douglas, Tenney) [1987]

NIDBA *New International Dictionary of Biblical Archaeology* (Blaiklock and Harrison) [1983]

NIDNTT *New International Dictionary of New Testament Theology* (4 vols., C. Brown) [1975–1985]

NIDOTTE *New International Dictionary of Old Testament Theology and Exegesis* (5 vols., W. A. VanGemeren) [1997]

PG *Patrologia Graecae* (J. P. Migne) [1857–1886]

PGM *Papyri graecae magicae: Die griechischen Zauberpapyri.* (Preisendanz) [1928]

TBD *Tyndale Bible Dictionary* (Elwell, Comfort) [2001]

TDNT *Theological Dictionary of the New Testament* (10 vols., Kittel, Friedrich; trans. Bromiley) [1964–1976]

TDOT *Theological Dictionary of the Old Testament* (8 vols., Botterweck, Ringgren; trans. Willis, Bromiley, Green) [1974–]

TLNT *Theological Lexicon of the New Testament* (3 vols., C. Spicq) [1994]

TLOT *Theological Lexicon of the Old Testament* (3 vols., E. Jenni) [1997]

TWOT *Theological Wordbook of the Old Testament* (2 vols., Harris, Archer) [1980]

UBS^3 *United Bible Societies' Greek New Testament* (3rd ed., Metzger et al.) [1975]

UBS^4 *United Bible Societies' Greek New Testament* (4th corrected ed., Metzger et al.) [1993]

WH *The New Testament in the Original Greek* (Westcott and Hort) [1882]

ABBREVIATIONS FOR BOOKS OF THE BIBLE

Old Testament

Gen	Genesis	Deut	Deuteronomy	1 Sam	1 Samuel
Exod	Exodus	Josh	Joshua	2 Sam	2 Samuel
Lev	Leviticus	Judg	Judges	1 Kgs	1 Kings
Num	Numbers	Ruth	Ruth	2 Kgs	2 Kings

1 Chr	1 Chronicles	Song	Song of Songs	Obad	Obadiah
2 Chr	2 Chronicles	Isa	Isaiah	Jonah	Jonah
Ezra	Ezra	Jer	Jeremiah	Mic	Micah
Neh	Nehemiah	Lam	Lamentations	Nah	Nahum
Esth	Esther	Ezek	Ezekiel	Hab	Habakkuk
Job	Job	Dan	Daniel	Zeph	Zephaniah
Ps, Pss	Psalm, Psalms	Hos	Hosea	Hag	Haggai
Prov	Proverbs	Joel	Joel	Zech	Zechariah
Eccl	Ecclesiastes	Amos	Amos	Mal	Malachi

New Testament

Matt	Matthew	Eph	Ephesians	Heb	Hebrews
Mark	Mark	Phil	Philippians	Jas	James
Luke	Luke	Col	Colossians	1 Pet	1 Peter
John	John	1 Thess	1 Thessalonians	2 Pet	2 Peter
Acts	Acts	2 Thess	2 Thessalonians	1 John	1 John
Rom	Romans	1 Tim	1 Timothy	2 John	2 John
1 Cor	1 Corinthians	2 Tim	2 Timothy	3 John	3 John
2 Cor	2 Corinthians	Titus	Titus	Jude	Jude
Gal	Galatians	Phlm	Philemon	Rev	Revelation

Deuterocanonical

Bar	Baruch	1–2 Esdr	1–2 Esdras	Ps 151	Psalm 151
Add Dan	Additions to Daniel	Add Esth	Additions to Esther	Sir	Sirach
Pr Azar	Prayer of Azariah	Ep Jer	Epistle of Jeremiah	Tob	Tobit
Bel	Bel and the Dragon	Jdt	Judith	Wis	Wisdom of Solomon
Sg Three	Song of the Three Children	1–2 Macc	1–2 Maccabees		
		3–4 Macc	3–4 Maccabees		
Sus	Susanna	Pr Man	Prayer of Manasseh		

MANUSCRIPTS AND LITERATURE FROM QUMRAN

Initial numerals followed by "Q" indicate particular caves at Qumran. For example, the notation 4Q267 indicates text 267 from cave 4 at Qumran. Further, 1QS 4:9-10 indicates column 4, lines 9-10 of the *Rule of the Community*; and 4Q166 1 ii 2 indicates fragment 1, column ii, line 2 of text 166 from cave 4. More examples of common abbreviations are listed below.

CD	Cairo Geniza copy of the *Damascus Document*	1QIsa[b]	Isaiah copy [b]	4QLam[a]	Lamentations
		1QM	*War Scroll*	11QPs[a]	Psalms
		1QpHab	*Pesher Habakkuk*	11QTemple[a,b]	*Temple Scroll*
1QH	*Thanksgiving Hymns*	1QS	*Rule of the Community*	11QtgJob	*Targum of Job*
1QIsa[a]	Isaiah copy [a]				

IMPORTANT NEW TESTAMENT MANUSCRIPTS

(all dates given are AD; ordinal numbers refer to centuries)

Significant Papyri (𝔓 = Papyrus)

𝔓1 Matt 1; early 3rd
𝔓4+𝔓64+𝔓67 Matt 3, 5, 26; Luke 1–6; late 2nd
𝔓5 John 1, 16, 20; early 3rd
𝔓13 Heb 2–5, 10–12; early 3rd
𝔓15+𝔓16 (probably part of same codex) 1 Cor 7–8, Phil 3–4; late 3rd
𝔓20 Jas 2–3; 3rd
𝔓22 John 15–16; mid 3rd
𝔓23 Jas 1; c. 200
𝔓27 Rom 8–9; 3rd
𝔓30 1 Thess 4–5; 2 Thess 1; early 3rd
𝔓32 Titus 1–2; late 2nd
𝔓37 Matt 26; late 3rd
𝔓39 John 8; first half of 3rd
𝔓40 Rom 1–4, 6, 9; 3rd

𝔓45 Gospels and Acts; early 3rd
𝔓46 Paul's Major Epistles (less Pastorals); late 2nd
𝔓47 Rev 9–17; 3rd
𝔓49+𝔓65 Eph 4–5; 1 Thess 1–2; 3rd
𝔓52 John 18; c. 125
𝔓53 Matt 26, Acts 9–10; middle 3rd
𝔓66 John; late 2nd
𝔓70 Matt 2–3, 11–12, 24; 3rd
𝔓72 1–2 Peter, Jude; c. 300
𝔓74 Acts, General Epistles; 7th
𝔓75 Luke and John; c. 200
𝔓77+𝔓103 (probably part of same codex) Matt 13–14, 23; late 2nd
𝔓87 Philemon; late 2nd
𝔓90 John 18–19; late 2nd
𝔓91 Acts 2–3; 3rd
𝔓92 Eph 1, 2 Thess 1; c. 300
𝔓98 Rev 1:13-20; late 2nd
𝔓100 Jas 3–5; c. 300
𝔓101 Matt 3–4; 3rd
𝔓104 Matt 21; 2nd
𝔓106 John 1; 3rd
𝔓115 Rev 2–3, 5–6, 8–15; 3rd

Significant Uncials

ℵ (Sinaiticus) most of NT; 4th
A (Alexandrinus) most of NT; 5th
B (Vaticanus) most of NT; 4th
C (Ephraemi Rescriptus) most of NT with many lacunae; 5th
D (Bezae) Gospels, Acts; 5th
D (Claromontanus), Paul's Epistles; 6th (different MS than Bezae)
E (Laudianus 35) Acts; 6th
F (Augensis) Paul's Epistles; 9th
G (Boernerianus) Paul's Epistles; 9th
H (Coislinianus) Paul's Epistles; 6th
I (Freerianus or Washington) Paul's Epistles; 5th
L (Regius) Gospels; 8th
P (Porphyrianus) Acts—Revelation; 9th
Q (Guelferbytanus B) Luke, John; 5th
T (Borgianus) Luke, John; 5th
W (Washingtonianus or the Freer Gospels) Gospels; 5th
Z (Dublinensis) Matthew; 6th
037 (Δ; Sangallensis) Gospels; 9th
038 (Θ; Koridethi) Gospels; 9th
040 (Ξ; Zacynthius) Luke; 6th
043 (Φ; Beratinus) Matthew, Mark; 6th
044 (Ψ; Athous Laurae) Gospels, Acts, Paul's Epistles; 9th
048 Acts, Paul's Epistles, General Epistles; 5th
0171 Matt 10, Luke 22; c. 300
0189 Acts 5; c. 200

Significant Minuscules

1 Gospels, Acts, Paul's Epistles; 12th
33 All NT except Rev; 9th
81 Acts, Paul's Epistles, General Epistles; 1044
565 Gospels; 9th
700 Gospels; 11th
1424 (or Family 1424—a group of 29 manuscripts sharing nearly the same text) most of NT; 9th-10th
1739 Acts, Paul's Epistles; 10th
2053 Rev; 13th
2344 Rev; 11th
f^1 (a family of manuscripts including 1, 118, 131, 209) Gospels; 12th-14th
f^{13} (a family of manuscripts including 13, 69, 124, 174, 230, 346, 543, 788, 826, 828, 983, 1689, 1709—known as the Ferrar group) Gospels; 11th-15th

Significant Ancient Versions

SYRIAC (SYR)

syr^c (Syriac Curetonian) Gospels; 5th
syr^s (Syriac Sinaiticus) Gospels; 4th
syr^h (Syriac Harklensis) Entire NT; 616

OLD LATIN (IT)

it^a (Vercellenis) Gospels; 4th
it^b (Veronensis) Gospels; 5th
it^d (Cantabrigiensis—the Latin text of Bezae) Gospels, Acts, 3 John; 5th
it^e (Palantinus) Gospels; 5th
it^k (Bobiensis) Matthew, Mark; c. 400

COPTIC (COP)

cop^{bo} (Boharic—north Egypt)
cop^{fay} (Fayyumic—central Egypt)
cop^{sa} (Sahidic—southern Egypt)

OTHER VERSIONS

arm (Armenian)
eth (Ethiopic)
geo (Georgian)

TRANSLITERATION AND NUMBERING SYSTEM

Note: For words and roots from nonbiblical languages (e.g., Arabic, Ugaritic), only approximate transliterations are given.

HEBREW/ARAMAIC

Consonants

א	*aleph*	= *'*	מ, ם	*mem*	= *m*
בּ, ב	*beth*	= *b*	נ, ן	*nun*	= *n*
גּ, ג	*gimel*	= *g*	ס	*samekh*	= *s*
דּ, ד	*daleth*	= *d*	ע	*ayin*	= *'*
ה	*he*	= *h*	פּ, פ, ף	*pe*	= *p*
ו	*waw*	= *w*	צ, ץ	*tsadhe*	= *ts*
ז	*zayin*	= *z*	ק	*qoph*	= *q*
ח	*heth*	= *kh*	ר	*resh*	= *r*
ט	*teth*	= *t*	שׁ	*shin*	= *sh*
י	*yodh*	= *y*	שׂ	*sin*	= *s*
כּ, כ, ך	*kaph*	= *k*	תּ, ת	*taw*	= *t, th* (spirant)
ל	*lamedh*	= *l*			

Vowels

ַ	*patakh*	= *a*	ָ	*qamets khatuf*	= *o*
חַ	*furtive patakh*	= *a*	ֹ	*holem*	= *o*
ָ	*qamets*	= *a*	וֹ	*full holem*	= *o*
ָה	*final qamets he*	= *ah*	ֻ	*short qibbuts*	= *u*
ֶ	*segol*	= *e*	ֻ	*long qibbuts*	= *u*
ֵ	*tsere*	= *e*	וּ	*shureq*	= *u*
ֵי	*tsere yod*	= *e*	ֲ	*khatef patakh*	= *a*
ִ	*short hireq*	= *i*	ֳ	*khatef qamets*	= *o*
ִ	*long hireq*	= *i*	ְ	*vocalic shewa*	= *e*
ִי	*hireq yod*	= *i*	ַי	*patakh yodh*	= *a*

GREEK

α	*alpha*	= *a*	ι	*iota*	= *i*
β	*beta*	= *b*	κ	*kappa*	= *k*
γ	*gamma*	= *g, n (before* γ, κ, ξ, χ*)*	λ	*lamda*	= *l*
			μ	*mu*	= *m*
δ	*delta*	= *d*	ν	*nu*	= *n*
ε	*epsilon*	= *e*	ξ	*ksi*	= *x*
ζ	*zeta*	= *z*	ο	*omicron*	= *o*
η	*eta*	= *ē*	π	*pi*	= *p*
θ	*theta*	= *th*	ρ	*rho*	= *r* (ῥ = *rh*)

σ, ς	*sigma*	= *s*	ψ	*psi*	= *ps*
τ	*tau*	= *t*	ω	*omega*	= *ō*
υ	*upsilon*	= *u*	ʻ	*rough breathing mark*	= *h (with vowel or diphthong)*
φ	*phi*	= *ph*			
χ	*chi*	= *ch*			

THE TYNDALE-STRONG'S NUMBERING SYSTEM

The Cornerstone Biblical Commentary series uses a word-study numbering system to give both newer and more advanced Bible students alike quicker, more convenient access to helpful original-language tools (e.g., concordances, lexicons, and theological dictionaries). Those who are unfamiliar with the ancient Hebrew, Aramaic, and Greek alphabets can quickly find information on a given word by looking up the appropriate index number. Advanced students will find the system helpful because it allows them to quickly find the lexical form of obscure conjugations and inflections.

There are two main numbering systems used for biblical words today. The one familiar to most people is the Strong's numbering system (made popular by the *Strong's Exhaustive Concordance to the Bible*). Although the original Strong's system is still quite useful, the most up-to-date research has shed new light on the biblical languages and allows for more precision than is found in the original Strong's system. The Cornerstone Biblical Commentary series, therefore, features a newly revised version of the Strong's system, the Tyndale-Strong's numbering system. The Tyndale-Strong's system brings together the familiarity of the Strong's system and the best of modern scholarship. In most cases, the original Strong's numbers are preserved. In places where new research dictates, new or related numbers have been added.[1]

The second major numbering system today is the Goodrick-Kohlenberger system used in a number of study tools published by Zondervan. In order to give students broad access to a number of helpful tools, the Commentary provides index numbers for the Zondervan system as well.

The different index systems are designated as follows:

TG	Tyndale-Strong's Greek number	ZH	Zondervan Hebrew number
ZG	Zondervan Greek number	TA/ZA	Tyndale/Zondervan Aramaic number
TH	Tyndale-Strong's Hebrew number	S	Strong's Aramaic number

So in the example, "love" *agapē* [TG26, ZG27], the first number is the one to use with Greek tools keyed to the Tyndale-Strong's system, and the second applies to tools that use the Zondervan system.

The indexing of Aramaic terms differs slightly from that of Greek and Hebrew. Strong's original system mixed the Aramaic terms in with the Hebrew, but the Tyndale-Strong's system indexes Aramaic with a new set of numbers starting at 10,000. Since Tyndale's system for Aramaic diverges completely from original Strong's, the original Strong's number is listed separately so that those using tools keyed to Strong's can locate the information. This number is designated with an S, as in the example, "son" *bar* [TA/ZA10120, S1247].

1. Generally, one may simply use the original four-digit Strong's number to identify words in tools using Strong's system. If a Tyndale-Strong's number is followed by a capital letter (e.g., TG1692A), it generally indicates an added subdivision of meaning for the given term. Whenever a Tyndale-Strong's number has a number following a decimal point (e.g., TG2013.1), it reflects an instance where new research has yielded a separate, new classification of use for a biblical word. Forthcoming tools from Tyndale House Publishers will include these entries, which were not part of the original Strong's system.

1–2 Chronicles

MARK J. BODA

INTRODUCTION TO
1–2 Chronicles

IT WAS DURING MY SEMINARY DAYS that I first took a serious look at the books of Chronicles. Up to that point my attitude had been that expressed by the title of these books in the Septuagint. There they are called *Paraleipomenōn* or "omissions," implying that they contain material that was not included in the books of Samuel and Kings. Chronicles was just "the leftovers"; Samuel—Kings was "the main course." But it was under the tutelage of Raymond Dillard that I saw for the first time that these "leftovers" could be "the main course." His riveting lectures left me on the edge of my seat as we discussed the significance of the Chronicler's version of Israel's story and its implications for theology.[1]

The first line of the work now known as 1 and 2 Chronicles begins with the words "The descendants of Adam" (1 Chr 1:1), while the final pericope of the work begins with the words "In the first year of King Cyrus of Persia" (2 Chr 36:22). These two citations reveal the scale of the accomplishment of this work: It is nothing short of a history of the world from the creation of humanity to the restoration of the Jews from Babylonian exile; it is, as Jerome once called it, "the chronicle of the whole of sacred history." Until recently, however, the work as a whole has often been maligned by (and, probably even worse, ignored in) critical scholarship.

Jerome's statement above is the most likely origin of the book's English name, "Chronicles." This name is closely aligned with the Hebrew tradition, which calls this work *dibre hayyamim*, or "events of the days," a title that is used to refer to the official royal histories used as a source in the book of Kings (1 Kgs 14:19; 15:31; 16:5, 14, 20, 27). The name in the Greek tradition (*Paraleipomenōn*, or "omissions"), however, does little to encourage its readership. As noted above, this title reflects a common attitude toward Chronicles: It is simply to be used as a supplement to the more important works of Samuel and Kings.

There are other reasons why Chronicles has been ignored and maligned in biblical studies, both on literary and historical levels. In terms of its literary character, although Chronicles reviews the "whole of sacred history," the vast majority of this "sacred history" is covered efficiently through the genre of genealogical lists, which fill the first nine chapters of the work (1 Chr 1–9)—not the most riveting introduction to capture the imagination of modern readers. When the Chronicler finally does get to the key narratives of David and Solomon in 1 Chronicles 10—2 Chronicles 9, he lessens the tension of the plot by removing nearly all references to the failures of these kings and inserts long lists of people (1 Chr 11–12, 23–27). In the rest of his account (2 Chr 10–36), the Chronicler excises from his source the story of the northern kingdom with its fascinating parallel plot to the enduring Davidic kingdom.

In addition, Chronicles is often ignored and maligned in biblical studies because of its perceived lack of historical worth. There is no question that the Chronicler was at some distance from the events he related, indicated by the final recorded incident in the book, which places it in the Persian period. The Chronicler raises questions for many historians in the way he rehearses the history of Israel. His results not only diverge from Samuel and Kings but also reflect a consistent agenda and style. In the sections that are not found in Samuel and Kings, one can discern a common vocabulary that reveals the personality of the Chronicler. This vocabulary occurs not only in the "direct narrative," that is, those sections where the Chronicler is describing events in the third person, but also in the "dramatic narrative," that is, those sections that cite speeches or prayers. Many have questioned the veracity of the *Paraleipomenōn* or "omissions" that the Chronicler has added into his account.

These critiques are the product of our modern fixation on literature and history. It may be difficult for us to appreciate a literary work in which long lists and genealogies form a key component, but this does not appear to be true for ancient writers and readers. Although not testing the limits of our modern patience, the New Testament Gospel of Matthew begins in similar fashion, drawing the reader into the story of Jesus by tracing his human origins in the line of Abraham and David. Modern readers may want the story of Israel to be told with more brilliant colors, but the Chronicler had an agenda that sought to capture the imagination of his own generation rather than a modern one. It is this agenda that has often

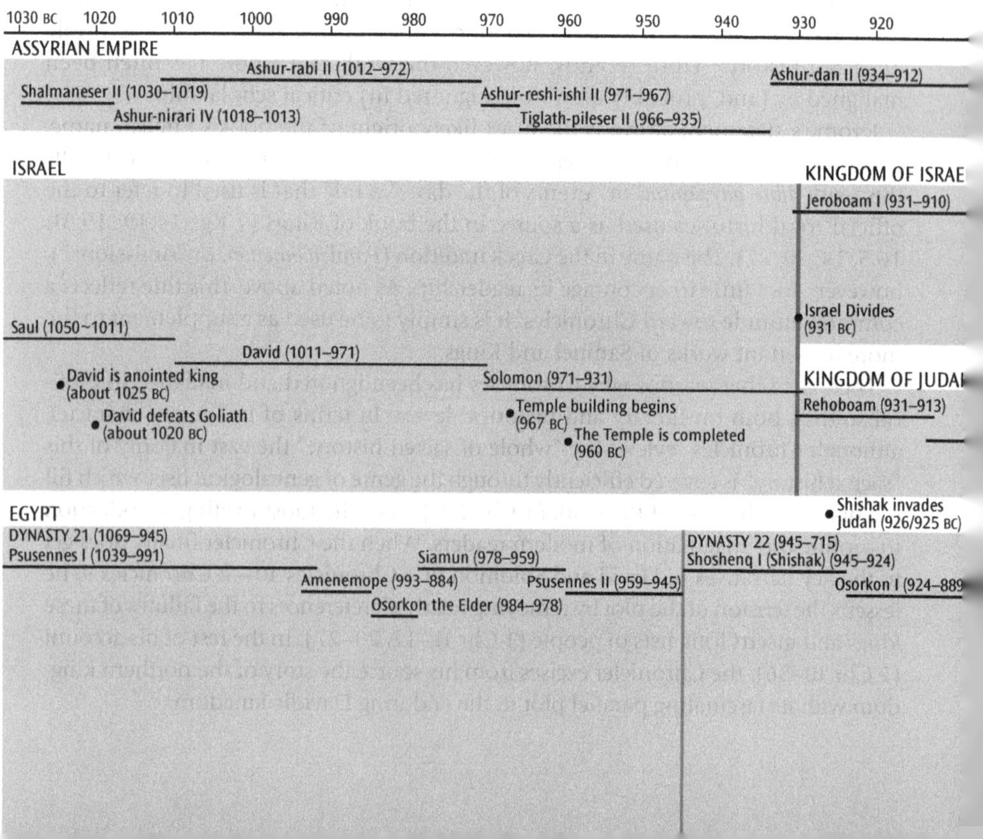

been the subject of modern debate over the historical character of the Chronicler, yet all the while the greatest detractors seem to think that modern historiography itself is devoid of an agenda. Fundamental to the task of writing history, whether in the ancient or modern world, is linking cause and effect and establishing a rationale for understanding events in a certain way. Throughout time, all history writing has highlighted certain themes by emphasizing particular parts of history over others through including or excluding various events. It is true that there are dimensions of ancient historiography, such as the creation and shaping of speeches to reflect the sentiments of a character (see Thucydides) or the inclusion of supernatural causes, which are seen as inappropriate for many modern historians, but these were accepted modes of historical writing in the ancient world and would not have been considered faulty or inferior.[2] The Chronicler has also shaped his historical presentation in a certain way to highlight historiographical principles that were key to his worldview and theology and helpful to his readers, who lived in a unique period in history. Understanding these principles is key to using Chronicles for reconstructing the history of Israel as well as for highlighting its theological significance for believers today. Some of these principles will be highlighted under "Major Themes" below (see also the introductions to 1 Chr 1–9, 10–29, 2 Chr 1–9, and 10–36 for historiographic principles key to each section of the work).

In order to investigate the Chronicler's work, we need to look more closely at introductory issues of history, text, and literature. First, we need to discover when

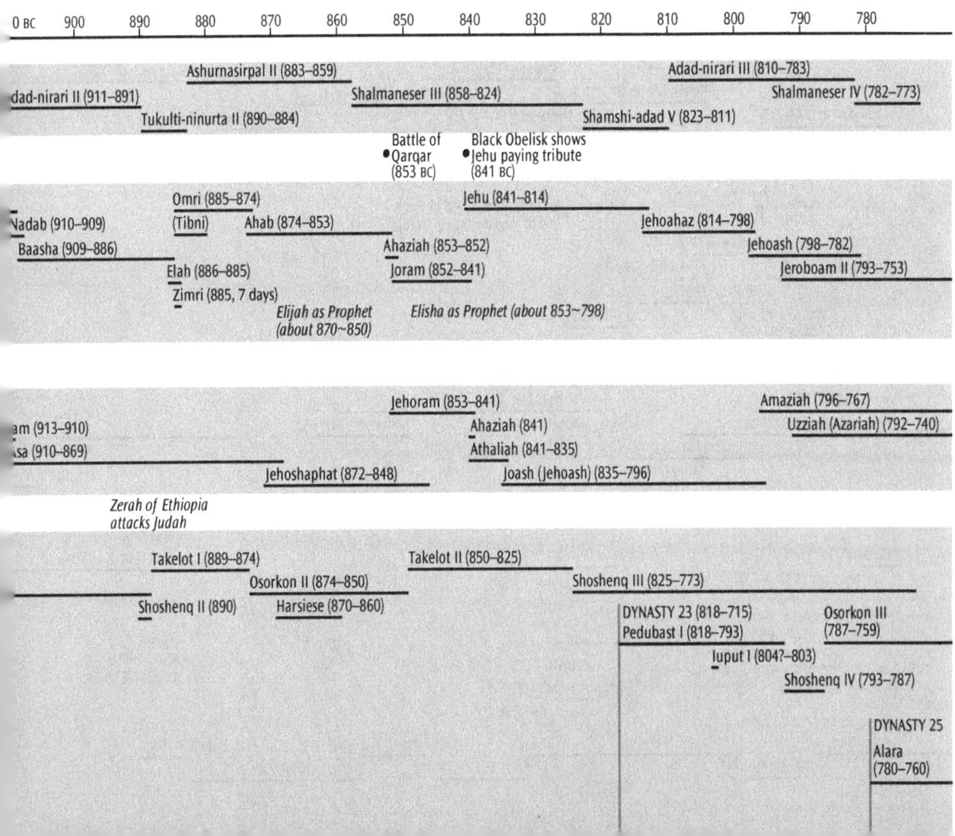

this work was written, who was responsible for it, and to whom it was written. Second, we need to evaluate the textual sources for the study of Chronicles, that is, evaluate the various ancient manuscripts in Hebrew and other languages that bear witness to the original text. Part of the textual study is to ascertain the textual limits of the work itself, whether it comprised 1 and 2 Chronicles or whether it included Ezra and Nehemiah as well. Finally, in light of this, we need to determine what evidence can be drawn from the resulting work that offers clues into the historiography of the writer, that is, what the agenda of the writer and the potential for theology is.

AUTHOR

Jewish tradition largely associated the authorship of Chronicles with Ezra. The Babylonian Talmud (*b. Bava Batra* 15a) claimed that Ezra wrote the book that bears his own name and the genealogies of the book of Chronicles up until his own time and that Nehemiah finished it. It is unclear what is meant here, whether Ezra just updated the genealogies in Chronicles or wrote beginning with the genealogies and up until Ezra 10. However, the identity of the author (or authors) of this work is never revealed in the book, a characteristic that is the rule rather than the exception for Old Testament books. Evidence within the book suggests that the author was closely associated with the Temple. The book emphasizes the Temple and its services and provides extensive detail about it. Further evidence for the author's close association with the Temple can be found in the fact that the Temple played a key

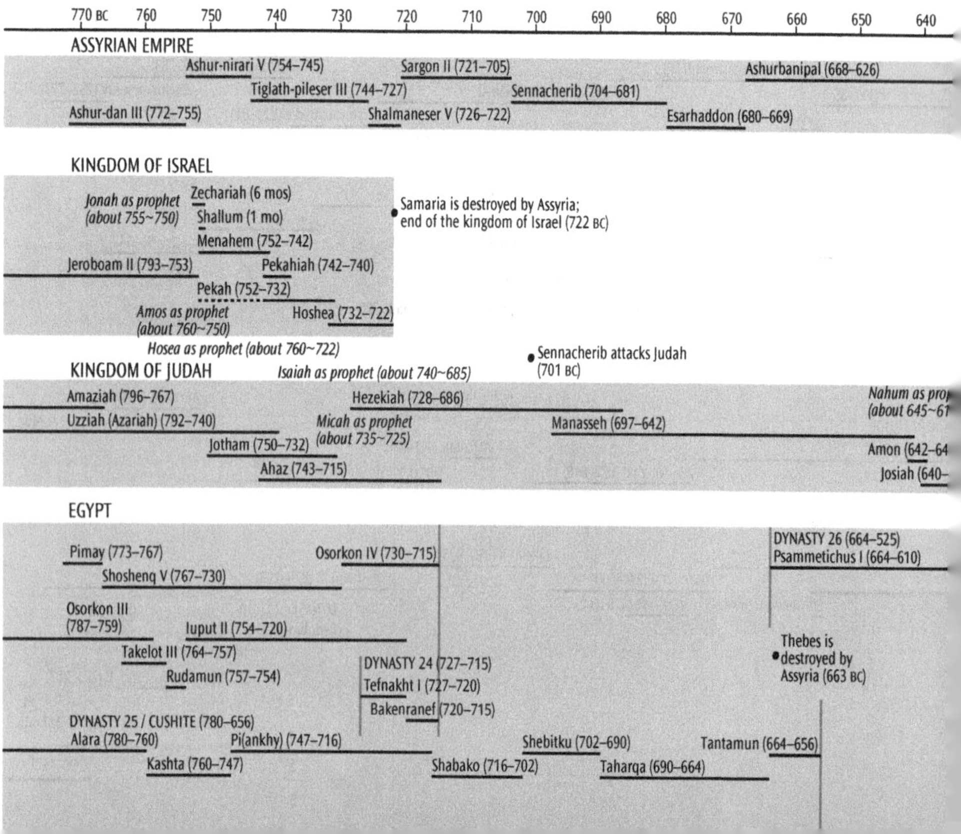

role in supporting the development of Jewish literature in the Second Temple period (the period in which Chronicles was written). Furthermore, the prominence given to Levites (and within that group to Levitical musicians) suggests someone among that sacred guild in the Second Temple period. The consistent focus on Jerusalem and the Temple suggests that those responsible for composing the Chronicles were living in the Persian province of Yehud (comprised primarily of Jerusalem and its surrounding suburbs).

DATE AND OCCASION OF WRITING

Chronicles offers only a few pieces of evidence for ascertaining the date of its origin. First, its extensive use of the books of Samuel and Kings means that it must have been written after the final event in that composition, which is cited in 2 Kings 25:27-30 as the 37th year of Jehoiachin's exile during the reign of Amel-Marduk (Evil-merodach) of Babylon (Nebuchadnezzar's son), who reigned from 562–560 BC. Second, the final pericope of Chronicles cites a proclamation that was written in the first year of the Persian King Cyrus, encouraging the Jews to return to their land and rebuild the Temple in Jerusalem. Although Cyrus rose to prominence in the ancient Near East in 553 BC, when he revolted against his grandfather, the Median king Astyages, and inherited his kingdom, it was not until 539 BC that Cyrus finally marched into Babylon and took full control of the ancient Near East from Nabonidus. On a famous cylinder discovered in Mesopotamia and written in the early months of Cyrus's control of the former Babylonian Empire,

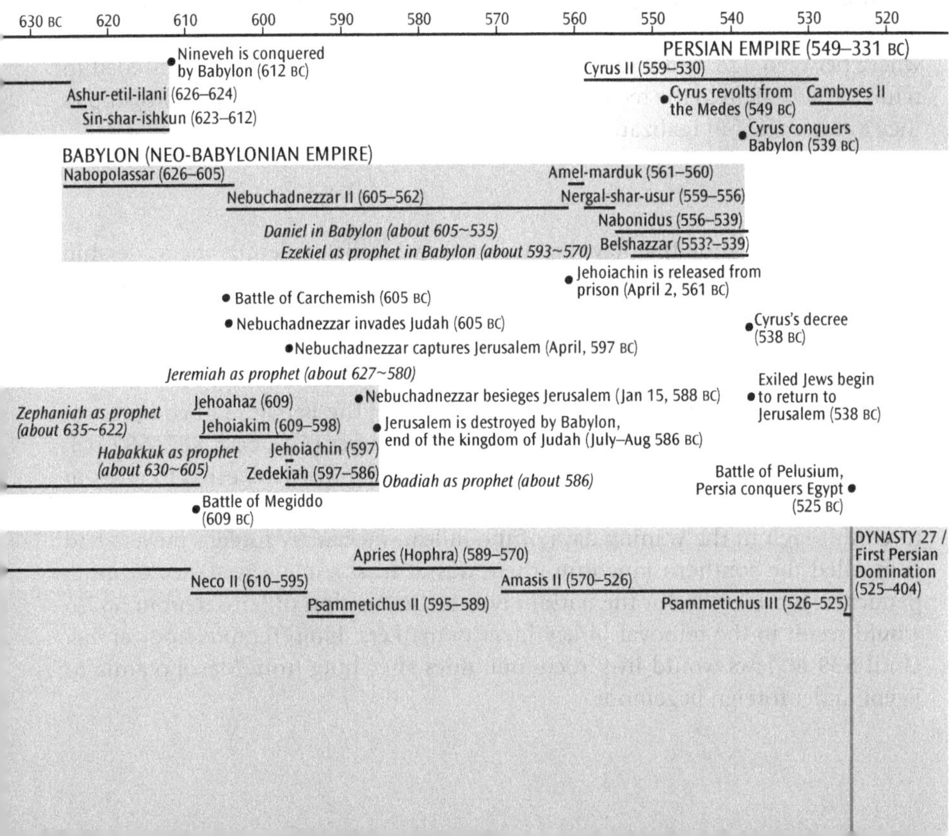

Cyrus not only describes his defeat of Nabonidus and enthusiastic acceptance by the residents of Babylon, but also his policy of returning various gods to their respective cities and rebuilding their sanctuaries. The proclamation now recorded in 2 Chronicles 36:22-23[3] reflects the policies of Cyrus in the period immediately after Cyrus's conquest of Babylon. Third, in 1 Chronicles 29:7 one of the valuable items ("10,000 gold coins") is referred to as "darics" (gold coins), a coin that was minted during the reign of Darius I no earlier than 515 BC and would not have reached the province of Yehud until some time after that. Fourth, the lack of details on Solomon's building project and the greater attention to the worship systems and services suggest that it was not written in the period when the Temple was being built, that is, during the period from 539–515 BC, but rather in a period when the Temple had been operational for a time (Dillard 1987:31; Knoppers 2004:111). Fifth, the genealogy of the Davidic royal line in 1 Chronicles 3:17-24 extends at least two generations after Zerubbabel, who was governor of Yehud in 520 BC (see Ezra 1–6, Haggai, Zechariah), and some have suggested that it extends as many as 14 generations after his time (see commentary on 1 Chr 3). This commentary will follow Klein (2006:113) in dating the final generation in this genealogy to the latter half of the fifth century BC.

These various pieces of evidence suggest that the earliest date for the writing of Chronicles is 425 BC. Regarding the latest possible date for the book's composition, there is strong evidence of the use of Chronicles in several books in the Second Temple period (Daniel, 1 Maccabees, Sirach, and various of the DSS). This, together with the fact that Chronicles is part of the Greek translation of the Old Testament (LXX), "points to a mid-third century date as the latest reasonable time for composition" (Knoppers 2004:111).[4] Thus, the Chronicler was at work somewhere between 425 and 250 BC, writing to a community of Jews who needed to return to Jerusalem to the reconstructed Temple and to participate in its worship as they awaited the full realization of the restoration of the kingdom of David.

AUDIENCE

The dates and location that have been given for Chronicles identify the readership as those who lived in the province of Yehud sometime during the Persian (539–333 BC) and early Hellenistic (333–250 BC) periods. Although this is a wide range, there are certain characteristics of this community that may help us understand the book.

One cannot overestimate the powerful impact of the Babylonian conquest of Judah in the early sixth century BC. In at least four waves (605, 597, 587, 582 BC), a portion of the upper echelon of the Judean kingdom was deported to areas in Mesopotamia, leaving behind a decimated community and destroyed infrastructure. Although in the waning days of the Judean monarchy foreign powers had controlled the southern kingdom, there was at least some semblance of independence and identity for the nation. But the destruction of Jerusalem in 587/6 would result in the removal of key identity markers: king, Temple, and capital. Until 539 BC Jews would live in communities stretching from Mesopotamia to Egypt under foreign hegemony.

With Babylonian control over the ancient Near East finally broken by Cyrus in 539 BC, the Jewish people began to return to the land in at least four waves to join those who had remained behind, first under Sheshbazzar in 539–537, then under Zerubbabel and Jeshua in 522–520, Ezra in 458, and Nehemiah in 445. Persian authorization for these returns is inextricably linked with the reconstruction of the Temple and the reinstitution of its worship, a project that was begun under Sheshbazzar's leadership (Ezra 1; 5:15-16) but only fully engaged under the leadership of governor Zerubbabel, the priest Jeshua, and the prophets Haggai and Zechariah (Ezra 2–6; Haggai; Zech 1–8). The Temple structure was completed in 515 BC (Ezra 6:15), even though temple services had begun as early as 520 with the reconstruction of the altar (Ezra 3:1-6).[5]

The return of Zerubbabel, with his Davidic lineage (1 Chr 3:17-24; Hag 2:20-23), to the land from Mesopotamia (*Zerubbabel* means "seed of Babylon") around 520 BC was an important signal of the restoration of the nation to its former state. That is, he represented the reinstatement of the royal identity marker, even if he was accountable to Persian authorities. His choice of Jerusalem as the capital of the province reinstated a second identity marker, while the reconstruction of the Temple represented the third and final identity marker. Thus, by 515 BC there would have been much hope that the community was on the brink of restoration; all that remained was independence from the Persian Empire. Some see evidence of rebellion in the language of Haggai (Hag 2:1-9, 20-23), but this is far from certain. What we do know is that by the end of the sixth century BC Zerubbabel was no longer governor of Yehud, let alone king of an independent Judah. In his place sat his son-in-law Elnathan, a man married to Zerubbabel's daughter Shelomith, who ruled until around 490 BC. After that point there is no evidence of a figure from Davidic descent involved in leadership in the province.

Little is known about the little province of Yehud during the era after the disappearance of Zerubbabel. Texts in Zechariah 9–14 and Malachi suggest that there were some tensions within the community. Two of these tensions likely revolved around the relationship between Jerusalem and the surrounding province (Zech 12–14) and the relationship between the functioning of the Temple and the priesthood (Malachi). Zechariah 11:4-16 may indeed point to Zerubbabel's demise as the cause for this tension.[6] Evidence from Ezra 4 suggests that the Jewish community in Yehud faced serious opposition in the first half of the fifth century in the period leading up to Ezra's arrival in 458 BC. Any progress that had been made in securing Jerusalem as the capital city was eradicated by adversarial forces within the empire. Ezra's return, enabled and empowered by the Persian court, was largely focused on renewal within the community, protecting the community from foreign influences, and securing any privileges that had been gained from the Persians (Ezra 7–10). With Nehemiah came even greater empowerment from the Persian court, finally securing Jerusalem as the provincial capital with its protective wall (Neh 1–7). In the wake of Nehemiah two of the key identity markers of the community were in place: Temple and capital, even if the third, the monarchy, was no longer a reality.

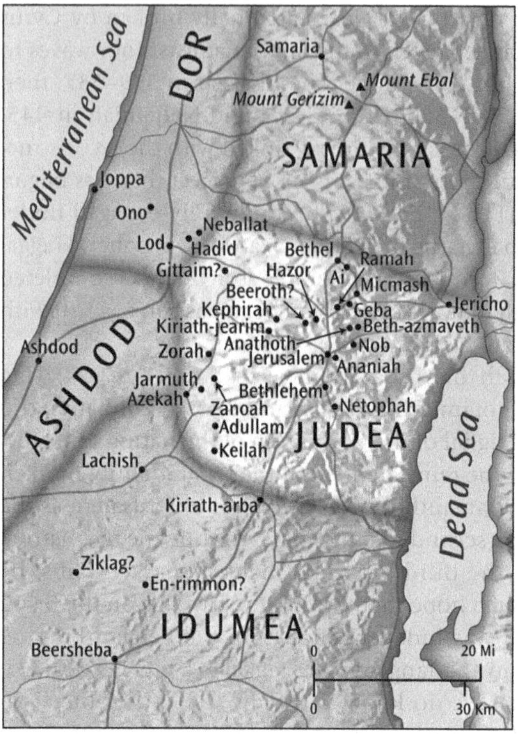

The Province of Yehud

Although evidence is slight for the period after the fifth century, it appears that the Temple in Jerusalem became the key center for Jewish community and identity in Yehud. However, even in the sixth century BC the Jewish temple at Elephantine in Egypt rivaled the Temple in Jerusalem, and as time progressed this Egyptian community showed signs of syncretism with local Egyptian religion.[7] In the late Persian/early Hellenistic period (latter half of the fourth century BC) another temple would be built on traditional Israelite soil, that is, the Samaritan temple on Mount Gerizim (Josephus *Antiquities* 9.288; 11.302-310; 13.74),[8] and some have suggested that sanctuaries were already present in the sixth and fifth centuries at Bethel (Zech 7:1-3), Lachish, and Casiphia (in Babylon; Ezra 8:17; Ezek 11:14-16; see Knoppers 2004:112). There is also evidence of a Jewish sanctuary built at Leontopolis in Egypt in the second century BC.[9] The limited size of Yehud during this period, however, meant that most of these various sanctuaries were not within the confines of the province, even if some of them were on traditional territory. Nevertheless, their presence was a problem for those who saw the Temple in Jerusalem as the fulfillment of the Deuteronomic legislation that centralized worship and sacrifice (Deut 12).

With the Temple at the core of the Persian-period community, the priestly orders clearly had a key role to play in identity formation for the community. They, along with their Temple and services, provided the only link to the ancient traditions of Israel. It is not surprising then that the priestly orders exerted considerable influence on Yehud from the Persian period until the destruction of the Second Temple in AD 70.

The readers of Chronicles, therefore, were a community dealing with the realities of life after the demise of their nation and independence. The failed reinstitution of the royal line, together with the successful reconstruction of the Temple, meant that at least for the time being the Temple and its sacred orders were the only hope for nurturing Jewish community and faith. Notwithstanding, this was a community that would have been dealing with considerable loss and in need of hope as they lived under the hegemony of foreign lords whose tenure appeared unending.

CANONICITY & TEXTUAL HISTORY

Textual Sources. The key extant ancient witnesses to the original text of Chronicles include the following: in Hebrew, the medieval Masoretic Hebrew manuscript tradition and the much earlier Hebrew fragment found at Qumran (Japhet 1993:29);[10] in Greek, the book called *Paraleipomenōn* (which largely follows the order of the book known from the Masoretic Hebrew tradition) and a later book called 1 Esdras (or *Esdras A*, as in the LXX), which is included in the "Apocrypha" found in some Protestant Bibles and is comprised of 1 Chronicles 35–36, Ezra 1–10, and Nehemiah 8 (with some additions, including a long narrative at 1 Esdr 3:1–5:6); in other ancient languages, most important of which include Latin (Old Latin, Vulgate traditions), Aramaic (Targums, Syriac Peshitta), Ethiopic and Arabic works. While these latter versions are of little help for establishing the original Hebrew text of Chronicles,[11] the Greek version cannot be ignored. *Paraleipomenōn* is a literal translation that in most cases reflects the same tradition as the Masoretic Text. At times, however, it reflects a better reading than the Masoretic Text.[12] Although reflecting "elegant and idiomatic Greek" and representing a later compilation of sections of Chronicles, Ezra, and Nehemiah, 1 Esdras is nevertheless a key resource as an early textual witness to Chronicles (Knoppers 2004:56).

Close study of the Masoretic Text of Chronicles, the Masoretic Text of Samuel—Kings, Qumran evidence of Samuel (4QSam[a], 4QSam[b], 4QSam[c]), and the Septuagint for Samuel has demonstrated that Chronicles drew on a text of Samuel closer to 4QSam[a] and the Septuagint than to the Masoretic Text of Samuel, but on a text of Kings closer to the Masoretic Text of Kings.[13] This latter point is very important because it reminds us that some of the "differences" between Chronicles and its key source, Samuel—Kings, are not due to editorial revision by the Chronicler but rather to textual revisions by scribes.

Textual Limits. One of the key debates over the past century of work on Chronicles has been over the limits of the work. Since the nineteenth century it was largely assumed that Chronicles, Ezra, and Nehemiah were a single work that traced the history of the world from Adam to Nehemiah. This view was based on textual data (the overlap between the end of 2 Chr 36 and the beginning of Ezra 1 and the shape of 1 Esdras, which stretches from 2 Chr 35 to Ezra 10 plus Neh 8), lexical data (long lists of vocabulary shared by these books), and thematic data (shared interests in genealogies and the Temple with its services and personnel).

Through the work of Sara Japhet and H. G. M. Williamson, however, the consensus was seriously challenged, and the majority of opinion has shifted justifiably to view Ezra-Nehemiah as a separate entity from Chronicles (Japhet 1968:330-371; Williamson 1977b:5-82).[14] Key to this shift are the following developments: First, similarities in language between Chronicles and Ezra-Nehemiah have been reevaluated in light of research on the history of the Hebrew language, which has shown that much of this shared language was merely a reflection of a general linguistic shift in the Hebrew language, a shift that resulted in a new type of Hebrew known as "Late Biblical Hebrew."[15] In other words, the similarities in language between Ezra-Nehemiah and Chronicles is likely due to their shared linguistic context, which stands in marked contrast to the linguistic context of earlier Old Testament books.

Additionally, Japhet has highlighted the absence in Ezra-Nehemiah of vocabulary key to Chronicles.[16] Second, and related to this last point, several scholars have noted significant differences between Chronicles and Ezra-Nehemiah on the thematic level, especially in their treatment of the traditions of David, mixed marriages, the Sabbath, Levites, the northern kingdom, and prophecy.[17] Third, the Chronicler's historiographic technique contrasts with that of the writer(s) of Ezra and Nehemiah, especially in the use of speech material to accentuate theological themes (Williamson 1982:11). Fourth, the repetition of the proclamation of Cyrus at the end of Chronicles (2 Chr 36:22-23) and the beginning of Ezra (Ezra 1:1-3) does not strengthen the bond between the books, but rather shows that the Chronicler was abbreviating the longer form in Ezra. Evidence for this can be seen in the way he stopped his citation awkwardly (but purposefully) midsentence (see commentary on 2 Chr 36:22-23); furthermore, by changing the Hebrew phrase *mippi* [TH4480/6310, ZH4946/7023] (from/through the mouth of) in Ezra 1:1 to *bepi* [TH871.2/6310, ZH928/7023] (through the mouth of) in 2 Chronicles 36:22, the Chronicler brought the text into line with the form in 2 Chronicles 36:21 (*bepi*). And finally, the evidence of 1 Esdras does not apply to this discussion because it originated after Chronicles and Ezra-Nehemiah had already reached their final forms.

Textual Editions. There have been many proposals concerning the editorial process that produced the form of Chronicles we possess today, including those which posit Priestly, Levitical, and Deuteronomistic redactions.[18] The issue is complicated, however, by the fact that the book appears to be an editorial masterpiece, drawing on a variety of sources (even on the fundamental level of all theories). As per Knoppers (2004:92), identifying redactions within a book such as Chronicles is rendered nearly impossible because of the nature of the Chronicler's compositional technique: "his adroitness in drawing upon originally disparate lemmata, his ability to acknowledge and negotiate different ideological perspectives, and his capacity for pursuing his own agenda as he engages a variety of earlier biblical traditions." Evidence of diversity should be seen not as "an indelible mark of literary disunity" but rather as "the author's concern to mediate different perspectives."

Canon. Seventeenth-century rationalist Baruch Spinoza once wrote of the books of Chronicles: "I have always been astonished that they have been included in the Bible by men who shut out from the canon the books of Wisdom, Tobit, and the others styled apocryphal" (2004:2.10.5).[19] This much later criticism of Chronicles, however, admits that such disdain was not shared by the ancients who affirmed and formed the Canon. In all ancient Hebrew manuscripts Chronicles appears in the third section of the Hebrew canon, called the Ketubim (or the Writings). Although some may argue that its presence within the Writings suggests its inferiority to the books of the other two sections, this cannot be sustained. According to Sanders, the first two sections (Torah and Prophets, the latter including Samuel—Kings) were probably "stabilized in content and order" by the sixth or fifth centuries BC (ABD 1.840), which is before the Chronicler completed his work. Most likely its location within the Writings is due to the period of its composition.

While the early list of biblical books in the Babylonian Talmud places Chronicles in the final position of the Writings (and thus the Hebrew Bible as a whole),[20] the

Hebrew textual tradition that ultimately dominated the transmission of the Hebrew Bible throughout the Medieval period (Masoretic) nearly always places Chronicles at the beginning of the Writings followed by the grouping Psalms/Proverbs/Job (in various orders).[21] The Writings include books that shaped and describe the worship of the community that endured exile and was instrumental in restoring worship and in assembling the Canon after the Exile. For instance, in this section one finds the Psalter with its record of and resource for the worship of the people of God. Here one also finds the five Megilloth or scrolls, each of which was read at one of the five major festivals in the Jewish liturgical year (Ruth = Pentecost; Song of Songs = Passover; Ecclesiastes = Shelters; Lamentations = ninth of Ab; and Esther = Purim). Finally, the Wisdom Literature is located in this section, offering instructions for wise living.

In contrast, in the Jewish Greek textual traditions (Septuagint), the traditions that have been most influential on the order of books in Christian Bible translations, Chronicles is found following the books of Kings (Kingdoms) and before the book of Ezra. It appears that those who created this order grouped books according to genre and tradition, thus emphasizing the historiographic dimension of the Chronicler's work. As already noted above, the name given to Chronicles in this tradition means "omissions." This suggests that its role in the shadow of the long history that stretches from Genesis to Kings is to fill in information that was missed. Its position prior to Ezra, Nehemiah, and Esther is also suggestive of its role to bridge the gap between Kings and Ezra, especially with its closing genealogy (1 Chr 9) and narrative (2 Chr 36).

While in the Jewish Greek tradition, Chronicles functions as a rereading of the story of Israel that stretches from Genesis to Kings, in the Jewish Hebrew tradition it forms a bridge to the worship rhythms of the community that arose out of the ashes of the Exile. These two ways of handling Chronicles reflect emphases that honor the intentions of the Chronicler.

LITERARY CONCERNS

The writer of Chronicles explicitly cited sources at several points in his account, and the names of these sources are different from those cited in the book of Kings for the kings of Judah (see chart on next page).[22]

The book of Kings cites in one place an account of Solomon's reign and in all other places a single source providing the accounts of all the kings of the southern kingdom. The Chronicler cited sources similar in name to the royal accounts in Kings: in two cases *The Book of the Kings of Israel* (*seper malke yisra'el;* 1 Chr 9:1; 2 Chr 20:34), in one case *The Events* (NLT, "Book") *of the Kings of Israel* (*dibre malke yisra'el;* 2 Chr 33:18), in one case *The Commentary on the Book of the Kings* (2 Chr 24:27), in four cases *The Book of the Kings of Judah and Israel* (2 Chr 16:11; 25:26; 28:26; 32:32), and in three cases *The Book of the Kings of Israel and Judah* (2 Chr 27:7; 35:27; 36:8; cf. 1 Chr 9:1). Interestingly, none of these names match the names of the sources cited throughout Kings. The Chronicler also cited accounts beyond those explicitly mentioning kings in their title, and all of these accounts are related to various prophets: Nathan the prophet (1 Chr 29:29; 2 Chr 9:29), Gad

CHRONICLES		KINGS	
1 Chr 29:29	*The Record of Samuel the Seer, The Record of Nathan the Prophet,* and *The Record of Gad the Seer*	–	–
2 Chr 9:29	*The Record of Nathan the Prophet,* and *The Prophecy of Ahijah from Shiloh,* and also in *The Visions of Iddo the Seer*	1 Kgs 11:41	*The Book of the Acts of Solomon*
2 Chr 12:15	*The Record of Shemaiah the Prophet* and *The Record of Iddo the Seer,* which are part of the genealogical record	1 Kgs 14:29	*The Book of the History of the Kings of Judah*
2 Chr 13:22	*The Commentary of Iddo the Prophet*	1 Kgs 15:7	*The Book of the History of the Kings of Judah*
2 Chr 16:11	*The Book of the Kings of Judah and Israel*	1 Kgs 15:23	*The Book of the History of the Kings of Judah*
2 Chr 20:34	*The Record of Jehu Son of Hanani,* which is included in *The Book of the Kings of Israel*	1 Kgs 22:45	*The Book of the History of the Kings of Judah*
–	–	2 Kgs 8:23	*The Book of the History of the Kings of Judah*
2 Chr 24:27	*The Commentary on the Book of the Kings*	2 Kgs 12:19	*The Book of the History of the Kings of Judah*
2 Chr 25:26	*The Book of the Kings of Judah and Israel*	2 Kgs 14:18	*The Book of the History of the Kings of Judah*
2 Chr 26:22	Events . . . recorded by the prophet Isaiah son of Amoz	2 Kgs 15:6	*The Book of the History of the Kings of Judah*
2 Chr 27:7	*The Book of the Kings of Israel and Judah*	2 Kgs 15:36	*The Book of the History of the Kings of Judah*
2 Chr 28:26	*The Book of the Kings of Judah and Israel*	2 Kgs 16:19	*The Book of the History of the Kings of Judah*
2 Chr 32:32	*The Vision of the Prophet Isaiah Son of Amoz,* which is included in *The Book of the Kings of Judah and Israel*	2 Kgs 20:20	*The Book of the History of the Kings of Judah*
2 Chr 33:18-19	*The Book of the Kings of Israel . . . The Record of the Seers*	2 Kgs 21:17	*The Book of the History of the Kings of Judah*
–	–	2 Kgs 21:25	*The Book of the History of the Kings of Judah*
2 Chr 35:27	*The Book of the Kings of Israel and Judah*	2 Kgs 23:28	*The Book of the History of the Kings of Judah*
2 Chr 36:8	*The Book of the Kings of Israel and Judah*	2 Kgs 24:5	*The Book of the History of the Kings of Judah*

the seer (1 Chr 29:29), Ahijah from Shiloh (2 Chr 9:29), Iddo the seer (2 Chr 9:29; 12:15) and prophet (2 Chr 13:22), Shemaiah the prophet (2 Chr 12:15), Jehu son of Hanani (2 Chr 20:34), the prophet Isaiah son of Amoz (2 Chr 26:22; 32:32), and the seers (2 Chr 33:18-19). While the royal accounts are nearly always referred to with the term "book," in 2 Chronicles 24:27 the royal record is referred to as *The Commentary on the Book of the Kings.* This term "commentary" (*midrash* [TH4097, ZH4535]) is also associated with one of the prophetic sources in 2 Chronicles 13:22. Other terms associated with the prophetic sources include: "record" (1 Chr 29:29; 2 Chr 12:15; 20:34; 33:19; cf. 2 Chr 26:22), "prophecy" (2 Chr 9:29), and "vision" (2 Chr 9:29; 32:32). At certain points the Chronicler notes that these prophetic sources were part of a larger piece of work, whether a genealogical record (2 Chr 12:15) or a royal account (2 Chr 20:34; 32:32).

It can probably be assumed that when the Chronicler incorporates material into his account not known from other extant literature (like Samuel—Kings), his citations name the source of this extra material. It is interesting that in every case these unique source citations replace the source citation found in the book of Kings (upon which the Chronicler is relying) and in two cases the citations in Kings are deleted without the Chronicler adding any of his own (2 Kgs 8:23; 21:25). Also interesting is that the Chronicler's additions to the account of Solomon in Kings constitute long lists of Temple and military personnel, not the kind of material one would expect in books related to prophets (2 Chr 9:29; cf. Knoppers 2004:124). The fact that the prophetic sources are viewed as originally part of a larger royal account (2 Chr 20:34; 32:32), may suggest that the Chronicler was referring merely to the account of that prophet within his source in Kings. However, this does not solve the problem of the reference to the records of Shemaiah and Iddo within a "genealogical record."

This evidence suggests that the Chronicler was relying on a royal account, described in various ways and probably referring to a form of the biblical books of Samuel—Kings (cf. Williamson 1982:18).[23] At times the Chronicler referred to prophetic material that appears within Samuel—Kings (2 Chr 20:34; 32:32); in another place this prophetic material appears within a genealogical record (2 Chr 12:15). But there appear to be still other sources, all but one drawn from prophetic sources. In that one case the Chronicler attests access to a commentary on the book of Kings (2 Chr 24:27).

While the focus of much study on these various citations has been on establishing the authenticity of these references and the existence of the sources themselves, one should not miss the rhetorical effect of these citations. The fact that the citations are dominated by references to prophetic works is important in the development of the narrative. The Chronicler was showing how both prophets and kings in Judah affirm the Temple and its services. Thus, citations of these sources play a role not only in bolstering the authenticity of the Chronicler's account, but also in strengthening the Chronicler's appeal to his generation to rally around the Temple. Furthermore, as Knoppers (2004:124-125) has observed, "References to prophets and prophetic figures in his source citations seem to fall into a larger pattern. Such references almost always occur for rulers whom the Chronicler appraises positively"[24] (1 Chr 29:29; 2 Chr 9:29; 13:22; 20:34; 26:22; 32:32) or in accounts where "prophecies or prophetic figures play major roles in turning around negative segments of their reigns" (2 Chr 12:14-15; 33:18-19).

Whether one can firmly link the citations of the royal sources (2 Chr 16:11; 20:34; 24:27; 25:26; 27:7; 28:26; 32:32; 35:27; 36:8) in Chronicles to a form of the present biblical book of Samuel—Kings, it is common knowledge that the main source for Chronicles (about 50 percent) is the account of Israelite history in Samuel and Kings.[25] In addition, the Chronicler also draws on the Torah, Joshua, Ruth, Ezra, Nehemiah, and Psalms.

The Chronicler was a master at combining sources together into a new entity, in some cases citing his source verbatim while in others removing and rearranging material found in his source. In some cases the Chronicler inserted material unknown from any extant source. This material may have come from a written source or from oral tradition. By contrasting the Chronicler's source material with his narrative (see "Textual Sources" above) and by comparing narrative sections throughout Chronicles that are unique to the Chronicler's work, one can discern the creative agenda of the Chronicler as he weaved a new history of Israel that was relevant to his own context and values.

It is apparent from studying this work that the Chronicler was not only writing "the facts" of the national history of Israel, but rather (as in all historical writing) he was also addressing burning issues in his own day. As discussed above, in all historical work there is interplay between the needs of the author's generation and the realities of history. This is true not only in the selection of the data for the historical work, but also in the presentation of this data.

The Chronicler viewed the history of Israel from his perspective not only after the Exile but also after the first phase of the restoration with its successes and failures. For the Chronicler the city of Jerusalem had been restored, the Temple rebuilt, and its services restored, but the political stature of Jerusalem and the Davidic monarchy had not reached the prophetic expectations of the Babylonian and early Persian periods. The concerns that result from this mixture of success and failure are subtly addressed by the Chronicler in his work. Israel's failure to regain its former status is to be linked to the enduring need for renewal among the community.[26]

MAJOR THEMES

Covenant Relationship and Obedience. The Chronicler gave close attention to covenant relationship with the Lord and obedience to Torah. Great emphasis is placed on God's willingness to act graciously in response to the penitential posture of his people, as well as on God's willingness to discipline justly in response to sin (see introduction to 2 Chr 10–36). This is exemplified most vividly in the Chronicler's portrayal of Manasseh. While in Kings Manasseh is depicted as the worst of all kings, in 2 Chronicles 33 Manasseh becomes an example of an exilic figure whose repentance led to his bringing restoration to the land and kingdom. Human responses encouraged throughout Chronicles include seeking God, humbling oneself, praying, and turning to God (see the programmatic statement of Yahweh in 2 Chr 7:14), while responses discouraged include abandoning God and being unfaithful to him (see the programmatic statement by the Chronicler in 2 Chr 12:1-2; Longman and Dillard 2006:199-200). Key also to this renewal was the enduring support of the Temple and its worship. This can be discerned in the Chronicler's close attention to the various kings' support or lack of support for the Temple. This is showcased most vividly in the Chronicler's treatment of the accounts of David and Solomon. While Samuel—Kings focuses considerable attention on their building the kingdom, Chronicles focuses almost exclusively on their building the Temple. The Chronicler depicts David as consumed with the transfer of the Ark into Jerusalem, and he devotes 1 Chronicles 22–29 to describe in detail David's preparations for the Temple construction and services. In Chronicles the gift to Solomon of wisdom (and the wealth and fame that accompanied it) is immediately linked to the Temple-building project (2 Chr 1–2), unlike Kings, where wisdom is related to his administration of justice and rule (1 Kgs 3–4).

For the Chronicler, those who embrace this renewal experience blessing (building construction, military resources and victory, royal offspring, popular support, long rule), while those who reject it suffer curse (lacking the above signs). Through this theme, the Chronicler sought to show his community the power of renewal and faithfulness in the present circumstances but also to warn them of the potential damage for a community that rejects his call. The new start for his community is made clear in the final chapter of the book. Second Chronicles 36:21 draws on the theology of Leviticus 25:4; 26:33-35 to highlight the renewal of the land and of its people in the Persian period. As they "go there" (2 Chr 36:23), that is, to Jerusalem, they are given a clean slate and a new opportunity. The call of the Chronicler is to obedience to the covenant and support of the Temple.

Legitimizing the Present by the Past. As noted above, the Chronicler offers consistent exhortations and examples from the monarchial past to guide the community in the kind of renewal that would lead to full restoration. Another way the Chronicler regularly uses the past is to legitimize the present community. This can be seen in his fixation with genealogies and lists throughout his account, especially in 1 Chronicles (1 Chr 1–9, 11–12, 23–27). These lists offer legitimacy to the people as a whole, reminding them of God's election of Israel from time immemorial, but also to the families who served in the Temple and its services. Such legitimacy is very important in the wake of the stain of the Exile and new circumstances of foreign hegemony (see Ezra 2:61-63).

The Chronicler offers such legitimization also through a technique called "recapitulative historiography" (Longman and Dillard 2006:198)—that is, he used an earlier incident in the story of Israel as a model for a later incident. Thus, David and Solomon are depicted through the model of Moses and Joshua (see commentary on 1 Chr 22), and later Solomon and his craftsman Huram-abi are depicted through the model of Bezalel and Oholiab (see introduction to 2 Chr 1–9) in order to legitimize a Temple and dynasty stained by the sin of the later monarchy. Additionally, for those who were being called to follow the example of David and Solomon in support for the Temple and its services, this clearly established the premonarchic Tabernacle as the theological foundation for the Temple. Legitimacy for the present is based on these links to the past.

Prophetic Office. Another feature of the Chronicler's account is the treatment of the prophetic office. At several junctures the Chronicler cites prophetic accounts as key sources for his work (1 Chr 29:29; 2 Chr 9:29; 12:15; 13:22; 32:32), lending credibility to his account. In addition, those associated elsewhere with classic prophecy, such as Jehu, Isaiah, and Jeremiah, are cited in the text (2 Chr 19:2; 32:20; 35:25). At the same time, however, the line of this classic prophetic witness is now broadened to include Levites (1 Chr 25:1-5; 2 Chr 20:14; 29:30; 34:30; 35:15), priests (2 Chr 24:20), and even foreign monarchs (2 Chr 35:22). The Chronicler treats the prophetic tradition of the past as authoritative revelation while expanding this tradition to include revelation through the sacred personnel attached to the Temple and to imperial figures who superintended the political structure of the province. In this way the Temple could function as a conduit for divine revelation to his people, and the present imperial situation could be seen as Yahweh's present will.

Limits of the Restoration Community. But there is more. The Chronicler sought to expand not only the people's view of prophecy but also their view of the limits of the restoration community. The Chronicler, rather than losing hope for a united Israel, engendered hope through his many references to "all Israel" (1 Chr 9:1; 11:1, 10; 12:38; 14:8; 15:3, 28; 18:14; 2 Chr 1:2; 7:8; 9:30; 10:3, 16; 12:1; 13:4, 15; 18:16; 24:5). His concern to include all the tribes is evident when he lists as many tribes as possible in his genealogies of 1 Chronicles 1–9 (leaving out only Zebulun and Dan). The omission of the history of the northern kingdom throughout the account is not intended as a slight against these tribes, but rather is used to play down the schism and to include them in "all Israel." For the community of Yehud (Judah) in the Persian period, this message was important. It was a subtle reminder that the proper vision of restoration must include Jews from both Yehud and Samaria, from the south as well as the north. There is plenty of evidence to suggest that there were tensions between the two provinces in the Persian Empire, seen best in the confrontation between people from the north and Zerubbabel (Ezra 4:1-5), as well as Sanballat's concerted effort to derail Nehemiah (Neh 2:19; 4:1-9; 6:1-14). The Chronicler, however, would have nothing to do with this separation between north and south. This does not mean that he would allow Jews from Samaria to control Yehud, but rather that there is only one option: a kingdom comprised of inhabitants from both north and south united around the Temple, King, and Jerusalem.

THEOLOGICAL CONCERNS

The historical context and historiographic agenda above lay the foundation for the potential of Chronicles as a source of Christian theological reflection. The Chronicler wrote for an audience living in the wake of the fall of Judah and its subsequent exile in the sixth century BC. This was an audience forced to reorient their faith and worldview to a post-kingdom reality, living as an insignificant Jewish colony on the edge of the mighty Persian Empire. The themes developed in this book would have provided a basis for this community to live faithfully through successive Greek and Roman empires, the soil in which Christianity took root. Christian readers often forget that the community to which the Chronicler wrote was a community that preserved the covenantal tradition upon which the church is founded. It is not surprising that Matthew's Gospel begins with a genealogy that continues the line traced by the Chronicler in 1 Chronicles 3 and then shows its fulfillment in the person of Jesus Christ. Luke's Gospel begins with stories of people who had gathered around the Temple courts (one of the objects of the Chronicler's passion), serving Yahweh faithfully and awaiting the appearance of the Messiah. The genealogies and narratives the Christian reader finds within the pages of Chronicles are thus to be seen first and foremost as the genealogies and narratives of their ancestors and traditions.

But Chronicles is more than just a record of the past. It is filled with theological potential for the church today, a church living in what is often described as a post-Christendom era in which the church has been pushed from its place of cultural privilege to the private margins of society. In this way the church today resonates with a community struggling to cope with life at these margins and can leverage not only the theology of the early church who saw themselves as aliens and strangers but also that of a book like Chronicles. Through this book the Chronicler speaks to those searching for identity as the people of God in an age when the surrounding culture (empire) dominated their lives so profoundly. Chronicles identifies key spiritual rhythms for individual and community living in this context, whether the call to revival and renewal through repentance, the invitation to make prayer a priority in their lives and communities, or the provision of a robust theology of worship—outlining David's innovations in verbal worship alongside the enduring Mosaic tradition of sacrifice.

For the committed and patient reader, there are immeasurable riches in this intricate book, which is far more than a collection of mere "omissions," as the Greek textual tradition treated it, but rather a vision for a community to live faithfully among the nations because they represent God's hope for the world.

OUTLINE OF 1 CHRONICLES

- I. Genealogies from Adam to Saul's Family (1:1–9:44)
  - A. Genealogies from Adam to Israel's Family (1:1–2:2)
  - B. Genealogies of Judah, Hezron, Caleb, David, Solomon, Jehoiachin, and Simeon (2:3–4:43)
  - C. Genealogies of Reuben, Gad, and the Transjordan Tribes (5:1-26)
  - D. The Priestly Line (6:1-81)
  - E. Genealogies of Issachar, Benjamin, Naphtali, Manasseh, Ephraim, and Asher (7:1-40)
  - F. Genealogies of Benjamin and Saul (8:1–9:1a)
  - G. List of Exilic Returnees and Saul's Genealogy (9:1b-44)
- II. The Account of David (10:1–29:30)
  - A. The Death of King Saul (10:1-14)
  - B. David Becomes King of All Israel, Conquers Jerusalem, and Is Joined by Mighty Warriors (11:1-47)

C. David's Military Support (12:1-40)
D. David Attempts to Move the Ark (13:1-14)
E. David's Family and Palace (14:1-17)
F. Moving the Ark to Jerusalem (15:1–16:3)
G. The Levites Lead Worship before the Ark (16:4-43)
H. The Lord's Covenant Promise to David (17:1-27)
I. David's Military Victories (18:1-17)
J. David Defeats the Ammonites and Arameans (19:1-19)
K. David Captures Rabbah; Battles against Philistine Giants (20:1-8)
L. David Takes a Census (21:1–22:1)
M. Preparations for the Temple (22:2-19)
N. David's Commission of the Levites: Gershonites, Kohathites, Merarites (23:1-32)
O. David's Commission of the Priests; List of Levitical Leaders (24:1-31)
P. David's Commission of Levitical Musicians: Asaph, Heman, Jeduthun (25:1-31)
Q. David's Commission of the Levitical Gatekeepers, Treasurers, and Administrators (26:1-32)
R. David's Commission of the Military; Lists of Tribal Leaders and Officials (27:1-34)
S. David's Instructions to Solomon (28:1-21)
T. David's Final Acts before Solomon Becomes King (29:1-30)

OUTLINE OF 2 CHRONICLES

I. The Account of Solomon (1:1–9:31)
   A. Solomon Asks God for Wisdom (1:1-17)
   B. Preparations for Building the Temple (2:1-18)
   C. Solomon Builds the Temple (3:1–4:22)
   D. After the Ark Is Brought, God's Presence Fills the Temple (5:1-14)
   E. Solomon's Praise and Prayer (6:1-42)
   F. The Dedication of the Temple and God's Message to Solomon (7:1-22)
   G. Solomon's Achievements (8:1-16)
   H. Solomon's Economic Achievement and International Fame (8:17–9:31)
II. The Account after Solomon (10:1–36:23)
   A. Division of the Kingdom (10:1–11:4)
   B. Rehoboam's Period of Success (11:5-23)
   C. Rehoboam's Rebellion and Repentance (12:1-16)
   D. Abijah's Reign (13:1–14:1a)
   E. Asa's Reign (14:1b–16:14)
      1. Asa's early years (14:1b-15)
      2. Asa's later years (15:1–16:14)

- F. The Reign of Jehoshaphat (17:1–21:1a)
    1. Jehoshaphat rules in Judah (17:1-19)
    2. Jehoshaphat's inappropriate alliance with Ahab of Israel (18:1-34)
    3. Jehoshaphat appoints judges (19:1-11)
    4. Jehoshaphat's victories and inappropriate alliance with Ahaziah of Israel (20:1–21:1a)
- G. Jehoram's Reign (21:1b-20)
- H. Ahaziah's Reign (22:1-9)
- I. Athaliah's Reign until Overthrown by Jehoiada (22:10–23:21)
- J. Joash's Reign (24:1-27)
- K. The Reign of Amaziah (25:1-28)
- L. The Reign of Uzziah (26:1-23)
- M. The Reign of Jotham (27:1-9)
- N. The Reign of Ahaz (28:1-27)
- O. The Reign of Hezekiah (29:1–32:33)
    1. Hezekiah takes the throne and reopens the Temple (29:1-36)
    2. Renewal of the Passover and Festival of Unleavened Bread (30:1–31:1)
    3. Reform of worship practices (31:2-21)
    4. Rescue from Assyrian attack (32:1-23)
    5. Hezekiah's sickness, pride, repentance, and later accomplishments (32:24-33)
- P. The Reigns of Manasseh and Amon (33:1-25)
- Q. The Reign of Josiah (34:1–35:27)
    1. Josiah's accession and reform of worship (34:1-33)
    2. Josiah's celebration of the Passover and Festival of Unleavened Bread (35:1-19)
    3. Josiah's death with a summary of his reign (35:20-27)
- R. The Reigns of Jehoahaz, Jehoiakim, Jehoiachin, Zedekiah, and the Fall of Jerusalem (36:1-23)

ENDNOTES

1. It was through Ray Dillard that I met H. G. M. Williamson, my first doctoral supervisor, under whose guidance I continued to hone my perspective on this rich corpus. It is to these two mentors that I dedicate this volume. As in all my books, I would like to give Augustine the final word: *Ego ex eorum numero me esse profiteor qui scribunt proficiendo, et scribendo proficient* (Augustine *Epistle* 143.2, via John Calvin).
2. Although Chronicles is often disparaged as useful for theology but not history, see discussion of the use of Chronicles for historical reconstruction in Dillard 1987; Japhet 1993:31-41 (with examples at 1002-1004); Knoppers 1997:178-203; Vaughn 1999. Japhet (2006:216) notes: "Although the Chronicler certainly adopts the theological framework within which Israel's history is conceived, he does provide some data that contribute to a better historical understanding of these issues." Furthermore, Knoppers (1997:202) cautiously writes: "It is also clear, however, that the unique evidence of

Chronicles, when compared with archeological or epigraphic evidence, is occasionally of some value for historical reconstruction." For a review of trends, see Japhet 1985:83-107; Peltonen 1996; Smelik 1998.

3. The complete version of this proclamation can be found in Ezra 1 and an official archival record in Aramaic in Ezra 6:3-5.
4. See the evidence in Knoppers 2004:105-111.
5. See further Boda 2004.
6. See further Boda 2003c:277-291.
7. "One document from Elephantine claims that the Jewish temple there was built during a period of native Egyptian rule before the Persian conquest under Cambyses (reigned 529–522 BC). That would give a date for the construction of the Elephantine temple by the mid-sixth century at the latest" (TBD 420). Clearly by the late fifth century the Elephantine temple had been destroyed (410 BC), because permission for its reconstruction is recorded in documents sent first to Johanan the high priest (Neh 12:22-23) and Bagoas governor of Yehud, and then three years later to Bagoas and to Delaiah and Shelemiah, the sons of Sanballat, the governor of Samaria (Neh 2:10, 19; 4:1, 7; 6:1, 2, 5, 12, 14; 13:28). The temple was rebuilt by 402 BC, even if permission for burnt offerings was denied.
8. Williamson (ABD 5.973-975) notes that the temple at Gerizim was built at the time of Darius III before the advance of Alexander the Great. According to Josephus (*Antiquities* 11.302-310 [11.8.2-4]) the governor of Samaria in the fourth century BC, Sanballat, promised a priest named Manasseh the priesthood and also a temple on Mount Gerizim to rival Jerusalem. This temple was destroyed by the Maccabean king John Hyrcanus in 128 BC (Josephus *Antiquities* 13.254-256 [13.9.1]; *War* 1.62-63 [1.2.6]). The temple is also mentioned in 2 Macc 5:23; 6:2.
9. Built by Onias (III or IV) sometime in the second century BC by permission of Ptolemy VI Philometor; see Josephus *War* 7.420-436; see ABD 3.1040.
10. Only four words of which are legible.
11. However, see the comments of Japhet (1993:30-31), who notes with Rudolph the helpfulness of the Old Latin as a witness to the LXX tradition and also as a witness to the original Hebrew text at three places (2 Chr 4:17; 20:2; 32:31). The Targum of Chronicles did not reach its final form until the eighth to ninth centuries AD.
12. See Japhet 1993:30; Allen (1999:168) argues that *Paraleipomenōn* is a "valuable witness" to the text of Chronicles in second-century BC Egypt.
13. See ABD 1.995; McKenzie 1985; Knoppers 2004:70; Klein 2006:28-30.
14. See Boda and Redditt 2008.
15. See Williamson 1977b:37-59; cf. Polzin 1976; Talshir 1988:165-193; Throntveit 1982:201-216.
16. Japhet 1968:330-371.
17. See Braun 1979:52-64; Williamson 1977b:60-69; 1982:9-11.
18. See Knoppers 2004:90-93 for a detailed review of this issue.
19. Cited by Ben Zvi (2002:262).
20. Within the tradition represented by the Babylonian Talmud (*b. Bava Batra* 14b; no earlier than second century AD), Chronicles appears at the end of the Writings (Knoppers 2004:135-136; ABD 1.840). Some medieval Hebrew manuscripts follow the Babylonian Talmud order.
21. See further Boda 2009d:4-10, 357-358, 506-514.
22. See Klein 2006:40; cf. Knoppers 2004:123. When dealing with the kings of Israel (who are largely ignored by the Chronicler), the writer of Kings cites the source *The Book of the History of the Kings of Israel* (e.g., 1 Kgs 14:19; 15:31; 16:5, 14, 20, 27; 22:39; 2 Kgs 1:18; 10:34; 13:8, 12; 14:15, 28; 15:11, 15, 21, 31).
23. See Klein (2006:41), who argues that although various names are used, they all refer to the same book.
24. So also Klein 2006:41.

25. For this see Kalimi 2005b:1. There has been great debate over whether the Chronicler and the writer of Samuel—Kings were each relying upon a third source (Halpern 1981:35-54). The majority of scholars see Samuel—Kings as the source for the Chronicler. There has also been debate over what form of Samuel—Kings the Chronicler relied upon as his source. Although it is true that in some cases the Chronicler appears to be relying on an earlier text form, this cannot account for all the differences.
26. See Boda 2009b.

COMMENTARY ON

1 Chronicles

INTRODUCTION TO 1 CHRONICLES 1–9

It is the genealogies at the outset of the book of Chronicles—lists that comprise 25 to 30 percent of the entire work (Knoppers 2004)—that have earned the book a notorious reputation among ancient and modern readers alike.[1] Genealogical lists elsewhere in the Old Testament are usually brief and placed within narratives, making them more palatable to the modern reader. The narrative of Genesis, for instance, is structured according to what are called *toledoth* [TH8435, ZH9352] (Gen 2:4; 5:1; 6:9; 10:1, 32; 11:10, 27; 25:12, 13, 19; 36:1, 9; 37:2), a word whose verbal root connotes bearing or siring a child (*yalad* [TH3205, ZH3528]). At the various junctures cited above, the narrative employs the term *toledoth* to signal the beginning of a new section of the book. In some cases the term is followed by genealogical information (e.g., Gen 10:1), while in others it is followed by simple narrative description (e.g., Gen 37:2). The term *toledoth* probably has its origins in genealogies as suggested by its use in Genesis 10:32; 11:10, 27; 25:12-13, 19; 36:1, 9, and thus shows the key role that genealogies can play in a narrative. For the first section of his work, the Chronicler has taken the many genealogies within Genesis and stripped them from their surrounding narratives. These lists introduce an elongated genealogy that stretches for nine chapters and tests the patience of even the most committed Hebrew scholar. But the Chronicler, by collating these lists and placing them at the outset of his grand narrative, shows that for him the lists were not only significant as ancient records of Israel but essential for the reading of the subsequent narrative in 1 Chronicles 10—2 Chronicles 36. This introduction to chapters 1–9 seeks to orient the modern reader to the sociology, rhetoric, sources, and purposes of the genealogies in the Chronicler's work.[2]

Sociology. Although literary in character, ancient genealogies presume an underlying sociological reality, not only in terms of the world of those represented in the genealogy, but more importantly, in terms of the world of those reproducing the genealogy. They are reflections, as well as projections, of sociological structure.

Structures. There is no question that genealogies are dominated by family structures, beginning with the *beth 'ab* (house of the father), each of which belonged to a "clan" (*mishpakhah* [TH4940, ZH5476]; Ruth 2:1; Gen 12:3), which in turn belonged to a "tribe" (*shebet* [TH7626, ZH8657] or *matteh* [TH4294, ZH4751]) and even a nation (*bene yisra'el* [TH1121, ZH1201], the "children of Israel"; Josh 7:16-18; Judg 6:15; 1 Sam 9:21; 10:20-21). The *beth 'ab* [TH1004/1, ZH1074/3] (house) was larger than the modern Western nuclear family, including up to four generations and often the families of multiple brothers from a common father who lived in two or three houses architecturally connected (see Gen 7:1, 7; 36:6; 45:10; cf. Gen 46:26; Exod 20:8-10, 17; Deut 5:12-15, 21; Josh 7:16-18; Judg 6:11, 27, 30; 8:20). This unit also included individuals who were not related by blood, such as debt servants, slaves, concubines, resident aliens, sojourners, and priests (see Judg 18:14-22, 25, 29). The diverse character of the core family unit helps the modern reader understand why the genealogies in the Old Testament may at times describe lines and link people who are not related by blood. At times geographical, social, economic, religious, and political relationships are also in view (cf. Braun 1986:4). This is evident in cases where the term "father" (*'ab* [TH1, ZH3]) is used for the founder of a city (see NLT mg on 2:24, 42, 55) or where a list reflects political succession (1:43-51a) or military organization (1:51b-54).

Values. The household in ancient Israel was patrilineal (descent was reckoned through the male line), patrilocal (the wife joined the household of her husband), patriarchal (the family was led by the eldest male), and patrimonial (land was transferred from father to sons, with the eldest son receiving the largest portion).[3] The dominance of these values in ancient Israelite sociology explains much of the content of the genealogies. Exceptions to these rules, then, should stand out to the reader and receive greater rhetorical attention. For instance, one should not miss cases where the one who is not firstborn carries on the line or is singled out within the line.

Most genealogies arising in patriarchal societies focus on the male line. The Chronicler, however, does not completely ignore women in his genealogies, a feature noted by Knoppers (2004:358) for the genealogy of Judah, which mentions wives (2:18, 24, 26, 29, 35; 3:3; 4:5, 7, 19), concubines (2:46, 48; 3:9; cf. 2:21, 24), sisters (2:16-17; 3:9, 19; 4:3, 19), daughters (2:4 [daughter-in-law], 21, 34, 35, 49; 3:2, 5; 4:18), and mothers (2:26; 4:9). Women appear in the genealogies for structural purposes, to differentiate between various children born to a patriarch (3:1-9), and/or for ideological purposes, to bring into view background narratives or developing themes for the line under discussion. For instance, the mention of Zerubbabel's daughter Shelomith in 3:19 emphasizes her role in the Persian period community (see also 3:9).

At points, however, the genealogies are matrilineal. For example, both 2:21-23 and 7:14-19 trace the line of the Transjordan Manasseh clan of Makir, and in both instances these lines intersect the key tribes of Judah and Benjamin. The use of such matrilineal structure probably reflects sociological patterns in this region, but they may also have been used by the Chronicler to show that a remnant of this half-tribe of Joseph survived in Judah and Benjamin.

Ethnicity. The fact that Israel is singled out from all the nations traced in chapter 1 may suggest to some a focus on exclusivity in the Chronicler's genealogy. However, the consistent mention of non-Israelites throughout the genealogies of Israel leads Knoppers (2004:358) to conclude that "the genealogy does affirm a range of humans—male and female, ancestor and slave, Israelite, Canaanite, Edomite, Moabite, Ishmaelite, and Egyptian—had a role to play in Judah's development." In this Japhet (1993:74) finds evidence that "one of the goals of these genealogies is the inclusion, rather than exclusion, of the non-Israelite elements in the people of Israel, by presenting them as an organic part of the tribes, mainly in the status of 'wives' or 'concubines.' It is geographical rather than ethnic affiliation which constitutes the unifying element, especially in Judah."

Rhetoric. Genealogies in the ancient world in general and the Old Testament in particular are not all cut from the same cloth. One can discern a diversity of rhetorical principles used for the genealogical lists of Chronicles. This diversity can be traced to a variety of factors, including the makeup of the family unit, the purpose of the genealogist, and the preference of a particular group or era.

Focus. Some genealogies in Chronicles have *breadth,* offering a comprehensive list of members of a single generation (intragenerational), while others restrict the focus by concentrating on *depth,* focusing the list on one individual each in multiple generations (intergenerational). Genealogies dominated by breadth are often called *segmented* genealogies, while those dominated by depth are called *linear.* Combinations of these two types are found (see below under "Purposes").

Order. Some genealogies in Chronicles (either linear or segmented) trace the generations in *descending* chronological order, from parent to child, from oldest child to youngest, while other genealogies trace them in *ascending* chronological order, from child to parent, from youngest to oldest child. Still other genealogies use an ordering principle other than chronology, related to ideological or narrative principles. As already noted, at times lists are employed that are not explicitly genealogical but rather related to political succession (1:43-51a) or military organization (1:51b-54).

Design. Usually genealogies of Chronicles are presented in sequential fashion, which is not surprising since lineage moves methodically from generation to generation. One can discern at times a penchant for symbolic enumeration, with focus on birth order (3:1-3) and patterns of three (e.g., 2:3, 9, 27; 3:23), six (3:4), seven (2:10-13a, 13b-15; 3:24), twelve (2:1-2), and fourteen (2:34-41). At times the sequence is punctuated with structural summaries (as in ch 1). Sometimes instead of a sequential design, one finds a chiastic design that identifies the importance of the figures placed at the beginning, middle, and end of the list. For example, Knoppers (2004:257) claims that there is a chiastic design in the priestly lists in 6:2-15 [5:28-41] that places Kohath (son of Levi) at the outset, Zadok (the high priest serving in the court of David-Solomon) in the center, and Jehozadak (the final high priest before the Exile) at the end.

Chiastic design can also be discerned on the macrolevel, even alongside sequential patterns. Knoppers (2004:260-265) highlights these in his work on the overall shape of chapters 1–9.[4] One can discern a sequential flow to the genealogy. First Chronicles 1 identifies Israel's relationship with the nations of the world, chapters 2–8 note its privileged place among the nations, and chapter 9 emphasizes continuity between privileged Israel and the restoration community centered around Jerusalem and the Temple. Furthermore, "If the universal lineage sets the stage for the appearance of Israel (1 Chr 2–8), the tribal lineages set the stage for the reestablishment of an Israel centered around Jerusalem (9:2-34)" (Knoppers 2004:264). At the same time, a chiastic pattern (see below) shows that for the Chronicler Levi stands at the center of the community and that Judah and Benjamin are related as the surviving tribes who now inhabit the province of Yehud, while the other tribes are not ignored (Simeon, Transjordan, and northern tribes). First Chronicles 1 and 9 both highlight Israel's emergence from the nations of the world, first in creation and second in restoration. The design is as follows:

A. The peoples of the world (1:1–2:2)
  B. Judah with Simeon (2:3–4:43)
    C. Transjordan tribes (5:1-26)
      D. Levi (6:1-81)
    C'. The northern tribes (7:1-40)
  B'. Benjamin (8:1-40)
A'. Persian-period inhabitants of Jerusalem (9:2-34)

Formula. In Chronicles, various formulae are used to introduce each generation within a genealogy. The most prevalent formula is "the son(s) of FATHER: SON 1 . . ." (Heb., *ben(ey)* [TH1121, ZH1201]; e.g., 1:28), with "daughter" (Heb., *bath* [TH1323, ZH1426]) replacing "son(s)" in limited cases (e.g., 2:49). At times the formula will be preceded by the demonstrative pronoun "these" (Heb., *'elleh* [TH428, ZH465]; "these are the son(s) of FATHER: SON 1 . . ."), and this secondary formula can also function to terminate a list (1:23b, 31b, 33b, 54b). Other formulae are also used, including:

"FATHER *sired* SON" (Hebrew root *yalad* [TH3205, ZH3528], Qal/Hiphil; e.g., 2:22)
"MOTHER *gave birth to* SON" (*yalad*, in Qal; e.g., 2:49)
"FATHER, *the father of* SON" (Heb., *'abi* [TH1, ZH3]; e.g., 2:49)
"SON, *son of* FATHER" (Heb., *ben* [TH1121, ZH1201]; e.g., 4:34)
"FATHER, *his son* SON" (Heb., *beno*; e.g., 3:10-14; 7:25-27)

One should keep in mind that the terms "father/mother" and "son/daughter" do not always signify immediately successive generations but can designate "ancestor" and "descendant" and even at times the "founder" of a city (see 2:24, 42, 55, NLT mg). The technique of telescoping generations (see 2:10-17; Klein 2006:95) may serve the purpose of creating literary structure,[5] conserving space, or bringing key generations into closer proximity.

Extranominal information. While the backbone of any genealogy is the bare list of names joined by one of the formulae, at times the genealogy will contain other material. This may be short descriptions (1:46, 50; 3:17), brief narratives (4:9-10), numbering (either ordinal or cardinal, 3:1-9),[6] or chronological information (1:19, 43).

In general, variations in these various structuring principles within a genealogy will serve a rhetorical purpose, and such variations should be noted by the reader.

Sources. In 4:22 the Chronicler makes the claim that "these names all come from ancient records." In some cases these records are most likely the books that now comprise the Old Testament canon. For example, chapter 1 relies heavily upon materials now found in the book of Genesis, if not the book of Genesis itself, while 3:1-4 relies on 2 Samuel 3:1-5. In other cases the source used by the Chronicler has not survived. Knoppers (2004:286) notes several key techniques employed by the Chronicler. Sometimes he would excise his lists from long narratives (1:1-4, 24-27). At other times, he would rearrange blocks of material from his source (1:29-31, 32-33, 35-54; 2:1-2). He was free to transform the original headings of the material and even create new transitions that would fit the new literary context better. He displays liberty in omitting or abridging details, whether geographical, anecdotal, or chronological.

Purposes. To introduce a discussion of the purpose of the genealogies in Chronicles, Armin Siedlecki (1999:235) relates the story, told by Charles Kraft (1979:229), of a discussion between a Jewish and Gentile university student:

> *The Gentile asked the Jewish student what his favorite passage of Scripture was. His immediate response was, 'The first eight chapters of First Chronicles'. These are Hebrew genealogies. From my (Gentile) point of view I have often wondered why God allowed so much space in his Word to be 'wasted' on such trivia. But to a Hebrew (and to many other kinship-oriented societies around the world) genealogical lists of this nature demonstrate in the deepest way the specificity of God's love and concern that lies at the heart of the Gospel.*

To many modern westerners these nine chapters may appear to be "wasted" space in revelatory history, but as the response of the Jewish student makes clear, such is not the view of many Jews today, nor was it of the Jewish community in the past. While Kraft has focused on one particular purpose of genealogy, there are probably a multitude of purposes for the use of genealogical lists in antiquity.

One purpose of genealogies was *to structure and validate sociological functions,* especially those related to war (military lists), worship (Temple personnel lists), and rule (royal lists). Thus, Ezra 2:62-63//Nehemiah 7:64-65 recounts how priests were required to prove their genealogy in order to serve, 1 Chronicles 27 records the military divisions that served in David's army, and 1 Chronicles 23–26 records the priestly and Levitical divisions for Israel's worship. Most note a difference in function between linear and segmented types of lists, with the former used to legitimize the terminal individual of the list by creating a link to a worthy ancestor, and the latter used to depict relationships between the various contemporaneous lines. So, for instance, a linear genealogy of priestly functionaries would be more useful for establishing the legitimacy of a later high priest (e.g., 6:4-15), while a segmented genealogy of priestly functionaries would be more useful for describing the roles played by the various priestly families for the maintenance of worship (e.g., 6:16-30).

These purposes of establishing legitimacy and demonstrating relationships through genealogies are not mutually exclusive. Since segmented genealogies often have a linear dimension and a single genealogy may employ both structuring principles, there may be a dual purpose at work. For instance, while the Davidic genealogy in chapter 3 is dominated by a linear focus, it begins with a segmented focus for David's family, revealing the abundant potential of the dynasty at the outset from which the line of Solomon was chosen. After a linear focus from Solomon to Josiah, there is a return at the end to a form that combines the segmented and linear foci. After Josiah, the breadth of successive generations is described, showing the enduring potential of the royal line, but in each generation one line is always identified and traced forward to the next, showing an enduring election within this royal line (see commentary on ch 3; cf. Knoppers 2001:35-50).

Although similar to their original function as lists created as records of the community and preserved in archives, the range of purposes for these lists expands when they are incorporated creatively into a narrative work. Such genealogies continue to play the roles of legitimizing single lines and relating multiple lines. For the Chronicler's community, tracing the lines of Israel would have provided much needed continuity and thus legitimacy for a community living under imperial hegemony in the wake of the Exile. In addition, the lists function to legitimize or envision legitimization for various sociological groups, including tribal units and Levitical clans.[7] The inclusion of a list of those who returned from exile in chapter 9, as well as the focus on the genealogies of key figures from the Chronicler's own time, legitimizes families involved in leadership in the Second Temple community (Knoppers 2004:251). In addition, the segmented genealogies of the world in chapter 1 and of Israel in chapters 2–8 *highlight Israel's relationship with their world, as well as the relationships between the various tribes.*[8] A community living with the reality of imperial hegemony, confirmed by the inclusion of the list of returning exiles in chapter 9,[9] would need to understand their place within this world.[10] A community consisting merely of the remnant of Judah, Benjamin, and Levi and limited to the tribal territories of the south would need to reflect carefully on their relationship with the other tribes and territories and be reminded that the present reality was not necessarily the preferred future.

But these lists function in other ways within these narratives.[11] First, they *create narrative movement* as they trace the period from Adam (1:1) to Saul (9:35-44) and as a result place this story of David's dynasty and kingdom within the larger history of the world and Israel.[12] In this way the Chronicler was able to cover in his single book the entire history of Israel that consumes Genesis—Kings and thus to earn for his work Jerome's description of being a "Chronicle of All Divine History."[13] Another dimension of this narrative movement is highlighted by Japhet (1993:8), who compares 1 Chronicles 1:1 with 2 Chronicles 36:22-23, a movement from what she calls "beginning to 'beginning,'" that is, from the beginning of human history to the new beginning of Israel's history after exile. Additionally, Knoppers (2004:264) argues for a close literary relationship between chapters 1–9 and chapter 10—2 Chronicles 36, both ending with exile (9:1; 2 Chr 36:17-21), both identifying the people's "unfaithfulness" (*ma'al* [TH4604, ZH5086]) as the cause of the Exile (9:1; 2 Chr 36:12-16), and both announcing a return to the land (9:2-34; 2 Chr 36:22-23).

Second, especially by including extranominal information (see above), but also by inserting certain lists (the various northern tribes, the royal line, the priestly line), the genealogies *foreshadow some of the key theological themes, rhetorical structures, and narrative characters* of the Chronicler's work. Three recent descriptions of evidence for this foreshadowing are worthy of note:

Oeming (1990), summarized so nicely by Kleinig (1994:57), details the effects of the Chronicler's genealogies:

> *True Israel is defined geographically as a land centered on Judah and Jerusalem, ethnically as twelve tribes coordinated around the tribe of Levi, politically as a nation unified by David and his descendants, theologically as a people obedient to God's law, cultically as a liturgical community participating in the sacrificial ritual at the temple*

> *in Jerusalem, and sacrally as a holy people linked personally to the temple sanctuary via the Levites scattered throughout its territory. The genealogies are therefore taken to encapsulate the main elements of the Chronicler's theology.*

Johnstone (1998:107-113, here 107) argues that the thematic term *ma'al* binds the genealogical section together: "From start to finish on West Bank and on East, Israel's history has been blighted by מעל (1 Chron. 2.7; 5.25; 9.1)." Johnstone notes how the genealogies in chapter 1 identify the universal context of Israel's life and the central genealogies in chapters 2–8 portray the ideal tribal ordering of Israel so that it can realize its destiny (especially with Levi at its center) while at the same time revealing how Israel vitiated its destiny (exemplified in the behavior of Reuben, Nadab and Abihu, the inclusion of the Transjordanian tribes, the omission of Dan, the mention of the Exile). Finally, however, chapters 8–9 provide the remedial action necessary for Israel to realize its destiny (especially in the interweaving of the failure of the Benjaminite king Saul and the redemption of Benjaminite Jerusalem). Johnstone (1998:113) says, "The reason that Benjamin appears last in the tribal genealogies is, therefore, not merely that Benjamin, as one of the last survivors, constitutes an enclosing bracket around the more vulnerable northern tribes; rather, it is that Benjamin provides the Chronicler with the double link of both guilt and atonement forward into this account of Israel's history."

Duke (1990:56) argues that the narrative statements throughout the genealogies (2:3; 4:10; 5:20, 22, 25-26; 9:1) "signal to the audience the laws operating within the world of the narrative," which he sees as a "maxim of divine blessing/punishment." In addition, the repetition of the genealogy of Benjamin (7:6-12; 8:29-40) directs attention to the surviving tribe associated with Judah and provides movement toward the opening of the narrative.

One should analyze such genealogies embedded within biblical narratives by giving attention to the sociological and literary sources and forms of the genealogy and then to its functions within the narrative context of Chronicles.

ENDNOTES

1. Dillard cites one writer who called it "Scriptural Sominex," a reference to a popular North American sleeping pill; cf. Longman and Dillard 2006:190.
2. This introduction is based in part on the superb treatments of genealogies in Braun 1986:1-12; M. Johnson 1988; Johnstone 1998:106-114; Klein 2006:80-81; Kleinig 1994:43-76; Knoppers 2003:13-31; 2004:245-265; Oeming 1990; Selman 1994a:85-89; Snyman 2003:32-60; Williamson 1979b:351-359; 1982:38-40; R. Wilson 1975:169-189; 1977.
3. I am thankful to Sandra Richter (Asbury) for first alerting me to these categories; cf. Bendor (1996); Perdue (1997); ABD 2.761-769.
4. My presentation modifies Knoppers slightly. Most of the implications he draws from the outer frame (chs 1, 9) are actually comments relevant to the sequential pattern of chapters 1–9, rather than to the chiastic pattern. Another proposal has been suggested by Oeming (1990:200), who sees in the flow of chs 1–9 concentric circles: the outer circle contains the nations (ch 1), the second circle contains the tribes of Israel (chs 2–8), and the innermost circle contains the holy city and inhabitants (ch 9); cf. Kalimi 2002:556-562; Klein 2006:265.

5. Especially in order to place key figures on certain numbers, especially seventh and tenth generations, as in 2:10-17; see further Sasson (1978:171-185), who identifies the fifth and seventh spots as key.
6. Japhet (1993:93) refers to "the author's propensity for numbers."
7. Aufrecht (1988:205-235) and Snyman (2003:32-60) both show how genealogies function sociologically to establish and validate present structures. Snyman highlights that genealogies are helpful for boundary maintenance, conflict resolution, elite justification, group solidarity, and social order; in Chronicles they are focused on domestic (determining social position), juridical (regulating relations and controlling land), and religious purposes. Also note Knoppers (2004:251-253), who cites the evidence of 28:4-5 (for the genealogical function of legitimization) and 2 Chr 13:4-8 (for the genealogical function of disqualification).
8. The dominant connection is through shared lineage, but also note the geographical character of these relationships, as Kartveit (1989) argued, noting that Israel is placed at the center of the world with Judah and Jerusalem at its center; on Jerusalem, see also Kalimi 2005a:92.
9. Also note Knoppers's chiastic connection between chs 1 and 9.
10. See also Knoppers (2004:256), who sees a more positive role for genealogies; comparing the Chronicler to Greek genealogies, he concludes that for the Chronicler, "The primary issue at stake is not so much the definition of the ethnos over against external groups as it is the relationships of the various groups who make up the ethnos."
11. Although some have questioned whether the genealogies were original to the Chronicler's work, evidence for these two additional purposes undermine this view; see especially Kartveit 1989; Knoppers 2004; and Oeming 1990 for ideological, stylistic and structural evidence for the unity of chapter 1—2 Chr 36; contra Cross 1975:4-18; Freedman 1961:436-442; Newsome 1975:201-217; cited in Williamson 1982:40.
12. See the evidence in Knoppers 2004:259 from ancient Greek biographers who begin accounts with an account of ancestry.
13. See Klein 2006:1; cf. Knoppers and Harvey 2002. Knoppers (2004:286) compares the genealogies of ch 1 to the ancient Greek genre of epitome, which represented "a short abridgement or compendium of an older work," in this case, the book of Genesis; cf. Japhet 1993:52.

◆ I. Genealogies from Adam to Saul's Family (1:1–9:44)

A. Genealogies from Adam to Israel's Family (1:1–2:2)

**The descendants of Adam were Seth,
Enosh, 2Kenan, Mahalalel, Jared, 3Enoch,
Methuselah, Lamech, 4and Noah.
The sons of Noah were* Shem, Ham, and
Japheth.
5The descendants of Japheth were Gomer,
Magog, Madai, Javan, Tubal, Meshech,
and Tiras.
6The descendants of Gomer were
Ashkenaz, Riphath,* and Togarmah.
7The descendants of Javan were
Elishah, Tarshish, Kittim, and
Rodanim.
8The descendants of Ham were Cush,
Mizraim,* Put, and Canaan.
9The descendants of Cush were Seba,
Havilah, Sabtah, Raamah, and Sabteca.
The descendants of Raamah were
Sheba and Dedan. 10Cush was also the
ancestor of Nimrod, who was the first
heroic warrior on earth.
11Mizraim was the ancestor of the
Ludites, Anamites, Lehabites,
Naphtuhites, 12Pathrusites, Casluhites,
and the Caphtorites, from whom the
Philistines came.***

[13]Canaan's oldest son was Sidon, the ancestor of the Sidonians. Canaan was also the ancestor of the Hittites,*
[14]Jebusites, Amorites, Girgashites,
[15]Hivites, Arkites, Sinites, [16]Arvadites, Zemarites, and Hamathites.

[17]The descendants of Shem were Elam, Asshur, Arphaxad, Lud, and Aram.

The descendants of Aram were* Uz, Hul, Gether, and Mash.*

[18]Arphaxad was the father of Shelah.

Shelah was the father of Eber.

[19]Eber had two sons. The first was named Peleg (which means "division"), for during his lifetime the people of the world were divided into different language groups. His brother's name was Joktan.

[20]Joktan was the ancestor of Almodad, Sheleph, Hazarmaveth, Jerah,
[21]Hadoram, Uzal, Diklah, [22]Obal,*
Abimael, Sheba, [23]Ophir, Havilah, and Jobab. All these were descendants of Joktan.

[24]So this is the family line descended
from Shem: Arphaxad, Shelah,* [25]Eber,
Peleg, Reu, [26]Serug, Nahor, Terah,
[27]and Abram, later known as Abraham.

[28]The sons of Abraham were Isaac and
Ishmael. [29]These are their genealogical records:

The sons of Ishmael were Nebaioth (the oldest), Kedar, Adbeel, Mibsam,
[30]Mishma, Dumah, Massa, Hadad,
Tema, [31]Jetur, Naphish, and Kedemah. These were the sons of Ishmael.

[32]The sons of Keturah, Abraham's concubine, were Zimran, Jokshan, Medan, Midian, Ishbak, and Shuah.

The sons of Jokshan were Sheba and Dedan.

[33]The sons of Midian were Ephah, Epher, Hanoch, Abida, and Eldaah.

All these were descendants of Abraham through his concubine Keturah.

[34]Abraham was the father of Isaac. The sons of Isaac were Esau and Israel.*

[35]The sons of Esau were Eliphaz, Reuel, Jeush, Jalam, and Korah.

[36]The descendants of Eliphaz were Teman, Omar, Zepho,* Gatam, Kenaz, and Amalek, who was born to Timna.*

[37]The descendants of Reuel were Nahath, Zerah, Shammah, and Mizzah.

[38]The descendants of Seir were Lotan, Shobal, Zibeon, Anah, Dishon, Ezer, and Dishan.

[39]The descendants of Lotan were Hori and Hemam.* Lotan's sister was named Timna.

[40]The descendants of Shobal were Alvan,* Manahath, Ebal, Shepho,* and Onam.

The descendants of Zibeon were Aiah and Anah.

[41]The son of Anah was Dishon.

The descendants of Dishon were Hemdan,* Eshban, Ithran, and Keran.

[42]The descendants of Ezer were Bilhan, Zaavan, and Akan.*

The descendants of Dishan* were Uz and Aran.

[43]These are the kings who ruled in the land of Edom before any king ruled over the Israelites*:

Bela son of Beor, who ruled from his city of Dinhabah.

[44]When Bela died, Jobab son of Zerah from Bozrah became king in his place.

[45]When Jobab died, Husham from the land of the Temanites became king in his place.

[46]When Husham died, Hadad son of Bedad became king in his place and ruled from the city of Avith. He was the one who destroyed the Midianite army in the land of Moab.

[47]When Hadad died, Samlah from the city of Masrekah became king in his place.

[48]When Samlah died, Shaul from the city of Rehoboth-on-the-River became king in his place.

[49]When Shaul died, Baal-hanan son of Acbor became king in his place.

[50]When Baal-hanan died, Hadad became king in his place and ruled

from the city of Pau.* His wife was
Mehetabel, the daughter of Matred
and granddaughter of Me-zahab.
51Then Hadad died.

The clan leaders of Edom were Timna,
Alvah,* Jetheth, 52Oholibamah, Elah,
Pinon, 53Kenaz, Teman, Mibzar,
54Magdiel, and Iram. These are the
clan leaders of Edom.

CHAPTER 2

The sons of Israel* were Reuben, Simeon,
Levi, Judah, Issachar, Zebulun, 2Dan,
Joseph, Benjamin, Naphtali, Gad, and
Asher.

1:4 As in Greek version (see also Gen 5:3-32); Hebrew lacks *The sons of Noah were.* **1:6** As in some Hebrew manuscripts and Greek version (see also Gen 10:3); most Hebrew manuscripts read *Diphath.* **1:8** Or *Egypt;* also in 1:11. **1:12** Hebrew *Casluhites, from whom the Philistines came, Caphtorites.* See Jer 47:4; Amos 9:7. **1:13** Hebrew *ancestor of Heth.* **1:17a** As in one Hebrew manuscript and some Greek manuscripts (see also Gen 10:23); most Hebrew manuscripts lack *The descendants of Aram were.* **1:17b** As in parallel text at Gen 10:23; Hebrew reads *and Meshech.* **1:22** As in some Hebrew manuscripts and Syriac version (see also Gen 10:28); most Hebrew manuscripts read *Ebal.* **1:24** Some Greek manuscripts read *Arphaxad, Cainan, Shelah.* See notes on Gen 10:24; 11:12-13. **1:34** *Israel* is the name that God gave to Jacob. **1:36a** As in many Hebrew manuscripts and a few Greek manuscripts (see also Gen 36:11); most Hebrew manuscripts read *Zephi.* **1:36b** As in some Greek manuscripts (see also Gen 36:12); Hebrew reads *Kenaz, Timna, and Amalek.* **1:39** As in parallel text at Gen 36:22; Hebrew reads *and Homam.* **1:40a** As in many Hebrew manuscripts and a few Greek manuscripts (see also Gen 36:23); most Hebrew manuscripts read *Alian.* **1:40b** As in some Hebrew manuscripts (see also Gen 36:23); most Hebrew manuscripts read *Shephi.* **1:41** As in many Hebrew manuscripts and some Greek manuscripts (see also Gen 36:26); most Hebrew manuscripts read *Hamran.* **1:42a** As in many Hebrew and Greek manuscripts (see also Gen 36:27); most Hebrew manuscripts read *Jaakan.* **1:42b** Hebrew *Dishon;* compare 1:38 and parallel text at Gen 36:28. **1:43** Or *before an Israelite king ruled over them.* **1:50** As in many Hebrew manuscripts, some Greek manuscripts, Syriac version, and Latin Vulgate (see also Gen 36:39); most Hebrew manuscripts read *Pai.* **1:51** As in parallel text at Gen 36:40; Hebrew reads *Aliah.* **2:1** *Israel* is the name that God gave to Jacob.

NOTES

1:4 *and Noah. The sons of Noah were Shem, Ham, and Japheth.* The Hebrew text does not contain the phrase "The sons of Noah were," but instead continues the list begun in 1:1: "Noah, Shem, Ham, Japheth." The NLT (see margin note) follows LXX at this point, versional evidence that may point to a scribal error (the eye skipping from a possibly original first occurrence of the word Noah to a second (in "sons of Noah"), thus leading to the loss of this phrase. While the list in 1:1-3 traces successive generations, the list in 1:4 is restricted to one generation, so that Shem, Ham, Japheth are brothers, not father, son, grandson.

1:10 *Nimrod.* He is variously identified as god (Ninurta, Marduk), hero (Gilgamesh, Lugalbanda), Mesopotamian archetypal royal, or historical person (Sargon I, Tukulti-Ninurta I, Hammurabi). While likely a historical figure lies behind this description, the lack of any clear connections to known historical figures means that he functions as an archetype. See further details in Gen 10:10-12 and his connection to Assyria and Babylon (ABD 4.1116; Westermann 1984:515-517; G. Wenham 1987:222-223; Walton 2001:367-371; Klein 2006:66).

1:12 *Casluhites, and the Caphtorites, from whom the Philistines came.* The NLT mg gives the reading from the Hebrew text, which suggests that the Philistines came from the Casluhites, rather than the Caphtorites. The NLT's switch is based on the evidence of Deut 2:23; Jer 47:4; Amos 9:7, each of which claims that the Philistines were related to the Caphtorites, a people group traditionally related to the island of Crete, with the possibility of association with Cyprus. For a defense of the Hebrew reading, see Rendsburg 1987:89-96, who argues that the Casluhites must be Egyptians who migrated to the coastal plain via Crete (ABD 1.877).

1:13-16 *Sidonians . . . Hamathites.* Here are eleven peoples listed based on Gen 10:13-18. Lists of Canaanite peoples vary in the OT from six nations in Exodus (Exod 3:8, 17; 33:2; 34:11), to seven in Deuteronomic literature (Deut 7:1; Josh 3:10; 24:11), to ten in Gen 15:19-21.

1:32-33 *The sons of Keturah, Abraham's concubine.* Abraham took Keturah as a concubine late in his life (Gen 25:1-6).

COMMENTARY

Sources. The Chronicler drew this first chapter from the substantial genealogical material he found in the book of Genesis. At times he summarizes the list, at others he excises historical and geographical material, and at still others he condenses and even slightly rearranges it. Williamson (1982:40-45) identifies the source of 1:1-4 as Genesis 5; 1:5-23 as Genesis 10 ("with the omission of historical and geographical material from 10:5, 9-12, 18b-21, 30-32"); 1:24-27 as Genesis 11:10-26; 1:29-31 as Genesis 25:13-16a; 1:32-33 as Genesis 25:1-4; 1:35-37 as Genesis 36:4-5, 10-14 ("condensed and slightly rearranged"); 1:38-42 as Genesis 36:20-28; 1:43-54 as Genesis 36:31-43 (with "few omissions and very slight changes"); and 2:1-2 as Genesis 35:23-26.

Structure and Content. The Chronicler begins his genealogy with the first human, Adam, and in 1:1–2:2 he traces the generations to the family of Israel (Jacob). This first major section of the genealogy, which stretches from chapters 1 to 9, begins with a linear genealogy that traces a single line from Adam through Seth to Noah (1:1-4). The line of Cain is ignored and unnecessary in light of the fact that Noah would become the founder of a new humanity after the Flood.

With Noah the Chronicler then begins employing a segmented genealogical structure, one that traces more than one subunit of a family in turn. Thus, 1:4b identifies Shem, Ham, and Japheth as the three sons of Noah, and this is followed by a listing of the descendants of these three sons in reverse order: Japheth (1:5-7), Ham (1:8-16), and Shem (1:17-26). This trend of using reverse order can be seen in each of these Noahic subfamilies. Japheth's sons are listed in 1:5, and then 1:6-7 lists the genealogies of two of these sons (Gomer and Javan). As can be seen with Japheth, Ham, and Shem, not all the subfamilies established by the sons of a father are traced: for Japheth, only Gomer and Javan; for Ham, only Cush, Egypt (Mizraim), and Canaan; and for Shem, only Aram and Arphaxad.

One can discern a structuring principle that first limits the descendant lines but also identifies the last lineage mentioned as having in each case greater relevance to the genealogist, as well as in some cases being the line that will be traced further.[1] For instance, in Noah's family it is Shem's line that is traced last because it will be traced throughout the rest of chapters 1–9. With the Noahic line of Japheth, it is not surprising that the descendants of Javan (Dan 8:21; 10:20; 11:2; Zech 9:13) are traced last, since their connections to the Greek world were so important in the Chronicler's day. Similarly with the line of Ham, the descendants of Canaan are traced last, since the Israelites would replace them in the land. For Shem, the descendants of Aram are traced before those of Arphaxad, and when his grandson Eber has two sons, Peleg and Joktan, it is Joktan who is reviewed first so that the Chronicler can move on to Peleg's line, from which came Abraham. So important is Abraham's line that the Chronicler incorporates a linear genealogy that moves methodically through Shem's line from Arphaxad to Abraham. With Arphaxad's line there is the employment of a closing formula for the non-chosen line, so Joktan's list ends in 1:23 with "all these were descendants of Joktan."

Similar principles can be discerned in the rest of the chapter. The sons of Abraham are listed (Isaac and Ishmael), before Ishmael is traced, followed by the "sons of Keturah, Abraham's concubine." The connection to Abraham for the latter sons is minimized by the Chronicler as he copied his source in Genesis 25:1-4, omitting the words "to him" (NASB) in Genesis 25:2 and clarifying the status of Keturah ("wife" in Gen 25:1) as concubine (based on Gen 25:5-6).[2] A terminal formula brings closure to these two non-chosen lines in 1:31 ("these were the sons of Ishmael") and 1:33b ("All these were descendants of Abraham through his concubine Keturah"). Following this, the Chronicler identifies the continuance of the line through Isaac's sons Esau and Israel.

While five sons are listed for Esau in 1:35, the families of only two of these sons are listed in detail (Eliphaz and Reuel). At this point the Chronicler has included other genealogical material related to the family of Esau; first, in 1:38-42 a segmented genealogy of the "sons of Seir"; second, in 1:43-51a a linear genealogy of the Edomite kings; and finally, a list of Edomite clan leaders in 1:51b-54. Exodus 15:15 suggests that Edom was ruled by chiefs (cf. literal rendering), while 1 Kings 11:14-15 shows it was ruled by a dynastic royal house. Klein (2006:77) notes that this non-dynastic royal list in chapter 1 "would fit typologically between these two types of government."[3] The Chronicler has slightly changed the transition at the beginning of the chieftain list in 1:51, suggesting that the chieftains followed the royal rule (see further below). These chieftains are pictured more like the premonarchial judges of Israel and probably ruled over parts of the territory of Edom. The signal that Esau's line is not chosen and that this final list of clan leaders brings closure to the genealogy of Esau is evident in the terminal formula in 1:54b: "These are the clan leaders of Edom." In summary, the chapter's overall structure is as follows:

1:1-4	From Adam to the sons of Noah
1:5-7	Descendants of Japheth
1:8-16	Descendants of Ham
1:17-23	Descendants of Shem
1:24-28	From Shem to the sons of Abraham
1:29-33	Descendants of Abraham
1:34	From Abraham to the sons of Isaac
1:35-37	Descendants of Esau
1:38-42	Descendants of Seir
1:43-51a	Kings of Edom
1:51b-54	Clan leaders of Edom

As expected, 2:1-2 identifies the one whose line will be traced further, namely, Israel (Jacob) and his 12 sons. The remainder of the genealogy in chapters 2–9 will unpack the lineage of the descendants of this family in 2:1-2. These two verses thus function as the conclusion to 1:1–2:2 and the introduction to chapters 2–9.[4]

While the chapter is dominated by segmented genealogies, at three points in the chapter linear genealogies break through: 1:1-4 (tracing from Adam to Noah's family), 1:24-28 (from Shem to Abraham's family), and finally 1:34 (from Abraham to Isaac's family).[5] At these three junctures in the first chapter a focusing summary statement picks up where the previous summary statement left off. This helps orient the reader and keeps the focus on the scarlet thread that moves from Adam to Israel.

Significance. The use of both linear and segmented forms of genealogical lists in this chapter reveals the multidimensional character of the chapter's function in the book of Chronicles. Its horizontal dimension (tracing at times contemporary subfamilies) establishes the relationship between Israel and its surrounding world. Israel shared some form of family connection with those who preceded them in the land of Canaan (1:13-16), with those who were their enemies in that land (1:11-12, 17, 34-54), and with those superpowers who would abuse them (1:5-7, 9-11, 17). The list thus offers information that reveals the web of ethnic relationships across the known world, showing that Israel had vested interest in the history of the world before and around them, but also that the nations of the world had vested interest in the story of Israel.

Klein (2006:81) highlights the positive aspect of these global relationships, noting how the "chapter implies the diversity *and* unity of the world; this suggests that Israel understood its role within the family of nations and as a witness to all humanity. While Johnstone (1998:107) is aware of this positive aspect ("Israel is to realize on behalf of humankind what humankind as a whole cannot"), he accentuates a negative implication: "But lurking in the background stands the world of the nations from which Israel springs and to which it is kin. Israel's pursuit of the ideal is constantly threatened by reversion to that 'wilderness of the nations,' from which it took its origins, or by invasion from these destructive nations."

The list's vertical dimension (tracing succeeding generations) grants it an orderly forward motion, moving the reader subtly from Adam to Israel. In general terms this serves a narrative role, initiating a plot that will end with the genealogy of Saul (9:35-44) to set up the narrative that will comprise the bulk of the book (ch 10—2 Chr 36). In this way chapter 1 makes possible the claim of Jerome that Chronicles is a "Chronicle of All Divine History."[6] It is also the beginning of a plot that will end with the list of those who returned to the land after exile (ch 9). Selman (1994a:87) argues that this shows that the genealogy is "not intended to be a historian's delight" but rather is designed for its relevance to the writer's contemporary context. In this way not only the story of Israel's kingdoms but also the story of Israel's remnant is rooted in the broader global story.

Although there is always a vertical dimension to a segmented genealogy, this dimension is accentuated (by ignoring the horizontal) in the linear form of genealogy that breaks through in 1:1-4, 24-28, 34. This highlights the selective purpose of this genealogy, that is, it functions to identify the chosen character of a particular line out of the nations of the world and rehearses this line at these three points so that it is not missed. Williamson (1982:40-41) wisely notes that the Chronicler emphasizes Israel (Jacob) as the founder of the nation more so than Abraham, probably foreshadowing the Chronicler's "stress on the full complement of twelve tribes as 'all Israel.'"[7] This selective purpose is also seen in the structuring principle of dealing first with the families unrelated to the ongoing list of the genealogy, a principle that echoes the emphasis of the linear genealogies by following the line relevant to Israel. So Klein (2006:80) has aptly written, "Israel is to understand itself within the circle of all the nations, at whose center Israel stands."[8]

Although the Chronicler has removed most of the anecdotal notes from his sources in Genesis, four remain (1:10, 12, 19 and 43). The reference to Nimrod (1:10) is abridged significantly from the source in Genesis 10, but the association with Assyria and Babylon was firmly established in Hebrew tradition. Johnstone (1997:1.30) argues that Nimrod and Nebuchadnezzar form a bracket of powerful Babylonian kings around the book of Chronicles. This connection to Babylon may also explain the note in 1:19 referring to the division of the world. The special note on the Philistines in 1:12 and the note on the Edomite kings in 1:43 highlight the role of the genealogies as a whole to provide a foundation for the emergence of the Davidic kingdom. The transitional note about the death of Hadad and the rise of clan leaders that the Chronicler inserts at 1:51 may also be designed to foreshadow the rise of the Davidic kingdom because Hadad is mentioned in 1 Kings 11:14-22 in a story of David's defeat of Edom and as an opponent who arose against Solomon. The Chronicler's report of his death suggests that Hadad was an unsuccessful adversary.

The opening genealogy in Chronicles sets Israel in the midst of the nations, revealing that Israel's significance is inextricably linked with the nations. This echoes the narrative shape of the Chronicler's source in Genesis, which begins with the story of creation and the development of nations (Gen 1–11) before the figure of Abram appears (Gen 12). Yahweh's speech to Abram in Genesis 12:1-3 reminds Israel that their destiny is to bring blessing to all the nations of the earth. The New Testament will apply this blessing to the gospel of Christ, which will spread from Jerusalem to the ends of the earth.

ENDNOTES

1. What Japhet (1993:53-54) calls a "concentric" process: "The peripheral elements are dealt with first, to form the background upon which the main genealogical line may be developed." She also notes that the closer one gets to Israel the more detailed the genealogy.
2. Williamson (1982:43) has argued that 1:32-33 appears to be a later addition to the genealogy, saying that someone striving for completeness drew on the genealogy in Genesis for the sons of Keturah. However, see Klein 2006:61 for recent defenses of the originality of this list to the chapter.
3. Many have attacked the biblical claim that kings ruled in Edom before Israel had kings. This has led some to translate this as "before an Israelite king ruled over them" (see NLT mg), a translation that is suspect; see Klein 2006:77. Recent archaeological work on this region has revealed evidence of earlier civilization than was at first envisioned; see especially Levy, Adams, Najjar, Hauptmann, Anderson, Brandl, Robinson and Higham 2004:863-876.
4. As also Japhet 1993:65; Klein 2006:59.
5. See also Wright 1999:136-155, here 148. By missing the function of the terminal element (sons: Shem, Ham, Japheth, Isaac, Ishmael) and the presence of a third linear

genealogy in 1:34, Japhet (1993:53-54) incorrectly identifies the first two linear genealogies as an inclusion around 1:1-27. Also notice that while the list of the kings of Edom has a linear quality, it is not a genealogy in that it does not speak of lineage but rather of succession of rule.

6. See Klein 2006:1; cf. Knoppers and Harvey 2002.
7. It is only at Israel's (Jacob's) generation that there is no longer a nonelect segment to be excluded. From that point on, all from Israel are part of the enduring line. See also Japhet 1993:60; contrast Knoppers 2004:277-278; also Oeming 1990:79, who notes that the name Abram/Abraham occurs five times in this chapter (1:27, 28, 32, 34).
8. See also Oeming 1990:90, who argued that ch 1 reveals Israel's position at the center of humanity.

◆ B. Genealogies of Judah, Hezron, Caleb, David, Solomon, Jehoiachin, and Simeon (2:3–4:43)

3 Judah had three sons from Bathshua, a
Canaanite woman. Their names were Er,
Onan, and Shelah. But the LORD saw that
the oldest son, Er, was a wicked man, so
he killed him. 4 Later Judah had twin sons
from Tamar, his widowed daughter-in-
law. Their names were Perez and Zerah. So
Judah had five sons in all.
5 The sons of Perez were Hezron and
Hamul.
6 The sons of Zerah were Zimri, Ethan,
Heman, Calcol, and Darda*—five in all.
7 The son of Carmi (a descendant of
Zimri) was Achan,* who brought
disaster on Israel by taking plunder
that had been set apart for the LORD.*
8 The son of Ethan was Azariah.
9 The sons of Hezron were Jerahmeel,
Ram, and Caleb.*
10 Ram was the father of Amminadab.
Amminadab was the father of
Nahshon, a leader of Judah.
11 Nahshon was the father of Salmon.*
Salmon was the father of Boaz.
12 Boaz was the father of Obed.
Obed was the father of Jesse.
13 Jesse's first son was Eliab, his second
was Abinadab, his third was Shimea,
14 his fourth was Nethanel, his fifth
was Raddai, 15 his sixth was Ozem, and
his seventh was David.
16 Their sisters were named Zeruiah
and Abigail. Zeruiah had three sons
named Abishai, Joab, and Asahel.
17 Abigail married a man named Jether,
an Ishmaelite, and they had a son
named Amasa.
18 Hezron's son Caleb had sons from his
wife Azubah and from Jerioth.* Her
sons were named Jesher, Shobab, and
Ardon. 19 After Azubah died, Caleb
married Ephrathah,* and they had a
son named Hur. 20 Hur was the father
of Uri. Uri was the father of Bezalel.
21 When Hezron was sixty years old, he
married Gilead's sister, the daughter
of Makir. They had a son named
Segub. 22 Segub was the father of Jair,
who ruled twenty-three towns in the
land of Gilead. 23 (But Geshur and
Aram captured the Towns of Jair*
and also took Kenath and its sixty
surrounding villages.) All these were
descendants of Makir, the father of
Gilead.
24 Soon after Hezron died in the town of
Caleb-ephrathah, his wife Abijah gave
birth to a son named Ashhur (the
father of* Tekoa).
25 The sons of Jerahmeel, the oldest son
of Hezron, were Ram (the firstborn),
Bunah, Oren, Ozem, and Ahijah.
26 Jerahmeel had a second wife named
Atarah. She was the mother of Onam.
27 The sons of Ram, the oldest son of
Jerahmeel, were Maaz, Jamin, and Eker.
28 The sons of Onam were Shammai and
Jada.

The sons of Shammai were Nadab and
Abishur.
29 The sons of Abishur and his wife
Abihail were Ahban and Molid.
30 The sons of Nadab were Seled and
Appaim. Seled died without children,
31 but Appaim had a son named Ishi.
The son of Ishi was Sheshan. Sheshan
had a descendant named Ahlai.
32 The sons of Jada, Shammai's brother,
were Jether and Jonathan. Jether died
without children, 33 but Jonathan had
two sons named Peleth and Zaza.
These were all descendants of Jerahmeel.
34 Sheshan had no sons, though he did
have daughters. He also had an
Egyptian servant named Jarha.
35 Sheshan gave one of his daughters
to be the wife of Jarha, and they had a
son named Attai.
36 Attai was the father of Nathan.
Nathan was the father of Zabad.
37 Zabad was the father of Ephlal.
Ephlal was the father of Obed.
38 Obed was the father of Jehu.
Jehu was the father of Azariah.
39 Azariah was the father of Helez.
Helez was the father of Eleasah.
40 Eleasah was the father of Sismai.
Sismai was the father of Shallum.
41 Shallum was the father of Jekamiah.
Jekamiah was the father of Elishama.
42 The descendants of Caleb, the brother
of Jerahmeel, included Mesha (the
firstborn), who became the father of
Ziph. Caleb's descendants also
included the sons of Mareshah, the
father of Hebron.*
43 The sons of Hebron were Korah,
Tappuah, Rekem, and Shema. 44 Shema
was the father of Raham. Raham was
the father of Jorkeam. Rekem was the
father of Shammai. 45 The son of
Shammai was Maon. Maon was the
father of Beth-zur.
46 Caleb's concubine Ephah gave birth to
Haran, Moza, and Gazez. Haran was
the father of Gazez.
47 The sons of Jahdai were Regem, Jotham,
Geshan, Pelet, Ephah, and Shaaph.
48 Another of Caleb's concubines, Maacah,
gave birth to Sheber and Tirhanah.
49 She also gave birth to Shaaph (the
father of Madmannah) and Sheva (the
father of Macbenah and Gibea). Caleb
also had a daughter named Acsah.
50 These were all descendants of Caleb.
The sons of Hur, the oldest son of Caleb's
wife Ephrathah, were Shobal (the
founder of Kiriath-jearim), 51 Salma
(the founder of Bethlehem), and
Hareph (the founder of Beth-gader).
52 The descendants of Shobal (the
founder of Kiriath-jearim) were
Haroeh, half the Manahathites, 53 and
the families of Kiriath-jearim—the
Ithrites, Puthites, Shumathites, and
Mishraites, from whom came the
people of Zorah and Eshtaol.
54 The descendants of Salma were
the people of Bethlehem, the
Netophathites, Atroth-beth-joab,
the other half of the Manahathites,
the Zorites, 55 and the families of
scribes living at Jabez—the Tirathites,
Shimeathites, and Sucathites. All
these were Kenites who descended
from Hammath, the father of the
family of Recab.*

CHAPTER 3

These are the sons of David who were born in Hebron:

The oldest was Amnon, whose mother
was Ahinoam from Jezreel.
The second was Daniel, whose mother
was Abigail from Carmel.
2 The third was Absalom, whose mother
was Maacah, the daughter of
Talmai, king of Geshur.
The fourth was Adonijah, whose
mother was Haggith.
3 The fifth was Shephatiah, whose
mother was Abital.
The sixth was Ithream, whose mother
was Eglah, David's wife.
4 These six sons were born to David in He-
bron, where he reigned seven and a half
years.

Then David reigned another thirty-three
years in Jerusalem. 5The sons born to Da-
vid in Jerusalem included Shammua,*
Shobab, Nathan, and Solomon. Their
mother was Bathsheba,* the daughter of
Ammiel. 6David also had nine other sons:
Ibhar, Elishua,* Elpelet,* 7Nogah, Nepheg,
Japhia, 8Elishama, Eliada, and Eliphelet.
9These were the sons of David, not in-
cluding his sons born to his concubines.
Their sister was named Tamar.
10The descendants of Solomon were
Rehoboam, Abijah, Asa, Jehoshaphat,
11Jehoram,* Ahaziah, Joash, 12Amaziah,
Uzziah,* Jotham, 13Ahaz, Hezekiah,
Manasseh, 14Amon, and Josiah.
15The sons of Josiah were Johanan (the
oldest), Jehoiakim (the second),
Zedekiah (the third), and Jehoahaz*
(the fourth).
16The successors of Jehoiakim were his
son Jehoiachin and his brother
Zedekiah.*
17The sons of Jehoiachin,* who was
taken prisoner by the Babylonians,
were Shealtiel, 18Malkiram, Pedaiah,
Shenazzar, Jekamiah, Hoshama, and
Nedabiah.
19The sons of Pedaiah were Zerubbabel
and Shimei.
The sons of Zerubbabel were Meshullam
and Hananiah. (Their sister was
Shelomith.) 20His five other sons were
Hashubah, Ohel, Berekiah, Hasadiah,
and Jushab-hesed.
21The sons of Hananiah were Pelatiah
and Jeshaiah. Jeshaiah's son was
Rephaiah. Rephaiah's son was Arnan.
Arnan's son was Obadiah. Obadiah's
son was Shecaniah.
22The descendants of Shecaniah were
Shemaiah and his sons, Hattush, Igal,
Bariah, Neariah, and Shaphat—six
in all.
23The sons of Neariah were Elioenai,
Hizkiah, and Azrikam—three in all.
24The sons of Elioenai were Hodaviah,
Eliashib, Pelaiah, Akkub, Johanan,
Delaiah, and Anani—seven in all.

CHAPTER 4

The descendants of Judah were Perez,
Hezron, Carmi, Hur, and Shobal.
2Shobal's son Reaiah was the father
of Jahath. Jahath was the father of
Ahumai and Lahad. These were the
families of the Zorathites.
3The descendants of* Etam were
Jezreel, Ishma, Idbash, their sister
Hazzelelponi, 4Penuel (the father
of* Gedor), and Ezer (the father of
Hushah). These were the descendants
of Hur (the firstborn of Ephrathah),
the ancestor of Bethlehem.
5Ashhur (the father of Tekoa) had two
wives, named Helah and Naarah.
6Naarah gave birth to Ahuzzam,
Hepher, Temeni, and Haahashtari.
7Helah gave birth to Zereth, Izhar,*
Ethnan, 8and Koz, who became the
ancestor of Anub, Zobebah, and all
the families of Aharhel son of Harum.
9There was a man named Jabez who
was more honorable than any of his
brothers. His mother named him
Jabez* because his birth had been so
painful. 10He was the one who prayed
to the God of Israel, "Oh, that you
would bless me and expand my
territory! Please be with me in all that
I do, and keep me from all trouble and
pain!" And God granted him his
request.
11Kelub (the brother of Shuhah) was the
father of Mehir. Mehir was the father
of Eshton. 12Eshton was the father of
Beth-rapha, Paseah, and Tehinnah.
Tehinnah was the father of Ir-nahash.
These were the descendants of Recah.
13The sons of Kenaz were Othniel and
Seraiah. Othniel's sons were Hathath
and Meonothai.* 14Meonothai was the
father of Ophrah. Seraiah was the
father of Joab, the founder of the
Valley of Craftsmen,* so called because
they were craftsmen.
15The sons of Caleb son of Jephunneh
were Iru, Elah, and Naam. The son of
Elah was Kenaz.

[16]The sons of Jehallelel were Ziph, Ziphah, Tiria, and Asarel.
[17]The sons of Ezrah were Jether, Mered, Epher, and Jalon. One of Mered's wives became* the mother of Miriam, Shammai, and Ishbah (the father of Eshtemoa). [18]He married a woman from Judah, who became the mother of Jered (the father of Gedor), Heber (the father of Soco), and Jekuthiel (the father of Zanoah). Mered also married Bithia, a daughter of Pharaoh, and she bore him children.
[19]Hodiah's wife was the sister of Naham. One of her sons was the father of Keilah the Garmite, and another was the father of Eshtemoa the Maacathite.
[20]The sons of Shimon were Amnon, Rinnah, Ben-hanan, and Tilon.
The descendants of Ishi were Zoheth and Ben-zoheth.
[21]Shelah was one of Judah's sons. The descendants of Shelah were Er (the father of Lecah); Laadah (the father of Mareshah); the families of linen workers at Beth-ashbea; [22]Jokim; the men of Cozeba; and Joash and Saraph, who ruled over Moab and Jashubi-lehem. These names all come from ancient records. [23]They were the pottery makers who lived in Netaim and Gederah. They lived there and worked for the king.
[24]The sons of Simeon were Jemuel,* Jamin, Jarib, Zohar,* and Shaul.
[25]The descendants of Shaul were Shallum, Mibsam, and Mishma.
[26]The descendants of Mishma were Hammuel, Zaccur, and Shimei.
[27]Shimei had sixteen sons and six daughters, but none of his brothers had large families. So Simeon's tribe never grew as large as the tribe of Judah.
[28]They lived in Beersheba, Moladah, Hazar-shual, [29]Bilhah, Ezem, Tolad, [30]Bethuel, Hormah, Ziklag, [31]Beth-marcaboth, Hazar-susim, Beth-biri, and Shaaraim. These towns were under their control until the time of King David. [32]Their descendants also lived in Etam, Ain, Rimmon, Token, and Ashan—five towns [33]and their surrounding villages as far away as Baalath.* This was their territory, and these names are listed in their genealogical records.
[34]Other descendants of Simeon included Meshobab, Jamlech, Joshah son of Amaziah, [35]Joel, Jehu son of Joshibiah, son of Seraiah, son of Asiel, [36]Elioenai, Jaakobah, Jeshohaiah, Asaiah, Adiel, Jesimiel, Benaiah, [37]and Ziza son of Shiphi, son of Allon, son of Jedaiah, son of Shimri, son of Shemaiah.

[38]These were the names of some of the leaders of Simeon's wealthy clans. Their families grew, [39]and they traveled to the region of Gerar,* in the east part of the valley, seeking pastureland for their flocks. [40]They found lush pastures there, and the land was quiet and peaceful.

Some of Ham's descendants had been living in that region. [41]But during the reign of King Hezekiah of Judah, these leaders of Simeon invaded the region and completely destroyed* the homes of the descendants of Ham and of the Meunites. No trace of them remains today. They killed everyone who lived there and took the land for themselves, because they wanted its good pastureland for their flocks. [42]Five hundred of these invaders from the tribe of Simeon went to Mount Seir, led by Pelatiah, Neariah, Rephaiah, and Uzziel—all sons of Ishi. [43]They destroyed the few Amalekites who had survived, and they have lived there ever since.

2:6 As in many Hebrew manuscripts, some Greek manuscripts, and Syriac version (see also 1 Kgs 4:31); Hebrew reads *Dara.* **2:7a** Hebrew *Achar;* compare Josh 7:1. *Achar* means "disaster." **2:7b** The Hebrew term used here refers to the complete consecration of things or people to the LORD, either by destroying them or by giving them as an offering. **2:9** Hebrew *Kelubai,* a variant spelling of Caleb; compare 2:18. **2:11** As in Greek version (see also Ruth 4:21); Hebrew reads *Salma.* **2:18** Or *Caleb had a daughter named Jerioth from his wife, Azubah.*

The meaning of the Hebrew is uncertain. **2:19** Hebrew *Ephrath*, a variant spelling of Ephrathah; compare 2:50 and 4:4. **2:23** Or *captured Havvoth-jair.* **2:24** Or *the founder of;* also in 2:42, 45, 49. **2:42** Or *who founded Hebron.* The meaning of the Hebrew is uncertain. **2:55** Or *the founder of Beth-recab.* **3:5a** As in Syriac version (see also 14:4; 2 Sam 5:14); Hebrew reads *Shimea.* **3:5b** Hebrew *Bathshua*, a variant spelling of Bathsheba. **3:6a** As in some Hebrew and Greek manuscripts (see also 14:5-7 and 2 Sam 5:15); most Hebrew manuscripts read *Elishama.* **3:6b** Hebrew *Eliphelet;* compare parallel text at 14:5-7. **3:11** Hebrew *Joram*, a variant spelling of Jehoram. **3:12** Hebrew *Azariah*, a variant spelling of Uzziah. **3:15** Hebrew *Shallum*, another name for Jehoahaz. **3:16** Hebrew *The sons of Jehoiakim were his son Jeconiah* [a variant spelling of Jehoiachin] *and his son Zedekiah.* **3:17** Hebrew *Jeconiah*, a variant spelling of Jehoiachin. **4:3** As in Greek version; Hebrew reads *father of.* The meaning of the Hebrew is uncertain. **4:4** Or *the founder of;* also in 4:5, 12, 14, 17, 18, and perhaps other instances where the text reads *the father of.* **4:7** As in an alternate reading in the Masoretic Text (see also Latin Vulgate); the other alternate and the Greek version read *Zohar.* **4:9** *Jabez* sounds like a Hebrew word meaning "distress" or "pain." **4:13** As in some Greek manuscripts and Latin Vulgate; Hebrew lacks *and Meonothai.* **4:14** Or *Joab, the father of Ge-harashim.* **4:17** Or *Jether's wife became;* Hebrew reads *She became.* **4:24a** As in Syriac version (see also Gen 46:10; Exod 6:15); Hebrew reads *Nemuel.* **4:24b** As in parallel texts at Gen 46:10 and Exod 6:15; Hebrew reads *Zerah.* **4:33** As in some Greek manuscripts (see also Josh 19:8); Hebrew reads *Baal.* **4:39** As in Greek version; Hebrew reads *Gedor.* **4:41** The Hebrew term used here refers to the complete consecration of things or people to the LORD, either by destroying them or by giving them as an offering.

NOTES

2:24 ***in the town of Caleb-ephrathah, his wife Abijah.*** The LXX and Vulgate translate here that Caleb "went into" Ephrath (a euphemism for sexual intercourse; so Klein 2006:84). The comment here on Hezron's wife Abijah may have originally been in 2:21, where no name is given for Hezron's partner (Williamson 1982:53-54). On the other hand, it may have originally specified the unnamed wife of Jerahmeel in 2:25.

3:10-14 ***Rehoboam, Abijah, Asa . . . Josiah.*** In Hebrew these names are all divided by the phrase "his son," which is left untranslated in NLT (see introduction to 1 Chr 1–9, "Formula").

3:12 ***Uzziah.*** In Hebrew the name is Azariah (NLT mg), the name of this king in 2 Kgs 15 (see NLT mg for 2 Kgs 15:1); but he is called Uzziah in 2 Chr 26 and Isa 6, possibly reflecting the Chronicler's fixation with the prophetic tradition as the basis for his history (see comments on 29:26-30). In addition, the Chronicler's negative evaluation of Uzziah, emphasizing divine judgment that led to his skin disease and ultimate death, is reminiscent of Isaiah, who only speaks of Uzziah's death (see Isa 6:1).

3:15 ***Jehoahaz.*** The name Shallum appears in the Hebrew text (NLT mg). Jeremiah 22:10-12 (see NLT mg) informs us that Shallum was the name of the king who succeeded Josiah, but 2 Chr 36:2, 4 as well as 2 Kgs 23:30-34 call him Jehoahaz or Joahaz. This must be the same person.

3:16 ***The successors of Jehoiakim were his son Jehoiachin and his brother Zedekiah.*** See NLT mg. "Successors" here is literally "sons." Zedekiah here is identified as "his son," thus a reference to another son of Jehoiakim (and thus brother of Jehoiachin), rather than to the King Zedekiah mentioned in 3:15.

3:17 ***Jehoiachin.*** Lit., "Jeconiah," a variant of Jehoiachin, which reverses the elements in the name: Jehoiachin = "Yahweh (Jeho-) appoints (-iachin)" while Jeconiah/Coniah = "Appointed (Jecon-/Con-) of Yahweh (-iah)." In Jeremiah he is called Coniah or Jeconiah (see NLT mg for Jer 22:24; 24:1). In Kings he is always Jehoiachin (2 Kgs 24:6). Second Chronicles 36:8-9 has Jehoiachin, here Jeconiah. Such a name reversal is also evident for Ahaziah (2 Kgs 8:25; 2 Chr 22:1), who is also called Jehoahaz (see NLT mg for 2 Chr 21:17; COS 2.174).

3:21 ***Jeshaiah's son was . . . Rephaiah's son was. . . Arnan's son was. . . Obadiah's son was.*** In each case, the MT reads *bene* (the sons of). The NLT (along with the LXX) interprets the last four names in this verse as a linear genealogy, as though it read *beno* (his son). It is better to understand these four figures as additional sons of Hananiah.

4:1 ***Carmi.*** Scholars are nearly unanimous in recognizing the word "Carmi" as a scribal error for "Caleb" (Klein 2006:124; Knoppers 2004:337).

4:17 ***Ezrah.*** This is most likely the same name that appears at the end of the Zerah family list in 2:8; thus read here "Azariah." The two names share the same Hebrew consonants except one: *'zryh* (Azariah, 2:8), *'zrh* (Ezrah, 4:17), the difference being the *mater lectionis* Yodh. See commentary on 4:17-20.

4:29 ***Bilhah . . . Tolad.*** Bilhah is probably the same town as the Baalah of Josh 15:29 and Balah of Josh 19:3, and Tolad is an abbreviated form of Eltolad in Josh 15:30; 19:4.

4:30 ***Bethuel.*** This is Bethul in Josh 19:4 and possibly Kesil in Josh 15:30.

4:31 ***Beth-marcaboth, Hazar-susim, Beth-biri, and Shaaraim.*** Beth-marcaboth appears in Josh 19:5, but as Madmannah in Josh 15:31. Hazar-susim is called Hazar-susah in Josh 19:5. Beth-biri is probably the same as the town called Lebaoth in Josh 15:32 and Beth-lebaoth in Josh 19:6. Shaaraim is probably not the Shaaraim in Josh 15:36, but rather the Shilhim in Josh 15:32, which is Sharuhen in Josh 19:6.

4:40 ***the land was quiet and peaceful.*** The Hebrew text reads here "the land was broad of hands and quiet and peaceful." The phrase "broad of hands" refers to spaciousness (cf. Gen 34:21; Judg 18:10; Neh 7:4; Ps 104:25; Isa 22:18; 33:21) and can refer to a land, city, sea, or river.

COMMENTARY

Sources. The Chronicler drew heavily upon the biblical accounts of the history of Judah to create the genealogy of the tribe of Judah in chapters 2–4. Although the Chronicler incorporated lists from biblical sources (cf. 2:5 with Gen 46:12; 2:10-12 with Ruth 4:18-22; and 3:1-9 with 2 Sam 3:3-5; 5:13-16), at other places he has mined names and notes from biblical narratives (cf. 2:3-8 with Gen 38; 3:10-16 and 1–2 Kings), and at still others he has apparently gathered material from extra-biblical sources (2:34-41; 3:19-24). This has been shaped into a genealogy with a theological message. For the account of the tribe of Simeon, the Chronicler has transformed the list of clans in Numbers 26:12-14 to create his list of the sons of Simeon in 4:24 and has used Joshua 19:1-9 for his list of towns in 4:28-33.

Structure and Content. The structure of the genealogy of Judah in 2:3–4:23 has been a matter of some debate. Williamson argued for the following chiastic design for the genealogy (1979b:351-359):

- Sons of Judah and Bathshua: Er, Onan, Shelah (2:3)
  - Descendants of Perez and Zerah (2:4-9)
    - Descendants of Ram (as far as David) (2:10-17)
      - Descendants of Caleb (2:18-24)
        - Descendants of Jerahmeel (2:25-33)
        - Supplementary material on Jerahmeel (2:34-41)
      - Supplementary material on Caleb (2:42-55)
    - Supplementary material on Ram (David's descendants) (3:1-24)
  - Supplementary material on the descendants of Perez and Zerah (4:1-20)
- Descendants of Shelah, only surviving son of Judah and Bathshua (4:21-23)

In contrast, Japhet and Knoppers have suggested a different chiastic structure, one that has the genealogy of Judah (2:3-55; 4:1-23) framing that of David (3:1-24). For Japhet (1993:68), this shows that "the house of David dominates the centre" and for Knoppers (2004:356) that "If Levi is central to Israel, David is central to Judah."[1] For Knoppers the validity of this chiastic structure is seen in the following elements in chapters 2 and 4, which are inverted:

Sons of Judah (2:3-4)
  Ashhur (2:24)
    Sons of Hur (2:50-55)
      Haroeh [=Reaiah] (2:52)
        David's family (ch 3)
      Reaiah [=Haroeh] (4:2)
    Sons of Hur (4:4)
  Ashhur (4:5)
Shelah (4:21-23)

A closer look at the genealogy, however, reveals some difficulties with these two schemes. Williamson's structure highlights some important literary relationships but at the same time minimizes others. First, while it is true that 2:18-24 deals with the descendants of Caleb, it is quite clear that 2:21-23 is unrelated to Caleb and traces another liaison of his father Hezron. Second, the first section of 4:1-20 is clearly related to the material at the end of chapter 2 (2:42-55), as it traces genealogies and stories related to the Caleb-Ephrathah clans, which were broken off by the inclusion of the Davidic genealogy. It appears that 4:1 is a summary statement placed after the Davidic genealogy of chapter 3 to remind the reader of the earlier material found in chapter 2 and to set up the continuation of the Caleb-Ephrathah material in 4:1-10. Thus, Caleb-Ephrathah material can be discerned at three points in the Judah genealogy: 2:18-20, 24; 2:42-55; and 4:1-10. The scheme shared by Japhet and Knoppers simplifies matters considerably and takes into account the observations above. Nevertheless, it minimizes a connection that was wisely highlighted by Williamson, that is, the genealogy of Ram in 2:10-17 that was interrupted and then continued with the genealogy of David in 3:1-24. It also does not explain the absence of any mention of Jerahmeel's lineage in chapter 4 after so much coverage in chapter 2. I have expressed my concerns elsewhere over elaborate chiastic designs, and it appears that work on this passage is another case in point (Boda 1996:55-70). The following is my explanation of the overall structure and flow of the genealogy of Judah.

I. Three Sons of Judah with Bathshua: Er, Onan, Shelah (2:3)
  II. Two Sons of Judah with Tamar: Perez, Zerah (2:4-8)
    III. Descendants of Perez through Hezron (2:9–4:16)
      A. Descendants of Hezron: Ram to David (2:10-17)
      B. Descendants of Hezron: Caleb with Ephrathah through Hur to Bezalel (2:18-20)
      C. Descendants of Hezron with Makir's daughter (2:21-23)
      B. Descendants of Hezron: Caleb with Ephrathah through Ashhur to Tekoa (2:24)

D. Descendants of Hezron: Jerahmeel through Ram and Onam (2:25-33)
D. Descendants of Hezron: Jerahmeel through Onam from Sheshan to Elishama (2:34-41)
B. Descendants of Hezron: Caleb through Mesha (Ziph), Mareshah (Hebron), and with concubines Ephah, Jahdai, Maacah (2:42-50a)
B. Descendants of Hezron: Caleb with Ephrathah through Hur to Shobal to Haroeh, and to Salma (2:50b-55)
A. Descendants of Hezron: Ram (after David) (3:1-24)
B. Descendants of Hezron: Caleb with Ephrathah through Hur (4:1-16)

II. Descendants of Zerah (4:17-20)

I. Descendants of Shelah (4:21-23)

First, the writer appears to employ a bracketing technique around the entire genealogy of Judah to demarcate its limits, and it is this that has probably motivated past scholarship to search for more complicated chiastic patterns. The very first and last units in the genealogy comprise the first bracket: 2:3 and 4:21-23. First Chronicles 2:3 begins the genealogy of Judah with the story of Judah's liaison with the Canaanite Bathshua, a liaison that produced three sons, the first of whom Yahweh put to death for his wickedness (see Gen 38). The main focus of the genealogy will shift away from the offspring of Judah and Bathshua to those of Judah and Tamar (2:4–4:20), but eventually the genealogy of Judah will return to the offspring of Judah and Bathshua by recounting their only descendants, which are those through Shelah (4:21-23).

The second and penultimate units in the genealogy comprise the second bracket: 2:4-8 and 4:17-20. First Chronicles 2:4-8 identifies the result of the Judah-Tamar relationship: the birth of the twins Perez and Zerah. Nearly the whole genealogy of Judah traces the descendants of Perez (2:9–4:16), but as was the pattern in chapter 1, 2:4-9 presents multiple sons of a father (2:4), followed by a short account of the non-favored line (2:6-8), which is then set aside to trace the favored line (2:9–4:16).

It will be argued below that this short genealogy of Zerah's line resumes at the end of the genealogy of Judah (4:17-20), thus functioning in a similar way to that of Shelah, reinforcing the bracket around the genealogy of Judah. The family of Azariah, which closes off the Zerah lineage in 2:8, becomes the starting point (Ezrah) for the continuation of the Zerah line in 4:17.

The core passage is 2:9–4:16. Clearly the Chronicler identifies the favored line as that of Perez, who had two sons, Hezron and Hamul (2:5). Hezron, in turn, produced three sons (Jerahmeel, Ram, Caleb) who founded key families in Judah (2:9), which are the focus of 2:10–4:16. The literary structure of this Hezron core, however, is not arranged chiastically. Hezron's second-born son Ram is given first exposure in 2:10-17, ending with the family of Jesse and focusing on his son David. Next, the line of Hezron's third-born son Caleb is recounted in 2:18-20, ending with a focus on Caleb's descendants through his wife Ephrathah. At this point an unanticipated (see 2:9) account of Hezron's Makirite descendants intrudes into the Caleb genealogy, which then resumes at 2:24 with a focus on more of Caleb's descendants with his wife Ephrathah (see note on 2:24). Then, the line of Jerahmeel, Hezron's firstborn, is recounted in the two lists of 2:25-33 and 2:34-41. In 2:42-55 the Chronicler returns to the Caleb-Ephrathah line of Hur, which he left off in 2:18-20. The first section (2:42-50a) traces the roots of Caleb's line through unnamed wives and named concubines, while the second section (2:50b-55) traces the Caleb-Ephrathah roots of the founder of Kiriath-jearim (Shobal) and the founder of Bethlehem (Salma). The latter's descendants also lived in a town named Jabez. The continuation of the account of Caleb's line in 2:50b-55 is certainly found in 4:1-10, but the Chronicler has severed this account in two by inserting the royal line of David in chapter 3, which is a continuation of the account of Ram's descendants (which had reached a hiatus at the end of 2:10-17).

Japhet has explained these interruptions in the accounts of Hezron's sons in chapter 2 in the following way: "Each of these three branches is unfolded, probably until they attained the age of David. This is explicitly illustrated by the line of Ram, and the genealogies of Jerahmeel and Caleb were therefore bound to follow suit" (1993:73). Although this is certainly the case for the line of Ram, as Japhet notes, and possibly for Caleb's line, it is certainly not the case for Jerahmeel's line, which continues in the list in 2:34-41 until the time of the Judean exile (Elishama, 2:41). Japhet does, however, provide a helpful insight by highlighting the way in which David's line is inserted into the midst of the account of a family associated with the founding of the community from which David would arise, and this explains why the accounts of both Ram and Caleb-Ephrathah have been interrupted.

In 1 Samuel 17:12 David is identified as "the son of a man named Jesse, an Ephrathite from Bethlehem in the land of Judah," while in Ruth 1:2 David's ancestral family from Bethlehem is identified again as "Ephrathites from Bethlehem in the land of Judah." In Ruth 4:11 Bethlehem and Ephrathah are identified as the same location, and in Micah 5:2 [1] "Bethlehem Ephrathah" is identified as a clan within the tribe of Judah. By inserting David's genealogy into the middle of one for the Caleb-Ephrathah line of Hur, the Chronicler is highlighting a role played by the Hezron-Caleb line, that is, the founding not only of towns throughout Judah that would become the power base of the royal line of Judah, but also of the key town (Bethlehem), which would nurture the royal line itself until David would arise. The Chronicler then suspends the line of genealogy of David at Jesse until he recounts the line of Caleb-Ephrathah, which will found Bethlehem. This is emphasized by the Chronicler with the repeated references to "Bethlehem" on both sides of chapter 3 (2:51, 54; 4:4).

Therefore, the Judahite genealogies not only highlight the importance of the Davidic line but also depict how the other Judahite clans were key to the origins and survival of the royal line. Special attention appears to be given to the Caleb clans who founded the communities that fostered and protected the Davidic line (2:50b-55; 4:1-4) and to the Shelah clans who "worked for the king" (4:23). The shape of the genealogy may suggest in a literary way Judah's lineal and physical role of nurturing the Davidic line in the past, present, and future.

In the chiastic structure of the genealogy section in chapters 1–9, the genealogy of Judah in 2:3–4:20 matches the genealogy of Benjamin in 8:1-40, and the account of the northern tribes to the east of the Jordan in chapter 5 matches the account of the northern tribes to the west of the Jordan in chapter 7. However, it is difficult to know where the genealogy of the tribe of Simeon fits into this overall structure. On one hand, the Chronicler may be including Simeon among those non-Judah/Benjamin tribes, tracing these tribes in a counterclockwise movement that begins in southern Judah with Simeon (4:24-43), then moves to the Transjordan tribes to the northeast (ch 5) and ends with the Cisjordan tribes to the north (ch 7). On the other hand, the Chronicler may be attaching Simeon to the end of the Judahite account before he recounts the northern tribes.

Three pieces of evidence suggest the latter option. First, the location of this tribe is clearly in the southern region of Judah, as the list of towns makes clear (e.g., Beersheba, Ziklag). Second, 5:1-2 appears to function as a major literary break in the genealogy, isolating the Simeon list in 4:24-43 from the northern tribes in chapter 5. Third, Old Testament tradition suggests a close relationship between the tribes of Judah and Simeon. Joshua 18–19 describes the areas that were distributed to the Cisjordan tribes after those claimed by the Joseph tribes (Ephraim and Manasseh) and Judah. The first lot fell to Benjamin (Josh 18:11) and the second to Simeon (Josh 19:1), whose inheritance is described in the Hebrew text of Joshua 19:1 (cf. Josh 19:9) as "in the midst of the inheritance of the sons of Judah" (NLT, "surrounded by Judah's territory") and in Joshua 19:9 as, literally, "from the portion of the territory/portion of the sons of Judah," because Judah's territory was too large for them alone. In Judges 1:1-4, when Judah is chosen as the tribe who will attack the Canaanites first, Judah invites the tribe of Simeon to join them (cf. Judg 1:17). These lists and narratives in Joshua and Judges appear to be designed to explain Simeon's presence in what many would consider traditional Judahite territory. Simeon almost functions as a clan within Judah, although the Chronicler was well aware that Simeon was a legitimate tribe in the nation of Israel. It is also possible that the Chronicler was tracing with Joshua and Judges the fulfillment of the judgment on Simeon delivered in Jacob's prophecy in Genesis 49:5-7, that he would share the fate of Levi in being scattered among the tribes of Israel due to their violent reaction to the rape of Dinah in Genesis 34. The violent character of Simeon is described in the stories that close his account in 4:38-43.

Three sons of Judah with Bathshua: Er, Onan, Shelah (2:3). The Chronicler has drawn material from the book of Genesis for information about the sons of Judah and Bathshua. Genesis 38 recounts how Judah left his brothers and moved to Adullam, where he lived with a man named Hirah and ended up with a Canaanite wife who was the "daughter of Shua" (= Bath-Shua). In the Joseph novella this is a crisis for the family; not only is it odd for Judah to abandon his *beth 'ab* (the patriarchal family unit), but the disasters that befall him at Adullam reveal that liaisons with the Canaanites were dangerous (and illustrate why Isaac and Jacob were sent back to Aram to find wives from Abraham's clan). By inserting this account into the Joseph story, the narrator offers perspective on Joseph's suffering, suggesting that Joseph was preparing a place of safety where the family of Israel (Jacob) would be able to grow into the promised nation without risking amalgamation into the cursed line of Canaan (Gen 9:25-27). The Chronicler deemphasizes this danger by only citing the negative example of the death of Er and leaving out that of his brother Onan.[2] Er's wickedness and subsequent death provides an early example of the retribution theology espoused by the Chronicler throughout his narrative (see commentary on 2 Chr 7:12-22).

Descendants through the Judah-Bathshua relationship will soon be ignored, with the focus shifting to those of the Judah-Tamar relationship through Perez. However, the line of Shelah—the only surviving line of Judah and Bathshua—will reemerge at the conclusion of the genealogy of Judah in 4:21-23.

Two sons of Judah with Tamar: Perez, Zerah (2:4-8). The Chronicler's focus is on the descendants of Perez and Zerah, the twins produced from the relationship between Judah and Tamar. The Chronicler largely abandons the pattern established in chapter 1 for recounting the various lines of a family, a pattern that recounted last the line that would be traced further. In 2:5-9 Perez's sons Hezron and Hamul are mentioned first (2:5) before the account of Zerah's sons (2:6-8) is given.

Little is said at this point about Zerah's line except for one descendant through Zerah's firstborn, Zimri, (Achan) and one son through Zerah's second-born, Ethan, (Azariah). The reference in 2:7 to Achan (Josh 7), the one who caused Israel's defeat and death at Ai, accomplishes two things. First, it confirms the wisdom of the line's continuance through Perez rather than Zerah. Second, by associating the sinful action of *ma'al* [TH4603, ZH5085] (unfaithfulness) with Zerah's clan through Achan, the Chronicler was again foreshadowing one of his key themes throughout his narrative (on this word and theme, see further in commentary on 10:13-14). Nevertheless, that 4:17-20 picks up the Zerah account with the line of Azariah from 2:8 (Ezrah, 4:17) may suggest the importance of non-Perez clans within Judah.

With 2:9 the Chronicler brings the focus back to the line of Perez by listing his three sons, Jerahmeel, Ram, and Caleb. At first he will trace their lines in an order different from their birth order, beginning with Ram (2:10-17), then Caleb (2:18-20, 24), and finally Jerahmeel (2:25-41) before returning to Caleb (2:42-55), Ram (3:1-24), and Caleb (4:1-16).

Descendants of Hezron: Ram to David (2:10-17). Although listed as the second son of Hezron, Ram is given first exposure in a genealogy that traces a single line until it reaches the terminal family (Jesse), placing David's generation in the favored seventh position of the entire line after Ram:

Ram fathered: Amminadab
Amminadab fathered: Nahshon
Nahshon fathered: Salmon
Salmon fathered: Boaz
Boaz fathered: Obed
Obed fathered: Jesse
Jesse fathered: Eliab, Abinadab, Shimea, Nethanel, Raddai, Ozem, David, Zeruiah, Abishai, Joab, Asahel, Abigail, Amasa

In addition, the full panoply of Jesse's children is then related with David in the favored seventh position there as well,[3] stated by the Chronicler (explicitly) by counting from the beginning of the account of Jesse (2:13-15, among his brothers, Eliab, Abinadab, Shimea, Nethanel, Raddai, Ozem, David) but also ordered by the Chronicler (implicitly) by counting from the end of the Jesse account (2:16-17, among his sisters and their descendants: Amasa, Asahel, Joab, Abishai, Abigail, Zeruiah, David). By creating a linear genealogy in this way, the Chronicler highlights the roots of David but also his special character as the perfect choice from within the clan of Ram (seventh) and within the family of Jesse (seventh). By depicting the abundance of children in Jesse's family, the Chronicler was also suggesting abundance of human resources for the royal court. The identification of Zeruiah here as David's sister and thus his key military leaders (Joab, Abishai, and Asahel) as his nephews foreshadows David's glorious reign. However, the Chronicler also identifies Abigail as his sister, who with the Ishmaelite Jether bore Amasa. This same Amasa would lead Absalom's army in rebellion against David (2 Sam 17:25), suggesting that the Chronicler was alluding not only to the instability of the kingdom and the need to rely on Yahweh alone, but possibly also to the danger of certain foreign marriages.

Descendants of Hezron: Caleb with Ephrathah through Hur to Bezalel (2:18-20). Leaving the line of Hezron's son Ram for a moment (to be resumed with David at 3:1), the Chronicler begins the first of three accounts of the line of Hezron's third-born, Caleb (2:18-20, 24; 2:42-55; 4:1-15). The first account begins by tracing the children of Caleb's wife Azubah. The reference to "her" sons in 2:18b and to the death of Azubah in 2:19a suggests that Jerioth was a maidservant of Azubah (thus bearing children for her), though it is possible that this is a scribal addition. Azubah bore three sons (Jesher, Shobab, and Ardon), whose lines are not traced further. Instead, the Chronicler's focus shifts to Caleb's marriage to Ephrath, which produced Hur. Hur's line will be picked up in the later Caleb accounts at 2:50b-55 and 4:1-4. For now, however, the Chronicler traces the line of Hur through Uri to Bezalel, a contemporary of Moses who assisted in crafting the Tabernacle and its furniture (Exod 31:1-11; 35:30-31; 36:1-2). The figure of Bezalel lies behind the Chronicler's presentation of the building of the Temple (see commentary on 2 Chr 1:5), and thus his lineage needed to be included at this point.

Descendants of Hezron with Makir's daughter (2:21-23). First Chronicles 2:9 identifies only three sons for Hezron, and the lineage of these three sons structures all of the material in chapter 2 except 2:21-23. In these verses the reader learns that at sixty years old, Hezron married a woman of the family of Makir (grandson of Manasseh and father of Gilead; see Num 26:29; 36:1). They bore another son (Segub), who had influence in the region of Gilead. The phrase at the end of 2:23 ("all these were descendants of Makir, the father of Gilead") suggests that this account was not originally part of the Hezron genealogy upon which the Chronicler drew, while the references to "Makir (the father of Gilead)" in 2:21 and 2:23 represent a literary technique (resumptive repetition) that signals a short aside in an ancient text (Knoppers 2004:307). Evidence from another genealogy of Makir that appears in 7:14-19 suggests that the Transjordan Manasseh clan of Makir was matrilineal (see commentary there); thus children born to a Makirite wife of Hezron could legitimately be called "descendants of Makir, the father of Gilead." Makir's family will also intersect the other key tribe of Benjamin (see 7:12, 15), and since Judah and

Benjamin are the two tribes that survived the Exile, the Chronicler may be implying that a remnant of the great Joseph half-tribe of Manasseh had been preserved.

Descendants of Hezron: Caleb with Ephrathah through Ashhur to Tekoa (2:24). The addition of 2:21-23 by the Chronicler proved confusing to later scribes in their preservation of 2:24, which is the continuation of 2:18-20. The phrase "his wife Abijah" is most likely an editorial or scribal gloss that originally provided the identity of the unnamed daughter of Makir in 2:21 or the unnamed wife of Jerahmeel in 2:25. The verse should read: "After the death of Hezron, Caleb went into Ephrathah and she gave birth to a son named Ashhur (the father of Tekoa)."[4] The Chronicler continues to build the line of Caleb-Ephrathah, here identifying for the first time a connection to a key town in Judah (Tekoa) that lay ten miles south of Jerusalem (see 2 Chr 11:6). Judean towns will regularly appear in connection with Calebite families in the Chronicler's genealogy: Ziph (2:42; cf. Josh 15:55), Hebron (2:42; cf. Josh 15:54; 2 Sam 2:3), Beth-zur (2:45; cf. Josh 15:58; 2 Chr 11:7; Neh 3:16), Madmannah (2:49; cf. Josh 15:31), Gibea(h) (2:49; cf. Josh 15:57), Kiriath-jearim (2:50; cf. 13:6; Josh 15:9), Bethlehem (2:51), Beth-gader (2:51), Zorah and Eshtaol (2:53; cf. Josh 15:33), and Jabez (2:55).

Descendants of Hezron: Jerahmeel through Ram and Onam (2:25-33). As the account of Caleb (2:18-20, 24) interrupted the account of Ram (2:10-17), so now the account of Jerahmeel interrupts the account of Caleb. Although the line of Jerahmeel runs from 2:25 until 2:41, the phrase "these were all descendants of Jerahmeel" (2:33b; lit., "These were the sons of Jerahmeel") is a summarizing conclusion and identifies 2:34-41 as an independent (though related, as we will see) genealogy. This first list of Jerahmeel's family introduces the children of two wives: five sons through an unnamed wife (Ram, Bunah, Oren, Ozem, Ahijah) and one son through Jerahmeel's second wife Atarah (Onam). Only the eldest from the first wife is traced further and then only for one generation to Ram's three sons (Maaz, Jamin, Eker). It is the line of the second wife (Atarah) that becomes the enduring focus through Onam, whose line is recounted through a robust segmented genealogy.

Descendants of Hezron: Jerahmeel through Onam from Sheshan to Elishama (2:34-41). The second list of Jerahmeel's family builds on one of the lines of Onam (2:26), picking up with the figure Sheshan, who was listed in the favored seventh position from Jerahmeel and tenth position from Judah in 2:31 (Klein 2006:85, 100-101). There, oddly, the Chronicler noted that Sheshan had a descendant (lit., "son") named Ahlai, and yet 2:34 makes the clear statement that Sheshan had "no sons." Most likely Ahlai was the daughter given to his Egyptian servant Jarha (2:35), a view bolstered by the claim in 11:41 that Zabad (see 2:36) was a descendant of Ahlai.[5] The practice of giving a daughter to a slave seems to combine emergency customs in a patriarchal society for tracing inheritance through servants (Gen 15:2-4) with emergency customs for tracing inheritance through daughters (Num 27; Josh 17).[6] The line of Sheshan is then traced for 14 generations to Elishama.

Although the length of Elishama's pedigree is bested only by those of David (3:1-24), Levi (6:1-15), and Saul (8:29-40; 9:35-44), his identity still remains a mystery. Counting generations, he probably lived at the time Jerusalem fell to the Babylonians (587/6 BC); some have identified him as the son of "Jekamiah the son of Meshullam," whose bullae dates from this period (Klein 2006:101).[7] As the Chronicler does not seem to mind intermarriage with foreigners, it does not appear that this genealogy, which relies on the intervention of an Egyptian slave, was meant to disqualify or discredit this family. Its length suggests the opposite and possibly recognizes a major Jerahmeelite family that survived the Exile.

Descendants of Hezron: Caleb through Mesha (Ziph), Mareshah (Hebron), and with concubines Ephah, Jahdai, Maacah (2:42-50a). First Chronicles 2:42 returns to the account of Hezron's son Caleb, which was broken off at 2:24. It takes into account the intervening genealogy of Jerahmeel (2:25-41) with its identification of Caleb as the "brother of Jerahmeel" (2:42). Like the Jerahmeel section in 2:25-41, the account is divided into two distinct parts by the identical summarizing conclusion in 2:50a: "These were all descendants of Caleb."[8] This is confirmed by the fact that 2:50b-55 is connected to the earlier Caleb genealogy (2:18-20, 24), while 2:42-50a is unconnected.

This list traces the origins of many key towns in Judah to the clan of Caleb. Caleb's partners in the case of the towns of Ziph and Hebron are not identified, but the rest of the towns are associated with concubines. This may suggest greater status for the towns associated with Hezron's wife Ephrathah, which will be traced in the following section.

Descendants of Hezron: Caleb with Ephrathah through Hur to Shobal to Haroeh, and to Salma (2:50b-55). First Chronicles 2:50b returns to the genealogy of Hur (son of Caleb and Ephrathah), which began in 2:19-20. There Hur's line was traced to the Tabernacle artisan Bezalel, foreshadowing the role the tribe of Judah would continue to play in the construction of holy space in the Chronicler's account (see commentary on 2 Chr 1). In this list, however, the Chronicler focuses on the role played by the family of Caleb and Ephrathah in the rise of Judahite royalty. The list traces the line of Hur to Shobal (who founded Kiriath-jearim), to Salma (who founded Bethlehem), and to Hareph (who founded Beth-gader). Since the latter town (Beth-gader) does not figure in the traditions of Israel, it is not surprising that Hareph's line is traced no further. The two other towns were key to the emergence of David. The first, Kiriath-jearim, is the town from which David brought the Ark to Jerusalem (13:6; cf. 2 Sam 6:2), while the second, Bethlehem, was his hometown (11:16-26; cf. 1 Sam 16). Here passing reference is made to the presence of scribal families of the descendants of Salma in the city of Jabez, a name that will reappear after the account of David's family (4:9-10).

Descendants of Hezron: Ram (after David) (3:1-24). With 3:1 the Chronicler returns to the genealogy of Ram, which had been on a hiatus since 2:17, and begins to trace the longest genealogy in Scripture (Knoppers 2004:331). In 2:10-17, the Chronicler traced a single line of Ram until it reached the family of Jesse, with his descendants as the honored seventh generation after Ram. Then the many male descendants of Jesse were listed with David in their midst. By leaving out one of Jesse's sons, the Chronicler reveals his intention to place David in the honored seventh position, both explicitly from the beginning of the list (with ordinal numbers to reinforce this position) and implicitly from the end (taking into account the names of David's two sisters and their four sons).

The continuing list of the Ram clan employs similar rhetorical technique. Now the family of the favored son, David, is traced. At first sight the list of sons appears to be structured into two groups, first the list of sons who were born in Hebron (3:1-4; see the summaries bracketing the section in 3:1a and 4a), then the list of sons born to his wives in Jerusalem followed by a note on his daughter Tamar (3:5-9; see the summaries bracketing the section in 3:4b-5a and 9a). The sons born in Jerusalem are subdivided further with those born to Bathsheba (3:5b) distinguished from "other sons" (3:6-8). This surface structure is based on the sources from which the Chronicler gathered these names, with the list in 3:1-3 drawn from 2 Samuel 3:2-5 and the list in 3:5-8 from 2 Samuel 5:13-16.[9] Two changes, however, to the second list reveal the Chronicler's purpose. First, the list in 2 Samuel 5:13-16 does not distinguish the sons born to Bathsheba, and second, the Chronicler expanded the list by two names. The result of these two changes is that Solomon now appears precisely at a seam in the surface structure, and in the overall scheme of the "sons of David" he appears now in the honored tenth spot (3:5). The Chronicler has given both David and Solomon special status within their immediate families in order to prepare the reader for the narrative account in which David and Solomon together will establish the dynasty, build the Temple, and institute its worship:

> Sons of **David**: Amnon, Daniel, Absalom, Adonijah, Shephatiah, Ithream, Shammua, Shobab, Nathan, **Solomon**, Ibhar, Elishua, Elpelet, Nogah, Nepheg, Japhia, Elishama, Eliada, Eliphelet.

One should not miss the appearance of the names of two women in this Davidic genealogy, that of Bathshua in 3:5 (NLT, "Bathsheba"; see NLT mg) and Tamar in 3:9. The inclusion of these names in David's genealogy strengthens the bond between David and his tribal founder, Judah, whose two wives are identified as Bathshua and Tamar (2:3-4). This technique, which at times involves the slight revision of names to strengthen the connection, will be employed by the Chronicler in his narrative presentation to link David and Solomon to the wilderness generation (see 22:6-16; 2 Chr 1–2). Here it is used to link David and Solomon to the patriarchal generation.

The list of Ram's clan that follows Solomon until Josiah (the next rhetorical break with "the sons of," 3:15) returns to the same pattern that preceded David in the first list of Ram in 2:10-12 by tracing a single line—that is, the illustrious royal succession that will be the focus of the Chronicler's narrative in chapter 10—2 Chronicles 35. Not surprisingly, the Chronicler leaves out the notorious Athaliah, who was neither a legitimate monarch nor a Davidic descendant (see 2 Chr 22:10–23:15).

The linear pattern found in 3:10-14, however, is broken at 3:15 with the introductory phrase "the sons of Josiah," which initiates a genealogical pattern that will structure the remainder of the list. Although the list from this point on will include individuals who reigned on Judah's throne after Josiah (Jehoahaz, Jehoiakim, Jehoiachin, Zedekiah), it is not presented as following the order of their reigns as was the case from Solomon to Josiah. Additionally, an individual called Johanan (identified as the firstborn of Josiah) is named first, yet he did not reign in Judah, creating a break in the list of monarchs that began with Solomon. For every generation following Josiah (except one Shemaiah, son of Shecaniah, 3:22), a list of multiple (at least two and sometimes up to seven) potential heirs is provided for each generation before the son of the chosen potential heir is then identified to carry the line to the next generation.

Son of **Solomon**: **Rehoboam** (3:10)
Abijah: his son
Asa: his son
Jehoshaphat: his son
Joram (NLT, Jehoram): his son
Ahaziah: his son
Joash: his son
Amaziah: his son
Azariah (NLT, Uzziah): his son
Jotham: his son
Ahaz: his son
Hezekiah: his son
Manasseh: his son
Amon: his son
Josiah: his son (3:14)
Sons of **Josiah**: Johanan, **Jehoiakim**, Zedekiah, Shallum (NLT, Jehoahaz)
Sons of **Jehoiakim**: **Jehoiachin** his son, Zedekiah his son
Sons of **Jehoiachin**: Shealtiel his son, Malkiram, **Pedaiah**, Shenazzar, Jekamiah, Hoshama, Nedabiah
Sons of **Pedaiah**: **Zerubbabel**, Shimei
Son (so MT) of **Zerubbabel**: Meshullam, **Hananiah**, Shelomith (daughter), Hashubah, Ohel, Berekiah, Hasadiah, Jushab-hesed
Son (so MT) of **Hananiah**: Pelatiah, Jeshaiah, sons of Rephaiah, sons of Arnan, sons of Obadiah, sons of **Shecaniah** (see note on 3:21)
Sons of **Shecaniah**: **Shemaiah**
Sons of **Shemaiah**: Hattush, Igal, Bariah, **Neariah**, Shaphat
Son (so MT) of **Neariah**: **Elioenai**, Hizkiah, Azrikam
Sons of **Elioenai**: Hodaviah, Eliashib, Pelaiah, Akkub, Johanan, Delaiah, Anani (3:24)

There is some debate over the list in 3:15-16. The name Johanan, which appears at the head of the list of Josiah's sons in 3:15, is unique to the Chronicler and is considered by many to be a firstborn son who was outlived by his father Josiah. The rest of the names in 3:15, however, do not follow birth order (Jehoiakim, Jehoahaz/Shallum, Zedekiah) or reign order (Jehoahaz/Shallum, Jehoiakim, Zedekiah). Some have suggested a complicated text-critical solution in which Johanan replaced two variants of Jehoahaz/Shallum at the beginning of the list and that this replacement pushed Shallum to the end of the verse. However, in keeping with classic text-critical reasoning, the more difficult reading in the present text is to be preferred and may be explained by the Chronicler's agenda to heighten the line of Jehoiakim-Jehoiachin over those of Zedekiah and Jehoahaz/Shallum. In 3:16 the NLT translates "sons of" as "successors of" and calls Zedekiah "his brother" rather than "his son" as it appears in the Hebrew text (see NLT mg). This translation suggests that the Zedekiah in 3:16 is Jehoiakim's brother Zedekiah, already listed in 3:15. However, the Chronicler identifies a son of Jehoiakim and brother of Jehoiachin whose name was Zedekiah (to name a son after a brother would not be an oddity, see 2:9, 25). This would follow the dominant pattern from 3:15-24 to identify a favored individual from a multiple list of potential heirs.

Archaeological work on Nebuchadnezzar's palace in Babylon has unearthed a tablet that records the rations provided for Jehoiachin (Ia-'-ú-kin below) and his sons while in exile in Babylon (cf. 2 Kgs 25:27-30).

> . . . t[o?] *Ia-'-ú-kin,* king . . .
>
> . . .
>
> 10 (*sila* of oil) to . . . [*Ia*]-'-*kin,* king of *Ia*[. . .]
> 2 ½ *sila* (oil) to [. . . so]ns of the king of Judah (*Ia-a-hu-du*)
> 4 *sila* to 8 men from Judah (*amel Ia-a-hu-da-a-a*)
> . . .
> 10 (*sila*) to *Ia-ku-ú-ki-nu,* the son of the king of *Ia-ku-du* (i.e., Judah)
> 2 ½ *sila* for the 5 sons of the king of Judah (*Ia-ku-du*) through Qana'a
> (ANET 308)

This confirms that Jehoiachin did enjoy a large number of progeny to carry on the Davidic line, but there has been significant debate over the identity and significance of these sons. First of all, some have identified the Shenazzar of 3:18 with the Sheshbazzar called a "governor of Judah," who led the first return to the land at the beginning of the Persian period (see Ezra 1:1-11; 5:13-16),[10] but most scholars have rejected this view because of the difficulty of equating these names.[11] Second, although the Chronicler places Shealtiel among Jehoiachin's sons in first position and highlights Shealtiel as his son (3:17-18), according to the Chronicler the line continues through Pedaiah, Jehoiachin's third son in the list (3:18), and then through Zerubbabel, who is identified as the first son of Pedaiah (3:19). While it is not that odd for someone other than the firstborn to carry on the line (as was true in the case of David, Solomon, Jehoiakim, Hananiah, and Neariah), it is odd that elsewhere in the Old Testament Zerubbabel is always identified as the son of Shealtiel (Ezra 3:2, 8; Neh 12:1; Hag 1:1, 12, 14; 2:2, 23). Although certainty is impossible to attain based on the present evidence, this anomaly has been explained by appeals to premature deaths of Shealtiel and Malkiram and subsequent clan reorganization through the promotion of Pedaiah and/or the practice of levirate marriage (Deut 25:5-10; cf. Gen 38; Ruth 4). In this way Zerubbabel was linked legitimately to both Shealtiel and Pedaiah.

Jehoiachin is given special status with the additional remark that he was "captive" (NLT, "who was taken prisoner by the Babylonians"). So also his grandson Zerubbabel is emphasized in the list by identifying his two key sons followed by their sister and then an additional list of five "other sons," the latter group possibly being those born after his return to the land (3:19-20). This description links him closely with his ancestor David, who in 3:1-9 is presented as having two groups of sons as well as a daughter. While Zerubbabel's name (meaning "seed of Babel") reflects the conditions of exile, Klein (2006:121) argues that the names of Zerubbabel's children signal the new day of restoration: Meshullam (meaning "recompensed" or "restored"), Hananiah (Yahweh is gracious), Shelomith (peace), Hashubah (consideration), Ohel (tent [of Yahweh]), Berekiah (Yahweh has blessed), Hasadiah (Yahweh has shown loyalty), Jushab-hesed (let covenant loyalty be restored).

While biblical texts from the early Persian period attest to the rule of Zerubbabel as governor of the Persian province of Yehud (Hag 1:1, 12, 14; 2:2, 21, 23; cf. Ezra 3:2, 8; Zech 4:6b-10a), there is no evidence that any of his sons listed in 3:19-20 followed him. Instead, archaeological evidence suggests that Zerubbabel was succeeded by his son-in-law Elnathan, who had married Zerubbabel's daughter Shelomith (see 3:19), thereby extending a leadership role for the Davidic line until around 490 BC.[12] After that there is no more evidence of a Davidic governor in the province of Yehud, even though Hattush (3:22) participated in the return of Ezra in 458 BC (Ezra 8:2).[13]

What was the Chronicler's purpose in shaping the final section of the genealogy in this way? First, the shift of the genealogical structure after Josiah suggests that the lists in 3:15-16 are seen by the Chronicler as having more in common with those in 3:17-24 than with the monarchs in 3:10-14. Through this the Chronicler may be implying that the death of Josiah brought an end to the kingdom of Judah. This appears to be borne out in his account of this era in the history of the kingdom in 2 Chronicles 35–36. Josiah was the only king who broke the pattern of a single offspring assuming the throne and then passing the throne on to one of his own sons; instead, three of his sons ascended the throne. Beginning with Josiah's sons, the Chronicler highlights the power of foreign emperors to enthrone and depose the kings of Judah (2 Chr 36:4-13); for all intents and purposes the kingdom had lost its independence and had become a vassal state within the Babylonian Empire. Beginning with that fateful encounter between Josiah and Pharaoh Neco in 2 Chronicles 35:20-23, the Chronicler depicts foreign emperors speaking (2 Chr 35:20-23; 36:22-23) and acting (2 Chr 36:5-6, 9-10, 12-13, 16-17) in accord with Yahweh's will (see Boda 2009b).

Second, the concern to trace only one individual's sons for the successive generation reveals that this genealogy has more in common with the linear genealogy that preceded it than with the segmented genealogies seen elsewhere in chapters 1–8.[14] In particular this pattern of listing multiple potential heirs and then identifying the favored individual is found in the Ram list in the two key generations of David (2:13-17) and Solomon (3:1-9), the two individuals who will figure so strongly in the Chronicler's account. This suggests that the list is designed to show the enduring and robust potential of the favored line to bring forth a royal line. Knoppers (2004:335) suggests this when he writes that the genealogy from 3:19b-24 is "hardly a neutral accounting of the progress of David's seed. It argues for a particular line of succession within the Davidic house (from Zerubbabel to Elioenai)."[15]

If the Chronicler was uninterested in the fulfillment of the promise of a royal heir and was interested merely in showing the great blessing on the Davidic line, he would have been better served by a segmented genealogy that traced various Davidic clans. The special designation in 3:17 of Jehoiachin as "the captive" (NLT, "who was taken prisoner by the Babylonians") emphasizes that it is his line that will carry forward the Davidic hope after the debacle of the fall of Judah and Jerusalem. This foreshadows the Chronicler's account in 2 Chronicles 36, where the fates of Jehoiakim and Jehoiachin are carefully traced to Babylon along with the Temple treasures (2 Chr 36:4-10), while Zedekiah's fate is completely ignored (2 Chr 36:13-20; cf. 2 Kgs 25:1-7).

The genealogy in chapter 3 probably extends into the late fifth century BC, if not beyond. If Zerubbabel was born in approximately 575 BC, counting 20 years for each generation from that point would place the birth of the generation of Anani (3:24) in approximately 455 BC. This date would confirm the evidence of the Elephantine papyri, which are dated to 407 BC and mention the name of Anani, who would have been 48 years old at that time (Klein 2006:113; COS 3.48).[16] It is interesting that the final individual in the list is this Anani and that he is in the honored seventh position among the sons of Elioenai, the same position held by his ancestor David in Jesse's family. This may suggest that great hopes were attached to this Davidic descendant at the time the list was composed.[17]

Descendants of Hezron: Caleb with Ephrathah through Hur (4:1-16). First Chronicles 4:1 functions as a summary statement orienting the reader to the resumption of the account of the family of Hur son of Caleb (see note on 4:1) son of Hezron son of Perez son of Judah,[18] an account that is interrupted by David's genealogy at the beginning of chapter 3.[19] It must be admitted that there is much uncertainty as to the lineal identity of much of 4:2-23, what Klein (2006:86) calls "genealogical fragments" and Knoppers (2004:344) calls "a collection of miscellaneous genealogies." Nevertheless, some connections can be made with a reasonable level of certainty. First, it is quite certain that 4:2-4 contains genealogies that continue to trace the line of Caleb-Ephrathah through Hur, especially since it begins with a reference to "Shobal" (4:2)[20] and ends with the summary conclusion "these were the descendants of Hur (the firstborn of Ephrathah), the ancestor of Bethlehem" (4:4b). Second, the list in 4:5-8 begins with "Ashhur (the father of Tekoa)" whose name came at the conclusion of the Caleb-Ephrathah account in 2:24 (see commentary above). Third, the account of Jabez is probably recounted because of the presence of descendants of Salma (Hur's son) in the town of Jabez (2:54-55).

The account of Jabez continues the trend seen already in the genealogy: It foreshadows theological points that the Chronicler will develop more fully in his narratives in chapter 10—2 Chronicles 36. This story about the namesake of the town Jabez is based on a play between the name Jabez and the Hebrew word *'atsab* (which actually reverses the second and third letters). The story shows how someone whose name means "he causes pain," and thus has a destiny of pain, experienced the very opposite in his life by being "more honorable than any of his brothers" (4:9). It was due to his prayer to the God of Israel both for the positive blessings of territorial expansion and divine active presence (lit., "may your hand be with me") and for the negative blessing of preservation from all trouble and pain. This foreshadows a strong emphasis in the Chronicler on prayer as a sign of human covenant fidelity and blessing. Such a prayer would have been significant for those living within the limited space of the Chronicler's Jewish province.

While 4:1-10 contains clear connections to the earlier Caleb lists in chapter 2, the next section (4:11-16) betrays none. Nevertheless, the fact that the name "Caleb" appears throughout 4:11-15 and "Ziph" appears in 4:16 probably indicates that the Chronicler was suggesting some familial connection. The Caleb, for instance, in 4:15 is the Caleb of the Exodus and Conquest generations, the spy from Judah who brought back a "good report" with Joshua (Num 13:6, 30; 14:6, 30, 38; 26:65; 34:19; Deut 1:36), who was given the city of Hebron in conquest (Josh 14:13-14; 15:13; 21:12). That this Caleb had a daughter named Acsah (Josh 15:16-17) and that Caleb son of Hezron had a daughter named Acsah (2:49) suggests not necessarily that they should be equated, but rather that there is a familial connection. By extension, then, Kenaz, who was the brother of Caleb (Josh 15:17), would be included in this family. Possibly also the Kelub of 4:11-12 was of the same clan and family as Ziph in 4:16 (cf. 2:42).

Descendants of Zerah (4:17-20). Since the beginning of the account of Shelah's descendants is clearly indicated in 4:21, and the accounts in 4:1-16 appear to be connected with the Perez-Hezron-Caleb group, the individuals in 4:17-20 are most likely related to families in other Perez-Hezron clans (Jerahmeel, Ram) or to families in the Perez-Zerah family, which was quickly covered in 2:6-8. It is improbable that these families are related to the Jerahmeel or Ram clans because the earlier accounts of both of those clans appear to be brought to closure by tracing an individual line into the exile of Judah (Jerahmeel's to Elishama in 2:25-41 and Ram's to Anani in 3:1-24). Additionally, the name "Ezrah" (*'ezrah*), which introduces the lists in 4:17-20, is strikingly similar to the name "Azariah" (*'azaryah*), which concluded the genealogy of Zerah's descendants in 2:8. The form of the name "Ezrah" here is unique in the Old Testament; elsewhere the final letter for this name would be the letter Aleph rather than the letter He (cf. Ezra 7:1, *'ezra'*). This may be evidence that the name in both cases was originally Azariah and that the letter Yodh (y) has dropped out of 4:17.

Descendants of Shelah (4:21-23). While 4:17-20 probably recounts the line of Zerah, returning to the non-favored line introduced briefly near the beginning of the genealogy of Judah in 2:6-8, now 4:21-23 recounts the line of Shelah, the non-favored line introduced briefly at the very outset of the genealogy of Judah in 2:3 and ignored for the rest of the account of Judah. Shelah is the only surviving member of Judah's family with Bathshua, his brothers Er and Onan having died before bearing a child through Tamar (Gen 38).

Shelah's first offspring is a boy named Er, suggesting the ultimate fulfillment by Judah of the levirate customs he had withheld from his eldest son Er (Gen 38:9). The final verse describes how descendants of Shelah "worked for the king" (4:23b). This final section may be designed by the Chronicler to bolster the reputation of the Shelah clan by showing how Shelah fulfilled his responsibility to his brother and also how his descendants were supportive of the Davidic royal house.

Descendants of Simeon (4:24-43). Before moving on to the first of two sections on the northern tribes (ch 5 on the Transjordan tribes and ch 7 on the Cisjordan tribes), the Chronicler first recounts the descendants of Simeon, who were considered within the orbit of the tribe of Judah. This section contains a significant amount of extranominal (non-name) material, possibly because the genealogical source material was sparse for this tribe.

The genealogy begins by listing eight generations of Simeon's tribe (see the list below that follows the Hebrew text, contra NLT), only listing multiple children within the first and last generations. For the first generation, see the lists in Genesis 46:10; Exodus 6:15; and Numbers 26:12-14. Shimei's children form the final generation. He was obviously greatly blessed with so many children and so is placed in the seventh generation from Simeon.

Sons of **Simeon**: Jemuel, Jamin, Jarib, Zohar, **Shaul** [Most likely Shallum is the son of Shaul (Klein 2006:146-147).]
Shallum, his son
Mibsam, his son
Mishma, his son
Sons of Mishma: Hammuel, his son
Zaccur, his son
Shimei, his son
Sons of **Shimei**: sixteen sons and six daughters

No names are recorded for the final generation, however, possibly due to lack of information, but possibly also due to the Chronicler's intent to minimize the line of Simeon, especially in light of the two statements that follow: "But none of his brothers had large families. So Simeon's tribe never grew as large as the tribe of Judah" (4:27b). This comment appears to be an attempt by the Chronicler to address any misconceptions about Judah's abundance in Joshua 19:9: "Their allocation of land came from part of what had been given to Judah because Judah's territory was too large for them." Simeon functions then as a foil against which the blessing of Judah may be seen more brilliantly.

The account of Simeon continues in 4:28-33 with a list of the towns inhabited by Simeon's descendants. These towns are all in the southern portion of Judah and are those listed in Joshua 19:1-9 as given to Simeon from Judahite territory (cf. Josh 15:26-32). Nehemiah 11:26-29 identifies Moladah, Hazar-shual, Beersheba, Ziklag, and En-rimmon as places where exilic returnees settled in the land in the Persian period. At the end of this list of towns the Chronicler includes the note: "These towns were under their control until the time of King David" (4:31), another instance which pictures Simeon functioning as a foil for the tribe of Judah, this time for the rise of David, who assumes control over the Simeonite towns. These allusions to Simeon within Judah and under David may be the Chronicler's attempt to show the fulfillment of Jacob's "blessing/curse" in Genesis 49:7—that is, that he "will scatter them among the descendants of Jacob . . . disperse them throughout Israel." The Chronicler stresses that Simeon did not enjoy control over its own tribal lands, as did the other tribes.

A further list of Simeonite names is provided in 4:34-37,[21] a list that is identified in 4:38 as "the names of some of the leaders" of the clans within Simeon and that introduces a lengthy extranominal note that closes off the account (4:38-43). These descendants are seen as enjoying great success as "the house of their fathers exploded greatly" (NLT, "their families grew"), a verb that is used in relation to an explosion of human population (Gen 28:14; Exod 1:12; 2 Chr 11:23; Isa 54:3; Hos 4:10) as well as of material wealth (Gen 30:30, 43; Job 1:10). Here both nuances are probably applicable: An expanding population was accompanied by expanding wealth (i.e., flocks, 4:39, 41) and thus led to the need for the tribe to find more land. In 4:39 we are told that they found lush and peaceful land in the region of what the Hebrew tradition calls Gedor and the Greek tradition calls Gerar. Gerar is between Beersheba and Gaza in the south of Judah, while Gedor is in the hill country of Judah (Josh 15:58). The Chronicler then shows how Simeon eradicated Hamites and Meunites who were in that region during the time of Hezekiah (probably related to Hezekiah's exploits in 2 Kgs 18:5-8). The form of this story in 4:39-41 is strikingly similar to that of the Danites who abandoned their tribal territory in the south (Judg 18), trekked north, conquered unsuspecting Laish, and settled down. In both accounts the land is "broad of hands" (4:40; Judg 18:10) and is "quiet" (see note on 4:40; Judg 18:7, 27).

The final story connected with Simeon (4:42-43) takes a significant group of these Simeonites into Edomite territory (Mount Seir), where they again attacked an ancient people group (Amalekites) and eradicated them from the land.[22] As the first section of Simeon's account (4:24-33) may represent an allusion by the Chronicler to Jacob's "blessing/curse" in Genesis 49:7, the same may be true for this second section (4:34-43). The reason that Simeon did not enjoy control over their own tribal lands is based in Genesis 49 on their violent cruelty (Gen 49:5-7). The final statement ("they have lived there ever since") suggests that the Chronicler was claiming that the Simeonite tribe did survive and had settled in the region of Mount Seir.[23]

Significance. The overall scheme of the genealogy of Judah in chapters 2–4 clearly identifies David as the key figure and his family as the key line for the tribe. The structure of the Davidic genealogy suggests enduring potential for the royal line, highlighting abundant progeny and tracing the elect line into the time of the Chronicler.

Caleb's family is important because it provides the infrastructure for the development of the towns of Judah, especially the towns that would house and support David's family line in the beginning. Thus, Ram in many ways is reliant on the Caleb clans, and David will emerge out of this group. By placing David in the middle of the Caleb/Shobal/Salma/Ashhur account (2:42-55; 4:1-8), the Chronicler shows the supportive role of these other clans.

There is a redemptive quality to this genealogy because it ends with the family of Shelah, showing that even Canaanite liaisons could be redeemed. The same is true for the Chronicler's presentation of the Zerah lines (if they indeed form an inclusion around the genealogy), showing that the Shelah and Zerah clans were still important within Judah. They played a supporting role to the Hezron clans, which produced the royal line (see 4:23).

Within the overall scheme of chapters 1–9 Judah is clearly given precedence by coming first and having the longest genealogy. This is confirmed by the note at 5:1-2 that says that while Joseph received the birthright from Reuben, Judah received the power. The Judah genealogy showcases the key tribe that will emerge from the pain of exile and carry on the promises given to the patriarchs. The identity of Judah is clearly linked to the royal line; in this the tribe is essential to the enduring royal hope within the postexilic community. For the New Testament community this royal hope finds its fulfillment in Jesus, whose lineage is carefully delineated at the outset of the Gospel of Matthew.

The beginning of the Judah genealogy brings to mind the horrendous stories found in Genesis 38, a chapter that relates the near extinction of the line of Judah. Through this, members of the tribe of Judah were reminded of God's grace to redeem their line. It is significant that from this line with such a dubious past Yahweh would raise a royal line to bring the blessing of Abraham to the entire world.

ENDNOTES

1. Cf. Knoppers 2001:35-50. Interestingly, Klein (2006:87, 142) embraces the views of both Williamson and Knoppers.
2. The Chronicler does not express concern in most cases over foreign elements within Israel (Japhet 1993:74). This is the first of six instances where intermarriages are recorded (or implied) without criticism (2:3, 17, 34-35; 3:2; 4:17, 22).
3. Although in 1 Sam 16 we are told there are eight sons, here one is left out to accentuate David.
4. See Klein 2006:82; Williamson 1979b:355.
5. See ABD 1.123.
6. Klein (2006:100-101) notes that in the slave laws of Lev 25, children from an Israelite slave remain with the Israelite slave, while children from a foreign slave are the property of the master.
7. Meshullam is interchangeable with Shallum.
8. This suggests that the list of Jerahmeel in 2:25-33 and the list of Caleb in 2:42-50a were taken from the same source by the Chronicler.
9. The Chronicler found Solomon in the fourth position in his source in 2 Sam 5:13-16. This is odd in that Solomon appears to have been the first son born to David and Bathsheba after that ill-fated child conceived in their tryst (2 Sam 12:13-25). Kalimi (2005a:87-88) suggests a principle by which the fourth position was identified as favored.
10. See, for example, Sacchi 2000:60.
11. See Klein 2006:120; Knoppers 2004:327-328.
12. Cf. Avigad 1976:11, 22; Boda 2003c:277-291; Meyers 1985:33*-38*.
13. Giving 20 years for each generation with Zerubbabel's birth in 575 would result in the following birth years: Hananiah in 555 (3:19), Shecaniah in 535 (3:21), Shemaiah in 515 (3:22), Neariah in 495 (3:22), Elioenai in 495 (3:23), and then Anani in 455 (3:24); see Klein (2006:113). Hattush, who was in Neariah's generation, would then be around 35 years old in 458 BC when Ezra returned. For discussion of this issue see further Klein 2006:121 and Knoppers 2003:322-323.
14. Contra Klein (2006:123), who calls this a segmented genealogy, which for him "makes it unlikely it was preserved with hope of the restoration of the Davidic throne."
15. Contra Klein 2006:112, 123. Klein stresses with Willi the uninterrupted inhabitation of Jerusalem by the Davidic family, as does Kalimi (2005a:85-89), who claims "It seems, however, that the Chronicler's main purpose was to depict Jerusalem as the ultimate and almost continual residential city of David's descendants." If the Chronicler wanted to emphasize this he could have made more of the name of the city in the list.
16. Knoppers (2004:322, 330) suggests this last generation should be placed around 426 BC if following the MT, but if following the LXX (which reads 3:21 as a linear genealogy, rather than as the sons of a single family; so also NLT), then 346 BC. Japhet (1993:94) suggests a range of 460–320 BC.

17. Knoppers (2004:332-333) highlights the messianic interpretation of the Targums in which Anani is linked to the Hebrew word for clouds in order to suggest a figure originating in the heavens and the appropriation of this list in NT genealogies of Jesus (Matt 1:1-7; Luke 3:23-28). See also Selman 1994a:99-101.
18. Chapter 2 covers the family units mentioned in 4:1 in this order: Judah (2:3-55); Perez (2:4-5, 9-55); Hezron (2:5, 9-55); Caleb (2:9, 18-20, 24, 42-55); Hur (2:19-20, 50b-55); Shobal (2:50b, 52-53). Shobal is listed last and so the Chronicler will pick up with his family.
19. For this literary function, see Knoppers 2004:128.
20. Reaiah in 4:2 is most likely the same person as Haroeh in 2:52.
21. The Hebrew text does not have the phrase "other descendants of Simeon included" at the beginning of 4:34. The list is defined by 4:38.
22. There is debate over whether Mount Seir is a designation limited to the eastern side of the Rift Valley, or whether it included territory west of the Rift Valley and south of Simeon's traditional lands (see ABD 5.1073; cf. Deut 1:44; 2:1).
23. So also Knoppers 2004:370-371, although it is possible this statement was merely copied from his source and not relevant to the Chronicler's day.

◆ C. Genealogies of Reuben, Gad, and the Transjordan Tribes (5:1-26)

The oldest son of Israel* was Reuben. But
since he dishonored his father by sleeping
with one of his father's concubines, his
birthright was given to the sons of his
brother Joseph. For this reason, Reuben is
not listed in the genealogical records as
the firstborn son. 2The descendants of Ju-
dah became the most powerful tribe and
provided a ruler for the nation,* but the
birthright belonged to Joseph.

3The sons of Reuben, the oldest son of
Israel, were Hanoch, Pallu, Hezron,
and Carmi.
4The descendants of Joel were Shemaiah,
Gog, Shimei, 5Micah, Reaiah, Baal,
6and Beerah. Beerah was the leader of
the Reubenites when they were taken
into captivity by King Tiglath-pileser*
of Assyria.
7Beerah's* relatives are listed in their
genealogical records by their clans:
Jeiel (the leader), Zechariah, 8and Bela
son of Azaz, son of Shema, son of Joel.
The Reubenites lived in the area that
stretches from Aroer to Nebo and
Baal-meon. 9And since they had so
many livestock in the land of Gilead,
they spread east toward the edge of
the desert that stretches to the
Euphrates River.
10During the reign of Saul, the
Reubenites defeated the Hagrites
in battle. Then they moved into the
Hagrite settlements all along the
eastern edge of Gilead.
11Next to the Reubenites, the descendants
of Gad lived in the land of Bashan as
far east as Salecah. 12Joel was the
leader in the land of Bashan, and
Shapham was second-in-command,
followed by Janai and Shaphat.
13Their relatives, the leaders of seven
other clans, were Michael, Meshullam,
Sheba, Jorai, Jacan, Zia, and Eber.
14These were all descendants of
Abihail son of Huri, son of Jaroah,
son of Gilead, son of Michael, son of
Jeshishai, son of Jahdo, son of Buz.
15Ahi son of Abdiel, son of Guni, was
the leader of their clans.

16The Gadites lived in the land of Gilead,
in Bashan and its villages, and throughout
all the pasturelands of Sharon. 17All of
these were listed in the genealogical re-
cords during the days of King Jotham of
Judah and King Jeroboam of Israel.

18There were 44,760 capable warriors in the armies of Reuben, Gad, and the half-tribe of Manasseh. They were all skilled in combat and armed with shields, swords, and bows. 19They waged war against the Hagrites, the Jeturites, the Naphishites, and the Nodabites. 20They cried out to God during the battle, and he answered their prayer because they trusted in him. So the Hagrites and all their allies were defeated. 21The plunder taken from the Hagrites included 50,000 camels, 250,000 sheep and goats, 2,000 donkeys, and 100,000 captives. 22Many of the Hagrites were killed in the battle because God was fighting against them. The people of Reuben, Gad, and Manasseh lived in their land until they were taken into exile.

23The half-tribe of Manasseh was very large and spread through the land from Bashan to Baal-hermon, Senir, and Mount Hermon. 24These were the leaders of their clans: Epher,* Ishi, Eliel, Azriel, Jeremiah, Hodaviah, and Jahdiel. These men had a great reputation as mighty warriors and leaders of their clans.

25But these tribes were unfaithful to the God of their ancestors. They worshiped the gods of the nations that God had destroyed. 26So the God of Israel caused King Pul of Assyria (also known as Tiglath-pileser) to invade the land and take away the people of Reuben, Gad, and the half-tribe of Manasseh as captives. The Assyrians exiled them to Halah, Habor, Hara, and the Gozan River, where they remain to this day.

5:1 *Israel* is the name that God gave to Jacob. **5:2** Or *and from Judah came a prince.* **5:6** Hebrew *Tilgath-pilneser,* a variant spelling of Tiglath-pileser; also in 5:26. **5:7** Hebrew *His.* **5:24** As in Greek version and Latin Vulgate; Hebrew reads *and Epher.*

NOTES

5:1 ***he dishonored his father by sleeping with one of his father's concubines.*** Lit., "he defiled the bed of his father." Although Gen 35:22 reveals that Reuben did sleep with his father's concubine Bilhah, this phrase is drawn from Gen 49:4, which uses the priestly terminology "to defile" or "to profane" (*khalal* [TH2490, ZH2725], Piel; e.g., Exod 20:25; Lev 19:8).

5:7 ***clans.*** The term is the plural of *mishpakhah* [TH4940, ZH5476] (clan), which is usually considered one step up sociologically from the *beth 'ab* [TH1004/1, ZH1074/3] (the patriarchal family unit).

5:8 ***Aroer to Nebo and Baal-meon.*** The proximity of these sites to Moabite territory is displayed in the late ninth-century BC inscription of King Mesha of Moab, who refers to them on his stela commemorating his victory against the northern kingdom (2 Kgs 3).[1] Interestingly, Mesha also talks about bringing flocks to Baal-meon.

5:9 ***the edge of the desert that stretches to the Euphrates River.*** The higher Transjordan region receives any rain gathered into clouds passing over the Jordan Valley, creating a region with potential for agricultural activity. As one moves east, however, the landscape quickly turns to desert. This "eastern desert" is the same desert that forms the western border of the Mesopotamian region.

5:13 ***clans.*** The term is *beth 'aboth,* which may be merely the plural of *beth 'ab* [TH1004/1, ZH1074/3] (the patriarchal family unit), but most likely for the Chronicler writing in the Persian period, this plural form has taken on the nuance of the term *mishpakhah* [TH4940, ZH5476] (clan); cf. Weinberg 1992.

5:16 ***pasturelands.*** Heb. *migrash* [TH4054, ZH4494] designates "the belt of land or open space outside a town or a sanctuary . . . that could be used for livestock, cattle, and other animals (Josh 14:4)" and is to be distinguished from residential and farmland used for growing crops (Knoppers 2004:388). In Num 35:1-8 a *migrash* was to extend 1,000 cubits (1,500 feet) from the outer wall of the town.

5:16 ***Sharon.*** The pasturelands of Sharon cannot refer to the area by that name on the Mediterranean coastal plain, but rather to a location in the Transjordan region mentioned by the Moabite King Mesha's inscription (see note above on 5:8).[2]

5:25 ***They worshiped.*** The Hebrew verb and preposition here are related to committing fornication or acting as a prostitute (to have illicit intercourse with), thus picturing a breach of the marriage covenant between Yahweh and his people (cf. Exod 34:15; Lev 17:7; 20:5; Deut 31:16; Judg 2:17; 8:27, 33; Ezek 6:9; 20:30; cf. Lev 20:6; Num 15:39; Jer 3:1-8; Ezek 16:15-17; 23:3, 19).

5:26 ***Halah, Habor, Hara, and the Gozan River.*** Halah, Habor, and Gozan are mentioned along with the cities of the Medes as the destination of the exiles of the northern kingdom after the fall of Samaria (2 Kgs 17:6; 18:11). Some suggest that the phrase "exiles of Israel" in Obad 1:20 (which translates the phrase "exiles of this host" in the Hebrew text) should be emended to read "exiles in Halah," but this is far from certain. Habor is a tributary of the Euphrates River that stretches up to the ancient city of Gozan. Assyrian documents from this region list Israelite personal names, confirming the presence of the exiles in this region (ABD 3.10). Sennacherib bragged to Hezekiah that he easily subjugated the Gozan region (2 Kgs 19:12; Isa 37:12). The referent of Hara is uncertain, especially since it is missing in 2 Kgs 17:6 and 18:11.

COMMENTARY

Sources. The Chronicler drew upon earlier sources for only a select portion of the genealogy in chapter 5. Knoppers (2004:393) identifies Genesis 35:22; 47:25–48:22; 49:3-4 as the source of 5:1-2; Exodus 6:14 or Numbers 26:5-6 as the source of 5:3; and 2 Kings 15:29; 17:6 as the source of 5:25-26. The genealogical records of these tribes are limited. The Chronicler, however, did have more information for the Transjordanian tribes in sources he used elsewhere (e.g., Gen 46:16; Num 26:15-17), but he does not include this.[3] This suggests that the Chronicler intentionally abridged and avoided the data for rhetorical effect.[4] The limited lists for the northern tribes accentuate the presentation of Judah, Levi, and Benjamin in his genealogy. Interestingly, the Chronicler does not follow Ezekiel's vision of the territory of Israel, which makes no mention of Transjordanian territory (see Ezek 47:13-23; 48:1-29; cf. Knoppers 2004:394).

Structure and Content. The account of Simeon was clearly overshadowed by that of Judah, but even Simeon's account is longer than the accounts of the northern tribes, which now follow in chapter 5. The Chronicler moves from south to north through the tribes that settled in the region to the east of the Jordan River (Josh 1:10-18). Although there is a general movement from south to north, at times the boundaries between these tribal units are fuzzy at best. This probably reflects sociological realities and echoes the fusion of these tribal units in military exploits in 5:18-22, 25-26. While the tribes of Reuben (5:1-10) and Gad (5:11-17) are reviewed at first, that of the "half-tribe of Manasseh" appears to be an afterthought, placed in the midst of an account of the military exploits of all three Transjordan tribes in 5:18-26. Klein suggests that the intrusion of the Manasseh account may reflect the Chronicler's desire "to put chronological distance" between the victory and blessing of 5:18-22 and the unfaithfulness and defeat of 5:25-26 (Klein 2006:158, note 155).[5] Possibly this abbreviated comment on Manasseh was deemed necessary to make sense of the account while not preempting the later, full genealogy of Manasseh in 7:14-19.

Descendants of Reuben (5:1-10). First Chronicles 5:1-2 functions as a summary note at the outset of the account of Reuben. The opening phrase (NLT, "the oldest son of Israel was Reuben") is actually the identical phrase in Hebrew as the one found at the beginning of 5:3: "the sons of Reuben, the oldest son of Israel." This is a literary technique in Hebrew called resumptive repetition; it introduces and concludes material off the main line of the text (here the genealogy).[6] The note explains Reuben's loss of his firstborn rights. Such rights were reserved for the first male offspring of a legitimate wife because, as the firstfruit of the father, this child symbolized, according to Genesis 49:3 (cf. Deut 21:17; Pss 78:51; 105:36), the father's "might" (*koakh* [TH3581, ZH3946]) and "generative power" (*'on* [TH202, ZH226]), the one who carried on his "dignity" (*se'et* [TH7613, ZH8420]) and "power" (*'az* [TH5794A, ZH6435]). In light of this the firstborn was to assume the father's resources and authority. First of all, the eldest would receive the birthright, which is described as a larger portion of the inheritance, twice that of the other brothers (Gen 48:21-22; Deut 21:15-17; cf. 2 Kgs 2:9). Second, the eldest was to carry on the responsibilities and exercise the authority of his father as the head of the clan.[7] These two aspects of firstborn rights and responsibilities were interconnected. In order to assume the patriarchal role within the family unit and its attendant responsibilities to support its various members, the firstborn would need a larger pool of resources.

Reuben forfeited his firstborn rights by committing incest with his father's concubine Bilhah (Gen 35:22), an act that here is simply called "defiling his father's bed" (lit., as per the Chronicler's source in Gen 49:1-4). His rights were distributed to two different brothers, Joseph and Judah, the two brothers whose blessings dominate Jacob's final words to his sons in Genesis 49 (Gen 49:8-12, 22-26). The firstborn right of resources (birthright) was assumed by Joseph, explaining why both of his sons (Ephraim, Manasseh) were given status as tribes equal with the other sons of Jacob (Gen 48:5) and why the Joseph tribes (especially Ephraim) dominated the northern tribes. The Chronicler's statement is a reminder of his inclusive attitude toward the northern tribes at whose core lay the Joseph tribes.

Reuben's firstborn right of authority was assumed by Judah. This explains why Judah was the tribe from which the royal leader would arise over the whole nation and in later years would dominate the southern kingdom. This allusion to Davidic kingship will be a consistent feature in the lists of non-Judahite/Benjaminite tribes throughout the genealogy: Simeon (4:31; cf. 4:41), Transjordan northern tribes (5:2), Levi (6:31-32), and Cisjordan northern tribes (7:2). This prepares the way for the Chronicler's ideal picture of a united Israel facilitated by a Davidic monarchy—a picture that will typify his narrative account.

The Chronicler used this opportunity to explain why Reuben was not listed first in his genealogy (the place taken by Judah, 2:3–4:23) and why Joseph was among the sons of Jacob in 2:1-2 and yet his two sons are listed as tribes in the genealogies (Ephraim, Manasseh, 5:23-24; 7:14-29). Reuben, however, does retain his place of status as "firstborn," even without the rights that accompanied it (5:3).

First Chronicles 5:3 records the sons of Reuben from Exodus 6:14 (cf. Gen 46:9;

Num 26:5-7). The list in 5:4-6 is not linked to any of Reuben's sons in 5:3 but appears to represent a linear genealogy that traces the descendants of a Reubenite clan leader named Joel for seven generations (contra NLT),[8] until it reached the generation that faced exile at the hands of the Assyrian king Tiglath-pileser III (ruling from 745 to 727 BC; see 2 Kgs 15:29-30; cf. 2 Kgs 15:19-20; 16:7-9). Again, the seventh generation is highlighted, but here in a negative way in that the clan leader is taken away. Other Reubenites ("Beerah's relatives"; lit., "his brothers") listed in 5:7-8 appear to have remained in the land and lived at various places in the Transjordan region in towns given to and conquered by the Reubenites at the time of the conquest: Aroer, Nebo, and Baal-meon (cf. Num 32:3, 34, 38; Josh 13:16-17).[9] This remnant community is considered greatly blessed with great livestock holdings that filled the region of Gilead on the Transjordanian plateau. In 5:10 the Chronicler also records Reubenite success in military exploits during the reign of Saul against the Hagrites, who are mentioned in Psalm 83:6 alongside Edomites, Ishmaelites, and Moabites, also Transjordanian peoples.

Although in the first half of this genealogy (5:1-6) the Chronicler was honest about Reuben's loss of firstborn status and blessing and did not hide the exilic nightmare his tribe faced in the Assyrian period, the second half (5:7-10) highlights signs of blessing with extensive tribal territory, accumulation of wealth, and success in battle.

Descendants of Gad (5:11-17). North of the Reubenites was the tribe of Gad, whose territory stretched from Heshbon to Mahanaim but who controlled territory even as far east as Salecah, which represented the edge of habitable territory before entering the eastern desert (cf. Deut 3:10; Josh 12:5; 13:11). Unlike the previous tribal genealogies, the first generation of sons of the tribal patriarch was not provided for Gad, a trend that will be seen also for the half-tribe of Manasseh in 5:23-24. The names that appear first are those of tribal leaders in the land of Bashan: Joel (leader), Shapham (second), then Janai and Shaphat. The last two are not numbered but merely listed after Shapham. As with the genealogy of Reuben, the initial list is followed by a list introduced by the phrase "his/their brothers" (5:13; cf. 5:7; NLT, "relatives"). In the case of Gad seven clan leaders are traced through a line that extends from Abihail back to Buz, who must be an early Gadite. While there has been some confusion over the relationship between 5:15 and the list in 5:14, the present Hebrew text appears to identify Ahi as the tribal head over the seven clan leaders. As with the Reubenites (5:9-10), the Gadites are placed in the region of Gilead, the northern extent of which is not precisely defined in the Old Testament (ABD 2.1020). The region of Bashan is the upper Transjordan north of the Yarmuk River and south of Mount Hermon. Bashan was known for agricultural fertility (Ps 22:12; Amos 4:1-3) and forests (Isa 2:13; Ezek 27:6).

The closing note of this section identifies one of the sources of the Gadite genealogy as a record dating from the reigns of Jotham in Judah (750–735 BC) and Jeroboam II in Israel (786–746 BC; Knoppers 2004:388). This means that it must have been recorded sometime between 750 and 746 BC. The Chronicler may be foreshadowing his account of Jotham, whose successful expedition against the Ammonites in 2 Chronicles 27:1-9 brought much tribute to Judah.

Transjordan tribes: Success in prayer and war (5:18-22). For some reason before introducing the half-tribe of Manasseh in 5:23-24, the Chronicler inserts in 5:18-22 the account of a combined military action by the two and a half Israelite tribes who lived in the Transjordan (Reuben, Gad, and the half-tribe of Manasseh). This account, strikingly similar to and possibly the same as Reuben's battle with the Hagrites in 5:10,[10] is designed to characterize these tribes positively and explain the phase of blessed existence in the land (as 5:22b makes clear). The account pits the Israelite tribes against the Hagrites, Jeturites, Naphishites, and Nodabites. Clearly, the Jeturites and Naphishites are descendants of Jetur and Naphish, two sons of Ishmael (1:31; Gen 25:15). Possibly the Nodabites are descendants of another son of Ishmael or Adbeel (Gen 25:13). The Hagrites are listed with Edomites, Ishmaelites, and Moabites in Psalm 83:6. The term may be based on the name of Ishmael's mother, Hagar (Gen 16; 21:8-21; 25:12). If this is the case, these peoples may all have Ishmaelite roots.

The narrative relates that the Israelite tribes were well endowed militarily both in quantity (large numbers of soldiers) and quality (skilled and armed soldiers; see 5:18). When they waged war, they cried out to God in prayer as an expression of trust in Yahweh (5:20), and it was Yahweh who brought victory (5:22). The victory brought Israel abundant spoil (5:21). This military narrative foreshadows battle descriptions that the Chronicler will provide in his narratives in chapter 10—2 Chronicles 36 and accentuates the key theological themes of blessing, prayer and trust, and divine war (for the large numbers cited here, see the commentary on 12:23-40).[11] But this is only half of the Chronicler's theological perspective. Before providing the flip side, which he will do in 5:25-26 (which represents the continuation of 5:18-22), the Chronicler inserts the belated account of the descendants of the half-tribe of Manasseh.

Descendants of the half-tribe of Manasseh (5:23-24). The Chronicler's comment that even the half-tribe of Manasseh was "very large" probably relates to his statement in 5:1-2 that the Joseph tribes (of which Manasseh was a part) received the blessing of the firstborn instead of Reuben. The other half of this tribe settled on the western side of the Jordan River (see 7:14-19; Josh 17:1-2). The Chronicler placed this half-tribe geographically in the farthest northern region of the Transjordan. With Reuben in southern Gilead between the Arnon River and the Wadi Heshbon and Gad in Bashan north of the Wadi Heshbon, the half-tribe of Manasseh was located in northern Bashan to the peaks of the Hermon range (Baal-hermon, Senir, and Hermon). Although this tribe was greatly blessed with descendants, the Chronicler has few genealogical resources for their account, listing only seven "heads of the house of their fathers" (NLT, "leaders of their clans"), without any indication as to the time period of these leaders. The only information provided is that they were widely known as "mighty warriors" (5:24).

Transjordan tribes: Failure in worship and war (5:25-26). The Chronicler picks up again the account he began in 5:18-22, explaining now the causes behind the final word in 5:22: "exile" (*haggolah* [TH1473, ZH1583]). The subject of the verb "were unfaithful" (*ma'al* [TH4603, ZH5085]) at the beginning of 5:25 is the "people of Reuben, Gad, and Manasseh" of 5:22 and not the clan leaders of Manasseh in 5:24, especially in light of 5:26, where "the people of Reuben, Gad, and the half-tribe of Manasseh" are taken away as captives. By linking the Exile to unfaithfulness (*ma'al*), the Chronicler is again foreshadowing one of the key themes in his narrative work (see commentary on ch 10 and the account of Manasseh in 2 Chr 33). Such unfaithfulness is consistently linked there as here to illicit worship of foreign gods, here described in terms of breaking marital vows (see note on 5:25). The result of such behavior throughout his narrative account is divine discipline, the ultimate expression of which is invasion by foreign armies and exile to foreign lands.

Important to note is that the "God of Israel" is seen as the cause of the invasion of Tiglath-pileser III, since Yahweh "stirred up the spirit of Pul" (NLT, "caused King Pul of Assyria . . . to invade"). This phrase will appear again at the end of Chronicles (2 Chr 36:22) as God stirs up the spirit of Cyrus to set in motion the restoration of the tribes to the land. This language is probably drawn from earlier prophetic material related to the restoration of Israel (Jer 51:11; Hag 1:14). The invasion by Tiglath-pileser III is probably the same as that of 5:6, which looked to the invasion of the Transjordan described in 2 Kings 15:29-30 (cf. 2 Kgs 15:19-20; 16:7-9). The destination of their exile (Halah, Habor, Hara, and the Gozan River, locations across northern Assyria) is similar to that of the exiles of the northern kingdom after the fall of Samaria to the Assyrians (2 Kgs 17:6; 18:11), although those deportations happened later under Shalmaneser V (727–722 BC) and his brother Sargon II (721–705).[12] The Chronicler stresses that in his own time they remained in the state of exile.

Significance. The fact that the Chronicler focuses his genealogy and narrative on the southern kingdom of Judah does not mean there is no place for the northern tribes in his vision of Israel. Although the northern kingdom will be deemed illicit (see introduction to 2 Chr 10–36), the northern tribes are still part of "all Israel." This openness to the north is shaped at the outset of chapter 5 with the reminder that the birthright belongs to the northern Joseph tribes, even if the power resides with Judah. This helps the reader understand the role of Judah as the mighty royal line and suggests that Judah could still play a role in realizing the return of the northern tribes (see commentary on 2 Chr 29–30; cf. Zech 9–11).

While the immoral behavior of the Transjordan tribes led ultimately to their exile by the Assyrians (5:6, 25-26), these tribes also provided for the Chronicler a normative example of the kind of trust in Yahweh he will highlight throughout his narrative in chapter 10—2 Chronicles 36. For those who will "[cry] out to God during the battle," God will "[answer] their prayer because they [trust] in him" (5:20).

ENDNOTES

1. See COS 2.23: "And I built Baal Meon, and I made in it a water reservoir. . . . And Kemosh said to me: 'Go take Nebo from Israel!' . . . I have built Aroer, and I made the military road in the Arnon. . . . And I have built . . . the House of Baal Meon, and I brought there . . . flocks of the land."
2. COS 2.23.13: "I made the men of Sharon live there, as well as the men of Maharith."
3. See the extensive lists in Knoppers 2004:393.
4. Of course, it is difficult to understand all of the purposes that lie behind this account. See the many questions raised by Klein (2006:158).

5. Similarly Japhet (1993:129-130) says this "avoids the theological questions which might be raised." However, it would seem that such questions would have been raised by 5:22b.
6. See Anbar 1988:385-398; Long 1987:390-392; Talmon 1978:9-26; cf. Williamson 1985:43-45.
7. See Bendor 1996 and Perdue 1997 for superb overviews of the sociological structure of family units in ancient Israel, with special focus on the smallest unit, the *beth-'ab* (house of the father), which consisted of the patriarchal figure, his wives, his sons and their families, his unmarried or divorced daughters, as well as servants and others (priests, visiting foreigners, etc.).
8. Read instead as in Hebrew: "The descendants of Joel: Shemaiah, his son, Gog, his son, Shimei, his son, Micah, his son, Reaiah, his son, Baal, his son, Beerah, his son."
9. Interestingly the names Joel and Jeiel sons of Nebo appear among the restoration community in Ezra's time (Ezra 10:43), suggesting some Transjordanian elements within Yehud; cf. Cogan 1979:37-39.
10. Japhet (1993:131) notes the contacts in language.
11. See, for instance, the motif of prayer and divine answer in battle (especially 2 Chr 20:5-12 and 32:20, which use the same vocabulary as here: *za'aq* [TH2199, ZH2410], "cry," and *'atar* [TH6279, ZH6983], "entreat"). For the Chronicler, battle is divine war, and success is dependent on God's participation (see also 2 Chr 20:15; 25:8; 32:8). See further Knoppers 2004:389-390.
12. See ANET 284 for Sargon's account of the fall of Samaria.

◆ D. The Priestly Line (6:1-81)

1*The sons of Levi were Gershon, Kohath, and Merari.
2The descendants of Kohath included Amram, Izhar, Hebron, and Uzziel.
3The children of Amram were Aaron, Moses, and Miriam.
The sons of Aaron were Nadab, Abihu, Eleazar, and Ithamar.
4Eleazar was the father of Phinehas.
Phinehas was the father of Abishua.
5Abishua was the father of Bukki.
Bukki was the father of Uzzi.
6Uzzi was the father of Zerahiah.
Zerahiah was the father of Meraioth.
7Meraioth was the father of Amariah.
Amariah was the father of Ahitub.
8Ahitub was the father of Zadok.
Zadok was the father of Ahimaaz.
9Ahimaaz was the father of Azariah.
Azariah was the father of Johanan.
10 Johanan was the father of Azariah, the high priest at the Temple* built by Solomon in Jerusalem.
11 Azariah was the father of Amariah.
Amariah was the father of Ahitub.
12 Ahitub was the father of Zadok.
Zadok was the father of Shallum.
13 Shallum was the father of Hilkiah.
Hilkiah was the father of Azariah.
14 Azariah was the father of Seraiah.
Seraiah was the father of Jehozadak,
15who went into exile when the LORD sent the people of Judah and Jerusalem into captivity under Nebuchadnezzar.
16*The sons of Levi were Gershon,* Kohath, and Merari.
17The descendants of Gershon included Libni and Shimei.
18The descendants of Kohath included Amram, Izhar, Hebron, and Uzziel.
19The descendants of Merari included Mahli and Mushi.

The following were the Levite clans, listed according to their ancestral descent:

20The descendants of Gershon included Libni, Jahath, Zimmah, 21Joah, Iddo, Zerah, and Jeatherai.

22 The descendants of Kohath included
Amminadab, Korah, Assir, 23 Elkanah,
Abiasaph,* Assir, 24 Tahath, Uriel,
Uzziah, and Shaul.
25 The descendants of Elkanah included
Amasai, Ahimoth, 26 Elkanah, Zophai,
Nahath, 27 Eliab, Jeroham, Elkanah, and
Samuel.*
28 The sons of Samuel were Joel* (the
older) and Abijah (the second).
29 The descendants of Merari included
Mahli, Libni, Shimei, Uzzah, 30 Shimea,
Haggiah, and Asaiah.

31 David assigned the following men to
lead the music at the house of the LORD
after the Ark was placed there. 32 They
ministered with music at the Tabernacle*
until Solomon built the Temple of the
LORD in Jerusalem. They carried out their
work, following all the regulations handed
down to them. 33 These are the men who
served, along with their sons:

Heman the musician was from the clan
of Kohath. His genealogy was traced
back through Joel, Samuel, 34 Elkanah,
Jeroham, Eliel, Toah, 35 Zuph, Elkanah,
Mahath, Amasai, 36 Elkanah, Joel,
Azariah, Zephaniah, 37 Tahath, Assir,
Abiasaph, Korah, 38 Izhar, Kohath, Levi,
and Israel.*
39 Heman's first assistant was Asaph
from the clan of Gershon.* Asaph's
genealogy was traced back through
Berekiah, Shimea, 40 Michael, Baaseiah,
Malkijah, 41 Ethni, Zerah, Adaiah,
42 Ethan, Zimmah, Shimei, 43 Jahath,
Gershon, and Levi.
44 Heman's second assistant was Ethan
from the clan of Merari. Ethan's
genealogy was traced back through
Kishi, Abdi, Malluch, 45 Hashabiah,
Amaziah, Hilkiah, 46 Amzi, Bani, Shemer,
47 Mahli, Mushi, Merari, and Levi.

48 Their fellow Levites were appointed to
various other tasks in the Tabernacle, the
house of God.

49 Only Aaron and his descendants
served as priests. They presented the of-
ferings on the altar of burnt offering and
the altar of incense, and they performed
all the other duties related to the Most
Holy Place. They made atonement for Is-
rael by doing everything that Moses, the
servant of God, had commanded them.

50 The descendants of Aaron were Eleazar,
Phinehas, Abishua, 51 Bukki, Uzzi,
Zerahiah, 52 Meraioth, Amariah, Ahitub,
53 Zadok, and Ahimaaz.

54 This is a record of the towns and terri-
tory assigned by means of sacred lots to
the descendants of Aaron, who were from
the clan of Kohath. 55 This territory includ-
ed Hebron and its surrounding pasture-
lands in Judah, 56 but the fields and outlying
areas belonging to the city were given to
Caleb son of Jephunneh. 57 So the descen-
dants of Aaron were given the following
towns, each with its pasturelands: Hebron
(a city of refuge),* Libnah, Jattir, Eshtemoa,
58 Holon,* Debir, 59 Ain,* Juttah,* and Beth-
shemesh. 60 And from the territory of Ben-
jamin they were given Gibeon,* Geba,
Alemeth, and Anathoth, each with its pas-
turelands. So thirteen towns were given to
the descendants of Aaron. 61 The remaining
descendants of Kohath received ten towns
from the territory of the half-tribe of Ma-
nasseh by means of sacred lots.
62 The descendants of Gershon received
by sacred lots thirteen towns from the
territories of Issachar, Asher, Naphtali,
and from the Bashan area of Manasseh,
east of the Jordan.
63 The descendants of Merari received by
sacred lots twelve towns from the territo-
ries of Reuben, Gad, and Zebulun.
64 So the people of Israel assigned all
these towns and pasturelands to the
Levites. 65 The towns in the territories of
Judah, Simeon, and Benjamin, mentioned
above, were assigned to them by means of
sacred lots.
66 The descendants of Kohath were given
the following towns from the territory of
Ephraim, each with its pasturelands:
67 Shechem (a city of refuge in the hill
country of Ephraim),* Gezer, 68 Jokmeam,

Beth-horon, [69]Aijalon, and Gath-rimmon.
[70]The remaining descendants of Kohath
were assigned the towns of Aner and
Bileam from the territory of the half-tribe
of Manasseh, each with its pasturelands.

[71]The descendants of Gershon received
the towns of Golan (in Bashan) and
Ashtaroth from the territory of the half-
tribe of Manasseh, each with its pasture-
lands. [72]From the territory of Issachar,
they were given Kedesh, Daberath, [73]Ra-
moth, and Anem, each with its pasture-
lands. [74]From the territory of Asher, they
received Mashal, Abdon, [75]Hukok, and Re-
hob, each with its pasturelands. [76]From
the territory of Naphtali, they were given
Kedesh in Galilee, Hammon, and Kiria-
thaim, each with its pasturelands.

[77]The remaining descendants of Merari
received the towns of Jokneam, Kartah,*
Rimmon,* and Tabor from the territory of
Zebulun, each with its pasturelands.
[78]From the territory of Reuben, east of the
Jordan River opposite Jericho, they re-
ceived Bezer (a desert town), Jahaz,* [79]Ke-
demoth, and Mephaath, each with its
pasturelands. [80]And from the territory of
Gad, they received Ramoth in Gilead, Ma-
hanaim, [81]Heshbon, and Jazer, each with
its pasturelands.

6:1 Verses 6:1-15 are numbered 5:27-41 in Hebrew text. **6:10** Hebrew *the house.* **6:16a** Verses 6:16-81 are numbered 6:1-66 in Hebrew text. **6:16b** Hebrew *Gershom,* a variant spelling of Gershon (see 6:1); also in 6:17, 20, 43, 62, 71. **6:23** Hebrew *Ebiasaph,* a variant spelling of Abiasaph (also in 6:37); compare parallel text at Exod 6:24. **6:27** As in some Greek manuscripts (see also 6:33-34); Hebrew lacks *and Samuel.* **6:28** As in some Greek manuscripts and the Syriac version (see also 6:33 and 1 Sam 8:2); Hebrew lacks *Joel.* **6:32** Hebrew *the Tabernacle, the Tent of Meeting.* **6:38** *Israel* is the name that God gave to Jacob. **6:39** Hebrew lacks *from the clan of Gershon;* see 6:43. **6:57** As in parallel text at Josh 21:13; Hebrew reads *were given the cities of refuge: Hebron, and the following towns, each with its pasturelands.* **6:58** As in parallel text at Josh 21:15; Masoretic Text reads *Hilez;* other manuscripts read *Hilen.* **6:59a** As in parallel text at Josh 21:16; Hebrew reads *Ashan.* **6:59b** As in Syriac version (see also Josh 21:16); Hebrew lacks *Juttah.* **6:60** As in parallel text at Josh 21:17; Hebrew lacks *Gibeon.* **6:66-67** As in parallel text at Josh 21:21. Hebrew text reads *were given the cities of refuge: Shechem in the hill country of Ephraim, and the following towns, each with its pasturelands.* **6:77a** As in Greek version (see also Josh 21:34); Hebrew lacks *Jokneam, Kartah.* **6:77b** As in Greek version (see also Josh 19:13); Hebrew reads *Rimmono.* **6:78** Hebrew *Jahzah,* a variant spelling of Jahaz.

NOTES

6:3 [5:29] ***Ithamar.*** See commentary on ch 24 for the Ithamar line of priests, which was connected to Eli in the time of Samuel and Abiathar in the time of David and Solomon (see also 1 Sam 2:27-36; 3:11-14; 14:3; 22:20; 1 Kgs 2:26-27).

6:4 [5:30] ***Phinehas.*** See Num 25:11-13 for the covenant made between Yahweh and Phinehas due to his decisive action to turn away God's wrath. The priestly line would play a key mediatorial role in averting such wrath through sacrifice.

6:8 [5:34] ***Zadok.*** For the background of this key priestly figure who served during the time of David and Solomon, see note on 15:11. For the debate over the origins of the priestly lines in Israel, see Knoppers 2004:405-406.

6:9 [5:35] ***Ahimaaz.*** See 2 Sam 15:27, 36; 17:17, 20; 18:19-29 for accounts of this priest.

6:11 [5:37] ***Amariah.*** See 2 Chr 19:11 for a high priest by this name at the time of Jehoshaphat.

6:13 [5:39] ***Hilkiah.*** See 2 Chr 34:9, 14-22; 35:8 for a high priest by this name at the time of Josiah.

6:14 [5:40] ***Azariah.*** Knoppers (2004:406) notes evidence of an Azariah son of Hilkiah in a late seventh/early sixth century BC bulla from Jerusalem and a seal from the same period.

Seraiah . . . Jehozadak. For the fate of Seraiah see 2 Kgs 25:18-21 and note his descendant Ezra (Ezra 7:1). Jehozadak's name will appear in the Persian period as the father of the reinstated Zadokite high priest Joshua/Jeshua (Ezra 3:2, 8; 5:2; Hag 1:1, 12, 14; 2:2; Zech 6:11).

6:20-30 [5-15] ***Libni, Jahath, Zimmah.*** The Hebrew reads literally "For these descendants of Gershon: Libni his son, Jahath his son, Zimmah his son." The same formula governs the list of the descendants of Kohath in 6:22-28 and the descendants of Merari in 6:29-30.

6:25 [10] ***Elkanah.*** First Samuel 1:1 traces Elkanah's lineage to the tribe of Ephraim through a different line. Either the Chronicler understood Elkanah as a Levite living within the boundaries of Ephraim or, more likely, that the gift of Samuel to the Tabernacle at Shiloh officially brought Samuel's lineage into the tribe of Levi.

6:32 [17] ***the Tabernacle.*** Lit., "the Tabernacle, the Tent of Meeting" (so NLT mg), a phrase also found in Exod 39:32; 40:2, 6, 29 (see Klein 2006:204). Here the Chronicler foreshadows his account in chs 15–16 of the phases of the movement of the Ark into Jerusalem. The Ark was first located at the Tabernacle at the high place at Gibeon and then was transferred to the Temple.

6:33-47 [18-32] ***His genealogy was traced back through Joel, Samuel.*** Lit., "the son of Joel, the son of Samuel," etc. The same formula governs the list of the ancestors of Asaph in 6:39-43 and the ancestors of Ethan in 6:44-47.

6:39 [24] ***first assistant.*** Lit., "the one who stands on his right."

6:44 [29] ***second assistant.*** Lit., "on the left."

Ethan. Lists in 16:41-42 and 25:1-3 replace the name Ethan with the name Jeduthun, while 15:17 supports the name Ethan used here. This is most likely related to a scribal error rather than conflicting traditions.

6:48 [33] ***appointed to various other tasks in the Tabernacle, the house of God.*** Lit., "assigned to all the service of the Tabernacle of the house of God." Knoppers notes that this terminology carries "broader connotations" in Chronicles and is used not only of Levites, as here, but also of priests in 9:13; 2 Chr 35:2 and of both priests and Levites in 28:13. Thus although the Chronicler has "some demarcation of duties," the emphasis is on "complementarity" rather than "hierarchy" (Knoppers 2004:424). Johnstone argues that this is a reference to sacrificial activity (1997:1.89).

6:49 [34] ***altar of burnt offering and the altar of incense.*** The former was located in the courtyard of the Tabernacle (Exod 27:1-8; 38:1-7; 40:29) and later in the Temple precincts (2 Chr 4:1; cf. 1 Kgs 8:64); the latter was located in the Holy Place of the Tabernacle (Exod 30:1-10; 40:5) and later in the Temple (1 Kgs 6:22).

6:55 [40] ***its surrounding pasturelands.*** See Num 35:1-8 for measurements that determined these "pasturelands" around a Levitical city.

COMMENTARY

Sources. While most of the material in chapter 6 is unique to the Chronicler, borrowing can be discerned at several places (Knoppers 2004:426, 442-448):

CHRONICLES PASSAGE	BORROWS FROM
6:1-4, 16-19 [5:27-30; 6:1-4]	Gen 46:11; Exod 6:16-18; Num 17–20
6:22-23 [7-8]	Exod 6:24
6:27, 34-35 [12, 19-20]	1 Sam 1:1
6:28, 33 [13, 18]	1 Sam 8:2
6:54-81 [39-66]	Josh 21 (although see Auld 2000a:132-140)

Structure and Content. The Chronicler placed the tribe of Levi at the center of his genealogical section and devoted an amount of space surpassed only by the tribe of Judah in chapters 2–4. One can discern two different systems for organizing the tribe of Levi. The first is based on lineage and is arranged according to the three sons of Levi: Gershon, Kohath, and Merari (6:1, 16). The second is based on function and is arranged according to the priestly function associated with the Kohath clan of Aaron and the Levitical function associated with the non-Aaronide families of Levi that arose from the clans of Gershon, Kohath, and Merari. The bulk of this genealogy in chapter 6 (6:1-53) is arranged in chiastic fashion, with high priestly lineage and duties covered in the first (6:1-15) and last (6:49-52) sections and Levitical (non-priestly) lineage and duties covered in the second (6:16-30) and second-to-last (6:31-48) sections.[1] First Chronicles 6:54-81 then deals with the territorial assignments for all the clans of Levi throughout the tribal regions of Israel, beginning with the priests (6:54-61) and then extending to the Levites (6:62-81).

Sons of Levi: The priestly line until exile (6:1-15). The record of the tribe of Levi gives initial attention to the priestly line through Aaron. While 6:1 and 6:16 are identical in the Hebrew text, 6:1 (along with 6:2-3) introduces a linear genealogy that focuses on the particular priestly line, while 6:16 introduces a segmented genealogy that expands the account to the various Levitical clans.

The priestly genealogy is introduced by four generations of segmented lineage, tracing Kohath out of Levi, then Amram out of Kohath, Aaron out of Amram, and finally Eleazar out of Aaron. Beginning with Eleazar, the structure shifts to a linear genealogy, identifying only one member of successive generations until the exile of Judah, where the list ends. The reason for these segmented lists at the outset of the genealogy is uncertain.

Citing all the children of Amram associates the priestly line with Moses in terms of genealogy, a connection that is made explicit in terms of duties later in the chapter (6:49). Citing all the children of Aaron brings to mind the disqualification of Nadab and Abihu (Lev 10) and subsequent choice of Eleazar (Num 20:25-28; Deut 10:6). The Chronicler will focus on these stories and lines in 24:1-18 and will preserve a role for the Ithamar priestly clan in Temple worship. However, in this genealogy and its corresponding section in 6:50-53, the Chronicler identifies the line of Eleazar as the leadership of the priestly clans. In this, the Chronicler follows a similar method to his treatment of Davidic kingship, using a segmented structure for David's family and beginning the linear structure only with Solomon (ch 3).[2]

Two extranominal (non-name) notes are included in the list. First Chronicles 6:10 speaks about Azariah as the high priest at the Temple built by Solomon, while 6:14-15 describes Jehozadak as the high priest who went into exile under Nebuchadnezzar. This structures the history of the priestly leadership into three phases: its founding under Eleazar, its role under Azariah in the Temple of Solomon, and its crisis under Jehozadak in the exile of Judah.

In light of the emphasis on the Zadokite line of priests during and after the Exile (Ezek 44; Zech 3), it is not surprising that Zadok is the center figure of the list that stretches from Kohath to Jehozadak (6:1, 14; see Knoppers 2004:411) and represents the tenth generation after Aaron (6:3-8). However, one may have expected that the note attached to Azariah would be better suited for Zadok (see 1 Kgs 2:35). Furthermore, the corresponding high priestly genealogy in 6:50-53 ends not with Zadok but with his son Ahimaaz. This final piece of evidence along with references to David and Solomon in 6:31-32 suggests that the focus in this section is on the ideal age of the united kingdom, an era that came to an end after Ahimaaz. Too great a fixation on Zadok puts the interpreter at odds with the emphasis of the Chronicler. Although Zadok will play a key role in the Chronicler's account of the first Temple (12:28; 15:11; 16:39; 18:16; 24:3, 6, 31; 27:17; 29:22), the Chronicler consistently presents a more inclusive depiction of priestly and Levitical service (Knoppers 2004:412-414). To focus on Zadok would be to miss the fact that the Chronicler is open to the involvement not only of non-priestly Levitical clans with the priests (see 6:48), but also of the other priestly clan descended from Aaron through Ithamar (6:3; 24:1-6).

While the genealogy of David is traced well after the Exile (ch 3), the genealogy of Aaron ends at the beginning of the Exile with Jehozadak. Although pride of place is given to the priestly line with its position at the outset of the genealogy of Levi and with the careful delineation of its responsibilities near the end (6:49), the extensive listing of the non-priestly Levitical families somewhat mutes the emphasis on the priests. Although the priestly line is not sidelined in the Chronicler's genealogy, it shares the field with the Levites and is possibly overshadowed by the Davidic line.[3]

Sons of Levi (6:16-30). With 6:16 the Chronicler returns to the original clans of Levi already introduced in 6:1, and he employs a segmented genealogy to show the breadth of Levitical clans. First Chronicles 6:16-30 is comprised of two lists with 6:16-19a introduced by the phrase "The sons of Levi were Gershon, Kohath, and Merari" (6:16) and the list in 6:19b-30 introduced by the phrase "The following were the Levite clans, listed according to their ancestral descent" (6:19b). The first list identifies the sons in the families of each of Levi's sons, Gershon bearing two sons, Kohath bearing four sons, and Merari bearing two sons. Kohath's number emphasizes again his favored status within the tribe. The second list then traces a linear genealogy for one Levitical line within each of the clans.[4] The clan of Gershon is traced seven generations through Libni (cf. 6:17) to a person named Jeatherai (6:20-21), the clan of Kohath ten generations through Amminadab to a figure named Shaul (6:22-24), and the clan of Merari also seven generations through Mahli (cf. 6:19) to Asaiah (6:29-30). The identity of these three figures (Jeatherai, Shaul, and Asaiah) is unclear, but Klein (2006:212) concludes, "These genealogies were no doubt designed to give legitimacy to these three heads, but in Chronicles they are used to provide a more robust genealogy for Levi himself."

There are some oddities, however, to the list of Kohath's clan, both in terms of the name at the outset of the list (Amminadab, 6:22) and the names at the conclusion to the list (Elkanah through Samuel's sons Joel and Abijah, 6:25-28). The name Amminadab is not found in either 6:2 or 6:18 as a son of Kohath. In 6:22, Amminadab is identified as the father of Korah, while in 6:37-38 and Exodus 6:18-21 Korah's father is identified as Izhar, who is named in 6:2, 18 as the second son of Kohath. Most likely, then, Amminadab is to be identified as the Izhar of

6:2, 18. Through Amminadab/Izhar the Chronicler is able to trace the non-priestly Kohathite line, first to a figure named Shaul (6:24), which represented the original ending to the list, and then on to Samuel and his sons (6:25-28).

While it appears that the list of Kohath concluded at first with the figure of Shaul, 6:25-28 represents an expansion of the list through the line of Elkanah mentioned in 6:23. This line continues to Samuel and his sons. It is interesting that in 1 Samuel, Samuel functions in priestly duties at the Tabernacle at Shiloh, and there are indications in 1 Samuel 1–3 (see especially 1 Sam 2:35-36) that Samuel was to establish an enduring leadership line for Israel.[5] In 1 Samuel 8, Samuel appointed his sons as leaders in Israel (1 Sam 8:1), but because of their wickedness the people asked for a king instead (1 Sam 8:5). By including the lineage of Samuel, the Chronicler again accentuates the favor of the Kohathite clan. At the same time he may also be affirming the claim of the Kohath-Amram line to priestly duties over against that of the Kohath-Izhar line (6:2). Furthermore, as Dillard (ABD 1.193) has suggested, this may lay the foundation for the prophetic function of the Levitical clans (cf. 25:1-8; 2 Chr 20:14; 29:25; 34:30; 35:15), especially because their key leader Heman (see 6:33) traces his ancestry to Samuel (cf. Japhet 1993:156).

Levites (6:31-48). In the next two sections (6:31-48, 49-53) of the genealogy, the Chronicler articulates first duties and then leadership of the two main divisions of the tribe of Levi. Although aware of a Levitical role related to "the Tabernacle, the house of God" (6:48), the Chronicler's main focus of 6:31-48 is on the musical function of the Levites. This is clearly linked to David's arrangements for the Temple worship (6:31) and Solomon's construction of the house (6:32), even though the Chronicler is careful to note that there was precedent for this even at the Tabernacle, using terminology associated in the Torah with the tent of Moses (see note on 6:32). These verses foreshadow a consistent theme of the Chronicler's presentation, namely the close association of the Levites with David, Solomon, and the Temple.

Klein (2006:213) has noted a key strategy that underlies the Chronicler's presentation of the Levites: "The Chronicler is trying to establish a niche for the Levites in the postexilic cult, since their role in carrying the ark had become obsolete." This strategy will be evident throughout the Chronicler's narrative account, as other tasks are associated with the Levites (Klein 2006:207), including:

stripping off the hide of animals in burnt offerings (2 Chr 29:34)
handing blood of sacrifices to the priests (2 Chr 30:16)
prophesying under the influence of the Spirit (25:1-3; cf. 2 Chr 20:14-17)
functioning as troops (12:26; 2 Chr 23:7)
serving as musicians, scribes, officials, gatekeepers (2 Chr 34:12-13)
judging (2 Chr 19:8)
functioning in Temple service and as officers/judges (23:4)
gathering Temple taxes (2 Chr 24:5-6)
teaching people the law (2 Chr 17:7-9)

The genealogy lays the foundation for the broader involvement envisioned for the Levites in "administrative, judicial, and political responsibilities (e.g., 1 Chr 26:29-32; 2 Chr 17:7-9; 19:4-9)" throughout the Chronicler's history (Knoppers 2004:448).

The Chronicler follows this description of duties with the names and genealogies of three leaders of the Levitical musicians at the time of the first Temple: Heman (6:33b-38), Asaph (6:39-43), and Ethan (6:44-47). The Chronicler provides a genealogy for each that links them back to Levi through one of his sons: Kohath (Heman), Gershon (Asaph), and Merari (Ethan). The Kohathite Heman is simply called "the singer" (or "musician"), while the Gershonite Asaph is said to "stand on his right" (see note on 6:39) and the Merarite Ethan, "on the left" (see note on 6:44); these latter two expressions designate their lower status in support of Heman. Heman's status is also elevated by the fact that the Chronicler traces his line through Samuel all the way back to "Israel" (the name the Chronicler prefers for Jacob, accentuating his "all Israel" theme). As the clan of Kohath supplied the priestly leadership line within Levi, so this clan supplied the leadership line among the Levitical clans, even though there was collegial leadership with the other clans.

Priests (6:49-53). Although the closing verse on Levitical duties (6:48) does leave open a role for the non-priestly Levites related to the "Tabernacle," 6:49 makes clear the functional focus of the priests from Aaron's line. As the authority of the Levites is traced to David and Solomon (6:31-32), so the authority of the priests is traced to "Moses, the servant of God" (6:49). The core of their role was to make atonement (*kapar* [TH3722, ZH4105]) on behalf of Israel (see Exod 30:10-16; Num 25:11-13). To accomplish this meant attention, first, to the presentation of offerings at the two altars in the sacred precincts: the altar of burnt offering, which lay in the courtyard, and the altar of incense, which lay within the Holy Place. It also meant performance of rites related to the Most Holy Place, a reference to the annual Day of Atonement ceremonies (Exod 30:10; Lev 16). This section ends by tracing the line of those who performed this atoning function until the end of the ideal period of the united kingdom (Aaron–Ahimaaz, 6:50-53), rounding off the section on genealogies of duties that began in 6:31.[6]

Levitical territory (6:54-81). The Chronicler devotes the final section of his account of the tribe of Levi to a list of the settlement patterns of the tribe. This follows his practice in the earlier genealogies of Judah, Simeon, Reuben, Gad, and Manasseh (chs 2–5). In the "blessing" of Jacob's sons (tribes) in Genesis 49, Simeon and Levi are implicated for their role in the slaughter of Shechem (Gen 34:25-30), resulting in the curse that they would be scattered throughout Israel. This was not lost on the Chronicler, who included the genealogy of Simeon in 4:24-43 as an appendix to that of Judah in chapters 2–4 (see commentary there) and recorded the well-known tradition of Levi's territorial claims throughout the tribal lands of Israel. Numbers 18:20, 24 make it clear that Levi would not have a tribal territory as the other tribes (cf. Deut 10:8-9; Josh 13:33; 18:7), but instead would have God as their inheritance. They would be given villages scattered throughout the land, six of which would be designated as cities of refuge (Josh 20–21; cf. Josh 14:4).

The Chronicler's account is comprised of two sections (6:54-65, 66-81) divided by the summarizing conclusion at 6:65. Both sections are structured according to the order Kohath (6:54-61, 66-70), Gershon (6:62, 71-76), Merari (6:63, 77-81). However, the first section subdivides the Kohath allotments into priestly (6:54-60) and non-priestly (6:61), while no such distinction is made in the second section

(6:66-70). Furthermore, the first section does not provide the names of the cities granted to the non-priestly Levitical clans (6:61-63), while the second account supplies this information (6:66-81).

It is with the Kohathite priestly line of Aaron that the Chronicler thus begins his account of the assignment of territory to Levi (6:54-60), rearranging this list from his source in Joshua 21:1-40, thus giving the priests pride of place again. He lists 13 towns in Judah and Benjamin that they received. The priestly assignment was restricted to the clans associated with the Persian period community and the tribal base for the Temple at Jerusalem, which lay on the border between Judah and Benjamin.

While the priestly Kohathite line was associated with Judah and Benjamin (6:54-60), the non-priestly Kohathite line (6:61, 66-70) was associated with the tribes of Manasseh and Ephraim. Because Transjordan Manasseh was associated with the clan of Gershon (6:62, 71), most likely the Manasseh territory here is on the west side of the Jordan. This again emphasizes the important role for this Levitical clan as it functioned within the favored and central tribes of the southern kingdom (Judah, Benjamin, Simeon) and the northern kingdom (Joseph: Ephraim, Manasseh; cf. 5:1-2).

In 6:69 the Chronicler has excised from his source in Joshua 21:23-24 the words "The following towns and pasturelands were allotted to the priests from the tribe of Dan: Eltekeh, Gibbethon . . . four towns," keeping only "Aijalon, and Gath-rimmon."[7] This then transfers the original allotment to Dan to the tribe of Ephraim, a situation that reflects reality after Dan's early abandonment of its tribal allotment for peaceful land in the far north (Judg 17–18).[8] This excision, however, leaves Dan out of the list of tribes in chapter 6, an absence that will be repeated in the genealogical lists of the Transjordan tribes in chapter 7.

The other two Levitical clans (Gershon, Merari) are associated with other minor tribes that formed part of the northern kingdom. Gershon was given land in Issachar, Asher, Naphtali, and Transjordan Manasseh (Bashan). Merari was given land in Reuben, Gad, and Zebulun.

Significance. This chapter provides insight into the Chronicler's view of Temple service within Israel. First, by placing this genealogy at the center of chapters 1–9, the Chronicler foreshadows the emphasis he will place on the functions of this tribe throughout his narrative account in chapter 10—2 Chronicles 36. For the Chronicler and his community living after the Exile and under colonial rule, the Temple and its personnel were essential to the community's spiritual and social survival. Lacking monarchy and the independent political status that results from it, survivors of the Exile would rally around the Temple to preserve their identity.

Second, priests and Levites were given particular duties within the Temple service. The priests were responsible for atonement rites by presenting offerings on the altars and performing duties in the Most Holy Place (6:49), and the Levites were responsible for music and "various other tasks in the Tabernacle" (6:32, 48).

Third, these duties were authorized by the key worship founders of the past. For the Levites it was the authority of David and Solomon (6:31-32); for the priests it was the authority of Moses, the servant of God (6:49).

Fourth, priests and Levites shared the same lineage, a reality that should encourage collaboration rather than competition. The Chronicler will continually focus on the duties of these two groups of sacred personnel throughout his narrative account, suggesting that he was seeking space for the non-priestly Levitical clans in Second Temple worship. As Japhet (1993:165) notes, the Chronicler shows that the Levites had rights independent of the priests.

Fifth, the clan of Kohath is the source of the leadership not only for the priestly order through Amram (6:1-3), but also for the Levitical order through Izhar (6:33-38). This emphasis on Kohath appears in the special treatment of the Kohathite Elkanah, the father of Samuel (6:25-28). It is interesting that the territory of the clan of Kohath (6:54-61, 66-70) lies within the tribal boundaries of Judah, Benjamin, Simeon, Ephraim, and Manasseh, tribes accentuated within the Chronicler's genealogies. This shows the ancient roots of the Levitical leadership but also the key role of the line of Kohath within worship leadership.

Sixth, the Chronicler lists the Levite clans twice—Gershon (6:17, 20-21), Kohath (6:18, 22-28), Merari (6:19, 29-30)—and then traces the genealogies of the three leaders of the Levitical musicians back to one of these three clan founders (6:33b-47: Heman to Kohath, Asaph to Gershon, Ethan to Merari). This double listing reveals his desire to show the importance of all three clans of the tribe of Levi to the Temple service.

Finally, although the Chronicler saw the Jerusalem Temple as the central place of worship for all Israel, this did not restrict the priestly tribe to this "sacred preserve" (Knoppers 2004:448). Instead, the tribe of Levi had a key role to play throughout the land, a role the Chronicler will highlight elsewhere in his narrative account (13:1-3; 2 Chr 11:13-14, 16-17; 31:19). Through this dissemination of priestly influence, the Chronicler develops not only his vision for the spiritual vitality of all the tribes of Israel, but also for the territorial reclamation of the entire land. As Klein (2006:213) observes, "By being spread throughout all twelve tribes, the Levites also represent an all-Israel theme. There may be incorporated in this list an implicit hope by the Chronicler for a restoration of Israel to a territory approximating the dimensions of Israel in the era of David and Solomon."

Christian interpretation has often denigrated priestly aspects of the Old Testament because of the negative characterization of various priestly figures in the Gospel narratives. However, the priestly figure of Zechariah, the father of John the Baptist, is cast as a normative character in Luke, and the Temple precinct is a positive location for the faithful remnant who recognized Christ's arrival (Luke 1–2) and for the early church to gather (Acts 2–5). It should be remembered that the priestly covenant established with the tribe of Levi and the family of Aaron was an eternal covenant (Num 18:19; 25:12-13), one that endured throughout the history of Israel (Exod 28–29; Lev 8–9; Num 18; 25:10-18; Deut 10:8; 33:9-10; 1 Sam 2:35; 1 Kgs 2:26-27, 35; Ps 106:30-31; Mal 2:1-6). The book of Hebrews reveals how Jesus has assumed the responsibilities of the Israelite priesthood, fulfilling its rituals in the heavenly sanctuary. As a priestly mediator lies at the heart of Christian faith, so at the heart of the Chronicler's vision for the community of God is the priestly role of the tribe of Levi.

ENDNOTES

1. Japhet (1993:158) identifies a similar chiastic structure but distinguishes between "singers" and "Levites" in 6:31-48; thus, Priests (6:1-15), Levites (6:16-30), Singers (6:31-47), Levites (6:48), Priests (6:49).
2. This evidence questions Knoppers's view that the focus in 6:1-15 is not on the high priestly line because the linear genealogy does not begin until Eleazar (Knoppers 2004:412-413). Knoppers concludes, "The point of such a generation is to legitimize a line of priests in Persian period Yehud rather than to provide a continuous list of chief priests" (2004:413).
3. Rooke (2000:199) notes that the purpose of this genealogy is to highlight the unbroken priestly line before the Exile, which was then resumed after the Exile (so also Klein 2006:212), but it is interesting that the line is not traced past the Exile.
4. This is not clear in the NLT. The Hebrew text reads "his son" between each of the members of the lists in 6:20-29.
5. Klein (2006:212) argues that the inclusion of Samuel "exonerates Samuel of any suspicion of inappropriate cultic activity."
6. Japhet (1993:159) and Klein (2006:176) consider this genealogy from Aaron to Ahimaaz as preparatory for the territorial account in 6:54-81. However, the structure of the duty list for Levites in 6:31-47 has a list of duties followed by a genealogy, just as in 6:49-53.
7. Contra Japhet (1993:160) and Klein (2006:210), who read into the lists the name "Dan."
8. The Chronicler's incorporation of Dan's Levitical cities into Ephraim may be based on Judg 1:35.

◆ E. Genealogies of Issachar, Benjamin, Naphtali, Manasseh, Ephraim, and Asher (7:1-40)

The four sons of Issachar were Tola, Puah,
Jashub, and Shimron.
2 The sons of Tola were Uzzi, Rephaiah,
Jeriel, Jahmai, Ibsam, and Shemuel.
Each of them was the leader of an
ancestral clan. At the time of King
David, the total number of mighty
warriors listed in the records of these
clans was 22,600.
3 The son of Uzzi was Izrahiah. The sons
of Izrahiah were Michael, Obadiah,
Joel, and Isshiah. These five became
the leaders of clans. 4 All of them had
many wives and many sons, so the
total number of men available for
military service among their
descendants was 36,000.
5 The total number of mighty warriors
from all the clans of the tribe of Issachar
was 87,000. All of them were listed in
their genealogical records.
6 Three of Benjamin's sons were Bela,
Beker, and Jediael.
7 The five sons of Bela were Ezbon, Uzzi,
Uzziel, Jerimoth, and Iri. Each of them
was the leader of an ancestral clan.
The total number of mighty warriors
from these clans was 22,034, as listed
in their genealogical records.
8 The sons of Beker were Zemirah, Joash,
Eliezer, Elioenai, Omri, Jeremoth,
Abijah, Anathoth, and Alemeth. 9 Each
of them was the leader of an ancestral
clan. The total number of mighty
warriors and leaders from these clans
was 20,200, as listed in their
genealogical records.
10 The son of Jediael was Bilhan. The sons
of Bilhan were Jeush, Benjamin, Ehud,
Kenaanah, Zethan, Tarshish, and
Ahishahar. 11 Each of them was the
leader of an ancestral clan. From these
clans the total number of mighty
warriors ready for war was 17,200.
12 The sons of Ir were Shuppim and
Huppim. Hushim was the son of Aher.

13 The sons of Naphtali were Jahzeel,*
Guni, Jezer, and Shillem.* They were
all descendants of Jacob's concubine
Bilhah.
14 The descendants of Manasseh through
his Aramean concubine included
Asriel. She also bore Makir, the father
of Gilead. 15 Makir found wives for*
Huppim and Shuppim. Makir had a
sister named Maacah. One of his
descendants was Zelophehad, who
had only daughters.
16 Makir's wife, Maacah, gave birth to
a son whom she named Peresh. His
brother's name was Sheresh. The
sons of Peresh were Ulam and Rakem.
17 The son of Ulam was Bedan. All
these were considered Gileadites,
descendants of Makir son of
Manasseh.
18 Makir's sister Hammoleketh gave
birth to Ishhod, Abiezer, and Mahlah.
19 The sons of Shemida were Ahian,
Shechem, Likhi, and Aniam.
20 The descendants of Ephraim were
Shuthelah, Bered, Tahath, Eleadah,
Tahath, 21 Zabad, Shuthelah, Ezer, and
Elead. These two were killed trying to
steal livestock from the local farmers
near Gath. 22 Their father, Ephraim,
mourned for them a long time, and
his relatives came to comfort him.
23 Afterward Ephraim slept with his
wife, and she became pregnant and
gave birth to a son. Ephraim named
him Beriah* because of the tragedy
his family had suffered. 24 He had a
daughter named Sheerah. She built
the towns of Lower and Upper Beth-
horon and Uzzen-sheerah.
25 The descendants of Ephraim included
Rephah, Resheph, Telah, Tahan,
26 Ladan, Ammihud, Elishama, 27 Nun,
and Joshua.

28 The descendants of Ephraim lived in
the territory that included Bethel and its
surrounding towns to the south, Naaran
to the east, Gezer and its villages to the
west, and Shechem and its surrounding
villages to the north as far as Ayyah and
its towns. 29 Along the border of Manasseh
were the towns of Beth-shan,* Taanach,
Megiddo, Dor, and their surrounding vil-
lages. The descendants of Joseph son of
Israel* lived in these towns.
30 The sons of Asher were Imnah, Ishvah,
Ishvi, and Beriah. They had a sister
named Serah.
31 The sons of Beriah were Heber and
Malkiel (the father of Birzaith).
32 The sons of Heber were Japhlet,
Shomer, and Hotham. They had
a sister named Shua.
33 The sons of Japhlet were Pasach,
Bimhal, and Ashvath.
34 The sons of Shomer were Ahi,* Rohgah,
Hubbah, and Aram.
35 The sons of his brother Helem* were
Zophah, Imna, Shelesh, and Amal.
36 The sons of Zophah were Suah,
Harnepher, Shual, Beri, Imrah, 37 Bezer,
Hod, Shamma, Shilshah, Ithran,* and
Beera.
38 The sons of Jether were Jephunneh,
Pispah, and Ara.
39 The sons of Ulla were Arah, Hanniel,
and Rizia.
40 Each of these descendants of Asher was
the head of an ancestral clan. They were
all select men—mighty warriors and out-
standing leaders. The total number of
men available for military service was
26,000, as listed in their genealogical
records.

7:13a As in parallel text at Gen 46:24; Hebrew reads *Jahziel,* a variant spelling of Jahzeel. **7:13b** As in some Hebrew and Greek manuscripts (see also Gen 46:24; Num 26:49); most Hebrew manuscripts read *Shallum.* **7:15** Or *Makir took a wife from.* The meaning of the Hebrew is uncertain. **7:23** *Beriah* sounds like a Hebrew term meaning "tragedy" or "misfortune." **7:29a** Hebrew *Beth-shean,* a variant spelling of Beth-shan. **7:29b** *Israel* is the name that God gave to Jacob. **7:34** Or *The sons of Shomer, his brother, were.* **7:35** Possibly another name for *Hotham;* compare 7:32. **7:37** Possibly another name for *Jether;* compare 7:38.

NOTES

7:3 ***These five.*** Uzzi's son was Izrahiah, who in turn had four sons: Michael, Obadiah, Joel, and Isshiah. The number five here must then refer to the recorded descendants of Uzzi, which included his son and four grandsons.

7:8 ***Anathoth, and Alemeth.*** These last two names are also the names of towns in Benjamin (6:60). Anathoth was the hometown of the prophet Jeremiah and the location of exile for the priest Abiathar (1 Kgs 2:26). Alemeth was also known as Almon (Josh 21:18).

7:15 ***Makir found wives for.*** See NLT mg. The Hebrew idiom here is *laqakh* [TH3947, ZH4374] (to take) *'ishah* [TH802, ZH851] (a wife) *l-*[TH3807.1, ZH4200] (for) someone. The preposition *l-* introduces the one for whom the wife is taken (Gen 4:19; 24:4), not the one from whom the wife is taken, so the NLT text is preferable over NLT mg.

Makir had a sister named Maacah. Lit., "and the name of his sister (was) Maacah." The antecedent for "his" may be Makir but may also be Shuppim, which may better explain why Maacah appears in the following verse as the wife of Makir.

One of his descendants was Zelophehad, who had only daughters. Lit., "and the name of the second (was) Zelophehad, and daughters were to Zelophehad." It is uncertain why Zelophehad is called "the second." In Num 27:1 Zelophehad is called the son of "Hepher son of Gilead, son of Makir, son[1] of Manasseh, son of Joseph." While Makir is the father of Gilead, Zelophehad is the grandson of Gilead. Thus, this reference to the "second" is not related to Manasseh's or Makir's families, but rather to Hepher's family.[2] For the story of Zelophehad and his daughters, see Num 27:1-11; 36:1-12; Josh 17:3-6.

7:17 ***All these were considered Gileadites, descendants of Makir son of Manasseh.*** Lit., "These (were) the sons of Gilead son of Makir son of Manasseh." Although the name Gilead most likely refers to the well-known Transjordan region of the same name, here Gilead is considered an ancestor in the line of Manasseh and Makir (Num 27:1). Gilead was at least the grandfather of Zelophehad.

7:18 ***Makir's sister.*** Lit., "his sister"; the antecedent may be Makir but also could be the Peresh of 7:16 or even the Gilead of 7:17 (if taken as a personal name—see note on 7:17), especially if the Iezer of Num 26:30 is Hammoleketh's son Abiezer here.[3]

Abiezer, and Mahlah. For Abiezer, see previous note. Gideon was from this clan (Judg 6:11, 34; 8:2). Mahlah may be the name of a daughter (notice how one of Zelophehad's daughters was called by this name, Num 26:33).

7:20-21 ***The descendants of Ephraim were Shuthelah, Bered, Tahath, Eleadah, Tahath, Zabad, Shuthelah, Ezer, and Elead.*** Lit., "And the sons of Ephraim were Shuthelah, and Bered his son, Tahath his son, Eleadah his son, Tahath his son, Zabad his son, Shuthelah his son, and Ezer and Elead." The repetition of the names Shuthelah, Tahath, and possibly Elead(ah), looks like a linear genealogy, but this seems to be rendered impossible by the fact that Ephraim himself mourns over the murder of the final two members, Ezer and Elead (7:22). However, the term "his son" is not connected to the first Shuthelah nor to Ezer and Elead. This evidence suggests that the Chronicler lists Shuthelah, Ezer, and Elead as the three original sons of Ephraim, and that the rest of the list (Bered, Tahath, Eleadah, Tahath, Zabad, Shuthelah) is the linear genealogy tracing seven generations down the line of Shuthelah.[4]

local farmers near Gath. Lit., "the men of Gath who were born in the land." Although Gath may refer to one of the five key Philistine city-states along the coastal plain, Knoppers (2004:484) suggests it may be Gath-gittaim, which guarded the western approach to the Aijalon valley.

7:25-27 ***The descendants of Ephraim included Rephah, Resheph, Telah, Tahan.*** Lit., "And Rephah his son, and Resheph, and Telah his son, and Tahan his son." These, then, are probably the descendants of Beriah, who was mentioned in 7:23 and whose daughter was Sheerah. Since this list ends with Non (Nun) and Joshua, it is most likely a linear genealogy tracing down through eight or nine generations.

7:28 ***south . . . east . . . west . . . north.*** The Hebrew text only has the terms east and west, although most likely Shechem and Bethel are the north and south boundaries. At the southern edge of Ephraim, Bethel was associated with both Benjamin (Josh 18:21-22) and Ephraim (Judg 1:22); and although Bethel usually lay within the northern kingdom (1 Kgs 12:29-30), it was vulnerable to southern conquest (2 Chr 13:19). Shechem lay in the pass between Mount Gerizim and Mount Ebal (thus its name means "shoulder"). Its association with both Manasseh (Josh 17:2, 7) and Ephraim (Josh 20:7) reveals its northern border position. The location of Ayyah is uncertain. Japhet (1993:184) associates it with Ai, but this would place it in the south near Bethel rather than in the north near Shechem.

COMMENTARY

Sources. Knoppers (2004:468) has provided a list of the extensive use of earlier biblical lists in chapter 7, noting especially the influence of Genesis 46 on 7:1, 6, 12, 14, 30-31; Numbers 26 on 7:6, 19-20; and Joshua 16–17 on 7:28-29. As with chapter 5, the Chronicler had much more potential material to include but limited himself because of his rhetorical purposes in the genealogy as a whole.

Structure and Content. The overall structure of the Chronicler's genealogies in chapters 1–9 is arranged in a chiasm that places the tribe of Levi at its center (ch 6), the northern tribes on either side of Levi (chs 5, 7), the southern tribes on either side of the northern tribes (chs 2–4, 8), and finally Israel as the final bracket (chs 1, 9).

While chapter 5 (a unit corresponding to ch 7 in the chiasm) covers the northern tribes east of the Jordan River (Transjordan), chapter 7 covers the northern tribes west of the Jordan River (Cisjordan). Although the names Dan and Zebulun appeared in the list of Jacob's sons in 2:1-2, no accounting of their descendants is provided in the Chronicler's genealogy.[5] Zebulun is mentioned in the list of Levitical allotments throughout the tribes of Israel in chapter 6 (6:63, 77), but Dan is also absent there. The Chronicler excised the name of Dan from his source material and associated some of the towns of Dan with Ephraim (see commentary on 6:69).

Half of the lists in this section (Issachar, Benjamin, Asher) contain the results of military enumeration,[6] a characteristic that links this section to the corresponding lists of northern tribes in chapter 5 (see 5:18-26). The first military enumeration list for Issachar is specifically linked to the time of David (7:2), implicitly connecting the rest of the lists in this chapter to that time period. Connections to the period of David and Solomon (the Davidic united kingdom) were also evident in the lists of Simeon (ch 4), the Transjordan tribes (ch 5), and Levi (ch 6).[7]

The tribes of Joseph are structured together as a unit, constituting almost half the chapter at its center (Japhet 1993:170; Klein 2006:218). These facts highlight the importance of Manasseh and Ephraim within the northern tribes, a point made explicit in the Chronicler's introduction to the northern tribes in 5:1-2.

Descendants of Issachar (7:1-5). Issachar's line is traced with a segmented/linear genealogy for five generations: through Issachar-Tola-Uzzi-Izrahiah to the sons of

Izrahiah. Although there is linear progression in the genealogy (one individual from each generation carries on the line), in the third (7:2b) and fifth (7:3b-4) generations the Chronicler notes that all the sons became "leaders" (*ra'shim* [TH7218, ZH8031]), a term that in both cases is followed by a reference to military enumeration. Similarly, the account as a whole ends in 7:5 with a summary note on the total number of military personnel available from Issachar. The connection to David stresses the purpose of the list for the Chronicler. Issachar represents a key military resource for the Davidic kingdom, foreshadowing their participation in David's army in the Chronicler's narrative in 12:32, where they will be singled out as those who "understood the signs of the times and knew the best course for Israel to take." Issachar is given the highest number of warriors in the genealogical accounts of the northern tribes, reflecting the Chronicler's high estimation of this tribe.

Descendants of Benjamin (7:6-12). The line of Benjamin is structured according to a segmented genealogy and is built around the material in 7:7-11. The three sons of Benjamin are named in 7:6: Bela, Beker, and Jediael. Bela had five sons; Beker, nine sons; and Jediael, only one (Bilhan), who in turn had seven. These segmented genealogies echo those of the clans of Issachar (7:1-5) by identifying these sons as "leaders" (*ra'shim* [TH7218, ZH8031]) of family units poised for battle. Through this the Chronicler pictures these tribes north of Judah as military units, and if the description of Issachar influences the reading of that of Benjamin, these were units available to bolster David's kingdom, again foreshadowing their participation in David's army in the Chronicler's narrative (ch 12).

The final verse (7:12), however, breaks this pattern, with names unrelated to the sons named in the introductory verse (7:6) and with no reference to military enumeration. Genesis 46:21 suggests that the names Shuppim (a common scribal error for Muppim) and Huppim are probably two other sons of Benjamin, added here for completeness. The name Ir is unattested elsewhere, but is possibly a shortened or defective form of the name Iri in 7:7. Here he is identified as the father of Shuppim and Huppim, who would then be considered grandsons of Benjamin (a legitimate translation of the Hebrew word in Gen 46:21, which usually means "sons"). To explain the final name, Hushim, many have noted that this is the name of the only son of Dan in Genesis 46:23, which follows the list of Benjamin there. Although the name Dan may have been lost due to scribal error,[8] this excision of Dan's name and inclusion into a tribe contiguous with Dan's original territory is strikingly similar to techniques already observed in 6:69, where two originally Danite cities, abandoned when Dan moved to the far north (Judg 17–18), were listed as incorporated into the tribe of Ephraim, which lay to the north of the original territory of Dan. In 7:12 the only clan of Dan is incorporated into the tribe of Benjamin, which lay directly east of the original Danite tribal allotment.

Descendants of Naphtali (7:13). This short account of Naphtali's descendants is clearly taken from Genesis 46:24-25, confirming the reliance of 7:12 on Genesis 46. In Genesis 46, the summary note about the children born to Jacob through his concubine Bilhah refers to both the sons of Dan and Naphtali.

Descendants of Joseph: Manasseh and Ephraim (7:14-29). In 7:14-28 the accounts of the tribes of Manasseh and Ephraim are treated separately; however, 7:29 suggests that these two are unified. At the end of the account of Ephraim, 7:29 clarifies the territorial holdings of the Cisjordan Manasseh tribe and concludes by mentioning the "descendants of Joseph son of Israel." Japhet (1993:170) argues for a chiastic design to the account of the tribe of Joseph (7:14-29).

A. Genealogy of Manasseh (7:14-19)
  B. Genealogy of Ephraim (7:20-27)
  B'. Settlements of Ephraim (7:28)
A'. Settlements of Manasseh (7:29)

In this way the reader is subtly reminded that Manasseh and Ephraim are the sons of the favored Joseph (see 5:1-2) and share a common lineage.

In Joshua 17:1-3 the Transjordan region (Gilead, Bashan) was given to Manasseh's firstborn son Makir, who was, in turn, the father of Gilead. The Cisjordan region was allotted to the Manasseh clans of Abiezer, Helek, Asriel, Shechem, Hepher, Shemida, and Zelophehad (the latter descended from a line of Manasseh-Makir-Gilead-Hepher). First Chronicles 7:14-19 contains several of the names linked to the Cisjordan region of Manasseh, in particular Asriel (7:14), Zelophehad (7:15), Abiezer (7:18), Shemida (7:19), and Shechem (7:19). In addition, the list of cities in 7:29 reflects Cisjordan Manasseh. Nevertheless, the influence of the Transjordan Makir, father of Gilead, can be discerned throughout the account.

The list of Manasseh is unlike those of Issachar (7:1-5), Benjamin (7:6-12), and Asher (7:30-40), which take the form of a military enumeration. It provides far more detail than that of Naphtali (7:13) and is not as focused on locations as that of Ephraim (7:20-29). Instead, it is dominated by the figure of Makir, who appeared earlier in the lists of chapter 2, where a daughter of Makir is listed as marrying into the family of Judah. Here in chapter 7 we are told that Makir married into the family of Benjamin as he found wives for the Benjaminites Huppim and Shuppim (see 7:12). This forges a close association between the Transjordan Manassehites and the key tribe of Benjamin, who would be united with Judah in the Chronicler's age.

What is distinctive about these Manasseh lists is that they emphasize lineage through women with the mention of wives for Huppim and Shuppim,[9] Makir's sister Maacah, Zelophehad's daughters, Makir's wife Maacah, who named Makir's son, and the children of Makir's sister Hammoleketh (without mention of a father). The consistent reference to women in the genealogy may suggest a matrilineal society, a proposal that may explain why the list of Judahite descendants of Hezron in 2:21-23 could be summarized as "descendants of Makir, the father of Gilead" in 2:23. This pattern of interlinking the genealogy of Makir with those of two key surviving tribes of Judah and Benjamin may be the Chronicler's way of highlighting the preservation of a remnant for the key Joseph tribe of Manasseh. However, the lack of patrilineage is the first sign of a crisis for the lineal endurance of the tribes of Joseph (especially seen in the reference to Zelophehad's daughters; see note on 7:15) that will reach a climax in the account of Ephraim.

The genealogy of Ephraim relates the original three sons of Ephraim as Shuthelah, Ezer, and Elead (see note on 7:20-21). Shuthelah's line is traced seven generations (Bered to Shuthelah II), but the lines of Ezer and Elead were cut short by the justifiable anger of Philistine farmers from Gath. The Chronicler inserted into Ephraim's account considerable extranominal (non-name) material at this point, which may prepare the way for the Philistine challenges that David will resolve as king (see 11:12-14; 18:1, 11 and compare 2 Sam 8:1, which follows, e.g., 1 Sam 18:27; 19:8; 2 Sam 5:25). More importantly, the material accentuates the lineal crisis faced by Ephraim.[10] The crisis is linked to illicit behavior ("trying to steal livestock") and its resolution to the birth of Beriah, whose name "in disaster" (NLT mg on 7:23 suggests "tragedy" or "misfortune") is enduring testimony to the crisis. From this Beriah comes a daughter, Sheerah, who was responsible for the building of three towns,[11] and a son, Rephah, whose line (see note on 7:25-27) produced that great leader of the conquest, Joshua son of Nun (Num 13:8, 16; Josh 1).

This material shows how a crisis caused by sinful behavior, which put the survival of the tribe of Ephraim at risk, was resolved through the provision of a child whose descendants would establish towns in the tribal allotment of Ephraim (Josh 16:3, 5) and lead the conquest of the land (Josh 1). The reference to Ephraim's "brothers" (NLT, "his relatives") coming to comfort him in his grief in 7:22 suggests an empathetic role to be played by the other tribes (possibly Judah and Benjamin) after the tragedy of the Exile. Interestingly, the Benjamin clans led by a certain Beriah (the same name given to Ephraim's new son) successfully routed the inhabitants of Gath according to 8:13. This is possibly the Chronicler's way of depicting vengeance for the Gittite attack and accentuating Benjamin's role on behalf of other tribes (see further commentary on ch 8).

The account of Ephraim concludes with a review of the territory inhabited by Ephraim, identifying first the southern region (Bethel), then eastern (Naaran), western (Gezer), and northern (from Shechem as far as Ayyah). In a note that forges unity between the tribes and accounts of Manasseh and Ephraim, the Chronicler turns to the northern boundary region of Manasseh. Here he identifies the towns of Beth-shan, Taanach, and Megiddo, which sat on the hills overlooking the Jezreel Valley from the south, and Dor, which was situated due west of Megiddo on the Mediterranean coast. These towns associated with Cisjordan Manasseh are listed in Joshua 17:11-12 and Judges 1:27 as those assigned to Manasseh that the tribe was unable to conquer. The Chronicler, however, emphasizes in his closing words that they were ultimately conquered by "the descendants of Joseph," possibly suggesting the role Ephraim would play in conquering these towns and at the same time reminding the reader of their shared identity as tribes of Joseph, who received the rights of the firstborn (5:1-2).

Descendants of Asher (7:30-40). The account of Asher is reminiscent of those of Issachar and Benjamin at the beginning of chapter 7, particularly in the connection of the genealogies to military leadership in 7:40, a feature that prepares the way for Asher's participation in David's army in chapter 12.

The genealogy itself is segmented, tracing the line of Asher through Beriah (7:31) to Heber (7:32). At least the children of Heber's first two sons, Japhlet (7:33) and Shomer (7:34), are recounted, and probably also his third son, Hotham (Helem of 7:35), whose line is then continued two more generations through Zophah (7:36-37) to Jether (7:38; Ithran of 7:37). The identity of the Ulla in 7:39 is unknown; it is most likely a scribal error for Heber's daughter Shua of 7:32,[12] which would mean that the lines of all of Heber's children mentioned in 7:32 would be reviewed in this account: Japhlet (7:33), Shomer (7:34), Hotham (7:35-38), and Shua (7:39).

Significance. Through the accounts in chapter 7 the Chronicler completes his review of the northern tribes begun in chapter 5. In a literary way the Chronicler's Israel is bounded by Judah (chs 2–4) and Benjamin (ch 8) and centered on Levi (ch 6). From the Chronicler's perspective, it is these three tribes whose lands and people survived the Exile, although there was confidence that the northern tribes and their territories would be included in an expanded Israelite political entity that would approximate the ideal united kingdom under David and Solomon. This inclusion of the northern tribes will be a regular feature of the Chronicler's narrative account, even if the political entity of the northern kingdom will be attacked and ignored as illegitimate (see especially 2 Chr 13 and the ubiquitous references to "all Israel").

The genealogies of three of the tribes in chapter 7 reveal an abundance of descendants, and each of these are connected to military enumerations (Issachar, Benjamin, Asher). The first of these is related to the "time of King David" (7:2), suggesting that these military records are linked to the military support of the northern tribes for David and preparing the way for the narrative of 1 Chronicles 12. By connecting the list to the period of David in 7:2, the Chronicler was subtly portraying the Cisjordan tribes as participants in the united Davidic kingdom, that ideal age and theme that will become the focus of his narrative to follow. Such allusions to Davidic kingship have been a consistent feature in the lists of non-Judah/Benjamin tribes throughout the genealogy: Simeon (4:31; cf. 4:41), Transjordan northern tribes (5:2), and Levi (6:31-32).

The genealogies of the other three tribes (Naphtali, Manasseh, and Ephraim), however, all share in common a lack of male descendants, which in patrilineal Israel would have been a point of concern. While Naphtali's future is ignored, Manasseh's crisis is solved by intermarriage with the favored tribes of Judah and Benjamin (2:21-23; 7:15). But what about Ephraim? In the earlier account of the northern tribes (ch 5) there were clear references to the exile of the northern tribes (Transjordan) due to their unfaithfulness (5:6, 25-26). In this second account of the northern tribes (Cisjordan), one can only discern a subtle allusion to the sin of Ephraimites Ezer and Elead (7:21), whose deaths led to crisis and mourning and ultimately to provision of another child (7:23). The subsequent reference to the founding of Ephraimite towns and the conquest of the land suggests a faint hope for a return of the northern tribes to their tribal allotments in the land after exile. Thus, the Chronicler makes clear that the northern tribes' crisis was brought on by their own unfaithfulness, but he held out hope for the endurance of their remnant and reinstatement in the land.

One cannot ignore the fact that Dan and Zebulun are omitted from the Chronicler's account. The Chronicler included Dan among the sons of Israel (Jacob) in 2:1-2, and so the omission here appears to be deliberate on the Chronicler's part, who excised references to Dan in his source material at both 6:69 and 7:12. These excisions ostensibly handed control of Danite territory to Ephraim (6:69) and Danite lineage to Benjamin (7:12).[13] It may be that Dan was singled out by the Chronicler because of its blatant abandonment of its territorial allotment, as well as its creation of a rival cult, which led the northern tribes astray (for both of these acts of Dan, see Judg 18; 1 Kgs 12:29-30; 2 Chr 11:14-15; 13:8-12).[14]

But this does not explain the absence of Zebulun, who does appear elsewhere in the Chronicler's account (2:1; 6:63; 12:33, 40; 2 Chr 30:10-11, 18; see Knoppers 2004:459). The absence of Zebulun cannot be attributed to a lack of source material, for the Chronicler had plenty at his disposal in the Torah (Klein 2006:217). It may be that Zebulun was lost through scribal error,[15] but it may also be that the Chronicler was reminding the northern tribes that one of the consequences of their disobedience was a loss of two of their tribes.

It is odd that Benjamin is mentioned among these northern tribes, especially in light of the considerable attention afforded this tribe in chapters 8–9. Williamson (1982:77) suggested that Benjamin was simply the next component after Issachar in the Chronicler's source list and so was copied as well (cf. Klein 2006:220). Curtis and Madsen (1910:147) sought to reconstruct the missing account of Zebulun from the Benjamin section with little success.[16] Oeming, however, has provided the best suggestion so far by tracing the relationship between the tribe of Benjamin and the northern tribes throughout the history of Israel (1990:161-163). There is some ambiguity over Benjamin's affiliation within Israel as a nation; at times it is affiliated with the north and at others with the south. This was not necessarily a negative situation for the Chronicler, who has shown a willingness to highlight relationships between the northern tribes and Judah and Benjamin in his references to Manasseh's son Makir. Benjamin's status as a "neutral" buffer tribe between Joseph and Judah granted it status as a go-between and possibly also as a legitimate remnant of the northern kingdom within the Chronicler's province of Yehud.

The Chronicler's inclusion of most of the Cisjordan northern tribes sent the message to his Judean audience that members of these northern tribes were to be considered as part of "Israel." This subtle call to unity was key in an era in which the territory of these tribes did not form a separate province in the Persian Empire. The omission of Zebulun and Dan, however, is a reminder of the devastating effects of the Exile on the community. The overall shape of the genealogy suggests that the Chronicler's Judah-Benjamin-Levi community had a role to play in preserving and encouraging faithful members of these northern tribes.

ENDNOTES

1. Better rendered "of the clans of" (*mishpekhoth* [TH4940, ZH5476]).
2. Edelman (1991:179-201) argues that "his sister" (*'akhotho* [TH269, ZH295]; NLT, "Makir had a sister") originally read "the first" (*ha'akhath* [TH259, ZH285]), thus making Maacah and Zelophehad two wives of Makir. The changes are too extensive and diverge too greatly from the Chronicler's known sources.
3. Demsky (1982:70-75) argued that Hammoleketh is to be identified as Zelophehad's daughter Milcah (Num 27:1), but Milcah was the great-great-granddaughter of Makir.
4. A comparison with Num 26:35-36 reveals that Ephraim also had sons by the name of Beker and Tahan, which some have connected to the names Bered and Tahath here in 7:20. If these connections can be sustained, it is possible that Num 26:36a is a concluding summary note related to the previous two families.
5. Williamson (1982:47-48, 78) suggests that possibly scribal error has caused the excision of the material on Zebulun, Dan, and Naphtali.

6. Japhet (1993:168) and Klein (2006:217) note common elements within these three sections of this chapter: (1) a genealogical citation from the Pentateuch (cf. Num 26); (2) references to the ancestral clans; (3) military terminology; and (4) absence of settlement notes.
7. Japhet (1993:73) suggests that this technique also explains the interruption of the various lists in chs 2–4, although this is far from certain (see commentary on chs 2–4).
8. Knoppers (2004:453) argues for the insertion of the phrase "the descendants of Dan" here.
9. Contra Edelman (1991:179-201), Japhet (1993:175), and Klein (2006:225), who see the reference to Huppim and Shuppim as a secondary scribal intrusion.
10. There is great debate over the historicity of this incident, because Ephraim was born in Egypt and died long before the exodus of Israel and conquest of the land. Either this account represents a personification of the tribe of Ephraim (which would need to be carried over into 7:23, where Ephraim has intercourse with his wife and conceives a son), like the personification of Rachel in Jer 31:15, or the account refers to a later Ephraim who was the father of Ezer and Elead (cf. Klein 2006:232-233).
11. There is a precedent for the involvement of females in the founding of towns; see 2:50-52, where the offspring of the woman Ephrathah founds three towns in Judah. Upper and Lower Beth-horon lay on the southern boundary of Ephraim with Benjamin (Josh 10:10-11; 18:13-14).
12. So Japhet 1993:187. She notes that the descendants of females are often placed at the end of accounts (see 2:16-17; 7:18).
13. The only time Dan is mentioned in the Chronicler's account (besides the common idiom "from Dan to Beersheba"—21:2; 2 Chr 30:5—and an Aramean conquest of the city of Dan—2 Chr 16:4) is in the list of the sons of Israel (Jacob) in 2:1-2 and the list of tribal officers in 27:16-22.
14. This does not explain why Bethel was not singled out as well, since it was the other cult center of the northern kingdom (see 1 Kgs 12:29-30).
15. See Williamson 1982:47-48, 78.
16. This position is attacked by Williamson (1982:77) and Klein (2006:221).

◆ F. Genealogies of Benjamin and Saul (8:1–9:1a)

Benjamin's first son was Bela, the second was Ashbel, the third was Aharah, 2the fourth was Nohah, and the fifth was Rapha.

3The sons of Bela were Addar, Gera,
Abihud,* 4Abishua, Naaman, Ahoah,
5Gera, Shephuphan, and Huram.

6The sons of Ehud, leaders of the clans living at Geba, were exiled to
Manahath. 7Ehud's sons were Naaman, Ahijah, and Gera. Gera, who led them into exile, was the father of Uzza and Ahihud.*

8After Shaharaim divorced his wives Hushim and Baara, he had children in
the land of Moab. 9His wife Hodesh gave birth to Jobab, Zibia, Mesha,
Malcam, 10Jeuz, Sakia, and Mirmah. These sons all became the leaders of clans.

11Shaharaim's wife Hushim had already given birth to Abitub and Elpaal. 12The
sons of Elpaal were Eber, Misham, Shemed (who built the towns of Ono and Lod and their nearby villages),
13Beriah, and Shema. They were the leaders of the clans living in Aijalon, and they drove out the inhabitants of Gath.

14Ahio, Shashak, Jeremoth, 15Zebadiah,
Arad, Eder, 16Michael, Ishpah, and Joha were the sons of Beriah.

17 Zebadiah, Meshullam, Hizki, Heber,
18 Ishmerai, Izliah, and Jobab were the
sons of Elpaal.
19 Jakim, Zicri, Zabdi, 20 Elienai, Zillethai,
Eliel, 21 Adaiah, Beraiah, and Shimrath
were the sons of Shimei.
22 Ishpan, Eber, Eliel, 23 Abdon, Zicri,
Hanan, 24 Hananiah, Elam, Anthothijah,
25 Iphdeiah, and Penuel were the sons
of Shashak.
26 Shamsherai, Shehariah, Athaliah,
27 Jaareshiah, Elijah, and Zicri were the
sons of Jeroham.
28 These were the leaders of the ancestral
clans; they were listed in their genealogical
records, and they all lived in Jerusalem.
29 Jeiel* (the father of* Gibeon) lived in
the town of Gibeon. His wife's name
was Maacah, 30 and his oldest son was
named Abdon. Jeiel's other sons were
Zur, Kish, Baal, Ner,* Nadab, 31 Gedor,
Ahio, Zechariah,* 32 and Mikloth, who
was the father of Shimeam.* All these
families lived near each other in
Jerusalem.
33 Ner was the father of Kish.
Kish was the father of Saul.
Saul was the father of Jonathan,
Malkishua, Abinadab, and Esh-baal.
34 Jonathan was the father of Merib-baal.
Merib-baal was the father of Micah.
35 Micah was the father of Pithon,
Melech, Tahrea,* and Ahaz.
36 Ahaz was the father of Jadah.*
Jadah was the father of Alemeth,
Azmaveth, and Zimri.
Zimri was the father of Moza.
37 Moza was the father of Binea.
Binea was the father of Rephaiah.*
Rephaiah was the father of Eleasah.
Eleasah was the father of Azel.
38 Azel had six sons: Azrikam, Bokeru,
Ishmael, Sheariah, Obadiah, and
Hanan. These were the sons of Azel.
39 Azel's brother Eshek had three sons:
the first was Ulam, the second was
Jeush, and the third was Eliphelet.
40 Ulam's sons were all mighty warriors
and expert archers. They had many
sons and grandsons—150 in all.

All these were descendants of Benjamin.

CHAPTER 9

So all Israel was listed in the genealogical
records in *The Book of the Kings of Israel.*

8:3 Possibly *Gera the father of Ehud;* compare 8:6. **8:7** Or *Gera, that is Heglam, was the father of Uzza and Ahihud.* **8:29a** As in some Greek manuscripts (see also 9:35); Hebrew lacks *Jeiel.* **8:29b** Or *the founder of.* **8:30** As in some Greek manuscripts (see also 9:36); Hebrew lacks *Ner.* **8:31** As in parallel text at 9:37; Hebrew reads *Zeker,* a variant spelling of Zechariah. **8:32** As in parallel text at 9:38; Hebrew reads *Shimeah,* a variant spelling of Shimeam. **8:35** As in parallel text at 9:41; Hebrew reads *Tarea,* a variant spelling of Tahrea. **8:36** As in parallel text at 9:42; Hebrew reads *Jehoaddah,* a variant spelling of Jadah. **8:37** As in parallel text at 9:43; Hebrew reads *Raphah,* a variant spelling of Rephaiah.

NOTES

8:1 *Benjamin's first son was Bela.* Lit., "Benjamin fathered Bela his firstborn." In Hebrew "his firstborn" is *bekoro* [TH1060, ZH1147], strikingly similar to what is considered the name of Benjamin's second son in 7:6 and Gen 46:21. It is uncertain whether this is the name of the second son or status of the first son.

8:6 *Ehud.* The judge Ehud was the son of Gera and a Benjaminite (Judg 3:12-30). If the Ehud in 8:6 is the same person as the Abihud of 8:3, then he is the son of Bela. It is possible, however, that the Ehud here is the son of one of the individuals named Gera in 8:3-4 and that he in turn named his own son after his father (8:7). It is also possible that the judge Ehud came much later in this line and that the presence of the names Ehud and Gera highlight traditional family names in this clan.

Geba. This Benjaminite Levitical city was six miles northeast of Jerusalem (Josh 18:24; 21:17). Some of the early returnees in the Persian period were from Geba (Ezra 2:26; Neh 7:30; 11:31). In the settlement traditions of Joshua, Geba, Gibeon, and Gibeah are all considered Benjaminite towns (Josh 18:21-28; though cf. Josh 15:1, 57), with Gibeon and Geba designated as Levitical cities (Josh 21:17). The dominant tradition about Saul's hometown is that it was called Gibeah, and it was from there that he ruled Israel (1 Sam 10:26; 11:4; 15:34; 22:6; 23:19; 26:1; 2 Sam 21:6). At times, however, there appears to be very close connections between Gibeah and Geba in the stories of 1 Samuel. First, both towns are called "of Benjamin": Gibeah of Benjamin (Judg 19–20, passim; 1 Sam 13:2, 15; 14:16; 2 Sam 23:29), Geba of Benjamin (1 Sam 13:16; 1 Kgs 15:22). Second, at times the towns are mentioned in the same events and appear to be referring to the same location. For instance, 1 Sam 13:2 relates how Saul had 3,000 men in Micmash and Bethel while Jonathan had 1,000 at Gibeah of Benjamin. In 1 Sam 13:3-4, Jonathan is depicted as leading a force against Geba, which has a Philistine outpost. Interestingly, back in 1 Sam 10:5 the Gibeah (of God) where Saul was anointed by the Spirit of the Lord is also identified as having a Philistine outpost. Additionally, in 1 Sam 14, while in the vicinity of Gibeah (1 Sam 14:2, 16), Jonathan crosses over to attack a Philistine garrison (1 Sam 14:1, 6, 11-12) that is related to Geba (1 Sam 14:5). First Samuel 13:15 records that Samuel went to Gibeah of Benjamin, and then the following verse continues the narrative concerning Saul and Jonathan and their army at Geba of Benjamin. In ch 8, however, although there is close attention to the tribe of Benjamin and to Saul's roots, there is not one mention of Gibeah, but rather only of Geba and Gibeon. It may be that Geba, Gibeah, and Gibeon were considered the same entity by the Chronicler, and this may explain why Saul was identified with Gibeon.

8:8 *Shaharaim divorced his wives.* The Hebrew verb here is *shalakh* [TH7971, ZH8938] (to send [away]), which is used for divorce in Deut 24:1 ("sends her away from his house"), Isa 50:1 ("was your mother sent away"), Jer 3:8 (lit., "I have sent her away and I have given the certificate of her divorce").

8:12 *their nearby villages.* Lit., "their daughters," a metaphor in which the larger city (often fortified) is the mother and its dependencies are considered the daughters.

8:13 *Gath.* Although this may refer to one of the key Philistine cities on the coastal plain, Knoppers (2004:484) suggests it may be Gath-gittaim, which guarded the western approach to the Aijalon valley.

8:21 *Shimei.* Klein (2006:252) suggests that Shimei is the Shema of 8:13.

8:27 *Jeroham.* Knoppers (2004:484) suggests that Jeroham is the Jeremoth of 8:14.

8:29 *Jeiel (the father of Gibeon) lived in the town of Gibeon.* The name Jeiel is missing in the Hebrew text (see NLT mg), but it can be reconstructed from the same list in 9:35. Here "father" may mean "founder" of the town, since the name Gibeon does not appear in Jeiel's family list. Gibeon lay about six miles northwest of Jerusalem in Benjaminite territory (ABD 2.1010). See note on 8:6.

8:32 *All these families lived near each other in Jerusalem.* Lit., "And also they (were) near their brothers (who) lived in Jerusalem with their brothers." The identity of these "brothers" is not clear but probably refers to the Benjaminite clans of 8:28 that lived in Jerusalem. The NLT suggests that this family that "lived in the town of Gibeon" (8:29) also lived in Jerusalem, but the Hebrew text does not clearly state this. Instead, the transition between 8:28 and 8:29 suggests a contrast between Saul's family and those in Jerusalem, since the final Hebrew construction in 8:28 is "in Jerusalem" and is followed immediately by "but in Gibeon" at the outset of 8:29.[1] Nevertheless, the Chronicler was making a connection between Saul's ancestors and Jerusalem but clearly placed them in Gibeon (see further below).

8:33 *Jonathan, Malkishua, Abinadab, and Esh-baal.* The Chronicler begins his account in ch 10 with a description of the death of these first three sons of Saul. Esh-baal, the youngest son of Saul and his heir (2 Sam 2:8), was also called Ishbosheth. Esh-/Ish- means either "man" or "gift" (ABD 2.615). The alternative name replaces the word "Baal" (lord) with the word "shame," and possibly represents a deliberate excision of the name of this god. See also the shift in the name of Mephibosheth (2 Sam 4:4), who was also known as Merib-baal (8:34; 9:40). Interestingly, the Chronicler used the term "baal" in association with Saul's family, possibly a subtle undermining of a king he considered illegitimate.

9:1a *So all Israel was listed in the genealogical records in* The Book of the Kings of Israel. This note at the beginning of ch 9 more properly belongs at the end of ch 8 (as it is set in the NLT). It serves as a summary note for the genealogy of Israel that began in 2:1-2 with the list of the sons of Israel. Here the Chronicler uses the phrase "all Israel," a ubiquitous phrase in his narrative account, which emphasizes his ideal of all the tribes of Israel united around the Davidic king in Jerusalem.

COMMENTARY

Sources. For Benjamin's genealogy, the Chronicler drew on earlier biblical sources. In particular, 8:1-3a draws on Genesis 46 and Numbers 26; 8:3b on Judges 3:15; 8:33 on 1 Samuel 31:2; and 8:34 on 2 Samuel 4:4; 9:12 (Knoppers 2004:487).

While the Chronicler mentioned generically some genealogical sources throughout his lists in chapters 2–8 (5:1, 17; 7:5, 7, 9, 40; 8:28), the summarizing source note in 9:1a (see note) identifies a key source as *The Book of the Kings of Israel.* This source is mentioned in 2 Chronicles 20:34 and 36:8 as his source for the reigns of Jehoshaphat and Jehoiakim. That this source is not related to the canonical book of Kings is evident from 2 Chronicles 20:34, which claims that *The Record of Jehu Son of Hanani* is part of this book. By mentioning a source used also for his narrative accounts, the Chronicler was creating a link to the narrative that follows in chapter 10—2 Chronicles 36. The citation also serves as a subtle reminder not only that the Israel of these genealogies is the foundation for the monarchy but also that Israel's identity is defined by the monarchy and especially the worship structures and rhythms created by the Davidic royal house at Jerusalem.

Structure and Content. As noted in the introduction to 1 Chronicles 1–9, the Chronicler structures his Israelite genealogies (chs 2–8) in a chiasm that places Levi at the center of Israel (ch 6) and Judah (chs 2–4) and Benjamin (ch 8) as the bracket around the northern tribes (chs 5, 7). It is the tribes of Judah and Benjamin who dominate the Chronicler's narrative section in chapter 10—2 Chronicles 36 because they were key groups who comprised the Jewish colony at the start of the Persian restoration period (Ezra 1:5).

Benjamin has already been reviewed in the account of the Cisjordan northern tribes in 7:6-12, reminding the reader of Benjamin's role as a tribe sandwiched between the northern and southern tribal units. These northern affiliations for this later southern tribe possibly can be discerned in chapter 8 with the allusions to exile (8:6-8) and the links to Ephraim (8:13). Benjamin's connection to Manahath (8:6), however, is a reminder of the close relationship between Benjamin and Judah.

The account of Benjamin provides genealogies of the main clans of the tribe

(8:1-28) and then the particular clan from which the first king of Israel, Saul, would arise (8:29-40).[2] The relationship of Saul's clan to the rest of Benjamin is not made explicit. The dominance of segmented genealogies in the account of the main clans (8:1-28) emphasizes the abundance of descendants in this tribe. Although dominated by linear genealogies, the account of Saul's clan begins and ends with a segmented genealogy (8:38-40), in contrast to the form of this genealogy found in 9:35-44, where the content in 8:39-40 has been excised. The form of this genealogy in chapter 8 points to its function of bolstering the size of the Benjaminite tribe.

Benjamin's ancestral clans (8:1-28). The first section of Benjamin's genealogy uses a segmented format to trace Benjamin's line down four generations from Benjamin through Bela to Abihud/Ehud, to Gera, to Gera's sons (Uzza, Ahihud). Multiple sons are listed for each generation, but the line of only one of these sons is then traced to the next generation. The account of this line ends with a reference to an exile to Manahath, but it is uncertain whether it was Benjaminites who were deported to Manahath, whether Benjaminites deported former non-Israelite inhabitants of Geba to Manahath, or whether Benjaminite clans deported other Benjaminite clans to Manahath.[3] Interestingly, Manahath is associated with the sons of the Calebite Salma in 2:54, among whom also are found the inhabitants of Bethlehem. It is possible that this exile to Manahath suggests Benjaminite inclusion in the heart of Judahite territory and identity, but this is not certain.

The second section introduces an individual named Shaharaim, whose connection to the previous material is uncertain.[4] The first information the Chronicler provides concerns Shaharaim's divorce of his two wives Hushim and Baara and the list of his seven sons through his new wife in Moab. His enduring legacy, however, is traced through one of his divorced wives, Hushim, who established a line that endured through Beriah and his sons Shashak and Jeremoth/Jeroham (8:14-16, 22-25, 26-27) and Elpaal with his son Shimei/Shema (8:12-13, 17-18, 19-21).

Both of these sections cast a shadow across Benjamin's past by noting Benjaminite foreign sojourns (8:6-8), which are always linked in Chronicles to some sinful cause (see 2 Chr 33; 36 and especially 2 Chr 6:36-39). The reference to the divorcing of wives (8:8) does not appear to be a positive feature, since it is followed by a marriage to a wife in a foreign land (8:9). The fact that the line of one of the divorced wives dominates the list suggests the Chronicler's disapproval.

Four towns are mentioned in the list at 8:12-13, those of Ono, Lod, Aijalon, and Gath. The first two are mentioned in the list of exilic returnees (Ezra 2:33//Neh 7:37; cf. Neh 11:35) and probably represented the border of the province of Yehud in the Chronicler's time.[5] Their mention here may be related to the extent of the province in which the Chronicler lived. However, there may be other reasons from Israelite tradition that explain the significance of these names in this list.

Oeming (1990:172) has noted that the boundaries of Joshua 16 would place Ono and Lod within the territory of Ephraim that originally was Danite territory.[6] Here towns originally within Danite territory, which were associated later with Ephraim, are linked to Benjamin. Similarly, Aijalon was a town within Dan's original allotment (Josh 19:42; 21:24), which was abandoned by the Danites because of its stubborn Canaanite inhabitants (Judg 1:34; 18:1-31). Here in chapter 8 Aijalon is related to the inhabitants of Gath, suggesting that the Benjaminites were those who displaced these Canaanites. It is probably not coincidental that the Chronicler mentions the towns of Aijalon and Gath in connection with the tribe of Ephraim in chapters 6–7.[7] In 6:69 Aijalon is identified as a Levitical city of Ephraim. In 7:20-24 Gath is the city of the "local farmers" who killed Ephraim's offspring, an action that (although justified) created a crisis for the continuance of the line of Ephraim. Now in 8:13 little Benjamin, which lay directly south of Ephraim and east of traditional Dan, enacts vengeance on the Gittites and conquers Aijalon.[8] Interestingly, Beriah, who in Benjamin's genealogy is a clan head who led this charge against Gath, has the same name as the son whom Ephraim fathered after the death of his two sons at the hands of these Gittites (7:23). This strengthens further the connection between these two passages, suggesting that Ephraim honored these Benjaminites by naming his new son after this ancestral head.

The summary note for the list in 8:28 establishes a link between the Benjaminite clans and the city of Jerusalem. This city lay on the boundary between the tribal allotments of Benjamin and Judah (Josh 15:8; 18:16), and thus in the books of Joshua and Judges is associated with both tribes: Benjamin (Judg 1:21) and Judah (Josh 15:63; Judg 1:8). Both tribes struggled to displace the Canaanite Jebusites who lived in the city. It is only with David that Jerusalem was fully integrated into the tribe of Judah and the united kingdom (ch 11). In chapter 3 Jerusalem was identified as the royal city in the tribe of Judah, and it reappears here in the treatment of the other remnant tribe, Benjamin. From antiquity the Benjaminites have been connected to Jerusalem.

Saul's genealogy (8:29-40). This genealogy focuses on the line of Saul, linking his ancestors to both Gibeon and Jerusalem, as well as tracing an enduring line of descendants after his death. It will be repeated in 9:35-44 (save 8:39-40), and there it will function to introduce the story of Saul, which begins in chapter 10. In chapter 8, however, it is used to bolster the size of the Benjaminite account, making it the third-longest account after Judah (chs 2–4) and Levi (ch 6).

Most of the genealogy is linear in structure, listing only one descendant in each generation, which then carries on the line. However, at five points a segmented genealogy is provided, listing multiple descendants from which the one descendant emerges. This happens at the outset of the list (8:29-32) with Jeiel, to whom ten sons are born; in 8:33b with Saul, to whom four sons are born; in 8:35 with Saul's great-grandson Micah, to whom four sons are born; in 8:36b with Micah's grandson Jadah, to whom three sons are born; and finally at the end of the list in 8:38-40 with Azel and his six sons and Azel's brother Eshek and his three sons. The use of the segmented format for the sons of Jeiel, Saul, and Azel/Eshek is understandable, highlighting the choice of Saul's line from this Benjaminite clan and the endurance of his line. But it is difficult to discern why the families of Micah and Jadah were also singled out. Possibly Micah's sons were listed to show the reemergence of the line after the precarious phase of Jonathan (who died in battle) and Merib-baal (the Mephibosheth who was physically handicapped; cf. 2 Sam 9).

Two things are odd about the Chronicler's association of Saul's family with Gibeon (about six miles northwest of Jerusalem) in 8:29. First, in the Chronicler's source in Samuel, Gibeah (three miles north of Jerusalem) is identified as the hometown of Saul (1 Sam 10:26; 15:34; 22:6; 23:19), and Gibeon, though within Benjaminite territory (Josh 18:25), is depicted as unfriendly to Saul (2 Sam 21:1-9). The Chronicler, however, regularly refers to Gibeon as the key worship center, which housed the Tabernacle and Ark prior to the Temple's construction (16:39; 21:29; 2 Chr 1:3, 13; cf. 14:16; Knoppers 2004:485). Second, although Gibeon is mentioned at the outset of the account of Saul, his family is associated with Jerusalem in 8:32, alluding to the link already established in 8:28 for all of Benjamin.[9] It is probably more than coincidence that the Chronicler associates Saul with both Gibeon and Jerusalem, the two worship centers of the united kingdom under David and Solomon.[10]

The list ends with a segmented genealogy of the two sons of Eleasah (Azel, Eshek), to whom are connected not only abundant descendants (150), but also skilled warriors ("mighty warriors and expert archers"). The length of Saul's line reveals enduring divine blessing not only through offspring but also through military prowess. Benjamin in general and Saul's line in particular had much to offer Judah and its royal city Jerusalem.

Significance. The Chronicler's account of Benjamin clearly exalts the status of this tribe that was considered insignificant within Israelite tradition, which is indicated by Benjamin's status as youngest son and by the size of its territory (cf. Ps 68:27). In chapter 8 the Chronicler includes the genealogy of Saul at the service of the tribe, rather than the house of Saul. The genealogy provides material necessary to bolster the size of the tribe and to show its endurance as a tribe into the Chronicler's day. Genealogies tracing lines at least to the time of the Exile are found only in the lists of Judah (2:25-41; 3:1-24), Levi (6:1-15), and Benjamin (8:29-40).[11]

Although not certain, references to exile in 8:6-8 and to divorce of wives (through whom lines are then traced in 8:8-28) cast a shadow on the tribe of Benjamin and possibly prepare the way for the negative evaluation of Saul at the outset of the Chronicler's narrative in chapter 10. But there is plenty to commend Benjamin in this chapter. Benjamin appears to play a role on behalf of mighty Ephraim and by association the northern tribes. Its potential as a military force possibly for Judah and certainly for Ephraim is evident in 8:13 and 40.

Finally, the close association between Jerusalem, Gibeon, and the Benjaminites is important. After the fall of Jerusalem, the capital of the new Babylonian province was Mizpah (2 Kgs 25:23-25; Jer 40–41) in Benjaminite territory (Josh 18:21-26), most likely due to the lack of damage to the Benjaminite region—in contrast to the damage to Jerusalem (see ABD 4.880). By associating Jerusalem from antiquity with all the clans of Benjamin (8:28) and then again with Saul's family (8:32), the Chronicler was reminding the Benjaminite community of the centrality of Jerusalem (and its Temple) in his own age. Similarly, Benjaminite Saul had roots in Gibeon, a city honored by the Chronicler as David's chosen intermediate location for the Tabernacle and Ark. The Tabernacle was ultimately superseded by the Temple, and thus the focus shifts from Gibeon to Jerusalem in the narrative of the Chronicler, and hopefully for the Benjaminites of the Chronicler's age. As Jerusalem was central to Judah's and David's genealogy in chapter 3, so it is now central to Benjamin's and Saul's genealogy in chapter 8. The importance of Jerusalem to the Chronicler's age will become clear in chapter 9; Jerusalem is the destination of those who returned from both northern and southern tribes (9:3, 34).

ENDNOTES

1. See especially Japhet 1993:195; Klein 2006:253.
2. Braun (1986:122, 142), Japhet (1993:189), and Klein (2006:245) all dissociate the genealogy of 8:29-32 (//9:35-38) from the genealogy of Saul in 8:33-40 (//9:39-44), identifying 8:29-32 as part of the list of returnees in 9:1-38, which was copied over to ch 8 with the Saul material. It is true that the phrase "all these families lived near each other in Jerusalem" (8:32b//9:38b) does create a break in the Saulide genealogy, but the phrase used here is not the same as that used of Jerusalem in ch 9 (see 9:3, 34), and the use of Saulide names like Ner and Kish in 8:29-32 (//9:35-38) establishes a clear link between the two sections.
3. Both times that exile is mentioned in 8:6-7 the phrase is "they/he exiled them." It is uncertain who the "them" is in each case. Klein (2006:248) suggests that the phrase "were exiled to Manahath" could mean that "a portion of the tribe of Benjamin was exiled or the Benjaminites exiled their opponents" (the latter identifying the "they" as "a circumlocution for the passive").
4. Japhet (1993:192) suggests that Shaharaim is the same person as Huram (8:5) or Aharah (8:1), but this is pure conjecture.
5. See Williamson 1985:254-255. Klein (2006:251) argues that Neh 6:2 places these towns outside the province.
6. Cited by Klein (2006:251, note 231).
7. Hopefully this answers the question of Klein (2006:252): "Is there any relationship between Beriah the son of Elpaal in this verse and Beriah the son of Ephraim mentioned in 7:23?"
8. Although this is probably a reference to Gath-gittaim (see note above on 8:13), the name Gath is also associated in Davidic tradition with the great warrior Goliath (1 Sam 17:4), whose defeat symbolized David's subjugation of the Philistines. This Benjaminite victory over "Gath" may suggest a similar role for the Benjaminites and is especially striking since the David-Goliath tradition is absent from the Chronicler's narrative.
9. The transition between 8:28 and 8:29 in the Hebrew text creates a structural link: *yashebu birushalaim. Ubegib'on yashebu* [TH3427, ZH3782]: "they all lived in Jerusalem" (end of 8:28), "lived in the town of Gibeon" (beginning of 8:29).
10. Japhet (1993:196) suggests that allusions to Jerusalem and Gibeon in Chronicles and here may indicate "rivalry" between these two centers. However, this does not appear to be the case for the Chronicler. Rather, what he may be doing is using Gibeon to invite Benjamin's greater participation in worship, noting how David honored Gibeon and that the worship that was once there has now been transferred to Jerusalem.
11. Japhet (1993:199) traces the extent of Saul's genealogy to the late seventh century BC.

◆ G. List of Exilic Returnees and Saul's Genealogy (9:1b-44)

The people of Judah were exiled to Babylon because they were unfaithful to the LORD. 2The first of the exiles to return to their property in their former towns were priests, Levites, Temple servants, and other Israelites. 3Some of the people from the tribes of Judah, Benjamin, Ephraim, and Manasseh came and settled in Jerusalem.

4One family that returned was that of Uthai son of Ammihud, son of Omri, son of Imri, son of Bani, a descendant of Perez son of Judah.

5Others returned from the Shilonite clan, including Asaiah (the oldest) and his sons.

6From the Zerahite clan, Jeuel returned with his relatives.

In all, 690 families from the tribe of Ju-
dah returned.

7 From the tribe of Benjamin came Sallu
son of Meshullam, son of Hodaviah,
son of Hassenuah; 8 Ibneiah son of
Jeroham; Elah son of Uzzi, son of Micri;
and Meshullam son of Shephatiah, son
of Reuel, son of Ibnijah.

9 These men were all leaders of clans, and
they were listed in their genealogical re-
cords. In all, 956 families from the tribe
of Benjamin returned.

10 Among the priests who returned were
Jedaiah, Jehoiarib, Jakin, 11 Azariah son
of Hilkiah, son of Meshullam, son of
Zadok, son of Meraioth, son of Ahitub.
Azariah was the chief officer of the
house of God.

12 Other returning priests were Adaiah
son of Jeroham, son of Pashhur, son of
Malkijah, and Maasai son of Adiel, son
of Jahzerah, son of Meshullam, son of
Meshillemith, son of Immer.

13 In all, 1,760 priests returned. They were
heads of clans and very able men. They
were responsible for ministering at the
house of God.

14 The Levites who returned were
Shemaiah son of Hasshub, son of
Azrikam, son of Hashabiah, a
descendant of Merari; 15 Bakbakkar;
Heresh; Galal; Mattaniah son of Mica,
son of Zicri, son of Asaph; 16 Obadiah
son of Shemaiah, son of Galal, son of
Jeduthun; and Berekiah son of Asa,
son of Elkanah, who lived in the area
of Netophah.

17 The gatekeepers who returned were
Shallum, Akkub, Talmon, Ahiman, and
their relatives. Shallum was the chief
gatekeeper. 18 Prior to this time, they
were responsible for the King's Gate
on the east side. These men served as
gatekeepers for the camps of the
Levites. 19 Shallum was the son of Kore,
a descendant of Abiasaph,* from the
clan of Korah. He and his relatives,
the Korahites, were responsible for
guarding the entrance to the sanctuary,
just as their ancestors had guarded the
Tabernacle in the camp of the LORD.

20 Phinehas son of Eleazar had been
in charge of the gatekeepers in earlier
times, and the LORD had been with
him. 21 And later Zechariah son of
Meshelemiah was responsible for
guarding the entrance to the
Tabernacle.*

22 In all, there were 212 gatekeepers in
those days, and they were listed according
to the genealogies in their villages. David
and Samuel the seer had appointed their
ancestors because they were reliable men.
23 These gatekeepers and their descen-
dants, by their divisions, were responsible
for guarding the entrance to the house of
the LORD when that house was a tent.
24 The gatekeepers were stationed on all
four sides—east, west, north, and south.
25 Their relatives in the villages came reg-
ularly to share their duties for seven-day
periods.

26 The four chief gatekeepers, all Levites,
were trusted officials, for they were re-
sponsible for the rooms and treasuries at
the house of God. 27 They would spend the
night around the house of God, since it
was their duty to guard it and to open the
gates every morning.

28 Some of the gatekeepers were as-
signed to care for the various articles used
in worship. They checked them in and out
to avoid any loss. 29 Others were respon-
sible for the furnishings, the items in the
sanctuary, and the supplies, such as choice
flour, wine, olive oil, frankincense, and
spices. 30 But it was the priests who blend-
ed the spices. 31 Mattithiah, a Levite and
the oldest son of Shallum the Korahite,
was entrusted with baking the bread used
in the offerings. 32 And some members of
the clan of Kohath were in charge of pre-
paring the bread to be set on the table
each Sabbath day.

33 The musicians, all prominent Levites,
lived at the Temple. They were exempt
from other responsibilities since they were
on duty at all hours. 34 All these men lived

in Jerusalem. They were the heads of Le-
vite families and were listed as prominent
leaders in their genealogical records.
35 Jeiel (the father of* Gibeon) lived in
the town of Gibeon. His wife's name
was Maacah, 36 and his oldest son was
named Abdon. Jeiel's other sons were
Zur, Kish, Baal, Ner, Nadab, 37 Gedor,
Ahio, Zechariah, and Mikloth.
38 Mikloth was the father of Shimeam.
All these families lived near each
other in Jerusalem.
39 Ner was the father of Kish.
Kish was the father of Saul.
Saul was the father of Jonathan,
Malkishua, Abinadab, and Esh-baal.
40 Jonathan was the father of Merib-baal.
Merib-baal was the father of Micah.
41 The sons of Micah were Pithon,
Melech, Tahrea, and Ahaz.*
42 Ahaz was the father of Jadah.*
Jadah was the father of Alemeth,
Azmaveth, and Zimri.
Zimri was the father of Moza.
43 Moza was the father of Binea.
Binea's son was Rephaiah.
Rephaiah's son was Eleasah.
Eleasah's son was Azel.
44 Azel had six sons, whose names were
Azrikam, Bokeru, Ishmael, Sheariah,
Obadiah, and Hanan. These were the
sons of Azel.

9:19 Hebrew *Ebiasaph,* a variant spelling of Abiasaph; compare Exod 6:24. **9:21** Hebrew *Tent of Meeting.* **9:35** Or *the founder of.* **9:41** As in Syriac version and Latin Vulgate (see also 8:35); Hebrew lacks *and Ahaz.* **9:42** As in some Hebrew manuscripts and Greek version (see also 8:36); Hebrew reads *Jarah.*

NOTES

9:1b *The people of Judah.* Lit., "Judah," accentuating the tribal forefather listed in 2:1-2.

9:2 *The first of the exiles to return.* Lit., "those first ones who lived who (were) in their possessions in their cities." The NLT is correct in assuming that this refers to the exiles mentioned in 9:1, but the emphasis is not on "returning" (as though the Hebrew word here were *shub* [TH7725, ZH8740]), but rather on "living" (Heb., *yashab* [TH3427, ZH3782]).

priests, Levites, Temple servants, and other Israelites. Lit., "Israel, the priests, the Levites, and the Temple servants" (*nethinim* [TH5411, ZH5987]). "Israel" here refers to all tribal identities besides the sacred orders, as the lists that follow reveal. By placing Israel first, the Chronicler emphasizes his "all Israel" theme, now in relation to the return from exile. The term *nethinim* (meaning "the given ones") probably refers to slaves dedicated to Temple service. They are mentioned through the books of Ezra and Nehemiah (Ezra 2:43, 58, 70; 7:7; 8:17, 20; Neh 3:26, 31; 7:46, 60, 73; 10:28; 11:3, 21); they are clearly a later group of Temple functionaries.

9:4, 5, 6, 10, 12, 13, 14, 17 Though not found in the Hebrew text, the words "returned" or "returning" (v. 12) were added by the translators (based on 9:1-2) to clarify the identity of these people.

9:6 *In all, 690 families from the tribe of Judah returned.* The Hebrew reads simply the number "690." A similar bare number appears at the end of Benjamin's list in 9:9. This is probably a tally of the list that immediately precedes, as the NLT indicates.

9:9 *leaders of clans.* Lit., "heads of the fathers to the house of their fathers." Preexilic sociology appears to have been structured according to the "house of the father" (*beth 'ab* [TH1004/1, ZH1074/3]) and then the clan (*mishpakhah* [TH4940, ZH5476]) and tribe (*shebet* [TH7626, ZH8657]) in ascending order. During the Babylonian exile this structure changes so that in the Chronicler's age the term for clan was replaced by the term "house of the fathers" (*beth 'aboth*).[1]

In all, 956 families from the tribe of Benjamin returned. The Hebrew reads simply the number "956." See note on 9:6.

9:11 ***Azariah was the chief officer of the house of God.*** Heb., *negid* [TH5057, ZH5592] *beth ha'elohim,* a title used in 2 Chr 31:13 of the Zadokite "chief priest" Azariah at the time of Hezekiah.

9:13 ***responsible for ministering at the house of God.*** Lit., "for the work of the service of the house of God." See note on 6:48.

9:16 ***in the area of Netophah.*** The word for "area" is *khatser* [TH2691, ZH2958] and refers to settled areas outside of the main cities (Josh 15:46). This included villages without walls (see Lev 25:31) but also could be just a circle of tents of nomads (Gen 25:16; Isa 42:11). Netophah was a town near Bethlehem (see 2:54) and is also mentioned in the returnee lists of Ezra 2:21-23; Neh 7:26.

9:18 ***the King's Gate on the east side.*** See Ezek 44:1; 46:1-2.

9:22 ***Samuel the seer.*** See 26:28; 29:29.

9:30 ***the priests.*** Lit., "the sons of the priests."

9:32 ***the bread to be set on the table each Sabbath day.*** See Lev 24:5-9.

9:33 ***all prominent Levites.*** Lit., "heads of the fathers," a reference to the leadership of the clan system within Levi. (See note on 9:9.)

COMMENTARY

Structure and Content. The final component of the Chronicler's intricate lists in chapters 1–9 is the list of returning exiles in 9:1-34. In the overall chiastic structure of the lists of chapters 1–9, Levi lies at the center of the Chronicler's ideal Israel (ch 6), while Judah (chs 2–4) and Benjamin (ch 8) function as protective brackets around the vulnerable northern tribes originally east (ch 5) and west (ch 7) of the Jordan River. In this chiastic structure the list of chapter 9 is related to the opening list in chapter 1, which traced Israel's origin from and position within the family of nations. The list of exilic returnees in 9:1-34 depicts Israel again coming out of the family of nations, that is, out of exile.

Although 9:35-44 is a genealogy like the rest of chapters 1–9, it is structurally distinct and functions as a transition between the lists of chapters 1–9 and the narrative of chapter 10—2 Chronicles 36. By repeating a list that was used earlier (8:29-38), the Chronicler shows how the narrative arises out of the genealogies, as the story of David's rise to power is cast against the dark backdrop of the failure of Saul's rule.

List of exilic returnees (9:1b-34). The Chronicler begins the genealogy with a summary note (9:1b-3). With 9:1b the Chronicler presents the awful truth of Judah's exile to Babylon. The cause is made clear: "They were unfaithful to the LORD." The Chronicler uses one of his favorite terms for disobedience: *ma'al* [TH4603, ZH5085] (see commentary on ch 10; cf. 2 Chr 33:19), a term that was used earlier in the genealogies to explain the exile of the northern tribes east of the Jordan (5:25-26). Such unfaithfulness is consistently linked to illicit worship of foreign gods. The result of such behavior throughout his narrative account is divine discipline, the ultimate expression of which was the invasion by foreign armies and exile to foreign lands. Second Chronicles 36 recounts the phases of deportations to Babylon that took place in this painful final phase of Judah's history (see commentary there).

But as the Chronicler's narrative does not leave the community hopeless in exile (2 Chr 36), so the Chronicler's genealogy turns immediately to the return of this community. The complete absence of any record of what happened in the land of Israel during the Exile or what happened in the land of exile matches the Chronicler's approach in 2 Chronicles 36:20-21 in which the people become servants to the king of Babylon and the land lies desolate for 70 years. In his narrative in 2 Chronicles 36, the Chronicler will accentuate the role played by Yahweh and Cyrus in bringing about this return, but the focus of the genealogy is simply on the faithful few who resettled the land in the earliest phases of the restoration.

In 9:2-3 the Chronicler provides a summarizing note concerning the restoration before citing his genealogical material. First, this summary note places emphasis on the reclamation of "their property" (*'akhuzzah* [TH272, ZH299]; cf. Josh 22:19) and "their towns." Throughout the genealogical lists the Chronicler has noted the settlement patterns of the various tribes and here reminds the reader that this information was not just for historical interest, but rather to provide a vision for the geographical shape of restored Israel.

Second, by employing the list "priests, Levites, Temple servants, and other Israelites," the Chronicler defines this community not only as a collaboration of laity (Israelites) and clergy (priests, Levites, Temple servants), but also as a collaboration of all religious orders (priests, Levites, Temple servants). Such a vision for Israel is evident in the presentation of the genealogies as a whole, which places a robust tribe of Levi at the center of lay Israel and provides the foundation for the Chronicler's description of the breadth of clerical orders founded by David at the First Temple (see commentary on chs 22, 23–27).

Third, by calling the laity "Israelites" (9:2) and then mentioning the return of "Judah, Benjamin, Ephraim, and Manasseh" (9:3), the Chronicler was emphasizing the return of representatives of both southern and northern tribes.[2] Ephraim and Manasseh were the two tribes of Joseph at the heart of the former coalition of northern tribes. Joseph is singled out as the inheritor of the firstborn rights from Jacob, with Judah the inheritor of the leadership of the family (5:1-2). Judah and Benjamin are the two tribes that form the core of the community restored from exile in Babylon (Ezra 1:5). Such a remnant of both northern and southern elements shows potential for the restoration of "all Israel."

Finally, even though reclamation of the various tribal allotments is important (9:2), the Chronicler notes that "some" from these tribes "settled in Jerusalem." This emphasis on Jerusalem as the geographical center of this new Israel was important to the Chronicler, for whom the Temple is the key identity marker in his own era. This explains his concern to record the lists of priests and Levites who returned and to conclude his lists with the note, "All these men lived in Jerusalem" (9:34).

Following this summary note, the Chronicler continues to cite from his source (see Neh 11), which was focused on the return of people from Judah, Benjamin, and the clerical orders (9:4-34). The lists of laity in Judah (9:4-6) and Benjamin (9:7-9) are concise, listing three individuals and clans from Judah (Uthai, Asaiah, Jeuel) and four from Benjamin (Sallu, Ibneiah, Elah, Meshullam). The three individuals from Judah are representative of the three main clans of the tribe (2:3-4): Perez (Uthai), Shelah (Asaiah), and Zerah (Jeuel). In each case summary numbers are provided with Judah (690) considerably lower in number than Benjamin (956).

The lists of clergy span 9:10-34 and incorporate not only names but also accounts of their worship duties. Only six priests are named in the list of 9:10-23 (Jedaiah, Jehoiarib, Jakin, Azariah, Adaiah, Maasai), but a total of 1,760 is given for the order. Three priests stand out from the list because of the extended lineage attached to their names.

Azariah is the most prominent of these three, not only because he is related to Zadok (son of Hilkiah, son of Meshullam, son of Zadok, son of Meraioth, son of Ahitub), but also because a function (chief officer of the house of God) is attached to his name. All the names in this lineage can be found in the list of the priestly line of Aaron in 6:1-15,[3] confirming Azariah's status within the core of the priestly clan. The term "chief officer" (see note on 9:11) points to his leadership of the priestly clan in the early Persian period probably prior to that of Jeshua son of Jehozadak (Ezra 3; Hag 1–2; Zech 3), but it also creates an allusion to the ideal era of Hezekiah when an earlier Azariah would facilitate a renewal of worship (see commentary on 2 Chr 31). Adaiah (son of Jeroham, son of Pashhur, son of Malkijah) and Maasai (son of Adiel, son of Jahzerah, son of Meshullam, son of Meshillemith, son of Immer) are both linked to key Aaronide priestly clans that were assigned regular priestly duties by David according to chapter 24 (Malkijah in 24:9 and Immer in 24:14).

The description of priestly duties in 9:13 is very general ("responsible for ministering at the house of God"), since phrases similar to this one are used elsewhere in Chronicles in reference to both priests and Levites (6:48; 28:13; 2 Chr 35:10). This more general description stands in contrast to the more detailed descriptions of the Levitical orders that follow (9:14-34), foreshadowing a regular trend throughout the Chronicler's narrative account.

Although the list in 9:14-34 distinguishes between Levites, gatekeepers, and musicians, notes throughout the list (9:26, 31, 33) and especially at its conclusion (9:34) place all of these as members of Levitical (as opposed to priestly; see 9:30) orders. The gatekeepers are given the most extensive coverage (9:17-29), while some reference is made to bakers (9:31-32) and musicians (9:33). The Levites facilitated the Temple worship by guarding the gates to the sacred precincts (9:19-25), overseeing rooms and treasuries on the sacred mount (9:26), controlling the inventory of worship utensils and supplies (9:28-29), baking bread for offerings (9:31-32), and creating music (9:33). The Chronicler's description suggests meticulous and vigilant attention to the physical environment and needs of the Temple, but also participation in worship through music. To accomplish this demanded the assistance of the Levitical families throughout the land (9:25), even though Levites were also stationed at the Temple, especially the musicians (9:33). The Chronicler makes constant references to the schedule that enabled the Levitical clans to accomplish this extensive work (9:25, 27, 32, 33), even though their numbers were not abundant (9:22; cf. Ezra 8:15 for low numbers of Levites).

The emphasis on the Levitical gatekeepers throughout this chapter is also evident in the fact that the Chronicler traces supervision of these orders to the priestly figure Phinehas (9:20, "and the LORD had been with him"; cf. 6:4) and their appointment to the figures of David and Samuel the seer. By mentioning Phinehas, the Chronicler depicts the priests as affirming the role of these gatekeepers. The reference to David and Samuel is used because the Chronicler consistently described the service of the gatekeepers in both the Tabernacle (9:19, 21, 23) and the Temple (9:23, 26, 27, 33). Samuel served at the Tabernacle at Shiloh, and David was the figure who, in the eyes of the Chronicler, was instrumental in moving Israel from Tabernacle to Temple. The authority of David will continue to be key to the Chronicler's bolstering of the function of the Levites in his narrative section (ch 10—2 Chr 36). Moreover, the Chronicler will leverage precedents within Tabernacle worship as key to his presentation of significant Levitical participation in Temple worship (see, for example, 9:19-21).

Although the Chronicler has described the Levitical gatekeepers as coming to the Temple in Jerusalem from their allotments throughout the land (9:25; see the account of these allotments in 6:61-81), he is careful to note that certain Levites lived in Jerusalem. The note in 9:27 may have referred, in an earlier version of this list, to the Levites listed in 9:14-18, but now it probably includes the comptrollers and bakers of 9:26-32, and certainly the musicians of 9:33. The lists of 1:1–9:34 come to an end with the account of Levites living in Jerusalem and participating fully in the Temple worship.

Saul's genealogy (9:35-44). First Chronicles 9:35-44 functions as a segue between the genealogical lists of chapters 1–9 and the narrative of 1 Chronicles 10—2 Chronicles 36. The same list can also be found in 8:29-40 (see commentary there), but slight differences between the two lists suggest their different functions. The fact that in chapter 9 the Chronicler did not include the final part of this genealogy, which now forms 8:39-40, suggests that the genealogy functions in chapter 8 to fill out the tribe of Benjamin and give it status as the tribe with the third most extensive coverage, behind Judah (first) and Levi (second). Here in chapter 9 the focus is on setting up the narrative in chapter 10, and so Saul's roots are provided, and then a simpler version of his descendants is included. By including his descendants, the Chronicler provides proof that David was not responsible for the murder of either Saul or his descendants.

Significance. By ending his series of lists with the account of Israel exiled to the nations and then returning from them, the Chronicler has come full circle back to where he began in chapter 1. As Israel came forth through birth from the nations (ch 1), so now it comes forth through discipline from the nations (ch 9). This is a sobering thought, reminding Judah that it was unfaithful as the northern tribes were (5:25). This return to Israel's original state suggests that there is hope that the small remnant will once again become the multitude of "all Israel," which includes all tribes. With 9:1-3 the Chronicler signals a new day by his mention of the Exile and the beginning of the restoration. The conclusion of his section of lists (chs 1–9) therefore foreshadows the end of his narrative section (1 Chr 10—2 Chr 36), which ends with the invitation to "go up" (2 Chr 36:22-23). The parallel references reinforce the final destination of the book as a whole. The Chronicler appears to have a message to those who have not returned to the land, encouraging them to return, but also a message to those who have already returned to accept those who do come (see Boda 2009b).

While there is a chiastic structure to 1 Chronicles 1–9, one can also discern a forward movement in the genealogies as it funnels the spatial dimension from the nations to the tribes to the holy city (Klein 2006:265; Oeming 1990:200). This destination of Jerusalem is foreshadowed by regular references to the city throughout the account (3:4-5; 6:10, 15, 32; 8:28, 32), and the name of the city now brackets this final list (9:3, 34).[4]

This focus on Jerusalem is soon linked to "the house of God" (9:13), that is, "the Temple" (9:33), in which the priests and Levites served and lived. Although the return of Judah and Benjamin was important to the Chronicler in and of itself, this return serves the greater purpose of the Temple and its service.[5] The stark contrast between the generic description of priestly duties and the elaborate delineation of Levitical duties suggests that for the Chronicler priestly duties were clearly articulated (and possibly entrenched) in his era, while Levitical duties needed more careful definition and theological foundation. This list then prepares the way for a major theme that will be developed throughout the Chronicler's narrative: the significant role the Levites would play in the Chronicler's Temple. The emphasis on the function of the gatekeepers suggests a great need to define their function more clearly. However, this emphasis may also reflect a concern in the Chronicler's age for the security of the city and its sacred precincts.

Finally, the length of Saul's genealogy cannot be overlooked. The commentary on chapter 8 concluded that this genealogy was employed there to show the enduring quality of Benjamin, which would form, with Judah and Levi, the core of the restoration province of Yehud. This is why genealogies stretching to the Exile are provided for the tribes of Judah, Levi, and Benjamin. However, the use of this genealogy in 9:35-44 is different. First and foremost, this genealogy functions to help the reader transition from the lists of chapters 1–9 to the narratives of chapter 10—2 Chronicles 36 by introducing the figure of Saul and his lineage. But this does not explain the continuation of the genealogy past 9:39. This is best explained by Klein (2006:256, 258) and Oeming (1990:179), who see here a response to any suggestion that David murdered the house of Saul (cf. 2 Sam 16:7-8; 21:1-14).[6] This is made clear as the narrative begins in 10:1-6. But there may be a third and darker purpose behind this genealogy. The naming of Ish-bosheth and Mephibosheth as Esh-baal and Merib-baal may subtly highlight a link between Saul and idolatry, an association that becomes explicit in the account of his death (10:8-14).[7]

ENDNOTES

1. See ABD 2.761-767 and especially Bendor 1996; Perdue 1997; Weinberg 1992:49-61.
2. The parallel list in Neh 11 makes no mention of Ephraim and Manasseh, a fact that shows the intention of the Chronicler to accentuate the "all Israel" theme.
3. Although Meraioth and Ahitub are switched, possibly due to the excision of a generation in the list in ch 6 and a case of papponymy (naming a son after one's father or ancestor).
4. Japhet (1993:218) notes the Hebrew bracket around the passage: *ubirushalaim yashebu. . . . yashebu birushalaim* ("Now in Jerusalem they dwelled [beginning of 9:3]. . . . They dwelled in Jerusalem" [end of 9:34]). See also Kalimi 2005a:83-94 for the importance of Jerusalem to the genealogies.
5. This becomes obvious upon a comparison of ch 9 with Neh 11, both of which draw from the same source. The Chronicler has expanded the coverage of the sacred personnel considerably (9:18-33); Knoppers 2004:512-513.

6. However, Klein thinks that the preservation of the genealogical source is related to hopes of Saulide families, noting Flanagan 1982:25.
7. Walters (1991:61-76), whose treatment of Saul is very negative, notes how Saul is depicted merely as a geographical, rather than an ethnic, Benjaminite, and is linked to a city (Gibeon) that has primarily negative connotations in Hebrew tradition. Klein (2006:258) is correct in his criticism that Gibeon is treated positively in the Chronicler's account.

INTRODUCTION TO 1 CHRONICLES 10-29: THE ACCOUNT OF DAVID

First Chronicles 10 marks the transition from the book's genealogical introduction to the narrative proper. The greatest contrast between the Chronicler and the writers of Samuel—Kings lies in the early phases of the narrative. Absent from the account in Chronicles is the long story of the rise of the monarchy as an institution and the extended struggle that marked the transition from the rule of Saul to that of David. This reveals first that the Chronicler assumed the readers' familiarity with the account of Samuel—Kings, especially in light of the sudden appearance of Saul and his army in chapter 10. Second, it reveals that the Chronicler assumed the legitimacy of the royal office in Israel. But third, it also reveals the Chronicler's avoidance of any events that would detract from the glory of the Davidic dynasty. Thus, in the transition to David's rule (chs 10–11) and later Solomon's (ch 29—2 Chr 1), any challenge to the transition was ignored (cf. 2 Sam 2–4; 1 Kgs 1–2).

The Chronicler's account of David is divided into two major sections: chapters 11–20 and chapters 22–29, separated by the key event in chapter 21, David's census. At the heart of the first major section lies David's work to establish Jerusalem as the center of Israel's worship by moving the Ark into the city and developing worship rituals (chs 13, 15–17). Surrounding this core are accounts of David's successful military exploits, which made this worship possible (chs 11–12, 14, 18–20).

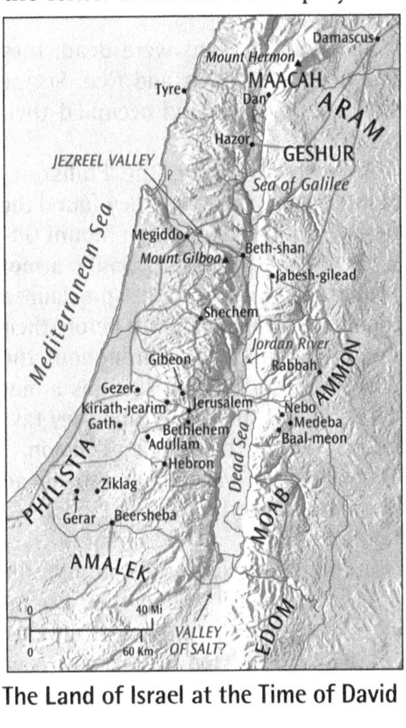

The Land of Israel at the Time of David

A similar structure can be discerned in the second major section, at the core of which is a series of lists of personnel necessary for worship in the city (chs 23–26) with some attention to military personnel at the end of this core (ch 27). Surrounding this core are two accounts that focus on David's provision for the Temple and the commissioning of Solomon as builder of the Temple (chs 22, 28–29).

What lies between these two major sections is chapter 21, the account that describes David's inappropriate census, which brought down judgment on the kingdom. This inattention to ritual procedures echoes an earlier blunder by David in chapter 13, but in each case the resolution of the mistake leads to positive developments for worship in Jerusalem: the movement of the Ark into Jerusalem (ch 13) and the identification of the site for the altar and Temple (ch 21).

The Chronicler's account of David is thus focused on securing the borders of the kingdom and developing worship in Jerusalem. His depiction extols the Davidic era as the ideal age, which lays the foundation for the construction of the Temple in Solomon's time and ultimately worship at the Temple in the time of the Chronicler. Even in his unfaithful acts, David is presented as a normative character. He learned from his folly in the Ark incident, inquiring of Yahweh and following appropriate ritual. Even his inappropriate census led to the provision of an altar and Temple to deal with the sin of Israel. Through these things David projects a model of the penitential king, one by which his descendants will be evaluated (Abadie 2003:89-104; Knoppers 1995:449-470).

As Longman and Dillard (2006:197) conclude, the Chronicler's account reflects a messianic historiography: "David and Solomon in Chronicles are not just the David and Solomon who were, but the David and Solomon of the Chronicler's eschatological hope. At a time when Israel was subject to the Persians, the Chronicler still cherished hope of a restoration of Davidic rule, and he describes the glorious rule of David and Solomon in the past in terms of his hope for the future." Such a concern for the future of the Davidic line has already been discerned in the genealogy of David in chapter 3 (see further Boda 2009b).

◆ II. The Account of David (10:1–29:30)
A. The Death of King Saul (10:1–14)

Now the Philistines attacked Israel, and
the men of Israel fled before them. Many
were slaughtered on the slopes of Mount
Gilboa. 2The Philistines closed in on Saul
and his sons, and they killed three of his
sons—Jonathan, Abinadab, and Malkishua.
3The fighting grew very fierce around
Saul, and the Philistine archers caught up
with him and wounded him.

4Saul groaned to his armor bearer,
"Take your sword and kill me before these
pagan Philistines come to taunt and tor-
ture me."

But his armor bearer was afraid and
would not do it. So Saul took his own
sword and fell on it. 5When his armor
bearer realized that Saul was dead, he fell
on his own sword and died. 6So Saul and
his three sons died there together, bring-
ing his dynasty to an end.

7When all the Israelites in the Jezreel
Valley saw that their army had fled and
that Saul and his sons were dead, they
abandoned their towns and fled. So the
Philistines moved in and occupied their
towns.

8The next day, when the Philistines
went out to strip the dead, they found the
bodies of Saul and his sons on Mount Gil-
boa. 9So they stripped off Saul's armor
and cut off his head. Then they proclaimed
the good news of Saul's death before their
idols and to the people throughout the
land of Philistia. 10They placed his armor
in the temple of their gods, and they fas-
tened his head to the temple of Dagon.

11But when everyone in Jabesh-gilead
heard about everything the Philistines
had done to Saul, 12all their mighty war-
riors brought the bodies of Saul and his
sons back to Jabesh. Then they buried
their bones beneath the great tree at
Jabesh, and they fasted for seven days.

13So Saul died because he was unfaith-

ful to the LORD. He failed to obey the LORD's command, and he even consulted a medium [14]instead of asking the LORD for guidance. So the LORD killed him and turned the kingdom over to David son of Jesse.

NOTES

10:1 ***Mount Gilboa.*** This mountain rises above the far eastern end of the Jezreel Valley (bordering the Jordan River basin), overlooking Beth-shan (on the valley floor to the northeast) and Jezreel (on the valley floor to the northwest). Saul's retreat into the mountain reveals that his army was no match for the Philistines in the large valley of Jezreel, which was ideally suited for a battle with chariots but not for a force accustomed to guerrilla warfare in mountainous terrain.

10:2 ***Jonathan, Abinadab, and Malkishua.*** Of these three sons of Saul, Jonathan is the most famous because of his close relationship to David (1 Sam 20). He served his father faithfully, functioning as his commander-in-chief. Little is known about the other two sons, even though it was ancient Near Eastern practice to have one's sons involved in military campaigns, not only to train the next generation of leadership, but also to have loyal lieutenants leading the ranks. In this list Abinadab comes second and Malkishua third, as is the case in the Chronicler's base text (1 Sam 31:2; cf. 14:49). However, in the genealogy of the Chronicler, the order is reversed (8:33; 9:39).

10:7 ***Jezreel Valley.*** First Samuel 29:1 records that the Philistines originally amassed their troops at Aphek with the Israelites at Jezreel. This Aphek may be in the Sharon or at the far western end of the Jezreel Valley. The Philistine traditional lands were on the coast in the south. For them to push this far north reveals the vulnerability of Saul's kingdom. That Ishbosheth (Saul's son and successor) would have to establish his throne at Mahanaim in the Transjordanian region (2 Sam 2:8-9) shows the completeness of the Philistine victory.

10:10 ***fastened his head to the temple of Dagon.*** First Samuel 31:10 tells us that Saul's body was attached to the wall of the city; the head, however, could have been impaled in the temple. Dagon was an ancient Semitic god, who in biblical tradition features as the chief god of the Philistines (Judg 16:21-23; 1 Sam 5:2-7), but he was worshiped throughout Canaan, as names of towns signify (e.g., Beth-dagon, Josh 15:41; 19:27) and archaeological evidence has revealed. His name appears in texts from Ugarit (north of Israel) as the father of Baal, god of fertility. Temples of Dagon have been discovered throughout the Middle East, for example, in Ugarit (twenty-second to fourteenth century BC) and Mari (eighteenth century BC). The temple in Ugarit was dedicated to the worship of Dagon, indicating that he was a deity in his own right. According to 1 Sam 31, the location of this temple was Beth-shan, which was situated at a key crossroads for travel north–south and east–west. Excavations on Level V at Beth-shan unearthed tombs consistent with Philistine presence, cult objects, and temples, one of which probably was the setting of 10:10 (NBD 251; Negev 1990:s.vv. "Beth-Shean," "Scythopolis").

10:11 ***Jabesh-gilead.*** The precise location of this city is uncertain, although the Wadi el-Yabis, which empties into the Jordan River just south of the Sea of Galilee, preserves its name. While Tell el-Maqereh, which lies 1.75 miles east of the Jordan and 9 miles east of Beth-shan is possible (TBD 660; NBD 535), probably better is Tell el-Maqlub, which lies even further east (ABD 3.594). It was the attack on Jabesh-gilead by Nahash the Ammonite that led to Saul's appointment and confirmation as king (1 Sam 11–12). Jabesh-gilead's loyalty to Saul may reflect a long-standing commitment to his tribe, Benjamin, for they were punished for their lack of participation in the war against Benjamin, according to the latter chapters of Judges (Judg 19–21).

10:12 *the great tree at Jabesh.* This is a terebinth tree, which is common in the lower hills of Israel. The sap of this tree is the source of turpentine. These large trees (along with oaks) are often linked to sacred sites in the OT and the ancient Near East. Abraham's first altar was built at "the oak of Moreh" (Gen 12:6-7) and his second "near the oak grove belonging to Mamre" (Gen 13:18). Near the latter site he would buy a family tomb. Of course, trees are also associated with idolatry in the OT, as evidenced in Ezekiel's prophetic indictment against idolatry "under every green tree and every great shade tree" (Ezek 6:13; DBI 891).

COMMENTARY

Rather than easing the reader into the story line, the Chronicler begins abruptly with the Philistines routing the army of Israel. The story is told in two phases, with the first describing the defeat of Saul and his army (10:1-7) and the second the fate of the remains of Saul and his sons after the battle (10:8-12). The chapter ends with a theological reflection on the significance of the story (10:13-14).[1]

The Defeat of Saul and His Army (10:1-7). From the opening words of the story, the Philistines have the upper hand, and Israel is in flight from their enemies. Vulnerable to their pursuers, many fall dead on Mount Gilboa. These fleeing "men of Israel" appear to be the main flank of Saul's army, with a back flank on the valley floor to protect the towns (10:7). Soon the narrative narrows in on Saul.[2] In 10:1 he loses the protection of his army, and by the end of 10:2, his right-hand men—his sons Jonathan, Abinadab, and Malkishua. This clearly leaves him alone and surrounded, and worst of all, the deadly archers overtake and wound him. The role of archers as sharpshooters commissioned to take out the general or king is evident in several stories in the Old Testament (1 Kgs 22:34; 2 Kgs 9:24; 2 Chr 35:23). In this case, however, many have noted a special irony, since the tribe of Benjamin, from which Saul hailed, was known for its skilled archers (Japhet 1993:223; cf. 12:2).

In 10:4 we finally hear the voice of Saul as the Chronicler employs dramatic narrative for effect. The wounded monarch commands his armor bearer to kill him in order to spare him abuse at the hands of the Philistines. The powerlessness of this tragic figure is highlighted by the fact that even his own armor bearer refuses the order, leaving Saul to carry out this final act himself.[3] While some have debated whether this act displays heroism or fear (Japhet 1993:224), it is better to see it as highlighting the tragedy of Saul's reign.

While the writer of Samuel emphasizes the deaths of Saul, his sons, his armor bearer, and his men (1 Sam 31:6), the Chronicler focuses attention exclusively on Saul and his three sons and then adds for emphasis, "bringing his dynasty to an end" (10:6). Noting what he calls the obvious "dynastic overtones" of the Chronicler's rendition, Williamson (1982:93) has highlighted the chiastic structure of the Hebrew text, with the verb "die" (*muth*) at the beginning and end and members of Saul's household in the center. The Chronicler was well aware that Saul's son Ishbosheth remained alive after this battle (8:33, Esh-baal), but his agenda was to emphasize that Saul's dynasty had come to an end and that the kingship had been transferred to David's family. The Chronicler would not even mention the civil war between the families of Saul and David that is described in detail at the beginning of 2 Samuel.

The Fate of the Remains of Saul and His Sons after the Battle (10:8-12). As is typical in ancient Near Eastern warfare, the corpses of dead warriors were stripped of their weaponry (for reuse by the victor in future battles) and buried or burned (to limit disease and odor). The leaders of the conquered army, however, were treated with great contempt, and their remains (body and armor) were paraded as symbols of victory. The account in 1 Chronicles emphasizes the idolatrous character of the celebration with the good news of the victory reaching many people and the remains enshrined in the foreign temple. Such desecration in an unholy site expresses the abhorrence of God toward one who committed such "unfaithfulness" against him (see further on 10:13-14).

The act of loyalty to Saul displayed by the inhabitants of Jabesh-gilead in 10:11-12 offers closure for the career of Saul, for it was his success in protecting the town of Jabesh-gilead in 1 Samuel 11:1-11 that led to full recognition of Saul's reign by the people. Once victory was secured by Saul in 1 Samuel 11, those who had supported Saul wanted to put to death those who questioned Saul's kingship. Interestingly, the fate of Jabesh-gilead is closely linked with the people's request for a king, a request that was fulfilled by the appointment of Saul (cf. 1 Sam 12:12). The bones of Saul and his sons were buried in a ceremony that lasted for seven days and included fasting. Such mourning rites were common (2 Sam 1:11-12, 17-27; 3:35; Ps 35:13-14).

The Chronicler's account is slightly different, however, from 1 Samuel 31. In 1 Samuel Saul's head is severed, the armor displayed in a temple, and his body hung on the wall of Beth-shan. First Chronicles 10 speaks of his armor and severed head, which are displayed in a temple of Dagon (Heb., *beth dagon*) at an unspecified location. The Chronicler leaves out 1 Samuel's account of the burning of the bodies prior to burial, an act that was probably linked to the desire not to defile the land through the burial of an accursed, hanged body (see Deut 21:22-23; Japhet 1993:228). Some have traced these differences to distinct traditions or textual sources, others to "a sophisticated reworking" of the source by the Chronicler.[4] The purpose behind this "reworking," however, is not as clear as one would expect. It may be that the focus on the head was to associate the death of Saul with that of Goliath in 1 Samuel 17 or with the fall of the Philistine god Dagon in 1 Samuel 5 (cf. Williamson 1982:93).

Japhet (1993:228) has noted that the change from Beth-shan to Beth-dagon (NLT, "temple of Dagon"; 10:10) plays down foreign possession of the Jezreel valley towns, but it appears that the Chronicler was not trying to hide foreign occupation in his account of Saul's demise. Rather, the Chronicler appears to have been focusing on Saul's association with impurity in life (consulting a medium, 10:13), as well as in death. It is true that the resultant text in Chronicles plays down the heroism of the men of Jabesh-gilead in 10:11-12, for the emphasis is no longer on bodies hanging on the wall of Beth-shan, the taking of which would indeed be a valiant deed. But this final difference may be merely the result of the earlier shift to a focus on the head.

Theological Reflection on the Significance of the Story (10:13-14). The final two verses of chapter 10 are unique to the Chronicler; they contain vocabulary that is found regularly in sections in Chronicles but not in Samuel—Kings. In this section, the narrator moves out of direct narrative into declarative narrative, offering an evaluation of the story for the reader. Since this is not common in Hebrew narrative, readers should take careful note. Here the Chronicler is able to offer explicitly his theological evaluation of the story.

The evaluation begins with the simple statement that "Saul died," but by the end of the reflection the ultimate cause behind this death is clearly delineated through the repetition of the same verb (*muth* [TH4191, ZH4637]), but now in the causative stem: "the LORD killed him" (i.e., the Lord caused him to die). The reason for the Lord's severe judgment is offered between these two appearances of the verb "to die." Fundamentally, the reason for this judgment was Saul's "trespass" (NLT, "he was unfaithful"; Heb., *ma'al* [TH4603, ZH5085]), a term that often appears in priestly literature in the Old Testament. Milgrom (1976) has defined this as "a sin against God" in contrast to a sin against humanity. Such sins can be categorized in two ways: the Sancta Trespass, which refers to inappropriate contact with that which is holy (Lev 5:14-19; 14:10-14, 21-25; 22:14-16; Num 6:12; Ezra 10:19; Jer 2:3), and the Oath Violation, that is the violation of God's name that was sworn in the oath (Lev 6:1-7; Num 5:6-8). For Milgrom, "*ma'al*, then, means trespassing upon the divine realm either by poaching on his sancta or breaking his covenant oath; it is a lethal sin that can destroy both the offender and his community" (1976:21; cf. Boda 2006a). Japhet (1993:229-230) distinguishes the use of *ma'al* in Chronicles from the technical priestly literature and defines it as "covering the whole range of man's sins against God, equivalent to 'forsaking God.'" But to reject God's counsel and accept that of an inappropriate spiritual medium is to violate Israel's covenant oath with God. The idolatrous connection may also be suggested by Saul's association in death with the temple of Dagon and his burial under the oak at Jabesh (see note on 10:12).

Three acts are associated with Saul's *ma'al* [TH4603, ZH5085]. First, he did not keep the word of the Lord that was delivered. On one level, this is an allusion to his failure to wait the appropriate days before sacrificing and going into battle (1 Sam 13) and/or to his failure to practice *kherem* [TH2764, ZH3051] on the Amalekites (1 Sam 15). This practice involved the irrevocable giving over of everything to God, which in acts of war involves the complete destruction of the inhabitants of a city and either destruction of or dedication of nonhuman objects to God (see Josh 6:17-21; 8:26; 10:1, 28-40; 11:11-21; ABD 3.244; cf. Lev 27:21, 28, 29; Num 18:14). However, on another level the Chronicler regularly used language related to keeping the Lord's word and seeking the Lord to describe the success or downfall of Israelite generations (2 Chr 12:1, 14; 13:11, 13; 14:4-5; 33:8; 34:2; 36:16; Williamson 1982:95). Second, he consulted a medium, an allusion to his association with the witch of Endor (1 Sam 28). Such an act was clearly forbidden in the Torah (Deut 18:9-14); it would lead to expulsion from the land. And third, he did not "inquire" (of the Lord), a word that is a favorite of the Chronicler, appearing some 40 times in his narrative. In Chronicles, the phrase used here ("inquire of the LORD") usually refers to the more general orientation of faithfulness toward God, but in the case of Saul in chapter 10, it also bears its more technical meaning of seeking God for a decision, often through a spiritual intermediary (1 Kgs 22:5//2 Chr 18:4; 2 Kgs 3:11; 8:8).

The final phrase of the evaluation brings into focus the main purpose of the chapter as a whole, that is, to describe how the kingship came to David. As the Lord was the subject of the action of judgment against Saul, so he was the subject of the transference of the kingship from Saul to David. This is a key reminder that this office was God's to appoint to one who was faithful to him. In this uneasy transition between dynasties, the reader is reminded who the true king was. At the same time the emphasis on God as actor does remove beyond question any conspiracy theory that would implicate David in the demise of Saul's dynasty (Zalewski 1989:449-467). The mention of David, the son of Jesse, at the end of chapter 10 clearly attests to the function of this chapter as providing the dark foil against which the reader will be able to see the brilliance of David and Solomon.[5]

Although functioning in many ways as a prelude to the narrative of David, this chapter is rich in theology. It reminds us of Yahweh's deep concern for pure modes of revelation. The ultimate form of revelation from God within Christian theology is unquestionably that of the Word become flesh. That is, the Son of God came to reveal God's character in the purest form possible (John 1:14-18). Furthermore, Jesus offered to us as Christians one he called "another Advocate" or "Comforter," that is, the Holy Spirit, who as the "Spirit of truth" will lead/guide us "into all truth" (John 14:16-17; 16:13), "will teach you everything and will remind you of everything I have told you" (John 14:26), and "will tell you whatever he receives from me" (John 16:15). These two resources are never seen in competition with the third enduring revelatory resource for Christians, that is, the Scriptures inspired by God, which testify to "the salvation that comes by trusting in Christ Jesus" and are "useful to teach us what is true and to make us realize what is wrong in our lives" (2 Tim 3:15-16).

Saul had similar resources in his own day. The prophetic voice of Samuel, the invitation to seek God directly, the royal Spirit's empowering presence in his life, and the Torah delivered through Moses. By not accessing these resources, he ultimately was thrown upon the inappropriate resources of the witch of Endor. No less today, Christians can be tempted to draw upon similar means of revelation, whether in the "religious" realm of horoscopes, new-age religion, or the occult, or the "secular" realm of self-help books and humanistic guides. Without losing sight of the many good sources of truth and knowledge that can be found in our world because of God's common grace to all humanity, as Christians we need to ensure that the priority of revelation is found in "asking the LORD for guidance" (10:14) in the person of Jesus, in the presence of the Spirit, and in the witness of Scripture.

ENDNOTES

1. Cf. Japhet 1993:221 for this structure.
2. Japhet (1993:223) says, "The description of the battle has the quality of a moving picture, coming ever closer to its focus on Saul."
3. This account is the same as 1 Sam 31, but it is interesting to hear the tale spun by the Amalekite in 2 Sam 1:10, who claimed to have killed Saul out of mercy, an act that earns him death at the hand of David.
4. For these see Japhet 1993:227; cf. Ackroyd 1977:5; Rudolph 1955:92.
5. One may also see here with Mosis (1973) the development of the paradigm of the exilic situation, the conditions of which are only rectified by the appearance of David; cf. Ackroyd 1977:3-9; Williamson 1982:92.

B. David Becomes King of All Israel, Conquers Jerusalem, and Is Joined by Mighty Warriors (11:1-47)

Then all Israel gathered before David at Hebron and told him, "We are your own flesh and blood. 2 In the past,* even when Saul was king, you were the one who really led the forces of Israel. And the LORD your God told you, 'You will be the shepherd of my people Israel. You will be the leader of my people Israel.'"

3 So there at Hebron, David made a covenant before the LORD with all the elders of Israel. And they anointed him king of Israel, just as the LORD had promised through Samuel.

4 Then David and all Israel went to Jerusalem (or Jebus, as it used to be called), where the Jebusites, the original inhabitants of the land, were living. 5 The people of Jebus taunted David, saying, "You'll never get in here!" But David captured the fortress of Zion, which is now called the City of David.

6 David had said to his troops, "Whoever is first to attack the Jebusites will become the commander of my armies!" And Joab, the son of David's sister Zeruiah, was first to attack, so he became the commander of David's armies.

7 David made the fortress his home, and that is why it is called the City of David. 8 He extended the city from the supporting terraces* to the surrounding area, while Joab rebuilt the rest of Jerusalem. 9 And David became more and more powerful, because the LORD of Heaven's Armies was with him.

10 These are the leaders of David's mighty warriors. Together with all Israel, they decided to make David their king, just as the LORD had promised concerning Israel.

11 Here is the record of David's mightiest warriors: The first was Jashobeam the Hacmonite, who was leader of the Three—the mightiest warriors among David's men.* He once used his spear to kill 300 enemy warriors in a single battle.

12 Next in rank among the Three was Eleazar son of Dodai,* a descendant of Ahoah. 13 He was with David in the battle against the Philistines at Pas-dammim. The battle took place in a field full of barley, and the Israelite army fled. 14 But Eleazar and David* held their ground in the middle of the field and beat back the Philistines. So the LORD saved them by giving them a great victory.

15 Once when David was at the rock near the cave of Adullam, the Philistine army was camped in the valley of Rephaim. The Three (who were among the Thirty—an elite group among David's fighting men) went down to meet him there. 16 David was staying in the stronghold at the time, and a Philistine detachment had occupied the town of Bethlehem.

17 David remarked longingly to his men, "Oh, how I would love some of that good water from the well by the gate in Bethlehem." 18 So the Three broke through the Philistine lines, drew some water from the well by the gate in Bethlehem, and brought it back to David. But David refused to drink it. Instead, he poured it out as an offering to the LORD. 19 "God forbid that I should drink this!" he exclaimed. "This water is as precious as the blood of these men* who risked their lives to bring it to me." So David did not drink it. These are examples of the exploits of the Three.

20 Abishai, the brother of Joab, was the leader of the Thirty.* He once used his spear to kill 300 enemy warriors in a single battle. It was by such feats that he became as famous as the Three. 21 Abishai was the most famous of the Thirty and was their commander, though he was not one of the Three.

22 There was also Benaiah son of Jehoiada, a valiant warrior from Kabzeel. He did many heroic deeds, which included killing two champions* of Moab. Another time, on a snowy day, he chased a lion down into a pit and killed it. 23 Once, armed only with a club, he killed an Egyptian warrior

who was 7½ feet* tall and whose spear
was as thick as a weaver's beam. Benaiah
wrenched the spear from the Egyptian's
hand and killed him with it. 24 Deeds like
these made Benaiah as famous as the
three mightiest warriors. 25 He was more
honored than the other members of the
Thirty, though he was not one of the
Three. And David made him captain of his
bodyguard.
26 David's mighty warriors also included:

Asahel, Joab's brother;
Elhanan son of Dodo from Bethlehem;
27 Shammah from Harod;*
Helez from Pelon;
28 Ira son of Ikkesh from Tekoa;
Abiezer from Anathoth;
29 Sibbecai from Hushah;
Zalmon* from Ahoah;
30 Maharai from Netophah;
Heled son of Baanah from Netophah;
31 Ithai son of Ribai from Gibeah (in the land of Benjamin);
Benaiah from Pirathon;
32 Hurai from near Nahale-gaash*;
Abi-albon* from Arabah;
33 Azmaveth from Bahurim*;
Eliahba from Shaalbon;
34 the sons of Jashen* from Gizon;
Jonathan son of Shagee from Harar;
35 Ahiam son of Sharar* from Harar;
Eliphal son of Ur;
36 Hepher from Mekerah;
Ahijah from Pelon;
37 Hezro from Carmel;
Paarai* son of Ezbai;
38 Joel, the brother of Nathan;
Mibhar son of Hagri;
39 Zelek from Ammon;
Naharai from Beeroth, Joab's armor bearer;
40 Ira from Jattir;
Gareb from Jattir;
41 Uriah the Hittite;
Zabad son of Ahlai;
42 Adina son of Shiza, the Reubenite leader who had thirty men with him;
43 Hanan son of Maacah;
Joshaphat from Mithna;
44 Uzzia from Ashtaroth;
Shama and Jeiel, the sons of Hotham, from Aroer;
45 Jediael son of Shimri;
Joha, his brother, from Tiz;
46 Eliel from Mahavah;
Jeribai and Joshaviah, the sons of Elnaam;
Ithmah from Moab;
47 Eliel and Obed;
Jaasiel from Zobah.*

11:2 Or *For some time.* **11:8** Hebrew *the millo.* The meaning of the Hebrew is uncertain. **11:11** As in some Greek manuscripts (see also 2 Sam 23:8); Hebrew reads *leader of the Thirty,* or *leader of the captains.* **11:12** As in parallel text at 2 Sam 23:9 (see also 1 Chr 27:4); Hebrew reads *Dodo,* a variant spelling of Dodai. **11:14** Hebrew *they.* **11:19** Hebrew *Shall I drink the lifeblood of these men?* **11:20** As in Syriac version; Hebrew reads *the Three;* also in 11:21. **11:22** Or *two sons of Ariel.* **11:23** Hebrew *5 cubits* [2.3 meters]. **11:27** As in parallel text at 2 Sam 23:25; Hebrew reads *Shammoth from Haror.* **11:29** As in parallel text at 2 Sam 23:28; Hebrew reads *Ilai.* **11:32a** Or *from the ravines of Gaash.* **11:32b** As in parallel text at 2 Sam 23:31; Hebrew reads *Abiel.* **11:33** As in parallel text at 2 Sam 23:31; Hebrew reads *Baharum.* **11:34** As in parallel text at 2 Sam 23:32; Hebrew reads *sons of Hashem.* **11:35** As in parallel text at 2 Sam 23:33; Hebrew reads *son of Sacar.* **11:37** As in parallel text at 2 Sam 23:35; Hebrew reads *Naarai.* **11:47** Or *the Mezobaite.*

NOTES

11:1 *Hebron.* In the account in 2 Samuel, Hebron was the city God directed David to establish as his capital after the death of Saul (2 Sam 2:1). There he was anointed king over the tribe of Judah and ruled for seven years until the civil war between the houses of Saul and David were completed (2 Sam 5:5). Hebron was one of the towns that harbored David during his flight from Saul (1 Sam 30:31). This close association between David and Hebron is most likely why Absalom initiated his revolt against his father at Hebron (2 Sam 15:7-10). Geographically, the town is 18.6 miles south-southwest of Jerusalem at a key east–west intersection on the road from Jerusalem to Beersheba. Topographically, it is at one of the highest elevations in Israel.

your own flesh and blood. Lit., "your bone and flesh."

11:2 ***the one who really led the forces of Israel.*** Lit., "You (were) the one going out and coming in with Israel," that is, in battle (for the explicit link to war, see 1 Sam 29:6).

11:4 ***Jerusalem (or Jebus, as it used to be called).*** The connection between Jerusalem and the Jebusites is found in Judg 19:10-11 and 2 Sam 24:16 (where David buys the Temple site from Araunah the Jebusite). This city was not taken in the conquest of Joshua (Josh 15:8; 18:16). Judges 1:8 claims that the warriors of Judah took the city and destroyed its inhabitants and burned it with fire; however, later in the chapter (Judg 1:21), the Benjaminites were unable to dislodge the Jebusites from Jerusalem, which lay on the boundary between the tribes of Benjamin and Judah. This failure of Benjamin appears to be supported by Judg 19:10-12. The city's location was determined by the presence of an adequate aquifer in the Kidron Valley below, which may have been the way the city was taken by David (2 Sam 5:8). The shift of capitals from Hebron to Jebus (Jerusalem) was politically brilliant for David.[1] Since the city itself was not under the control of any tribe, it was neutral. Furthermore, the Benjaminite territory was medial territory between the northern (Ephraim) and southern (Judah) power blocks in Israel, a factor that probably influenced the choice of the first king of Israel from this relatively insignificant tribe. Jerusalem, on the edge of Benjamin, was as far north in Judah as one could go, placing the new king within close physical proximity to the northern tribal coalition, which had rallied around the house of Saul in the civil war and would ultimately form the northern kingdom after Solomon's reign.

11:5 ***fortress of Zion.*** The Jebusite city was quite small, occupying 11 acres on the southeastern ridge (by the eighth century BC it would comprise over 130 acres), an area that now lies outside the present "Old City" of Jerusalem (TBD 1333). However, this may be a reference to a fortification that lay within this old city. For a recent survey of evidence for the city of Jerusalem in the tenth century BC, see Mazar 2006:255-272, who concludes, "The city at the time of David emerges as a city that was small in size but included a stronghold unique to the period, and it could have functioned as a power base of a political entity."

11:8 ***the supporting terraces.*** Lit., "Millo" (see NLT mg). This was apparently a location in Jerusalem (1 Kgs 9:15, 24; 11:27; 2 Kgs 12:20; 2 Chr 32:5). The term is related to the Hebrew root that means "to fill," suggesting landfill, earthwork, terraced hill, or rampart. Most likely it refers to artificial platforms built on top of earthwork (fill and retaining walls), evidence of which has been noted in excavations on Shechem and, notably, Jerusalem on the east slope of the Temple Mount (NBD 766).

to the surrounding area. This could also be translated "all around" or "to the perimeter" (cf. 2 Sam 5:9).

rebuilt. This verb usually means "to give life" but in later Hebrew could be used for the restoration of a city (cf. Neh 4:2).

11:11 ***300.*** Second Samuel 23:8 reads "800." The higher number is more likely, considering the status of Jashobeam in comparison to Abishai, who "used his spear to kill 300" (11:20).

11:13 ***Pas-dammim.*** This is called Ephes-dammim in the valley of Elah in 1 Sam 17:1, the site of the Philistine camp in the famous encounter between David and Goliath. This most likely refers to a different battle that took place at this location.

11:15 ***cave of Adullam.*** David hid from Saul in this cave near the city of Adullam in the territory of Judah and used this as a fortification against the Philistines (11:15-19; 1 Sam 22:1; 2 Sam 23:13-17; cf. Josh 12:15; 15:35; 2 Chr 11:7; Neh 11:30; Mic 1:15). It is located two-thirds of the way on the southwestern journey from Jerusalem to Lachish.

valley of Rephaim. This is a valley running southwest of Jerusalem where David defeated the Philistines (2 Sam 5:18, 22; 23:13). This was a key battle as the Philistines sought to snuff out the newly anointed king's reign. The valley may be named after early inhabitants of Canaan (Gen 14:5; 15:20) who were tall in stature (Deut 2:20-21), but it also appears in contexts that suggest "ghosts" (Job 26:5; Ps 88:10 [11]; Prov 2:18; 9:18; 21:16; NBD 1008).

The Three . . . the Thirty. References to three and thirty in 11:11-25 have been much debated, mostly on text-critical grounds. These two numbers look very similar and could easily be confused, so one must be careful when weighing the evidence. The "Thirty" probably referred to a group of about thirty (whose number would fluctuate from time to time) who were in the inner circle of David's military. Names of military units are often based on numbers in ancient societies, but this does not mean the unit matched the number. Roman centurions rarely commanded 100 men (even though centum = 100), and the troop called "thousand" in Hebrew literature probably did not number 1,000 (see Selman 1994a:142).

11:16 *the stronghold.* Heb., *metsudah* [TH4686A, ZH5181]. The same word is used in 11:5 to refer to the "fortress of Zion." Second Samuel 23:13-14 shows us that the "stronghold" here is the cave of Adullam.

Bethlehem. Nine kilometers south of Jerusalem and also called Ephrath (Gen 35:19; Ruth 1:1-2), Bethlehem was the ancestral home of David and the location of his anointing by Samuel (1 Sam 16). Its importance to the Philistines lay in its location on the north–south central ridge trade route that ran through Jerusalem to Hebron and ultimately on to Egypt.

11:22 *two champions of Moab.* Lit., "two Ariel of Moab." Suggestions include "two sons of Ariel of Moab," "two warriors of Moab," and "two oracle priests of Moab" (see Williamson 1982:103).

lion. An Asian species of lion once roamed Israel (and also Asia Minor, Syria, Mesopotamia, and Iran) and is mentioned in relationship to the Jordan River's thickets (Jer 49:19; 50:44; Zech 11:3). It was distinguished from the African lion by its "scantier mane, thicker coat, and longer tail tassel" (Achtemeier 1996:563). In ancient times the mark of a great hunter and warrior was his ability to defeat a lion (Judg 14:6; 1 Sam 17:34-36), but lions could also be deadly (1 Kgs 13:24-26). Ancient kings were often depicted in the midst of a lion hunt, which were in reality staged events in which a lion was captured and then sent into a ring of warriors where the king could safely kill the lion without much effort.

11:23 *spear was as thick as a weaver's beam.* Lit., "spear as the beam of a weaver." The image may not be related to "thickness," but rather to appearance. There was a type of loom used in Egypt, Greece, and Canaan whose two long posts anchored in the ground supported a third horizontal post to which were tied warp threads held down by clay or stone weights. The weaving was done in the upper part of the loom, and fabric rolled on top of the beam. The weaver's beam would be this horizontal post (Achtemeier 1996:989). There was an ancient weapon called the "Aegean loop javelin" because of the loop, which was wound around its shaft, thereby increasing the distance of one's throw.

COMMENTARY

All Israel Anoints David as King (11:1-3). In the aftermath of the death of Saul, the book of Samuel depicts the anointing of David as king of Judah with his capital at Hebron and the bitter civil war between forces loyal to Saul and those loyal to David. In contrast, the Chronicler moves immediately to the story of the northern tribes approaching David at Hebron to embrace him as king. The Chronicler refers to this group as "all Israel," a term that plays down distinctions between north and south. Additionally, he used the verb "gathered" (*qabats* [TH6908, ZH7695], 11:1) instead of "went" (*bo'* [TH935, ZH995], 2 Sam 5:1), emphasizing their unity.

The Chronicler appears to skip 2 Samuel 5:4-5, which provides chronological information on David's reign, distinguishing between his reign in Hebron over Judah and his reign in Jerusalem over all Israel. This would be understandable in light of the Chronicler's emphasis on David's acceptance by the entire nation. However, an early manuscript of Samuel at Qumran (4QSam) also lacks these verses. Furthermore, 3:4-5 speaks of the two stages of kingship.

The words "all Israel" reveal the people's recognition that long before Saul died, David displayed the qualities of kingship. They link this to two factors: first, his function as leader even during the reign of Saul, portrayed in his leadership in battle; and second, God's declaration that he was shepherd and leader, a divine election that had been communicated through Samuel. The image of shepherd for a royal figure is well attested in the ancient Near East, displayed in an Egyptian text originating before 2000 BC, which describes a god-king who delivers Egypt as a shepherd (ANET 443), and in Hammurabi's declaration that he is a shepherd (ANET 164). The shepherd metaphor is a strong stream within the Davidic tradition. The link between David's early shepherding activities and his later royal function is made explicit in Psalm 78:70-72, which traces David's rise from "tending the ewes and lambs" to becoming "the shepherd of Jacob's descendants." His care for sheep honed qualities necessary for leading the kingdom. This pastoral image also emphasizes the vulnerability of a people without a leader, for sheep are notorious followers in need of direction.

The word for "leader" (11:2) is the Hebrew term *nagid* [TH5057, ZH5592], one that often appears on the mouth of Yahweh when speaking of royal figures in the books of Samuel—Kings (1 Sam 9:16; 10:1; 13:14; 25:30; 2 Sam 5:2; 6:21; 7:8; 1 Kgs 1:35; 14:7; 16:2; 2 Kgs 20:5). It may be significant that this is the term God used when he first alerted Samuel to Saul as the answer to the people's request in 1 Samuel 9:16 and 10:1 and when David was introduced as his successor in 1 Samuel 13:14. Mettinger (1976:182) has argued for a semantic link between Bathsheba's call for David "to announce" (*lehaggid* [TH5046, ZH5583]) Solomon as his successor (1 Kgs 1:20) and David's declaration of Solomon as *nagid* (1 Kgs 1:35). This would make *nagid* the Qal passive participle of the root *nagad* ("to proclaim"/"designate"), thus rendering "the one designated." If this meaning can be sustained, then *nagid* is a term emphasizing God's appointment of the royal figure.

The appointment to royal office (or better, dynasty) in the books of Samuel consists of four steps: private divine election/anointing (1 Sam 10:1-8; 16:1-13), Spirit endowment (1 Sam 10:9-13; 16:13-16), great feat (1 Sam 11:1-11; 17:1-58), and public confirmation (1 Sam 11:12-15; 2 Sam 2:1-7; 5:1-5). The Chronicler reminds his readers of the broader narrative of the book of Samuel by alluding to the role of Samuel at the very end of 11:3. The steps in Samuel reveal both private/divine and public/human dimensions to the appointment of the monarch. This is not surprising since this figure is portrayed as a mediatorial figure in the Old Testament, one who represents God before the people (Ps 2), but this figure also represents (and some would say embodies) the people before God (Lam 4:20). The influence of these broader phases of appointment is evident in the short episode in 11:1-3, as the people rehearse the human dimension of appointment (his military exploits and their acceptance of his leadership) and the divine dimension (God's words of election). Reference is made here to a "covenant" between David and the leaders of Israel before God. This covenant is not the "Davidic covenant" established between Yahweh and David for a perpetual dynasty, but rather an agreement between David and the people. Such agreements that bring together king, people, and God are found elsewhere, such as at the beginning of the reign of Joash (Jehoash) in 2 Kings 11:17 and Josiah in 2 Kings 23:1-3.

The emphasis on David's kingship as a result of the Lord's promise through Samuel is a consistent emphasis in chapters 11–12 (see also 11:10; 12:23) and reflects the Chronicler's view that the prophetic word controls history (see Williamson 1982:97).

David Conquers and Fortifies Jerusalem (11:4-9). As in his source (2 Sam 5:1-10), the Chronicler next relates the story of David's capture of Jerusalem. This story could not be left out, for Jerusalem (which would become the center of Israelite worship) will play an important role in the book of Chronicles with its focus on the Temple and its services. At the time of David's ascension to the throne, however, Jerusalem was not under Israelite control (see note on 11:4). The Chronicler changes the description of the Jebusites slightly from his source text in 2 Samuel 5:6, making it explicit that Jebusite control was limited to the city of Jebus. The Chronicler's account also emphasizes the unity of all Israel, by replacing "David then led his men to Jerusalem" with "David and all Israel went to Jerusalem" (11:4).[2] Surely these two descriptions can be harmonized, but one should not miss that the change makes the conquest of Jerusalem the result of a concerted action of the entire nation (not just David and his men) and illustrates the claim of 11:2 that David was a leader of all Israel in battle. The Chronicler also brings greater focus onto Joab (whose exploits are not mentioned in 2 Sam 5), tracing the appointment of David's key general to Joab's bravery in the battle at Jerusalem.[3] With the conquest of the city, its name is changed to reflect its new master, who would embark immediately with his newly appointed general on a building program to strengthen the fortifications in the capital. The Chronicler is careful to retain 11:9, the short piece of declarative narrative from his source that explains that the secret of David's increasing power was nothing less than the presence of the "LORD of Heaven's Armies" (*yhwh tseba'oth* [TH3068/6635, ZH3378/7372]) with him. This term for God is one that is closely associated with Jerusalem-Zion theology and the motif of battle and divine war as it depicts God as king with a mighty army, even if it is not a typical idiom for the Chronicler (Japhet 1989:24-25).[4]

The List and Exploits of David's Mighty Men (11:10-47). The rest of chapter 11, except for 11:10 and 11:41b-47, is drawn from 2 Samuel 23:8-39, where it forms an appendix near the end of the account of David. By shifting it to the beginning of David's reign, the Chronicler needed to add 11:10 in order to connect it more clearly with the narrative concerning David's ascension to the throne. This verse is carefully worded to show that the support of David by the mighty men was in concert with that of "all Israel" (cf. 11:1), and, furthermore, in accordance with the word of the Lord through

Samuel (cf. 11:3). The phrase "concerning Israel" reminds the reader that David's appointment was not ultimately about David but rather for the sake of Israel.

The "account" (NLT, "record") of David's warriors (11:11-19) begins with a review of the exploits of the most famous group, "the Three," who were considered "the mightiest warriors among David's men" (11:11). The Hebrew text of 2 Samuel 23 identifies these warriors as Josheb-basshebeth (a Tahkemonite), Eleazar (son of Dodai, a descendant of Ahoah), and Shammah (son of Agee from Harar). The text of 1 Chronicles 11:1-14, however, appears to reflect a scribal error that resulted in the loss of Shammah and the assignment of his account to Eleazar, whose account in turn was lost. Thus, it appears appropriate to replace 1 Chronicles 11:13b-14 with 2 Samuel 23:9b-12a (in italics below):

> Next in rank among the Three was Eleazar son of Dodai, a descendant of Ahoah. He was with David in the battle against the Philistines at Pas-dammim. *Once Eleazar and David stood together against the Philistines when the entire Israelite army had fled. He killed Philistines until his hand was too tired to lift his sword, and the LORD gave him a great victory that day. The rest of the army did not return until it was time to collect the plunder!*
>
> *Next in rank was Shammah son of Agee from Harar. One time the Philistines gathered at Lehi and attacked the Israelites in a field full of lentils. The Israelite army fled, but Shammah held his ground in the middle of the field and beat back the Philistines.* So the LORD saved them by giving them a great victory.

The resulting text credits each of "the Three" with a major victory against overwhelming odds.

In two of the cases (Eleazar and Shammah) their victory was against the Philistines and was attributed to the direct action of God. The section closes with the description of the daring act of all three together, when they sought to fulfill the longing of David for water from the well at Bethlehem.[5] While this act displays the level of loyalty and respect that David received from his soldiers, David's refusal to drink the water expresses the depth of his respect and affection for his men. The language used here, however, suggests sacrifice with the allusion to the "blood" and the phrase "poured it out as an offering to the LORD," which is used to refer to offering a drink offering to a god (Gen 35:14; Exod 25:29; Num 28:7; 2 Kgs 16:13; cf. Ps 16:4; Jer 7:18; 19:13; 32:29; 44:17-19, 25; Ezek 20:28).

In 11:20-25 we are told of the exploits of two additional, superior members of "the Thirty." The Hebrew text calls Abishai the "leader of the Three" in 11:20-21, even though "he was not one of the Three." One might suggest changing this to "leader of the Thirty" (as NLT) or leaving it as is and interpreting this as a political move by Joab to control "the Three." In the Hebrew text of 11:21 there is an additional phrase that is left untranslated in the NLT: *bashenayim* [TH8147, ZH9109], which could be rendered either as "doubly" (as in "he was honored doubly above the three") or "in the second." If the latter is in view, this phrase indicates that there was a "second" group of three,[6] over which Abishai exercised leadership.

The final warrior to be singled out with accompanying stories is Benaiah son of Jehoiada, who was renowned among the Thirty but never attained to the Three. Interestingly, Benaiah is afforded the most space in this account. Japhet (1993:247) suggests that this may offer an insight into the time of the compilation of this account, for Benaiah rose to great prominence after the accession of Solomon when he replaced Joab as chief commander (1 Kgs 1–2). Additionally, his exploits do not mention the Philistines as the others do. Many have noted how the Chronicler's account stresses the similarity between Benaiah's slaying of the giant Egyptian and David's slaying of Goliath (cf. 11:23; 1 Sam 17:7; 2 Sam 23:21). Benaiah came from Kabzeel, a remote southern town in the Negev (Josh 15:21). David expressed his favor and trust in Benaiah by setting him over his bodyguard.

The chapter concludes (11:25-47) with a long list of mighty men who probably comprised some of "the Thirty," the inner core of warriors loyal to and protective of David.

ENDNOTES

1. Flanagan (1979:223-244) sees this move as politically motivated but religiously devastating. This latter conclusion is not supported by the persistent Jerusalemite worship traditions in the Old Testament.
2. Notice a similar trend in 14:12 of the use of 2 Sam 5:21, where "David and his men" becomes merely "David."
3. Japhet (1993:241) has probably unearthed the reason for this focus on Joab: "In Chronicles, where the list of the 'mighty men' is found at the beginning of David's reign, Joab's absence is conspicuous indeed. His role in the conquest of Jerusalem fills the gap and explains his position as 'commander'." However, Williamson notes that the Chronicler could have added a section on Joab in the list if he wanted to (1982:99).
4. Williamson (1982:101) goes as far as to speak of the Chronicler's "dislike" for this term. For the idiom, see Hess and Wenham 1999; Ollenburger 1987.
5. See Japhet (1993:245), who argues that two events have been telescoped in this case, one with David near the cave of Adullam and the Philistines encamped in the valley of Rephaim, and the other with David in the stronghold and the Philistines in Bethlehem. However, this need not be the case, as both the valley and Bethlehem could be part of a common military campaign and the stronghold could be a reference to the protection he enjoyed in the cave.
6. With NASB, contra Japhet (1993:246), who sees this as reflecting on the relationship between Abishai and Benaiah.

C. David's Military Support (12:1–40)

The following men joined David at Ziklag
while he was hiding from Saul son of
Kish. They were among the warriors who
fought beside David in battle. 2 All of
them were expert archers, and they could
shoot arrows or sling stones with their
left hand as well as their right. They were
all relatives of Saul from the tribe of
Benjamin. 3 Their leader was Ahiezer son
of Shemaah from Gibeah; his brother
Joash was second-in-command. These
were the other warriors:

Jeziel and Pelet, sons of Azmaveth,
Beracah;
Jehu from Anathoth;
4 Ishmaiah from Gibeon, a famous
warrior and leader among the
Thirty;
***Jeremiah, Jahaziel, Johanan, and**
Jozabad from Gederah;
5 Eluzai, Jerimoth, Bealiah, Shemariah,
and Shephatiah from Haruph;
6 Elkanah, Isshiah, Azarel, Joezer, and
Jashobeam, who were Korahites;

7 Joelah and Zebadiah, sons of Jeroham
from Gedor.

8 Some brave and experienced warriors
from the tribe of Gad also defected to Da-
vid while he was at the stronghold in the
wilderness. They were expert with both
shield and spear, as fierce as lions and as
swift as deer on the mountains.

9 Ezer was their leader.
Obadiah was second.
Eliab was third.
10 Mishmannah was fourth.
Jeremiah was fifth.
11 Attai was sixth.
Eliel was seventh.
12 Johanan was eighth.
Elzabad was ninth.
13 Jeremiah was tenth.
Macbannai was eleventh.

14 These warriors from Gad were army
commanders. The weakest among them
could take on a hundred regular troops,
and the strongest could take on a thou-
sand! 15 These were the men who crossed
the Jordan River during its seasonal flood-
ing at the beginning of the year and drove
out all the people living in the lowlands
on both the east and west banks.

16 Others from Benjamin and Judah
came to David at the stronghold. 17 David
went out to meet them and said, "If you
have come in peace to help me, we are
friends. But if you have come to betray me
to my enemies when I am innocent, then
may the God of our ancestors see it and
punish you."

18 Then the Spirit came upon Amasai,
the leader of the Thirty, and he said,

"We are yours, David!
We are on your side, son of Jesse.
Peace and prosperity be with you,
and success to all who help you,
for your God is the one who helps
you."

So David let them join him, and he made
them officers over his troops.

19 Some men from Manasseh defected
from the Israelite army and joined David
when he set out with the Philistines to
fight against Saul. But as it turned out,
the Philistine rulers refused to let David
and his men go with them. After much
discussion, they sent them back, for they
said, "It will cost us our heads if David
switches loyalties to Saul and turns
against us."

20 Here is a list of the men from Ma-
nasseh who defected to David as he was
returning to Ziklag: Adnah, Jozabad, Jedi-
ael, Michael, Jozabad, Elihu, and Zillethai.
Each commanded 1,000 troops from the
tribe of Manasseh. 21 They helped David
chase down bands of raiders, for they
were all brave and able warriors who be-
came commanders in his army. 22 Day after
day more men joined David until he had a
great army, like the army of God.

23 These are the numbers of armed war-
riors who joined David at Hebron. They were
all eager to see David become king instead
of Saul, just as the LORD had promised.

24 From the tribe of Judah, there were
6,800 warriors armed with shields
and spears.
25 From the tribe of Simeon, there were
7,100 brave warriors.
26 From the tribe of Levi, there were
4,600 warriors. 27 This included
Jehoiada, leader of the family of
Aaron, who had 3,700 under his
command. 28 This also included Zadok,
a brave young warrior, with
22 members of his family who were
all officers.
29 From the tribe of Benjamin, Saul's
relatives, there were 3,000 warriors.
Most of the men from Benjamin had
remained loyal to Saul until this time.
30 From the tribe of Ephraim, there were
20,800 brave warriors, each highly
respected in his own clan.
31 From the half-tribe of Manasseh west
of the Jordan, 18,000 men were
designated by name to help David
become king.
32 From the tribe of Issachar, there were

200 leaders of the tribe with their relatives. All these men understood the signs of the times and knew the best course for Israel to take.
33From the tribe of Zebulun, there were 50,000 skilled warriors. They were fully armed and prepared for battle and completely loyal to David.
34From the tribe of Naphtali, there were 1,000 officers and 37,000 warriors armed with shields and spears.
35From the tribe of Dan, there were 28,600 warriors, all prepared for battle.
36From the tribe of Asher, there were 40,000 trained warriors, all prepared for battle.
37From the east side of the Jordan River—where the tribes of Reuben and Gad and the half-tribe of Manasseh lived—there were 120,000 troops armed with every kind of weapon.

38All these men came in battle array to
Hebron with the single purpose of making
David the king over all Israel. In fact,
everyone in Israel agreed that David
should be their king. 39They feasted and
drank with David for three days, for prep-
arations had been made by their relatives
for their arrival. 40And people from as far
away as Issachar, Zebulun, and Naphtali
brought food on donkeys, camels, mules,
and oxen. Vast supplies of flour, fig cakes,
clusters of raisins, wine, olive oil, cattle,
sheep, and goats were brought to the cel-
ebration. There was great joy throughout
the land of Israel.

12:4 Verses 12:4b-40 are numbered 12:5-41 in Hebrew text.

NOTES

12:1 ***Ziklag.*** This was a town on the southern edge of Judah (Josh 15:31), identified with remains at sites nearly 14 miles northeast of Beersheba. Ziklag was David's command center during his flight from Saul and after his defection to the Philistines until he was directed to go to Hebron (2 Sam 2) and finally Jerusalem (2 Sam 5). Ziklag was given to David by King Achish of Gath (1 Sam 27).

12:2 ***sling stones with their left hand as well as their right.*** Judges 20:13-16 also relates how left-handed Benjaminites and in particular men from Gibeah were accurate stone slingers. There appears to be a play here on the name of Benjamin, "son of the right hand," a pun that is also seen in the story of Ehud, the "left-handed" judge (Judg 3).

12:8 [9] ***the stronghold in the wilderness.*** This is a reference to a fortification of David in the wilderness. The cave of Adullam (1 Sam 22:1-5), En-gedi (1 Sam 23:29), and Jerusalem/Zion (2 Sam 5:7, 9) are all associated with strongholds of David (as well as unnamed ones in 1 Sam 24:22; 2 Sam 5:17). This could be either the cave of Adullam or En-gedi or another that was used by David. Some scholars have suggested that this was the fortress of Masada, which means "stronghold" (Beitzel 1985:116; Aharoni 2002:73).

fierce as lions and as swift as deer on the mountains. Lit., "their faces (were) faces of a lion and as swift as deer on the mountains." The focus in the first half of the phrase appears to be on their appearance, although to appear as a lion suggests the common association of strength and courage. The deer (or gazelle) image suggests the qualities of speed and agility. Such qualities (strength, courage, speed, agility) were key for warriors.

12:14 [15] ***hundred . . . thousand.*** This appears to be terms for a leader or grouping of troops, which may not designate 100 or 1,000 (similar to "centurion," which technically means a commander of 100, but in Roman times a centurion rarely commanded 100 troops).

12:15 [16] ***crossed the Jordan River during its seasonal flooding at the beginning of the year.*** Joshua 3:15 describes the Jordan overflowing its banks, a phenomenon related to the melting of snow in the Lebanon mountain range, especially Mount Hermon. The event referred to in this verse must have been severe flooding that left certain settlements near the Jordan vulnerable.

12:17 [18] ***we are friends.*** Lit., "I will have toward you a heart for unitedness."

12:18 [19] ***the Spirit came upon.*** Lit., "the Spirit clothed," a phrase also found in Judg 6:34; 2 Chr 24:20. In Judges this results in Gideon's great military feat and in 2 Chr 24 in Zechariah's prophetic speech. In this passage, one would expect the former (since it is describing warriors), but instead the warrior Amasai breaks into a speech.

Peace and prosperity be with you, and success. Peace, prosperity, and success are all the same word in Hebrew (*shalom* [TH7965, ZH8934]), playing off of David's request in 12:17 [18].

12:20 [21] ***Each commanded 1,000 troops.*** Lit., "chiefs of thousands." The "thousands" could also be "clan" or "military group" (see commentary below).

12:22 [23] ***a great army, like the army of God.*** Sometimes the name of God (*'elohim* [TH430, ZH466]) is used in Hebrew to designate the superlative. But here the preposition Kaph [TH3509.1, ZH3869] (like) signals a simile. The same phrase as here for "army of God" (*makhaneh* [TH4264, ZH4722] *'elohim*) is used in Gen 32:1-3 by Jacob after he was met by the angels of God.

12:23 [24] ***just as the Lord had promised.*** This was promised through Samuel (11:3; cf. 1 Sam 16).

12:38 [39] ***In fact, everyone in Israel agreed that David should be their king.*** The Hebrew text uses the phrase *kol-sherith yisra'el*, that is, "all the rest/remnant of Israel." The term *sherith* [TH7611, ZH8642] (remnant) may have links to the identity of the community that went into and returned from exile (see 2 Chr 36:20; NLT, "the few who survived").

COMMENTARY

First Chronicles 12, which is unique to the Chronicler, continues to develop the picture of David as military leader. While the lists in the previous chapter were more general in character, cataloguing those warriors who determined to make David king, chapter 12 records the list of those who joined David during his flight from Saul (while in Ziklag and before that in the wilderness strongholds) and after the death of Saul.

According to 12:1-40, David was a magnet for those disaffected with Saul's rule. The account is structured into two basic sections: those who supported David prior to (12:1-22) and after (12:23-40) his enthronement at Hebron. Statements emphasizing this support introduce each of the subparagraphs in the first section (12:1, 8, 16, 19) and close off the first section as a whole (12:22; Williamson 1982:104).[1] The same vocabulary introduces the second main section (12:23), which then shifts to the theme of support for his kingship at Hebron, bringing closure to the account of David's enthronement that began at 11:1.[2]

David's Support prior to Hebron (12:1-22). This section begins with relatives from Saul's own tribe (Benjamin) and even his own town (Gibeah) who were both expert archers and stone slingers, showing that there was discontent within Saul's own power base. They came to Ziklag, a town on the southern border of Judah's traditional territory, which was held by the Philistines during the reign of Saul. At that time it had been given to David as reward for his defection from Saul and loyalty to the Philistine king Achish of Gath (1 Sam 27:1-6). It would become the base of his operations until Saul's death (2 Sam 1:1), when David's base would move to Hebron (2 Sam 2:1).

Next, the Chronicler relates the defection of warriors from Gad who were experts with shield and spear. They approached David while at an unnamed "stronghold in the wilderness" (see note on 12:8). Only then does the Chronicler introduce defectors from David's own tribe of Judah, who, together with others from Saul's tribe Benjamin, approached David at the stronghold to join him. Here the Chronicler (or his source) incorporates powerful dramatic narrative. David's speech challenged them to reveal their loyalties; it oriented the discussion theologically by calling on "the God of our ancestors" to judge the answer. The response was given by Amasai (12:18), who would later become a leader in "the Thirty" (see commentary on 11:10-47 for a discussion of "the Thirty") and is probably the later Amasa of Absalom's revolt (2 Sam 17:25; cf. 1 Chr 2:17).[3] He functions in this narrative as a Spirit-inspired spokesperson ("the Spirit came upon Amasai"). The terms used by Amasai echo those used in David's, especially "peace," "help," and "God." His words express their loyalty to David ("We are on your side") and their hope for his prosperity and success ("Peace and prosperity be with you, and success to all who help you"). The last phrase, "for your God is the one who helps you," grounds this pledge theologically.

The final group, which defected from Saul's army to David's prior to the Philistine defeat of Saul (ch 10), is from Manasseh. At the time David was encamped with his protector Achish of Gath. But the other Philistine leaders mistrusted David, so Achish reluctantly sent him back to Ziklag (1 Sam 29). At some point on David's journey home to Ziklag after leaving the Philistine encampment at Aphek, seven leaders from Manasseh joined David's troop, bringing with each of them a troop of a thousand. It appears from 12:19 that it was news of their defection that prompted the distrust of the Philistines, who smelled a ruse.

David's Support at Hebron (12:23-40). The four examples in 12:2-21 (Benjamin/ Gibeah, Gad, Judah/Benjamin, Manasseh) provide qualitative evidence of broad support for David's leadership, even before the death of Saul. This evidence is then supported by quantitative evidence with the precise number of warriors from each of the 13 tribes (12:24-37), who not only joined David at Hebron, but affirmed his kingship. The phrase used to introduce this section ("David become king instead of Saul"; lit., "to turn over the kingdom of Saul to him") is identical to the one used in 10:14 ("turned the kingdom over to David"), which signaled the beginning of the transition.

The numbers given in this section for the armed warriors who joined David at Hebron are inordinately large. Much has been written on the large numbers found in the book of Chronicles; four streams of interpretation have arisen.[4] First, many early conservative interpreters considered these numbers as precise figures corresponding to historical reality, even though some of the discrepancies in the numbers may have been explained as the writer rounding off numbers or scribal errors. Second, some have suggested that the term used for 1,000 in the Hebrew text is a word that also designates a military unit. Although this unit may have originally contained a thousand soldiers, the term became associated in time with large military units that numbered less than a thousand (see Num 1:16; Judg 6:15; 1 Sam 10:19-21; Mic 5:1). Related to this is a third view that revocalizes the word (changing the vowels but not the original consonants) found in the Hebrew text to match the word used in Hebrew for a commander or leader of a military unit. According to this view the armed forces are counted by numbers of leaders rather than soldiers. The final view is that the Chronicler used these numbers hyperbolically.

The first view is difficult to sustain in light of the fact that most estimates of the size of Judah at its height in the eighth century BC place the population at 250,000, with the population of the combined kingdoms during this century under 1,000,000 (see Klein 1997:270). The greatest difficulty often cited for the second and third views is that although they may solve the problem of high numbers related to human beings, they are not applicable to instances where large numbers are used for precious metals (22:14; 29:4) and animals (5:21; 2 Chr 30:24; 35:7-9; cf. Knoppers 2004:570). For many, the fourth view appears more in keeping with patterns discerned elsewhere in Chronicles. For instance, in the genealogies in chapters 1–9 one can discern at times a penchant for symbolic enumeration (see introduction to chs 1–9). Additionally, the Chronicler's depiction of the era of David-Solomon is highly stylized, shaping this period into the idyllic and normative era of Israel's history (see introductions to chs 10–29 and 2 Chr 1–9). The massive numbers used by the Chronicler seem to reflect both of his historiographic techniques, using symbolic numbers to heighten the rhetorical effect of his depiction of the idyllic past. If this is the case, it may be related to what Longman and Dillard (2006:197) call the Chronicler's "messianic historiography," a technique obvious to the Chronicler's audience who would have had access to his source text in Samuel—Kings.

It may, however, be inappropriate to limit the answer to just one of these streams of interpretation. In some cases the numbers that are found in Chronicles simply echo those found in Samuel—Kings or are considered appropriate by most and thus should be read as precise figures. If the second and third views are correct, there is no reason that this could not be used to explain the high numbers of human beings alone without the need to deal with the nonhuman enumeration. However, it is also possible that at times the Chronicler was engaging in hyperbole, much as he does in his idyllic presentation of the reigns of David and Solomon.[5] The answer to this dilemma, therefore, may entail a combination of these various solutions—that is, in some cases the Chronicler was indeed speaking of actual numbers, in others of troop groups/leaders, and in still others in hyperbolic fashion. In the present case of chapter 12, it appears that the Chronicler was speaking of military groupings.

The list is structured geographically, starting with the tribes in the southern half of the land (Judah, Simeon, Levi), then moving north (Benjamin, Ephraim, Manasseh, Issachar, Zebulun, Naphtali, Dan and Asher) before crossing the Jordan and moving from south to north (Reuben, Gad, Manasseh; see Japhet 1989:285-286; 1993:259).[6] The movement from south to north may reflect an eastern geographical orientation for the ancient Israelites combined with a right (south) to left (north) movement. The pattern from south to north is also evident throughout the book of Judges. Judah was an obvious starting point not only because of its southern location, but because this was the tribe from which David came and the tribe that first embraced his leadership. The strong tradition of a close relationship between the tribes of Judah and Simeon is reflected in Judges 1:3, when the tribe of Judah invited the tribe of Simeon to accompany them on their initial expedition against the Canaanites. The Chronicler emphasized the role the tribe of Levi played in the army and focused particular attention on the support of the family of Aaron and within that family, in particular, a young warrior named Zadok, a figure who would emerge as a chief priest for David and Solomon. The loyalty of the Benjaminites ("Saul's relatives") to Saul was probably not intended as a knock against his tribe, but rather as a sign of faithfulness (12:29). Such support would be assumed, but after the death of Saul they expressed their commitment to David. The Chronicler recorded much larger numbers for the tribes in 12:30-37, revealing not only the reality of the demographic weight of the northern tribes, but also emphasizing the level of support from this region for David's rule. Pride of place is given to the powerful tribes of Joseph: Ephraim and Manasseh.

Along with the numbers, the Chronicler included a statement about each group, affirming either their prowess in battle (Ephraim, Zebulun, Naphtali, Dan, Asher, Reuben/Gad/eastern Manasseh) or their loyalty to David (western Manasseh, Zebulun). For the men of Issachar, however, neither of these is mentioned. Instead, the Chronicler recorded that "All these men understood the signs of the times and knew the best course for Israel to take" (12:32). Japhet (1993:268) identifies this as a conflation of two idioms: "those who have (gain, are endowed with) understanding" (2 Chr 2:11-12; Job 38:4; Prov 4:1) and "those who know the times" (Esth 1:13). While Japhet suggests this may be related to some form of astrological discernment, the texts above only suggest that the men of Issachar were wise and provided good counsel to the nation.

The final picture of chapter 12 is that of the community as a whole gathered at Hebron joyfully to eat and drink with David for three days. Japhet (1993:269) notes the "secular" tone of this section, especially in contrast to Solomon's enthronement in 29:22, where joyful eating and drinking are depicted "in the LORD's presence" and the ceremony anoints Solomon "before the LORD as their leader" and Zadok as priest. The reason for this different tone is because the Chronicler wanted to stress Jerusalem's role as spiritual center for the nation, a role that still lay in the future when the celebration of chapter 12 took place.

All of this evidence was mustered by the Chronicler to support the picture of the progressive growth ("day after day more men joined David," 12:22) and comprehensive scope ("everyone in Israel agreed that David should be their king," 12:38) of those who joined David's side and who were eager to replace Saul with David. The resulting force, beginning at Ziklag and continuing at Hebron, created an army that the Chronicler called "a great army, like the army of God." To equate David's army with the hosts of heaven at Yahweh's disposal certainly legitimized David's rule. As has been noted at several points in the lists of warriors, David was appointed by divine election ("just as the LORD had promised," 12:23) and confirmed by communal acceptance ("everyone in Israel agreed that David should be their king,"

12:38). The emphasis throughout this section is clearly on the unified purpose of Israel: "They were all eager" (12:23), "all these men . . . with the single purpose" (12:38), "everyone in Israel agreed" (12:38), and "throughout the land of Israel" (12:40). The phrase "everyone in Israel agreed that David should be their king" (12:38) is literally, "all Israel (was) of one heart concerning the enthronement of David." Here, as with the declaration of David in 12:17, those who accepted and helped David were unified in heart (see note on 12:17). As Japhet (1993:258) has concluded, "The underlying presupposition of the list is the view that the accession of David was celebrated in an impressive, all-Israelite ceremony."

Through chapters 11–12, with their lists and short accounts of military exploits, the Chronicler emphasized the unity of the tribes of Israel around David as their royal leader. The final scene (12:39-40) depicts the tribes, even the more remote people of Issachar, Zebulun, and Naphtali, celebrating the enthronement of David. This is a very different emphasis from that found in 1–2 Samuel with its depiction of David's struggle for power and legitimacy. In portraying the events this way, the Chronicler was not trying to deceive his readers, for the accounts of Samuel were readily available to them. Rather, likely using other sources and traditions, the Chronicler focused on evidence for unity in the early years of David's rule. This technique is described by Williamson (1982:97) in the following way: "The Chronicler is seen to regard history from the point of view of its outcome as determined by God, in the light of which the intervening material may be passed over as irrelevant." The resulting picture presents an idealized portrait of David and his rule, a consistent trend throughout Chronicles in relationship to David and Solomon as cofounders of a new dynasty.

What was the Chronicler seeking to accomplish through his rendition of David's rise to power? Some have suggested that the presentation of David was merely used to provide legitimacy for the Temple, which was so intimately linked with the Davidic house in the tradition of Israel. By beginning with Saul's demise and David's enthronement and presenting David in idealized ways, the Chronicler was trying to legitimize the Temple at which he served. The difficulty with this approach is the lack of attention in these chapters to the Temple and its cultus, in particular in the account of the capture of Jerusalem.[7] It appears that Davidic kingship is more than just a subtheme supporting the Temple motif for the Chronicler. On three occasions in chapters 11–12, the Chronicler linked the appointment of David with the promise of God through his prophet with the word of the Lord (11:2, 10; 12:23; cf. 2 Sam 5:2; 7:8).

Writing in a period when there was little hope in the reemergence of the Davidic line, the Chronicler's idealized portrait suggests that he was concerned not merely with leveraging the past to legitimate the present, but rather with leveraging the past to stimulate hope for the future. In other words, he was writing a portrait of the ideal future David, employing a messianic historiography. David called for help, for oneness of heart. This is repeated at the end of the passage in 12:38, as the people became one in heart and supported David. In particular the message is directed to the "remnant of Israel," the group that had returned from exile (2 Chr 36:20), to join together in unity and support of Davidic kingship.

ENDNOTES

1. Selman (1994a:144) notes that "help" is a leitmotif in Chronicles, "expressing commitment and co-operation rather than merely assistance." Notice how God also "helps" in 12:18.
2. Selman (1994a:144) argues for a chiastic structure in chs 11–12: Hebron (11:1-3), Ziklag (12:1-7), stronghold (12:8-15), stronghold (12:16-18), Ziklag (12:19-22), Hebron (12:23-40), but he can only accomplish this by dropping out 11:4-47 (see Boda 1996:55-70). It may be that the unit 12:1-22 is structured chiastically; surely 11:1-3 forms a bracket with (at least) 12:38-40 around the entire unit of chs 11–12.
3. See the argument of Japhet (1993:266).
4. A sampling of this diversity can be drawn from Dillard 1987:106, Klein 1997:270-282, Knoppers 2004:569-571, Payne 1979:109-128, 206-220, and J. Wenham 1993:116-120.
5. The strongest case for this is ch 22, which speaks of 100,000 talents of gold and 1,000,000 talents of silver. Throughout this section, which is unique to Chronicles, one finds the regular use of the Hebrew phrases *'en mishqal* [TH4948, ZH5486] (NLT, "more . . . than could be weighed/it cannot be weighed," 22:3, 14) and *'en mispar* [TH4557, ZH5031] (NLT, "innumerable," 22:4), phrases that suggest the hyperbolic character of the numbers in this section.
6. Contrast Williamson (1982:110), who says the list is ordered "not strictly geographically."
7. So Williamson (1982:98), contra Mosis (1973), on lack of attention to temple/cult here. This shows that for the Chronicler the Davidic kingship had status independent from the Temple.

◆ D. David Attempts to Move the Ark (13:1-14)

David consulted with all his officials, in-
cluding the generals and captains of his
army.* 2Then he addressed the entire as-
sembly of Israel as follows: "If you ap-
prove and if it is the will of the LORD our
God, let us send messages to all the Isra-
elites throughout the land, including the
priests and Levites in their towns and
pasturelands. Let us invite them to come
and join us. 3It is time to bring back the
Ark of our God, for we neglected it during
the reign of Saul."

4The whole assembly agreed to this, for
the people could see it was the right thing
to do. 5So David summoned all Israel, from
the Shihor Brook of Egypt in the south all
the way to the town of Lebo-hamath in
the north, to join in bringing the Ark of
God from Kiriath-jearim. 6Then David and
all Israel went to Baalah of Judah (also
called Kiriath-jearim) to bring back the
Ark of God, which bears the name* of the
LORD who is enthroned between the cher-
ubim. 7They placed the Ark of God on a
new cart and brought it from Abinadab's
house. Uzzah and Ahio were guiding the
cart. 8David and all Israel were celebrating
before God with all their might, singing
songs and playing all kinds of musical
instruments—lyres, harps, tambourines,
cymbals, and trumpets.

9But when they arrived at the threshing
floor of Nacon,* the oxen stumbled, and
Uzzah reached out his hand to steady the
Ark. 10Then the LORD's anger was aroused
against Uzzah, and he struck him dead
because he had laid his hand on the Ark.
So Uzzah died there in the presence of
God.

11David was angry because the LORD's
anger had burst out against Uzzah. He
named that place Perez-uzzah (which
means "to burst out against Uzzah"), as it
is still called today.

12David was now afraid of God, and he
asked, "How can I ever bring the Ark of
God back into my care?" 13So David did
not move the Ark into the City of David.

Instead, he took it to the house of Obed-edom of Gath. 14The Ark of God remained there in Obed-edom's house for three months, and the LORD blessed the household of Obed-edom and everything he owned.

13:1 Hebrew *the commanders of thousands and of hundreds.* 13:6 Or *the Ark of God, where the Name is proclaimed—the name.* 13:9 As in parallel text at 2 Sam 6:6; Hebrew reads *Kidon.*

NOTES

13:1 *the generals and captains of his army.* Lit., "the commanders of thousands and of hundreds" (so NLT mg). The terms "thousands" and "hundreds" may signify military units within David's army. They may have their origins in precise numbers but most likely have lost this connotation and are merely terms for divisions and subdivisions of an army (much like "centurion" in Roman times). See commentary on 12:23-40.

13:2 *if it is the will of the LORD our God.* Lit., "from the LORD our God," translated in the LXX as "from the Lord there will be success/prosperity." In either case, it refers to the will of God.

let us send messages. Hebrew has two verbs here: *parats* [TH6555, ZH7287] (break through) and *shalakh* [TH7971, ZH8938] (send), both cohortative in form. The first verb is used in 2 Chr 31:5 to refer to the word spreading, which was due to Hezekiah's "sending" (*shalakh*) letters inviting Israel to meet in Jerusalem (2 Chr 30:1).

in their towns and pasturelands. This is a reference to the Levitical cities with their surrounding pasturelands (Num 35:1-7; Josh 14:4; 21:2; cf. 1 Chr 6:54-81; Japhet 1979:205-218).

come and join us. Communal gathering is an important leitmotif throughout Chronicles. This is the second time that a new section of the book is signaled by the use of the Hebrew verb *qabats* [TH6908, ZH7695] (cf. 11:1). In the Persian period, with the community's very existence in question due to the overshadowing presence of the empire, the Chronicler encourages the communal bond in his presentation of David.

13:5 *from the Shihor Brook of Egypt . . . to the town of Lebo-hamath.* As noted in the translation, the Shihor is a brook in the south and Lebo-hamath a town in the north. Joshua 13:3 says the Shihor is "on the border" (lit., "on the face of," often meaning "east") of Egypt. In Isa 23:3 and Jer 2:18 it is closely associated, if not equated, with the Nile (*ye'or* [TH2975, ZH3284]). In 1 Kgs 8:65 the assembly that is drawn to the Temple dedication came from "Lebo-hamath in the north and the Brook of Egypt in the south." This evidence suggests that the various terms "Shihor," "Brook of Egypt," and "Nile" are closely associated, if not identical, and represent the ideal southern boundary of Israel's land (see Gen 15:18). Lebo-hamath, which means "entrance of Hamath," is on the northern frontier of Syria on the eastern side of the Orontes River. This city was the promised northern boundary of Israel (Num 13:21; Josh 13:5; Ezek 47:15, 20).

13:6 *Baalah of Judah (also called Kiriath-jearim).* Baalah was on the border of Philistia and Judah; it is where the Ark was taken after it was abandoned by the Philistines following their tragic possession (1 Sam 6:21; cf. Josh 15:9, 60; 18:14).

13:7 *Uzzah and Ahio.* These were Abinadab's sons (2 Sam 6:3).

13:8 *before God.* Second Samuel 6:5, a parallel passage, reads, "before the LORD." Chronicles often has "God" (*'elohim* [TH430, ZH466]) where Samuel has "the LORD" (*yhwh* [TH3068, ZH3378]). This may be evidence of the increasing distancing of God from human affairs seen in the Second Temple era, but even if so, it may have more to do with scribal practice than with the Chronicler, since "the LORD" is used regularly in Chronicles. See further Williamson 1982:116.

13:9 ***the threshing floor of Nacon.*** This is the location in the MT account of 2 Sam 6:6 (see NLT mg). In Chronicles it is "Kidon"; in 4QSam[a], "Nodan"; and in LXX[B], "Nodav." A threshing floor was a large flat surface used for removing extraneous material from grain. It was often located on higher ground to take advantage of the natural winds to blow away the chaff, although forks were used to speed the process (Isa 30:24; Jer 15:7; Matt 3:12). The grain would be beaten with small (Judg 6:11; Ruth 2:17) or large (Isa 28:27; 41:15) instruments.

the oxen stumbled. This is better translated as "the oxen let [it] drop"—referring to the Ark.

COMMENTARY

First Chronicles 13 is an important section in the Chronicler's presentation of the reign of David. In this chapter the Chronicler makes it clear that David's military prowess and popular support were for the grander purpose of the worship of God in Jerusalem. However, the Chronicler heightens tension in the narrative by including the story of the failed attempt to bring the Ark from Kiriath-jearim to Jerusalem, an event that in the book of Samuel follows David's Philistine victories (cf. ch 14 with 2 Sam 5). Williamson (1982:113) attributes this order to the Chronicler's concern for "theme and theology rather than strict chronology." Although this story reveals David's lack of attention to ritual detail, it is essential to the development of the Chronicler's depiction of David as the great champion of the Levites and catalyst for the worship of God in Jerusalem.

David Consults the People about Moving the Ark (13:1-4). The chapter begins with a section unique to the Chronicler, echoing the strong theme of unity that has been clear throughout chapters 11–12. He consults "all his officials" (13:1), exhorts them to call together "all the Israelites throughout the land" (13:2), assembles "all Israel" (13:5) in order that "all Israel" (13:6) may bring the Ark to Jerusalem. This agenda is seen clearly in the contrast between 13:5 and 2 Samuel 6:1, the former focusing on all Israel from the ideal southern boundary to the ideal northern boundary (see note on 13:5) and the latter on David with his army. Thus, the worship of the nation around the Temple is "understood as the inheritance of all the people" (Williamson 1982:113).

In the opening verses, the Chronicler uses dramatic narrative to draw the reader's attention to David's speech (13:2-3). The phrase "if it is the will of the LORD our God" (see note on 13:2) introduces the theme of David's concern to take his lead from God's action (just as he will inquire of God before his battles in 14:10, 14). But the emphasis in this speech is on his desire to consult and motivate his assembly of officials. This emphasis is evident throughout Chronicles, in which "the people are not limited to playing the role of accompanying crowd or the audience at a performance; rather, they are full partners—in consultation and decision-making" (Japhet 1993:274).[1] Phrases like "if you approve" and verbs rendered in the cohortative mood ("let us") reveal a far more democratized portrait of David than in Samuel, where the emphasis is on the actions of David and his army.[2] Two key aspects to this portrait are the balance between consultation and persuasion—that is, the openness to consult and the skill to persuade. Such leadership values appear to be rewarded as the assembly agrees with his wise counsel (13:4).

This royal speech also foreshadows other emphases of the theology of Chronicles. David encouraged the assembly to send messages "to all the Israelites throughout the land." This paraphrases a Hebrew clause that reads literally, "Our brothers, the remainder, in all the lands of Israel." The plural "lands" is odd, but often noted as a feature of Late Biblical Hebrew (cf. 2 Chr 11:23; 34:33; see Japhet 1993:275). The term "remainder" (from the verb *sha'ar* [TH7604, ZH8636]) probably originally referred to the remainder of the community that was not present with David, but for the Chronicler, writing in the early Persian period with many Israelites still in "exile" from the land, this term takes on the expanded nuance of the "remnant" (cf. 12:38; 2 Chr 36:20; Hag 1:12, 14; 2:2).[3] In light of this, "lands" may suggest the broad spread of this remnant throughout the earth. But if it refers to the land of Israel, it limits the remnant to those who have taken the faithful risk of returning to the land.[4] In either case, the Chronicler rallies the exilic community to the worship of God in the Temple (Braun 1971:502-514).

Not only is this "remnant" to be the recipient of the call, but also "priests and Levites in their towns and pasturelands" (13:2). This phrase reveals a priesthood that was comprised of "priests," those of the tribe of Levi who were descendants of Aaron and provided leadership, and "Levites," the rest of the tribe who played a subsidiary role. After the conquest of the land, the tribe of Levi was to be given cities and their surrounding pastureland to inhabit (i.e., the Levitical cities). Although not ignoring the role the priests must play in Israel's worship, the Chronicler brings great focus on the role the rest of the tribe must play and presents David as the champion of this group. This will become very clear in the chapters that follow. At present, however, the Chronicler includes the reference to the priests and Levites because ultimately they will play a key role in the successful transfer of the Ark to Jerusalem (15:13).

The final words of David's speech remind the reader again of the stark contrast between David and Saul who "neglected" the Ark. Although the Ark technically had been within Judean territory (cf. 13:6), David was passionate to restore ("it is time to bring back") the Ark to its rightful place at the center of Israel's life and worship (Japhet 1993:276). Japhet (1993:276) and Williamson (1982:115) both identify this as another key "turn" in the story of Israel with the appearance of the same verb (*sabab* [TH5437, ZH6015]) as was used in the transfer of rule from Saul to David in 10:14.

Ironically, although David had consulted the people and hoped for divine blessing, he did not directly inquire of God to discover the appropriate way to transport the Ark (15:13).[5] The Chronicler presents David in one respect as a normative character with his intense passion to bring the Ark into Jerusalem, yet in another respect as a developing character, still in need of much wisdom as to how to approach the holy God of Israel.

David Moves the Ark with Joy and Praise (13:5-8). Using the ideal boundaries of Israel for the definition of his kingdom (from the Shihor of Egypt to Lebo-hamath; see note on 13:5), David drew together "all Israel" (13:5).[6] The parallel account in 2 Samuel 6:1 focuses the account on David's military, while Chronicles emphasizes the involvement of all Israel in war. Ultimately, it will be to Jerusalem and its Ark that these tribes must go to worship the Lord. Their involvement at this seminal moment foreshadows and encourages future calls to worship in the City of David, an important emphasis for the Chronicler writing in the Persian period when the Temple became the unifying symbol for those who returned to the land.

And so the Chronicler describes David and all Israel going to Kiriath-jearim to retrieve the Ark. The Ark was the most holy object in Israel's worship. According to the Tabernacle instructions, it was to be placed in the "Most Holy Place" and was constructed of the finest materials (Exod 25:10-22). Its cover was called the "place of atonement," revealing its key role on the Day of Atonement (Lev 16:14) when the holy objects were purified and Israel's sins confessed before the Lord. Upon this cover were crafted two cherubim. The angelic symbolism signals the close association between this object and the presence of God, something made explicit in Exodus 25:22 when God tells Moses, "I will meet with you there and talk to you from above the atonement cover between the gold cherubim that hover over the Ark of the Covenant" (cf. Lev 16:2, 13). This helps orient the reader to the description of the Ark in 13:6: "which bears the name of the LORD who is enthroned between the cherubim." This Lord enthroned between the cherubim reveals the royal association of the Ark: It was a throne (or some would say a footstool) for the divine King of Israel, Yahweh. The name of the Lord signifies the person of God, something made clear when Moses asks for God to reveal his "glorious presence" and God promises, "I will make all my goodness pass before you, and I will call out my name, Yahweh, before you" (Exod 33:18-23). The Ark was intimately associated with the divine King whose terrifying presence (Exod 20:18-19) descended from the mountain into the center of the Israelite camp (Exod 25:8; 40:34-35).

The Ark had originally been housed at Shiloh, the central sanctuary of Israel before Saul's reign (1 Sam 4:4), but was lost to the Philistines in the infamous battle of 1 Samuel 4. After seven months it was promptly returned to the Israelites because of the toll it was taking on the Philistine idols and people (1 Sam 5–6). The Philistines sent it off to the Israelite town of Beth-shemesh on a "new cart" pulled by cows (1 Sam 6:7-8). Several Israelites at Beth-shemesh were struck down for looking upon the Ark, so they sent it off to Kiriath-jearim to the house of Abinadab, who consecrated his son Eleazar to superintend its care (1 Sam 7). There it remained until David brought it to Jerusalem.[7] To transport the Ark, however, the people appeared to follow the precedent set by the Philistine priests, placing the Ark again on a "new cart" (13:7; 1 Sam 6:7-8). Guiding the cart were Uzzah and Ahio, the sons of Abinadab, who had established a shrine for the Ark at Kiriath-jearim (2 Sam 6:3). The Chronicler describes the scene as one of great joy and worship, as David and "all Israel" (13:8; cf. 2 Sam 6:5) celebrated passionately with a variety of musical instruments, a foreshadowing of the musical tone of David's worship in the chapters that will follow.

The Celebration's Tragic Ending: Uzzah's Death (13:9-12). The celebration, however, was cut short when the oxen stumbled and Uzzah sought to steady the Ark. He was immediately struck dead. The initial description that Uzzah "reached out his hand" (13:9, *shalakh . . . 'eth-yado* [TH853, ZH906]) is subtly changed when the death is explained in 13:10 to "stretched his hand against" (*shalakh yado 'al-* [TH5921, ZH6584];

NLT, "he had laid his hand on"), a phrase that carries a negative nuance of offense against the Ark (cf. Exod 24:11, NASB; Japhet 1993:280). But lest one think that it was just the touching of the holy object that was in view, the Chronicler wrote that the death occurred "in the presence of God" (rather than "beside the Ark of God"; 2 Sam 6:7).

The site of this deadly incident is clearly marked as "the threshing floor," a foreshadowing of the ultimate destination of the Ark, which would also be a threshing floor (21:18) discovered in connection with a foolish act of David (a census).[8] David's initial response was one of anger (13:11), ironically matching the anger of God in 13:10, but this soon turned to fear (13:12) as he considered the mysterious action of this "holy" other, Yahweh. The human monarch must bend to the divine King, and yet he still voiced the sincere question of 13:12,[9] one that is left unanswered until 15:11-13, where it becomes clear that a new cart drawn by oxen and attended by laity was not appropriate for transporting the manifest presence of God. David must follow the careful instructions Yahweh had given to Moses at Sinai or risk the destruction of his people.

The Ark Remains with Obed-edom: God's Blessing (13:13-14). The resolution of the dilemma expressed in David's question in 13:12 was left aside in the Chronicler's account, creating tension for the reader. For the time being, the Ark would remain at the home of Obed-edom of Gath. Obed-edom did not hail from the Philistine city of Gath, but rather the Levitical city of Gath-rimmon (a Kohathite city that was in the tribe of Dan according to Josh 19:45; 21:24, but in the tribe of Ephraim according to 6:69). Nevertheless, there may be some irony in this tradition (also found in Samuel) that when David failed the first time to bring the Ark into Jerusalem, it ends up at the "house" (*beth* [TH1004, ZH1074]) of someone from "Gath" (ironic allusion to those who stole the Ark in the first place). Furthermore, God blessed his "household" (*beth* [TH1004, ZH1074]). The name Obed-edom reappears in a later Levitical list in Chronicles (26:4-8) with a reference to God's blessing, confirming that the same Obed-edom of chapter 13 was in view.

This incident is a subtle reminder that God sets the agenda for his worship; he must be worshiped in the way he has required. Religion was consistently manipulated by royal houses in the ancient Near East to achieve their own ends. David and his people must realize that they served God and not vice versa. This is the same lesson that Joshua learned prior to the Jericho battle. Encountering the "commander of the LORD's army" outside Jericho, the leader of Israel called out, "Are you friend or foe?" only to receive the reply, "Neither one" (Josh 5:13-15). God does not serve Israel, but rather Israel serves God. This God cares for those who submit themselves to his rule, but those who do not (and Israel soon found out about this) are his foes. Joshua's response, falling on his face and crying, "I am at your command," was the appropriate response. Later, when it was Saul's turn to submit to God's command as he moved to war, he became impatient and disobeyed this command and ultimately forfeited the throne.

For the Chronicler, this chapter prepares the way for the key role the priests and especially the rest of the Levites will play in Israel's worship. They were invited to join the march to Kiriath-jearim, but they are not explicitly used to transport the

Ark. Nonetheless, this event secures their position in the worship of Israel. The Levites (who will be addressed in ch 15) are the answer to David's question in 13:12: "How can I ever bring the Ark of God back into my care?"

ENDNOTES

1. See further positive examples in Solomon (2 Chr 1:2), Jehoshaphat (2 Chr 20:21), and Hezekiah (2 Chr 30:2; 32:3) and negative ones in Rehoboam (2 Chr 10:6-14) and Amaziah (2 Chr 25:16-17); cf. Selman 1994a:151.
2. Notice Japhet (1993:274), who says, "The term 'democratization' is probably the most appropriate."
3. With Mosis (1973:51ff), contra Japhet (1993:275) and Williamson (1982:114).
4. As Japhet (1993:275) puts it, "historical-theological penchant to describe the territory of the Israelites in its broadest possible scope."
5. This does not undermine the Chronicler's "democratized" tone for David, since this is a regular feature in the Chronicler's presentation (cf. Japhet 1989:416-427).
6. Japhet (1993:278) notes, "The Chronicler takes this very picture, the broadest boundaries of the land, to depict the territory in which the people of Israel are actually settled; not at the end of David's rule and after all his military campaigns, but at the very beginning of his reign."
7. There is some confusion over where the Tabernacle was located at this time, in Jerusalem or Gibeon; see especially 2 Chr 1:1-13, but also 16:39-42; 21:29-30 and commentary at 2 Chr 1.
8. See also Selman (1994a:150), who argues that although "the Chronicler omits several details from earlier accounts of David's private life, including the Bathsheba incident (2 Sam 11-12), he certainly does not whitewash David's reputation, as some have alleged."
9. Contra Japhet (1993:281), who sees here a rhetorical question, implying it must stay where it is.

◆ E. David's Family and Palace (14:1-17)

**Then King Hiram of Tyre sent messengers
to David, along with cedar timber, and
stonemasons and carpenters to build him
a palace. [2]And David realized that the
LORD had confirmed him as king over Is-
rael and had greatly blessed his kingdom
for the sake of his people Israel.**

**[3]Then David married more wives in Je-
rusalem, and they had more sons and
daughters. [4]These are the names of Da-
vid's sons who were born in Jerusalem:
Shammua, Shobab, Nathan, Solomon, [5]Ib-
har, Elishua, Elpelet, [6]Nogah, Nepheg,
Japhia, [7]Elishama, Eliada,* and Eliphelet.**

**[8]When the Philistines heard that David
had been anointed king over all Israel,
they mobilized all their forces to capture
him. But David was told they were com-
ing, so he marched out to meet them. [9]The
Philistines arrived and made a raid in the
valley of Rephaim. [10]So David asked God,
"Should I go out to fight the Philistines?
Will you hand them over to me?"**

**The LORD replied, "Yes, go ahead. I will
hand them over to you."**

**[11]So David and his troops went up to
Baal-perazim and defeated the Philistines
there. "God did it!" David exclaimed. "He
used me to burst through my enemies like
a raging flood!" So they named that place
Baal-perazim (which means "the Lord who
bursts through"). [12]The Philistines had
abandoned their gods there, so David gave
orders to burn them.**

[13]But after a while the Philistines re-
turned and raided the valley again. [14]And
once again David asked God what to do.
"Do not attack them straight on," God re-
plied. "Instead, circle around behind and
attack them near the poplar* trees. [15]When
you hear a sound like marching feet in the
tops of the poplar trees, go out and attack!
That will be the signal that God is moving
ahead of you to strike down the Philistine
army." [16]So David did what God command-
ed, and they struck down the Philistine
army all the way from Gibeon to Gezer.
[17]So David's fame spread everywhere,
and the LORD caused all the nations to
fear David.

14:7 Hebrew *Beeliada*, a variant spelling of Eliada; compare 3:8 and parallel text at 2 Sam 5:16. 14:14 Or *aspen*, or *balsam;* also in 14:15. The exact identification of this tree is uncertain.

NOTES

14:1 ***King Hiram of Tyre.*** Tyre (meaning "rock") was the lead city among the Phoenician people, who lived on the border of northern Israel. The city of Tyre was founded on the mainland but soon spread to an island close to shore. Under Hiram's rule (969–939 BC, although it could be earlier; Selman 1994a:156), this island was expanded by uniting it with an adjoining island, the larger entity ultimately becoming a fortress, impregnable to even the greatest forces (see Ezek 26). Hiram would also provide help in the building of the Solomonic Temple, in return for which Solomon ceded 20 cities in Galilee (1 Kgs 9:11-13; see commentary on 2 Chr 8). Tyre and surrounding Phoenicia were famous throughout the ancient Near East for two things: maritime trade and cedar forests.

14:2 ***greatly blessed.*** Better, "greatly exalted."

14:4-7 ***Shammua, Shobab, Nathan, Solomon, Ibhar, Elishua, Elpelet, Nogah, Nepheg, Japhia, Elishama, Eliada, and Eliphelet.*** This is the same list as that found in 3:5-8 (cf. 2 Sam 5:14-16). The sons born to David in Hebron are listed in 3:1-3: Amnon, Daniel, Absalom, Adonijah, Shephatiah, Ithream.

14:8 ***all Israel.*** Second Samuel 5:17, a parallel verse, reads only "Israel." The Chronicler's theme of a unified Israel gathered around David and Jerusalem is emphasized.

14:9 ***valley of Rephaim.*** This is a shallow valley running southwest from Jerusalem (see note on 11:15).

14:11 ***Baal-perazim.*** This was a few miles southwest of Jerusalem.

14:13 ***the valley.*** A parallel verse (2 Sam 5:22) reads "the valley of Rephaim."

14:15 ***poplar trees.*** Heb., *baka'* [TH1057, ZH1132]. This obscure term has been associated with trees (usually poplar, balsam, aspen, mastic-terebinth; in LXX "pear trees"), but the definition is based on similarity of the sound with other Hebrew and Arabic words.

14:16 ***Gibeon to Gezer.*** Gibeon was just over 5 miles northwest of Jerusalem, and Gezer was about 20 miles west of Jerusalem. The Hebrew text of 2 Sam 5:25 records Geba instead of Gibeon (see NLT mg); Geba was about 6 miles northeast of Jerusalem. Williamson (1982:119) attributes the change from Geba to Gibeon in the Chronicler's *Vorlage* to the influence of Isa 28:21.

COMMENTARY

In the Chronicler's source, the events in chapter 14 were placed prior to those in chapter 13. The Chronicler presents the events in chapter 14 at a spot in 2 Samuel 6:11-12 where there is a break of three months in the activity surrounding the Ark. By doing this, the Chronicler was not necessarily claiming these events occurred during this break (the beginning of 14:1 does not necessarily have to be translated "then"). Rather, by shifting these events into this space, the Chronicler elongates the resolution of the dilemma over the transportation of the Ark in order to introduce a key rhythm for royal rule (inquiring of God) while also ensuring the reader that divine blessing had not been removed from David. Furthermore, while chapters 11–12 showcase David's internal respect and support, chapter 14 showcases David's international respect and support, a leitmotif highlighted in the Chronicler's short declarative narrative in 14:17.

International Recognition and Building Project (14:1). The exaltation of David's kingdom is most intimately related to Hiram's sending of messengers in 14:1a, a move that signals the establishment of diplomatic relations with David's emerging court. As Japhet (1993:285) writes, this "implies some kind of a treaty between David and Hiram." At the outset at least, Hiram was clearly the more powerful partner in this relationship, ruling a major Canaanite city-state that predated the rise of David's kingdom and controlled the Phoenician region, including its ports and timber resources. Possibly this action by the Tyrian king was to establish an alliance with David against the Philistines, whose military tactics as far north as the Jezreel Valley (cf. ch 10) may have threatened the Phoenicians. Hiram also could have held out hope that David would become a vassal of the Phoenician state and so supported David; however, the text identifies Hiram as the one bringing tribute (Williamson 1982:116).

But Hiram's action entailed not only sending messengers, but also providing the materials and workers for the construction of a palace. This action is the first of a series of signs of blessing in this chapter that often appear in Chronicles in relation to royal figures. While 2 Samuel 6 links the renewal of David's desire to bring the Ark into Jerusalem to the blessing of Obed-edom (2 Sam 6:12), the Chronicler left this fact aside and focused instead on the enduring blessing on David. The consistent signs of such blessing are five Bs (buildings, babies, battles, business, and beliefs), four of which are highlighted in chapter 14.

First of all, as already noted, Hiram built David a palace in Jerusalem, providing for the first time for the emergence of a stable royal court through which the new king would extend his rule over his nation. Under Saul the first signs of kingship (that is, the development of a standing army) could be discerned in contrast to the armies in the book of Judges, which were tribal and called up as the need arose. The standing-army system was effectively employed by the royal courts of the nations that surrounded Israel. But Saul did not have a clearly defined capital city and thus he did not have a developed royal court. Hiram's gift enabled David to develop a court. Such a building project was a sign confirming David as king.

David Confirmed as King (14:2). The key verse in this chapter is 14:2 because it informs the reader that David realized God had confirmed him as king over Israel. In the Hebrew text the cause of this "realization" is clearly identified as "his kingdom was highly exalted" (NLT, "had greatly blessed his kingdom"), the two phrases linked to one another by the Hebrew causal particle *ki* [TH3588, ZH3954] (because).[1] One final phrase in this verse reminds us that the focus was not exclusively on David. The confirmation through exaltation of his kingdom was "for the sake of his people Israel" (14:2). This is a reminder that Israel's royal house functioned as a mediatorial figure, serving both as vice-regent of the Lord in Israel and on earth (Ps 2), but also as the one who ensured righteousness, justice, and even blessing for the people of God. Any exaltation for the human monarch found its source in the divine kingdom and was for the sake of the people he represented and served.

Dynastic Progeny (14:3-7). Second, the Chronicler provided an extensive list of the children born to David in Jerusalem, another key sign of blessed kingship, since the birth of children secured the king's dynasty, especially with the higher mortality rates of the ancient Near East. Noticeably, the children born in Hebron were not mentioned because the focus of this account is on Jerusalem. In this aspect of numerous children, David transcended Saul, whose dynasty came to an end with the loss of his house (10:6).

Military Campaigns (14:8-16). Third, the Chronicler (following his source in Samuel) provided two accounts of David's military victories over the Philistines, furthering the contrast between Saul and David.[2] It is clear that the motivation for this Philistine attack was David's ascendancy to the throne of Israel. In the later period of his flight from Saul, David received protection from one of the Philistine city-state kings. His break with the Philistines came in the decisive battle that resulted in Saul's death. David was sent home by the Philistine kings lest he turn against them in the battle against Israel (1 Sam 29). His elevation to replace Saul as king would have confirmed the Philistines' fears. Knowing firsthand David's prowess as military commander (1 Sam 29:4-5) and possibly also the recent Phoenician alliance caused the Philistines to move quickly to end the young king's reign.

Both of the battles were prompted by a preemptive Philistine strike in the valley of Rephaim, which runs southwest of Jerusalem (14:9, 13). In both cases, however, David did not engage them immediately in battle.[3] Instead, he asked (*sha'al* [TH7592, ZH8626]) God for direction first (14:10, 14),[4] and in both cases God told him that they were to enter battle and that God would win the battle for David. David's obedience to the divine answer is stated explicitly in 14:16: "So David did what God commanded."[5] The emphasis in both accounts is clearly on David as inquirer of God and the Lord as victorious Divine Warrior.

This pattern for kingship must be seen against the backdrop of the evaluation of Saul in 10:13-14, where the unfaithfulness of Saul is directly linked to the issue of inquiring of the Lord, rather ironically because Saul's name is based on the verb "ask" (*sha'al* [TH7592, ZH8626]). However, this pattern also must be placed in the larger context of the narrative about the Ark (chs 13–16) and especially David's actions in chapter 13. There he spoke of God's will but did not ask God about moving the Ark. However, when he finally brought the Ark into Jerusalem in chapter 15, he identified the earlier problem as the failure "to ask God how to move it properly" (15:13), in this case using the closely related Hebrew term *darash* [TH1875, ZH2011]. While presenting chapter 14 as an account confirming David's kingship, the Chronicler was also using it to reveal the pattern of proper kingship—that is, a king must be one who asks God and seeks his will.

In the first battle, David encountered the Philistines at Baal-perazim. David's response identifies the true victor of the battle: "God did it!"—even if he is aware of human agency ("He used me," 14:11). The name David gives to this battlefield creates a clear contrast with chapter 13 (Selman 1994a:155; Williamson 1982:114). There, after removing the Ark from Baalah (13:6) without divine consultation, David's plans were thwarted by a death at a place he named Perez-uzzah (explicitly explained, "which means 'to burst out against Uzzah,'" 13:11). Here, after entering battle with divine consultation, David's plans were accomplished by God at a place he named Baal-perazim (explicitly explained, "which means 'the Lord who bursts through,'" 14:11). The image in chapter 14 is drawn from the sudden rush of water in the rainy season, which can produce flood conditions in Israel. In this way the military accounts serve a purpose within the Ark narrative.

In 2 Samuel 5:21, a parallel passage, David's men removed the abandoned Philistine idols, but the Chronicler, knowing the temptation to capitalize on the economic value of idols (with their precious metals and stones; see Japhet 1993:289), made it clear that this removal resulted in the destruction of the idols (14:12; cf. Deut 7:5, 25; 12:3). According to the Chronicler, David would not tolerate idolatry, an attitude that qualified his city for the presence of the Holy One, who has no rivals. This destruction of the idols accentuates further the contrast between David and Saul, the armor and head of the latter ending up as "trophies to 'the temple of their gods'" (Williamson 1982:118).

In the second skirmish David was offered detailed military instructions: He was not to attack the Philistines directly but rather from their rear flank. Although this tactical move appeared to be preparation for a brilliant surprise attack by David's forces, in the end the focus is not on the surprise tactic of human soldiers but of a heavenly force. They were to listen for God's signal, namely, the sound of the heavenly army marching ahead of them through the tops of what are often assumed to be trees (see note on 14:15). As with the earlier battle, it is not David's army but rather God and his army who are credited with the decisive win. The Israelites functioned more as a cleanup operation after the enemy army had already been routed.

This kind of victory echoed God's view of kingship (see Boda 2007a). The appointment of a "king" over Israel was clearly controversial, according to the first part of Samuel. When the people asked Samuel for a king, God told Samuel explicitly that this represented a rejection not of Samuel but of God himself (1 Sam 8:7). Some have interpreted this to mean that God was not in favor of royal leadership in Israel. However, the expectations for such leadership expressed in passages like Genesis 17:6, 49:8-12, Deuteronomy 17:14-20, and 1 Samuel 2:1-10 suggest otherwise. Rather, at issue are two different conceptions of royal leadership. The Israelites' vision was of a king "like all the other nations have" (1 Sam 8:5), one that would "lead us into battle" (1 Sam 8:20; cf. 1 Sam 12:12-13). This explains the close association between kingship and war in God's warning through Samuel in 1 Samuel 8:10-18. This association is also key to understanding God's vision of kingship. For him kingship was directly related to battle, and that is why he saw himself as the only King. This is demonstrated in the powerful song that Moses and the people sang after God's paradigmatic battle against Egypt at the Red Sea. Notice how Exodus 15 begins by celebrating God as the triumphant Divine Warrior:

"I will sing to the LORD,
for he has triumphed gloriously;
he has hurled both horse and rider
into the sea. . . .
The LORD is a warrior;
Yahweh is his name!"

Since the sign of kingship in the ancient Near East was successful battle, God retains the royal prerogative of leadership in battle. However, Israel wanted a king they could see, one like the other nations, who would lead them into battle, and thus God was grieved. It is not surprising that the king that they received initially was one that matched their view of the royal house. He was great in stature, a man who displayed great potential as a military man (1 Sam 9:1-2). But the irony in the end is that this giant of Israel cowered before the giant of the Philistines, and it was the smaller David who defeated the foe, not because of greater military prowess but because he battled in the name of the Lord of hosts (1 Sam 17).

Thus, the battle accounts in chapter 14 emphasize a theology of kingship that sees the human royal figure merely as a catalyst of faith within the nation. The "king," or better, "prince," would lead the people to inquire of and rely upon this Lord of hosts, who is the true and almighty King of Israel.

International Recognition of David's Kingdom (14:17). The chapter closes in similar fashion to its beginning—with a declarative comment from the Chronicler that emphasizes that all these signs (buildings, babies, battles, business, and beliefs) not only confirmed to David that he was king over Israel but also declared to the surrounding nations that David's kingship over Israel was not to be taken lightly. As Japhet (1993:290) puts it, "David's greatness has reached its zenith: It is not only he who knows that 'the Lord had established him as king' (14:2), but all the nations around." Although news of David's fame spread through natural means, the accompanying fear was nothing short of divine work.

In chapter 14 David continues to reveal that he is the royal figure of Yahweh's choosing. David displays the core values that the Chronicler will espouse throughout this history of Israel, especially the values of seeking and trusting in God. God's reward is success in battle and international fame.

ENDNOTES

1. Following Japhet (1993:286), who notes that 2 Sam 5:12 has a Waw before the second occurrence of the Hebrew word *ki* [TH3588, ZH3954], which is omitted in Chronicles. This could be a scribal mistake, but the change is in keeping with the Chronicler's agenda: "It is a leading theme of the Chronicler's historical view that the exaltation of the kingdom, in political and material terms, is a sign of God's election."
2. Japhet (1993:287) doubts these battles took place after the capture of Jerusalem and suggests that they came prior to it, when David was still at Hebron, confirmed according to her by the reference to David's going down to the stronghold in 2 Sam 5:17.
3. Second Samuel 5:17 tells us that "he went into the stronghold," while 14:8 indicates that "he marched out to meet them." The Chronicler plays down the sense of flight in the Samuel account.

4. The Chronicler stresses this asking by adding in 14:14 "again," which is missing in his source (cf. literal rendering of 2 Sam 5:23 [contra NLT]).
5. Notice the close echo in the rhetoric of human question, divine answer, and human response: "Should I go (*'alah* [TH5927, ZH6590]) out to fight the Philistines? Will you hand them over to (*nathan beyad*) me? . . . Yes, go (*'alah*) ahead. I will hand them over to (*nathan beyad*) you. So David and his troops went up (*'alah*). . . . God has broken through my enemies by my hand (*beyad* [TH3027, ZH3338])"; cf. Japhet 1993:288.

◆ F. Moving the Ark to Jerusalem (15:1–16:3)

David now built several buildings for himself in the City of David. He also prepared a place for the Ark of God and set up a special tent for it. 2Then he commanded, "No one except the Levites may carry the Ark of God. The LORD has chosen them to carry the Ark of the LORD and to serve him forever."

3Then David summoned all Israel to Jerusalem to bring the Ark of the LORD to the place he had prepared for it. 4This is the number of the descendants of Aaron (the priests) and the Levites who were called together:

5From the clan of Kohath, 120, with Uriel as their leader.
6From the clan of Merari, 220, with Asaiah as their leader.
7From the clan of Gershon,* 130, with Joel as their leader.
8From the descendants of Elizaphan, 200, with Shemaiah as their leader.
9From the descendants of Hebron, 80, with Eliel as their leader.
10From the descendants of Uzziel, 112, with Amminadab as their leader.

11Then David summoned the priests, Zadok and Abiathar, and these Levite leaders: Uriel, Asaiah, Joel, Shemaiah, Eliel, and Amminadab. 12He said to them, "You are the leaders of the Levite families. You must purify yourselves and all your fellow Levites, so you can bring the Ark of the LORD, the God of Israel, to the place I have prepared for it. 13Because you Levites did not carry the Ark the first time, the anger of the LORD our God burst out against us. We failed to ask God how to move it properly." 14So the priests and the Levites purified themselves in order to bring the Ark of the LORD, the God of Israel, to Jerusalem. 15Then the Levites carried the Ark of God on their shoulders with its carrying poles, just as the LORD had instructed Moses.

16David also ordered the Levite leaders to appoint a choir of Levites who were singers and musicians to sing joyful songs to the accompaniment of harps, lyres, and cymbals. 17So the Levites appointed Heman son of Joel along with his fellow Levites: Asaph son of Berekiah, and Ethan son of Kushaiah from the clan of Merari. 18The following men were chosen as their assistants: Zechariah, Jaaziel,* Shemiramoth, Jehiel, Unni, Eliab, Benaiah, Maaseiah, Mattithiah, Eliphelehu, Mikneiah, and the gatekeepers—Obed-edom and Jeiel.

19The musicians Heman, Asaph, and Ethan were chosen to sound the bronze cymbals. 20Zechariah, Aziel, Shemiramoth, Jehiel, Unni, Eliab, Maaseiah, and Benaiah were chosen to play the harps.* 21Mattithiah, Eliphelehu, Mikneiah, Obed-edom, Jeiel, and Azaziah were chosen to play the lyres.* 22Kenaniah, the head Levite, was chosen as the choir leader because of his skill.

23Berekiah and Elkanah were chosen to guard* the Ark. 24Shebaniah, Joshaphat, Nethanel, Amasai, Zechariah, Benaiah, and Eliezer—all of whom were priests—were chosen to blow the trumpets as they marched in front of the Ark of God. Obed-edom and Jehiah were chosen to guard the Ark.

25Then David and the elders of Israel and the generals of the army* went to the house of Obed-edom to bring the Ark of the LORD's Covenant up to Jerusalem with a great celebration. 26 And because God was clearly helping the Levites as they carried the Ark of the LORD's Covenant, they sacrificed seven bulls and seven rams.

27 David was dressed in a robe of fine linen, as were all the Levites who carried the Ark, and also the singers, and Kenaniah the choir leader. David was also wearing a priestly garment.* 28 So all Israel brought up the Ark of the LORD's Covenant with shouts of joy, the blowing of rams' horns and trumpets, the crashing of cymbals, and loud playing on harps and lyres.

29 But as the Ark of the LORD's Covenant entered the City of David, Michal, the daughter of Saul, looked down from her window. When she saw King David skipping about and laughing with joy, she was filled with contempt for him.

CHAPTER 16

They brought the Ark of God and placed it inside the special tent David had prepared for it. And they presented burnt offerings and peace offerings to God. 2 When he had finished his sacrifices, David blessed the people in the name of the LORD. 3 Then he gave to every man and woman in all Israel a loaf of bread, a cake of dates,* and a cake of raisins.

15:7 Hebrew *Gershom,* a variant spelling of Gershon. **15:18** As in several Hebrew manuscripts and Greek version (see also parallel lists in 15:20; 16:5); Masoretic Text reads *Zechariah ben Jaaziel.* **15:20** Hebrew adds *according to Alamoth,* which is probably a musical term. The meaning of the Hebrew is uncertain. **15:21** Hebrew adds *according to the Sheminith,* which is probably a musical term. The meaning of the Hebrew is uncertain. **15:23** Hebrew *chosen as gatekeepers for;* also in 15:24. **15:25** Hebrew *the commanders of thousands.* **15:27** Hebrew *a linen ephod.* **16:3** Or *a portion of meat.* The meaning of the Hebrew is uncertain.

NOTES

15:1 *a place.* The term "place" (*maqom* [TH4725, ZH5226]) is a key leitmotif in Chronicles for the location that God showed David for the Temple site (21:22, 25) and where Solomon built the sanctuary (2 Chr 3:1; Knoppers 2004:612). This place is referred to in a verse that also speaks of David constructing buildings for himself in the City of David. Second Chronicles 8:11 confirms this, indicating that the Ark had been brought to David's palace.

special tent. The tent structure should not be confused with the Tabernacle, which was located at Gibeon (see 16:39-40; 21:29-30), where sacrifice continued to be offered. Thus, the Ark alone was brought into the city to signify God's presence, but the sacrificial services continued at the high place at Gibeon, awaiting the construction of the Temple by Solomon (2 Chr 6). For evidence of the use of temporary sanctuaries while awaiting (re)construction of a new sanctuary, see Boda 2006c:223; Hurowitz 1992:328-329; 1993:37-50; Novotny 2003:60-64.

15:4 *the descendants of Aaron (the priests) and the Levites.* The distinction between these two groups among Israel has been a matter of great debate. In the genealogies of Chronicles a clear distinction is made between the "Levites," who "were appointed to various other tasks in the Tabernacle, the house of God" (6:48) and "Aaron and his descendants," who alone "served as priests"—i.e., presented offerings on the altar and other duties related to the Most Holy Place (6:49). Clearly in the priestly genealogy Aaron's line is given priority (6:3-15), followed by the Levite clans in the order "Gershon, Kohath, and Merari" (6:16). Here notice the order: Kohath, Merari, Gershon. The term "Levites" is used in two senses even in this chapter, both of those of the tribe of Levi who are not "priests" (15:4, 11, 14) as well as of all members of the tribe of Levi, including "priests" (15:11-12). There is some ambiguity, then, in 15:15-16 (see Japhet 1993:300).

15:5-7 *From the clan of Kohath . . . Merari . . . Gershon.* In the desert traditions of Israel, these are the three core Levitical clans (see 6:1 [5:27]; 6:16 [6:1]; 23:6; cf. Exod 6:16). Zadokite priests trace their descent from Aaron, whose father Amram was the eldest son of Kohath.

15:8-10 ***Elizaphan . . . Hebron . . . Uzziel.*** These three groups, which are placed on the same level as the main clan groupings in 15:5-7, are technically subgroups within the clan of Kohath. The second and third names (Hebron, Uzziel) are the third and fourth sons of Kohath (Exod 6:18). The first name (Elizaphan), however, is actually a further subgroup within the subclan of Uzziel. It is interesting that the families of Hebron and Uzziel are given special status alongside the main clans and that Elizaphan is singled out as a sub-subgroup. This heightened status may be due to the fact that members of this clan would be chosen to carry the Ark (15:10-11).

15:11 ***Zadok and Abiathar.*** These were the two chief priests under David's administration. Although the story is not recounted in Chronicles, Abiathar will make a disastrous mistake in championing the candidacy of Adonijah to succeed David (1 Kgs 1). Zadok's line will ultimately emerge in the highest position, while Abiathar will be banished to Anathoth (1 Kgs 2:16-27). Zadok's lineage was clearly linked to the Levitical clan of Kohath via Aaron (6:3-15), while Abiathar was linked in tradition to the house of Eli (1 Kgs 2:27) and (with some debate) to Aaron via Ithamar (24:3; 1 Sam 14:3; 22:9, 11, 20; see ABD 2.456). In any case, Abiathar is never mentioned in the genealogies, while Zadok is a key figure.

15:12 ***purify yourselves.*** Heb. *qadash* (Hitpael) [TH6942, ZH7727] means to set apart for use in the realm of the divine. In Chronicles it is used when preparing for a major sacred event (2 Chr 5:11; 29:5, 15, 34; 30:3, 15, 24; 31:18; 35:6; Knoppers 2004:617). The process is not described here, but Exod 19:14-15; 29:21, 37; 30:29 suggest rituals associated with blood, water, and oil were integral to this, besides careful avoidance of any contact or activity that would jeopardize one's holiness (Hill 2003:235).

15:13 ***properly.*** Heb., *kammishpat* [TH4941, ZH5477], "according to the regulation," also found in 6:32; 23:31; 24:19; 2 Chr 4:7, 20; 8:14; 30:16; 35:13 usually in cultic context, similar to terminology in priestly legislation in Torah (Lev 5:10; 9:16; Num 15:24; 29:6, 18, 21, 24, 27, 30, 33, 37; Knoppers 2004:618).

15:15 ***carrying poles.*** The Ark, gold table, incense altar, and altar of burnt offering had rings attached to them to facilitate their transportation (Exod 25, 30, 37, 38). The term in Exodus for these poles is *baddim* [TH905B, ZH964], while in 15:15 it is *mototh* [TH4133, ZH4574], a term in the Torah that refers to some kind of "'carrying frame' used for the transport of the smaller and more precious vessels of the tabernacle" (Japhet 1993:302). The *mototh* is associated regularly with "yoke" (Lev 26:13; Jer 27:2; 28:10, 13; Ezek 34:27) and thus appears to refer to a more advanced form of pole that probably replaced the *baddim*.

15:17 ***Heman . . . Asaph . . . Ethan.*** These three men are identified as key leaders of the new musical tradition established by David. Heman and Ethan should not be confused with Heman the Ezrahite and Ethan, two of the sons of Mahol (1 Kgs 4:31; cf. Pss 88, 89) who were associated with the wisdom tradition. Asaph, however, is to be associated with the Psalter tradition (Pss 50, 73–83). These three individuals are each linked by the Chronicler in 6:31-48 [16-33] to one of the core Levitical clans: Heman (Kohath), Asaph (Gershon), and Ethan (Merari)—although see in 16:41-42; 25:1-3 how Ethan is replaced by Jeduthun, possibly due to a scribal error.

15:18 ***gatekeepers.*** These were the ones responsible for guarding the sanctuary from violation of its sanctity by the common or unclean.

15:20-21 ***play the harps . . . play the lyres.*** Here the underlying text includes a phrase that modifies the musical act with obscure terms that may indicate a musical pattern or tune (see NLT mg).

16:1 ***the special tent David had prepared for it.*** See note on 15:1.

they presented burnt offerings. Here the Chronicler carefully nuances David's role in sacrificial acts, leaving his name out (cf. 2 Sam 6:17) and replacing it with the nebulous third-person plural subject ("they"), even though he does allow that David was responsible for the acts (16:2). It is possible that the subject is the people as a whole, but more likely it is a reference to the subject of the preceding verb in 16:1 ("They brought the Ark of God and placed it"), which is the group of Levites moving the Ark.

COMMENTARY

Knoppers (2004:629-631) highlighted the close affinity between the accounts narrating David's transfer of the Ark of God into Jerusalem and ancient Near Eastern texts and ceremonies associated with the introduction of a national god into a new royal city: "These ceremonies consisted of a royal invitation of the gods and goddesses into the city, feasting, royal dedicatory gifts, royal sacrifices, and the participation of the populace in a large celebration." This showcases not only the importance of this event in the history of Israel in general, but also its importance in the history of the monarchy in particular. This event marks the approval of the royal city that will be graced by the presence of the Lord God.

First Chronicles 15 begins with a significant account not found in Samuel (15:1-24), and even when the later sections do parallel events in Samuel (2 Sam 6:12-19a), the Chronicler makes significant changes. The Chronicler began his unique account by noting that while David was building palaces for himself, he was also preparing a sanctuary for the Ark, even if it was only a tent (15:1). This brings the reader back to the issue of the Ark, which had remained in the background as the Chronicler related the events of chapter 14.

In the commentary on chapter 14, it was observed that the Chronicler had switched events in the story line of his source. By doing this, information about the international character of David's rule and especially the spread of his fame and fear throughout the surrounding nations (ch 14) precedes the resolution of the Ark incident in chapter 15. This serves first of all to elongate the resolution of the Ark incident begun in chapter 13 and thus to build tension, and, second, to relate the more "secular" pursuits of his tenure to the underlying project of the Ark's transport to Jerusalem. The fear and fame of David caused by the Lord is now placed at the service of the development of the Temple and worship.

In the Chronicler's account, David's motivation for completing the transport of the Ark to Jerusalem is not directly related to the blessing of the household of Obed-edom as in 2 Samuel 6:12 (cf. Williamson 1982:120). Instead, David is portrayed as a leader concerned with cultic ceremony, speaking in the idiom of Torah. He notes that all others are barred from carrying the Ark because of the Lord's election (15:2), using phrases echoing the language of Deuteronomy 10:8 and 18:5.[1] He also instructs the Levites to purify themselves (15:12). This legislation is linked to God's election of the Levites (15:2) and to God's legislation communicated through Moses (15:13, 15). While the account in 2 Samuel does not even identify who carried the Ark in the second attempt (2 Sam 6:13), David is clear about the fact that it was inappropriate cultic procedures that led to the judgment upon Uzzah.[2] David is first and foremost a figure who learned his lesson on cultic matters and rectified the situation with precision.

The Chronicler portrays David as going far beyond the "letter" of the law.[3] First, in the book of Numbers (Num 3:30; 4:4-6, 15) it was the Kohathites who were to carry the Ark, and among the Kohathites it was Elizaphan son of Uzziel. This may explain why the clan of Kohath and the descendants of Elizaphan and Uzziel were listed.[4] Second, David not only appointed the two priests[5] and six Levites to carry the Ark (15:11-15) but also commanded the head of the Levites to appoint personnel for the purpose of aural praise (15:16). In this the Chronicler highlights the role the Levites would play once the Ark was in a permanent dwelling and their previous function of transporting the Ark became superfluous (Williamson 1982:120). The Hebrew text speaks of appointing Levites as "singers" (*meshorerim* [TH7891A, ZH8876]), but the appointments made in 15:17-21 are focused on instrumentalists, with three principal musicians playing bronze cymbals (Heman, Asaph, and Ethan; 15:17, 19), as well as fourteen other associates, drawn from the Levites and gatekeepers, playing either harps or lyres (15:18, 20-21).[6] Possibly the "singers" were drawn from a larger pool of unnamed Levites; only the instrumentalists are mentioned because they were essential to the leadership of the music group. This would explain the mention of Kenaniah in 15:22, who would have been responsible for the group of Levites serving as the choir.[7] This final character is chosen to lead the choir because he possessed "understanding" (NLT, "skill"). This musical entourage was commissioned to produce "joyful songs" to accompany the transport of the Ark, the terminology here being typical of the Chronicler's presentation of cultic music (cf. 15:28; 16:5, 42; 2 Chr 5:13; Japhet 1993:303). Therefore, although the Chronicler portrays David as adhering closely to the Tabernacle legislation for transporting the Ark, he also highlights David as an innovator who builds on that legislation and produces a powerful worship scene that resonates with the worship in the Second Temple.

Three final groups are listed in 15:23-24. Two Levites were appointed as gatekeepers (see NLT mg) of the Ark, most likely figures who would guard the entrance to the tent when the Ark was safely in Jerusalem. Seven priests were chosen to announce the movement of the Ark by blowing trumpets at the front of the procession. Finally, two Levites were chosen as a military escort.

In 15:25 the Chronicler comes back to the story line, as David now moves from preparation to action. While the writer of 2 Samuel focuses on David alone, the Chronicler speaks also of "the elders of Israel" and "the generals of the army" (lit., "commanders of thousands") who visited Obed-edom to return the Ark. This phrase not only emphasizes the "participation of all Israel" (Williamson 1982:126), but also reminds the reader of the outset of the Ark narrative complex in 13:1-3, where similar vocabulary was used. Finally, the plot is coming to resolution. Japhet (1993:301) has noted the echo of 13:3 ("we didn't seek it," *darash* [TH1875, ZH2011]; NLT, "we neglected it") in 15:13 when David admits that "we failed to ask [*darash*] God how to move it properly." For Japhet (1993:301), this indicates a development in the people's approach to God: "In the days of Saul they did not seek the ark at all; in the first attempt to transfer the ark they did not seek it 'as ordained.'"

What, then, made the difference between this attempt to bring the Ark into Jerusalem and the earlier one? First, it is because David followed the ordained legislation laid out by Moses—that is, the Levitical clans played their proper role, and

David deferred to them (15:2, 12-13). Second, it is because the Levites purified themselves (15:12). Third, it is because David and the community inquired properly of God for his will (15:13). Finally, it is because God recognized these acts of obedience and "was clearly helping the Levites" (15:26). As Japhet (1993:306) has summarized it, "Nothing can be achieved without the help of God, which is granted to those who seek him 'as ordained.'"

The writer of 2 Samuel has the sacrifice of an ox and a fatling every six paces (2 Sam 6:13) and David dancing before the Lord with all his might. In contrast, the Chronicler speaks of the sacrifice of seven bulls and rams at one time[8] and completely leaves out the first reference to David's dancing (in 15:27) and tones down the second reference to his dancing (in 15:29), where the dancing is no longer "before the LORD" (cf. 2 Sam 6:14). Instead, he accentuates David's more dignified "robe of fine linen" that matched those of the Levites, singers, and choir leader (15:26-27). Both chapter 15 and 2 Samuel 6 have David in "a linen ephod" (NLT mg), an allusion to his priestly character and role. This priestly depiction of David, however, is carefully presented so as not to suggest that David crossed the line between laity and clergy, as did his descendant Uzziah (2 Chr 26:16-21). The Chronicler has expanded this section in such a way that David nearly disappears among the group of Levites in 15:27 and then is swallowed up in "all Israel" in 15:28 (cf. 2 Sam 6:15, where it is "David and all the people of Israel"). The Chronicler accentuates far more the musical character of the event, expanding the simple "with shouts of joy and the blowing of rams' horns" to include "trumpets, the crashing of cymbals, and loud playing on harps and lyres" (15:28). Although more demure, the scene is also more spectacular and communal.[9]

The end of the first phase of the transportation of the Ark episode is marked by the scene depicting the response of Michal, the daughter of Saul, to David's burst of praise. Although the Chronicler has shortened the Michal incident from his source (leaving out the dramatic scene in 2 Sam 6:20b-23), he retained at least this verse, even though it intrudes into the story and focuses on David's "dancing," which the Chronicler downplays.[10] It was important for the Chronicler to retain this short scene, for he began his story with the death of Saul and his dynasty. Here the reader is reminded again of the qualities that set David apart from Saul.[11] David was truly a catalyst of worship among the people of God. At the same time, by leaving out the dramatic encounter between David and Michal in 2 Samuel 6:20b-23, the Chronicler "ends climactically with the communal banquet" (Knoppers 2004:629).[12]

In chapter 16 reference is made to two different types of sacrifice (16:1), both voluntary offerings for Israelites. The first ("burnt offerings") signifies the offering of oneself in devotion to God (Lev 1), and the second ("peace offerings") celebrates covenant relationship with God (Lev 3). They foreshadow the role of Jerusalem and its sanctuary as the place that will sustain covenant relationship with the Lord through sacrifice and praise. The reader is left with the scene of David blessing his people in the name of Yahweh and distributing to "all Israel." This latter phrase replaces the phrase, lit., "all the people, the whole multitude of Israel" from his source in 2 Samuel 6:19 and reflects a larger trend in Chronicles to use the phrase "all Israel" to speak of the people unified around the Davidic king. The Chronicler drew from his source this vision of harmony between monarch and a united people.

In the final three verses (16:1-3) the reader is reminded of the mediatorial role that David played in Israel. Although reliant on the priestly and Levitical orders, he was a catalyst for the blessing of God through sacrifice and praise. At the same time, he was also a source of blessing for God's people, providing for them here in tangible ways through bread, meat (see NLT mg), and raisins.

Japhet has noted the striking similarity between David's preparations in chapter 15, Hezekiah's Temple cleansing in 2 Chronicles 29, and Josiah's Passover celebration in 2 Chronicles 35 (Japhet 1993:299). In each case the project is (1) initiated by the king, (2) the priests and Levites (Levites in primary role and priests in secondary) are summoned with an appeal for their cooperation, (3) the king delivers a speech to explain their activity, and (4) the participants are sanctified. David is thus setting a precedent for royal activity related to the Temple and worship.

The Chronicler accentuated David's passion for the presence and worship of Yahweh at the heart of his kingdom. His reckless abandonment in worship at the end of the chapter is balanced by careful attention to proper rituals throughout the chapter. It is such passionate pursuit of worship that lies at the heart of the Davidic dynasty, the city of Jerusalem, and the kingdom of Israel. Through this account the Chronicler seeks to motivate his own audience to passionately pursue worship.

ENDNOTES

1. So Japhet (1993:297). Knoppers (2004:614) notes that the Chronicler presents a perspective on the Levites that lies between the Deuteronomic and Priestly codes in that in his presentation, "the priests and the Levites have their distinct responsibilities, but both minister to Yahweh (1 Chr 6:17 [32 in English Bible]; 16:4, 37; 23:13; 26:12; 2 Chr 5:14; 8:14; 13:10; 23:6; 29:11; 31:2)."
2. Hill (2003:235) notes that the term *parats* [TH6555, ZH7287] (which is used to speak of God breaking out against Uzzah in ch 13) is the same term used to speak of God breaking out against the Israelites if ritual purity was ignored at Mount Sinai (Exod 19:24). Thus priestly ritual is key to the successful transfer.
3. Knoppers (2004:619) notes that the "official appointment of singers and musicians is a case in which the Chronicler goes beyond Deuteronomic and Priestly precedent." As he cogently argues, however, this is not an "invention" of the Chronicler, since ancient Near Eastern and biblical evidence points to the existence of musical personnel not only in ancient temples but in the Jerusalem Temple in particular (2 Sam 19:35; 1 Kgs 10:12; Ezek 40:44 mg; Sennacherib's tribute list in COS 2.119A). As he concludes, "It may be the better part of wisdom to say that he took a special interest in Levitical singers," noting Kleinig 1993.
4. However, this does not explain the expansion to include the clans of Merari and Gershon and the descendants of Hebron.
5. Following Japhet (1993:298), who sees these two priestly names as original, rather than as "priestly additions" as, e.g., Williamson (1982:123). Japhet (1993:298) says, "There is no doubt that the Levites play a more prominent role in Chronicles than the priests, and that their interests are closer to the Chronicler's heart. Nevertheless, there is no reason to assume that this observation should be pushed to an extreme 'all or nothing' position. It is hardly likely that the Chronicler would ignore the priesthood altogether, or deny its well-established rights."
6. Compare the list in 15:18 and those in 15:20-21. One name (Azaziah) is added at

the end of the list in 15:21. Possibly his name had dropped out from 15:18, where he would have been the last of the gatekeepers (Japhet 1993:303).

7. Petersen (1977:63) presents three other translations for 15:22. First, "Chenaniah, leader of the Levites in carrying, shall be in charge of carrying because he is expert at it." Second, "Chenaniah, leader of the Levites in music, should direct the music." Third, "Chenaniah, leader of the Levites in oracles, since he was skillful at the art of giving oracles." Although he can see the validity of the third option in light of Levitical prophecy in Chronicles (see ch 25), he opts for the first option because of the strong emphasis in this passage on the Ark and the use of the same term here ("carrying") for the Levites' role of transporting the Ark in 2 Chr 35:3. Petersen's argument is a strong possibility.
8. Japhet (1993:306) evaluates 2 Sam 6:13 as "non-priestly," while Chronicles as "distinctly priestly." The change, however, is found in 4QSam[a], so possibly the Chronicler's source had this priestly terminology.
9. As Japhet (1993:294) says, "The changes introduced into the Chronistic description of the transfer itself are calculated to conform to the letter with the implications of the broader section, introduced in vv. 1-24." That is, the last section is reworked to conform to the new piece the Chronicler has created.
10. See how Japhet (1993:307-308) defends the Chronicler at this point, contra Curtis's evaluation that this is "a mark of the unskillful art of the Chronicler" (Curtis and Madsen 1910:219).
11. See Williamson 1982:120, who notes that the present shape of the Michal affair focuses on "the differing approaches of Saul and David to the ark."
12. Knoppers (2004:633) observes that the "royalism shines through" in this passage and additionally that "the author reclaims the temple and its cultus for the Davidides."

◆ G. The Levites Lead Worship before the Ark (16:4-43)

**4David appointed the following Levites to
lead the people in worship before the Ark
of the LORD—to invoke his blessings, to
give thanks, and to praise the LORD, the
God of Israel. 5Asaph, the leader of this
group, sounded the cymbals. Second to
him was Zechariah, followed by Jeiel,
Shemiramoth, Jehiel, Mattithiah, Eliab,
Benaiah, Obed-edom, and Jeiel. They
played the harps and lyres. 6The priests,
Benaiah and Jahaziel, played the trumpets regularly before the Ark of God's
Covenant.**

7On that day David gave to Asaph and his fellow Levites this song of thanksgiving to the LORD:

**8 Give thanks to the LORD and proclaim
his greatness.
Let the whole world know what he
has done.
9 Sing to him; yes, sing his praises.
Tell everyone about his wonderful
deeds.
10 Exult in his holy name;
rejoice, you who worship the LORD.
11 Search for the LORD and for his
strength;
continually seek him.
12 Remember the wonders he has
performed,
his miracles, and the rulings he has
given,
13 you children of his servant Israel,
you descendants of Jacob, his
chosen ones.
14 He is the LORD our God.
His justice is seen throughout
the land.
15 Remember his covenant forever—
the commitment he made to a
thousand generations.
16 This is the covenant he made with
Abraham**

and the oath he swore to Isaac.
17 He confirmed it to Jacob as a decree,
and to the people of Israel as a never-ending covenant:
18 "I will give you the land of Canaan
as your special possession."

19 He said this when you were few in number,
a tiny group of strangers in Canaan.
20 They wandered from nation to nation,
from one kingdom to another.
21 Yet he did not let anyone oppress them.
He warned kings on their behalf:
22 "Do not touch my chosen people,
and do not hurt my prophets."

23 Let the whole earth sing to the LORD!
Each day proclaim the good news that he saves.
24 Publish his glorious deeds among the nations.
Tell everyone about the amazing things he does.
25 Great is the LORD! He is most worthy of praise!
He is to be feared above all gods.
26 The gods of other nations are mere idols,
but the LORD made the heavens!
27 Honor and majesty surround him;
strength and joy fill his dwelling.

28 O nations of the world, recognize the LORD,
recognize that the LORD is glorious and strong.
29 Give to the LORD the glory he deserves!
Bring your offering and come into his presence.
Worship the LORD in all his holy splendor.
30 Let all the earth tremble before him.
The world stands firm and cannot be shaken.

31 Let the heavens be glad, and the earth rejoice!
Tell all the nations, "The LORD reigns!"
32 Let the sea and everything in it shout his praise!
Let the fields and their crops burst out with joy!
33 Let the trees of the forest rustle with praise,
for the LORD is coming to judge the earth.

34 Give thanks to the LORD, for he is good!
His faithful love endures forever.
35 Cry out, "Save us, O God of our salvation!
Gather and rescue us from among the nations,
so we can thank your holy name
and rejoice and praise you."

36 Praise the LORD, the God of Israel,
who lives from everlasting to everlasting!

And all the people shouted "Amen!" and praised the LORD.

37 David arranged for Asaph and his fel-
low Levites to serve regularly before the
Ark of the LORD's Covenant, doing what-
ever needed to be done each day. 38 This
group included Obed-edom (son of Jedu-
thun), Hosah, and sixty-eight other Le-
vites as gatekeepers.

39 Meanwhile, David stationed Zadok the
priest and his fellow priests at the Taber-
nacle of the LORD at the place of worship
in Gibeon, where they continued to minis-
ter before the LORD. 40 They sacrificed the
regular burnt offerings to the LORD each
morning and evening on the altar set aside
for that purpose, obeying everything writ-
ten in the Law of the LORD, as he had com-
manded Israel. 41 David also appointed
Heman, Jeduthun, and the others chosen
by name to give thanks to the LORD, for
"his faithful love endures forever." 42 They
used their trumpets, cymbals, and other
instruments to accompany their songs of
praise to God.* And the sons of Jeduthun
were appointed as gatekeepers.

43 Then all the people returned to their
homes, and David turned and went home
to bless his own family.

16:42 Or *to accompany the sacred music;* or *to accompany singing to God.*

NOTES

16:5 ***Asaph.*** Asaph is well-known from the Psalter, where his name appears in superscription in the phrase "sons of Asaph," most likely a reference to the Asaphite clan that assumed responsibility for composing psalms, as 16:4-6 suggests (Pss 50, 73–83). Asaph traced his Levitical lineage through Levi's son Gershon (6:31-48).

cymbals. Cymbals were played by the leaders of the group (see 15:19), most likely because they could be heard above the sound of the other instruments and because percussion would set the beat.

16:7 ***On that day David gave to Asaph and his fellow Levites this song of thanksgiving to the Lord.*** Better, "on that day David first assigned the activity of giving thanks to the Lord to Asaph and his fellow Levites" (see Hill 2003:238; Thompson 1994:140). The words "this song of" are not found in the Hebrew text.

16:38 ***Obed-edom (son of Jeduthun).*** Not to be confused with the Obed-edom (the Gittite) in whose house the Ark was stored prior to coming to Jerusalem (ch 13), nor with the Obed-edom who was a Levite from the sons of Korah (26:1-19), whose family served as gatekeepers on the south gate of the Temple precinct. Whether the Obed-edom of 16:5 was the same as this Obed-edom is unclear, although it appears that the figure in 16:5 was a musician and the figure in 16:38 was a gatekeeper.

16:39 ***Zadok the priest.*** Zadok is identified as high priest (lit., "the priest") elsewhere in Chronicles (16:39; 24:6; 29:22), a term only necessary when other priests are in view (Knoppers 2004:652).

Gibeon. Identified with el-Jib (ABD 2.1010), approximately 6 miles northwest of Jerusalem. The sanctuary proper may have been atop Nebi Samwil, 1 mile south of Gibeon. Solomon would go here at the outset of his reign to offer sacrifices and pray to God for wisdom (1 Kgs 3; 2 Chr 1). The Chronicler connects this site to the Benjaminite Saul in 8:29, suggesting an early royal connection between the royal house and the sacred sites of Gibeon (and also Jerusalem).

16:40 ***regular burnt offerings.*** This legislation is described in Exod 29:38-43; Num 28:1-8.

16:41 ***Jeduthun.*** There is some debate over the identity of Jeduthun. The triumvirate of worship leaders in 15:17, 19 is Heman, Asaph, and Ethan, while in 16:5, 37 and 25:1 it is Heman, Asaph, and Jeduthun. Japhet (1993:324) suggests that the original form "Ethan" was corrupted into "Jeduthun," which is very similar orthographically. Notice the appearance of Jeduthun in the superscriptions to Pss 39, 62, 77. In Ps 77 Jeduthun appears with Asaph.

COMMENTARY

The episode of the Ark entering Jerusalem is divided into two phases: first, the preparations for and fulfillment of the conveying of the Ark from the house of Obed-edom to Jerusalem (ch 15), and second, the entrance of the Ark into Jerusalem and provisions for its regular care (ch 16).[1] The incident concerning Michal serves as a segue between the two phases (15:29). Chapter 16 then opens with the Ark of God placed into the tent David had prepared for it. Interestingly, David does not do all the appointments of personnel in this chapter directly. According to 15:16, he delegates the appointment process to the Levitical leadership. Although the Chronicler portrays Davidic sanction for Temple activities, he is careful to highlight the necessary role played by the Levitical orders.

Levites Led by Asaph Appointed to Lead Regular Worship before the Ark (16:4-37). The Chronicler now depicts David's appointments for regular worship (see 16:37, "regularly . . . each day"). This establishes firmly the tradition that aural worship was to be an integral facet of Temple worship in Jerusalem and defends the full status of singers as Levites.[2] In chapter 15 similar appointments were made, but there David commissioned Levitical leaders to make the musical appointments, and these appointments were limited to the transport of the Ark to Jerusalem. Now, David makes the appointments directly, and these appointments are now activities that are established and regularly occurring.[3] The Levites were appointed as "ministers" (Heb., *mesharetim* [TH8334, ZH9250]; NLT, "to lead the people in worship"), hearkening back to David's recitation of the special role the Levites would play in the worship of God in 15:2 ("to serve"). Notice there, however, that this "ministry" is to the Lord (lit.), even if it is on behalf of the people of God.

This ministry is to be enacted "before the Ark of the LORD" (16:4, 37). Two things are worthy of note here. First, these Levites were given responsibility in the manifest presence of God. The Torah had allowed a priestly figure into the Most Holy Place, but this was restricted to the high priest from Aaron's line and only on one day of the year (Lev 16). Second, the activity of these Levites is described as verbal worship. When the high priest from Aaron's line entered the Most Holy Place, it was for the purpose of sacrificial atonement with blood being sprinkled on the Ark. One should not miss the innovative character of David's appointments.

Those who were appointed are named in 16:5-6. In the list of personnel for the transport of the Ark, the Levites had appointed Heman, Asaph, and Ethan as the Levitical leaders of music (15:17), each of whom played cymbals (15:19). These leaders were split up for this new phase of worship at the Ark in Jerusalem. Asaph, still playing his cymbals, was to lead the group commissioned to serve at the tent assembled for the Ark in Jerusalem (16:5, 37), while Heman and Jeduthun (Ethan)[4] would lead the group serving at the Tabernacle at Gibeon (16:39, 41). Asaph was given nine Levitical musical assistants to play harps and lyres (16:5), two priestly assistants to play trumpets (16:6), and seventy Levitical gatekeepers to guard the sacred tent (16:38).

The Chronicler provides more detail on this new ministry of verbal worship (see further Boda 2007a). These Levites were "to invoke his blessings, to give thanks, and to praise the LORD, the God of Israel" (16:4). The first term, *zakar* (Hiphil) [TH2142, ZH2349] (NLT, "invoke his blessings"), is often translated as "make known" or "report" (lit., "cause to remember"). Japhet (1993:315) sees here an allusion to the priestly duty of "invoking" (Num 10:10), but there the term is different (*zikkaron* [TH2146, ZH2355]). In Old Testament contexts of speech directed to God, it is often difficult to discern if *zakar* (Hiphil) is restricted to a particular kind of expression, either praise or prayer. In some contexts it is used in connection with expressions of praise (Ps 71:16; Isa 12:4; 26:13), while in others it refers to prayer (Isa 62:6). Other cases are uncertain; it may be praise or prayer, especially when used in relationship to serving other gods (Exod 23:13; Josh 23:7; Ps 45:17 [18]; Isa 48:1; Amos 6:10). Nevertheless, in the superscriptions of Psalms 38 and 70 the very same form that is found here in 16:4 is used with reference to the psalm as a whole. In both cases, the psalm it introduces is a prayer for help connected with David. Although it is possible that here we merely have another term for praise (to be placed alongside the other two, praise and thanks), it is significant that the only times this term is used in the Psalter in the infinitive construct (as here) is in association with a psalm of prayer.[5]

The second term, *yadah* [TH3034A, ZH3344], is the Hebrew term for giving thanks, a term that can be used in general for the praise of God but is closely associated with thanking God for blessings bestowed upon his people. In Psalm 122:4, within a psalm focused on the gathering of the tribes in Jerusalem for festal celebration, the psalmist reveals that the purpose of this gathering at the time of harvest with tithes and offerings in hand was to give thanks to the Lord for his bountiful care of his people. The third term, a Piel stem of *halal* [TH1984A, ZH2146], is the common Hebrew term for giving praise to God. It is the base of the English term "*hallelu*-jah" (*Praise* Yahweh) and is used to express the praise of God as Creator, King, and Redeemer.

In this commission the Levites are instructed to lead the people in a variety of expressions to God: from the cry of help, to the exclamation of thanks, to the shout of praise. Such a diversity of worship expression is evident in the Psalter. Westermann (1981) categorized ancient Israelite worship expressions into two basic types: praise and lament. He noted, however, that even in lament the impulse was always toward praise, a point demonstrated by the regular appearance of the element of praise in laments in the Psalter. For Westermann, however, there were two types of praise in the Psalter: declarative praise (thanksgiving) and descriptive praise (hymns). This more nuanced categorization has been captured brilliantly by Brueggemann's typology of Psalm forms (1984; Brueggemann and Miller 1995). For Brueggemann, the Psalter is comprised of psalms of Orientation, Disorientation, and New Orientation. Brueggemann draws this vocabulary from the earlier work of Ricoeur, who described the rhythm of human experience with these terms. According to Brueggemann, the types of psalms then match the reality of human life and offer us expressions for dialogue with God in the ebb and flow of life experience (see Boda 2005a:806-811; 2006b:181-192).

Following the appointment of the Levites to this new commission, the Chronicler includes a composition that offers an example of the kind of expressions David had in mind.[6] In order to insert this material into his narrative, the Chronicler uses a technique called "resumptive repetition," in which vocabulary used at the outset of the insertion is repeated when the insertion is complete. Thus, the phrases "Asaph and his fellow Levites" and "regularly before the Ark of the LORD's Covenant" appear in both 16:6-7 and 16:37. The inserted piece is actually an amalgamation of three psalms from the Psalter: Psalm 105:1-15 (16:8-22); Psalm 96:1-13 (16:23-33); Psalm 106:1, 47-48 (16:34-36). What is interesting is that these three psalms represent the three basic types of psalms: Psalm 105 is a psalm of thanksgiving (New Orientation), Psalm 96 is a psalm of praise (Orientation), and Psalm 106 is a psalm of penitence (Disorientation). These represent the diversity of liturgical speech that was acceptable among the people of God.

Since the Chronicler used the term "thanksgiving" (16:7) to describe the kind of material showcased in 16:8-36, it is not surprising that an excerpt from Psalm 105 comes first (Ps 105:1-15). This Psalm gives thanks to God for the covenant established with Abraham, Isaac, and Jacob; it traces the story of God's faithfulness through the narratives related to Joseph and Moses in the Exodus and wilderness; and it ends with an allusion to the conquest of the land. The focus of Psalm 105 is entirely on the grace and faithfulness of God toward Israel founded firmly on the Abrahamic covenant, ending with a clear emphasis on the response of Israel as obedience to the law (Ps 105:45). The Chronicler included only the first section of the psalm with its strong tone of praise and its focus on the establishment of a covenant with the patriarchs that would last for a thousand generations. So also this section views Israel when it was but "few in number" while emphasizing the promise of the inheritance of the land and protection from the nations among whom they walked.[7] This part of the drama resonates with the vulnerable remnant living in the Chronicler's time with the land still ruled by other nations even as they longed for the reconquest of the land (Ps 105:45).

The second section of the composition in 16:8-36 incorporates nearly all of Psalm 96.[8] This is a psalm of orientation, calling the entire creation, both animate and inanimate, to sing praise to God. While the citation of Psalm 105 focuses on the grace and faithfulness of their covenant God to this insignificant people wandering among the nations, the citation from Psalm 96 focuses on the power and glory of their cosmic God who demands the submission and praise of the nations among whom his people wander. To those who lived vulnerably among the nations the declarations "the LORD reigns" (16:31) and "the LORD is coming to judge the earth" (16:33) were essential to sustain faith.

Based on these recitations of faith focused on the faithfulness of the covenant God and the rule of the cosmic God, the Chronicler returns to a psalm (Ps 106:1, 47-48) that not only signals the legitimacy of petition in the worship of Israel but also shows how such petition is intricately linked to the other two forms of prayer—that is, God's answer to their deepest plea will result in both thanksgiving and praise to God ("so we can thank . . . and praise you," 16:35). The Chronicler picks up on the theme introduced in the first psalm citation (16:19-22) from Psalm 105 where the people were wandering from nation to nation. Now he turns this into a cry to "Save . . . gather . . . rescue us from among the nations" (16:35).[9] This looks not only to the return of others who have not yet joined the remnant in the Promised Land but also to the release of those who have returned from the hegemony of the nations; as Knoppers (2004:651) so aptly puts it, "The plea to Yhwh to 'liberate us from the nations' is an appeal for freedom from the tyranny of others."

The Chronicler drew together an assortment of psalms to highlight the Davidic roots of the worship of his day and in the process constructed "a skillful and artfully arranged composition" that is nothing short of "a new work" (Knoppers 2004:644). This new composition reveals the role of the Temple as a place for the people to cry to God for help in the midst of their new predicament among the nations and to announce the reign of God to the nations who foolishly believe they rule the cosmos.

Priests and Levites Worship at the Tabernacle in Gibeon (16:39-42). Meanwhile, worship was to continue at the Tabernacle site in Gibeon, where the priests, led by Zadok (descendant of Aaron), were to sacrifice twice daily the burnt offerings demanded in the Torah (cf. Exod 29:38-43; Num 28:1-8). Alongside these priests were the rest of the musical Levites led by Heman and Jeduthun (Ethan), who were commissioned to offer thanksgiving to the Lord accompanied by trumpets, cymbals, and other instruments. The content of their "songs of praise" is even cited: "Give thanks to the LORD, for 'his faithful love endures forever'" (16:41), a refrain that pervades the worship of ancient Israel (2 Chr 5:13; 7:3; Ezra 3:11; Ps 136). This refrain will bracket the Chronicler's account of the dedication of the Temple in 2 Chronicles 6–7 (2 Chr 5:13; 7:3). So important is this phrase that it signifies all expressions of worship (1 Chr 16:7). In addition to these sacrificing priests and Levitical musicians were Levitical gatekeepers.

The Chronicler makes clear what is only implicit in Samuel—Kings, that is, that there were two worship centers for Israel during David's reign, one in Gibeon and one in Jerusalem (Knoppers 2004:652; cf. Blenkinsopp 1972:102). The Chronicler associates the one in Jerusalem with the Ark and the one in Gibeon with the Tabernacle sanctuary. This "temporary bifurcation in Israel's national cult" (Knoppers 2004:651) allowed the Chronicler to showcase the Davidic innovation of Levitical aural worship while continuing the traditional sacrificial role reserved for the priests at the Tabernacle.

The Chronicler's presentation in chapter 16 reveals that he considered the Gibeon shrine as legitimate for this period before the Temple was built.[10] However, considering the Deuteronomic demand (Deut 12) for centralized worship, this situation could not persist; ultimately the Ark and the Tabernacle would be reunited in the sanctuary Solomon built (Knoppers 2004:660). The Chronicler here may be suggesting why the Temple was necessary, although it is difficult to discern why the entire shrine could not have been transported from Gibeon to Jerusalem from the outset.

While the account fulfills the Deuteronomic demand by having a single site for sacrifice, it also reveals that Jerusalem worship began under the leadership of the Levites, who were musicians performing before the Ark without sacrificial activity. This emphasizes the innovative contribution of David to the worship life of Israel while also legitimizing the service of the Levitical musicians. As Knoppers has noted, "Both the allocation of coverage and the details of that coverage point toward the great importance of thanksgiving, music, and song in the Chronicler's vision of Yahwistic worship" (2004:661). Thus, for those living in the Persian period, this account legitimizes elements of their worship by seeking their roots in the ancient initiative of David.

People and King Return to Their Homes (16:43). The Chronicler brings his account of the Ark narrative to a close by returning to his source and citing 2 Samuel 6:19b, where David and the people part ways, each going home. However, while 2 Samuel 6:20-23 uses David's return as a segue to highlight the contrast between David and

Saul via Michal's outburst, the Chronicler leaves the idyllic scene undisturbed. In the Chronicler's account, then, the final words of chapter 16, "to bless his own family" (*lebarek* [TH1288A, ZH1385] *'eth-betho;* "to bless his house"), echo the closing words of the earlier failed attempt to move the Ark, an attempt that led to the blessing of Obed-edom's house (13:14; *wayebarek yhwh 'eth-beth 'obed-'edom;* NLT, "blessed the household of Obed-edom") and foreshadows the leitmotif of "house" (*bayit* [TH1004, ZH1074]) that will run throughout chapter 17 (see commentary on chapter 17; Japhet 1993:324).

In chapter 16 the Chronicler highlights David's meticulous provision for worship of God at the newly installed Ark. The Chronicler focuses on both tradition and innovation—that is, the ways in which David continues the worship rituals established by Moses, but also the ways in which David develops the worship of Israel, especially through the incorporation of verbal and musical forms of worship. This depiction of David would have supported the rituals used in the Chronicler's age, rituals that would endure throughout the Second Temple period. It is not surprising, then, that this Davidic legacy would be picked up by the early church and incorporated into their worship (see Eph 5:18-20; Col 3:16-17; Jas 5:13).

ENDNOTES

1. That ch 16 is a phase distinct from ch 15 is confirmed by the observations of Japhet (1993:312) that 16:1-3 and 16:43 are dependent on the source material in Samuel and form an *inclusio* around the Chronicler's account. I do not, however, find her chiastic structure for the entire passage convincing (cf. Boda 1996:55-70), especially in light of her awkward separation of 16:38 from 16:37.
2. Knoppers (2004:658-659) says, "The authors of Chronicles stand very much in defense of the singers, classifying the singers, musicians, and gatekeepers as full-fledged Levites. Within the larger tribe, the singers stand alongside other Levites, including the priests, as participants in major cultic activities."
3. See the close affinity in the language of 15:24 and 16:6, and yet the presence of the term "regularly" in 16:6 highlights the contrastive situation (Japhet 1993:315).
4. See previous note.
5. See also Williamson 1982:127, who interprets this verb as "invoke through the Psalms of lament."
6. See Knoppers 2004:654-659 for scholarly debate over this composition as the work of the Chronicler or some later editor.
7. The Abrahamic covenant was important to those living in the wake of the destruction of Jerusalem and the exile of its people. See Neh 9; cf. Boda 1999:85-87, 101-114.
8. First Chronicles 16:23 does not incorporate two lines from Ps 96:1-2, and although 16:30-33 does include nearly all the material from Ps 96:10-13, the order of the lines is slightly changed. It is possible that the source used by the Chronicler was slightly different from Ps 96 in the extant textual witnesses.
9. Japhet (1993:319) argues that the LXX preserves the original form of 16:35 with its lack of the verb "gather." She says return from exile is not common in Chronicles and is found elsewhere only in 2 Chr 30:9 (see absence in 2 Chr 6:39). Even the LXX, however, has the phrase "save us from the nations."
10. This legitimacy is assured by the authoritative revelation of Yahweh to Solomon at Gibeon (1 Kgs 3:4-5//2 Chr 1:5-7).

◆ H. The Lord's Covenant Promise to David (17:1-27)

When David was settled in his palace, he
summoned Nathan the prophet. "Look,"
David said, "I am living in a beautiful
cedar palace,* but the Ark of the LORD's
Covenant is out there under a tent!"
2Nathan replied to David, "Do what-
ever you have in mind, for God is with
you."
3But that same night God said to
Nathan,

4"Go and tell my servant David, 'This
is what the LORD has declared: You
are not the one to build a house for
me to live in. 5I have never lived in a
house, from the day I brought the
Israelites out of Egypt until this very
day. My home has always been a tent,
moving from one place to another in
a Tabernacle. 6Yet no matter where I
have gone with the Israelites, I have
never once complained to Israel's
leaders,* the shepherds of my people.
I have never asked them, "Why
haven't you built me a beautiful
cedar house?"'
7"Now go and say to my servant
David, 'This is what the LORD of
Heaven's Armies has declared: I took
you from tending sheep in the pasture
and selected you to be the leader of
my people Israel. 8I have been with
you wherever you have gone, and I
have destroyed all your enemies
before your eyes. Now I will make your
name as famous as anyone who has
ever lived on the earth! 9And I will
provide a homeland for my people
Israel, planting them in a secure place
where they will never be disturbed.
Evil nations won't oppress them as
they've done in the past, 10starting
from the time I appointed judges to
rule my people Israel. And I will defeat
all your enemies.
" 'Furthermore, I declare that the
LORD will build a house for you—a
dynasty of kings! 11For when you die
and join your ancestors, I will raise up
one of your descendants, one of your
sons, and I will make his kingdom
strong. 12He is the one who will build
a house—a temple—for me. And I will
secure his throne forever. 13I will be his
father, and he will be my son. I will
never take my favor from him as I took
it from the one who ruled before you.
14I will confirm him as king over my
house and my kingdom for all time,
and his throne will be secure forever.'"

15So Nathan went back to David and told
him everything the LORD had said in this
vision.

16Then King David went in and sat be-
fore the LORD and prayed,

"Who am I, O LORD God, and what is
my family, that you have brought me
this far? 17And now, O God, in addition
to everything else, you speak of giving
your servant a lasting dynasty! You
speak as though I were someone very
great,* O LORD God!
18"What more can I say to you about
the way you have honored me? You
know what your servant is really like.
19For the sake of your servant, O LORD,
and according to your will, you have
done all these great things and have
made them known.
20"O LORD, there is no one like you.
We have never even heard of another
God like you! 21What other nation on
earth is like your people Israel? What
other nation, O God, have you redeemed
from slavery to be your own people?
You made a great name for yourself
when you redeemed your people from
Egypt. You performed awesome miracles
and drove out the nations that stood in
their way. 22You chose Israel to be your
very own people forever, and you,
O LORD, became their God.
23"And now, O LORD, I am your
servant; do as you have promised
concerning me and my family. May it
be a promise that will last forever.

[24]And may your name be established
and honored forever so that everyone
will say, 'The LORD of Heaven's Armies,
the God of Israel, is Israel's God!' And
may the house of your servant David
continue before you forever.
[25]"O my God, I have been bold
enough to pray to you because you
have revealed to your servant that you
will build a house for him—a dynasty of
kings! [26]For you are God, O LORD. And
you have promised these good things
to your servant. [27]And now, it has
pleased you to bless the house of your
servant, so that it will continue forever
before you. For when you grant a
blessing, O LORD, it is an eternal
blessing!"

17:1 Hebrew *a house of cedar.* 17:6 As in Greek version (see also 2 Sam 7:7); Hebrew reads *judges.* 17:17 The meaning of the Hebrew is uncertain.

NOTES

17:1 *a beautiful cedar palace . . . under a tent.* The Hebrew term here is "a house of cedar" (as NLT mg), introducing the play on the word "house" (*bayit* [TH1004, ZH1074]) throughout this chapter. The tent here is the temporary structure where David housed the Ark before the Temple was built (15:1; 16:1). The Tabernacle remained at Gibeon (see 16:39). The building of temples in honor of one's deity, especially after ascending the throne or attaining military success, was a common activity in the ancient Near East (Boda 2006c:211-249).

17:7 *the LORD of Heaven's Armies.* This is the translation of the Hebrew *yhwh tseba'oth* [TH3068/6635, ZH3378/7372], a name closely associated with the Davidic and Jerusalem/Zion traditions in the OT. It points to the Lord's role as Divine Warrior leading his heavenly armies into battle (12:22; Josh 5:13-15; see Kang 1989; Longman and Reid 1995; Sherlock 1993).

tending sheep in the pasture. The shepherd motif is common in ancient Near Eastern literature related to kings (1 Sam 16:11; 17:12-20, 34; Ps 23; see Knoppers 2004:668).

17:10 *I appointed judges.* Their stories are in the book of Judges.

17:11 *one of your descendants, one of your sons.* This is a reference to Solomon.

17:13 *the one who ruled before you.* This is a reference to Saul, whose rule was rejected by the Lord and whose dynasty was never confirmed (1 Sam 13:13-14; cf. 1 Sam 15:26, 28, 35; 16:1). Although the Chronicler did not include the earlier narratives of the rejection of Saul as king, he used Saul and his family as the dark foil against which the brilliance of David shone brightly (10:13-14; 13:3; 15:29).

17:15 *told him everything.* The Hebrew text emphasizes Nathan's full disclosure of this prophetic encounter with God, placing these words at the outset of the verse: "according to all these words and according to all this vision."

this vision. Key avenues of revelation to prophets were dreams and visions in the night (Num 12:6-8; Joel 2:28; Amos 7:1, 7; 8:1; 9:1; Zech 1:7-8; 4:1).

17:16 *what is my family.* David situated himself within his family, thereby displaying ancient Hebrew social consciousness in which a person's status was determined by his or her place within the broader clan and tribal context (see also Gideon in Judg 6; cf. Bendor 1996).

17:17 *in addition to everything else.* This is a reference to the earlier blessings of the throne, military victories, and progeny (chs 11–12, 14).

17:24 *The LORD of Heaven's Armies.* See note on 17:7.

COMMENTARY

David's Concern for the Houseless Ark (17:1-2). The initial crisis created by David's passion to bring the Ark into Jerusalem was the death of Uzzah (ch 13). This was no sooner resolved by proper attention to Levitical law (chs 15–16) when a new crisis arose pertaining to the presence of the Ark in Jerusalem (ch 17). David mourned the fact that he was settled in his own "house" (his palace) made of cedar, while the Ark was merely housed in a fabric tent. The contrast here was probably both one of quality—that is, a grand palace versus a humble tent—as well as one of permanence, a settled palace versus a transient tent.

David's realization marks one of the key milestones in the grand story of Israel's redemption, for this would lead to the establishment of a covenant between Yahweh and David.[1] This is true not only in the introduction of a new covenant relationship between Israel and God, now through their leader David, but also in the key shift it signaled between a transient people to a settled nation. Thus, with this royal covenant came the move from Tabernacle to Temple worship, from Sinai to Davidic covenant, from wilderness to Promised Land.

This event, however, merely marks the beginning of a phase of transition that would only be completed by David's son Solomon—as Japhet (1993:335) notes, "Not David's day, indeed, but the combined reign of David and Solomon constitutes the climax of Israel's history."[2] The Chronicler left out the phrase from his source "and the LORD had given him rest from all the surrounding enemies" (2 Sam 7:1b) in 17:1 and changed the phrase "I will give you rest from" (2 Sam 7:11) to "I will defeat" in 17:10.[3] Japhet (1993:328) convincingly argues that this omission was related to the Chronicler's desire to accentuate Solomon as the "man of peace," a trait that will qualify his reign as the appropriate time for building the Temple (22:9). (See introduction to 2 Chronicles 1–9 for the discussion on building sanctuaries.)

David's initial words to Nathan (merely a statement of fact) betray a deeper intention (his desire to build a temple) that the prophet ascertained. Nathan, sensing God's presence with David, quickly affirmed his passion, only to be confronted by God in a dream that very night.

The Lord's Vision to David through Nathan (17:3-15). Using classic prophetic formula to introduce the speech, the Lord commanded Nathan to relay a message to David. The message is divided into two sections, each marked by the phrase "go and tell/say to my servant David" (17:4, 7) followed by the phrase "this is what the LORD has declared." The first section is negative in tone, the second positive (Knoppers 2004:667).

First, in 17:4-6 David is told that he is not the one who will build a house for God (i.e., the Temple).[4] Rehearsing the history of his past relationship with Israel as a nation, God questioned even the necessity of such a project, considering that he had always dwelled in the Tabernacle and had never requested a "house." God's initial inquiry questions David's Jerusalemite innovation, placing the emphasis on the Sinai tradition with its Tabernacle instruction.

In the second part of the speech (17:7-14), God moved from his past history with Israel to his past history with David. Focus on the past relationship between two parties is typical of covenant literature in the ancient Near East.[5] God reminded David of his humble roots as shepherd boy and of his election by God to be leader.

With this election had come God's presence and protection from all his enemies. The future was bright for David because God would make him famous and provide a secure homeland for his people. This new royal phase is seen as the answer to the oppression faced by Israel in the period of the judges, echoing the message of the final edition of the book of Judges (see also the refrains in Judg 17:6; 18:1; 19:1; 21:25; cf. Dragga 1987:39-46; O'Connell 1996).

In this, the intricate interrelationship between David and Israel is demonstrated. The covenant with David could not be dissociated from the larger covenantal history of the Lord with Israel; rather, it was a further development in that broader relational story that began with the patriarchs and continued at Sinai. These earlier covenantal moments were not supplanted by the new one but rather were foundational to a new phase. As God makes clear in 17:9-10 of this vision, David's key role would be to secure the promise of land offered to Abraham (Gen 15, 17), a promise that proved elusive after the initial conquest of the land by Joshua (see the book of Judges).

At the climax of the second section of the speech, marked by the phrase "Furthermore, I declare that" (17:10b), God echoes his initial words of the speech in 17:4 by promising that "the LORD will build a house for" David. The play on words is clear: living in a grand "house" (palace), David desired to build a "house" (Temple) for the Lord, but God denied him this task, promising instead to build David a "house" (dynasty) and that this "house" (dynasty) will build a "house" (Temple) for the Lord. God was referring to David's son Solomon, who would build that Temple (see the early chapters of 2 Chronicles).

The phrase at the core of this covenant ceremony is found in 17:13: "I will be his father, and he will be my son." This phrase reflects the reciprocity that is central to all covenants in the Old Testament. Thus, to the Sinai generation God declared, "I will be your God, and you will be my people" (cf. Exod 6:7; Lev 26:12; Deut 29:13; cf. Lev 11:44-45; 22:33; 25:38; Num 15:41), and to Abraham he promised to "be your God and the God of your descendants after you. . . . I will be their God" (Gen 17:7-8). Ultimately, in the new covenant the Lord repeats, "I will be their God, and they will be my people" (Jer 31:33). The language here, however, is slightly different from that of the Abrahamic, Sinaitic, and new covenants, which place the emphasis on the national character of the covenant (God with his people).[6] With David, the terms are far more intimate, emphasizing the unbreakable bonds of family relationship with its depth of loyalty.

The close association between sonship and royalty is evident in the literature of the ancient Near East. In Egypt the pharaoh was considered a son of the gods, but this sonship was achieved through conception (the god Amon begat the pharaoh with the queen mother), while in Israel it was through adoption, captured in the declaration of Psalm 2:7, "You are my son. Today I have become your Father."

Close attention to the Chronicler's use of his source in Samuel reveals that he incorporated a couple of changes. First, in 17:13 he excised the words "If he sins, I will correct and discipline him with the rod, like any father would do" from 2 Samuel 7:14b. In Chronicles Solomon is presented as a leader without sin, bringing the focus on his faithful act of building the Temple. Second, in 17:14 the Chronicler changed the source from "Your house and your kingdom will continue before me for all time, and your throne will be secure forever" in 2 Samuel 7:16 to "I will confirm him as king over my house and my kingdom for all time, and his throne will be secure forever." The covenantal focus subtly shifts here from David to Solomon, a shift that some have seen as an indication that the covenant was being established with both David and Solomon and that it was actually the faithful acts of Solomon that would establish and confirm the covenant expressed.[7] At the same time the focus shifted from the Davidic line to God as king, as the text shifts from "your [David's] house and your [David's] kingdom" to "my [God's] house and my [God's] kingdom." This is an important reminder that the kingdom was never the possession of David but rather of God, for whom the Davidic line functioned as vice-regent on earth (see Ps 2). Nevertheless, the Chronicler's presentation retains a strong emphasis on the enduring quality of the Davidic covenant, suggesting that the Chronicler retained hope for royal reinstatement.[8]

David's Response to the Lord (17:16-27). Key to the structure of covenant forms and texts in the Old Testament is the value of reciprocity. This has already been ascertained in the core expression of the Davidic covenant in 17:13, "I will be his father, and he will be my son," but it is also expressed in that David responded to God's vision through Nathan with a prayer to the Lord.[9] The exact location where David offered this prayer is not identified. One might assume it was in the tent where the Ark was then stationed in Jerusalem, but another viable option is the Tabernacle at Gibeon, where it appears David did inquire of God even when the Ark was in Jerusalem (see 21:29-30).

The prayer is divided into three sections based on theme. In 17:16b-19, David expresses that he was overwhelmed by God's promise to him. Such self-deference was typical of Hebrew interactions with the divine, marking the formalization of the relationship with God. David's response echoes those of Moses (Exod 3–4), Gideon (Judg 6), Isaiah (Isa 6), and Jeremiah (Jer 1). The mood of such personal depreciation is normally the inquisitive, asking questions that probe the worth or ability of the human. In the end the focus is always placed on the superior (the divine) who was calling or granting the gift, with particular emphasis on God's grace and greatness. David's humility is also expressed through his self-designation as "your servant," a title first given him by the Lord himself (17:4) and one that appears three times in this first section (17:17, 18, 19). This clearly defines the relationship as one of master-servant, suggesting his submission to God. Ironically, throughout the Old Testament it is the ones who submit themselves to such a relationship who are ultimately honored the most (Moses, Joshua, the prophets), for the worth of the servant is derived from the worth of his master, and in this case this worth is infinite.

In the second part of the prayer (17:20-22), David's focus shifts from himself to the nation as a whole. God is praised for his uniqueness among the gods of the nations ("We have never even heard of another God like you"), and this uniqueness grants to Israel special status among the nations of the earth ("What other nation on earth is like your people Israel?"). David rehearsed the way in which God had distinguished himself and his nation on earth by reciting the fundamental story of salvation, which includes the Exodus ("redeemed from slavery . . . redeemed your people from Egypt"),[10] Conquest ("drove out the nations"), and events that confirm God's election of his people ("You chose Israel") into covenant relationship ("your very own people . . . their God"). This covenant relationship is described as enduring forever. This middle section of the prayer is an important reminder that the Davidic covenant is significant because of its role within the broader scheme of Israelite history and theology: "If the chosen heir succeeds and Yhwh fulfills the pledges made through Nathan, the promises to David will join the Exodus and Conquest as formative events in Israelite history" (Knoppers 2004:688). While in the first section David's significance is based upon the God he served, in the second section David's significance is based upon the people he represented.

In the third part of the prayer (17:23-27), signaled by the phrase "And now," David returns to the main issue at hand: the promises God made to him. Although he had expressed his unworthiness of such an honor, David was not rejecting the offer but rather asking God to fulfill his promise. Having just emphasized the eternal character of the covenant between Israel and God (17:22), David asked four times for these divine promises for his dynasty to be eternal as well (17:23-24, 27),[11] an endurance based upon the eternal character of the praise due the Lord (17:24). Again, David's rule is immediately related to the broader interests of the covenant relationship between Israel and God ("The LORD of Heaven's Armies, the God of Israel, is Israel's God," 17:24).

This final part of both major sections of this chapter—God's prophecy to David and David's prayer to God—places great emphasis on the endurance of the Davidic line and covenant within Israel. Interestingly, the Chronicler included David's response to the Lord, even though the prayer says nothing about the Temple. This suggests that the prayer had been retained to express the Chronicler's hope for an enduring Davidic line (Knoppers 2004:673).

ENDNOTES

1. Although God's promise to David is referred to elsewhere as a covenant using the more technical term *berith* [TH1285, ZH1382] (e.g., 2 Chr 13:5; 21:7; cf. Ps 89:3; Isa 55:3; Jer 33:21), here the term is not employed.
2. So also Knoppers (2004:674) says, "Slightly recasting the dynastic oracle and David's prayer, the Chronicler employs these texts to tie David's career closely to that of his son."
3. However, see McKenzie 1985:63, who denies that the phrase in 2 Sam 7:1 was part of the Chronicler's source.
4. There is a slight shift in the Chronicler's account. In 2 Sam 7 the emphasis is on the viability of building a Temple at all, while in Chronicles this shifts to the question of who is the legitimate builder, the answer to which is Solomon rather than David (Schniedewind 1999).
5. See Hillers 1964, 1969; Kline 1963; McCarthy 1978.
6. It is true that there is an allusion to sonship in the Sinai covenant (Deut 1:31; 8:5), but this is not as core to the Sinai covenant as it is to the Davidic.
7. See Williamson 1976:351-361; 1983:305-318.
8. See Williamson 1977a:115-154; cf. Boda 2009b. Note Japhet (1993:333), who says, "David's time is the preparatory stage, the vestibule. The inner sanctum of peace, quiet and rest—with all that these imply—will be reached only in Solomon's day."
9. The comments by De Vries (1989:155) that this is "an aimless anxiety-ridden prayer" are completely inappropriate since a response is demanded (cf. Knoppers 2004:687).

10. Japhet (1989:379ff) has noted that the Chronicler plays down the Exodus even in this chapter, noting the omission of "Egypt" in the Hebrew text of 17:5 from the source in 2 Sam 7:6. However, the Chronicler does not avoid the Exodus here in David's prayer.
11. The Chronicler appears to accentuate the focus on the eternal character of the Davidic covenant by adding "May it be a promise that will last forever" (see 2 Sam 7:25).

◆ I. David's Military Victories (18:1-17)

After this, David defeated and subdued
the Philistines by conquering Gath and its
surrounding towns. 2David also conquered
the land of Moab, and the Moabites who
were spared became David's subjects and
paid him tribute money.
3David also destroyed the forces of Ha-
dadezer, king of Zobah, as far as Hamath,*
when Hadadezer marched out to strength-
en his control along the Euphrates River.
4David captured 1,000 chariots, 7,000
charioteers, and 20,000 foot soldiers. He
crippled all the chariot horses except
enough for 100 chariots.
5When Arameans from Damascus arrived
to help King Hadadezer, David killed 22,000
of them. 6Then he placed several army gar-
risons* in Damascus, the Aramean capital,
and the Arameans became David's subjects
and paid him tribute money. So the LORD
made David victorious wherever he went.
7David brought the gold shields of Ha-
dadezer's officers to Jerusalem, 8along
with a large amount of bronze from Ha-
dadezer's towns of Tebah* and Cun. Later
Solomon melted the bronze and molded it
into the great bronze basin called the Sea,
the pillars, and the various bronze articles
used at the Temple.
9When King Toi* of Hamath heard that
David had destroyed the entire army of
King Hadadezer of Zobah, 10he sent his
son Joram* to congratulate King David for
his successful campaign. Hadadezer and
Toi had been enemies and were often at
war. Joram presented David with many
gifts of gold, silver, and bronze.
11King David dedicated all these gifts to
the LORD, along with the silver and gold
he had taken from the other nations—
from Edom, Moab, Ammon, Philistia, and
Amalek.
12Abishai son of Zeruiah destroyed
18,000 Edomites in the Valley of Salt.
13He placed army garrisons in Edom, and
all the Edomites became David's subjects.
In fact, the LORD made David victorious
wherever he went.
14So David reigned over all Israel and did
what was just and right for all his people.
15Joab son of Zeruiah was commander of
the army. Jehoshaphat son of Ahilud was
the royal historian. 16Zadok son of Ahitub
and Ahimelech* son of Abiathar were the
priests. Seraiah* was the court secretary.
17Benaiah son of Jehoiada was captain of
the king's bodyguard.* And David's sons
served as the king's chief assistants.

18:3 The meaning of the Hebrew is uncertain. **18:6** As in Greek version and Latin Vulgate (see also 2 Sam 8:6); Hebrew lacks *several army garrisons.* **18:8** Hebrew reads *Tibhath,* a variant spelling of Tebah; compare parallel text at 2 Sam 8:8. **18:9** As in parallel text at 2 Sam 8:9; Hebrew reads *Tou;* also in 18:10. **18:10** As in parallel text at 2 Sam 8:10; Hebrew reads *Hadoram,* a variant spelling of Joram. **18:16a** As in some Hebrew manuscripts, Syriac version, and Latin Vulgate (see also 2 Sam 8:17); most Hebrew manuscripts read *Abimelech.* **18:16b** As in parallel text at 2 Sam 8:17; Hebrew reads *Shavsha.* **18:17** Hebrew *of the Kerethites and Pelethites.*

NOTES

18:1 *subdued.* Heb., *kana'* [TH3665, ZH4044] (Hiphil), as promised in 17:10, where the same word appears (NLT, "defeat").

Gath. This was one of the five Philistine city-states situated on the coastal plain to the west of Judah and southwest of Jerusalem. Gath was a traditional enemy of Judah.

18:2 ***land of Moab, and the Moabites.*** This was one of three kingdoms situated on the Transjordanian plateau to the east of Judah and Jerusalem on the other side of the Dead Sea. Ruth, ancestor of King David, was a Moabite (Ruth 1).

became David's subjects and paid him tribute money. Lit., "became servants, bearing tribute." This is the language of hegemony over foreign territories in the ancient Near East (so also 18:6).

18:3 ***Zobah, as far as Hamath.*** Zobah was north of Damascus. The phrase "as far as Hamath" is important because Hamath will appear in 18:9.

Hadadezer marched out to strengthen his control along the Euphrates River. The subject of this sentence is not designated in the Hebrew text and could refer to David. Additionally, the action could be that he was marching out "to set up his stela at the Euphrates River"—that is, a monument designating his control over a certain area. Such stelae have been discovered in the Levant, most notable being the Mesha Stela (or Moabite Stone), which not only marked Moabite territory but celebrated the defeat of their former lord, Israel (see ANET 320-321; COS 2.137-138; Knoppers 2004:695-696).

18:6 ***became David's subjects and paid him tribute money.*** See note on 18:2.

18:8 ***Tebah and Cun.*** Hadadezer's control extended beyond Zobah to include other towns and cities. Both these towns are in the area near Zobah.

the great bronze basin called the Sea. This was a large basin located in Solomon's Temple court, variously called the "molten sea," "the sea," and the "bronze sea" (1 Kgs 7:23-24; 2 Kgs 16:17). It was to be used for priestly washing, while 10 other basins were used for rinsing the burnt offerings (2 Chr 4:6).

the pillars. The two pillars, called "Jakin" (meaning "he establishes") and "Boaz" (meaning "in him is strength"), are described in 2 Chr 3:15-17. The bronze may have been used for the "interwoven chains" on the tops of the pillars and/or for the "decorative pomegranates."

18:9 ***Hamath.*** This was located on the River Orontes, north of Zobah.

18:12 ***Abishai son of Zeruiah.*** He was the brother of Joab and Asahel. Their mother was Zeruiah, who is identified as the sister of David (2:16; 2 Sam 17:25).

Edomites. This was the southernmost kingdom on the Transjordanian Plateau, to the southeast of Jerusalem and across the Dead Sea from southern Judah.

Valley of Salt. This is an uncertain location, but most likely south of the Dead Sea, either in the Rift Valley itself or in a valley that led out of the region of Judah or into the region of Edom.

18:17 ***David's sons served as the king's chief assistants.*** Lit., "the first sons of David were at the king's side" (so Knoppers 2004:704). This refers to the eldest sons of David's wives who participated in the court as they trained for royal service.

COMMENTARY

The depiction of the establishment of the covenant between Yahweh and David serves as a major juncture in the Chronicler's account. Following chapter 17, the Chronicler drew upon his source in Samuel to focus on David's victories over the surrounding nations. At the same time, however, the Chronicler excised a large quantity of material in Samuel, the focus of which is mainly on the sin of David and the resulting consequences within his family (2 Sam 11:2–12:25; 13:1–21:17). This presentation accomplishes several things for the Chronicler. First, the inclusion and piecing together of the military narratives showcase God's fulfilling his promises (see 17:8, 10; Knoppers 2004:740). Second, the focus on David's battles shows why David was not the one to build the Temple. He was truly a man of blood and war, while his son Solomon would be a man of peace and rest (22:8-10). Third, these military battles serve as a segue to the key chapter, chapter 21, which will identify the site on which Solomon will build the Temple, a narrative based on the need for a census for military purposes. Finally, the exclusion of the narratives related to the sin of David and to the threats to his kingdom produces a picture of stability and prosperity for the king who laid the foundation for Solomon's rule and the Temple's construction.[1] The Chronicler and his audience are well aware of the dark side of the Davidic tradition, an aspect of the tradition that was very important to the exilic Deuteronomic historian with his concern for admission of guilt and repentance in heart and deed. The Chronicler, however, had a slightly different focus as he wrote to an audience with the Second Temple and its services in view.

Chapters 18–20 are divided into four basic sections, the beginning of three of the sections signaled by the discourse marker "(some time) after this" (each time the Hebrew is the same: *wayehi 'akhare-ken,* lit., "And it was after this"; 18:1; 19:1; 20:4; cf. Japhet 1993:344), and the beginning of one section (20:1) signaled by the simple "In the spring of the year" (*wayehi le'eth teshubath hashanah* [TH6256, ZH6961], lit., "It was at the time of the turn of the year"). The first major section, chapter 18, consists of four major subsections, each containing a summary statement that is used to structure the subsections. These summaries are usually found at the end of their respective section, but the final one begins with a statement summarizing the quality of David's rule.

David's Victories over Philistia, Moab, Zobah, and Damascus (18:1-6). The account begins with a nebulous temporal designation, "After this," referring to some indeterminate time after the encounter between the Lord and David. The account of David's victories begins with the people group that had been nearly the exclusive enemy of Israel to this point in Chronicles: the Philistines (ch 10; 11:16; 14:8-17). The focus of the military action is on Gath, one of the five traditional cities of the Philistines located on the coastal plain to the southwest of Jerusalem. Since Philistine territory consisted of city-states ruled by petty kings, the phrase "its surrounding towns" is a reference to those towns, villages, and farms within the sphere of influence of Gath. Next David conquered Moab, a kingdom to the east of Jerusalem on the Transjordanian Plateau (just across the Dead Sea). Moab was placed under David's control and had to pay him tribute money. These first two military moves were strategic economically. For much of its pre-monarchial history, Israel was sequestered safely in the higher regions of the hill country of Judah, Samaria, and Galilee, the geographical backbone of the land of Israel. Although safe from the more powerful kingdoms of Philistia, Phoenicia, and the Transjordan, this location isolated Israel from the economy of the ancient Near East. Two major ancient highways ran through the strip of land called the Levant (Syria-Sinai), both joining the major route on the Fertile Crescent at Damascus. On the western edge ran the Great Trunk Road and on the eastern edge, the King's Highway (ABD 2.976; TBD 1272). By conquering Philistia and Moab, David was capturing the key to economic development in the Levant: the trade routes, which could be taxed as trade moved between Africa, Europe, and Asia. This economic advantage is suggested by the assertion in 18:2 that Moab "paid him tribute money."

The account then moves to the far north to tell of David's defeat of the powerful Aramean kingdom of Zobah, which during the eleventh century BC controlled a substantial portion of the northern Levant, from the Lebanon mountains to the region of Bashan and to the Euphrates River (ABD 6.1108). Since Zobah was located north of Damascus, David also gained control over Damascus, either because it was under the control of Hadadezer or was an ally. Damascus was another key control point on the ancient trade routes. Both the Great Trunk Road and the King's Highway met at Damascus before heading north to join routes to Asia and Europe. Again, the Chronicler made note of the Arameans paying David "tribute money" (18:6).

The language of this section echoes the world of international diplomacy and control. In the ancient Near East there were several levels of control by a foreign state: (1) A major power could occupy a land and incorporate it into its own country or empire as a province. (2) A major power could defeat the nation and set up a suzerain-vassal relationship, which involved the regular relay of tribute from the vassal to the suzerain while retaining some form of political autonomy with leadership drawn from its own populace. (3) A major power could defeat the nation and demand tribute while not demanding an ongoing relationship with the conquered land. First Chronicles 18 contains examples of the second and third types but, interestingly, not the first type. The designation of the lands as "servants" (18:2, 6, 13; see note on 18:2) who bear tribute (18:2, 6; see note on 18:2) and must accept Israelite garrisons (18:6, 13) is common language for these types of arm's-length arrangements in the ancient Near East (Knoppers 2004:700-703).

All of these victories, representing control over territories to the west, east, and north of Israel, are evaluated in the summary statement of 18:6, which links them to the action of the Lord on David's behalf: "So the LORD made David victorious wherever he went."

David's Spoils Dedicated to the Lord (18:7-11). With the Chronicler's interest in David's role in preparing for Temple construction, this next section, drawn from his Samuel source with some changes, was extremely helpful. Here he found accounts of valuables that were "dedicated . . . to the LORD" (18:11). First, the spoils from David's victory over Hadadezer are described, and the Chronicler inserts an extra sentence to emphasize that these spoils were the ones used by Solomon to fashion various bronze articles in the Temple, including the Sea and the pillars (2 Chr 3:15–4:2, 12, 15).[2] Second, King Toi of Hamath (another city in the northern Levant), fearful after David's defeat of neighboring Zobah, sent gifts of gold, silver, and bronze with the crown prince Joram to congratulate David, an indication of his desire to appease and show submission to the Israelite king. These gifts, along with the spoils of the battles against Edom, Moab, Ammon, Philistia, and Amalek, were all "dedicated . . . to the LORD," proof in the Chronicler's account of David's provision for the Temple and its furnishings. The battle against Edom is presented next (see below on 18:12-13), and the one against Ammon in chapter 19, but there is no account of a battle against Amalek in Chronicles or Samuel—Kings (although cf. 1 Sam 14:48; 15:1-9; 27:8; 30:1-31).

Abishai's Victories for David over Edom (18:12-13). One final military exercise is described in 18:12-13. In this case, the subject of the action is Abishai. Abishai is known in Samuel as the one who saved his uncle David's life from the giant Ishbi-benob, an incident that led to David's retirement from battle (2 Sam 21:16-17). Abishai was the commander of the elite troop called "the Thirty" and rose to leadership in the army, second only to his brother Joab, who will be featured in the next chapter. Here in 18:12-13, Abishai defeats the Edomites in the Valley of Salt, the location of which is uncertain but is often linked to the area south of the Dead Sea, which leads to the hill country of Edom (TBD 1152). Abishai's victory brings the Edomites under David's control. The closing line is identical to the summary statement that closed 18:1-6 (18:6b), making these two accounts of military success form a bracket around the central pericope concerned with the dedication of the gifts and spoils from battle to the Lord.

David's Administration over Israel (18:14-17). The chapter concludes with a section that shifts the focus for a moment from the external exploits of David against the surrounding nations to the internal administration of David within Israel. A literary signal of this shift from external to internal is found in the incorporation of the summary statement at the outset, emphasizing both the extent and quality of David's reign: His rule encompassed "all Israel" and was "just and right." The final phrase is literally "he enacted justice and righteousness," qualities related to the proper administration of justice, which was a key role for the king in ancient Israel as vice-regent of the Lord (Pleins 2001; Weinfeld 1995). These qualities typify conformity to an ethical standard or norm set by God and his law (see Ps 72:2-4, 12-14). Those who benefit from such righteous justice are the vulnerable of society, often listed as the poor, the needy, the widow, and the fatherless. Such justice has both a positive and a negative quality, that is, it involves frustrating the schemes of the oppressor as well as protecting the rights of the oppressed (see Ps 72:4). Such characteristics of royal justice ultimately find their source in the character and action of the High King of Israel, the Lord (Ps 146:7-10).

This summary of David's just and righteous rule is followed by a list of the administration that was appointed to ensure proper internal organization of the royal court and national state. Joab was the general of the army, a position he earned by leading the attack against Jerusalem (11:6). The precise role of Jehoshaphat as "royal historian" (Heb., *mazkir* [TH2142C, ZH4654]; 18:15) is uncertain, with suggestions ranging from "secretary of state" to "official spokesperson" to "registrar" (ABD 3.666; Knoppers 2004:707). If this was a "royal secretary" (similar to a registrar), it is difficult to discern how this position relates to that of Seraiah, who was the "court secretary" (*soper* [TH5608A, ZH6221]; 18:16). "Secretary of state" and "official spokesperson" presuppose the influence of the Egyptian court (where such roles are attested), but there is no clear evidence that the Judean court was patterned after the Egyptian court. Zadok and Ahimelech served together as chief priests in David's court. Earlier the Chronicler related that the two priests of David were Zadok and Abiathar (15:11). In 1 Kings 1:7, 19, 25-27 it is recorded that Abiathar was deposed by Solomon for supporting the coronation of Adonijah. It is possible that Ahimelech succeeded his father Abiathar and that the Abiathar of 1 Kings 1 is the son of Ahimelech, but it may be best to see here a scribal error and to read this as "Abiathar son of Ahimelech" (ABD 1.117; Japhet 1993:351-352; McCarter 1984:253). Benaiah son of Jehoiada was the perfect choice to lead the "Kerethites and Pelethites" (NLT, "king's bodyguard"; 18:17). The Kerethites and Pelethites were a mercenary unit separate from the regular army, commissioned to guard David (see 2 Sam 15:18; 20:7; 1 Kgs 1:38, 44; ABD 1.898). Benaiah, the son of a priest from Judah, distinguished himself as a faithful warrior throughout the reign of David and Solomon (27:5-6; 2 Sam 20:23; 23:20-22; 1 Kgs 1:8, 32-40; 2:25, 34-35, 46; 4:4). He was responsible for eliminating all challengers to Solomon's claim to the throne (1 Kgs 2:25-46). Finally, we are told that David's eldest sons served at David's side (see note on 18:17), a typical function of princes in ancient Near Eastern royal courts (see 2 Chr 11:23; Knoppers 2004:709). Their familial connection secured loyalty to their father; in the court they would learn the affairs of state in preparation for future rule.

ENDNOTES

1. Contra Japhet (1993:343), who sees the omission of these chapters as typical of the Chronicler, revealing "his reluctance to relate the private affairs of his protagonists, and his preference to stress the public and political aspects of their lives."
2. There is some debate over whether this statement about Solomon was an addition by the Chronicler or whether it was found in his source material (see Japhet 1993:348-349).

◆ J. David Defeats the Ammonites and Arameans (19:1-19)

Some time after this, King Nahash of the
Ammonites died, and his son Hanun* be-
came king. [2]David said, "I am going to
show loyalty to Hanun because his father,
Nahash, was always loyal to me." So David
sent messengers to express sympathy to
Hanun about his father's death.

But when David's ambassadors arrived
in the land of Ammon, [3]the Ammonite
commanders said to Hanun, "Do you re-
ally think these men are coming here to
honor your father? No! David has sent
them to spy out the land so they can come
in and conquer it!" [4]So Hanun seized Da-
vid's ambassadors and shaved them, cut
off their robes at the buttocks, and sent
them back to David in shame.

[5]When David heard what had hap-
pened to the men, he sent messengers to
tell them, "Stay at Jericho until your
beards grow out, and then come back."
For they felt deep shame because of their
appearance.

[6]When the people of Ammon realized
how seriously they had angered David,
Hanun and the Ammonites sent 75,000
pounds* of silver to hire chariots and
charioteers from Aram-naharaim, Aram-
maacah, and Zobah. [7]They also hired
32,000 chariots and secured the support
of the king of Maacah and his army. These
forces camped at Medeba, where they
were joined by the Ammonite troops that
Hanun had recruited from his own towns.
[8]When David heard about this, he sent
Joab and all his warriors to fight them.
[9]The Ammonite troops came out and drew
up their battle lines at the entrance of the
city, while the other kings positioned
themselves to fight in the open fields.

[10]When Joab saw that he would have to
fight on both the front and the rear, he
chose some of Israel's elite troops and
placed them under his personal command
to fight the Arameans in the fields. [11]He left
the rest of the army under the command

of his brother Abishai, who was to attack
the Ammonites. 12 "If the Arameans are too
strong for me, then come over and help
me," Joab told his brother. "And if the Am-
monites are too strong for you, I will help
you. 13 Be courageous! Let us fight bravely
for our people and the cities of our God.
May the LORD's will be done."
14 When Joab and his troops attacked,
the Arameans began to run away. 15 And
when the Ammonites saw the Arameans
running, they also ran from Abishai and
retreated into the city. Then Joab returned
to Jerusalem.
16 The Arameans now realized that they
were no match for Israel, so they sent
messengers and summoned additional
Aramean troops from the other side of the
Euphrates River.* These troops were under
the command of Shobach,* the command-
er of Hadadezer's forces.
17 When David heard what was happen-
ing, he mobilized all Israel, crossed the
Jordan River, and positioned his troops in
battle formation. Then David engaged the
Arameans in battle, and they fought
against him. 18 But again the Arameans
fled from the Israelites. This time David's
forces killed 7,000 charioteers and 40,000
foot soldiers, including Shobach, the
commander of their army. 19 When Hada-
dezer's allies saw that they had been
defeated by Israel, they surrendered to
David and became his subjects. After that,
the Arameans were no longer willing to
help the Ammonites.

19:1 As in parallel text at 2 Sam 10:1; Hebrew lacks *Hanun.* 19:6 Hebrew *1,000 talents* [34,000 kilograms]. 19:16a Hebrew *the river.* 19:16b As in parallel text at 2 Sam 10:16; Hebrew reads *Shophach;* also in 19:18.

NOTES

19:1 ***King Nahash of the Ammonites.*** He was infamous for his siege on Jabesh-gilead, the breaking of which launched Saul's career (1 Sam 11:1-2). Possibly David's good relationship with Nahash is related to their mutual enemy Saul.

19:2 ***messengers.*** Royal messengers were key to communication between courts (2 Sam 11:19; Isa 18:2). For a similar scenario, see the overture of Hiram of Tyre toward Solomon just after David's death (1 Kgs 5:1).

19:3 ***Ammonite commanders.*** These could be military leaders or royal advisers.

19:4 ***shaved them, cut off their robes at the buttocks.*** The loss of facial hair and body covering caused great shame in the ancient Near East (see Isa 7:20; 47:2-3).

19:6 ***how seriously they had angered David.*** Lit., "they had made themselves odious to David." The Hebrew verb is *ba'ash* [TH887, ZH944] (Hitpael). See Knoppers 2004:712; cf. NASB.

Aram-naharaim, Aram-maacah, and Zobah. Aram-naharaim means "Aram of the two rivers," a reference to its location between the Tigris and Euphrates. Aram-maacah was located in the Golan, northeast of the sea of Galilee and on the northern boundary of traditional Israel tribal territory. Zobah was north of Damascus (see 18:3; cf. Knoppers 2004:720).

19:7 ***Maacah.*** This is the same place as Aram-maacah (19:6).

Medeba. This city lay at the northeast corner of the Dead Sea. While within traditional Moabite lands, this city was conquered by the Israelites (Num 21:25-30; Josh 13:9, 16). While the Omride kings of the northern kingdom would control this region, the Mesha Stela claims that the Moabites freed it from Israelite control in the latter third of the ninth century BC (cf. 2 Kgs 3; see ANET 320-321; ANEP 274; COS 2.137-138).

19:10 ***Israel's elite troops.*** Joab chose from the "choice" troops.

19:11 ***his brother Abishai.*** See note on 18:12.

19:16 ***the other side of the Euphrates River.*** The Hebrew text has only "the river" (see NLT mg). With the involvement of Aram-naharaim, it is possible that this is a reference to the Euphrates River, which often is designated simply as "the river."

19:18 ***David's forces killed.*** Lit., "David killed," bringing greater focus on the king himself.

Shobach. He was the general of Hadadezer's forces (see 18:3-4).

19:19 ***they surrendered to David.*** Lit., "They made peace with David," signaling a formal agreement between the two peoples, which included some form of vassal submission ("became his subjects"). See note on 18:2.

COMMENTARY

Chapter 19 begins with the second of three appearances of the phrase *wayehi 'akhare-ken* (some time after this), which introduces three of the four sections in chapters 18–20 (18:1; 19:1; 20:4; so Japhet 1993:344). Chapters 18 and 19 contain two key contrasts. First, chapter 18 presents David on the offensive, moving out to exert his power, while chapter 19 presents David on the defensive, drawn into war by the arrogant Ammonites and fearful Arameans. Second, while chapter 18 reads more like annals of the exploits of David with shorter descriptions of various battles unrelated to one another, chapter 19 contains a narrative with its own integrity. The original tension is produced by the folly of King Hanun's rebuff of David's sympathy at the death of Hanun's father, the Ammonite king Nahash. This led to a battle between Israel and Ammon that also involved the Arameans.

King Hanun of Ammon Shuns David (19:1-5). A king's death always ushered in a period of uncertainty in the ancient Near East (see Isa 6:1; 14:28). Ancient annals record that such transitions could prompt a response from enemies of the royal family, both in the form of rebellions from inside and attacks from outside the former king's nation. Additionally, overlords, allies, and subjects of the former king would need to delineate their relationship with the new monarch. Thus, David's initiative to send a delegation to the Ammonite court in the wake of Nahash's death is not surprising. It was, as Japhet called it, "a political act of recognition and a declaration of peaceful intentions" (1993:356). Likewise, the Ammonites' suspicion about David was well-founded in light of ancient Near Eastern history.

The Chronicler (following his source in Samuel) presented David as innocently desiring to "show loyalty" to the new king in light of the historic relationship he had enjoyed with his father, Nahash. The language here ("loyalty," Heb., *khesed* [TH2617, ZH2876]) expresses the vocabulary of ancient Near Eastern state relations (Knoppers 2004:719) and reveals that Nahash and David were allies. Nahash was well-known for his attacks on Israel in the period just prior to the appointment of Saul as king (1 Sam 11:1-11). Interestingly, it was Nahash who was the prototype of the kind of king the Israelites wanted (1 Sam 12:12), a king that would go out before Israel in battle (1 Sam 8:19-20). God's answer to their request was to give them Saul, who would prove his claim to kingship by defeating none other than the prototype, Nahash. When David established friendly relations with Nahash is not known. The motivation may have been that they shared a mutual enemy: Saul.

Unfortunately, Nahash's son Hanun would not continue his father's loyalty to David, and he rebuffed David's show of loyalty. His officials (either military or political) suspected that David was up to something and had sent messengers as spies to evaluate the vulnerabilities of Ammon. Of course, the events of the previous chapter in Chronicles show there were reasons why David was to be feared by his neighbors. The immature Hanun foolishly listened to his advisers (cf. 2 Chr 10:6-14) and proceeded to shave the men and cut their garments in half. As Isaiah 7:20 shows, this shaving probably included all forms of hair on the men's bodies from head to toe; it was a form of official humiliation.[1] By cutting their garments in half they revealed their private areas, another form of shame (see Isa 47:2-3). Hanun's actions were symbolic of his repudiation of David's gesture. The messenger-ambassadors represented David, so what Hanun did to them he did to David. Showing kindness to his messengers, David had them remain in Jericho until their hair grew back. Jericho, which lay just north of the Dead Sea, would have been on the road back from Ammon to Jerusalem.

The First Battle: Joab Defeats the Ammonites and Aramean Mercenaries (19:6-15). Hanun's treatment of these messengers was not just for sport; it was nothing short of a call to war. So immediately the story moves to the preparation for battle. Hanun, however, did not appear to have enough resources to take on David, seen not only in that he had to recruit forces from his towns (19:7) but also because he sent money to hire mercenaries from the Aramean states to the north (Aram-naharaim, Aram-maacah, and Zobah).[2] He was able to secure from the Arameans a significant group of mercenary chariots, as well as the services of the king and army of Aram-maacah. The staging ground for the Ammonite-led expedition was Medeba, which was located in traditional Moabite territory on the Transjordanian Plateau at the same level as Jerusalem (on level with the top of the Dead Sea). This region had been conquered by Israel and would only return to Moabite control in the late ninth century BC (see note on 19:7). In contrast to the depiction of Hanun, the account is silent on any preparations that David needed to undertake to face Hanun, stating simply that David sent Joab and the army to fight the battle.

In 19:9 the narrative moves to the battlefield where the Ammonite-Aramean coalition had taken up their positions, with the mercenaries placed in the open fields and the Ammonites near the entrance to the city. The Arameans would need the open fields to use their chariots to their greatest advantage, while the Ammonites would have wanted the proximity to the city where they could find safety if need be. This positioning, however, also appeared to have been strategic militarily because by spreading out the forces there was the possibility of surrounding Joab's army.

While the depiction of the Ammonites focuses mostly on the gathering of sufficient personnel for the battle, the depiction of the Israelites focuses mostly on the creation of a military strategy. Joab divided his army into two groups. He would lead a group of elite troops into the open fields against the powerful Aramean mercenaries with their chariots, while his brother Abishai (see 18:12-13) would lead the rest of the army against the Ammonites outside the gates of Medeba. The use of dramatic narrative draws us into this section of the story as the two brothers pledge support for one another and for their nation (19:12-13). The final words of Joab in 19:13 highlight the divine dimension of this battle: "May the LORD's will be done."

The battle, however, does not live up to the great expectations of the narrative.

In two short verses we are told that the Arameans retreated, which prompted a retreat into the city by the Ammonites. Without even a drop of blood (at least in the description), the sons of Zeruiah have defeated their enemy; and rather than besiege the city of Medeba, the Israelites return to Jerusalem.

The Second Battle: David Defeats the Arameans (19:16-19). The conflict was not finished because the mercenary Arameans decided to take on David's troops. Realizing the increasing power of their southern enemies, they decided to engage David rather than wait for him to return to their region. The Aramean coalition appeared to be led by the Aramean king Hadadezer of Zobah, who had already suffered defeat at the hands of David (18:3-8). Summoning help from other Aramean kingdoms beyond the Euphrates River, Hadadezer placed the troops under the leadership of his general, Shobach.

This time it appears that the threat to Israel was more serious, because instead of just sending Joab with the standing army, David himself led the army and conscripted troops from the population. The narrator says that they crossed, lit., "the river." While it is possible that David marched all the way to the Euphrates River where the Arameans lived, most likely the Arameans had come down the King's Highway along the Transjordanian Plateau, and David went out to meet them before they crossed the Jordan River to threaten Jerusalem.[3] The battle was a clear victory for David and his troops, as evidenced in the retreat of the Arameans, the death toll of both army and commander, and the surrender and submission of the Arameans to David.

Chapter 19 continues the portrait of David's success in battle. Although this activity will ultimately disqualify him (as a "man of blood") from building the Temple (22:8), these battles secured the peace so Solomon could build the Temple (see further commentary on 22:6-16). These accounts continue to develop the picture of Yahweh's blessing on David but also provide a model for courageous trust in Yahweh, seen especially in the speech of Joab in 19:13: "Be courageous! Let us fight bravely for our people and the cities of our God. May the LORD'S will be done."

ENDNOTES

1. Although David only makes reference to their "beards" growing out in 19:5, this may be just representative of all the hair growing again, avoiding any uncomfortable references.
2. It does not appear that the Ammonites were allies of the Arameans, since Hanun must "hire" them.
3. This is also suggested by the closing words of ch 19, which describe the second battle as also related to Aramean assistance for the Ammonites.

◆ K. David Captures Rabbah; Battles against Philistine Giants (20:1-8)

**In the spring of the year,* when kings nor-
mally go out to war, Joab led the Israelite
army in successful attacks against the
land of the Ammonites. In the process he
laid siege to the city of Rabbah. However,
David stayed behind in Jerusalem.
2When David arrived at Rabbah, he re-
moved the crown from the king's head,*
and it was placed on his own head. The
crown was made of gold and set with
gems, and he found that it weighed
seventy-five pounds.* David took a vast
amount of plunder from the city. 3He also
made slaves of the people of Rabbah and**

forced them to labor with saws, iron picks, and iron axes.* That is how David dealt with the people of all the Ammonite towns. Then David and all the army returned to Jerusalem.

4After this, war broke out with the Philistines at Gezer. As they fought, Sibbecai from Hushah killed Saph,* a descendant of the giants,* and so the Philistines were subdued.

5During another battle with the Philistines, Elhanan son of Jair killed Lahmi, the brother of Goliath of Gath. The handle of Lahmi's spear was as thick as a weaver's beam!

6In another battle with the Philistines at Gath, they encountered a huge man with six fingers on each hand and six toes on each foot, twenty-four in all, who was also a descendant of the giants.
7But when he defied and taunted Israel, he was killed by Jonathan, the son of David's brother Shimea.

8These Philistines were descendants of the giants of Gath, but David and his warriors killed them.

20:1 Hebrew *At the turn of the year.* The first day of the year in the ancient Hebrew lunar calendar occurred in March or April. **20:2a** Or *from the head of Milcom* (as in Greek version and Latin Vulgate). Milcom, also called Molech, was the god of the Ammonites. **20:2b** Hebrew *1 talent* [34 kilograms]. **20:3** As in parallel text at 2 Sam 12:31; Hebrew reads *and cut them with saws, iron picks, and saws.* **20:4a** As in parallel text at 2 Sam 21:18; Hebrew reads *Sippai.* **20:4b** Hebrew *descendant of the Rephaites;* also in 20:6, 8.

NOTES

20:1 *In the spring of the year.* Heb., *le'eth* [TH6256, ZH6961] *teshubath hashanah* (lit., "at the time of the turning of the year")—that is, according to the ancient Hebrew calendar, in which the new year occurred in March/April, as opposed to the later calendar adopted from the Babylonians, in which the new year occurred in August/September.

Rabbah. This was the capital of the ancient kingdom of Ammon, just over 40 miles northeast of Jerusalem on the Transjordanian Plateau.

20:2 *the king's head.* As the NLT mg suggests, this could also be a reference to the chief god of the Ammonites, Milcom/Molech, whose name shares the same consonants as the Hebrew word for "king." Molech is mentioned eight times in the OT, often in relationship to an idolatrous cultic rite in which one would sacrifice a child to Molech through fire.

20:4 *Gezer.* In 2 Sam 21:18 the name of this city is "Gob." Possibly this was originally Gibbethon, a site of Philistine-Israelite conflict, near Gezer (1 Kgs 15:27; 16:15; see ABD 2.1041). Gezer was situated in the Judean Shephelah approximately 20 miles west of Jerusalem. The Shephelah was an area often cited in interactions between Philistia and Israel (Samson and Delilah, David and Goliath) because it was the transitional territory between the low-lying Coastal Plain (typically dominated by the Philistines) and the higher Judean Hills (occupied by Israelites). Gezer would be given to Solomon as a dowry gift by Pharaoh (1 Kgs 9:16), and it would become one of Solomon's key fortified cities (1 Kgs 9:15-17) because of its location on a key west-east route and proximity (7 miles) to the key north-south route (Great Trunk Road).

Sibbecai from Hushah killed Saph. Hushah was probably located about 4 miles west of Bethlehem on a ridge overlooking the Shephelah; it was home also of Mebunnai (2 Sam 23:27, NLT mg), one of the "Thirty." Sibbecai's feat qualified him to be a commander in David's army (27:1, 11).

giants. Heb., *repa'im* [TH7497, ZH8328]. This term is used for two different groups in the OT: (1) for departed spirits in the underworld (Job 26:5; Isa 14:9); (2) for a tall people group in Palestine (Gen 14:5; 15:20; Deut 2:11, 20; 3:11; Josh 12:4; 13:12). It is this latter group that is in view here, but it is not certain whether this term came to be associated with tall people in general or whether there was a belief that they were literal descendants of the Rephaim.

were subdued. Heb., *kana'* [TH3665, ZH4044]. See note on 18:1.

20:5 ***Lahmi, the brother of Goliath.*** Second Samuel 21:19, a parallel verse, reads only "Goliath." Some have explained this as the Chronicler's attempt to harmonize two claims found in Samuel regarding the death of Goliath (Knoppers 2004:736). In 1 Sam 17:50 David kills Goliath, while in 2 Sam 21:19 (see NLT mg) Elhanan killed Goliath. However, it may be that 20:5 preserves the original reading and 2 Sam 21:19 contains a scribal error that turned the name of Goliath's brother (Lahmi) into the town Bethlehem (*beth hallakhmi* [TH1022, ZH1095]).

Gath. This was one of the five Philistine cities that controlled the Coastal Plain. In the Davidic traditions it is associated with tall warriors, including Goliath, Lahmi, as well as unnamed others.

weaver's beam. See note on 11:23.

20:6 ***giants.*** See note on 20:4.

COMMENTARY

First Chronicles 20:1 is unlike the previous two section introductions in chapters 18–20. First Chronicles 18:1 and 19:1 begin with *wayehi 'akhare-ken* [TH310/3651A, ZH339/4027] (some time after this), a phrase that will also be used in 20:4. In 20:1, however, the introductory phrase is simply *wayehi* [TH1961, ZH2118] (and it was), followed by the designation of time: "in the spring of the year, when kings normally go out to war." In this the Chronicler was following his source material in Samuel.

David Captures Rabbah in Ammon (20:1-3). The war instigated by Hanun in chapter 19 is finally brought to a conclusion here at the outset of chapter 20. In the first phase (19:6-15) David had sent Joab and his brother Abishai to deal with the Ammonites' rejection of David's gesture of goodwill at the death of Hanun's father, King Nahash. Hanun quickly mobilized a combined force of Ammonite warriors and Aramean mercenaries, but they were no match for the skilled Israelite force. With the Arameans retreating to the north and the Ammonites taking cover behind city walls, Joab simply returned to Jerusalem. He probably did not have the men or resources to chase the Arameans into their own territory nor to sustain a prolonged siege of the city. Now, however, under the ideal conditions at the turn of the year in the spring, with his forces rested, Joab returned to Ammon to complete his mission. The Chronicler retained the note that David remained in Jerusalem, a note that in his source (2 Sam 11–12) introduced the intrigue of the Bathsheba incident. This incident, however, is left out by the Chronicler, who was presenting a pristine portrait of the victorious David. Also left out of this account is the message Joab sent back to David, calling the king to join him in Ammon lest he take the capital city of Rabbah and receive the glory (2 Sam 12:27-29).[1] For the Chronicler's depiction of David there can be no challenge to David's glory in victory.[2]

Upon his arrival at Rabbah, royal seat of Ammon, David took the crown and placed it on his own head. It is uncertain whether this crown was found on the head of the king (Hanun) or on the head of an idol dedicated to Molech, their chief god. In either case, this action was symbolic of his new control over the Transjordanian kingdom. The crown and other valuables were taken as spoil from the city. David, however, did more than just plunder the city. He made the people of the city his slaves for menial labor with saws, iron picks, and iron axes.

The account ends in similar fashion to the earlier Ammonite episode, but this time it was David rather than Joab at the head of an army returning to Jerusalem (19:15; 20:3).

David Battles the Giants of Philistia (20:4-8). In the transition from 20:3 to 20:4, the Chronicler skipped over a substantial portion of his source in the book of Samuel (2 Sam 13:1–21:14). This section of the book of Samuel recites the aftermath of David's sin with Bathsheba, dire consequences that would involve incest, murder, and treason within the house of David. Also excised is 2 Samuel 21:15-17, a section that exposes David's weakness as a warrior and relates his men prohibiting him from the battlefield. These omissions by the Chronicler keep the focus on the positive aspects of David's reign. As Knoppers (2004:739) has so aptly written:

> *The author's work does not minimize David's private, familial, and state struggles; it gives no attention to them whatsoever. . . . This means that David never faces a domestic challenge to his authority. Nor does the body politic ever divide into factions. Once acclaimed by all Israel at the inception of his rule (11:1-3), David never loses his people's undivided support.*

The final section of chapters 18–20 focuses on the ability of David's men to defeat the mighty Philistine giants, first Saph at Gezer, then Lahmi (brother of Goliath) at an unspecified location, and finally an unnamed Philistine giant at Gath. This is a fitting end to the entire military section that followed the covenant ceremony between God and David in chapter 17. The section began (18:1) with David's conquering Gath and its towns, and now it ends (20:6) with his defeat of the mightiest of the Philistine warriors—with the final episode at the city of Gath again. The intertwining of the fates of David and Gath's giants are key to the Davidic tradition in the Old Testament; from this comes one of the most memorable of all stories, that of David and Goliath.

As in chapters 18–19, so here in chapter 20 the Chronicler continues to highlight the success of David's military exploits. The Chronicler presents David's rule over the nations, with the closing focus on giants, thereby reminding the reader that those who trust in Yahweh need not fear even the most powerful human forces. The military accounts in these chapters are not only essential to build a picture of a peaceful kingdom in which Solomon will be free to build the Temple, but also to provide background for chapter 21, where David will foolishly request a census of his fighting forces. By the end of chapter 21 David will face a divine foe, Yahweh, who will discipline him for his folly.

ENDNOTES

1. Knoppers (2004:729-730) argues that the account of Joab's message to David in Jerusalem was lost in the scribal tradition (based on the LXX cursive manuscripts i and j and the MT 2 Sam 12:27-29). However, Japhet (1993:362-363) favors the shorter version.
2. The phrase "When David arrived at Rabbah" is not found in the Hebrew text but is added by the translators of the NLT to smooth the transition from 20:1 to 20:2.

◆ L. David Takes a Census (21:1–22:1)

Satan rose up against Israel and caused
David to take a census of the people of
Israel. 2So David said to Joab and the
commanders of the army, "Take a census
of all the people of Israel—from Beersheba
in the south to Dan in the north—and
bring me a report so I may know how
many there are."
3But Joab replied, "May the LORD in-
crease the number of his people a hun-
dred times over! But why, my lord the
king, do you want to do this? Are they not
all your servants? Why must you cause
Israel to sin?"
4But the king insisted that they take the
census, so Joab traveled throughout all Is-
rael to count the people. Then he returned
to Jerusalem 5and reported the number of
people to David. There were 1,100,000
warriors in all Israel who could handle a
sword, and 470,000 in Judah. 6But Joab did
not include the tribes of Levi and Benjamin
in the census because he was so distressed
at what the king had made him do.

7God was very displeased with the cen-
sus, and he punished Israel for it. 8Then
David said to God, "I have sinned greatly
by taking this census. Please forgive my
guilt for doing this foolish thing."
9Then the LORD spoke to Gad, David's
seer. This was the message: 10"Go and say
to David, 'This is what the LORD says: I will
give you three choices. Choose one of these
punishments, and I will inflict it on you.'"
11So Gad came to David and said, "These
are the choices the LORD has given you.
12You may choose three years of famine,
three months of destruction by the sword
of your enemies, or three days of severe
plague as the angel of the LORD brings
devastation throughout the land of Israel.
Decide what answer I should give the LORD
who sent me."
13"I'm in a desperate situation!" David
replied to Gad. "But let me fall into the
hands of the LORD, for his mercy is very
great. Do not let me fall into human
hands."
14So the LORD sent a plague upon Israel,
and 70,000 people died as a result. 15And
God sent an angel to destroy Jerusalem.
But just as the angel was preparing to de-
stroy it, the LORD relented and said to the
death angel, "Stop! That is enough!" At
that moment the angel of the LORD was
standing by the threshing floor of Arau-
nah* the Jebusite.
16David looked up and saw the angel of
the LORD standing between heaven and
earth with his sword drawn, reaching out
over Jerusalem. So David and the leaders
of Israel put on burlap to show their deep
distress and fell face down on the ground.
17And David said to God, "I am the one
who called for the census! I am the one
who has sinned and done wrong! But
these people are as innocent as sheep—
what have they done? O LORD my God, let
your anger fall against me and my family,
but do not destroy your people."

18Then the angel of the LORD told Gad
to instruct David to go up and build an
altar to the LORD on the threshing floor of
Araunah the Jebusite. 19So David went up
to do what the LORD had commanded him
through Gad. 20Araunah, who was busy
threshing wheat at the time, turned and
saw the angel there. His four sons, who
were with him, ran away and hid. 21When
Araunah saw David approaching, he left
his threshing floor and bowed before Da-
vid with his face to the ground.
22David said to Araunah, "Let me buy
this threshing floor from you at its full
price. Then I will build an altar to the LORD
there, so that he will stop the plague."
23"Take it, my lord the king, and use it as
you wish," Araunah said to David. "I will
give the oxen for the burnt offerings, and
the threshing boards for wood to build a
fire on the altar, and the wheat for the
grain offering. I will give it all to you."
24But King David replied to Araunah,
"No, I insist on buying it for the full price.
I will not take what is yours and give
it to the LORD. I will not present burnt

offerings that have cost me nothing!"
[25]So David gave Araunah 600 pieces of
gold* in payment for the threshing floor.
[26]David built an altar there to the LORD
and sacrificed burnt offerings and peace
offerings. And when David prayed, the
LORD answered him by sending fire from
heaven to burn up the offering on the al-
tar. [27]Then the LORD spoke to the angel,
who put the sword back into its sheath.
[28]When David saw that the LORD had
answered his prayer, he offered sacrifices
there at Araunah's threshing floor. [29]At
that time the Tabernacle of the LORD and
the altar of burnt offering that Moses had
made in the wilderness were located at
the place of worship in Gibeon. [30]But
David was not able to go there to inquire
of God, because he was terrified by the
drawn sword of the angel of the LORD.

CHAPTER 22

Then David said, "This will be the location for the Temple of the LORD God and the place of the altar for Israel's burnt offerings!"

21:15 As in parallel text at 2 Sam 24:16; Hebrew reads *Ornan*, another name for Araunah; also in 21:18-28. **21:25** Hebrew *600 shekels of gold*, about 15 pounds or 6.8 kilograms in weight.

NOTES

21:2 ***Beersheba . . . Dan.*** These are the traditional southern and northern extents of the land of Israel. Beersheba, approximately 45 miles south of Jerusalem, is the farthest south that will sustain agriculture before the water dissipates into the dry Negev. Dan, approximately 105 miles north of Jerusalem, is situated at one of the water sources of the Jordan.

21:9 ***Gad, David's seer.*** The key terms for prophets in the OT are "man of God" (*'ish ha'elohim* [TH376/430, ZH408/466]), "prophet" (*nabi'* [TH5030, ZH5566]), and "seer" (*khozeh* [TH2374, ZH2602] and *ro'eh* [TH7200A, ZH8014]). The first term reveals the close contact the prophet enjoyed with the divine realm, the second most likely is related to the prophet's spoken ministry, and the last to the means of revelation through sight. Here Gad is referred to as *khozeh,* but the fact that he is "David's" reveals his role within the court setting.

21:15 ***Araunah the Jebusite.*** The Jebusites were the inhabitants of Jerusalem prior to David's conquering of the city. His threshing floor was located on a higher hilltop outside the city walls.

21:18 ***threshing floor.*** The process of threshing involved drying the cut grain, beating with flails (Judg 6:11; Ruth 2:17) or crushing with a threshing sledge (Isa 28:27; 41:15), and finally winnowing the grain to separate the husks (chaff) from the grain (Isa 30:24; Jer 15:7). Ideal for a threshing floor was a flat rock surface able to accommodate driving a threshing sledge over the grain prior to winnowing. The location of Araunah's floor on a hilltop above the original City of David would have been ideal for this process because the natural wind flow could assist in the threshing process, blowing away the lighter chaff (cf. Gen 50:10; Judg 6:37; Ruth 3:14; 2 Sam 24:21).

21:26 ***fire from heaven.*** This was a sign of God's acceptance of the sacrifice. See other instances of God sending fire from heaven in Lev 9:24; 1 Kgs 18:37-38.

21:29 ***Tabernacle of the LORD.*** See 16:39-42.

Gibeon. See note on 16:39 and commentary on 8:29-40.

COMMENTARY

In the substantial presentation of the successful military exploits of David in chapters 18–20, the Chronicler provides the first evidence that God's promises in the dynastic oracle of chapter 17 are being fulfilled. Chapter 21 continues the martial focus, as

David forces his general Joab to take a census of his people, an enumeration that has as its purpose military strategy (see 21:5). This military focus, however, is soon left behind as the Chronicler begins the transition to his substantial presentation of David's preparing for the Temple building.

Most researchers have noted the way in which the Chronicler eliminated David's personal, family, and national crises in his account (cf. chs 18–20 with 2 Sam 8–21 and see my comments on 20:4-8). Thus, it may seem odd to some that the Chronicler would include David's census debacle. However, it is actually one of two failures of David that the Chronicler includes in his account, the first being the failed attempt to bring the Ark into Jerusalem (ch 13).[1] In that case, the Chronicler located the failure of David in his naive inattention to priestly ritual when transporting the Ark. In the end David acted as a priestly leader who sacrificed burnt and peace offerings (16:1-2). In the present case in chapter 21, which also leads to death among the people, the Chronicler again locates the failure of David in his naiveté over a matter of priestly ritual related to a census. So, again, David acts as a priestly leader who again sacrifices burnt and peace offerings (21:26). David fails twice in the Chronicler's account, but both times these failures are key to the development of Jerusalem as Israel's central place of worship, and in both cases David emerges as a royal priest who intercedes on behalf of the people. These two incidents are essential to David's preparation of Jerusalem as the central place of worship in Israel. First Chronicles 21 is particularly important because this incident isolates the location of the Temple and its altar, with their attendant practices of prayer and sacrifice. For the Chronicler, even David's failure turns to gold (Duke 1990:59-60).

David Enticed to Count the People (21:1-6). The account opens with Satan's causing David to count his people. A comparison with the Chronicler's source in 2 Samuel 24 reveals significant changes that can be seen more clearly by observing the two side by side in literal translation (author's translation):

Then Satan took a stand against Israel, and he incited/enticed David to count Israel. (1 Chr 21:1)	Again the anger of the Lord burned against Israel, and he incited/enticed David against them, saying, "Go, count Israel and Judah." (2 Sam 24:1)

The book of Samuel traces the ultimate cause of this enumeration to the Lord, whose anger moved him to incite David against Israel. For God's anger to burn against Israel assumes that Israel had disobeyed the Lord, even if no evidence of such disobedience is offered in 2 Samuel. This statement in 2 Samuel 24:1 is theologically awkward for many because of its depiction of God inciting someone to sin in order to bring punishment on others. It may be this very awkwardness that led to the Chronicler's version. The Chronicler removed all references to the Lord and replaced them with a figure called "Satan," who took his stand against Israel so that David was incited/enticed to count Israel.

Much controversy has raged around the identity of this "Satan" figure in 21:1. The word *satan* is actually a Hebrew word that means "adversary." It appears in the Old Testament usually in connection with both military and legal contexts, that is, the figure called *satan* functions either as a military opponent (1 Sam 29:4; 1 Kgs 5:4

[18]; 11:14, 23, 25) or as an opponent in court, possibly even the ancient equivalent of the prosecuting attorney (Ps 109:6; cf. 2 Sam 19:22-23).

This word, however, is also linked to heavenly beings in the Old Testament. In the early narratives of Job, one of the "sons of God" (heavenly beings with access to the divine court) is called *satan* (Job 1:6-9, 12; 2:1-4, 6-7). There this figure fulfills the role of moving throughout the earth as the other heavenly beings. His report to God, however, reveals a strong negative stance toward the human being named Job. In contrast, God defends Job. In similar fashion, a figure called *satan* appears in what seems to be a divine legal court scene in Zechariah 3. Jeshua the high priest is standing before the angel of the Lord, and to Jeshua's right is a figure accusing him, while God defends the human. Finally, Numbers 22:22-23 describes God's anger toward Balaam for responding to Balak's request to curse Israel. As a result of his displeasure with Balaam, God sends the angel of the Lord "as a satan" to block Balaam's way.

This evidence reveals that the term *satan* can be used of either human or divine beings and indicates a role of opposition, usually in military or legal contexts. It is not surprising, then, that interpreters of 21:1 have identified here two options for understanding the *satan* figure. First, it may refer to a human military adversary whose opposition prompted David to count his troops as a preparation for an imminent military battle.[2] Key evidence for this view is the fact that the previous three chapters in 1 Chronicles have been focused on descriptions of David's military exploits and, additionally, that the phrase "rose up against" in 21:1 (*'amad* [TH5975, ZH6641] + *'al* [TH5921, ZH6584]) is used in 2 Chronicles 20:23 to describe a military maneuver. Second, the *satan* figure in 21:1 may refer to a heavenly being who enticed David to count the people.[3] Key evidence for this view is the fact that the phrase *'amad* + *'al* ("rose up against," 21:1) is used in connection with the heavenly *satan* figure in Zechariah 3, and the verb *suth* [TH5496, ZH6077] ("entice/incite"; NLT, "caused") is used in connection with the same figure in Job 1–2 (Job 2:3). In addition, the angel of the Lord in Numbers 22:22-23 is sent as a *satan* against Balaam as an expression of the "anger" (*'ap* [TH639, ZH678]) of God, which "burned" (*kharah* [TH2734, ZH3013]), and in 21:1, the Chronicler has replaced the term "anger" (*'ap*) of the Lord (which "burned," *kharah*) from 2 Samuel 24 with *satan*. This evidence, along with the fact that there is no evidence for an impending battle in chapter 21, strongly suggests that the Chronicler, uncomfortable with the theological implications of his source, reworked the text guided by Numbers 22:22-23.

This conclusion, however, does not give clarity to the identity of this figure. It is not certain if this figure is a heavenly being or whether it is the "Satan" that later Second Temple Judaism and Christianity identified as the archenemy of God.[4] In Numbers 22 the "satan" is clearly identified as the "angel of the LORD," who is carrying out God's wrathful judgment. In Zechariah 3 and Job 1–2, the figure takes a negative stance toward human beings, challenging and accusing them before God, and as a result is rebuked by God. Nevertheless, the figure has access to God's divine court and presence and appears to have some kind of function within it. In the case of chapter 21, it appears that the Chronicler saw this figure as the one who carried out the will of God, in this case his judgment.

Another controversy surrounding this passage has centered on the evaluation of the census that was undertaken. Traditionally, it has been argued that the very act of counting the people was against God's will and that David was wrong to undertake this action. Wright, however, offers a radically different perspective on this issue, arguing that there was nothing wrong with David's desire to count the people. The cause of divine displeasure was Joab's failure to complete David's command to count the people. By leaving out the Benjaminites and Levites, Joab endangered Israel, for Benjamin comprised "one-half of the military strength of the Davidic king" and Levi comprised the "theological heart" of Israel (Wright 1993:96). Thus, while many see chapter 21 as unique in Chronicles for its depiction of David's failure, Wright is able to claim:

> *The David of 1 Chronicles 21, therefore, is not an aberration in the Chronicler's idealized picture of Judah's founding king. Divinely-chosen, crowned by popular acclaim, cultically beyond suspicion, victorious in battle, the David of 1 Chronicles heroically offers to accept undeserved divine wrath to save the people of Israel. David's reign falls short of no one's in the history of Judah. (1993:104)*

The strength of Wright's argument lies in his revelation that counting people and military personnel is viewed as normative behavior throughout Chronicles (7:2, 40; 9:1; 11:11 [using the same term as 21:5]; 12:24; 23:3; 2 Chr 2:17; 17:13b-19; 25:5; 26:11-13).[5] Thus, he concludes, "The Chronicler never attaches culpability to the royal right to enroll the citizenry into a military force. Indeed, the ability of the king to take a census indicates the king's firm control over the army that is necessary to pursue the military interests of the kingdom" (Wright 1993:92).

The weakness, however, lies in how Wright shifts the blame from David to Joab. Wright is correct that the phrase in 21:7, translated in the NLT as "God was very displeased with the census," is not so specific, merely saying, "God was very displeased with this thing" (*haddabar hazzeh*). The referent of "this thing," he argues, is the failure of Joab to complete the count in 21:6, rather than (as assumed in the NLT) David's command to count. However, in 21:8 this exact phrase is used again (*haddabar hazzeh;* NLT, "by taking this census"), but "this thing" is clearly identified as something that David did (lit., "I have sinned when I did this thing, but now, take away the guilt of your servant because I have behaved very foolishly").[6] Furthermore, David's confession in 21:17 clearly identifies him as the guilty party and his call for the census as the cause of the judgment (Bailey 1994:89).

It appears, then, that David was presented as guilty for ordering the census in this passage. But why would this be wrong in this case, while it is not wrong in the rest of Chronicles, as Wright contends? One answer may be that there was concern over counting all Israel because they were, according to the promise to Abraham, "uncountable" (Gen 15:5). Another answer may be that to count them would be putting one's trust in human military might rather than in the assistance of the Lord of Heaven's Armies, who fights on behalf of Israel. These concerns, however, do not appear to be the case according to the Chronicler's later comments on the event in 27:23-24.

The answer to this dilemma has been offered by the recent work of Johnstone, who maintains that the error was not in counting, but rather in failing to perform the appropriate rituals (Exod 30:11-16; Johnstone 1998:128-140). The Torah is clear that when a census is taken in Israel, atonement money of a half shekel was required for each person over 20 years old who was counted. This offering was to be used for the service of the Tent of Meeting. According to the legislation, lack of attention to this ritual would risk a plague among the people. The Chronicler incorporated the census incident into his account from his Samuel source with the assumption of these priestly rituals.[7]

Joab was instructed to count "all the people of Israel" from the far south (Beersheba) to the far north (Dan) and to return to David with the numbers. Joab acted as a foil for David, one who reminded him that this course of action was folly and would lead to sin. Notice that the one who was in danger of sinning is identified as "Israel" (21:3), a reference to the legislation that each Israelite was responsible for the ransom price in the case of a census.

David refused to listen to the warning and sent Joab on his way throughout the land. He returned to the king with a figure of those "who could handle a sword," an indication that this census was for military purposes, in line with the martial context of this phase of the Chronicler's account. The Chronicler noted that Joab sought to avert the wrath of God by secretly leaving out two tribes in his numbering. This reveals his ignorance of the priestly legislation, which demands ransom money (Exod 30:12). Possibly he was concerned that the census might decimate the army, and thus he left out the tribes of Benjamin and Levi to ensure a sufficient remnant for the army (see Wright's approach above).

God's Judgment on David's Sin (21:7-14). First Chronicles 21:7 appears to function as a proleptic description of 21:8-15—that is, it is not describing an initial punishment in 21:7, which is then followed by further punishment in 21:8-15, but rather offers a global description of God's punishment, the details of which are then offered in 21:8-15.[8] How David was informed of God's displeasure is uncertain, but the narrative presents David as approaching God for forgiveness. He admits his sin and begs for God's forgiveness, a powerful example of piety (cf. Knoppers 1995:449-470).[9] David's cry is answered immediately by the Lord through the prophet Gad, who is identified as one of David's court prophets ("David's seer"). The verses in 21:9-10 are distinct from 21:11-13. They describe the speech God gave Gad to declare to David. Here we see the direct speech of command ("choose") and the use of first person ("I") for God and second person ("you") for David. In contrast, 21:11-12 describes Gad's subsequent interaction with David in which God is now spoken about in the third person. Here we see an example of the prophetic revelatory process in action (Boda 2001:186-197). The prophet's responsibility was to approach God for messages for his people. These were then relayed to the person/people. Although it appears that usually these messages were relayed verbatim back to the person/people, in this case it appears that the prophet offered a summary of the message.

Gad offered David three options for God's judgment: three years of famine, three months of military defeat by his enemies, or three days of plague by the angel of the Lord. These three forms of judgment are typical in Chronicles, appearing in both Solomon's prayer in 2 Chronicles 6:28 and Jehoshaphat's prayer in 2 Chronicles

20:9. Rather than choosing one of the three, David eliminates only one and allows God to choose between the first and third options, deciding to throw himself upon the character of God ("for his mercy is very great"), a decision that is not disappointed. God followed through on his word, sending a plague that has a devastating effect on Israel. This third option is temporally the shortest of the three, but is also the most lethal because its source was the mighty angel of the Lord. This incident reveals the serious ramifications of sin and the impact that such sin had upon the entire community of Israel.

To some readers, God's response with choices of punishment is at odds with David's request for forgiveness. However, there is plenty of precedence elsewhere in the Old Testament for this. For instance, in Numbers 14 Moses pleads for forgiveness from Yahweh (Num 14:17-19) because of the people's refusal to conquer the land. Yahweh responded with the promise to pardon them as requested (Num 14:20), but then declares his punishment on the rebels (Num 14:21-23; cf. Exod 32:30-35). Sklar (2005:91-92) explains, "The Lord does forgive them: he does not wipe them out completely . . . this forgiveness does not mean the remission of all penalty . . . a mitigated penalty is placed upon the people: instead of completely wiping them out, the Lord 'smites' some of them." In the same way, David's sin had serious consequences for his kingdom, but there is forgiveness, which is a mitigation of the penalty deserved (cf. Sklar 2005:53, see his notes 33-34).[10]

David's Intercession for Jerusalem (21:15-27). As the angel of the Lord was about to destroy Jerusalem, the Lord relented and stopped the plague. First Chronicles 21:15a functions in the same way as 21:7, offering a proleptic overview of what is to come in 21:15b-27. The overview in 21:15a describes God's commanding the death angel to stop, but this is actually the outcome of the story, and it is repeated at the very end in 21:27. What is provided in 21:15b-26 (beginning with "at that moment") is the event that prompted the outpouring of God's mercy.

God's great mercy is manifested at the moment the death angel was hovering with sword drawn over Jerusalem. That God's compassion wells up at this very moment points to the preciousness of Jerusalem to the Lord. This may be linked to the Ark of his presence now being housed in this city or that the king after his own heart was enthroned there. In either case, it is indicative of an enduring tradition of Jerusalem's special status before the Lord (Zech 1:12-17; 2:12; 3:2). This is important to the theology of the Chronicler, who was addressing a community whose key unifying symbol was Jerusalem and its Temple.

The precise location of the angel of the Lord was "the threshing floor of Araunah the Jebusite," which was located above Jerusalem on a hill that overlooked the city. This location is very important because on this spot the Temple would be built. The position of the angel is described as "between heaven and earth." In Hebrew this phrase is actually "between earth and heaven," an expression that occurs in two other cases in the Old Testament: Zechariah 5:9 and Ezekiel 8:3. "In all three cases this region appears to designate a neutral zone where heavenly beings are able to carry out their mission unimpeded by earth's inhabitants" (Boda 2004:307).

Thus, with the angel poised and equipped for destruction, David and the leaders of Israel don the clothing ("burlap") and assume the posture ("fell face down on the ground") of prayer to God in distress. Although the leaders were there, David's voice alone was heard. He admitted his responsibility for the fiasco and confessed his sin. Exonerating the people, David asked for God's anger to fall upon him and his family. This intercessory cry reveals David's role as mediator between God and his people, even though it meant great risk to himself and his family.

Instead of striking down David and his family, the angel of the Lord informed Gad of God's plan.[11] As the prophet had offered insight into God's judgment, so now the same one offers guidance for mercy. David was to build an altar at the same spot where the angel of the Lord was presently poised to bring destruction on Jerusalem. David approached Araunah and his four fearful sons, and he bought his threshing floor from him at full price. There David built the altar where he sacrificed both burnt and peace offerings, the same offerings he offered in Jerusalem when the Ark finally came to a rest (16:1). The sacrifice was accompanied by prayer, reminding the reader that the Temple will ultimately be a location of both prayer and sacrifice. God's answer through fire from heaven not only reveals his acceptance of the offering on the altar, but also identifies this altar with the Tabernacle altar. Leviticus 9:24 reveals that when the priests first used the new altar at the Tabernacle, the Lord sent fire to consume the offering (see Knoppers 2004:759). First Chronicles 21:27-28 shows that the reason behind God's halting of the plague was his mercy prompted by David's prayer and sacrifice to him. This account underscores the overall scheme of the Chronicler's plan to reveal David as an exemplary figure of repentance; it also accentuates the role of Temple services for penitence. As Knoppers (2004:764) has noted, "The David of the census story is a person of confession and supplication par excellence, a human sinner who repents, seeks forgiveness, intercedes on behalf of his people, and ultimately secures the site of the future Temple."

From the Tabernacle in Gibeon to the Temple in Jerusalem (21:28–22:1). The Chronicler employs the story in chapter 21 to highlight David's role in the preparations for building the Temple. Although David was barred from building the Temple (see ch 17) because he was a man of blood and war (chs 18–20), the Chronicler will show the ways in which David's passion for the Temple could not be repressed. David's involvement in the choice of the site for the Temple is depicted in chapter 21; this will be followed in the succeeding chapters with many other details related to his preparations.

First Chronicles 21:28–22:1 is a key segue in the Chronicler's work. It functions both as a postscript to the census debacle as well as an introduction to the material that will consume the rest of 1 Chronicles. The Chronicler acknowledges the extraordinary nature of David's offering sacrifices away from the altar of burnt offering at the Tabernacle at Gibeon. This sacrifice was necessary because of the events that unfolded in chapter 21. It was this exceptional action of sacrifice that was key to the identification of the site for Temple building, as David declares in 22:1: "This will be the location for the Temple of the LORD God and the place of the altar for Israel's burnt offerings!"

The only two passages in the Chronicler's account of David that depict the king's failures are chapter 21 and chapter 13. Both cases are related to key phases in Jerusalem's becoming the location of Yahweh's Temple. In the first (ch 13), it is the transportation of the Ark into the city. Here, in the second instance, David's failure leads to the identification of the site of the altar and Temple. What this account reminds the reader of is the centrality of sacrifice and prayer for the Temple. In addition, even in his failure David is presented as normative for the Chronicler's audience: a repentant sinner who seeks atonement through sacrifice.

ENDNOTES

1. See the superb interlinking of chs 13 and 21 by Bailey (1999:358-359).
2. See Knoppers 2004; Wright 1993:93. Wright identifies the *satan* as "an anonymous enemy that attacks Israel, an unanticipated foe who threatens Israel's national security." For a direct critique of Wright, see Bailey 1994:83-90.
3. See the excellent treatment of P. Evans 2005:545-558.
4. See further Boda 2004:249-269. Even this needs to be carefully nuanced. In the NT "Satan" is used by God to fulfill his purposes. Jesus tells Peter that Satan has asked permission to sift him as wheat and that Jesus has allowed such. Paul speaks about a thorn in the flesh that was given to him by God, but which is described as "a messenger of Satan." Notice also how Jesus refers to Peter as "Satan" in Matt 16:23.
5. Also note Numbers 1, 26, where counting is not a problem.
6. Wright calls the use of *haddabar hazzeh* in 21:8 "very generic" after making it very specific in his evaluation of 21:7.
7. See also Bailey (1999:337-359), who draws on the earlier work of Elmslie (1916) to explain why the sin of David stained the people as well. Elmslie points to Lev 4:3, which resonates with the vocabulary of 21:3. This would strengthen the Chronicler's presentation of David as a priestly figure.
8. So also De Vries 1989:171; Williamson 1982:145, much like the function of Gen 1:1 in the account of creation; see Waltke 1991:2-10; Waltke and Fredricks 2001.
9. Abadie (2003:96) notes how Manasseh reflects this piety in a later generation (see 2 Chr 33).
10. Sklar (2005) leverages this understanding of forgiveness through mitigated penalty for understanding the role of sacrifice within ancient Israel.
11. P. Evans (2005:551) wisely highlights this change by the Chronicler to his Samuel source. The Chronicler emphasizes the role of heavenly intermediaries.

◆ M. Preparations for the Temple (22:2-19)

**2 So David gave orders to call together the
foreigners living in Israel, and he assigned
them the task of preparing finished stone
for building the Temple of God. 3 David
provided large amounts of iron for the
nails that would be needed for the doors
in the gates and for the clamps, and he
gave more bronze than could be weighed.
4 He also provided innumerable cedar logs,
for the men of Tyre and Sidon had brought
vast amounts of cedar to David.
5 David said, "My son Solomon is still
young and inexperienced. And since the
Temple to be built for the LORD must be a
magnificent structure, famous and glorious throughout the world, I will begin
making preparations for it now." So David
collected vast amounts of building materials before his death.
6 Then David sent for his son Solomon
and instructed him to build a Temple for
the LORD, the God of Israel. 7 "My son, I
wanted to build a Temple to honor the
name of the LORD my God," David told him.**

8"But the LORD said to me, 'You have killed many men in the battles you have fought. And since you have shed so much blood in my sight, you will not be the one to build a Temple to honor my name. 9But you will have a son who will be a man of peace. I will give him peace with his enemies in all the surrounding lands. His name will be Solomon,* and I will give peace and quiet to Israel during his reign. 10He is the one who will build a Temple to honor my name. He will be my son, and I will be his father. And I will secure the throne of his kingdom over Israel forever.'

11"Now, my son, may the LORD be with you and give you success as you follow his directions in building the Temple of the LORD your God. 12And may the LORD give you wisdom and understanding, that you may obey the Law of the LORD your God as you rule over Israel. 13For you will be successful if you carefully obey the decrees and regulations that the LORD gave to Israel through Moses. Be strong and courageous; do not be afraid or lose heart!

14"I have worked hard to provide materials for building the Temple of the LORD—nearly 4,000 tons of gold, 40,000 tons of silver,* and so much iron and bronze that it cannot be weighed. I have also gathered timber and stone for the walls, though you may need to add more. 15You have a large number of skilled stonemasons and carpenters and craftsmen of every kind. 16You have expert goldsmiths and silversmiths and workers of bronze and iron. Now begin the work, and may the LORD be with you!"

17Then David ordered all the leaders of Israel to assist Solomon in this project. 18"The LORD your God is with you," he declared. "He has given you peace with the surrounding nations. He has handed them over to me, and they are now subject to the LORD and his people. 19Now seek the LORD your God with all your heart and soul. Build the sanctuary of the LORD God so that you can bring the Ark of the LORD's Covenant and the holy vessels of God into the Temple built to honor the LORD's name."

22:9 *Solomon* sounds like and is probably derived from the Hebrew word for "peace." **22:14** Hebrew *100,000 talents* [3,400 metric tons] *of gold, 1,000,000 talents* [34,000 metric tons] *of silver.*

NOTES

22:2 *foreigners.* These were temporary foreign dwellers in the land with limited rights protected under the law.

finished stone. Lit., "stones of hewing," that is, stones that have been hewed. Although banned from use on altars in Israel (Exod 20:25; Deut 27:5-6), nothing is said of their use in temples.

22:4 *Tyre and Sidon.* Acquiring cedar logs from the Phoenicians is not only a prominent theme in temple-building texts in the OT but also throughout the ancient Near East (Boda 2006c). Their cedar forests were legendary.

22:5 *young and inexperienced.* Lit., "young and frail" (cf. 29:1). At his accession Solomon was around 20 years old. The same phrase is used of Solomon's son Rehoboam in 2 Chr 13:7.

22:14 *nearly 4,000 tons of gold, 40,000 tons of silver.* Cf. NLT mg. The numbers here are extravagant to highlight the great expense to which David went to support the project. Interestingly, the Letter of Gilgamesh speaks of a request for 120,000 talents (about 4,800 tons) of some kind of metal (see Gurney 1957:127-136; Kraus 1980:109-121). Concerning the high numbers, see commentary on 12:23-40.

22:19 *the holy vessels of God.* Better, "the vessels of the sanctuary of God" (cf. Num 3:31). These vessels (or utensils) were all those items that were dedicated to God and placed within the sanctuary or surrounding courts (Num 4:15; 18:3; 31:6).

COMMENTARY

With David's declaration of the identification of the site of the Temple and altar still ringing in his readers' ears (22:1), the Chronicler quickly moves on to highlight David's preparations for the Temple-building project. These preparations will drive the remainder of the Chronicler's account of David's reign. The section is introduced in chapter 22 and forms a bracket with chapters 28–29 around the many lists of personnel found in chapters 23–27 (see also notes at the beginning of the commentary on chs 23 and 28).

As in chapters 28–29, chapter 22 focuses on (1) David's provision of the raw building materials for the project (22:2-5), (2) his commissioning Solomon to build the Temple (22:6-16), and (3) his commissioning the leaders of Israel to assist Solomon (22:17-19). In this chapter the Chronicler not only returns the focus completely to David's preparations for the worship of God in Jerusalem, but he also highlights the unity of both the Davidic ruler and the people around this central activity. From this point until the end of the account of David, the Chronicler provides unique material not found in his Samuel source. These sections provide a clear vision of the Chronicler's view of David and the Temple (see introduction to 2 Chr 1–9 and the connection to the pattern of accounts on building sanctuaries).

David's Provision of Materials for the Temple (22:2-5). The Chronicler presents David in action from the moment the Temple site is identified. This first paragraph is structured in a way similar to the one that brought closure to the events in chapter 21 (21:28–22:1). In the previous paragraph descriptive material was provided at the outset, leading to a dramatic declaration by David near the end. In the present paragraph the declaration of David in 22:5 expresses David's inner passions reflected in the descriptive narrative of 22:2-4 and summarized in 22:5b. By presenting the material in this way, the Chronicler sets David's preparations in action from the outset (22:2-4) and describes how this was his passion until the day of his death (22:5b).

The Chronicler first lists David's preparation of the raw building materials for the Temple. His description includes the great variety of materials provided (stone for the walls, iron for the hardware, bronze for decorative work, and cedar logs for the roof), as well as the vast quantity of these materials. The text repeats the Hebrew phrase *larob* [TH7230, ZH8044] three times (NLT, "large amounts," "more," "vast amounts") and phrases for "beyond enumeration" twice (*'en mishqal* [TH4948, ZH5486] and *'en mispar* [TH4557, ZH5031], respectively, "more . . . than could be weighed"; and "innumerable"). This description paints in broad strokes and brilliant colors a vivid portrait of David's preparations in order to accentuate the glory of the Temple project. The Chronicler's characterization of David through verbalization of his inner thoughts makes this clear, noting that the Temple must be "a magnificent structure, famous and glorious throughout the world." Set between the external description of 22:2-4 and the internal declaration of 22:5 is the contrasting statement "My son Solomon is still young and inexperienced." David made it clear why he set to work on the Temple project and from this moment on inseparably links himself and his son together into a dynamic duo of sanctuary construction.

While in Kings the building project is focused on Solomon, in Chronicles Solomon merely assembles the building materials that David has gathered together and merely institutes the liturgical services carefully organized by his father.

David Instructs Solomon to Build the Temple (22:6-16). The next scene begins with a proleptic statement (22:6) summarizing the speech of David to Solomon in 22:7-16. David begins by rehearsing for Solomon his encounter with God recorded in 17:7-10. In this rehearsal, however, the Chronicler has David provide more details than are found in chapter 17, details based on the later rehearsals of the dynastic oracle in 1 Kings 5:3-4 and 8:17-19, which, among other things, provide further insight into why David was disqualified from building the Temple. David's great success in battle ("shed so much blood in my sight"), with its attendant condition of uncleanness (Num 31:19-24; cf. Num 19:16), had disqualified him from the holy task of building the sanctuary (see also 28:3; cf. Knoppers 2004:773-775).[1] Instead, David informed Solomon that he was that son who would build the Temple because God would grant him peace from his enemies, an idyllic condition suggested by his name, which is derived from the Hebrew word for "peace" (*shalom* [TH7965, ZH8934]).[2] Solomon was also the one who would enter into a covenant relationship with the Lord, who promised to secure his throne over Israel forever. This speech is very important in the Chronicler's account and continues the message found in 22:5—that is, not only must David play a part in the construction of the Temple by providing the materials for its construction, but Solomon would play the key role of bringing the construction to conclusion and securing the enduring character of the Davidic dynasty.

After his rehearsal of his encounter with God, David offered a series of commissions that are expressed in the language of blessing (22:11-13). The key priorities, according to David, are that Solomon follow the instructions of the Lord as he builds the Temple and that he follow the law of the Lord as he rules the land. Such obedience secures success ("may the LORD . . . give you success . . . for you will be successful") and is predicated on God's provision of both his presence ("may the LORD be with you") and his wisdom ("may the LORD give you wisdom and understanding"). In the Chronicler's account, the gift of wisdom to Solomon at the outset of his reign is related directly to the building of the Temple (2 Chr 1–2), while in Kings it is related first to the proper administration of justice (1 Kgs 3). David calls Solomon not only to obedience but also to courage ("Be strong and courageous; do not be afraid or lose heart!").

Many have noted striking similarities between David's commissioning speech to Solomon here in chapter 22 and the speeches of Moses to Joshua in Deuteronomy and of God in Joshua (Deut 1:6–3:29 [especially 1:37-38]; 31:2-8; and Josh 1:1-9).[3] These resonances are apparent immediately with respect to genre, because in both cases the basic building blocks of a literary form called "installation to an office" are evident (encouragement, description of task, assurance of divine aid). Related to this, however, is the use of vocabulary typical of this genre and unique to these passages. This includes phrases such as:

be strong and take courage (22:13; *khazaq we'emats* [TH553/2388, ZH599/2616]) cf. Deut 31:7, 23; Josh 1:6-9 with 1 Chr 22:13; 28:20; cf. Deut 31:6 with 1 Chr 28:10
do not be frightened or dismayed (22:13; *'al-tira' we'al-tekhath* [TH3372/2865, ZH3707/3169]) cf. Deut 31:6-8; Josh 1:9 with 1 Chr 22:13; 28:20
The LORD *your God is with you* (22:18; *yhwh 'elohekem 'immakem* [TH5973, ZH6640]) cf. Deut 31:6-8, 23; Josh 1:5, 9 with 1 Chr 22:11, 16; 28:20; 2 Chr 1:1
He will never leave you nor forsake you (28:20; *lo' yarpeka welo' ya'azbeka* [TH7503/5800, ZH8332/6440]) cf. Deut 31:6, 8; Josh 1:5

In addition to genre and vocabulary, there are other points of comparison. In both cases the senior leader

- establishes enduring key institutions in Israel's history (Moses for people, covenant, land; David for monarchy, dynasty, Temple)
- is disqualified from achieving his chief goal, which is then realized through his successor (Moses not entering the land; David not building the Temple (cf. Deut 1:37-38; 31:2-8 with 1 Chr 22:5-13; 28:2-8)
- undertakes much preparation that secures the success of the successor (Moses defeats Transjordan kingdoms and leads people to Jordan; David gathers the resources and organizes the personnel for the Temple)
- lays great stress on prospering through observance of the law (cf. Deut 31:5; Josh 1:7-8 with 1 Chr 22:12-13; 28:7-9)
- makes double announcements regarding the appointment of his successor (one private, one public; cf. Deut 31:23 with 1 Chr 22:6 and cf. Deut 31:2-8 with 1 Chr 28:8)
- is vigorous until the end of his ministry (cf. Deut 34:7 with 1 Chr 28:2, contrasting 1 Kgs 1)[4]

Furthermore, in both cases, the successor

- enjoys the immediate and wholehearted support of the people (cf. Deut 34:9; Josh 1:16-18 with 1 Chr 29:23-24; cf. 22:17-19)
- is "magnified" (Piel of *gadal* [TH1431, ZH1540]) by God (cf. Josh 3:7; 4:14 with 1 Chr 29:25; 2 Chr 1:1)
- leads the Israelites into "rest" (cf. Josh 11:23; 21:44 with 1 Chr 22:8-9)[5]

This technique of the Chronicler has been appropriately labeled "recapitulative historiography," meaning he took an earlier incident from the history of Israel and employed it as a model for a later situation (see introduction to 2 Chr 1–9; cf. Longman and Dillard 2006:198). By drawing this parallel, the Chronicler accomplished several things. First, he highlighted the importance of this transition from David to Solomon, placing it on level with the transition between the two greatest leaders in Israel's past (cf. Knoppers 2004:785). Second, he legitimized the Temple itself by linking it so closely with those who were responsible for the first sanctuary in Israel's foundational narrative. With the destruction of the Davidic kingdom and Temple at the fall of Jerusalem and the exile of the king and the people, the monarchy would have faced serious criticism. The close link between the monarchy and the Temple may have caused some to question the legitimacy of the Temple itself. By linking the monarchy to the pre-monarchic leadership of Israel, the Chronicler was not only strengthening the validity of the monarchy, but in turn the Temple for which they were responsible. Third, through these parallels the Chronicler bound David and Solomon together more closely, identifying the way in which as a team they realized the Temple construction and confirmed the dynastic covenant promised in chapter 17 (see Williamson 1976:351-361).

Not only does this section of David's speech echo the earlier experience of Moses and Joshua, but the language of this part of David's speech employs core themes of the Chronicler's work. The Chronicler links success to obedience to God's instruction, whether the instructions for building the Temple revealed through David (28:12, 19) or the decrees and regulations of the Torah revealed through Moses. Furthermore, key to success throughout Chronicles is the accompanying presence of God.

In the final part of his speech (22:14-16), David highlighted the preparations he made for the Temple project, including the raw materials (gold, silver, iron, bronze, timber, stone) and the skilled labor (stonemasons, carpenters, craftsmen, goldsmiths, silversmiths, workers of iron and bronze). While the closing words of the second section of David's speech (22:11-13) address issues of inner passion and resolve (22:13b), the closing words of this final section (22:14-16) call Solomon to external action ("begin the work"), based on the promise of God's presence ("may the LORD be with you").

David's Speech to the Leaders (22:17-19). David addressed "all the leaders of Israel," commanding them to assist Solomon. As in the last part of David's speech to Solomon, David began by highlighting his preparations for the Temple building. This time the preparations are focused on David's gift of peace through his success in battle. Employing vocabulary typical of Chronicles, David called the people to "seek" the Lord, an action expressed through building the Temple. David stated that the Temple affords an opportunity to bring under one permanent roof both the Ark of God and the holy vessels of God. This construction finds its ultimate purpose in its desire to "honor the LORD's name."

In chapter 22 the Chronicler highlights one of the main purposes of the Davidic dynasty, a purpose that will consume the reign of David's son Solomon. David told Solomon of his encounter with Yahweh and informed his son that his destiny had been determined by Yahweh himself. The leaders were all commanded to assist Solomon in this grand project. With his death in view (22:5), David is depicted as devoting all of his remaining energy to preparing for the Temple construction project, which will commence upon his death. For the Chronicler's audience this account is a reminder of the priority that lay at the core of their community, that is, the maintenance of the Temple and its worship services.

ENDNOTES

1. Another view on the meaning of the connection between David's disqualification and blood is that the shedding of blood only refers to the larger role of David in completing the conquest so that centralization of worship may be attained (see Deut 12). However, the fixation on the shedding of blood here in 1 Chr 22:8 favors the ritual uncleanness view argued here. Furthermore, if it was merely rest from enemies that was in view here, it is not clear why David could not build the Temple once he had secured the land before he died.

2. Solomon's other name was Jedidiah (see 2 Sam 12:24-25).
3. Williamson 1976:351-361; see also Braun 1976:581-590; Dillard 1987:3-4; Japhet 1993:498-499; Mason 1990:25. Knoppers (2004:784) adds Num 27:15-23.
4. For this last point, see Japhet 1993:486.
5. All these items are unique elements drawn in by the Chronicler. He retains two elements from his source in Samuel–Kings that also bolster these connections: Both successors conscript alien labor for construction of the Tabernacle and Temple (cf. 2 Chr 2:2, 17-18; 8:7-10 with Josh 9:26-27); both receive a divine endowment of wisdom (cf. 2 Chr 1 with Deut 34:9).

◆ N. David's Commission of the Levites: Gershonites, Kohathites, Merarites (23:1-32)

When David was an old man, he appointed
his son Solomon to be king over Israel.
2David summoned all the leaders of Israel,
together with the priests and Levites. 3All
the Levites who were thirty years old or
older were counted, and the total came to
38,000. 4Then David said, "From all the
Levites, 24,000 will supervise the work at
the Temple of the LORD. Another 6,000 will
serve as officials and judges. 5Another
4,000 will work as gatekeepers, and 4,000
will praise the LORD with the musical in-
struments I have made." 6Then David di-
vided the Levites into divisions named after
the clans descended from the three sons of
Levi—Gershon, Kohath, and Merari.

7The Gershonite family units were
defined by their lines of descent
from Libni* and Shimei, the sons of
Gershon. 8Three of the descendants of
Libni were Jehiel (the family leader),
Zetham, and Joel. 9These were the
leaders of the family of Libni.

Three of the descendants of Shimei were
Shelomoth, Haziel, and Haran. 10Four
other descendants of Shimei were
Jahath, Ziza,* Jeush, and Beriah.
11Jahath was the family leader, and
Ziza was next. Jeush and Beriah were
counted as a single family because
neither had many sons.

12Four of the descendants of Kohath
were Amram, Izhar, Hebron, and Uzziel.

13The sons of Amram were Aaron and
Moses. Aaron and his descendants
were set apart to dedicate the most
holy things, to offer sacrifices in the
LORD's presence, to serve the LORD, and
to pronounce blessings in his name
forever.

14As for Moses, the man of God,
his sons were included with the
tribe of Levi. 15The sons of Moses
were Gershom and Eliezer. 16The
descendants of Gershom included
Shebuel, the family leader. 17Eliezer
had only one son, Rehabiah, the
family leader. Rehabiah had numerous
descendants.

18The descendants of Izhar included
Shelomith, the family leader.

19The descendants of Hebron included
Jeriah (the family leader), Amariah
(the second), Jahaziel (the third),
and Jekameam (the fourth).

20The descendants of Uzziel included
Micah (the family leader) and Isshiah
(the second).

21The descendants of Merari included
Mahli and Mushi.

The sons of Mahli were Eleazar and Kish.
22Eleazar died with no sons, only
daughters. His daughters married their
cousins, the sons of Kish.

23Three of the descendants of Mushi
were Mahli, Eder, and Jerimoth.

24These were the descendants of Levi
by clans, the leaders of their family
groups, registered carefully by name.
Each had to be twenty years old or older
to qualify for service in the house of the

LORD. 25For David said, "The LORD, the God
of Israel, has given us peace, and he will
always live in Jerusalem. 26Now the Le-
vites will no longer need to carry the Tab-
ernacle and its furnishings from place to
place." 27In accordance with David's final
instructions, all the Levites twenty years
old or older were registered for service.

28The work of the Levites was to assist
the priests, the descendants of Aaron, as
they served at the house of the LORD. They
also took care of the courtyards and side
rooms, helped perform the ceremonies of
purification, and served in many other
ways in the house of God. 29They were in
charge of the sacred bread that was set
out on the table, the choice flour for the
grain offerings, the wafers made without
yeast, the cakes cooked in olive oil, and
the other mixed breads. They were also
responsible to check all the weights and
measures. 30And each morning and eve-
ning they stood before the LORD to sing
songs of thanks and praise to him. 31They
assisted with the burnt offerings that
were presented to the LORD on Sabbath
days, at new moon celebrations, and at
all the appointed festivals. The required
number of Levites served in the LORD's
presence at all times, following all the
procedures they had been given.

32And so, under the supervision of the
priests, the Levites watched over the Tab-
ernacle and the Temple* and faithfully
carried out their duties of service at the
house of the LORD.

23:7 Hebrew *Ladan* (also in 23:8, 9), a variant spelling of Libni; compare 6:17. **23:10** As in Greek version and Latin Vulgate (see also 23:11); Hebrew reads *Zina*. **23:32** Hebrew *the Tent of Meeting and the sanctuary.*

NOTES

23:4-5 ***Then David said . . . I have made.*** Ancient witnesses do not have "David said," but this is supplied because in the Hebrew text there is the later comment "I have made," suggesting that this is being spoken by someone other than the narrator. This may be a textual error, because the LXX has the third person expression "he has made for the praising of the Lord."

23:14 ***Moses, the man of God.*** This is most likely a reference to Moses's prophetic role (see 2 Kgs 4:9; cf. Deut 18:15; 34:10).

23:28 ***the priests, the descendants of Aaron.*** Lit., "the descendants of Aaron."

the courtyards and side rooms. It appears that the Temple had two courtyards, the inner and outer (cf. 1 Kgs 6:36; 7:12; 2 Kgs 23:12; 2 Chr 4:9). The bronze altar and laver ("the Sea") were located in the inner court (1 Kgs 7:23-26; 8:22). This area was distinguished from the building structure with its Holy Place and Most Holy Place by the porch (2 Chr 3:4). There were three stories of side rooms on three sides of the sacred building (1 Kgs 6:5, 10).

ceremonies of purification. Lit., "the purification of all holy things." The term "purification" is used in relation to ceremonial cleanness (Lev 13:7; Num 6:9).

23:29 ***the sacred bread.*** Often called the "Bread of the Presence" (Exod 25:30; 35:13), here it is called, lit., the "bread in row" (9:32; 23:29; 2 Chr 29:18; Neh 10:33), one time even, lit., "row of bread" (2 Chr 13:11) due to the fact that in Lev 24:5-7 the bread was to be put in two rows of six cakes on the bread table in the Holy Place.

choice flour. This is finely milled flour made from wheat, associated with luxury (Gen 18:6; Ezek 16:13, 19). The grain offering demanded this kind of flour (Lev 2:1). The grain offering accompanied other offerings, including the burnt offering and the peace offering (Num 15; cf. Lev 7:12-14).

the wafers made without yeast. Unleavened wafers were used in the grain offering ceremony (Lev 2:4), in the Nazirite rituals (Num 6:15, 19), and in the consecration of priests (Exod 29:2, 23).

the cakes cooked in olive oil. Lit., "griddle," but by extension the cakes that were cooked with oil on the griddle in preparation of the grain offering (Lev 2:5; 6:21; 7:9).

the other mixed breads. Lit., "the well-mixed things," referring to the bread made for the grain offering (Lev 6:21; 7:12).

weights and measures. The first Hebrew word refers to measure of capacity (related to water; Lev 19:35; Ezek 4:11, 16), the second of length (Exod 26:2, 8; cf. Neh 3:11, 19; Jer 22:14).

23:31 ***Sabbath days, at new moon celebrations, and at all the appointed festivals.*** Cf. Lev 23; Num 28–29.

The required number of Levites served in the LORD's presence at all times, following all the procedures they had been given. "The required number" most likely refers to the burnt offerings and not the Levites (as in the NLT). Thus, it should read, "with the number (being set) according to the procedures concerning them [the burnt offerings] continually in the Lord's presence." This is the opinion of Knoppers (2004:816) and Japhet (1993:420), who note Num 28:18, 21, 24.

23:32 ***the priests.*** Lit., "the descendants of Aaron."

COMMENTARY

David Gathers the Leaders (23:1-2). In chapter 22 the beginning of the royal transition from David to Solomon is implicitly signaled with the account of David's preparations for the Temple building and the two key addresses to Solomon and the leaders of Israel. With 23:1, however, this transition becomes explicit with the identification of David as "an old man." This initial verse functions as a proleptic summary of chapters 23–29, that is, the process by which David handed over the kingdom to his son Solomon and which reached fulfillment in 29:28.[1]

Chapters 23–29 are divided into two basic sections.[2] The first, introduced by the statement in 23:2 ("David summoned all the leaders of Israel, together with the priests and Levites"), includes chapters 23–27, while the second, introduced by the statement in 28:1 ("David summoned all the officials of Israel to Jerusalem"), includes chapters 28–29. Although the NLT translates the verb with the same English word ("summoned"), the Hebrew verb in 23:2 is *'asap* [TH622, ZH665] and in 28:1 is *qahal* [TH6950, ZH7735] (Hiphil). Wright (1991:231) has argued convincingly that these terms are not synonymous in Chronicles because *'asap* is used when the Chronicler "wishes to portray the gathering of officials to receive specific assignments," while *qahal* is used when he "describes the gathering of a civil and cultic national assembly." Thus, these two verbs introduce two distinct sections. The first introduces David's creation of the infrastructure for a kingdom that supports the Temple, and the second introduces David's assembling these officials for the official handing over to Solomon of both these entities as well as the authority of the throne.

David's Organization of the Levites (23:3-5). As has been typical throughout the Chronicler's work, the Levites and their role are addressed first. These verses identify the results of a census of the Levites, with the careful note that only those "thirty years old or older were counted," even though those qualified for service were "twenty years old or older" (23:24). Although some suggest different traditions at work here (twenty in Ezra 3:8; twenty-five in Num 8:24; thirty to fifty in Num 4:3, 23, 30) or textual corruption (Japhet 1993:412), this note may reflect the concern over counting the people without ransom money, which was so important in chapter 21 (see commentary). According to the Chronicler, David then identifies from this larger group those who would be responsible for various duties, with the bulk commissioned to supervise the construction of the Temple (the same phrase, *mele'keth beth-yhwh*, "work of Yahweh's Temple," occurs in 23:4 and Ezra 3:8). The rest were given roles ranging from serving as officials and judges to gatekeeping and singing praises.

David's Commission of the Levites: Gershon, Kohath, Merari (23:6-32). The Chronicler then relates that David organized the Levites into three divisions according to ancient clan affiliations within the tribe of Levi (Gershon, Kohath, and Merari), offering first a summary (23:6), followed by a delineation of the specific families within each clan (Gershon in 23:7-11; Kohath in 23:12-20; Merari in 23:21-23), before ending with another summary (23:24). The number of families total 24: Gershon (10), Kohath (9), and Merari (5). Although not made explicit, this matches the consistent use of the number 24 in the Levitical and priestly lists (chs 24–25).

These lists are followed immediately by a justification for and delineation of the elevated role of the Levites in the Davidic Temple worship. The Chronicler justifies this through David's assertion that God had not only granted Israel peace (that is, Israel will no longer need to go out in war), but God has also chosen to remain in Jerusalem forever. Thus, because God had chosen a permanent resting place for the Ark and because imminent war did not require the evacuation of the Ark, the role of the Levites to transport the Ark was no longer necessary. So all Levites were now focused on other aspects of Temple worship, which are defined in 23:24-32.

The Levites were commissioned to work in the Temple to assist the descendants of Aaron. The priests in Aaron's line are envisioned in chapter 23 as supervising the Temple worship (23:28, 32).[3] This is made explicit in the "digression" in the Kohathite list in 23:13, where the Chronicler recounts that Aaron and his descendants were commissioned for four purposes. The first purpose is actually a status and would be better translated as "to consecrate him as most holy," an allusion to the Lord's call to Moses to consecrate the priests as such (Exod 30:29-30).[4] Those who will serve in the most holy places with the most holy things must themselves be most holy. The second purpose moves from status to function, for it is to offer sacrifices in the Lord's presence, a function authorized in the Torah (Exod 29:38-42; 30:1-10; Lev 8:1–9:24; 16:1-28). As 23:31 shows, the Levites also served "in the LORD's presence"; the key here is that the priests were to take leadership in the sacrificial acts. The third purpose, "to serve the LORD," is a more general reference to the various activities required of the priests. The final purpose, to pronounce blessings, is the function of the Aaronic priesthood according to Numbers 6:22-27.

Nevertheless, the other members of the tribe of Levi were to play a role as well by (1) caring for the courtyards and side rooms, (2) performing purification ceremonies, (3) providing for the various baked goods in the Temple, and (4) calibrating the weights and measures. Beyond these menial tasks,[5] they were also involved in worship service directly through their musical worship to God in the morning and evening (23:30) and in their assistance of the priests in burnt offerings on various weekly, monthly, and yearly worship events (23:31).[6] Japhet (1993:419) has noted how the list of Levitical duties in 23:28-31 are the tasks of three suborders of the Levites: gatekeepers (23:28a), Levites (23:28b-29), and musicians (23:30-31), who are in focus in chapters 23–26.[7]

In this section Chronicles grants the non-priestly Levites space in the worship of Israel. They are legitimized through the voice of David himself, who links this transition in their role to the transition from Tabernacle to Temple ("In accordance with David's final instructions," 23:27). Thus, to have the Temple is to afford the Levites these roles in the new worship phase. Here the Chronicler emphasizes this space further through such phrases as "served in many other ways in the house of God" (23:28) and "served in the LORD's presence at all times" (23:31). Chronicles also stresses the faithfulness of the Levites to this new calling, reminding the reader that the Levites followed "all the procedures they had been given" (23:31) and "faithfully carried out their duties of service at the house of the LORD" (23:32). The non-priestly Levites, therefore, were legitimated by the authority of David, as well as by their faithful response to this royal commission. Interestingly, this duty in which "the Levites watched over the Tabernacle and the Temple" (lit., "the Tent of Meeting and the sanctuary," see NLT mg), is a responsibility granted to them in Numbers 3:28, but Numbers 18:1-7 makes it clear that they did this under the authority of the Aaronide priests.[8] The stress, then, in the book of Chronicles is on what Knoppers (2004:822, 826) has called "cooperation and complementarity, not competition and hierarchy," so that "the author does not always distinguish where Levitical duties end and Priestly duties begin" (9:10-34; 28:12-13; 2 Chr 5:2-14; 7:1-10; 13:9-12; 23:1-11; 29:3-36; 31:2-21; 34:8-13; 35:1-19).

ENDNOTES

1. It does not, then, suggest coregency for Solomon with David.
2. Much debate has raged around chs 23–27 and whether it was original to the Chronicler or a later addition; see Williamson 1979a:23-27; Williamson 1982:157-159. Recent work by Wright (1991:229-242), Japhet (1993:409), and Knoppers (2004:791) has argued for the authenticity of the basic core of this section and especially the role that it plays in the Chronicler's account in general, especially in light of contemporary Persian-period material in Egypt (the accounts of Udjahorresnet [Persian official] and Petosiris [an Egyptian high priest]) and in Yehud (Nehemiah Memoir in Neh 1:1–2:20; 4:1–7:5; 12:31-43; 13:6-31; cf. Boda 2008). Williamson argued that 23:3-6a represents the Chronicler's summary of the original content of chs 23–27 and anything in addition to this represents the work of a later ("pro-Priestly") editor. It appears, however, that the summary in 23:3-6a is restricted to the Levitical sections and that 23:2 functions as the introduction to the content of chs 23–27.
3. There has been much debate over whether 23:13-14 and 23:28-32 were original to the Chronicler's account, or whether they were later additions by a pro-Priestly redactor; see Braun 1986:235-236; Williamson 1979a:251-268. This debate cannot be resolved with certainty (see Introduction, "Canonicity and Textual History"). While 23:13-14 may appear to be an intrusion into a list, and 23:27 could have been the original ending of ch 23, Knoppers (2004:808) has argued that such "digressions" are a common feature of genealogies in the ancient Near East and, in particular, in the Israelite genealogy of Num 1, where a digression on the role of the excluded tribe of Levi is found in Num 1:50-53.

4. So Japhet (1993:415), who argues with NEB marginal note, and contra Knoppers (2004:808), who sees this as a reference to the function of the priests to consecrate, that is, to set apart items for sacred use. These items, called "most holy things" (*qodesh qadashim* [TH6944, ZH7731]), could refer to food (Lev 2:3), offerings (Lev 21:22), or furnishings (Exod 28:1–30:10; 40:10; Num 4:4-15, 19; 2 Chr 31:14), but here most likely refers to the latter (Num 4:4-20).
5. This is what Myers (1965:161) long ago meant when he called the Levites in Chronicles "janitors."
6. The Hebrew text is not as clear that this was merely "assisting" the priests, for it speaks of the Levites "standing morning by morning to sing songs of thanks and praise to the Lord, likewise in the evening" and then "to offer burnt offerings to the Lord for the Sabbath, for the new moon, and for the appointed feasts." So also in 23:32, the Hebrew text reads, "And they kept the charge of the tent of meeting, and the charge of the holy place, and the charge of the sons of Aaron, their brothers for the service of the house of the Lord." The Levites may have had more freedom than is usually envisioned (contra, for instance, Knoppers [2004:816], who translates here "and whenever burnt offerings are offered"). However, it is possible that 23:32 is referring to the Levitical function of guarding the tent of meeting, the holy place/objects, and the priests (cf. Knoppers 2004:817) or is an allusion to the helping function the Levites performed for the priests as outlined in Num 3:5-8 and 18:2-7 (cf. Japhet 1993:420-421).
7. Japhet also sees integrity to 23:28-32 with the opening "served at the house of the LORD" (23:28b) and the closing "service at the house of the LORD" (23:32b).
8. See the superb discussion on the relationship between ch 23 and the Priestly view of offices in Numbers by Knoppers (2004:821-826).

◆ O. David's Commission of the Priests; List of Levitical Leaders (24:1-31)

This is how Aaron's descendants, the priests, were divided into groups for service. The sons of Aaron were Nadab, Abihu, Eleazar, and Ithamar. [2]But Nadab and Abihu died before their father, and they had no sons. So only Eleazar and Ithamar were left to carry on as priests.

[3]With the help of Zadok, who was a descendant of Eleazar, and of Ahimelech, who was a descendant of Ithamar, David divided Aaron's descendants into groups according to their various duties. [4]Eleazar's descendants were divided into sixteen groups and Ithamar's into eight, for there were more family leaders among the descendants of Eleazar.

[5]All tasks were assigned to the various groups by means of sacred lots so that no preference would be shown, for there were many qualified officials serving God in the sanctuary from among the descendants of both Eleazar and Ithamar. [6]Shemaiah son of Nethanel, a Levite, acted as secretary and wrote down the names and assignments in the presence of the king, the officials, Zadok the priest, Ahimelech son of Abiathar, and the family leaders of the priests and Levites. The descendants of Eleazar and Ithamar took turns casting lots.

[7]The first lot fell to Jehoiarib.
The second lot fell to Jedaiah.
[8]The third lot fell to Harim.
The fourth lot fell to Seorim.
[9]The fifth lot fell to Malkijah.
The sixth lot fell to Mijamin.
[10]The seventh lot fell to Hakkoz.
The eighth lot fell to Abijah.
[11]The ninth lot fell to Jeshua.
The tenth lot fell to Shecaniah.

12 The eleventh lot fell to Eliashib.
The twelfth lot fell to Jakim.
13 The thirteenth lot fell to Huppah.
The fourteenth lot fell to Jeshebeab.
14 The fifteenth lot fell to Bilgah.
The sixteenth lot fell to Immer.
15 The seventeenth lot fell to Hezir.
The eighteenth lot fell to Happizzez.
16 The nineteenth lot fell to Pethahiah.
The twentieth lot fell to Jehezkel.
17 The twenty-first lot fell to Jakin.
The twenty-second lot fell to Gamul.
18 The twenty-third lot fell to Delaiah.
The twenty-fourth lot fell to Maaziah.

19 Each group carried out its appointed duties in the house of the LORD according to the procedures established by their ancestor Aaron in obedience to the commands of the LORD, the God of Israel.

20 These were the other family leaders descended from Levi:

From the descendants of Amram, the leader was Shebuel.*
From the descendants of Shebuel, the leader was Jehdeiah.
21 From the descendants of Rehabiah, the leader was Isshiah.
22 From the descendants of Izhar, the leader was Shelomith.*
From the descendants of Shelomith, the leader was Jahath.
23 From the descendants of Hebron, Jeriah was the leader,* Amariah was second, Jahaziel was third, and Jekameam was fourth.
24 From the descendants of Uzziel, the leader was Micah.
From the descendants of Micah, the leader was Shamir,
25 along with Isshiah, the brother of Micah.
From the descendants of Isshiah, the leader was Zechariah.
26 From the descendants of Merari, the leaders were Mahli and Mushi.
From the descendants of Jaaziah, the leader was Beno.
27 From the descendants of Merari through Jaaziah, the leaders were Beno, Shoham, Zaccur, and Ibri.
28 From the descendants of Mahli, the leader was Eleazar, though he had no sons.
29 From the descendants of Kish, the leader was Jerahmeel.
30 From the descendants of Mushi, the leaders were Mahli, Eder, and Jerimoth.

These were the descendants of Levi in their various families.
31 Like the descendants of Aaron, they were assigned to their duties by means of sacred lots, without regard to age or rank. Lots were drawn in the presence of King David, Zadok, Ahimelech, and the family leaders of the priests and the Levites.

24:20 Hebrew *Shubael* (also in 24:20b), a variant spelling of Shebuel; compare 23:16 and 26:24. **24:22** Hebrew *Shelomoth* (also in 24:22b), a variant spelling of Shelomith; compare 23:18. **24:23** Hebrew *From the descendants of Jeriah;* compare 23:19.

NOTES

24:5 ***sacred lots.*** See also Lev 16:8; for the Persian period, see Neh 10:34; 11:1.

for there were many qualified officials serving God in the sanctuary. Lit., "for they were officers of holiness, officers of God." Most likely these are not two different designations but rather descriptive of one another—that is, these sacred officers were officers of God.

24:6 ***the officials.*** These may be princes or military officers (as 25:1), but most likely refer to the "officers of holiness, officers of God" (see note on 24:5)—that is, priestly figures.

COMMENTARY

David's Commission of the Priests (24:1-19). The next list focuses attention on the Aaronic priestly line in Israel, explaining first that the two oldest sons of Aaron had died without progeny, an allusion to the punishment that befell Nadab and Abihu because they offered "the wrong kind of fire" in their incense burners (see Lev 10:1-2; Num 3:4). It is through the two remaining sons of Aaron, Eleazar and Ithamar, that Aaron's priestly line was to continue.

The Chronicler highlights the two heads of these Aaronide lines in the time of David as assisting the king in the organization of the Temple service, linking certain family lines with specific priestly duties. The larger Eleazar line was headed by Zadok, while the smaller Ithamar line was led by Ahimelech. Ahimelech was the son of Abiathar, who joined Zadok and the Levites in transporting the Ark to Jerusalem (15:11). In 18:16, the Chronicler identifies Abiathar's son Ahimelech as priest alongside Zadok in David's court. The Chronicler's account depicts Abiathar as disappearing from the royal court at some point and his son Ahimelech replacing him. This ultimate denigration of the Ithamar line is reflected in the much smaller number of family units (8) compared to those of Eleazar's line (16). Increased progeny is a key sign of blessing in the Chronicler's account. However, the Chronicler stresses carefully the lack of preferential treatment by David of any one line, identifying God as the one who linked family with duty through the use of sacred lots and recording that each family line (Eleazar, Ithamar) cast the lots in turn. The Chronicler also stresses that Levites were involved in this selection process, one acting as a recording secretary (Shemaiah son of Nethanel) and others present as the heads of Levitical families. As the Chronicler linked Levites with priests in the descriptions of the duties of the Levitical clans in chapter 23, so again here he links priests with Levites in the descriptions of the duties of the priestly clans.

After listing the results of the sacred-lot process, the Chronicler concludes this section with a summarizing note declaring that each family group fulfilled their "appointed duties in the house of the LORD" (24:19) without, however, listing the specific duties for which each family was responsible. These duties must have been well-known and established for the Chronicler's audience. The 24 divisions of priests depicted in this chapter appear to have been a necessity in the Persian period in light of the high numbers of priests reflected in the early returns (see Ezra 2, which records 4,289 priests, 74 Levites, 128 singers, and 139 gatekeepers). The use of the 24 divisions would have been "expedient for the situation, a time-sharing device by which all the priests were enabled to serve in the Temple, but not all the time; each group of priests served for a limited time, on a rotation basis" (Japhet 1993:424). If the rotation was completed annually, then each division would have served half a month, or if biannually, an entire month.[1]

Nevertheless, the key for the Chronicler is that these families followed the "procedures" Aaron had established based on the command of the Lord. As with the Levites, so with the priests, faithful obedience to God's revelation is key to this new phase of Israelite worship. However, it is interesting to note that the appointment of the Levites is orchestrated by David alone and based by the Chronicler upon the authority of "David's final instructions" (23:27), while the appointment of the priests is accomplished by David with the help of Zadok and Ahimelech and based by the Chronicler upon the authority of "the procedures established by their ancestor Aaron in obedience to the commands of the LORD, the God of Israel" (24:19).

A comparison of chapters 23 and 24 with their stress on the interaction between priest and Levite, the careful delineation of the duties of each, and the careful presentation of the choice of the various priestly family heads suggests some tension among these groups in the period of the Chronicler. Japhet has noted that in the overall presentation of chapters 23–26, the priests receive the least attention and are even placed second to the Levites (in ch 24, after ch 23). At the same time, however, the priests are clearly identified as the highest order (24:5; Japhet 1993:425). It appears that the Chronicler assumes the primacy and functioning of the priestly line but also that he is seeking through these lists and accounts to bring greater focus on the non-priestly lines of Levi, providing space for them to function in the Temple.[2] This is not intended to denigrate the priestly line or authority but rather to heal any rift between Levite and priest and even between the two Aaronide priestly lines. All have been appointed by God and his designates to perform services in the house of the Lord.

David's Commission and Organization of the Levites: Kohath, Merari (24:20-31). This section closes a Levitical bracket (23:6-32; 24:20-31) around the priestly appointments in 24:1-19.[3] Here the Chronicler focuses only on a select group of the Levitical families mentioned in the lists of 23:6-23, tracing only families from the line of Kohath (cf. 23:12-20) and Merari (23:21-23). The list is slightly expanded from the information provided in 23:12-23, including a few more families and in a few places another generation. The key to this section is its echo of the description of the steps taken for the appointment of the priests in 24:5-6. The Chronicler makes clear that the Levites also were assigned duties in the presence of David, Zadok, and Ahimelech, as well as priestly and Levitical leaders, through the use of the sacred lots without preferential treatment, now defined more carefully as "without regard to age or rank."

ENDNOTES

1. The impact of these 24 divisions can be seen in the Qumran community, where the rotations of the orders are mentioned in some calendrical documents (Knoppers 2004:841-842; cf. VanderKam 1998:71-90).
2. As Japhet (1993:425) concludes, "The definition of the priestly roles, rights and authority is so apparent as to require no elucidation. The Chronicler takes cognizance of all this—yet his sympathy still lies with the Levites."
3. Japhet (1993:423, 432-433) probably is wisest in her assertion that 24:20b-30 comprises an updated list (the list reflects one generation beyond the lists in ch 23) that has been inserted between 24:20a and 24:31. Why or how this list left out the Gershonites is uncertain.

◆ P. David's Commission of Levitical Musicians: Asaph, Heman, Jeduthun (25:1-31)

David and the army commanders then appointed men from the families of Asaph, Heman, and Jeduthun to proclaim God's messages to the accompaniment of lyres, harps, and cymbals. Here is a list of their names and their work:

2From the sons of Asaph, there were Zaccur, Joseph, Nethaniah, and Asarelah. They worked under the direction of their father, Asaph, who proclaimed God's messages by the king's orders.

3 From the sons of Jeduthun, there were
Gedaliah, Zeri, Jeshaiah, Shimei,*
Hashabiah, and Mattithiah, six in all.
They worked under the direction of
their father, Jeduthun, who proclaimed
God's messages to the accompaniment
of the lyre, offering thanks and praise
to the LORD.
4 From the sons of Heman, there were
Bukkiah, Mattaniah, Uzziel, Shubael,*
Jerimoth, Hananiah, Hanani, Eliathah,
Giddalti, Romamti-ezer, Joshbekashah,
Mallothi, Hothir, and Mahazioth. 5 All
these were the sons of Heman, the
king's seer, for God had honored him
with fourteen sons and three
daughters.

6 All these men were under the direction
of their fathers as they made music at the
house of the LORD. Their responsibilities
included the playing of cymbals, harps,
and lyres at the house of God. Asaph,
Jeduthun, and Heman reported directly to
the king. 7 They and their families were all
trained in making music before the LORD,
and each of them—288 in all—was an ac-
complished musician. 8 The musicians were
appointed to their term of service by
means of sacred lots, without regard to
whether they were young or old, teacher
or student.

9 The first lot fell to Joseph of the Asaph clan and twelve of his sons and relatives.*

The second lot fell to Gedaliah and twelve of his sons and relatives.

10 The third lot fell to Zaccur and twelve of his sons and relatives.

11 The fourth lot fell to Zeri* and twelve of his sons and relatives.

12 The fifth lot fell to Nethaniah and twelve of his sons and relatives.

13 The sixth lot fell to Bukkiah and twelve of his sons and relatives.

14 The seventh lot fell to Asarelah* and twelve of his sons and relatives.

15 The eighth lot fell to Jeshaiah and twelve of his sons and relatives.

16 The ninth lot fell to Mattaniah and twelve of his sons and relatives.

17 The tenth lot fell to Shimei and twelve of his sons and relatives.

18 The eleventh lot fell to Uzziel* and twelve of his sons and relatives.

19 The twelfth lot fell to Hashabiah and twelve of his sons and relatives.

20 The thirteenth lot fell to Shubael and twelve of his sons and relatives.

21 The fourteenth lot fell to Mattithiah and twelve of his sons and relatives.

22 The fifteenth lot fell to Jerimoth* and twelve of his sons and relatives.

23 The sixteenth lot fell to Hananiah and twelve of his sons and relatives.

24 The seventeenth lot fell to Joshbekashah* and twelve of his sons and relatives.

25 The eighteenth lot fell to Hanani and twelve of his sons and relatives.

26 The nineteenth lot fell to Mallothi and twelve of his sons and relatives.

27 The twentieth lot fell to Eliathah and twelve of his sons and relatives.

28 The twenty-first lot fell to Hothir and twelve of his sons and relatives.

29 The twenty-second lot fell to Giddalti and twelve of his sons and relatives.

30 The twenty-third lot fell to Mahazioth and twelve of his sons and relatives.

31 The twenty-fourth lot fell to Romamti-ezer and twelve of his sons and relatives.

25:3 As in one Hebrew manuscript and some Greek manuscripts (see also 25:17); most Hebrew manuscripts lack *Shimei.* **25:4** Hebrew *Shebuel,* a variant spelling of Shubael; compare 25:20. **25:9** As in Greek version; Hebrew lacks *and twelve of his sons and relatives.* **25:11** Hebrew *Izri,* a variant spelling of Zeri; compare 25:3. **25:14** Hebrew *Jesarelah,* a variant spelling of Asarelah; compare 25:2. **25:18** Hebrew *Azarel,* a variant spelling of Uzziel; compare 25:4. **25:22** Hebrew *Jeremoth,* a variant spelling of Jerimoth; compare 25:4. **25:24** Hebrew *Joshbekasha,* a variant spelling of Joshbekashah; compare 25:4.

NOTES

25:1 *Jeduthun.* Called Ethan in 15:17, 19; see note on 16:41.

25:5 *for God had honored him.* Lit., "in the words of God to raise a horn." Knoppers translates this phrase as "in divine matters to exalt his cause" (2004:843). However, in light of the prophetic allusion here ("seer"), the translation "in divine matters" is not as attractive as "in/by the words of God." This would then be a reference to the exaltation of the king (called "horn" elsewhere) because of the faithful prophetic ministry of the Levite.

25:8 *young or old, teacher or student.* Hebrew, lit., "small or great, learned or learning."

COMMENTARY

In chapter 23 David is depicted as acting alone in the appointment of the Levites alongside the priests. In chapter 24, however, the Chronicler depicts David working together with Zadok, Ahimelech, and the family heads of the priests and Levites to make his appointments. This trend continues in chapter 25 as David "and the army commanders" (25:1) together appoint the musicians. It does appear odd at first that military leaders would be involved in this appointment process, but clear lines between the sacred and secular, the church and the state, are not evident in the ancient Near East (Knoppers 2004:846-847).

The Chronicler has prepared the way for the commission and organization of the Levitical musicians in chapters 15–16 with (1) his descriptions of the appointments for musical accompaniment to the transportation of the Ark (15:16-22) and (2) his descriptions of the appointments for musical worship at the Jerusalem tent (under the leadership of Asaph, 16:37) and the Gibeonite Tabernacle (under the leadership of Heman and Jeduthun, 16:41-42). The description of the purpose behind these musicians' appointment is fascinating. The Chronicler says they were appointed "to proclaim God's messages" (25:1), using a term from a Hebrew root usually associated with prophecy in the Old Testament (*naba'*). The lists in 25:2-5 not only contain the names of the children of Asaph, Jeduthun, and Heman but also a short description of the family heads; in each case this description uses vocabulary associated with prophecy: Asaph, "who proclaimed God's messages" (*naba'* [TH5012, ZH5547] in the Niphal), Jeduthun, "who proclaimed God's messages" (*naba'* Niphal), and Heman, "the king's seer," with the words of God (*khozeh* [TH2374, ZH2602] *hammelek bedibre ha'elohim*). This Levitical prophetic proclamation is closely associated with the royal house ("by the king's orders," 25:2; "the king's," 25:5), making these Levites prophets in the royal court. At the same time the medium by which this prophecy is delivered is unquestionably music, evident in the reference to instruments (25:1, 3) and to "offering thanks and praise to the LORD" (25:3). Both the link to the royal house and the link to prophecy strengthen the claim of superior status for the Levitical singers among the Levitical orders. This broader view of prophecy, however, is reflected elsewhere for Levites in 2 Chronicles 20; 29; 34:30; and 35:15.[1] First Chronicles 25 is thus the first of a series of texts in Chronicles that will contribute to the tracing of a prophetic function for the Levites. In this chapter the Chronicler presents royal validation in David's commissioning and ordering of the Levitical singers. In 2 Chronicles 20 the Levite Jahaziel would function as prophet on the battlefield, and Levitical singers would sing praise as prophetic utterance to secure victory (2 Chr 20:19). In 2 Chronicles 29, during Hezekiah's reforms, Asaph is called a "seer," and later in 2 Chronicles 35:15, during Josiah's reforms, Jeduthun is called a "seer," showing the importance of the Levitical singers as prophetic figures to the renewal and purity of worship in Israel. Thus, for the Chronicler the function of prophecy is fulfilled in and through the Levitical (and even the priestly) orders.[2]

These emphases on the royal and musical dimensions of the Levites' service are continued in 25:6-7, where the children of the three lead Levitical musicians "made music" (playing "cymbals, harps, and lyres"), and their fathers "reported directly to the king." The excellence of their music is stressed in 25:7: They "were all trained" and each "was an accomplished musician." The location of this ministry is placed at the "house of the LORD . . . the house of God," emphasizing again that with this new sacred space has come new sacred service for the Levitical orders.

As with the priests and then the other Levites in chapter 24, so now with the musicians, the appointments are made through "sacred lots" without preferential treatment, here defined as discrimination on the basis of age ("young or old") or expertise ("teacher or student"). As with the priestly divisions, 24 lots were cast for 24 families, and in each case the leader of the family was accompanied by 12 relatives (25:9-31).

ENDNOTES

1. See Petersen 1977:55-87. Also note the expansion of prophecy coming from the priest Zechariah in 2 Chr 24:19-22. Note, however, Dillard (1987:155, 157), who responds to Petersen's claim that this prophetic function for Levites is in tension with other postexilic prophetic materials and thus is not a carryover from preexilic cultic prophecy but rather late redactional activity on the singer traditions and an innovation on the part of the Chronicler.
2. The distance between priestly and prophetic activity, however, should not be overstated in order to make the Chronicler's view appear out of place. Notice, for instance, the tradition of cult prophecy in ancient Israel (cf. Boda 2001:186-197; see especially A. Johnson 1962, 1979). One should also note the tradition preserved in 1 Sam 10:5, where a band of prophets are playing instruments and prophesying (cf. 2 Kgs 3:15).

◆ Q. David's Commission of the Levitical Gatekeepers, Treasurers, and Administrators (26:1-32)

These are the divisions of the gatekeepers:

From the Korahites, there was Meshelemiah son of Kore, of the family of Abiasaph.* 2The sons of Meshelemiah were Zechariah (the oldest), Jediael (the second), Zebadiah (the third), Jathniel (the fourth), 3Elam (the fifth), Jehohanan (the sixth), and Eliehoenai (the seventh).

4The sons of Obed-edom, also gatekeepers, were Shemaiah (the oldest), Jehozabad (the second), Joah (the third), Sacar (the fourth), Nethanel (the fifth), 5Ammiel (the sixth), Issachar (the seventh), and Peullethai (the eighth). God had richly blessed Obed-edom.

6Obed-edom's son Shemaiah had sons with great ability who earned positions of great authority in the

clan. 7Their names were Othni,
Rephael, Obed, and Elzabad. Their
relatives, Elihu and Semakiah, were
also very capable men.
8All of these descendants of Obed-
edom, including their sons and
grandsons—sixty-two of them in all—
were very capable men, well qualified
for their work.
9Meshelemiah's eighteen sons and
relatives were also very capable men.

10Hosah, of the Merari clan, appointed
Shimri as the leader among his sons,
though he was not the oldest. 11His
other sons included Hilkiah (the
second), Tebaliah (the third), and
Zechariah (the fourth). Hosah's sons
and relatives, who served as gate-
keepers, numbered thirteen in all.

12 These divisions of the gatekeepers
were named for their family leaders, and
like the other Levites, they served at the
house of the LORD. 13They were assigned
by families for guard duty at the various
gates, without regard to age or training,
for it was all decided by means of sacred
lots.
14The responsibility for the east gate
went to Meshelemiah* and his group. The
north gate was assigned to his son Zecha-
riah, a man of unusual wisdom. 15The
south gate went to Obed-edom, and his
sons were put in charge of the storehouse.
16Shuppim and Hosah were assigned the
west gate and the gateway leading up to
the Temple.* Guard duties were divided
evenly. 17Six Levites were assigned each
day to the east gate, four to the north
gate, four to the south gate, and two pairs
at the storehouse. 18Six were assigned
each day to the west gate, four to the
gateway leading up to the Temple, and
two to the courtyard.*
19These were the divisions of the gate-
keepers from the clans of Korah and
Merari.

20Other Levites, led by Ahijah, were in
charge of the treasuries of the house of
God and the treasuries of the gifts dedi-
cated to the LORD. 21From the family of
Libni* in the clan of Gershon, Jehiel* was
the leader. 22The sons of Jehiel, Zetham
and his brother Joel, were in charge of the
treasuries of the house of the LORD.
23These are the leaders that descended
from Amram, Izhar, Hebron, and Uzziel:

24From the clan of Amram, Shebuel
was a descendant of Gershom son of
Moses. He was the chief officer of
the treasuries. 25His relatives through
Eliezer were Rehabiah, Jeshaiah,
Joram, Zicri, and Shelomoth.
26Shelomoth and his relatives were
in charge of the treasuries containing
the gifts that King David, the family
leaders, and the generals and
captains* and other officers of the
army had dedicated to the LORD.
27These men dedicated some of the
plunder they had gained in battle to
maintain the house of the LORD.
28Shelomoth* and his relatives also
cared for the gifts dedicated to the
LORD by Samuel the seer, Saul son of
Kish, Abner son of Ner, and Joab son
of Zeruiah. All the other dedicated
gifts were in their care, too.
29From the clan of Izhar came Kenaniah.
He and his sons were given
administrative responsibilities*
over Israel as officials and judges.
30From the clan of Hebron came
Hashabiah. He and his relatives—1,700
capable men—were put in charge of
the Israelite lands west of the Jordan
River. They were responsible for all
matters related to the things of the
LORD and the service of the king in
that area.
31Also from the clan of Hebron
came Jeriah,* who was the leader
of the Hebronites according to the
genealogical records. (In the fortieth
year of David's reign, a search was
made in the records, and capable men
from the clan of Hebron were found at
Jazer in the land of Gilead.) 32There

were 2,700 capable men among the relatives of Jeriah. King David sent them to the east side of the Jordan River and put them in charge of the tribes of Reuben and Gad and the half-tribe of Manasseh. They were responsible for all matters related to God and to the king.

26:1 As in Greek version (see also Exod 6:24); Hebrew reads *Asaph.* **26:14** Hebrew *Shelemiah,* a variant spelling of Meshelemiah; compare 26:2. **26:16** Or *the gate of Shalleketh on the upper road* (also in 26:18). The meaning of the Hebrew is uncertain. **26:18** Or *the colonnade.* The meaning of the Hebrew is uncertain. **26:21a** Hebrew *Ladan,* a variant spelling of Libni; compare 6:17. **26:21b** Hebrew *Jehieli* (also in 26:22), a variant spelling of Jehiel; compare 23:8. **26:26** Hebrew *the commanders of thousands and of hundreds.* **26:28** Hebrew *Shelomith,* a variant spelling of Shelomoth. **26:29** Or *were given outside work;* or *were given work away from the Temple area.* **26:31** Hebrew *Jerijah,* a variant spelling of Jeriah; compare 23:19.

NOTES

26:1 ***Abiasaph.*** See 6:23; 9:19; Exod 6:24.

26:15 ***storehouse.*** This is mentioned elsewhere in Neh 12:25, again in conjunction with gates and gatekeeping. The supply rooms would be placed near the entrance away from the area of worship activity, near the place of delivery but also near the military guard for the Temple precinct, that is, the gatekeepers. These, however, were more than simply storehouses, actually functioning as vaults for precious items (cf. 2 Chr 25:24).

26:16 ***Shuppim.*** This name (*shuppim* [TH8206, ZH9157]), missing in the LXX and awkward in this verse, should possibly be deleted as a scribal error, representing a repetition of the last word in 26:15, "storehouse" (*ha'asuppim* [TH624, ZH667]).

the west gate and the gateway leading up to the Temple. The "west gate" and the "gate of Shalleketh on the upper road" (see NLT mg) should not be viewed as two different structures, but the same. Lit., "to the west, by the gate of Shalleketh on the upper road."

COMMENTARY

David's Commission of the Levitical Gatekeepers: Kohath, Merari (26:1-19). Following the organization of the musicians, the Chronicler lists the gatekeepers. As has been the trend so far in this section of Chronicles, the list is inserted at the outset (26:1b-11), followed by notes on the selection process and their vocational function (26:12-19).

The list in 26:1b-11 reveals a tripartite division of gatekeepers. First, from the Levitical line of Kohath was the Korahite Meshelemiah, whose seven sons are listed in 26:2-3. Meshelemiah's line will reappear in 26:9 following the long focus on Obed-edom in 26:4-8.[1] This statement appears to offer some balance to the clan that was listed in the prominent first place, noting that Meshelemiah not only had a considerable number of relatives (18), but that they were also "valiant men" (26:9; see further below). While the Chronicler, as will be seen, takes the opportunity with Obed-edom to emphasize the key theme of divine blessing, he does not want to undercut Meshelemiah's authority. Meshelamiah's status as "firstborn" is made clear in the distribution of gates in 26:14 when his division is given "two portions," that is, two gates (Japhet 1993:459).

Second, Obed-edom was from the Levitical line of Kohath and possibly also the clan of Korah (26:19), not surprising in light of his earlier function as gatekeeper in the Chronicler's account of the transport of the Ark to Jerusalem in 15:24. Although called, lit., "the Gittite" in 13:13, Obed-edom did not come from the Philistine city of Gath but rather the Levitical city of Gath-rimmon, which was in the tribe of Dan according to the book of Joshua (Josh 19:45; 21:24), but in the tribe of Ephraim according to the Chronicler (6:69). The Chronicler, drawing on his source in Samuel, is well aware of the tradition that Obed-edom had been highly blessed by God because of the presence of the Ark in his home for three months (13:14). This blessing is nowhere more evident than here in the record of his division of gatekeepers, which records eight sons followed by the explanatory note, "God had richly blessed Obed-edom" (26:5). The description of Obed-edom continues for three more verses, double the length of the other divisions. In these verses the Chronicler includes the record of Obed-edom's grandsons, whose ability earned them great authority. Such ability is also extended to the entire clan of Obed-edom, 62 in number. The phrase translated here as "very capable men" is in Hebrew *bene-khayil* [TH1121/2428, ZH1201/2657] in 26:7, 9 ("sons of strength" or "valiant sons") and *'ish-khayil* [TH376, ZH408] in 26:8 ("men of strength" or "valiant men"). The first phrase is used in all cases outside of 1 Chronicles 26 (except possibly one) to refer to those capable in military affairs (5:18; Deut 3:18; Judg 18:2; 1 Sam 14:52; 18:17; 2 Sam 2:7; 13:28; 17:10; 2 Kgs 2:16; 2 Chr 28:6).[2] The second phrase can refer to "capable men" (see Gen 47:6 for shepherds; Exod 18:21, 25 for judges; 1 Kgs 1:42 for a counselor), but it is most often linked to agility in war (10:12; 11:22; Judg 3:29; 20:44, 46; 1 Sam 31:12; 2 Sam 11:16; 24:9; Ps 76:5; Jer 48:14; Nah 2:4). This description of the gatekeepers along with the reference to "head warriors" in 26:12 (NLT, "family leaders") shows that, as Wright (1990:69) has argued, "rather than minor clerical functionaries, the Chronicler portrays the gatekeepers as a paramilitary inner city security force." These descriptions, thus, are lauding the ability of these gatekeepers to protect the sanctuary from trespassing by the common or unclean.

The final division of gatekeepers the Chronicler lists is that of Hosah from the Merari clan of Levi. Little is said of Hosah's clan except for a listing of four sons, enumeration of thirteen relatives, and the odd note that his eldest son did not assume the mantle of leadership in the family. The latter is not a positive signal in an ancient context, implying that either the eldest son had died (or worse, had been judged as Aaron's sons) or was unfit (as Eli's and Samuel's). This may justify the lack of numbers attached to the Hosah clan.

The list of gatekeepers contains two divisions from the Levitical line of Kohath and one division from Merari but fails to list a member from the Levitical line of Gershon. Interestingly, the Gershonites were also left out of the second rendering of the Levitical lists in 24:20b-31.[3]

Following the list of divisions, the Chronicler then provides a note on the selection process and vocational function. As with the other Levitical and priestly figures in chapters 24–25, the gatekeepers were chosen by "sacred lots," whether they were "small" or "great" (NLT, "without regard to age or training"). Thus, the decision on their assignments was left to the God who controls the "sacred lots." Meshelemiah's division was offered two gates (east and north), with the special note that Meshelemiah's son who was given charge of the north gate was a man of "unusual wisdom"—that is, "one who counsels with insight" (*yo'ets besekel* [TH3289/7922, ZH3619/8507]), an allusion to his role as political adviser (see Wright

1990:76). Additionally, Obed-edom was offered one gate (south) and the storehouse, while Hosah was offered one gate (west).[4]

The various clans were responsible to protect the gates to the Temple precincts, with six assigned by Meshelemiah to the prominent east gate,[5] four by Zechariah to the north gate, and four by Obed-edom to the south gate, with an additional pair at the storehouse.[6] The western side required eight gatekeepers[7] with four assigned to the main gate, two to the "upper road" (NLT, "the gateway leading up to the Temple") and two to the "courtyard," an area the referent of which is not clear but which most likely is mentioned in 2 Kings 23:11.[8] This brings the total number of gatekeepers to 24, not surprising in light of the regular use of this number for the enumeration of Levitical and priestly duties throughout chapters 24–25. The rotation of duty is not specified in this passage, but 9:24-25 offers details that specify that they were for "seven-day periods."

This passage links the gatekeepers to the control of access to the Temple area, a role that, according to 9:23, 27, included guarding the entrance, patrolling in the night, and opening the gates each morning and thus (as we have seen in the vocabulary of this chapter) one that demanded military acumen (see 2 Chr 23:1-21). However, throughout Chronicles the gatekeepers did more than merely maintain law and order (Wright 1990:69-81). As Wright (1990:74) has noted in his review of the function of gatekeepers in Chronicles, "The gatekeepers' tasks . . . embrace three chief areas in Chronicles: (1) the political administration of the state; (2) the administration of temple revenues; and (3) the custodial care of the Temple and its paraphernalia" (cf. 9:17-19, 26-32; 26:12, 14; 2 Chr 3:14; 31:14-17; 34:8-13).

David's Commission of Levitical Treasurers: Gershon, Kohath (26:20–28). The next section enumerates the list of Levites who were in charge of the treasuries.[9] The list is structured according to both personnel and responsibility (26:21-22, 23-28). Two types of treasuries are mentioned from the outset: "the treasuries of the house of God" and "the treasuries of the gifts dedicated to the LORD" (26:20; see also 28:12). Two Levitical groups were chosen for this task: one group from the Levitical line of Gershon and the other from Kohath. Thus, 26:21-22 links the leader Jehiel (from the family of Libni [Ladan] of the Levitical line of Gershon) to the care of the treasuries of the house of God, and 26:23-28 links the leaders Shebuel and Shelomoth (from the clan of Amram of the Levitical line of Kohath) to the administration of the treasuries of the gifts dedicated to the Lord. Little is said of what was in the "treasuries of the house of God," but 26:26-28 reveals that the "treasuries of the gifts dedicated to the LORD" contained plunder dedicated to maintain the house of the Lord. Mention is made of David and his officials but also of great warriors in the past, highlighting Samuel (cf. 1 Sam 7:7-14), Saul, Abner, and Joab. Although these verses give prominence to David and his military exploits as the foundation of these treasuries, it is interesting that others are included as well. This may have been an attempt to show the participation of all Israel in the care of the Temple, both past (Samuel, Saul) and present (David), whether north (Abner) or south (Joab). The establishment of these treasuries and their administration was very important to the Chronicler, who placed more emphasis on the treasuries than his source throughout the ensuing narratives.[10]

David's Commission of Levitical Administrators, the Kohathites (26:29-32). With 26:29 there is a departure from Levitical tasks related to the Temple Mount. The focus is on groups drawn from the Levitical line of Kohath (see 23:18-19; Exod 6:21). The first group mentioned, the clan of Izhar led by Kenaniah, was appointed to "external" duties (see NLT mg), or duties outside the Temple Mount. They functioned as "officials and judges" (see 23:3-5), terms or offices that Deuteronomy 16:18-20 links to the administration of local justice throughout the towns of Israel. While in Deuteronomy the people appointed these offices in their towns, in Chronicles it is David who appoints these to ensure proper justice. Two further groups are mentioned, both from the clan of Hebron and both placed over the affairs of Israelite territory. The one was led by Hashabiah over the area west of the Jordan (26:30) and the other by Jeriah over the area east of the Jordan River (26:31-32). The role of these two Hebron clans is not clear, but 26:30 and 26:32 list both "matters related to God/the things of the LORD" as well as "matters related to the king/service of the king." They clearly had a "sacred" role to play as Levites, but they also played a "secular" role, representing royal interests in the regions.

Clarity as to these roles can be gained from a close look at the reforms of Jehoshaphat in 2 Chronicles 19:5-11 (Japhet 1993:463-464). There the Chronicler depicts Jehoshaphat appointing "judges" to whom were assigned "officers" in order to consider cases related to the matters of the Lord (NLT, "involving the LORD") as well as the king (NLT, "civil disputes"). The same vocabulary appears here in 26:29-32 and suggests that Kenaniah and his clan functioned as officials and judges in all of Israel with the assistance of the clans of Hebron led by Hashabiah and Jeriah, who were divided between the two sections of the nation. The nature of this assistance is unclear, that is, whether the Hebronites were over the Izharites or vice versa, although primacy was given to the Izrahites in the list.

ENDNOTES

1. It is this that has led many to see 26:4-8 as an intrusive addition to this list, mainly because of the way these verses split up 26:3 and 9 and the way in which these verses begin and end with the same phrase (26:4, 8). Although it is possible that the list in 26:4-8 has been combined with the other list material, this does not mean that 26:9 was originally joined to 26:2-3. Verse 9 appears to incorporate similar vocabulary to 26:4-8 and may reflect the Chronicler's sensitivity to the various groups responsible for worship in his time. For this debate, see Knoppers (2004:869-870), who views it as an intrusion, and Japhet (1993:451), who views it as part of the literary structure of the lists.
2. The one possible exception is 1 Kgs 1:52. See Wright (1990:70), who notes that of 40 occurrences of *khayil* in Chronicles that unambiguously originated with the Chronicler, 36 are related to military contexts.
3. Japhet (1993:453-456) claims that the total number of family divisions comes to 24: Shelemiah (7), Obed-edom (13), and Hosah (4), matching the motif of 24 in the lists in chs 24–25. But this involves ignoring Shemaiah in Obed-edom's list.
4. See note on 26:16, "Shuppim."
5. The east gate is identified in 9:17-18 as the "King's Gate," a designation well established in the Persian and early Hellenistic periods (see Dan 2:49; Xenophon *Cyropaedia* 8.1, 6-9; cf. Wright 1990:75).

6. The phrase at the end of 26:17 in Hebrew is *shenayim shenayim* [TH8147, ZH9109] (lit., "two two"; cf. NLT's "two pairs"). It is possible that the extra "two" is the one missing from the awkward ending to 26:18. Even if both "twos" were originally present, the resulting phrase only appears elsewhere in Gen 7:9 and 15, where it refers to the animals going onto the ark two by two or in pairs.
7. The NLT translates here only six, but the Hebrew is awkward at this point. To this point in the enumeration the number of guards has always been placed after the reference to the location. Thus 26:18 should be translated as "at the west, four, at the upper road, two, at the *parbar*" [TH6503, ZH7232]. What is missing is a number after the final location, and this number probably was the "two" that is extra at the end of 26:17.
8. Here the Hebrew is *parbar* [TH6503, ZH7232]; in 2 Kgs 23:11 the word is *parwar* [TH6503A, ZH7247]. Knoppers (2004:866) points to the Qumran Temple Scroll (11QT), which identifies the *parwar* as a colonnade porch on the west of the Temple.
9. Here we should probably follow the LXX reading, "the Levites, their brothers," rather than the MT's "the Levites, Ahijah" (as in NLT).
10. See Knoppers (2004:883-890), who notes three aspects of the Chronicler's presentation of the treasuries: (1) The Chronicler dwells on the establishment and endowment of the treasuries in the united monarchy. (2) The Chronicler overtly posits times of economic renewal for Jerusalem and Judah, marked by the construction of new treasuries or storehouses. (3) The Chronicler plays down the destruction of the Temple, in contrast to his source.

◆ R. David's Commission of the Military; Lists of Tribal Leaders and Officials (27:1-34)

This is the list of Israelite generals and captains,* and their officers, who served the king by supervising the army divisions that were on duty each month of the year. Each division served for one month and had 24,000 troops.

2 Jashobeam son of Zabdiel was commander of the first division of 24,000 troops, which was on duty during the first month. 3 He was a descendant of Perez and was in charge of all the army officers for the first month.

4 Dodai, a descendant of Ahoah, was commander of the second division of 24,000 troops, which was on duty during the second month. Mikloth was his chief officer.

5 Benaiah son of Jehoiada the priest was commander of the third division of 24,000 troops, which was on duty during the third month. 6 This was the Benaiah who commanded David's elite military group known as the Thirty. His son Ammizabad was his chief officer.

7 Asahel, the brother of Joab, was commander of the fourth division of 24,000 troops, which was on duty during the fourth month. Asahel was succeeded by his son Zebadiah.

8 Shammah* the Izrahite was commander of the fifth division of 24,000 troops, which was on duty during the fifth month.

9 Ira son of Ikkesh from Tekoa was commander of the sixth division of 24,000 troops, which was on duty during the sixth month.

10 Helez, a descendant of Ephraim from Pelon, was commander of the seventh division of 24,000 troops, which was on duty during the seventh month.

11 Sibbecai, a descendant of Zerah from Hushah, was commander of the eighth division of 24,000 troops, which was on duty during the eighth month.

12 Abiezer from Anathoth in the territory of Benjamin was commander of the ninth division of 24,000 troops, which was on duty during the ninth month.
13 Maharai, a descendant of Zerah from Netophah, was commander of the tenth division of 24,000 troops, which was on duty during the tenth month.
14 Benaiah from Pirathon in Ephraim was commander of the eleventh division of 24,000 troops, which was on duty during the eleventh month.
15 Heled,* a descendant of Othniel from Netophah, was commander of the twelfth division of 24,000 troops, which was on duty during the twelfth month.

16 The following were the tribes of Israel and their leaders:

Tribe	*Leader*
Reuben	Eliezer son of Zicri
Simeon	Shephatiah son of Maacah
17 Levi	Hashabiah son of Kemuel
Aaron	(the priests) Zadok
18 Judah	Elihu (a brother of David)
Issachar	Omri son of Michael
19 Zebulun	Ishmaiah son of Obadiah
Naphtali	Jeremoth son of Azriel
20 Ephraim	Hoshea son of Azaziah
Manasseh (west)	Joel son of Pedaiah
21 Manasseh in Gilead (east)	Iddo son of Zechariah
Benjamin	Jaasiel son of Abner
22 Dan	Azarel son of Jeroham

These were the leaders of the tribes of Israel.

23 When David took his census, he did
not count those who were younger than
twenty years of age, because the LORD had
promised to make the Israelites as numer-
ous as the stars in heaven. 24 Joab son of
Zeruiah began the census but never fin-
ished it because* the anger of God fell on
Israel. The total number was never record-
ed in King David's official records.

25 Azmaveth son of Adiel was in charge of the palace treasuries.
Jonathan son of Uzziah was in charge of the regional treasuries throughout the towns, villages, and fortresses of Israel.
26 Ezri son of Kelub was in charge of the field workers who farmed the king's lands.
27 Shimei from Ramah was in charge of the king's vineyards.
Zabdi from Shepham was responsible for the grapes and the supplies of wine.
28 Baal-hanan from Geder was in charge of the king's olive groves and sycamore-fig trees in the foothills of Judah.*
Joash was responsible for the supplies of olive oil.
29 Shitrai from Sharon was in charge of the cattle on the Sharon Plain.
Shaphat son of Adlai was responsible for the cattle in the valleys.
30 Obil the Ishmaelite was in charge of the camels.
Jehdeiah from Meronoth was in charge of the donkeys.
31 Jaziz the Hagrite was in charge of the king's flocks of sheep and goats.
All these officials were overseers of King David's property.

32 Jonathan, David's uncle, was a wise
counselor to the king, a man of great in-
sight, and a scribe. Jehiel the Hacmonite
was responsible for teaching the king's
sons. 33 Ahithophel was the royal adviser.
Hushai the Arkite was the king's friend.
34 Ahithophel was succeeded by Jehoiada
son of Benaiah and by Abiathar. Joab was
commander of the king's army.

27:1 Hebrew *commanders of thousands and of hundreds.* **27:8** Hebrew *Shamhuth,* a variant spelling of Shammah; compare 11:27 and 2 Sam 23:25. **27:15** Hebrew *Heldai,* a variant spelling of Heled; compare 11:30 and 2 Sam 23:29. **27:24** Or *never finished it, and yet.* **27:28** Hebrew *the Shephelah.*

NOTES

27:2-3 *Jashobeam . . . descendant of Perez.* Jashobeam shared a common ancestor with David (see Ruth 4:18-22). This explains why he was given the prominent first month.

27:6 ***the Thirty.*** See note on 11:15.

27:7 ***Asahel was succeeded by his son Zebadiah.*** Abner killed this brother of Joab when David was still in Hebron (2 Sam 2:23); so the list honors Asahel but notes that it was really Zebadiah who commanded this division.

27:23 ***Israelites as numerous as the stars in heaven.*** See Gen 22:17.

27:24 ***King David's official records.*** Lit., "the account of the matters of the days of King David," which is probably a reference to a particular book recording the events of David's reign. Similar references in the OT to source materials can be found in 1 Kgs 14:19; Esth 10:2.

COMMENTARY

David's Commission of the Military (27:1-15). With chapter 27 the Chronicler leaves behind the enumeration of the Levitical families, moving to the "secular" leadership of his kingdom. He begins with the military (27:1-15), then moves to the tribes (27:16-22), and finally, after a short note on the census, concludes with the property managers (27:25-31) and royal advisers (27:32-34).

Because this chapter, as part of the unit of chapters 23–27, stands out as the only one unconcerned with sacred personnel, some have suggested it was a later addition.[1] However, although the Chronicler's focus has been on the commissioning and organization of the sacred orders due to his concern for the Temple, the royal secular infrastructure of the kingdom is also important for sustaining the Temple worship. In addition, in the discussion of 23:1-2 it is noted that the term "summoned" (*'asap* [TH622, ZH665]) in 23:2 is a literary signal from the Chronicler that summarizes the content of chapters 23–27. There David is depicted as assembling "all the leaders of Israel" (*kol-sare yisra'el*), a term that is distinguished in the list from "the priests and Levites." Thus, it is now in chapter 27 that the Chronicler presents the "leaders" of Israel, with the term "leader" (*sar* [TH8269, ZH8569]) used seven times in the chapter (27:1, 3, 5, 8, 22, 31, 34). Finally, the national assembly that David convenes in chapters 28–29 is comprised of the very groups introduced in chapter 27. Thus, chapter 27 is not only appropriate in a work focused on the Temple but is expected both by the introduction to chapters 23–27 and also the introduction to chapters 28–29.

The first section of chapter 27 focuses on the organization of the army. The term "list" here (*mispar* [TH4557, ZH5031]) is the one used regularly throughout chapters 23–27 for "numbering" (23:3, 24, 27, 31; 25:1, 7; 27:1). It is also the term used in 21:5 when Joab presents the results of the census to David, an event reflected in 27:23-24, where again the term appears twice. The initial list of personnel in 27:1 appears to reflect organization of groups through a chain of command, moving from the Israelites to "heads of the fathers" (not reflected in NLT) to generals and captains (lit., "[the leaders of] thousands and hundreds") to their officers. The role of this chain of command was to supervise the army divisions, and they did this under the authority of the king. This is an important development in the sociology of Israel, signaling that the army was no longer linked to tribal chieftains and tribal authority but rather to a centralized royal figure and that military affairs would no longer be conducted ad hoc but would be directed by a standing army.[2]

These army divisions are identified as those who "went in and went out" (*habba'ah wehayyotse'th* [TH935/3318, ZH995/3655]; NLT, "on duty"), a phrase related to the ancient "changing of the guard," which is illustrated in 2 Kings 11:9 and 2 Chronicles 23:8. These latter passages identify the Sabbath as the time of the changing of the Levitical guard; they distinguished between "men reporting for duty that Sabbath" and "those who were going off duty [on the Sabbath]," a process dependent on an act of dismissal ("Jehoiada the priest did not let anyone go home after their shift ended," 2 Chr 23:8). The specific duties of these troops is not made clear, although it obviously would have entailed battle in times of war, and in times of peace, as Japhet (1993:469) notes, "These reserves would be given the duty of guarding the kingdom's borders, doing police service and maintaining order in conquered territories, manning strongholds and castles, attending to the weapons and equipment—chariots, horses, etc." For the royal army in chapter 27, the cycle was monthly rather than weekly, a fact reinforced by the list in 27:2-15. Although the list is based on the principle of 12 units, it is interesting that the division is not based on the 12 tribes, further evidence of the social transformation under David's reign. The number 12, however, also bolsters the Chronicler's presentation of this perfect kingdom and echoes the earlier divisions in chapters 24–26, which were based on the number 24. However, the fact that it is only half the number may privilege the role and organization of the sacred orders.

Leaders of the Tribes of Israel (27:16-22). The second list in chapter 27 focuses on the tribal leaders of Israel. Two tribes are missing (Gad, Asher; cf. Gen 49), while Aaron is separated out from Levi, and the tribes of Joseph are divided into three: Ephraim, Manasseh (west), and Manasseh (east), resulting in 13 units. Japhet does not find this odd in Chronicles, arguing that the preference of the Chronicler is "for a comprehensive view of the tribes of Israel rather than the stereotyped number twelve" (1993:471). However, in light of the regular use of 12 in the lists in 27:1-15 and 27:25-31, it appears that the excision of Gad and Asher[3] was intentional (not a scribal error), and that the addition of Aaron was a quick note to highlight the distinction of the priests within Levi.[4]

At the beginning of the list the leaders are called *nagid* [TH5057, ZH5592], while at the end they are called *sar* [TH8269, ZH8569]. The first term is a favorite of the Chronicler, who uses it to refer to David (5:2; 11:2; 17:7; 2 Chr 6:5) but also to rulers in various capacities, whether over a tribe (27:16; 2 Chr 19:11), clan (9:20), priestly militia (12:28), army division (13:1; 27:4; 2 Chr 11:11; 32:21), treasury (26:24), or palace (2 Chr 28:7). These two terms are used together in 2 Chronicles 32:21 to refer to leadership in the Assyrian army. However, this list of leaders of tribes is important for the Chronicler, preparing the way for the appearance of tribal leaders in chapters 28 and 29 in support of Solomon and the Temple project (28:1; 29:6).

Note on the Census (27:23-24). A short note follows the listing of the army and the tribal leaders. These two verses have often mystified commentators who see no reason for its inclusion in a chapter presenting lists.[5] However, it appears to play an important function for the Chronicler, justifying his inclusion of the previous list of the leaders of the tribes without the numbers that were included in the army organization. The census of the people was incomplete ("never finished"), and thus the full number was unavailable ("never recorded"). The number provided in 21:5 was only the number of the incomplete census. The Chronicler also informs his readers that David's error was not related to breaking the priestly rule of counting only those over 20 years of age (Num 1:3, 45), basing this restriction on the Abrahamic promise of countless descendants (Gen 22:17). The problem, as noted in the commentary on chapter 21, must therefore have been that he did not provide the appropriate offering for conducting a census.

Overseers of David's Property (27:25-31). The next list in this chapter focuses on those in charge of royal property, a list that contains exactly 12 members. At the head of those in charge of royal property were the officials over the treasuries (27:25), one to control the main treasuries in Jerusalem (Azmaveth) and one to control the subsidiary treasuries spread throughout the kingdom (Jonathan). The royal house controlled a large portion of the agricultural activity in the land and needed supervisors for these many activities (27:26-31), whether that was the care of domestic plants (crops, vineyards, olive groves, sycamore-fig trees) and the control of their products (grapes, wine, olive oil), or the care of domestic animals (cattle, camels, donkeys, sheep, goats). Such holdings were necessary not only to support an expansive royal court but also to support the standing army.

According to 1 Kings 4, Solomon developed this system even further. While 27:25-31 records a centralized system controlled by royal officials, 1 Kings 4 reveals a system of royal maintenance closer to the model of military service seen in 27:1-15. Solomon developed a system in which 12 officers, each over different geographical sectors of the kingdom, were responsible for maintenance of the court one month each year (1 Kgs 4:7-18). Although it is difficult to ascertain the process of development from David to Solomon, it is interesting that the Chronicler did not incorporate this account of Solomon in his history, bringing the focus entirely on David as the one who organized provisions for the endurance of the court.

Advisers to David (27:32-34). Finally, the Chronicler turns to key wisdom figures in David's court, including David's uncle Jonathan, who also served as a scribe, and Ahithophel, Jehoiada, and Abiathar, who served as royal advisers. His good friend Hushai and Joab, the commander of his army, were also named. Even the one who attended to the princes is listed. The sum of this final list is 7, short of the 12 that is used regularly for the secular leadership in this chapter but identical to the number of advisers key to the Persian throne (see Esth 1:14), and if nothing else a complete number (Japhet 1993:480). This final list accentuates the resources of wisdom that were present in David's court. Interestingly, when he came to the reign of Solomon, the Chronicler focused little attention on his wisdom as well as on the administration of his court. As with the former list, this may be another case in which the Chronicler was accentuating David as the one who developed the royal court, freeing Solomon to focus on one task alone: building the Temple.

In chapters 23–27 the Chronicler once again provides a series of long lists akin to the genealogies that began his work. To the Western reader such lists test the mettle of the most devoted scholar, but to the Chronicler these lists were significant to his story. They not only highlighted David's meticulous care in preparing for the construction of the first Temple and maintenance of its services but also provided the foundation for the worship in the second Temple in his own time. Through this the reader is given a vision for the kind of commitment and involvement necessary to sustain the worship of Yahweh. And in this the glory of David's God was further enhanced.

ENDNOTES

1. See the defense of the originality of this chapter in Japhet 1993:468-469.
2. Note the contrast between this organization and that found in the book of Judges (e.g., Judg 1:3, 21-22, 27, 29-33).
3. These two tribes were named after the two sons of Leah's maid Zilpah (Gen 30:9-13); in 2:2 they are placed last in the list of tribes.
4. The piece "Aaron . . . Zadok" is distinct from the rest of the list with the lack of "son of X." Another option is that this piece is part of a later, pro-Priestly edition of Chronicles, but this is not necessary (see Introduction).
5. See Japhet 1993:473-474, who calls it "an interpolation, loosely linked to its context. Different in both genre and subject matter, it disturbs the sequence of the lists and deviates from the overall structure of the chapter, as well as from the Chronicler's historical and theological views." She concludes that it is "a 'theological corrective' of a midrashic nature based on ch 21. Its purpose is to present the census narrative in a new light and offer a new evaluation of David's image."

◆ S. David's Instructions to Solomon (28:1-21)

David summoned all the officials of Israel to Jerusalem—the leaders of the tribes, the commanders of the army divisions, the other generals and captains,* the overseers of the royal property and livestock, the palace officials, the mighty men, and all the other brave warriors in the kingdom. 2David rose to his feet and said: "My brothers and my people! It was my desire to build a temple where the Ark of the LORD's Covenant, God's footstool, could rest permanently. I made the necessary preparations for building it, 3but God said to me, 'You must not build a temple to honor my name, for you are a warrior and have shed much blood.'

4"Yet the LORD, the God of Israel, has chosen me from among all my father's family to be king over Israel forever. For he has chosen the tribe of Judah to rule, and from among the families of Judah he chose my father's family. And from among my father's sons the LORD was pleased to make me king over all Israel. 5And from among my sons—for the LORD has given me many—he chose Solomon to succeed me on the throne of Israel and to rule over the LORD's kingdom. 6He said to me, 'Your son Solomon will build my Temple and its courtyards, for I have chosen him as my son, and I will be his father. 7And if he continues to obey my commands and regulations as he does now, I will make his kingdom last forever.'

8"So now, with God as our witness, and in the sight of all Israel—the LORD's assembly—I give you this charge. Be careful to obey all the commands of the LORD your God, so that you may continue to possess this good land and leave it to your children as a permanent inheritance.

9"And Solomon, my son, learn to know the God of your ancestors intimately. Worship and serve him with your whole heart and a willing mind. For the LORD sees every heart and knows every plan and thought. If you seek him, you will find him. But if you forsake him, he will reject you forever. 10So take this seriously. The LORD has chosen you to build a Temple as his sanctuary. Be strong, and do the work."

11 Then David gave Solomon the plans
for the Temple and its surroundings, in-
cluding the entry room, the storerooms,
the upstairs rooms, the inner rooms, and
the inner sanctuary—which was the place
of atonement. 12 David also gave Solomon
all the plans he had in mind* for the
courtyards of the LORD's Temple, the out-
side rooms, the treasuries, and the rooms
for the gifts dedicated to the LORD. 13 The
king also gave Solomon the instructions
concerning the work of the various divi-
sions of priests and Levites in the Temple
of the LORD. And he gave specifications
for the items in the Temple that were to
be used for worship.

14 David gave instructions regarding
how much gold and silver should be used
to make the items needed for service.
15 He told Solomon the amount of gold
needed for the gold lampstands and
lamps, and the amount of silver for the
silver lampstands and lamps, depending
on how each would be used. 16 He desig-
nated the amount of gold for the table
on which the Bread of the Presence
would be placed and the amount of silver
for other tables.

17 David also designated the amount of
gold for the solid gold meat hooks used to
handle the sacrificial meat and for the
basins, pitchers, and dishes, as well as the
amount of silver for every dish. 18 He des-
ignated the amount of refined gold for
the altar of incense. Finally, he gave him
a plan for the LORD's "chariot"—the gold
cherubim* whose wings were stretched
out over the Ark of the LORD's Covenant.
19 "Every part of this plan," David told
Solomon, "was given to me in writing
from the hand of the LORD.*"

20 Then David continued, "Be strong and
courageous, and do the work. Don't be
afraid or discouraged, for the LORD God, my
God, is with you. He will not fail you or
forsake you. He will see to it that all the
work related to the Temple of the LORD is
finished correctly. 21 The various divisions of
priests and Levites will serve in the Temple
of God. Others with skills of every kind will
volunteer, and the officials and the entire
nation are at your command."

28:1 Hebrew *the commanders of thousands and commanders of hundreds.* **28:12** Or *the plans of the spirit that was with him.* **28:18** Hebrew *for the gold cherub chariot.* **28:19** Or *was written under the direction of the LORD.*

NOTES

28:1 ***the leaders of the tribes.*** This is a reference to those enumerated in 27:16-22, using the precise language of 27:22b.

the commanders of the army divisions, the other generals and captains. This is a reference to those enumerated in 27:1-15, sharing most of the language of the list in 27:1.

the overseers of the royal property and livestock. Lit., "the officials of the property and livestock belonging to the king and his sons," a reference to those enumerated in 27:25-31. Although these terms are not used in ch 27, it is interesting that this assumes some holdings by the princes.

the palace officials. Heb., *saris* [TH5631, ZH6247]. This title is often used for eunuchs (Esth 1:10, 12, 15; 2:21; 4:4; Isa 56:3-4), but it may be also used for a high official in the court (Gen 40:2, 7; 2 Kgs 18:17; 23:11; 24:12, 15; 25:19; Dan 1:3, 7-11, 18). Thus, it may be a reference to the advisers described in 27:32-34, although this term is not used in ch 27.

28:2 ***God's footstool.*** The Ark is depicted as the footstool for the feet of God, who is enthroned in heaven but whose feet are visible in the earthly sanctuary (cf. Ps 132:7). See how Isaiah catches a glimpse of the hem of his robe in Isa 6.

28:4 ***he has chosen the tribe of Judah to rule.*** For the wording here, see 5:2; Ps 78:68 (Knoppers 2004:927), but also note Gen 49:8-12; Judg 1:1-2; 20:18; Isa 11:1.

among my father's sons. See 1 Sam 16.

28:5 ***the LORD has given me many.*** In Chronicles progeny is a sign of God's blessing (3:1-9; 14:2-7; 25:5; 26:4-5; 2 Chr 11:18-22; 13:21; 21:1-3).

28:8 ***I give you this charge.*** The pronoun "you" here is plural, as are the verbs that follow, revealing that this is addressed to the assembly.

28:11 ***entry room.*** Heb., *'ulam* [TH361, ZH395] (also called *'elam* [TH197/361, ZH221/395]), a term for the enclosed porch that served as an entrance hall to the first Temple and measured about 30 feet by 15 feet (1 Kgs 6:3; 7:19; see also Ezek 40–48; cf. Ezek 40:7-8). The next four words in the Hebrew text all are modified by a possessive suffix, "its" (not represented in the NLT), suggesting that the *'ulam* is representative of the entire Temple complex (cf. 2 Chr 8:12; 15:8; 29:7, 17).[1] Missing in the NLT is a translation of the next term in the Hebrew text, *bayit* [TH1004, ZH1074] ("houses"). This could refer to rooms in the *'ulam* or nearby, but none are described elsewhere. Possibly it means that the Temple structure (Holy Place, Most Holy Place) lay behind the *'ulam*, but this is described later on.

storerooms. One might think these "storerooms" (*ganzak* [TH1597, ZH1711]), a loanword from Persian (see closely related *genez* [TH1595, ZH1709] in Esth 3:9; 4:7), referred to the treasuries (*'otsar* [TH214, ZH238]) of the Temple mentioned in 26:20 and administered by the Levites, but these are mentioned in the following verse.

upstairs rooms. The "upstairs rooms" were roof chambers in Solomon's Temple (2 Chr 3:9; 2 Kgs 23:12), also found above large ancient houses (Judg 3:20; Jer 22:13) and at the gates (2 Sam 18:33) and corners (Neh 3:31, 32) of walls.

inner rooms, and the inner sanctuary. These terms are "inner rooms" (*khadarayw happenimim* [TH2315/6442, ZH2540/7164]; lit., "its rooms, the inner ones") and "inner sanctuary" (*beth hakkapporeth* [TH3727, ZH4114]; lit., "the house of the atonement"). The term *happenimim* (toward the inside, inner) is used for the Most Holy Place in 1 Kgs 6:27; 7:12, but also for the court beyond the *'ulam* [TH197/361, ZH221/395] in Ezek 8:3, 16; 41:17. These last two phrases probably further define the term "its rooms" (*khadarayw* [TH2315, ZH2540]) to include the entire inner area of the house structure as well as the Most Holy Place—that is, the house of atonement where the Ark with its atonement cover was located (Exod 25:17-22; 26:34).

28:12 ***the courtyards of the LORD's Temple.*** There were two courts in the first Temple, the inner (1 Kgs 6:36; 7:12) and the outer or great court (cf. 2 Kgs 21:5; 23:12; 2 Chr 33:5). Second Chronicles 4:9 speaks of these two courts as the court of the priests and the great court (see also 2 Kgs 20:4 for a possible middle court).

the outside rooms. These were rooms connected to Solomon's Temple, where the Recabites were asked to drink wine (Jer 35:2, 4), Levites lived (9:33), and gifts were stored (2 Chr 31:11). They functioned similarly to those in the second Temple (Ezra 8:29; 10:6; Neh 10:38-39; 13:5, 8).

the treasuries, and the rooms for the gifts dedicated to the LORD. Although not translated the same in NLT, the Hebrew terms used here are identical to those used for the structures the Levites administered in 26:20. The contents of the first of these are never specified, while the second contained plunder from war (see commentary on 26:20-28). The relationship between these treasuries and those mentioned in 28:11 ("the storerooms") is uncertain.

28:15 ***lampstands and lamps.*** The Tabernacle contained a single branched lampstand (Exod 25:31-40; 37:17-24), which was placed in the Holy Place. The first Temple contained 10 lampstands arranged on each side in front of the inner sanctuary (1 Kgs 7:49; 2 Chr 4:7; 13:11), with no evidence that they were branched but rather seven-spouted bowl lamps (see Zech 4).

28:16 ***the table on which the Bread of the Presence would be placed.*** This table and its accompanying bread were features in the Tabernacle (Lev 24:5-9; cf. Exod 26:35), placed in the Holy Place with the lampstand as a reminder of the covenant between Israel and the Lord. It was incorporated into the Temple plans as well (23:29; 2 Chr 2:4; 13:11; 29:18).

other tables. Second Chronicles 4:8 speaks of ten tables (five on each side) in the first Temple. Ezekiel 40:39 speaks of two tables for sacrifice in the future Temple.

28:17 ***meat hooks.*** These were implements for sacrifice (*mizlag* [TH4207A, ZH4656]); see Exod 27:3; 38:3; Num 4:14; 2 Chr 4:16. A closely related word in 1 Sam 2:13 (*mazleg* [TH4207, ZH4657]) depicts that utensil with "three teeth" (three prongs), thus a three-pronged fork.

the basins, pitchers, and dishes. These "basins" were used for sacrifice in the Tabernacle (Exod 27:3; 38:3; Num 4:14), the first Temple (1 Kgs 7:40, 45; 2 Chr 4:8, 11, 22; Jer 52:18) and the second Temple (Neh 7:70). Along with the basins, the "pitchers" were used to pour out drink offerings (Exod 25:29; 37:16; Num 4:7). The "dishes" are mentioned elsewhere only in the list of utensils brought back from Babylon (Ezra 1:10; 8:27).

28:18 ***altar of incense.*** This was used in the Tabernacle (Exod 30:1, 27; 40:5; Lev 4:7). Two incense altars have been found in excavations at Arad, both on the steps ascending to the Holy of Holies in an Israelite sanctuary (see ABD 3.409).

the LORD's "chariot"—the gold cherubim whose wings were stretched out over the Ark of the LORD's Covenant. This designation of the Ark as a chariot may be under the influence of Ezekiel (Ezek 1:4-24; 10:1-22; 11:22), but it probably has its roots in the ancient theology of "the LORD of Heaven's Armies, who is enthroned between the cherubim" (2 Sam 6:2; Japhet 1993:497). The reference to the heavenly armies of God makes it understandable that he would sit in a chariot. For the description of the Ark, see Exod 25:10-22; 37:1-9.

28:19 ***David told Solomon.*** These words are not in any ancient text but are supplied here because the MT has "me," suggesting that the speech left off at 28:10 has now been taken up again. However, the speech appears to resume in 28:20, where "David said" (NLT, "Then David continued") is found in the ancient witnesses. Interestingly, LXX has "him" in place of "me," which is preferred in this context.

COMMENTARY

As noted earlier in the commentary, 23:2 ("David summoned all the leaders of Israel, together with the priests and Levites") serves as an introduction to the entire section of lists that stretches from chapter 23 to 27. The Hebrew word used there for "summoned" is *'asap* [TH622, ZH665], a term employed by the Chronicler when he portrays "the gathering of officials to receive specific assignments" (Wright 1991:231). In contrast, at 28:1 the Chronicler employs the term *qahal* [TH6950, ZH7735] (NLT, "summoned"), which is used when he "describes the gathering of a civil and cultic national assembly" (Wright 1991:231). This introduction at the outset of chapter 28 signals a new section of the Chronicler's work, distinct from the long lists that have preceded it in chapters 23–27.

The final phrase of David's prayer in 29:19, "for which I have made these preparations" (*kun* [TH3559, ZH3922] in the Hiphil), signals the conclusion of a long process that began back in 22:5 with David's declaration: "'I will begin making preparations [*kun* Hiphil] for it now.' So David collected [*kun* Hiphil] vast amounts of building materials before his death." Now just prior to his death (29:28), this process is brought to conclusion. This evidence highlights the way in which chapters 22 and

28–29 form a bracket around the second major section of the Chronicler's account of David, which comprises chapters 22–29 (see introduction to chs 10–29 and commentary on 22:1; 23:1). David's preparations for the Temple building are catalogued in chapters 22–29; these preparations are bracketed by the two ceremonies enthroning Solomon (see introduction to 2 Chr 1–9 and the connection to the pattern of accounts on building sanctuaries).

In contrast to chapter 22, chapters 28–29 focus more on Solomon's election. Here David builds a case for Solomon to construct the Temple. The account is dominated by David's addresses to the assembly and to Solomon, arranged in chiastic order around a central narrative in which David gives plans for the Temple to Solomon:

Address to Assembly 1 (28:2-8)
  Address to Solomon 1 (28:9-10)
    Direct Narrative of David Giving Plans to Solomon (28:11-18)
  Address to Solomon 2 (28:19-21)
Address to Assembly 2 (29:1-5)

The greater focus of this narrative is on the assembly, rather than on Solomon, evidence for which can be seen in the greater length of the addresses to the assembly (28:2-8; 29:1-5; contrast 28:9-10, 19-21) and in that it was the assembly that responded after the addresses (29:6-9) while Solomon played a passive role in this episode. [2] This is further evidence that the Chronicler was using this narrative to address his own generation, cajoling them to join David and Solomon of old in support of the Temple.

Solomon's passivity is accentuated by David's role as the key actor and catalyst in the chapter, something seen "through the style and syntax which places him as subject at the beginning of all the major units" (Japhet 1993:483). In contrast, as Japhet (1993:484) has noted of Solomon, "He neither does nor says anything" (except in 29:23). David's dominance is also seen in the way in which activities associated with Solomon in the book of Kings are associated by the Chronicler with David (Japhet 1989:229-232, 485-489). This is especially seen in David's extensive preparations for the Temple and its service, as Japhet (1989:485) notes: "Chronicles credits David with all the preparations; Solomon merely puts David's plan into operation."

Introduction (28:1). Having organized the necessary personnel for both Temple and kingdom (chs 23–27), David summoned the secular leadership of the kingdom, just enumerated in chapter 27,[3] to ensure their support of the crown prince Solomon and the Temple project he will undertake. The lack of reference to the Levites and priests is not surprising since their support of the Temple project and services is assumed.[4] The sacred personnel are part of the Temple infrastructure that David had prepared to hand over to Solomon and that must be supported by the rest of Israel.

David Addresses the Leaders (28:2-8). With this great assembly of leaders gathered, the Chronicler depicts David delivering an impassioned speech to both the leaders and Solomon. The first part of the speech (28:2-8) addresses the assembly as a whole ("my brothers and my people," 28:2), depicting David as rising to his feet to deliver the speech. By depicting David in this way, the Chronicler played down the portrayal of David's final days in Samuel—Kings, where David is presented as the weak and frail monarch, and the Chronicler also provides another link between David and Moses, whose physical powers were strong until death (Deut 34:7; Japhet 1993:486). As he stood up, David reviewed the history of the covenant God had established with him. The core of this speech is an echo of the one delivered to Solomon in 22:7-16. However, greater emphasis is placed in this speech on the divine election of Solomon, not surprising since it will form the foundation of the speech and actions of David to Solomon in 28:9-21. In addition, after several chapters of lists, this part of the speech reminds the readers of the covenantal foundation for the entire Temple-building project. David noted that the genesis of the covenant lies in David's desire to build a permanent sanctuary for the Ark, a desire that was rejected because David was a warrior. In spite of this, God had chosen David to be king over Israel and Solomon to be his successor who would build the Temple.

The flow of 28:4-5 binds David and Solomon together into a covenantal team. The list of election (Israel, Judah, David's father's family, David, Solomon) focuses on David's appointment as king and Solomon's appointment as his successor. Even greater emphasis is placed on Solomon in this speech, as he is the one who will sit "on the throne of Israel," "rule over the LORD's kingdom" (28:5), build the Temple, and gain the distinction of God's calling him "my son" (28:6). The Chronicler mentioned Solomon's election four times (28:5, 6, 10; 29:1), developing further his theme that "the process of divine choice is finalized not in David but in his son" (Japhet 1993:488). In this, greater emphasis is placed on the one who must successfully complete the Temple with obvious resonances to the Chronicler, who addressed a community that needed to support the Temple and its services in their time.

Tracing the lineage of kings was important in the ancient Near East in order to legitimize their reign before all contenders. Persian monarchs continued this tradition. There was no greater example of this than Darius I. In his great Behistun Inscription he constructs a lineage for himself that links him to the legendary Persian monarch Achaemenes and through this establishes his claim to the throne.[5] David also traced a link to earlier figures but did so using an election formula that stresses divine sanction of the choice of each generation, rather than human worthiness. While it is stressed that Judah-David-Solomon have been chosen "to be king over Israel forever . . . to rule . . . to make me king over all Israel . . . to succeed me on the throne of Israel" (28:4-5), Solomon was reminded in the end that such rule is ultimately "over the LORD's kingdom" (28:5). This is a careful reminder that the monarch's role was one of vice-regent for the Lord on earth (Ps 2).

With the privilege now declared for Solomon, however, comes great responsibility; this is clarified in the conditional clause of 28:7: "If he continues to obey my commands and regulations as he does now, I will make his kingdom last forever."[6] The Chronicler placed great weight on Solomon's shoulders in the sight of all the leaders of the nation. It was Solomon who must confirm the promises given to David (Williamson 1976:351-361; 1977a:115-154; 1983:305-318). However, instead of the conditional clause of 28:7 being a natural segue to the address of

Solomon individually, the speech first turns to the leaders as a group and addresses them.[7] David called them (with both human observers and divine hearer to ensure compliance)[8] to obey the Lord's commandments in order to secure their lives and the lives of their descendants in the blessed Promised Land. This exhortation is an unmistakable echo of the conditional promise of 28:7 that was delivered to Solomon. In this, the Chronicler declared the importance of the dynastic condition for the people of his own time. Those who first read Chronicles were being exhorted to confirm the promise of the land forever through their obedience to the commands of God.

David Charges Solomon (28:9-10). After addressing the leadership as a whole in 28:2-8, David finally addressed his own son Solomon in 28:9-10. He did not focus initially on the building of the Temple, choosing rather to emphasize spiritual issues that would prove foundational to the success of a reign able to sustain such a project. David called Solomon to "know the God of your ancestors,"[9] reminding him that the God the new king must know is the one who had accompanied his father throughout his reign. Knoppers (2004:929) has demonstrated that such "knowing" is covenantal in orientation—that is, it "finds its home in the world of international diplomacy . . . in which the command to 'know' someone, usually a superior, denotes legal recognition." Thus, to know is to submit to the authority of the superior alone. David also called Solomon to "serve" this God with his entire being ("whole heart"), that is, a heart wholly committed to God (12:38; 29:9, 19; 2 Chr 15:17; 19:9; 25:2). The Chronicler used this collocation in 12:38 to refer to the united action of the warriors when they came to Hebron to make David king. This action is parallel to that of the rest of Israel in the next phrase of 12:38, which describes Israel as having "one mind" (NLT, "everyone in Israel agreed"). Solomon was also called to serve God with his entire passion ("willing mind"), the term "willing" here often being used for "taking pleasure." David's exhortation was for all of Solomon's being, with all of his passion, to be focused on the pursuit of the knowledge and worship of God.

Such an exhortation is based on God's omniscience, searching (NLT, "sees") all hearts and knowing "all intent of thoughts" (NLT, "every plan and thought"). God is active in his omniscience, searching out the heart and thus gaining full knowledge. In divine view is even the very "intent" of the thoughts of humanity (see also Gen 6:5; 8:21). David will return to this in his prayer in 29:18, applying it to the people as a whole.

The exhortations to know and worship God completely are motivated first by the complete knowledge that God possesses of Solomon and second by the conditional character of the dynastic covenant. Solomon's pursuit of knowledge and worship, summed up in this charge and throughout Chronicles as "seek him" (*darash* [TH1875, ZH2011]),[10] will be rewarded by God allowing himself to be found (lit., "He will be found by you"; cf. 2 Chr 15:2, 4, 15). However, if Solomon rejected God, an action described throughout Chronicles as forsaking or abandoning God (*'azab* [TH5800, ZH6440]),[11] God would reject Solomon "forever." This verse thus reminds Solomon of the vulnerability of the dynastic covenant and the responsibility that lay on his shoulders.

One might have expected the Chronicler, in light of the great focus on the Temple and its services throughout the account of David's reign in Chronicles, to have included in David's charge much more on the call to build the Temple. However, David merely states the fact of God's election of Solomon to construct the sanctuary and declares one imperative related to building: *'aseh* [TH6213, ZH6913] (do the work). In this dramatic presentation of David's charge to Solomon, the Chronicler places greater emphasis on Solomon's wholehearted, passionate seeking of God than merely doing a work.

David Gives the Plans to Solomon (28:11-19). After the speech, the Chronicler moved from dramatic to direct narrative, describing David's provision of the detailed plans, which included everything from architectural plans for the Temple area (28:11-12), to work assignments for sacred personnel (28:13a), to specifications for the worship utensils (28:13b-19).

The claims of the Chronicler in 28:12 and in 28:19 as to the source of these plans are fascinating. In 28:12 the Chronicler spoke of the plans that emanated either from David's spirit or God's Spirit within him (see NLT mg). The divine source of "all" these plans is identified in 28:19: They have come "from the hand of the LORD" in written form. This strongly suggests that the "spirit" of 28:12 (NLT mg) is none other than the Spirit of God.[12] This would then place these plans for the Temple on the level of the two most direct forms of revelation in the Old Testament. It was by the Spirit that the Lord spoke his word to Israel through the prophets of old (Neh 9:30; Zech 7:12), and it was by directly writing the text that the Lord revealed the core of the law, the Ten Commandments, to his people (Exod 24:12; 32:15-16).[13] The medium of the revelation of these plans places David in great company and provides a solid foundation for this new phase of worship for Israel in Jerusalem (De Vries 1988:619-639; Mason 1990:25).

As observed in the commentary on chapter 22, the Chronicler established strong links between David and Moses as founders of worship in Israel's history. This link to the wilderness generation that created the first sanctuary for the worship of the Lord in the nation would also be observed in the Chronicler's presentation of Solomon. Here the Chronicler accentuates the divine origin of the Temple plans, suggesting that there may have been some questions in the Persian period as to the legitimacy of the Temple as a worship structure. Concerns over legitimacy could have been raised due to at least two factors. First, the Temple was instituted and sustained by Davidic monarchs whose misbehavior ultimately led to the demise of the kingdom and the destruction of the Temple. With the waning of royal hope in the Persian period, there may have been questions over the legitimacy of the Temple as an institution. Second, the Temple in Jerusalem was not the only temple of Judaism of this period. Temples would be built by Samaritan Jews at Mount Gerizim and Egyptian Jews at Elephantine and Leontopolis, developments that reveal a lack of commitment to a central sanctuary for Jewish worship (cf. Knoppers 2004:940-941). By tracing intimate links between the Tabernacle and Temple and the figures who were responsible for each and by highlighting the divine origin of the plans, the Chronicler was arguing for the legitimacy of the Temple in his own day. The Temple in Jerusalem is the only true heir to the sanctuary tradition of Israel (see further Boda 2009c).

David's Final Charge to Solomon (28:20-21). The Chronicler returns to dramatic narrative after David handed to Solomon all the written plans for the Temple. In 28:20 David picked up where he left off in 28:10 ("Be strong, and do the work"), calling Solomon to face the great tasks that lie ahead, both the building of the Temple and the institution of its services, with courage ("Be strong and courageous. . . . Don't be afraid or discouraged"). The speech form used here is called an "Encouragement for a Task," fitting for this context where David charges his successor (see Mason 1990:24-25, 31). But the use of this speech form at this juncture continues the trend, first observed in chapter 22, of presenting David and Solomon as a second Moses and Joshua, in particular because the same speech form is found in the transfer of leadership from Moses to Joshua (Deut 31:7, 23; Josh 1:6, 7, 9, 18; see further discussion in the commentary on ch 22; Braun 1976:581-590; Mason 1990:24-25; Williamson 1976:351-361).

As is typical in the "Encouragement for a Task," the initial call to courage is linked immediately to the promised presence of the Lord God, who will not fail or forsake the one called. This has the effect of shifting the focus from human response and ability ("do the work") to divine presence and enablement ("God . . . is with you"). The promise of God's unfailing presence is said to continue until the work is completed. In David's speech, however, there is more: In the closing verse (28:21), David points (Heb., *wehinneh* [TH2009, ZH2180], "now behold")[14] to his provision of an entire workforce to assist Solomon in the project, from the sacred personnel who would serve in Temple worship to other skilled laborers, officials, and even the entire nation, who would respond to his every command. This list highlights the fact that David's provision for the Temple included not only its construction but also its subsequent operation (cf. Japhet 1993:499-500).

David's speech places great expectations on Solomon, calling for obedience to God to fulfill the building project. At the same time, it accentuates the divine origin of the project and the divine presence that will accompany it, alongside the abundant resources that have been provided by David. The conditions had been set for success. However, while one might think that the Chronicler was awaiting the response of the young royal, the focus immediately shifts not to Solomon but to the assembly to ensure the success of the project.

ENDNOTES

1. See Japhet (1993:494), who notes that LXX regularly translates *'ulam* [TH361, ZH395] as *naos* [TG3485, ZG3724] (sanctuary).
2. Japhet (1993:483-484) provides a detailed comparison of the accounts in chs 28–29 and 1 Kgs 1–2. She notes how in 1 Kgs 1–2 the people play a part in only one verse (1 Kgs 1:39b-40), while in Chronicles: (1) The enthronement takes place in the presence of all the people—nothing is done in secret, with the assembly described in detail; (2) the bulk of David's words are addressed to the people and to God with Solomon in third place; (3) David's disposition is "people-oriented"—he directly addresses them, feels a need to explain his actions and justify his choice, and places the people's loyalty and skill at Solomon's disposal (28:21); (4) there is an emphasis on the people's participation in the freewill offering; and (5) the people participate in blessing and worship.

3. The language of the list in 28:1 is much closer to the language of ch 27 than the NLT suggests.
4. Japhet (1993:486) says they are represented in other ways: leaders of the tribes and various officials.
5. See Knoppers 2004:938-939 for this link between the Chronicler and Darius. There are some who have questioned the validity of Darius's link to this royal line and whether Achaemenes is actually a creation of Darius's propaganda machine, which was subtly applied to Cyrus and Cambyses (see Boda 2005b:22-41; Briant 2002:138; Waters 1996:11-18).
6. Japhet (1993:490) says this is a regular feature of the Chronicler, who omits the unconditional clause in 2 Sam 7:14 (see 17:13) and includes a conditional clause in the first charge to Solomon in 22:13.
7. The Hebrew imperative ("Be careful to obey"), subjunctives ("you may continue to possess . . . leave"), and second-person pronouns ("you"), are all plural in 28:8, thus addressing the assembly, not Solomon. This verse marks a key turning point in the speech with its introductory "so now" (*we'attah* [TH6258, ZH6964]).
8. In the Hebrew text 28:8 reads "before the eyes of all Israel, the assembly of the Lord, and the ears of our God."
9. In the Hebrew text, "father" is singular, referring to David (see one other similar occurrence of this phrase in 2 Chr 21:12). The LXX has "fathers," which is common in Chronicles. However, in chs 22, 28, 29, there is a regular emphasis on Solomon as the son of David (28:5, 6, 9, 11, 20; 29:1, 19, 22, 28; see Japhet 1993:492).
10. 10:13, 14; 13:3; 15:13; 21:30; 22:19; 28:8, 9; 2 Chr 12:14; 14:4 [3], 7 [6]; 15:2, 12, 13; 16:12; 17:3, 4; 18:4, 6, 7; 19:3; 20:3; 22:9; 25:15, 20; 26:5; 30:19; 31:21; 32:31; 34:3, 21, 26.
11. 28:9, 20; 2 Chr 7:19, 22; 12:1, 5; 13:10-11; 15:2; 21:10; 24:18, 20, 24; 28:6; 29:6; 34:25.
12. So also Knoppers (2004:931), who argues that if the Chronicler had meant "he had in his mind" he would have written *hayah 'im-lebabo* [TH3824, ZH4222] (22:7; 28:2; 2 Chr 6:7) rather than *hayah baruakh 'immo* [TH7307, ZH8120].
13. Interestingly the "plans" for the Tabernacle are shown to Moses (Exod 25:9, 40; 26:30; 27:8), while David is given a written text. Ezekiel is shown as well as instructed to write down the instructions (Ezek 40:2; 43:11; see Knoppers 2004:934-935).
14. At the beginning of 28:21, not represented in the NLT, however.

◆ T. David's Final Acts before Solomon Becomes King (29:1-30)

Then King David turned to the entire assembly and said, "My son Solomon, whom God has clearly chosen as the next king of Israel, is still young and inexperienced. The work ahead of him is enormous, for the Temple he will build is not for mere mortals—it is for the LORD God himself!
2 Using every resource at my command, I have gathered as much as I could for building the Temple of my God. Now there is enough gold, silver, bronze, iron, and wood, as well as great quantities of onyx, other precious stones, costly jewels, and all kinds of fine stone and marble.

3 "And now, because of my devotion to the Temple of my God, I am giving all of my own private treasures of gold and silver to help in the construction. This is in addition to the building materials I have already collected for his holy Temple.
4 I am donating more than 112 tons of gold* from Ophir and 262 tons of refined silver* to be used for overlaying the walls of the buildings
5 and for the other gold and

silver work to be done by the craftsmen.
Now then, who will follow my example
and give offerings to the LORD today?"

6Then the family leaders, the leaders of
the tribes of Israel, the generals and cap-
tains of the army,* and the king's adminis-
trative officers all gave willingly. 7For the
construction of the Temple of God, they
gave about 188 tons of gold,* 10,000 gold
coins,* 375 tons of silver,* 675 tons of
bronze,* and 3,750 tons of iron.* 8They also
contributed numerous precious stones,
which were deposited in the treasury of the
house of the LORD under the care of Jehiel,
a descendant of Gershon. 9The people re-
joiced over the offerings, for they had
given freely and wholeheartedly to the
LORD, and King David was filled with joy.

10Then David praised the LORD in the
presence of the whole assembly:

"O LORD, the God of our ancestor
Israel,* may you be praised forever and
ever! 11Yours, O LORD, is the greatness,
the power, the glory, the victory, and
the majesty. Everything in the heavens
and on earth is yours, O LORD, and this
is your kingdom. We adore you as the
one who is over all things. 12Wealth
and honor come from you alone, for
you rule over everything. Power and
might are in your hand, and at your
discretion people are made great and
given strength.

13"O our God, we thank you and
praise your glorious name! 14But who
am I, and who are my people, that we
could give anything to you?
Everything we have has come from
you, and we give you only what you
first gave us! 15We are here for only a
moment, visitors and strangers in the
land as our ancestors were before us.
Our days on earth are like a passing
shadow, gone so soon without a trace.

16"O LORD our God, even this
material we have gathered to build
a Temple to honor your holy name
comes from you! It all belongs to you!
17I know, my God, that you examine
our hearts and rejoice when you find
integrity there. You know I have done
all this with good motives, and I have
watched your people offer their gifts
willingly and joyously.

18"O LORD, the God of our ancestors
Abraham, Isaac, and Israel, make your
people always want to obey you. See
to it that their love for you never
changes. 19Give my son Solomon the
wholehearted desire to obey all your
commands, laws, and decrees, and to
do everything necessary to build this
Temple, for which I have made these
preparations."

20Then David said to the whole assem-
bly, "Give praise to the LORD your God!"
And the entire assembly praised the LORD,
the God of their ancestors, and they
bowed low and knelt before the LORD and
the king.

21The next day they brought 1,000
bulls, 1,000 rams, and 1,000 male lambs
as burnt offerings to the LORD. They also
brought liquid offerings and many other
sacrifices on behalf of all Israel. 22They
feasted and drank in the LORD's presence
with great joy that day.

And again they crowned David's son
Solomon as their new king. They anointed
him before the LORD as their leader, and
they anointed Zadok as priest. 23So Solo-
mon took the throne of the LORD in place
of his father, David, and he succeeded in
everything, and all Israel obeyed him. 24All
the officials, the warriors, and the sons of
King David pledged their loyalty to King
Solomon. 25And the LORD exalted Solomon
in the sight of all Israel, and he gave Sol-
omon greater royal splendor than any
king in Israel before him.

26So David son of Jesse reigned over all
Israel. 27He reigned over Israel for forty
years, seven of them in Hebron and
thirty-three in Jerusalem. 28He died at a
ripe old age, having enjoyed long life,
wealth, and honor. Then his son Solomon
ruled in his place.

29 All the events of King David's reign, from beginning to end, are written in *The Record of Samuel the Seer, The Record of Nathan the Prophet,* and *The Record of Gad the Seer.* 30 These accounts include the mighty deeds of his reign and everything that happened to him and to Israel and to all the surrounding kingdoms.

29:4a Hebrew *3,000 talents* [102 metric tons] *of gold.* 29:4b Hebrew *7,000 talents* [238 metric tons] *of silver.* 29:6 Hebrew *the commanders of thousands and commanders of hundreds.* 29:7a Hebrew *5,000 talents* [170 metric tons] *of gold.* 29:7b Hebrew *10,000 darics* [a Persian coin] *of gold,* about 185 pounds or 84 kilograms in weight. 29:7c Hebrew *10,000 talents* [340 metric tons] *of silver.* 29:7d Hebrew *18,000 talents* [612 metric tons] *of bronze.* 29:7e Hebrew *100,000 talents* [3,400 metric tons] *of iron.* 29:10 *Israel* is the name that God gave to Jacob.

NOTES

29:1 *young and inexperienced.* Lit., "young and frail." See note on 22:5.

29:4 *gold from Ophir.* See 1 Kgs 9:26-28; 10:11; 2 Chr 8:18; 9:10, where Solomon also attains gold from Ophir. Its location, however, is unclear. That this gold was imported through the port of Ezion-geber on the Red Sea has given rise to suggestions ranging from Arabia to southern Africa to India (ABD 5.26-27). Japhet queries whether this reference to Ophir is another instance of the Chronicler's strategy to "put David and Solomon on an equal footing" (1993:507). On the large amounts of precious metal here, see commentary on 12:23-40.

29:7 *gold coins.* Heb., *'adarkonim* [TH150, ZH163] (see also Ezra 8:27), the Persian coin called the "daric," named after Darius I and minted in the late sixth century BC. Briant (2002:408-409) says these coins were called "archers" by the Greeks because they depicted the king as an archer (see drawing in Briant 2002:214, fig. 217).

29:8 *Jehiel, a descendant of Gershon.* See 23:7-11 and his duties related to the treasuries in 26:21-22.

29:18 *the God of our ancestors Abraham, Isaac, and Israel.* The dominant version of this formula is "Abraham, Isaac, and Jacob." This form is used elsewhere only in Exod 32:13 (NLT mg); 1 Kgs 18:36 (NLT mg); 2 Chr 30:6. For the Chronicler, this version facilitated his "all Israel" theme.

29:21 *liquid offerings.* These were drink offerings (Num 15:1-10), which accompanied the daily (Exod 29:40-41), weekly (Num 28:9), and monthly (Num 28:14) offerings, and were even offered at some of the festivals (Num 29:18, 21).

29:22 *again they crowned.* Lit., "a second time"; see 23:1, where Solomon was first appointed.

COMMENTARY

David's Charge to the Assembly (29:1-5). Following his short second charge to Solomon, David finally turned to the entire assembly to invite their participation with Solomon. His speech began with an honest evaluation of the challenges ahead, a key first step in a speech that will ultimately implore the assembly to join the project (29:1). Although emphasizing that Solomon was clearly the one chosen by God (lest anyone would think from this introduction that he was disqualified from the job), David contrasted the immaturity of Solomon ("young and inexperienced") with the enormousness of the task (building the Temple "for the LORD God himself"). The structure referred to here is *habbirah* [TH1002, ZH1072], "the palace or citadel" (NLT, "Temple"; also found in 29:19), a term that appears to encompass a much larger complex of buildings that included the Temple. The enormousness of the task, however, was not linked by David ultimately to the size of the job but rather to the greatness of the one for whom it was being built. If it was merely for a human king, then the new king was qualified, but because it was for the divine king, "the LORD God himself," the task was immeasurable. David here offers important theological orientation for the task, even as he lays the foundation for his appeal to the assembly.

In the second part of the speech (29:2), David highlights his past work of gathering resources for the Temple, "using every resource at my command." But there was yet more. In the third part of the speech, David pledges all his own private treasures to the project, beyond what he has already collected for the Temple (29:3-5b). This gift opens the way for the end of this speech, which closes in a similar mood to the first address of David to the assembly in 28:8. Whereas in 28:8 David called the people to obedience to God's commands, now he shifts the request to the Temple project, imploring the assembly to follow his example and give of their treasures for the work of the Temple. David's final request in 29:5b reads like this in the Hebrew text: "Who is willing to fill his hand today to the LORD?" The phrase "to fill his hand" is used for consecrating oneself to the Lord, most often in connection with consecration to the priesthood (Exod 28:41; 29:9, 29, 33, 35; 32:29; Lev 8:33; 16:32; 21:10; Num 3:3; Judg 17:5, 12; 1 Kgs 13:33; 2 Chr 13:9), but in one other place, also in Chronicles, for consecration to God by lay people (2 Chr 29:31). In 2 Chronicles 29:31 the people bring sacrifices to the Lord in this consecration, while here in chapter 29 it is contributions to the treasury.

The Response of the Assembly (29:6-9). Guidance for the Chronicler's community was provided not only through David's exhortations but also through the direct narrative that follows David's searching question to the assembly in 29:5b. The entire assembly "gave willingly" (*nadab* [TH5068, ZH5605]), a Hebrew verbal root associated with freewill offerings given for the construction of the Tabernacle by the wilderness community (all in the Qal stem; Exod 25:2; 35:21, 29), as well as with the gifts for the reinstitution of worship at the Temple site in the early Persian period (all in the Hitpael stem; Ezra 2:68; 3:5). The "willing" character associated with these gifts is emphasized again in 29:9, where the Chronicler relates that not only did the people give "willingly," but they also gave "wholeheartedly," using the same phrase that David employed in his speech to Solomon in 28:9 when he called him to "serve him with your *whole heart,"* (italics added), that is, with the entirety of one's being. The Chronicler is thus suggesting here that the community's response parallels that intended by David for Solomon.

The gifts were not only given "willing[ly]" and "wholehearted[ly]," they were also enormous. The Chronicler depicts a community that had fully embraced this project and was able to outdo even David himself. The scene ends on a tone of joy as both people and king (David) rejoice over this response.

David's Praise and Prayer to God (29:10-19). The notification of the joy of both people and king in 29:9 prepares the way for David's outburst of praise in 29:10-19, after which the king prompts the entire assembly to join in praise to the Lord (29:20).

David's prayer to God is divided into four basic sections. The first section (29:10b-13) offers general praise to God, introduced by the phrase "O LORD, the God of our ancestor Israel."[1] Central to this praise is the phrase in 29:11b: "Everything in the heavens and on earth is yours, O LORD, and this is your kingdom." Greatness, power, glory, victory, majesty, wealth, and honor all find their origin in the Lord God, who is praised "forever and ever." Lest anyone think—after his final address to the assembly (29:1-5) and their subsequent response (29:6-9)—that the honor and praise is due these human participants, David's prayer sets the record straight.

This is made clear in the second section of the prayer (29:14-15), which begins with the rhetorical question: "But who am I, and who are my people, that we could give anything to you?" At the core of this section is the declaration (echoing 29:11b above): "Everything we have has come from you, and we give you only what you first gave us!" Human beings stand in stark contrast to the God they praise. God's resources encompass all of creation, while humanity's resources are only those that he has first given to them (29:14). God's nature is "forever and ever," while humanity's is "for only a moment . . . like a passing shadow, gone so soon without a trace" (29:15; see also Job 8:9; Ps 39:12).

While the first two sections of the prayer introduce key general concepts about God and his people, the final two sections apply these to the particular situation at hand. In the third section (29:16-17) David places the gifts that have been given for the Temple project in theological perspective. First, as has been developed in the previous sections of the prayer, all the gifts both he and his people have offered find their source originally in God himself ("this material . . . comes from you! It all belongs to you!" 29:16b). Second, these gifts had been given for the praise of God ("to honor your holy name"). Lest anyone doubt the motives of the givers, David declared the truth of God's omniscience, which will confirm the appropriate motives of both king and people.

In the final section of the prayer (29:18-19), David continues to speak to the particular situation at hand while repeating the opening address of the first section with a slight expansion: "O LORD, the God of our ancestors Abraham, Isaac, and Israel." Having praised the Lord (29:10b-13) and having declared to God his own unworthiness (29:14-15) and his motives (29:16-17), the king concludes with requests for his people and his son. First, David made two requests for his people. He asks God to, lit., "preserve this forever in the intentions of the thoughts of the heart of your people" (NLT, "make your people always want to obey you"). In this phrase David builds up a series of terms that point to the inner affections of the human being, using vocabulary first addressed to Solomon in David's charge in 28:9 (NLT, "every plan and thought"). The "this" that David wanted God to preserve was the willing and joyous offering of gifts just reviewed in 29:17b. David also asked God to, lit., "make firm their heart to you" (NLT, "See to it that their love for you never changes"), that is, he asks not only for purity of motives but also for endurance of commitment.

Second, Solomon also had many needs, so David returned to the two main emphases of his charge to Solomon in 28:9-10, 19-21. He asked God to give Solomon that "whole heart" that was key to his charge in 28:9. This whole heart should be focused on two activities: obeying God's law and building God's Temple.

David's prayer to God reflects a strong theocentricity, consistently placing God as the subject of actions that must be performed by human characters. In this prayer, human decision and action dissipates at the expense of divine decision and action. As Japhet (1993:511) has said, "Confidence in God's justice and benevolence is so complete that it is only [humanity's] part in the relationship which needs to be assured."[2] It is God to whom belong all the resources of the world that human beings are able to give. It is God who must make his people obey him and see to it that their love never changes. It is God who must give Solomon the desire to obey and to do everything necessary to build the Temple. In the Chronicler's view humanity shrinks in the presence of this almighty God. Although much is made of David's grand preparations, his prayer deflates even this human action when he asks, "Who am I?"

The Assembly's Praise to God (29:20-22a). David's prayer becomes a catalyst of praise among the people as he turns to them and prompts them to give praise. They immediately responded both aurally ("praised") and physically ("bowed low and knelt"), signaling not only their praise to God but also their submission to the Lord. Interestingly, they also knelt before "the king," a reference most likely to David, which reflects the belief that the king was vice-regent of the Divine King, Yahweh (Ps 2).

This aural and physical praise was matched the following day with a great sacrifice to the Lord.[3] The time interval may seem odd to some readers, who think that the assembly of chapters 28–29 was gathered together with the coronation of Solomon in view.[4] However, the importance of the event is actually increased by having it spread over two days, showing the necessity of preparations for the grand celebrations on the second day. The main focus is on the huge number of burnt offerings that were sacrificed, and also on drink offerings and "sacrifices of great number" (29:21, lit.; NLT, "many other sacrifices") for all Israel. These sacrificial acts were accompanied by much joyous feasting, an action that creates strong links between this day of coronation and that of David's (12:38-40 [39-41]), as well as this day of commission to build the Temple and the experience of those who would receive the instructions for the Tabernacle (Exod 24:1-11; cf. Knoppers 2004:955). The people are presented as having fully embraced David's agenda of worship. This led to exuberant praise to God but also to respectful homage; it involved extravagant sacrifices for sin but also enthusiastic feasting in fellowship with God. The Chronicler wanted his audience to see the potential of this kind of response to God. For him it leads to joyous celebration.

Solomon Crowned King (29:22b-25). It is in this exuberant context of explosive praise that the people crown Solomon as king. The text reads "a second time" (NLT, "again"), pointing back to David's private appointment of Solomon in 23:1.[5] To have two appointments to office is not odd in the Old Testament but actually follows the pattern established with both Saul and David, who were appointed in private (1 Sam 10:1; 16:13) and then in public (1 Sam 11:12-15; 2 Sam 2:1-7; 5:1-5). The enthronement of Solomon is particularly described as the taking of "the throne of the LORD in place of his father, David," a description that is slightly different from that found in 1 Kings 2:12, where it is the "throne of David his father." This change echoes the theme of 28:5, where David claims that Solomon is "to rule over the LORD's kingdom," a reminder that the kingship and kingdom do not belong to the dynasty but rather to the Lord, who chose to express his rule with and through the dynasty.

In 23:1 the subject of the action (of appointment) is David, while here in 29:22b it is the people who made him king and then anointed him. Anointing is attested throughout the Old Testament and serves as a sign of God's consecration of an individual, object (altar, vessel), or building (Tabernacle, Temple) for divine use. Individuals who are consecrated through an anointing ceremony include royalty (1 Sam 10:1; 1 Kgs 1:34, 39, 45), priests (Exod 28:41; 29:7, 29; 30:30; 40:13, 15), and, in one place at least, prophetic figures (1 Kgs 19:16; cf. 16:22; Ps 105:15; Isa 61:1). The significance of this ceremony is not made explicit in the Old Testament but may be associated with the use of perfumed oils during celebrations in ancient societies (Ruth 3:3; 2 Sam 12:20; Pss 23:5; 45:7; Isa 61:3; cf. 2 Sam 14:2; Dan 10:3) and/or with the symbolism of the blessing of God upon an individual (Ps 133).

In this ceremony not only was Solomon anointed to serve as king, but also Zadok was anointed as priest.[6] This is a key note, reminding the readers of the sacred nature of Solomon's kingship. He has been nurtured and commissioned to institute the worship of God at the Temple in Jerusalem, and thus Zadok's anointing is key to his reign.

What is obvious to most is the stark contrast between Chronicles and Samuel—Kings in their accounts of the transition between David and Solomon. In Samuel—Kings this transition is fraught with difficulties as Solomon's brother Adonijah engineered his own enthronement while the decrepit David lay in bed. Solomon's rights to the throne must be protected by none other than the much-maligned Bathsheba. The struggle between Solomon and Adonijah for the throne is matched by a struggle for the priesthood between Zadok and Abiathar. In the end Solomon and Zadok are installed legitimately, but the whole affair accentuates the vulnerability of David's kingdom, a theme that plagues the Samuel account since the Bathsheba affair in 2 Samuel 11. But not so for the Chronicler, who described a smooth transition between David and Solomon, a careful preparation of the infrastructure of the kingdom for such a transition, and orchestrated ceremonies (chs 22, 28–29) to facilitate the transition of kingship. As Knoppers (2004:956-957) has written:

> *The succession in Chronicles is a methodical, deliberate, and well-organized operation, a careful mixture of private and public events. . . . In Chronicles David acts proactively. The public ceremony ratifying and celebrating Solomon's ascent takes place after David has created the necessary conditions to ensure Solomon's acclamation.*

This presentation continues a trend that has been evident throughout the Chronicler's account of David and will be accentuated even more in the account of Solomon. The David-Solomon era is presented as the ideal. As noted in the introduction to chapters 10–29, this is what Longman and Dillard (2006:197-198) call a messianic historiography:

> *David and Solomon in Chronicles are not just the David and Solomon who were, but the David and Solomon of the Chronicler's eschatological hope. At a time when Israel was subject to the Persians, the Chronicler still cherished hope of a restoration of Davidic rule, and he describes the glorious rule of David and Solomon in the past in terms of his hope for the future.*

Summary Note on the Reign of David (29:26-30). The Chronicler signals the end of his account of David by reminding his readers that David reigned over "all Israel," a theme that is consistent throughout Chronicles and appears to remind the community in the Chronicler's day of the need for a united front for the people of God. The review of 29:28 accentuates the Chronicler's vision of blessing: enjoying long life, wealth, and honor. David was truly an exemplar of rule in the Chronicler's account.

The final verses (29:29-30) offer notes on the resources used by the Chronicler for his account. All three sources mentioned are the records of prophetic figures, using the three key titles associated with prophets in the Old Testament: "*Samuel the Seer* (*ro'eh* [TH7200A, ZH8014]) . . . *Nathan the Prophet* (*nabi'* [TH5030, ZH5566]) . . . *Gad the Seer* (*khozeh* [TH2374, ZH2602])." This link to the prophets offers increased credibility for this account to his readers, as well as increased credibility to David's reign (Knoppers 2004:958; cf. Glatt-Gilad 2001:184-209). The note, however, cannot be merely a source citation list, because it includes the chronicle of Samuel, which is not relevant to the part of the history that the Chronicler has recounted. Thus, this also may be a note that acknowledges that this history is only a portion of the exploits of David and that to find more information these other books may be consulted.

With chapters 28–29 the Chronicler comes to the end of his account of David. The founder of the dynasty has been depicted as one passionate for the worship of Israel at Jerusalem and now hands the rei(g)n over to his son Solomon, who will perfectly fulfill the vision Yahweh gave to David in chapter 17. It is fitting that the Chronicler would close his account of David with the long prayer in 29:10-19 and that this prayer would be followed immediately by David's exhortation to the assembly to give praise to Yahweh. This summarizes one of the central elements in the Chronicler's depiction of David—that is, David as catalyst of faithful worship in Israel. Against this brilliant backdrop, all the kings that follow in his line will be evaluated.

ENDNOTES

1. The opening phrase of this song resonates with the doxological tradition found at the "seams" between the "books" of the Psalter (Pss 41:13; 72:18; 89:52; 106:48); cf. Boda 2009a; Japhet 1993:503; McCann 1993; G. Wilson 1985.
2. Japhet (1993:511) notes that "in order to reach perfection in the service of God, man needs divine help." This theme is found several times in Chronicles (22:12; 2 Chr 30:12; probably also 2 Chr 29:36).
3. LXX has David as the subject of the verbs in 29:21.
4. Japhet (1993:513) sees this as "a gloss." However, there is no textual evidence for this assertion.
5. Contra Japhet (1993:514). Williamson (1982:187) sees the "first" as the events of 1 Kgs 1–2.
6. This reference to Zadok's anointing in a passage that is focused entirely on Solomon has been identified by some as the work of the pro-Priestly editor, but there is no need to posit this redactional level in Chronicles (see Introduction; Williamson 1982:187).

INTRODUCTION TO 2 CHRONICLES 1–9: THE ACCOUNT OF SOLOMON

The Chronicler's Solomon: Past, Present, and Future. In the account of the initial phase of Solomon's reign in the book of Kings, the writer immediately highlighted Solomon's alliance with Pharaoh symbolized in his marriage to Pharaoh's daughter as well as his practice of visiting high places (1 Kgs 3:1-3). This short note about a foreign wife and the high places at the outset of the account forms a bracket with another short note that occurs at the very end of the account in 1 Kings 11:1-8, picking up precisely where 1 Kings 3 left off ("besides Pharaoh's daughter," 1 Kgs 11:1). This final note introduces a series of foreign wives who were instrumental in turning his heart away from the Lord to worshiping their gods at high places. This literary bracket around the account of Solomon's reign in Kings offers insight into the division of the kingdom and the ultimate spread of idolatry throughout the land (1 Kgs 11–12).

The Chronicler, however, leaves out 1 Kings 3:1-3, the first of many omissions that highlight the interests and themes of the Chronicler in his presentation of Solomon. The Chronicler presents a Solomon untarnished by the fatal flaw of his foreign wives and idolatry. At no place is a sinful action connected to Solomon. Even the schism in the nation following the death of Solomon is blamed on Jeroboam's sedition and Rehoboam's youth (13:6-7) rather than on Solomon's idolatry (1 Kgs 11:9-13).

A similar trend is evident in the Chronicler's presentation of David in 1 Chronicles 10–29, an account that omits the seven-year schism in the nation at the outset of David's reign. It also omits the subsequent revolts by Absalom, Shimei, and Adonijah, as well as the sins against Bathsheba and Uriah, which were followed by the rape of Tamar and the murder of Amnon. In the account of David, however, the Chronicler did include two errors of the dynastic founder: the death of Uzzah due to inattention to ritual procedures related to the transport of the Ark (1 Chr 13; cf. 1 Chr 15:13) and the plague on the nation due to inattention to ritual procedures related to the census (1 Chr 21). David's errors in ritual judgment reveal the immaturity of the monarch in such affairs and were events essential to the establishment of worship in Jerusalem. Nevertheless, they do leave the image of David slightly tarnished. For Solomon, the one who, according to the Deuteronomic historian, was responsible for splitting the kingdom and laying the foundation for idolatrous behavior that would prompt the Exile, there is not a single description of error or sin. He is, as Dillard describes, "a glorious, all-conquering"

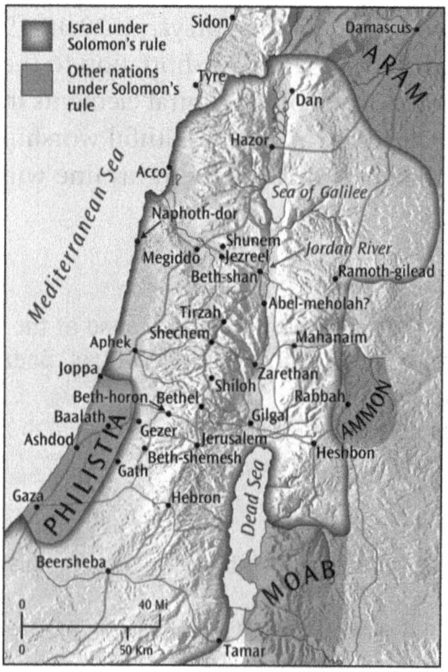

Israel during Solomon's Reign 971–931 BC

figure who enjoys "divine blessing and support of the nation" (Longman and Dillard 2006:197).

There has been much debate over the purpose of this "sanitized" Solomon in Chronicles. The Chronicler provides an idealized portrait of the past, highlighting the Davidic-Solomonic era as the idyllic past. This ideal past is not constructed, however, as mere fantasy over past glory. In doing this the Chronicler highlights the key era that laid the foundation for the Second Temple community to whom he writes his narrative. Thus, an ideal past provides foundation and direction for present realities. Longman and Dillard (2006:197), however, see an additional purpose behind the Chronicler's portrait of Solomon, calling it an example of "messianic historiography," that is,

> *David and Solomon in Chronicles are not just the David and Solomon who were, but the David and Solomon of the Chronicler's eschatological hope. At a time when Israel was subject to the Persians, the Chronicler still cherished hope of a restoration of Davidic rule, and he describes the glorious rule of David and Solomon in the past in terms of his hope for the future.*[1]

For the Chronicler, the people were to find their past, present, and future in Solomon.

Solomon and Recapitulative Historiography. The character of the Chronicler's account of Solomon, however, is defined by more than just its omissions of Solomon's flaws. Rather, the material provided reveals that the Chronicler was forging links between Solomon and earlier figures in the history of Israel, a technique that has been named by Dillard "recapitulative historiography" (see commentary on 1 Chr 22:6-16).[2]

First, as already noted in the commentary on the account of David in 1 Chronicles 22–29, Solomon was intimately linked with his father David. The Chronicler reminds the reader of this at the outset of the account of Solomon in 1:1 when he adds to his source the phrase "son of David" (cf. 1 Kgs 2:46). Braun (1973:511) has offered the most compelling evidence for this, highlighting how the "Chronicler had obviously designed his narrative to present two kings of equal standing before Yahweh and Israel and of equal devotion to the cult. Neither is exalted or denigrated at the expense of the other, but the reigns of both are presented according to the same general framework." Both are presented as kings by divine choice (1 Chr 17:11; 22:7-10; 28:6), as kings ruling with the unanimous consent of all Israel (1 Chr 11:2; 29:22b-25a), and as kings dedicated fully to the Temple and its services. Braun even suggests that Solomon seems to surpass David in that Solomon is presented as completely without fault and as the builder of the Temple and, along with David, responsible for the institution of its worship (7:10; 11:17; 30:26; 35:3-4; 1 Chr 22, 28–29).

Second, this link between Solomon and David is accentuated further by the Chronicler's link between David-Solomon and Moses-Joshua, a technique highlighted especially by Williamson (1976:351-361) and described in detail in the commentary on 1 Chronicles 22 and 28–29. The evidence is also apparent in this opening pericope in the Chronicler's account of Solomon with the link between

David and Moses (see 1:3-4) and the use of vocabulary associated with Joshua's assumption of the mantle of leadership: the statements that the "LORD his God was with him" (cf. Deut 31:6, 8, 23; Josh 1:5, 9 with 2 Chr 1:1; 1 Chr 22:11, 16; 28:20) and the Lord "made him very powerful" (Piel of *gadal* [TH1431, ZH1540]; cf. Josh 3:7; 4:14 with 2 Chr 1:1; 1 Chr 29:25). In doing this, the Chronicler accentuated the role that David and Solomon played in the history of Israel and highlighted the importance of the transfer of leadership from David to Solomon, but he also revealed that without Solomon David's quest for a Temple and dynasty would have been in vain.

Third, it appears that the Chronicler links Solomon to another figure in the history of Israel, that of Bezalel in the book of Exodus.[3] Bezalel was the craftsman responsible for the creation of the Tabernacle and its furnishings in the wilderness (Exod 31:1-11) and, with Oholiab working alongside him (Exod 38:23), instructed other laborers in the skills necessary for building the Tabernacle (Exod 35:30–36:7). Dillard (1987:4) notes that the only two books in the Bible to show any interest in the character of Bezalel are Exodus and Chronicles (1:5; Exod 31, 35, 36; 1 Chr 2:20). The Chronicler depicts Solomon's reception of wisdom from God at the very site of the bronze altar "made by Bezalel" (1:5), who in Exodus is described as one endowed "with the Spirit of God, giving him great wisdom" (Exod 35:30-31).[4] Both Solomon and Bezalel are members of the tribe of Judah (Exod 35:30). This link to Bezalel is accentuated further by the Chronicler's description of the figure of Huram in his account of the construction of the Temple. According to the account of the building of the Temple in 1 Kings 7:13-47, Huram was a craftsman responsible for decorations. Dillard has noted several key modifications that the Chronicler has made to his source account in Kings. While in Kings Huram appears at the completion of the Temple (1 Kgs 7:13), in Chronicles he is present from the beginning (2:7, 13), similar to the appearance of Oholiab in the Tabernacle account. Furthermore, the skill list attributed to Huram in Kings ("a craftsman in bronze," 1 Kgs 7:14), is expanded in Chronicles ("a master craftsman who can work with gold, silver, bronze, and iron, as well as with purple, scarlet, and blue cloth . . . a skilled engraver," 2:7; "skillful at making things from gold, silver, bronze, and iron, and . . . stone and wood . . . purple, blue, and scarlet cloth and fine linen . . . an engraver," 2:14) in line with the talents of Bezalel and Oholiab in Exodus 35:31–36:1 ("a master craftsman, expert in working with gold, silver, and bronze . . . skilled in engraving and mounting gemstones and in carving wood . . . engravers, designers, embroiderers in blue, purple, and scarlet thread on fine linen cloth, and weavers"). Additionally, the name of this craftsman in the Kings account is Hiram (see 1 Kgs 7:13 mg) or Hirom (1 Kgs 7:40), while in Chronicles it is Huram (4:11, though NLT has Huram-abi) and Huram-abi (2:13; 4:16). This slight revision brings Huram's name in line with that of Oholiab, each ending with the Hebrew word *'ab* [TH1, ZH3] (father). Finally, in 1 Kings 7:14 this figure is identified as the child of a "widow from the tribe of Naphtali," while in 2:14 the mother is a widow from the tribe of Dan, a lineage he shares with Oholiab (Exod 35:34). Through these various links the Chronicler successfully identifies Solomon and Huram-abi, men associated with the first Temple, with Bezalel and Oholiab, those responsible for work on the Tabernacle. In doing this, the Chronicler legitimizes the work on the Temple by appealing to the Tabernacle in the wilderness.[5]

Thus, Solomon in Chronicles is a second David, a figure intricately linked with David and upon whom was placed the task of building the Temple and securing the dynasty. He is also a second Joshua, receiving the commission from his predecessor and surpassing his accomplishments. And thirdly he is a second Bezalel, applying his gift of wisdom to the work of the Temple. Through this Solomon's reign is linked to earlier periods of grandeur in the life of Israel, to the glories of the early monarchy, to the challenge of the conquest of the land, and finally to the awesome task of building a dwelling place for God. In an age when people knew well the failings of the monarchy and had reason then to question the legitimacy of the Temple and its services, which owed their existence to the royal house, this reshaping of the Solomonic narrative was important because it showed that the characters and impulses of those responsible for the Temple were identical to those who first built the Tabernacle and conquered the land.

Solomon and Temple Building in the Ancient Near East. The narrative at the end of 1 Chronicles has been building toward the story of Solomon and the building of the Temple since the dynastic oracle from God in 1 Chronicles 17. This oracle informed David that he would not be the one to build the Temple. Instead, his son was the monarch chosen for this task. The tension has built throughout the ensuing account with repetitions of this oracle in 1 Chronicles 22 and 28.

The Chronicler's account of Solomon is bracketed by sections focusing on Solomon's wealth and wisdom (1:1-17; 9:13-28) and his interaction with foreign, Gentile royalty (2:1-16; 8:17–9:12).[6] Common to the sections on wealth and wisdom is a focus on Solomon's trade in horses and chariots, while common to the sections on his interaction with foreign Gentile royalty is the declaration by the foreign monarch that Solomon's enthronement is an expression of God's love for his people (2:11; 9:8). The Chronicler punctuated his account of Solomon at regular intervals with summarizing notes about the progress of the Temple project (2:1; 3:1-2; 5:1; 7:11; 8:1, 16).

This overall structure brings even greater focus on the Temple-building account than the source in 1 Kings from which the Chronicler has drawn his account. In addition, the key themes of wealth and wisdom now surround the Temple-building project, emphasizing that they were given to Solomon to enable the project rather than to assist Solomon in his royal rule. The connection between wisdom and Temple building is made explicit in 2:12 in the mouth of Hiram of Tyre, who describes Solomon as "a wise son, gifted with skill and understanding, who will build a Temple for the LORD" (see Japhet 1993:523). Further evidence can be discerned by comparing Chronicles with its source in Kings. In Kings, wisdom was given to Solomon to rule justly, and this is evidenced in the account of his wise judgment and ruling of the kingdom, which follows the theophany at Gibeon (1 Kgs 3:16–4:34).[7] The Chronicler, however, set aside these accounts and moved immediately to Solomon's construction projects in Jerusalem.

Ancient Near Eastern kings did not undertake the (re)construction of a Temple lightly. Scholars have uncovered a tradition for (re)constructing sanctuaries that stretches over two millennia in the ancient Near East (for details see Boda and Novotny 2009).

This tradition was preserved not only through ritual and oral tradition, but also through inscriptions consistently deposited in the foundations of the various buildings.

Among others, Kapelrud (1963) was instrumental in noting links between this tradition and Hebrew texts related to the construction of sacred space (Exodus, 1 Kings, Ezekiel). Hurowitz (1985, 1992, 1993) provides far more detail, focusing his attention on connections to 1 Kings, with some discussion of Exodus—Numbers and Ezra-Nehemiah. Working exclusively with the non-Hebrew ancient Near Eastern materials and focusing on foundation deposits, Ellis (1968) provides more detail on the earlier phases in Temple (re)construction. In recent work I have focused attention on the implications of Ellis's work for the texts of Haggai and Zechariah 1–8 (Boda 2006c; Boda and Novotny 2009).

Hurowitz (1992:25) largely ignored Chronicles in his work, expressing skepticism for an account that was "demonstrably a tendentious reworking and expan-

Kapelrud 1963	Chronicles (texts identified by Dillard/Riley)		Ellis 1968 (with texts from Haggai and Zech 1–8 identified by Boda [2006c])	Hurowitz 1992
	David	Solomon		
Some indication that a Temple has to be built (Exod 25:1-8)	1 Chr 17:1; 28:11-21		The Decision to Build (Hag 1:1-11; Zech 1:7-17)	(1) a reason to build or restore a building along with the command or consent of the gods to the proposed project (1 Kgs 5:1-5 [15-19]; cf. Exod 24:15–31:18; Exod 34:29–35:19)
The king visits a Temple overnight (Exod 24:12-18; cf. 1 Kgs 3:5)		2 Chr 1:2-13		
A god tells him what to do, indicates plans (Exod 25:8–30:38)	1 Chr 28:2-3, 11-19	2 Chr 1:7-12		
The king announces his intention to build a Temple (Exod 35:4-10)	1 Chr 22:1, 7-10; 28:1-6	2 Chr 2:1-10		
Master builder is engaged, cedars from Lebanon, building stones, gold, silver, etc., procured for the task (Exod 31:1-6; 35:4-29; 36:3-7)	1 Chr 22:1-5, 14-15; 29:1-9	2 Chr 2:7-17	The Preparation of the Building Site (Hag 2:1-5; Zech 4:6b-7a[7b?])	(2) preparations for the project including enlisting workers, gathering and manufacturing building materials, and laying the foundations of the building (1 Kgs 5:1-12 [15-26]; cf. Exod 35:20–36:7)
			Preparing the Building Materials (Hag 2:6-9)	
			Laying the Foundations (Hag 2:10-23; Zech 4:[7b?], 8-10a; 8:9a, 10-13)	

sion of an earlier story." Dillard (1987:10) and Riley (1993), however, provide some comment on the relationship between these ancient (re)building rituals and Chronicles. This may not appear significant since the Chronicler relied so heavily upon Kings, an account that Kapelrud had long ago connected to the ancient Near Eastern rituals. A closer look at the differences between Chronicles and its source in Kings, however, provides important insight into the Chronicler's historiography (see further Boda 2009c). The following table presents three series of elements of Temple construction processes proposed by Kapelrud, Ellis, and Hurowitz, along with the Scriptures correlated with those elements by various scholars. A separate column shows the identification of passages from Chronicles with these elements by Dillard and by Riley.

The Temple finished according to plan (Exod 39:42-43)		2 Chr 3:1–5:1; 6:10	Later Stages of Construction, Including the Dedication of the Finished Building	(3) a description of the building process and of the edifice under construction (1 Kgs 6:1–8:11; cf. Exod 36:8–39:43)
Offerings and dedication, fixing of norms (Exod 40:9-11)	1 Chr 23:2–26:32	2 Chr 6:1-42; 7:4-10		(4) dedication of the building by populating it, along with celebrations and rituals (1 Kgs 8:1-11, 62-66; cf. Exod 40:1-38; Lev 8:12-13; 9:1–10:19; Num 7)
Assembly of the people (Exod 39:32-33, 42-43)		2 Chr 5:2-14		
The god comes to his new house (Exod 40:34-35)		2 Chr 5:13-14; 7:1-3		
The king is blessed and promised everlasting dominion (1 Kgs 9:5)	1 Chr 17:10-14, 23-27	2 Chr 7:12-22		(5) a prayer or a blessing meant to assure a good future for the building and the builder (1 Kgs 8:12-61; Lev 9:22-23; Num 7:89)
				Optional element: (6) conditional blessings and curses addressed to a future king who will repair the building (1 Kgs 9:1-9)

While the ancient (re)building pattern is restricted in Samuel—Kings to the period of Solomon, in Chronicles it can be discerned in the account of David and Solomon. Riley (1993:61) concludes, "The Chronicler has taken the role of Temple-builder (which the Deuteronomistic historian had given to Solomon) and divides it between David for its inauguration and Solomon for its completion." Not only does this mixing of the various activities between these two characters bind their reigns together into a unified complex, but so also do the two incidents of fire falling from heaven. In the first (1 Chr 21:26), David sacrifices on his newly built altar on the Temple site; in the other (7:1), Solomon utters his dedicatory prayer at the completed Temple (Riley 1993:84).

There are other differences between Kings and Chronicles. At certain points the story of Temple construction in Chronicles appears to be more closely allied with the ancient ritual structure than its source in Kings. First of all, Dillard (1987:10) notes that in Kings the hiring of a wise master builder occurs at the end of the account (1 Kgs 7), while in Chronicles this occurs at the outset (ch 2). Second, the Chronicler lays greater stress on the divine origin of the plans for the Temple, noting in 1 Chronicles 28:11-19 that David had received "plans" (*tabnith* [TH8403, ZH9322]) for the Temple directly from Yahweh (1 Chr 28:11-12, 19; cf. Hurowitz 1992:169). Third, in contrast to his source in Kings, which places a considerable literary interval between the theophany at Gibeon in 1 Kings 3 and the building of the Temple in 1 Kings 5, the Chronicler places the Temple building directly after the visit to Gibeon. In this he echoes the broader ancient Near Eastern pattern of Temple building following a revelation to the royal figure. Fourth, while the account in Kings does depict an exchange of messages (through ambassadors) between Solomon and Hiram of Tyre (1 Kgs 5:1-2, 7-8), the Chronicler makes explicit mention of the use of a written letter for the exchange (2:11), the form used for acquiring building materials in the ancient Near Eastern construction texts (see Hurowitz 1992:131-223). Finally, while the account in Kings says nothing about the laying of the foundation, the Chronicler appears to be aware of its significance to the Temple-construction project, expanding his account at 3:3 and then noting it again in his summary at 8:16 (see commentary at 3:3 and 8:16).

In light of the Chronicler's close attention to ritual throughout his work, it would not be surprising if he wrote his account with an eye on such ancient patterns. However, it is more likely that these connections are due to other factors. First, his fixation on the Temple and its services explains why he brought the theophany into such close connection with the Temple construction. For the Chronicler Yahweh appeared to Solomon and endowed him with wisdom mainly for building the Temple. Second, most of the connections established above are more likely due to the Chronicler's technique of linking his story to patterns established in the construction of the Tabernacle. This probably explains the shift in the appearance of the master builder (see above) and may also explain the reference to David's reception of divine "plans," a term (*tabnith* [TH8403, ZH9322]) also used for Yahweh's revelation of the Tabernacle to Moses (Exod 25:9, 40; cf. Hurowitz 1992:168-169). Third, although the Chronicler does explicitly mention a letter in his account, Hurowitz (1992:181) has argued cogently that the form of address used in the messages between Hiram and Solomon in the book of Kings "reveal very strong similarities in both language and content between the words of these two kings and a number of authentic ancient letters."[8] Thus, the Chronicler was merely making explicit what is implicit in his source. Finally, the inclusion of a reference to the laying of the foundation may be related to patterns used in the reconstruction of the second Temple in the early Persian period (see especially Hag 2:15-19; Zech 4:6b-10a; 8:9-13; cf. Boda 2006c).

Therefore, although the Chronicler may have been drawing on the broader ancient Near Eastern patterns of Temple construction, it appears that this was mediated to him through the biblical accounts of the construction of the Tabernacle and the second Temple. In this the Chronicler legitimized the Temple through links to the past but also made it relevant through links to the present of his audience. The second Temple, through which his audience encountered their covenant God, was a sanctuary linked to the first Temple built in that ideal age of David and Solomon, which in turn was built in ways that resonate with the Tabernacle of old.

ENDNOTES

1. This view has not been accepted by all. Japhet (1993:48) sees these trends in Chronicles as the author's aversion to providing personal details in the lives of his characters.
2. For this evidence, see especially the superb review of Dillard (1981:289-300); cf. Braun 1973:503-516; 1976:581-590; Dillard 1987:2-4; Williamson 1976:351-361.
3. See Dillard 1981:289-300; 1987:4; Japhet 1993:540-541, 544-546.
4. Japhet (1993:545) notes a point of discontinuity between Exodus and Chronicles on this point: "According to Chronicles, craftsmanship is certainly 'wisdom,' but definitely not divine inspiration."
5. As Japhet (1993:526) says, "This, then, is an important feature of Chronistic theology: the continuity linking the desert Tabernacle with Solomon's Temple. Gibeon, where the Aaronide Zadok was officiating, is seen as a transitional stage."
6. There have been a few proposals on the literary structure of chs 1–9, often with a chiastic structure, the most convincing of which is offered by Dillard (1984a:85-93; 1987:5-6); cf. De Vries 1989:233; Selman 1994b:285-286. Dillard's work on the inclusion that enfolds the account of Solomon (1:1–2:16; 8:17–9:28) is convincing, while the rest is not (see Boda 1996:55-70). Williamson (1982:192-193, 232) suggests that 2:1 and 8:16 function as brackets around the account, and Dillard (1987:17) and Japhet (1993:537) indicate that 2:1 and 7:11 function this way, but as I note, such summarizing notes on the progress of the project can be found throughout the Chronicler's account.
7. See especially the evidence of Japhet (1993:531): "In Kings, the main task anticipated by Solomon upon accession to the throne, is to 'judge the people'" (cf. 1 Kgs 3:9). She notes that the verb *shapat* [TH8199, ZH9149] (judge), recurs in Kings six more times, a total of seven (cf. 1 Kgs 3:9, 28; 7:7; 8:32; 2 Kgs 15:5; 23:22).
8. Hurowitz (1992:181) also notes the Chronicler's penchant for highlighting written materials in his account.

◆ I. The Account of Solomon (1:1–9:31)
A. Solomon Asks God for Wisdom (1:1-17)

Solomon son of David took firm control of his kingdom, for the LORD his God was with him and made him very powerful.

[2]Solomon called together all the leaders of Israel—the generals and captains of the army,* the judges, and all the political and clan leaders. [3]Then he led the entire assembly to the place of worship in Gibeon, for God's Tabernacle* was located there. (This was the Tabernacle that Moses, the LORD's servant, had made in the wilderness.)

[4]David had already moved the Ark of God from Kiriath-jearim to the tent he had prepared for it in Jerusalem. [5]But the bronze altar made by Bezalel son of Uri and grandson of Hur was there* at Gibeon in front of the Tabernacle of the LORD. So Solomon and the people gathered in front of it to consult the LORD.* [6]There in front of the Tabernacle, Solomon went up to the bronze altar in the LORD's presence and sacrificed 1,000 burnt offerings on it.

[7]That night God appeared to Solomon and said, "What do you want? Ask, and I will give it to you!"

[8]Solomon replied to God, "You showed faithful love to David, my father, and now you have made me king in his place. [9]O LORD God, please continue to keep your promise to David my father, for you have made me king over a people as numerous as the dust of the earth! [10]Give me the wisdom and knowledge to lead them properly,* for who could possibly govern this great people of yours?"

[11]God said to Solomon, "Because your greatest desire is to help your people, and you did not ask for wealth, riches, fame, or even the death of your enemies or a long life, but rather you asked for wisdom and knowledge to properly govern my people—[12]I will certainly give you the wisdom and knowledge you requested. But I will also give you wealth, riches, and fame such as no other king has had before you or will ever have in the future!"

[13]Then Solomon returned to Jerusalem from the Tabernacle at the place of worship in Gibeon, and he reigned over Israel.

[14]Solomon built up a huge force of chariots and horses.* He had 1,400 chariots and 12,000 horses. He stationed some of them in the chariot cities and some near him in Jerusalem. [15]The king made silver and gold as plentiful in Jerusalem as stone. And valuable cedar timber was as common as the sycamore-fig trees that grow in the foothills of Judah.* [16]Solomon's horses were imported from Egypt* and from Cilicia*; the king's traders acquired them from Cilicia at the standard price. [17]At that time chariots from Egypt could be purchased for 600 pieces of silver,* and horses for 150 pieces of silver.* They were then exported to the kings of the Hittites and the kings of Aram.

1:2 Hebrew *the commanders of thousands and of hundreds.* 1:3 Hebrew *Tent of Meeting;* also in 1:6, 13. 1:5a As in Greek version and Latin Vulgate, and some Hebrew manuscripts. Masoretic Text reads *he placed.* 1:5b Hebrew *to consult him.* 1:10 Hebrew *to go out and come in before this people.* 1:14 Or *charioteers;* also in 1:14b. 1:15 Hebrew *the Shephelah.* 1:16a Possibly *Muzur,* a district near Cilicia; also in 1:17. 1:16b Hebrew *Kue,* probably another name for Cilicia. 1:17a Hebrew *600 [shekels] of silver,* about 15 pounds or 6.8 kilograms in weight. 1:17b Hebrew *150 [shekels],* about 3.8 pounds or 1.7 kilograms in weight.

NOTES

1:1 ***took firm control.*** It is common in Chronicles to refer to the consolidation of the power of a new king (12:13; 13:21; 27:6; see David in 1 Chr 11:10).

1:3 ***Gibeon.*** See note on 1 Chr 16:39 and commentary on 1 Chr 8:29-40.

Tabernacle. Instructions for the Tabernacle are given in Exod 25–31, and the construction of the Tabernacle occurs in Exod 35–40.

1:4 ***from Kiriath-jearim to . . . Jerusalem.*** These events were recounted by the Chronicler in 1 Chr 13–15.

1:5 ***the bronze altar.*** Used for sacrifice prior to the construction of the Temple, it was located in the courtyard in front of the bifurcated sacred sanctuary, which housed the Holy Place and Most Holy Place.

by Bezalel son of Uri and grandson of Hur. Bezalel (along with Oholiab) was a craftsman gifted by the Spirit of wisdom to create the Tabernacle and its furniture.

1:9 ***numerous as the dust of the earth.*** See the promise to Abraham in Gen 13:16; 28:14 (cf. Num 23:10).

1:10 ***to lead them properly.*** Lit., "to go out and come in before this people" (see NLT mg), a phrase that is used in military contexts to refer to breaking camp and making camp (23:7; Josh 14:11; 1 Sam 29:6; 2 Kgs 19:27) but was also a general term for the work and business of life (Deut 28:6; 2 Kgs 19:27; Ps 121:8; Isa 37:28) or conduct in general (1 Kgs 3:7). When it is used with "before" (*lipne* [TH3807.1/6440, ZH4200/7156]), it refers to military leadership (Num 27:17; 1 Sam 18:16). Here it appears parallel to "govern."

1:13 ***Gibeon.*** See note on 1:3.

1:15 ***cedar timber . . . sycamore-fig trees.*** In the ancient Near East cedar was a valuable resource often linked to the forests of Lebanon, which were controlled by the Phoenicians. The sycamore tree (*Ficus sycomorus*; Heb., *shiqmah* [TH8256, ZH9204]) flourished in lower areas of Israel including the Shephelah (NLT, "foothills of Judah"), the region between the high hills of Judah and the coastal plain, but also Lower Galilee and the Jordan Valley. This evergreen, which produces fruit (inferior to the fig tree, but edible) several times each year, could grow to heights of 60 feet. This tree was the traditional source of lumber for building.

1:16 ***Cilicia.*** Heb., *qewe'* [TH4723C, ZH7745] (elsewhere spelled *qeweh*). Kue was a neo-Hittite kingdom that existed in Asia Minor (southeast Turkey) during the first half of the first millennium BC (ABD 4.102).

1:17 ***Hittites . . . Aram.*** The Hittite kingdom flourished in the second millennium BC in Asia Minor, just prior to Solomon's rise to power. Their sphere of influence extended into the Aramean city-states to the north of Israel, chief among which was Damascus.

COMMENTARY

Summary Note: Solomon Took Firm Control of the Kingdom (1:1). At the outset of 2 Chronicles, David, the dominant character of the Chronicler's work to this point, now leaves the stage. However, there are still reminiscences of the great king in this opening chapter, which describes the initial stages of Solomon's kingship over Israel.

In the opening note the Chronicler places Solomon at the helm of the kingdom. In stark contrast to how Solomon was characterized throughout the Chronicler's presentation of David in 1 Chronicles 22–29, the Chronicler now has Solomon as the subject of the initial verb, introducing a slight change to his source in 1 Kings 2:46, which renders this action in the passive: "So the kingdom was now firmly in Solomon's grip." Additionally, the Chronicler inserts into his account the patrimonial note "son of David." As we have already seen in the Chronicler's presentation of 1 Chronicles 22–29, Solomon is key to the confirmation of the covenant between the Lord and the Davidic dynasty, and here the Chronicler reminds us that Solomon will act as representative co-covenant partner with his father throughout his reign. However, lest the Chronicler emphasize too much the role of these human participants, he qualifies Solomon's actions immediately by providing the divine cause that lay behind his establishment: the presence and action of God with Solomon. This initial evidence of the Chronicler's reworking of his main source in Kings is but the beginning of a trend that will be consistent throughout 2 Chronicles 1–9.

Solomon Gathers an Assembly at Gibeon (1:2-12). While his source focused attention only on Solomon's journey to Gibeon at the outset of his rule (1 Kgs 3:4), the Chronicler widened his lens to include the community as a whole. The account begins with Solomon speaking to "all Israel" (NLT, "all the leaders of Israel"). While only the leaders followed Solomon to Gibeon, the Chronicler wanted to emphasize that they were representative of the entire nation, which had embraced Solomon as their new king. The practice of listing leaders alongside the king continues a trend observed throughout the Chronicler's account of David (see especially 1 Chr 27:1; 28:1; 29:6; cf. 1 Chr 22:17; 23:2).

The Chronicler has been preparing for this encounter between God and Solomon at Gibeon for some time. Throughout the account of David he has carefully explained that while the Ark of God was brought into Jerusalem early in David's reign, the rest of the ancient sanctuary and its utensils remained at Gibeon (1 Chr 16:39; 21:29). These two earlier explanations were placed strategically at two key moments in the Davidic account: the first following the conveyance of the Ark into Jerusalem and its accompanying worship and sacrifice (1 Chr 16:39), and the second following the identification of the threshing floor as the site of the new Temple and its accompanying worship and sacrifice (1 Chr 21:29). Now as the Chronicler moves into the third and final phase of the Jerusalem sanctuary construction account, he again makes note of Gibeon and carefully highlights the Mosaic origins of this sanctuary (1:3b), as well as the Davidic innovations that were presently in play (1:4).[1] The reference to Bezalel is the beginning of a motif that will link Solomon's work intimately with that of the Tabernacle in the wilderness (see introduction to 2 Chr 1–9, "Solomon and Recapitulative Historiography"). Furthermore, it accentuates further the link between David and Moses that had been broached in 1:3b-4.

With the Ark in Jerusalem, it appears that the most important item in the Tabernacle at Gibeon had become the bronze altar, which was located in the courtyard in front of the sacred tent. It is there that Solomon and the people gathered to seek God and to worship "in the LORD's presence" (1:6). The Chronicler emphasizes that Solomon and the assembly gathered "to consult" or seek (*darash* [TH1875, ZH2011]) the Lord (1:5). Here he uses a key term that appears throughout his account to refer to those who are in proper relationship with the Lord. Saul was judged as one who consulted a medium rather than the Lord (1 Chr 10:13-14). In contrast to Saul, David brought the Ark into Jerusalem so that he could seek the Lord (1 Chr 13:3). In his charge to Solomon, David was concerned that Solomon would be a person who sought the Lord (1 Chr 22:19; 28:9) and his commandments (1 Chr 28:8). Thus, the Chronicler began his account with Solomon and the people journeying to Gibeon to seek the Lord.

Like his father in earlier scenes of worship, Solomon played the role of priest, sacrificing a large number of offerings on the bronze altar. These sacrificial acts appear to occur in the presence of the people during the day. However, beginning with 1:7, the text indicates that Solomon encountered a theophany in the night, most likely in the sacred precincts. God began the dialogue, promising to give Solomon whatever he asked. As God appeared to David and gave him the dynastic oracle found in 1 Chronicles 17, so God now appeared to Solomon. The final appearance of God will occur at the end of the Temple-building project in 7:12-22; ironically, this will signal the end of the Tabernacle, where Solomon first encountered God, who commissioned him to fulfill the promises articulated in David's encounter with God in 1 Chronicles 17.

Solomon began his response to God in classic covenant form, reviewing the history of the relationship between God and himself. Although the NLT translates the first sentence of the speech as referring to two different actions, one toward David and the other toward Solomon, most likely this is one and the same action: God expressed great covenant fidelity to David by placing Solomon on the throne (1:8). This historical review, accentuating the grace of God toward the house of David, lays the foundation for the request of 1:10, where Solomon asks God for wisdom to lead "this great people" who are as "numerous as the dust of the earth." This final phrase, which is not found in 1 Kings 3:8, echoes words spoken in the dream experienced by Jacob (Israel) in Genesis 28:14 (cf. Gen 13:16; Dillard 1987:12). This dream, which took place at "Bethel" (lit., "house of God"), envisioned an access point to God's presence through a stairway. Solomon encountered God at night at a sanctuary as he embarked on the mission of building a house for God in Jerusalem. This is an important link to the one from whom "all Israel" descended.

For God's response the Chronicler draws largely on his source in 1 Kings 3. God declares that since Solomon did not ask for those items that would benefit him as an individual (wealth, riches, fame, military victory) but rather asked for a quality (wisdom) that could only help his people through his leadership, God would grant him not only wisdom but also all of these benefits. While the writer of Kings accentuates Solomon's incomparability among the kings of his own generation (1 Kgs 3:13), the Chronicler stresses Solomon's incomparability among all kings before or after him. This is further evidence that the Chronicler places Solomon's reign on a higher plane than even David's, most likely because of Solomon's intimate link with the inauguration of the Temple and its services. However, the Chronicler's presentation carefully notes that the people and kingdom over which Solomon ruled were not his own but rather the Lord's ("my people"; Dillard 1987:12).

Summary Note: Solomon Returns to Jerusalem and Reigns over Israel (1:13). The end of the initial section of the account of Solomon is signaled in 1:13. Having sought God at Gibeon and experienced God's presence firsthand, Solomon returned to Jerusalem to reign. While the writer of Kings depicts Solomon's returning to Jerusalem to stand before the Ark and offer sacrifices, the Chronicler simply declares that he returned to rule over Israel. This omission may be related to the fact that throughout his account of David, the Chronicler made sacrifice the focus at the Gibeon shrine and oral praise the focus at the Jerusalem shrine (see especially 1 Chr 16:37-42; Japhet 1993:532).

By providing summary notes on both ends of this section the Chronicler isolates it as a key and foundational event in the story of Solomon. In this event Solomon exemplifies the core values of the Chronicler in that he consults the Lord and receives blessing from this encounter with God. In this account the Chronicler subtly depicts Solomon as one who had taken the baton from David through subtle allusions including the reference to "son of David" (1:1), the list of officials (1:2), the gathering of a worship assembly as the first act of kingship (1:3),[2] the reference to David's earlier actions to bring the sanctuary to Jerusalem (1:4), and the reference to the dynastic oracle (1:8-9). At the same time, however, the Chronicler's depiction shows Solomon superseding his father, especially in that Solomon consulted the Lord at Gibeon (1:5; cf. 1 Chr 21:29-30), that Solomon would now confirm the dynastic oracle (1:8-9), and that Solomon's wealth, riches, and fame would exceed that of his father (1:12).

Solomon Prospers (1:14-17). For the last four verses of the chapter, the Chronicler focuses on the prosperity of Solomon, drawing on material from 1 Kings 10:26-29. Much of this material is repeated at the end of the account of Solomon in Chronicles (9:25-28), revealing that the Chronicler was intentionally creating a literary bracket around the entire account. Prosperity here is exemplified by possession of the most advanced military resources available (chariots and horses). These were stationed in the fortified cities that protected Solomon's kingdom,[3] most of them set at the heads of valleys, protecting the interior from opposing forces. Prosperity was also evident in the abundance of precious metals like silver and gold, compared to the abundance of the common stone, as well as the abundance of precious wood like cedar, compared to the abundance of the common sycamore-fig tree. In addition to these things, Solomon is depicted as deeply involved in the import-export business, moving trade in chariots and horses between Egypt and kings from the northern border of Israel (Damascus) to Asia Minor. The new king took advantage of his control of the key routes between Africa, Arabia, Asia, and Europe (see commentary on 1 Chr 18:1-6).

This introduction to the account of Solomon showcases the new king as one dedicated to the same values of his father (consulting the Lord) and receiving the same privilege of God's theophanic presence. The king was granted the wisdom he asked for and much more. The key distinction between the Chronicler's account and that of his source is actually in what follows. Rather than how this gift of wisdom and wealth was used to enhance Solomon's ability to rule and judge (as suggested in the exchange between Solomon and God in 1:8-12), the Chronicler will show how these gifts were used for the purpose of constructing the Temple.

ENDNOTES

1. Japhet (1993:526-528) has wisely noted a key difference in emphasis between the Priestly Torah traditions and those of the Deuteronomistic History with regard to the Tabernacle and Ark, the former focusing on the Tabernacle and the latter on the Ark. The Chronicler brings these two together through the Gibeon-Jerusalem notes throughout, showing that both are essential to Temple theology.
2. See Williamson 1982:11 and Japhet 1993:526, who compare this to David's actions in 1 Chr 13.

3. While several of the fortified cities in Israel have shown evidence of stables, this has been a point of great debate; see Dillard 1987:13. The evidence suggests that the stables found at Megiddo and Hazor (for instance) were from a slightly later period in the monarchy. This does not preclude that these stables were later adaptations of earlier structures.

◆ B. Preparations for Building the Temple (2:1-18)

1*Solomon decided to build a Temple to honor the name of the LORD, and also a royal palace for himself. 2*He enlisted a force of 70,000 laborers, 80,000 men to quarry stone in the hill country, and 3,600 foremen.

3Solomon also sent this message to King Hiram* at Tyre:

"Send me cedar logs as you did for my father, David, when he was building his palace. 4I am about to build a Temple to honor the name of the LORD my God. It will be a place set apart to burn fragrant incense before him, to display the special sacrificial bread, and to sacrifice burnt offerings each morning and evening, on the Sabbaths, at new moon celebrations, and at the other appointed festivals of the LORD our God. He has commanded Israel to do these things forever.

5"This must be a magnificent Temple because our God is greater than all other gods. 6But who can really build him a worthy home? Not even the highest heavens can contain him! So who am I to consider building a Temple for him, except as a place to burn sacrifices to him?

7"So send me a master craftsman who can work with gold, silver, bronze, and iron, as well as with purple, scarlet, and blue cloth. He must be a skilled engraver who can work with the craftsmen of Judah and Jerusalem who were selected by my father, David.

8"Also send me cedar, cypress, and red sandalwood* logs from Lebanon, for I know that your men are without equal at cutting timber in Lebanon. I will send my men to help them. 9An immense amount of timber will be needed, for the Temple I am going to build will be very large and magnificent. 10In payment for your woodcutters, I will send 100,000 bushels of crushed wheat, 100,000 bushels of barley,* 110,000 gallons of wine, and 110,000 gallons of olive oil.*"

11King Hiram sent this letter of reply to Solomon:

"It is because the LORD loves his people that he has made you their king! 12Praise the LORD, the God of Israel, who made the heavens and the earth! He has given King David a wise son, gifted with skill and understanding, who will build a Temple for the LORD and a royal palace for himself.

13"I am sending you a master craftsman named Huram-abi, who is extremely talented. 14His mother is from the tribe of Dan in Israel, and his father is from Tyre. He is skillful at making things from gold, silver, bronze, and iron, and he also works with stone and wood. He can work with purple, blue, and scarlet cloth and fine linen. He is also an engraver and can follow any design given to him. He will work with your craftsmen and those appointed by my lord David, your father.

15"Send along the wheat, barley, olive oil, and wine that my lord has mentioned. 16We will cut whatever timber you need from the Lebanon mountains and will float the logs in rafts down the coast of the Mediterranean Sea* to Joppa. From

there you can transport the logs up to
Jerusalem."

17Solomon took a census of all foreigners in the land of Israel, like the census his
father had taken, and he counted 153,600.
18He assigned 70,000 of them as common
laborers, 80,000 as quarry workers in the
hill country, and 3,600 as foremen.

2:1 Verse 2:1 is numbered 1:18 in Hebrew text. **2:2** Verses 2:2-18 are numbered 2:1-17 in Hebrew text. **2:3** Hebrew *Huram*, a variant spelling of Hiram; also in 2:11. **2:8** Or *juniper;* Hebrew reads *algum*, perhaps a variant spelling of *almug;* compare 9:10-11 and parallel text at 1 Kgs 10:11-12. **2:10a** Hebrew *20,000 cors* [3,640 kiloliters] *of crushed wheat, 20,000 cors of barley.* **2:10b** Hebrew *20,000 baths* [420 kiloliters] *of wine, and 20,000 baths of olive oil.* **2:16** Hebrew *the sea.*

NOTES

2:3 [2] ***Tyre.*** This was a key Phoenician city northwest of Israel along the Mediterranean coast.

2:4 [3] ***incense.*** See Exod 30:1-10; 37:25-29; 40:27; Lev 16:13.

special sacrificial bread. See Exod 25:23-30; 40:22-24; Lev 24:5-9.

burnt offerings each morning and evening, on the Sabbaths, at new moon celebrations, and at the other appointed festivals. See Num 28:1–29:39.

2:11 [10] ***this letter of reply.*** Requests for acquiring building materials were typically done via a letter (see introduction to chs 1–9; cf. Hurowitz 1992:131-223).

2:16 [15] ***Lebanon mountains.*** This means "white" mountains, which is most likely a reference to the snow coverage (Jer 18:14). The Phoenicians controlled many of the forests there, which were a source of income along with their maritime trade.

float the logs in rafts down the coast. Katzenstein (1973:243) speaks of reliefs in the Assyrian King Sargon's buildings in Khorsabad that portray Phoenician ships transporting logs on boats as well as on rafts pulled by ships (cf. Dillard 1987:21).

Joppa. This was the only significant seaport on the Mediterranean coast between Acco (just north of Mount Carmel) and Egypt. It was about 35 miles to the west of Jerusalem and the closest harbor for shipping goods (see Jonah 1:3). Reefs just over 300 feet offshore create a natural breakwater for the port. It was exploited by the Egyptians, then the Philistines, and finally Israel (TBD 734-735).

2:18 [17] ***foremen.*** Extrabiblical evidence for this is seen in the seal of "Pela'yahu (son of) Mattiyahu, who is over the corvée" (cf. 2 Sam 20:24; 1 Kgs 4:6; 5:14; 12:18; Avigad 1980:170-173; Dillard 1987:22).

COMMENTARY

In the first chapter the Chronicler depicted Solomon's support by the people and his reception of wisdom from God at Gibeon. The sign of this wisdom is seen in the power and wealth listed in 1:14-17, a list that will be repeated at the end of the account of Solomon in 9:13-28. With chapter 2, however, the Chronicler begins his consideration of the Temple-building project, or at least the preparations for the project. By moving directly to the project (in contrast to his source in Kings, which first outlines examples of Solomon's justice and leadership), the Chronicler highlights "the *raison d'être* for Solomon's accession and his first priority of action" (Japhet 1993:536). This chapter will bring into focus Hiram, a Gentile king, who will not only reappear at the close of the account in 8:17–9:12 but also affirm Solomon's reign in identical ways to the Gentile Queen of Sheba, who is featured in 8:17–9:12.

Summary Note: Solomon's Command to Build a Temple and Palace (2:1). The opening note of chapter 2 signals the official beginning of a building project that includes a Temple and palace. The inclusion of the "royal palace for himself" as part of the building project does seem odd in light of the focus to this point on the Temple and in light of the omission of any significant account of the palace building in Chronicles. However, the building of the palace is mentioned three more times in the account of Solomon (7:11; 8:1; 9:11).[1] By citing the construction of the palace, the Chronicler may be linking Solomon to his father David, who also built a palace with Phoenician cedar at the outset of his rule. Besides its function as a sign of royal succession, one should not miss that it was placed alongside the Temple, which served as the palace of the Lord in the capital city. These two buildings, housing the two royals in Israel—divine and human—are physical reminders that God's rule is distinct from and yet intricately linked with that of the Davidic dynasty (see Ps 2; cf. Boda 2007a). This suggests that the Chronicler retains some hope for renewal of Davidic royal rule in the Persian period (Boda 2009b).

Solomon's Census and Organization of Israelite Workers for the Project (2:2). Following 2:1, the Chronicler includes evidence of Solomon's organization of the workforce for the Temple project. This verse (2:2) resonates with the final verses of the chapter (2:17-18), both speaking of Solomon's "numbering" (Heb., *sapar* [TH5608, ZH6218]; NLT, "enlisted," 2:2; "took a census," 2:17) workers and dividing them into the same three groups: "laborers" (burden bearers), "men to quarry stone in the hill country," and "foremen." Together these two lists form a literary bracket around the request of and response from Hiram of Tyre.[2] In this way the Chronicler reminds the reader that the vast majority of resources for the Temple project came from sources at Solomon's command. It is not, however, until 2:17-18 that the Chronicler informs the reader that these workers were actually foreigners temporarily living in the kingdom. In 8:9 he makes it clear that no Israelites were used as corvée laborers in the Temple construction (cf. 1 Kgs 5:13-14).

Solomon's Letter of Request to Hiram of Tyre (2:3-10). The Chronicler described earlier interaction between Hiram of Tyre and David in 1 Chronicles 14:1-2. There Hiram approached David with gifts of cedar and skilled workers to construct a palace for David. It is this act of friendship and submission that signaled to the Chronicler that God had confirmed and blessed David's kingship. Now at the outset of Solomon's reign, the Chronicler includes another interaction between royal houses, again a sign confirming a new king's reign and signaling blessing from God.

Evidence for the Phoenician kingdom of Hiram is largely restricted to the Old Testament and the later works of Josephus (*Against Apion* and *Antiquities*), which claim to draw also on Tyrian records and the works of Dius and Menander of Ephesus (see ABD 3.203-205). Tyre was situated on an island just off the Mediterranean shoreline northwest of Israel. It was well-known for maritime traffic, as well as logging in the Lebanon mountains to the east of Tyre and north of Israel. The biblical depiction of Hiram's relationship with Solomon reveals significant interaction and codependence. First Kings 5:9-14 offers details of a treaty that was struck between the two leaders, with Hiram supplying timber to Solomon and Solomon supplying food to Hiram's court, a practice that continued year by year (1 Kgs 5:11). The two kings were involved together in maritime trade ventures (8:17-18; 9:10, 21; 1 Kgs 9:26-28; 10:11, 22). However, 1 Kings 9:10-14 reports that Solomon had to cede 20 cities in Galilee to Hiram, evidence of economic troubles for Solomon in the latter part of his career. Dillard (1987:21) has demonstrated that the relationship between Tyre and Israel was one of "parity, not vassalage," evident because of the facts that (1) the term "brother" is used (1 Kgs 9:13; cf. 1 Kgs 20:33), (2) there was payment expected for the delivery of goods (1 Kgs 5:9), and (3) the treaty did not suggest subordination (1 Kgs 5:9).[3] Of course, the Chronicler does not focus on most of these aspects of the relationship between Hiram and Solomon; instead, he limits his material to that which is concerned with the building project. Nevertheless, Japhet (1993:546) has discerned a development in the Chronicler's account of this relationship, one that moves from parity at the outset to Hiram's subordination near the end of this unit (in 2:14 Hiram says, "my lord David, your father"; in 2:15, "my lord"). This trend is not discernible in Kings.

Solomon began his letter to Hiram by requesting cedar logs.[4] A common motif throughout temple-building texts in the ancient Near East was the acquisition of the raw materials for the project at hand (see Boda 2006c; Boda and Novotny 2009). For instance, the neo-Babylonian king Nabopolassar speaks of gathering and preparing baskets, spades, wood, stone, and bricks for his temple project (Harper 1904:131-133). A regularly repeating motif is highlighted by Hurowitz (1992:205-220), who cites evidence from the reigns of many kings from Gudea to Nabonidus reporting that they acquired wood (often cedar) for building sacred buildings.[5] Notable is the claim of Nebuchadnezzar when he was rebuilding Esagila in Babylon that he did so with cedar trees from Lebanon.

As is typical of exchanges between treaty partners in the ancient Near East, emphasis is placed on the history of the relationship between the two kingdoms and royal families.[6] The request, thus, was based on the long relationship that David had enjoyed with Hiram. It is also, however, based on the legitimacy of the task of building a Temple to the Lord. At this point the Chronicler expands the material of his source. Whereas 1 Kings 5:5 speaks only of building a house for God's name, 2:4-6 adds significant details on the worship practices that will take place in this sanctuary, following the order of these practices in the Torah (burning of incense, Exod 30:1-8; offering of showbread, Lev 24:5-9; as well as the daily, weekly, monthly and yearly sacrifices, Num 28–29; see Japhet 1993:540) and an emphasis on the need for the greatness of the house to match the greatness of its divine inhabitant, even if the house itself could never contain the Deity. The expressions of humility in Solomon's message to Hiram are meant to echo those of David in his prayer in 1 Chronicles 29:14 and link Solomon with his pious father.

With this foundation for the project in mind, Solomon finally asked for specific resources from Hiram (2:7-10). While 1 Kings 5:6 only includes a request for timber in Solomon's message, 1 Kings 7:13-14 records that Solomon also asked for a craftsman to assist with the project. This request is recorded by the Chronicler as part of the original letter to Hiram in 2:7. The request carefully notes that this craftsman would work alongside the human resources David had already provided for the project, a key for the Chronicler, who painstakingly listed the many preparations of David for the Temple building (1 Chr 22:14-16; 28:21; 29:5). Besides this skilled worker, Solomon also asked for timber (cedar, cypress, and red sandalwood logs) from the forests Hiram exploited in Lebanon. Solomon offered to send coworkers to assist Hiram's loggers and along with them payment for the use of Tyrian loggers and their wood. This offer is reflected in 1 Kings 5:10-12, even though it is not part of the message of Solomon to Hiram proper in 1 Kings 5.

One piece the Chronicler left out from his source in Kings is the introductory reference to David's disqualification from building the Temple (cf. 2:3 with 1 Kgs 5:3). This disqualification is the same in both Kings and Chronicles, related to David's involvement in war. But the Chronicler links it more closely with the shedding of blood (1 Chr 22:8; 28:2-3), suggesting that the large quantity of spilled blood in war by David led to his ritual disqualification from building the Temple (cf. Dillard 1987:23).

Hiram's Reply to Solomon (2:11-16). Hiram reciprocated with a letter to Solomon, announcing that Solomon's enthronement was an expression of the Lord's love for his people. This statement will match the later expression of another Gentile royal figure, the Queen of Sheba, in 9:8. Although this affirms Solomon, it reminds the reader that the Davidic dynasty was ultimately a benefit for the people of Israel—that is, the covenant with David was not merely about the royal house but was also about the nation as a whole in keeping with the Abrahamic and Sinai covenants of earlier generations.

Hiram offered his praise to this Lord (2:12, "Praise the LORD, the God of Israel"), echoing the purpose of this Temple that Solomon has already declared to be "to honor the name of the LORD my God" (2:4). The Chronicler adds the divine descriptive "who made the heavens and the earth," an important declaration for a foreigner and one that helps justify Hiram's participation in the construction of a Temple for the Lord.

At this point Hiram's speech again resonates with an earlier statement by a royal figure, this time David, who in his first commission to Solomon in 1 Chronicles 22:12 declared, "May the LORD give you *wisdom and understanding*" (*sekel ubinah* [TH7922/998, ZH8507/1069]; my italics; cf. Dillard 1987:20; Japhet 1993:544). Through Hiram the Chronicler signals the fulfillment of this hope in Solomon: "He has given King David a wise son, gifted with *skill and understanding*" (*sekel ubinah*; 2:12; my italics). Not surprisingly, this wisdom for the Chronicler was almost exclusively focused on the building project: "who will build a Temple for the LORD and a royal palace for himself" (2:12).

Hiram responded directly to the two requests of Solomon (cf. 1 Kgs 5). First, he would send a craftsman, Huram-abi by name, to assist in the project, and second, he would provide the timber needed and transport it by sea to the port of Joppa in order for it to be transported by land to Jerusalem. As noted in the introduction to 1–9, the Chronicler introduced slight modifications to his source in his description of the craftsman sent from Tyre to assist Solomon. By making his name "Huram-abi" (2:13) instead of "Hiram" (1 Kgs 7:13 mg),[7] by linking Huram-abi's lineage to the tribe of Dan instead of Naphtali (2:14; 1 Kgs 7:14), and by expanding the list of Huram-abi's skills (2:14; 1 Kgs 7:14), the Chronicler was forging a link between this craftsman and the craftsman Oholiab, who assisted Bezalel in the construction of Israel's first sanctuary, the Tabernacle (Exod 35:31–36:1). This example of "recapitulative historiography" (see also commentary on 1 Chr 22) was part of the Chronicler's strategy of legitimizing the Temple in Jerusalem as the rightful successor to the Tabernacle. The Chronicler, however, did not allow this Tyrian craftsman to overshadow David's preparations, reminding the reader through Hiram's speech that the work of Huram-abi would take place alongside that of the craftsmen of Solomon and (or, that are) the craftsmen arranged by David.

Solomon's Census and Organization of Foreign Workers for the Project (2:17-18). The chapter ends in a fashion similar to its beginning, by listing again the three categories of workers who were enlisted for the project: laborers, men who quarried stone in the hill country, and foremen (see 2:2). However, the list this time is identified as a numbering of "all foreigners" who were presently in the land. The term "foreigner" (Heb., *ger* [TH1616, ZH1731]) denotes a temporary dweller in a foreign nation. The rights of such individuals were limited; in this case it appears they were conscripted by Solomon to assist in the Temple construction. Here the Chronicler makes an explicit link to Solomon's father David, who enumerated foreigners in 1 Chronicles 22:2. There is, however, a more subtle link here to Joshua, who forced the Gibeonites to serve at the sanctuary (Josh 9:26-27; cf. Dillard 1987:4, 21).

In 2 Chronicles 2 the Chronicler emphasizes Solomon's immediate passion to build the Temple. It is this task for which Yahweh had chosen him (see 1 Chr 28–29), and he used the wisdom granted in the previous chapter to begin preparing for the project. The appearance of foreigners in these early stages reminds the Chronicler's audience of something suggested by the shape of the genealogies that began the book—that is, that Israel and its worship were not irrelevant to the surrounding world. As the palace of the God who created the cosmos, all nations had a vested interest in its construction.

ENDNOTES

1. Dillard (1987:18) calls these references infrequent, and Japhet (1993:538) incorrectly identifies only 2:1, 12; and 7:11 as places where the palace is mentioned. Instead, the palace is mentioned in many of the key notations tracking the building project throughout the account. In this way they are significant junctures in the account.
2. This should not be considered a gloss, as do Japhet (1993:538); Rudolph (1955:201); and Williamson (1982:198). For its literary quality, see Dillard 1987:17-18.
3. Mention is made in 1 Kgs 11:1, 5 of Solomon's marriage to a Phoenician princess; however, Sidon is the city mentioned, not Tyre.
4. It must be noted that the account in Chronicles does not resemble the epistolary genre known from ancient Israel; see Pardee and Sperling 1982:180. Some elements of this genre can be discerned in the account in 1 Kings; see Japhet 1993:539. See Hurowitz 1992:131-223 for connections between the underlying Kings source of these exchanges and ancient Near Eastern epistolary tradition.
5. Notice also this motif in the Baal texts: After his victory, his house was built on Zaphon with precious metals from mountains (silver, gold, pure lapis lazuli) and trees and cedars from Lebanon and Sirion (cf. Kapelrud 1963:59). See Nebuchadnezzar's account of rebuilding Esagila with cedar trees from Lebanon in Harper 1904:137;

cf. Harper 1904:147-150 for Nebuchadnezzar's use of Lebanon cedars in the roof of his palace in Babylon; see Harper 1904:150-152 for rebuilding of Ezida in Borsippa; and see Harper 1904:163-168 for Nabonidus also using cedar.

6. See Hillers 1964, 1969; Kline 1963; McCarthy 1978.
7. Japhet (1993:544) is not convincing in her argument that the change from Hiram to Huram-abi is to distinguish this individual from the king of Tyre.

◆ C. Solomon Builds the Temple (3:1–4:22)

So Solomon began to build the Temple of the LORD in Jerusalem on Mount Moriah, where the LORD had appeared to David, his father. The Temple was built on the threshing floor of Araunah* the Jebusite, the site that David had selected. [2]The construction began in midspring,* during the fourth year of Solomon's reign.

[3]These are the dimensions Solomon used for the foundation of the Temple of God (using the old standard of measurement).* It was 90 feet long and 30 feet wide.* [4]The entry room at the front of the Temple was 30 feet* wide, running across the entire width of the Temple, and 30 feet* high. He overlaid the inside with pure gold.

[5]He paneled the main room of the Temple with cypress wood, overlaid it with fine gold, and decorated it with carvings of palm trees and chains. [6]He decorated the walls of the Temple with beautiful jewels and with gold from the land of Parvaim. [7]He overlaid the beams, thresholds, walls, and doors throughout the Temple with gold, and he carved figures of cherubim on the walls.

[8]He made the Most Holy Place 30 feet wide, corresponding to the width of the Temple, and 30 feet deep. He overlaid its interior with 23 tons* of fine gold. [9]The gold nails that were used weighed 20 ounces* each. He also overlaid the walls of the upper rooms with gold.

[10]He made two figures shaped like cherubim, overlaid them with gold, and placed them in the Most Holy Place. [11]The total wingspan of the two cherubim standing side by side was 30 feet. One wing of the first figure was 7½ feet* long, and it touched the Temple wall. The other wing, also 7½ feet long, touched one of the wings of the second figure. [12]In the same way, the second figure had one wing 7½ feet long that touched the opposite wall. The other wing, also 7½ feet long, touched the wing of the first figure. [13]So the wingspan of the two cherubim side by side was 30 feet. They stood on their feet and faced out toward the main room of the Temple.

[14]Across the entrance of the Most Holy Place he hung a curtain made of fine linen, decorated with blue, purple, and scarlet thread and embroidered with figures of cherubim.

[15]For the front of the Temple, he made two pillars that were 27 feet* tall, each topped by a capital extending upward another 7½ feet. [16]He made a network of interwoven chains and used them to decorate the tops of the pillars. He also made 100 decorative pomegranates and attached them to the chains. [17]Then he set up the two pillars at the entrance of the Temple, one to the south of the entrance and the other to the north. He named the one on the south Jakin, and the one on the north Boaz.*

CHAPTER 4

Solomon* also made a bronze altar 30 feet long, 30 feet wide, and 15 feet high.* [2]Then he cast a great round basin, 15 feet across from rim to rim, called the Sea. It was 7½ feet deep and about 45 feet in circumference.* [3]It was encircled just below its rim by two rows of figures that resembled oxen. There were about six oxen per foot* all the way around, and they were cast as part of the basin.

4The Sea was placed on a base of twelve bronze oxen, all facing outward. Three faced north, three faced west, three faced south, and three faced east, and the Sea rested on them. 5The walls of the Sea were about three inches* thick, and its rim flared out like a cup and resembled a water lily blossom. It could hold about 16,500 gallons* of water.

6He also made ten smaller basins for washing the utensils for the burnt offerings. He set five on the south side and five on the north. But the priests washed themselves in the Sea.

7He then cast ten gold lampstands according to the specifications that had been given, and he put them in the Temple. Five were placed against the south wall, and five were placed against the north wall.

8He also built ten tables and placed them in the Temple, five along the south wall and five along the north wall. Then he molded 100 gold basins.

9He then built a courtyard for the priests, and also the large outer courtyard. He made doors for the courtyard entrances and overlaid them with bronze. 10The great bronze basin called the Sea was placed near the southeast corner of the Temple.

11Huram-abi also made the necessary washbasins, shovels, and bowls.

So at last Huram-abi completed everything King Solomon had assigned him to make for the Temple of God:

12 the two pillars;
the two bowl-shaped capitals on top of the pillars;
the two networks of interwoven chains that decorated the capitals;
13 the 400 pomegranates that hung from the chains on the capitals (two rows of pomegranates for each of the chain networks that decorated the capitals on top of the pillars);
14 the water carts holding the basins;
15 the Sea and the twelve oxen under it;
16 the ash buckets, the shovels, the meat hooks, and all the related articles.

Huram-abi made all these things of burnished bronze for the Temple of the LORD, just as King Solomon had directed. 17The king had them cast in clay molds in the Jordan Valley between Succoth and Zarethan.* 18Solomon used such great quantities of bronze that its weight could not be determined.

19Solomon also made all the furnishings for the Temple of God:

the gold altar;
the tables for the Bread of the Presence;
20 the lampstands and their lamps of solid gold, to burn in front of the Most Holy Place as prescribed;
21 the flower decorations, lamps, and tongs—all of the purest gold;
22 the lamp snuffers, bowls, dishes, and incense burners—all of solid gold;
the doors for the entrances to the Most Holy Place and the main room of the Temple, overlaid with gold.

3:1 Hebrew reads *Ornan,* a variant spelling of Araunah; compare 2 Sam 24:16. **3:2** Hebrew *on the second day of the second month.* This day of the ancient Hebrew lunar calendar occurred in April or May. **3:3a** The "old standard of measurement" was a cubit equal to 18 inches [46 centimeters]. The new standard was a cubit of approximately 21 inches [53 centimeters]. **3:3b** Hebrew *60 cubits* [27.6 meters] *long and 20 cubits* [9.2 meters] *wide.* **3:4a** Hebrew *20 cubits* [9.2 meters]; also in 3:8, 11, 13. **3:4b** As in some Greek and Syriac manuscripts, which read *20 cubits* [9.2 meters]; Hebrew reads *120 [cubits],* which is 180 feet or 55 meters. **3:8** Hebrew *600 talents* [20.4 metric tons]. **3:9** Hebrew *50 shekels* [570 grams]. **3:11** Hebrew *5 cubits* [2.3 meters]; also in 3:11b, 12, 15. **3:15** As in Syriac version (see also 1 Kgs 7:15; 2 Kgs 25:17; Jer 52:21), which reads *18 cubits* [8.3 meters]; Hebrew reads *35 cubits,* which is 52.5 feet or 16.5 meters. **3:17** *Jakin* probably means "he establishes"; *Boaz* probably means "in him is strength." **4:1a** Or *Huram-abi;* Hebrew reads *He.* **4:1b** Hebrew *20 cubits* [9.2 meters] *long, 20 cubits wide, and 10 cubits* [4.6 meters] *high.* **4:2** Hebrew *10 cubits* [4.6 meters] *across . . . 5 cubits* [2.3 meters] *deep and 30 cubits* [13.8 meters] *in circumference.* **4:3** Or *20 oxen per meter;* Hebrew reads *10 per cubit.* **4:5a** Hebrew *a handbreadth* [8 centimeters]. **4:5b** Hebrew *3,000 baths* [63 kiloliters]. **4:17** As in parallel text at 1 Kgs 7:46; Hebrew reads *Zeredah.*

NOTES

3:6 *Parvaim.* The precise location is not known, possibly to be identified with *Sâk el Farwain* in northeast Arabia or *Farwa* in Yemen (see ABD 5.171).

3:8 *Most Holy Place.* In the OT this area of the sanctuary is either called *debir* [TH1687, ZH1808] ("inner sanctuary," 1 Kgs 6:5, 16) or *qodesh haqqodashim* [TH6944, ZH7731] ("holy of holies," Exod 26:34). The Chronicler uses both terms for this area (Japhet 1993:556).

3:16 *a network of interwoven chains.* Lit., "chains in the inner sanctuary." The phrase "in the inner sanctuary" (*baddebir* [TH1687, ZH1808]) most likely is a gloss that was incorporated into the text by a scribe, or a scribal error for *kerabid* [TH7242, ZH8054] ("as a necklace"; cf. Gen 41:42; Ezek 16:11; Japhet 1993:558).

4:7 *according to the specifications that had been given.* This could be a reference to the Tabernacle instructions in Exod 25:31-40; 37:17-24, but it is more likely the instructions of David in 1 Chr 28:11-19.

4:11 *washbasins, shovels, and bowls.* The "washbasins" should be translated as "pails," which were used for gathering ashes. Shovels were used for the removal of ashes from the altar after sacrifice. Bowls caught the blood of sacrificial victims (Exod 27:3; 38:3; Num 4:14; 1 Kgs 7:40, 45; Jer 52:18-19).

COMMENTARY

While 2:1 related Solomon's decision to embark on the Temple-building project (a decision that led to the description of the arrangements for a master craftsman and timber for the Temple project for the rest of ch 2), 3:1 signals the beginning of the Temple project. Chapters 3 and 4 were compiled as a continuous section, as indicated by the regular use of the verb *wayya'as* [TH6213, ZH6913] ("and he made/did") in 3:8, 10, 14, 15, 16; 4:1, 2, 6, 7, 8, 9, 11, 18, 19. This becomes a "*Leitmotif,* lending the pericope a touch of uniformity" (Japhet 1993:563; cf. Williamson 1982:208). The section begins with a summary note (3:1-2), a structuring signal that matches others found throughout the Chronicler's account of the Temple building (1:1; 2:1; 3:1-2; 5:1; 7:11; 8:1, 16). It then presents the building account in two parts: first, the construction of the building structures (3:3-17) and, second, the fashioning of the furnishings and utensils within those structures (4:1-22).

In this section the Chronicler abridges his source in Kings, providing much less detail on the construction. This suggests that the Chronicler's concern is merely the "fact" of the construction rather than the "process" itself. In abridging his account of Solomon's greatest accomplishment, the Chronicler preserves the emphasis he placed on David's role in the Temple project. This fixation on David is evident from the outset, because David is depicted as a second Abraham, to whom God appeared at Moriah (Gen 22:2; cf. 2 Chr 3:1), designating the site of the sanctuary. Solomon is not lost in all of this, however. The Chronicler continues his depiction of the son of David as the second Bezalel and Huram-abi as the second Oholiab (see introduction to chs 1–9). They worked with the bronze that was contributed by David in immeasurable quantities (4:18). The many words used for gold in this chapter (pure gold, fine gold, gold from the land of Parvaim, solid gold, purest gold) highlight the quality of the project that involved materials close to the manifest presence of God. Furthermore, the careful attention to imagery and handiwork reveals that artistry and creativity are also appropriate for the God of the Temple.

Summary Note (3:1-2). The information provided in 3:1-2 was carefully chosen to place Solomon's project in a broader context. First of all, the Temple would be built on "Mount Moriah." The only other reference to this mountain (or better, range of hills) in the Old Testament is found in Genesis 22, the story of Abraham's near sacrifice of Isaac at God's command.[1] The Chronicler (or others before him) may have come to associate Moriah with Mount Zion, where the Temple was located because of two comments in Genesis 22. The first is that it took Abraham three days to reach the "land of Moriah" from the land of the Philistines (Gen 22:4). This fits with the 45-mile distance from southern Philistia to Jerusalem. The second comment is that after God provided a ram for a burnt offering in place of Isaac, "Abraham named the place Yahweh-Yireh (which means 'the LORD will provide'). To this day, people still use that name as a proverb: 'On the mountain of the LORD it will be provided'" (Gen 22:14). With the exception of one reference to Sinai in the Old Testament (Num 10:33), the vast majority of the references to "the mountain of the LORD" is to Mount Zion, that is, the Temple Mount in Jerusalem (Ps 24:3; Isa 2:3; 30:29; Zech 8:3).[2]

The Chronicler also linked the Temple-building project to the tradition he had recorded in 1 Chronicles 21, where the Lord appears to David on the threshing floor of Araunah the Jebusite. In this the Chronicler was moving beyond the evidence of his own source text, for the account of this theophany in 2 Samuel 24 and that of the building of the Temple in 1 Kings 6–7 do not make any explicit connection between the threshing floor and the Temple site.

In both the Davidic tradition of 1 Chronicles 21 (paralleled in 2 Sam 24) and the Abrahamic tradition of Genesis 22, the angel of the Lord appears and stops the destruction of human life and instructs an individual to offer an animal sacrifice in place of the human life. With this initial note, then, the Chronicler was linking the Temple site in Jerusalem with two key traditions of God's provision of sacrifice for his people at the Temple site, one Abrahamic and the other Davidic.[3] In this case it may depict David as a second Abraham at Moriah bringing to fulfillment God's designs for Moriah as his chosen place for sacrifice. It may even suggest that David "superseded" Abraham.[4] If nothing else, it is a reminder that the activities that take place at the Temple, in this case especially the sacrificial activities, are deeply rooted in the tradition of Israel and predate even David.

Furthermore, the Chronicler continues a trend already seen in 1 Chronicles of emphasizing David over Solomon in the Temple construction. Not only did David provide all the plans and materials for the construction, he also identified the very location on which it would be built. These introductory verses remind the reader of the imposing figure of David at the outset of the building project. There is no question that the Chronicler tends to highlight David as the key architect of the Temple project. This emphasis on David and de-emphasis on Solomon probably also lies behind the way the Chronicler significantly abridges the account of Temple construction found in his source text in 1 Kings 6–7.

The Foundation (3:3). The laying of foundations for temples in the ancient Near East was an important stage in the building project (see introduction to chs 1–9; see Ezra 3; Isa 28:16; Hag 2:15-19; Zech 4:6b-10a). It was accompanied by a special religious ceremony, often with the royal figure enacting the laying of the first brick in the new foundation. The king would bury foundation deposits including written texts (with blessings and curses for future monarchs who might rebuild the temple), precious metals, stones, and even fragrant plants. The foundation was seen as key to the endurance of the structure. The Chronicler continued this tradition by at least mentioning the laying of the foundation of the Temple (something unique to the Chronicler and not found in 1 Kgs 6:2), but he did not offer any details beyond its dimensions (see also the summary note in 8:16). Great focus is placed on the later stages of building the Temple, something that reflects his source in Kings but also reflects that the Chronicler was writing to an audience who could see the completed second Temple. The Chronicler then focused on those elements that were evident to all and traced the source to Solomon.

The dimensions of the entire structure are given in terms of what the Chronicler considered "the old standard of measurement." There were, indeed, two measurements for the cubit: short (17.4 inches) and long (20.4 inches); this variation is also evident in Egypt, where the cubit could be six or seven hand widths (Ezek 40:5; 41:8; 43:13). It appears here that the older cubit is the shorter cubit, thus placing the dimensions of the entire structure at about 90 feet long by 30 feet wide.

Entry Room and Main Room (3:4-7). Just outside the main structure of the Temple lay an entry area or porch that ran the entire width of the Temple structure. This area was overlaid with pure gold, signaling to the worshiper that one was approaching the holiness of deity.[5] In this area were positioned two pillars (3:15-17). These pillars do not appear to have been used to hold up the roof of the porch, but rather were freestanding.

Leaving the entrance area, the Chronicler then described the main room within the Temple structure.[6] Here he left out a significant portion of his source in 1 Kings 6 (1 Kgs 6:4-20a), revealing his lack of emphasis on the details of the construction of the Temple structure itself (see above). The equivalent area to this main room in the ancient Tabernacle structure was the "Holy Place" (Exod 26:33). As with the entry room, this room (beams, thresholds, walls, doors) was constructed from wood that was then overlaid with gold.[7] The walls were filled with iconography, carved images of palm trees, chains, and angelic beings (cherubim), as well as jewels and special gold from the land of Parvaim. Chapter 4 will reveal that this main room contained ten gold lampstands and ten tables, five of each along the north and south walls.

Most Holy Place (3:8-14). The description finally moves to the Most Holy Place, where again the Chronicler abridges the description from his source, leaving out 1 Kings 6:28-32 with its detailed description of this inner sanctuary. Solomon is the subject of the verbs throughout this section, revealing the fulfillment of God's promise to David in 1 Chronicles 17. The verb used throughout ("made," *'asah* [TH6213, ZH6913]; 3:8, 10, 14, 15, 16) echoes the account of the Tabernacle construction in Exodus 36:8–39:32, linking the Temple with the ancient sanctuary (Williamson 1982:27).

The dimensions reveal that this room was a perfect square (30 x 30 feet), the walls of which were lined with fine gold. The abundance of the gold used for this room reflects the Chronicler's emphasis on the sanctity of this space. The nails would not have been pure gold but rather coated with gold. The reference to "upper rooms" is not developed any further and is unknown from other sources.[8]

The focus of the description of the Most Holy Place is on the cherubim, whose presence dominated the room. The account clearly distinguishes these cherubim in the Temple from the cherubim that were part of the Ark in the Tabernacle (Japhet 1993:556). In the Tabernacle the cherubim were connected to the mercy seat, which formed the lid of the Ark (Exod 25:10-21) and faced each other, while in the Temple the cherubim were standing on their feet side by side and facing the entrance to the room.

They signified the presence of deity, as well as heavenly protection of the Most Holy Place. While later in his enumeration of the work of Solomon (4:22) the Chronicler does note that doors were placed between the main room and the Most Holy Place (cf. 1 Kgs 6:33-35), at this place the Chronicler notes that the entrance area was covered by a curtain. Although some have suggested that this feature in the Chronicler's account is an anachronistic imposition of a feature of the second Temple, it may just as easily be another example (see the use of "made" above) of the Chronicler alluding to the construction of the Tabernacle, which also had a fabric veil between the two areas of the sanctuary (Exod 26:31-33; see also Japhet 1993:556). The fabric of this curtain was not only of the finest quality, it was also carefully decorated with different colored threads and embroidered with the cherubim that could be observed on the walls of the main room and seen in the Most Holy Place.

Pillars at the Front of the Temple (3:15-17). After moving from the entrance area outside the Temple to the Most Holy Place, the Chronicler returned to the entrance area of the structure to describe the two pillars that stood before the Temple. These pillars, a common feature of temples in the ancient world, were constructed with much creativity and would attract the attention of Nebuchadnezzar when he sacked Jerusalem in 587 BC and removed them from the Temple as spoil (2 Kgs 25:13). The two pillars were given the names Jakin ("he will establish") and Boaz ("in strength"), possibly together forming a declaration to the enduring quality of the Temple. They were constructed in the Jordan Valley (1 Kgs 7:46) as hollow structures (Jer 52:21) and then transported to Jerusalem for placement before the Temple as freestanding structures.

Interestingly, the Chronicler does not explicitly mention Huram as the one who created the pillars as his source does at 1 Kings 7:13-22. The last subject to be mentioned was Solomon in 3:3, and it is not until 4:11 that Huram-abi is introduced into the account. At that point, Huram-abi is clearly identified as the one who completed the work assigned him by Solomon and that this encompassed the work described in the previous section, but the effect of the Chronicler's account is to give Solomon an implicit role in the crafting of the furnishings and utensils for the Temple. This fits the Chronicler's depiction of Solomon and Huram-abi as a second Bezalel and Oholiab (see introduction to chs 1–9 and commentary on ch 1). Not only is the emphasis on Solomon's role as craftsman, but also Huram-abi is placed in a role subordinate to Solomon in the account.

Account of Furnishings and Utensils for the Temple (4:1-8). For the remainder of his account of the building, the Chronicler focuses his attention on the furnishings and utensils that would be placed within the sanctuary and used for worship. Although assumed in the account of 1 Kings (see 1 Kgs 8:64; 9:25), the construction of the bronze altar is not provided in the present form of Kings, although it may have been lost through scribal error (Dillard 1987:34; Japhet 1993:564). The dimensions of the altar reveal it had the same footprint as the Most Holy Place. This altar replaced the temporary altar built by David on the threshing floor of Araunah the Jebusite (1 Chr 21:26) as well as the altar of burnt offering in the Tabernacle (Exod 27:1-8), dwarfing the latter altar in size (it was four times larger with sixteen times the surface area). The altar was placed in the inner court (1 Kgs 8:22, 64; 9:25), where the people would offer their various sacrifices.

A second major furnishing within the courtyard outside the Temple structure was the large round basin called "the Sea." This furnishing, which replaced the basin (often called the "laver") in the Tabernacle (Exod 30:17-21; 38:8; 40:30-32), was constructed of bronze and placed on a base of twelve oxen with three facing each direction. In place of the reference in his source in 1 Kings 7:24 to the "gourds" serving as decorations under the lip of the basin, the Chronicler depicts "oxen."[9] The Chronicler accentuates the link to the Tabernacle and its laver by adding to his source in Kings the note that "the Sea" was used for ritual cleansing (4:6; cf. Exod 30:18-21; Dillard 1987:34-35; Japhet 1993:565-566).[10] Besides this massive basin, ten smaller basins were constructed to wash the utensils for the offerings on the bronze altar.[11]

Along the wall of the main room of the sanctuary were placed not only these ten smaller basins but also ten gold lampstands and ten tables, with five of each furnishing on the north side and five on the south side. This was an innovation of the Tabernacle's lone lampstand and possibly led to the Chronicler's careful note, "according to the specifications that had been given."[12] The list in 4:12-16 tells us that the basins were supported by individual stands ("water carts," 4:14). The tables here must have held the Bread of the Presence, as 4:19 suggests.

Courtyards (4:9-10). Before providing the lists of furnishings and utensils created by Huram-abi (4:11-17) and by Solomon (4:18-22), the Chronicler describes the creation of the courtyards that surrounded the sanctuary structure and into which the bronze altar and basin ("the Sea") would be placed. The Chronicler depicts two courtyards, one for the priests and a larger outer courtyard, both of which had entrances with doors overlaid with bronze. Although the reference to two courtyards at this point in the building report is unique in Chronicles, 1 Kings 7:12 distinguishes between the "great courtyard" and the "inner courtyard." The term used here for "courtyard" reflects later terminology (also used in 6:13; cf. Ezek 43:14, 17, 20; 45:19 where the term appears to refer to a ledge around the altar; see Hurvitz 1982:78-81).

Lists of Furnishings and Utensils for the Temple (4:11-22). The account closes with the enumeration of the furnishings and utensils created by Huram-abi and Solomon. In the first section (4:11-18), the Chronicler describes the accomplishments of Huram-abi, reminding the reader that he thoroughly and faithfully worked ("completed everything," 4:11; "made all these things," 4:16) under the authority of Solomon ("had assigned him," 4:11; "had directed," 4:16). As one can see, the main focus of Huram-abi's work was on the pillars (4:12-13), the basins (4:14-15), and the utensils used for sacrifice (4:16; ash buckets, shovels, meat hooks). The items listed were all made of bronze and were destined for areas of the sacred precincts removed from the sanctuary proper. In contrast, Solomon's list in the second section (4:19-22) contains items made of gold that were destined for the sanctuary itself. The list is divided into three parts with 4:19-20 listing the three main furnishings (altar, table, lampstand), 4:21-22a listing the utensils and decorations used with the three main furnishings, and 4:22b listing the doors. The gold altar in 4:19 refers to an altar of incense (1 Chr 28:18), a furnishing that was also included in the Tabernacle (Exod 30:1-10). Interestingly, the lone table of the Bread of Presence (Exod 25:23-30; 26:35) and the single lampstand (Exod 25:31-40; 26:35), which were found in the Tabernacle, were each replaced by ten such furnishings, most likely due to the larger size of the building. The flowers, lamps, tongs, and snuffers in 4:21-22 are all associated with lampstands (Exod 25:38; 37:23; Num 4:9; 1 Kgs 7:50; 2 Kgs 12:13; 25:14; Jer 52:18), the bowls with altars (Exod 27:3; 38:3; Num 4:14; 1 Kgs 7:40, 45), the dishes with the table of the Bread of the Presence (Exod 25:29-30), and the incense burners (better, "trays") with the lampstand (Exod 25:38; 37:23; Num 4:9). The distinction between "bronze" and "gold" not only symbolizes the distinction between regions of sacred space and relative proximity to the manifest presence of the Lord but also the distinction between Solomon and Huram-abi. Solomon as the lead craftsman was associated with the gold items, while Huram-abi was his assistant and worked in bronze. Furthermore, Japhet has noted that the items of bronze were all David's innovations, while those of gold were all original to the ancient Tabernacle sanctuary (1993:570).

ENDNOTES

1. While the Chronicler emphasizes the connection to Abraham as he begins his description of the building project proper, he leaves out the reference to the Exodus that was found in his source in 1 Kgs 6:1. It has often been noted in scholarship that the Chronicler deemphasizes the Exodus, leaving out references to it from his sources (cf. 1 Chr 17:5, NASB with 2 Sam 7:6; 6:11 with 1 Kgs 8:21; 6:39-40 with 1 Kgs 8:50-53), and places greater stress on the patriarchal traditions. See Dillard 1987:28; Japhet 1979:205-218; 1989:322-327; Williamson 1977b:64-66.
2. This connection between Gen 22 and the Temple is assumed in later Jewish exegesis; see *Targum Jonathan* for Gen 22:14; Rashi on Gen 22:2; see Japhet 1993:551.
3. Dillard (1987:27) has highlighted the use of the verbal root *r'h* [TH7200, ZH8011] in Gen 22:8, 14 and in 2 Chr 3:1. This root is dominantly translated as "to see" in the active Qal and "to appear" in the passive Niphal, although in Gen 22 it seems to have the meaning "to provide" (so traditional translations). Just as the Lord appeared (provided) on Mount Moriah to Abraham, so he appeared to David.
4. Japhet (1993:552) says, "Davidic authority also superseded the ancient traditions of the Abrahamic cult."
5. Dillard (1987:28) suggests that this may be overlay but also could be gold inlaid in designs in wood.
6. Here the Chronicler uses the term *habbayith haggadol* [TH1004/1419, ZH1074/1524] (the great house), which interestingly is the original meaning of the term *é-gal*, a Sumerian equivalent of the Hebrew *hekal* [TH1964, ZH2121] (4:22), the term used to refer to the Temple in the OT (Japhet 1993:554).

7. There is a curious disjuncture between Kings and Chronicles on the type of wood used for the Temple. Kings speaks of cedar wood, while Chronicles of cypress wood. Whether the terminology for these woods had shifted by the Chronicler's time is not known.
8. Japhet (1993:555) claims this reference to upper rooms is related to the entire Temple structure and not to the Most Holy Place alone, but the flow of this section suggests that the description is still of the Most Holy Place. Better is the suggestion of Dillard (1987:29) that the height of the Most Holy Place was given as 20 cubits in 1 Kgs 6:2, 20, even though the building height was 30 cubits. If the Most Holy Place was on a raised platform of 5 cubits, this would leave 5 cubits above the sanctuary for upper rooms.
9. Some have suggested that this is a scribal error of *beqarim* [TH1241, ZH1330] (oxen) for *peqa'im* [TH6497, ZH7225] (gourds), others that the original is to be found in Chronicles because the writer of Kings was uncomfortable with the idolatrous associations of bovine imagery (Dillard 1987:35).
10. The significance of "the Sea" is not identified in the account in Kings, although many scholars have noted its association with the ancient tradition of the Chaos Sea over which God has exerted his dominion through creation (Gen 1) and redemption (Exod 15). In Chronicles the significance is linked to ritual cleansing, and in Ezekiel the Sea is replaced with a river of living water (Ezek 47:1-12).
11. It is unclear what the 100 gold basins mentioned in 4:8 were used for.
12. See Japhet 1993:570. This reference to ten lampstands and then to ten tables of the Bread of Presence are odd in light of 13:11, which refers to one lampstand and one table of the Bread of Presence (cf. 29:18; 1 Chr 9:32; 23:29). First Kings 7:48 refers to only one table of the Bread of the Presence, like in the Tabernacle.

◆ D. After the Ark Is Brought, God's Presence Fills the Temple (5:1-14)

So Solomon finished all his work on the Temple of the LORD. Then he brought all the gifts his father, David, had dedicated—the silver, the gold, and the various articles—and he stored them in the treasuries of the Temple of God.

2Solomon then summoned to Jerusalem the elders of Israel and all the heads of tribes—the leaders of the ancestral families of Israel. They were to bring the Ark of the LORD's Covenant to the Temple from its location in the City of David, also known as Zion. 3So all the men of Israel assembled before the king at the annual Festival of Shelters, which is held in early autumn.*

4When all the elders of Israel arrived, the Levites picked up the Ark. 5The priests and Levites brought up the Ark along with the special tent* and all the sacred items that had been in it. 6There, before the Ark, King Solomon and the entire community of Israel sacrificed so many sheep, goats, and cattle that no one could keep count!

7Then the priests carried the Ark of the LORD's Covenant into the inner sanctuary of the Temple—the Most Holy Place—and placed it beneath the wings of the cherubim. 8The cherubim spread their wings over the Ark, forming a canopy over the Ark and its carrying poles. 9These poles were so long that their ends could be seen from the Temple's main room—the Holy Place*—but not from the outside. They are still there to this day. 10Nothing was in the Ark except the two stone tablets that Moses had placed in it at Mount Sinai,* where the LORD made a covenant with the people of Israel when they left Egypt.

11Then the priests left the Holy Place. All the priests who were present had

purified themselves, whether or not they were on duty that day. [12]And the Levites who were musicians—Asaph, Heman, Jeduthun, and all their sons and brothers—were dressed in fine linen robes and stood at the east side of the altar playing cymbals, lyres, and harps. They were joined by 120 priests who were playing trumpets. [13]The trumpeters and singers performed together in unison to praise and give thanks to the LORD. Accompanied by trumpets, cymbals, and other instruments, they raised their voices and praised the LORD with these words:

"He is good!
His faithful love endures forever!"

At that moment a thick cloud filled the Temple of the LORD. [14]The priests could not continue their service because of the cloud, for the glorious presence of the LORD filled the Temple of God.

5:3 Hebrew *at the festival that is in the seventh month.* The Festival of Shelters began on the fifteenth day of the seventh month of the ancient Hebrew lunar calendar. This day occurred in late September, October, or early November. 5:5 Hebrew *the Tent of Meeting;* i.e., the tent mentioned in 2 Sam 6:17 and 1 Chr 16:1. 5:9 As in some Hebrew manuscripts and Greek version (see also 1 Kgs 8:8); Masoretic Text reads *from the Ark in front of the Most Holy Place.* 5:10 Hebrew *Horeb,* another name for Sinai.

NOTES

5:2 ***the City of David, also known as Zion.*** When Jerusalem was taken by David, it was called the "fortress of Zion" (2 Sam 5:7). Although there is a distinction here between Zion and the Temple area, eventually Zion would designate the entire city and Temple area (Pss 74:2; 76:2; 135:21). The name Zion would become a popular choice for referring to Jerusalem in the poetic and prophetic tradition of Israel (Ps 51:18; Isa 31:8-9; Jer 26:18; Amos 1:2; cf. Hess and Wenham 1999; Hoppe 2000; Ollenburger 1987).

5:3 ***Festival of Shelters.*** The Hebrew text merely says "the festival that is in the seventh month" (see NLT mg), here identified by the NLT as the Festival of Shelters (Tabernacles) based on 7:8. However, see commentary on 7:8 for the debate.

5:5 ***special tent.*** Lit., "the Tent of Meeting," a reference to the Tabernacle structure that was located at that time in Gibeon (cf. 1:3, 6, 13; cf. 1 Chr 6:32 [16]; 9:21; 23:32). This was the name by which it was identified in the wilderness accounts (Exod 27:21; 28:43; 29:4, 10-11).

5:12 ***Asaph, Heman, Jeduthun.*** For these musicians and their appointment by David, see 1 Chr 16 and 25.

COMMENTARY

With the summary note at the outset of chapter 5, the Chronicler moves into a new phase of his account of the Temple building, a section that will continue until the end of chapter 7. While the Chronicler abridged the previous section from his source in Kings (see commentary on chs 3–4), in the present section he expands his account. The result is that greater emphasis is placed on the dedication of the Temple than on the construction of the Temple. This suggests that the Chronicler was more interested in the functioning of the Temple and its services than in its construction, as he addressed readers after the second Temple was completed.

This section of the Chronicler's work is constructed chiastically—that is, the events in the second half of the account are related in reverse order to those in the first. All the events take place at the Festival of Shelters (Tabernacles).

Summary Note (5:1)
  Transferring the Ark Accompanied by Sacrifice at the Festival of Shelters (5:2-10)
    The Levites and Priests Worship (5:11-13a)
      God's Presence Fills the Temple; Priests Cannot Enter (5:13b-14)
        Solomon's Speeches and Prayers (6:1-42)
      God's Presence Fills the Temple; Priests Cannot Enter (7:1-2)
    The Levites and Priests Worship (7:3)
  Dedicating the Temple Accompanied by Sacrifice at the Festival of Shelters (7:4-10)
Summary Note (7:11)
  God's Speech to Solomon (7:12-22)

The pivot or center point of the section is the series of speeches by Solomon in chapter 6. After the final summary note, which closes off the section and declares definitively the completion of the Temple and palace projects, the Chronicler records God's response to Solomon's accomplishments (7:12-22).

The first half of the chiastic structure is represented in verse 5 and is concerned with the Ark's transfer to the Temple from the tent David had set up for it in Jerusalem and the Tent of Meeting's transfer from Gibeon. The chapter ends climactically with the glorious presence of God filling the Temple.

Summary Note (5:1). This section begins with a summary note, a structuring signal that is a regular feature in the Chronicler's account of the Temple building (1:1; 2:1; 3:1-2; 5:1; 7:11; 8:1, 16). In this case, it functions as a transition between the construction of the Temple (3:1–4:22) and the dedication of the completed Temple that follows. This summary note will be matched by another at the end of the dedication account (7:11), forming a bracket around the entire account.

At the outset of 5:1 there is a wordplay between the verb "finished" (*shalem* [TH7999, ZH8966]) and the name Solomon (*shelomoh* [TH8010, ZH8976]), reminding the reader that Solomon brought to completion the hopes and preparations of his father David (Dillard 1987:37; McConville 1984a:125). It is not surprising that David again features prominently in this summary note, as was the case in 1:1 and 3:1-2 and in the speech that followed the summary note in 2:1. Here the Chronicler notes that the gifts David had dedicated to the Temple (1 Chr 18:10-11; 26:26-27; 29:1-5) were now transferred safely to the Temple treasuries, emphasizing Solomon's careful attention to his father's legacy.

Transferring the Ark (5:2-10). The Chronicler found in his source in Kings a scene that resonated with his own account to this point—that is, the assembly of a group of leaders and priests around a royal figure, signaling the beginning of a key phase in the narrative (1:2; 1 Chr 11:1; 13:1; 15:3; 23:1-2; 28:1). The initial grouping ("elders of Israel") probably refers to the entire group of leaders, which is then broken down into "all the heads of tribes" and then "the leaders of the ancestral families," the latter being subdivisions within the tribal units. The purpose of this assembly was "to bring the Ark of the LORD's Covenant to the Temple" (5:2). The Chronicler had related the transfer of the Ark from Kiriath-jearim to Jerusalem in

1 Chronicles 13–16 and the identification of the Temple site in 1 Chronicles 21. Now the Ark would make its final journey into the Temple's inner sanctuary with the affirmation of the nation's leadership and priestly officials. In addition, the Tabernacle located at Gibeon was now also transferred along with its furnishings to the Temple site. The term used in 5:5, "the special tent" (lit., the Tent of Meeting, see NLT mg), is only used elsewhere in the Solomonic narrative for the Tabernacle structure at Gibeon (see 1:3, 6, 13; cf. 1 Chr 6:31-32; 9:21; 23:32).[1] The completion of the Temple spelled the end for the ancient Tabernacle and any role for sanctuaries outside of Jerusalem.

The transfer of the Ark and the dedication of the Temple took place in a festival in the seventh month.[2] There were three festivals during the seventh month of the year: the Festival of Trumpets on the first of the month, probably marking the beginning of the civil year (Lev 23:24; Num 29:1), the Day of Atonement on the tenth of the month (Lev 16:29; 23:27; Num 29:7), and the Festival of Shelters (Tabernacles) from the fifteenth to the twenty-first of the month (Lev 23:34, 39; Num 29:12-34). Most assume that the festival referred to here is the Festival of Shelters, and interestingly 7:8-10 refers to a "closing ceremony" on the eighth day (twenty-second of the month), which matches the priestly legislation in Leviticus 23:39; Numbers 29:35 (cf. 1 Kgs 8:2, 65-66). This festival was one of the three key festivals (Passover/Unleavened Bread, Weeks/Pentecost, Tabernacles) that coincided with the three harvest periods in Canaan and to which all Israelites were to journey to Jerusalem to offer their tithes and offerings (Exod 23:14-17; Deut 16:16). It is not surprising that Solomon would plan his dedication to coincide with a major festival with so many people gathering in Jerusalem to celebrate the harvest. (Concerning some confusion over the precise festival on which the transfer of the Ark took place, see commentary on 7:4-10.)

Most of the account in this chapter is taken directly from the Chronicler's source in 1 Kings 8:1-9. The scene is a powerful depiction of Solomon in the midst of his people sacrificing animals beyond number (5:6) as priests transferred the Ark to its new location under the outspread wings of the cherubim in the Temple's inner sanctuary (5:7-10). The precise location is emphasized by the employment of three statements: "into the inner sanctuary of the Temple—the Most Holy Place . . . beneath the wings of the cherubim." Both accounts note the presence of the two tablets of the Decalogue within the Ark as evidence of the covenant between the Lord and his people at the exodus from Egypt (5:10; 1 Kgs 8:9). This reference will provide an important foundation for Solomon's speech reviewing the history of the Davidic covenant (6:5, 11). It also creates another important link to the earlier generation responsible for the creation of the Tabernacle, which has been an important prototype for the Chronicler's depiction of the Temple construction (see introduction to chs 1–9). The Chronicler, however, made one change to his source in Kings in this account. He defined the priestly figures who picked up the Ark to transport it to the new site as "Levites" (5:4; cf. 1 Kgs 8:3). This modification continues the Chronicler's emphasis on the role of the Levites in the Temple services. In 1 Chronicles 15, the Chronicler showed through David that the reason for the disaster in the first transfer of the Ark in 1 Chronicles 13 was that the Levites had not carried the Ark (1 Chr 15:13). Thus, the Chronicler was careful to note that the priestly figures who carried the Ark were "Levites." This not only is an example of his careful attention to sacred regulations and his accentuation of the Levitical orders, but also creates a link to the earlier work of David in 1 Chronicles 15 and identifies this ceremony as the final phase of the transfer of the Ark.

The Levites and Priests Worship (5:11-13a). When the transfer of the Ark was completed, the presence of God filled the Temple, making it impossible for the priests to carry out their ministry in the Temple (5:11-14). The Chronicler provides here material (5:11b-13a) not found in his source. This pericope offers an explanatory note and a short narrative. In the explanatory note the Chronicler states that the priests had sanctified themselves and were all present whether or not they were on duty that day, a note that must be understood against the backdrop of the schedule for priestly duty in 1 Chronicles 24. In the short narrative the Chronicler describes the Levitical musicians' offering oral praise to the Lord at the end of the ceremony of transfer. Immediately following their articulation of praise (5:13a), the house was filled with the cloud of God's manifest presence.[3] In 1 Chronicles 16 the Chronicler shows how David appointed the Levites to perform music before the Ark (1 Chr 16:4-6). As the Ark was transferred to its new site, the Chronicler gave pride of place to the Levites, who both carried the Ark and sang praises. In all of this, however, the Chronicler did not allow the Levites to overstep their bounds. Following his source, it is the priests who carried the Ark into the Most Holy Place, which the Levites were forbidden to enter (see 29:16; see Japhet 1993:575).

The declaration of praise that the Levites offer in 5:13 ("He is good! His faithful love endures forever!") appears again in 7:3, bracketing the Temple-dedication account and setting the tone for the event. This declaration of praise is a favorite of the Chronicler (5:13; 7:3, 6; 20:21; 1 Chr 16:34, 41) and one that regularly appears in the book of Psalms (Pss 100:5; 106:1; 107:1; 118:1, 29; 136:1-26). Ezra 3:11 relates that it was also used in the praise service at the foundation of the second Temple. This phrase links God's characteristic goodness with the enduring quality of his love. The term "faithful love" (Heb., *khesed* [TH2617, ZH2876]) refers to God's faithfulness to the covenant he had established with Israel. Before God favored Israel with his manifest presence in the first Temple, the Levites rehearsed the covenant values that made this experience possible.

God's Presence Fills the Temple (5:13b-14). With the expression of praise by the Levites, a cloud filled the Temple. This is an important detail for the Chronicler to retain from his source because it supports the parallels he has been developing throughout his account between the Tabernacle in the wilderness and the Temple in Jerusalem (cf. Exod 40:34-35). Clouds are often used to signify the divine presence (see HALOT 858). They function as the Lord's veil (Lam 3:44) and the dust beneath his feet (Nah 1:3). They reveal his presence, while at the same time concealing him from human view. God accompanied Israel on the wilderness journey in a pillar of cloud (Exod 13:21-22; 14:19-20, 24; 16:10; 19:9, 16; 24:15-16, 18; 33:9-10; 34:5; 40:34, 38; Pss 78:14; 99:7; 105:39).

For God to fill the Temple with his manifest presence was a declaration of divine approval of this as his permanent resting place. This was an issue when David first declared his desire to build a Temple (in 1 Chr 17:4-6) and is celebrated at the end of Solomon's prayer (in 6:41-42). The careful attention to the appointment of personnel and the construction of the building and its furnishings is witness to the difficulty of the holy God's descending into the midst of an unholy and common people. In the end, it is nothing short of grace that makes this possible, symbolized through the sacrifices offered by Solomon on that day and celebrated in the praise song of the Levites.

With God's manifest presence filling the Temple, the priests were unable to enter the inner sanctuary to conduct their sacred duties. This is reminiscent of the Tabernacle account, where Moses was unable to enter the Tabernacle because of the glory of the Lord in the cloud (Exod 40:35). For the Chronicler, however, Moses was replaced with the priests, who were the only sacred personnel allowed into the Most Holy Place.

ENDNOTES

1. Contra Japhet (1993:576), who sees the terms "Tent of Meeting" and "Tabernacle" used for both the Mosaic and Davidic tents.
2. The Chronicler left out the name of the month that was given in his source in 1 Kgs 8:2 (Ethanim), something he did also when citing 1 Kgs 6:1 in 3:2 (see Dillard 1987:41).
3. See Dillard 1987:40-41 for arguments defending the originality of 5:13b-14 to the Chronicler, based on rhetorical (its function in the chiastic arrangement of the account), thematic (its function within the Chronicler's development of the Levitical orders), and source-critical (its appearance in 1 Kgs 8:11 and assumption in the response of Solomon in 6:1-2) grounds.

◆ E. Solomon's Praise and Prayer (6:1-42)

Then Solomon prayed, "O LORD, you have said that you would live in a thick cloud of darkness. [2]Now I have built a glorious Temple for you, a place where you can live forever!"

[3]Then the king turned around to the entire community of Israel standing before him and gave this blessing: [4]"Praise the LORD, the God of Israel, who has kept the promise he made to my father, David. For he told my father, [5]'From the day I brought my people out of the land of Egypt, I have never chosen a city among any of the tribes of Israel as the place where a Temple should be built to honor my name. Nor have I chosen a king to lead my people Israel. [6]But now I have chosen Jerusalem as the place for my name to be honored, and I have chosen David to be king over my people Israel.'"

[7]Then Solomon said, "My father, David, wanted to build this Temple to honor the name of the LORD, the God of Israel. [8]But the LORD told him, 'You wanted to build the Temple to honor my name. Your intention is good, [9]but you are not the one to do it. One of your own sons will build the Temple to honor me.'

[10]"And now the LORD has fulfilled the promise he made, for I have become king in my father's place, and now I sit on the throne of Israel, just as the LORD promised. I have built this Temple to honor the name of the LORD, the God of Israel. [11]There I have placed the Ark, which contains the covenant that the LORD made with the people of Israel."

[12]Then Solomon stood before the altar of the LORD in front of the entire community of Israel, and he lifted his hands

in prayer. [13]Now Solomon had made a bronze platform 7½ feet long, 7½ feet wide, and 4½ feet high* and had placed it at the center of the Temple's outer courtyard. He stood on the platform, and then he knelt in front of the entire community of Israel and lifted his hands toward heaven. [14]He prayed,

"O LORD, God of Israel, there is no God like you in all of heaven and earth. You keep your covenant and show unfailing love to all who walk before you in wholehearted devotion. [15]You have kept your promise to your servant David, my father. You made that promise with your own mouth, and with your own hands you have fulfilled it today.

[16]"And now, O LORD, God of Israel, carry out the additional promise you made to your servant David, my father. For you said to him, 'If your descendants guard their behavior and faithfully follow my Law as you have done, one of them will always sit on the throne of Israel.' [17]Now, O LORD, God of Israel, fulfill this promise to your servant David.

[18]"But will God really live on earth among people? Why, even the highest heavens cannot contain you. How much less this Temple I have built! [19]Nevertheless, listen to my prayer and my plea, O LORD my God. Hear the cry and the prayer that your servant is making to you. [20]May you watch over this Temple day and night, this place where you have said you would put your name. May you always hear the prayers I make toward this place. [21]May you hear the humble and earnest requests from me and your people Israel when we pray toward this place. Yes, hear us from heaven where you live, and when you hear, forgive.

[22]"If someone wrongs another person and is required to take an oath of innocence in front of your altar at this Temple, [23]then hear from heaven and judge between your servants—the accuser and the accused. Pay back the guilty as they deserve. Acquit the innocent because of their innocence.

[24]"If your people Israel are defeated by their enemies because they have sinned against you, and if they turn back and acknowledge your name and pray to you here in this Temple, [25]then hear from heaven and forgive the sin of your people Israel and return them to this land you gave to them and to their ancestors.

[26]"If the skies are shut up and there is no rain because your people have sinned against you, and if they pray toward this Temple and acknowledge your name and turn from their sins because you have punished them, [27]then hear from heaven and forgive the sins of your servants, your people Israel. Teach them to follow the right path, and send rain on your land that you have given to your people as their special possession.

[28]"If there is a famine in the land or a plague or crop disease or attacks of locusts or caterpillars, or if your people's enemies are in the land besieging their towns—whatever disaster or disease there is—[29]and if your people Israel pray about their troubles or sorrow, raising their hands toward this Temple, [30]then hear from heaven where you live, and forgive. Give your people what their actions deserve, for you alone know each human heart. [31]Then they will fear you and walk in your ways as long as they live in the land you gave to our ancestors.

[32]"In the future, foreigners who do not belong to your people Israel will hear of you. They will come from distant lands when they hear of your great name and your strong hand and your powerful arm. And when they pray toward this Temple, [33]then hear from heaven where you live, and grant what they ask of you. In this way, all

the people of the earth will come to
know and fear you, just as your own
people Israel do. They, too, will know
that this Temple I have built honors
your name.
34 "If your people go out where you
send them to fight their enemies, and
if they pray to you by turning toward
this city you have chosen and toward
this Temple I have built to honor your
name, 35 then hear their prayers from
heaven and uphold their cause.
36 "If they sin against you—and who
has never sinned?—you might become
angry with them and let their enemies
conquer them and take them captive
to a foreign land far away or near.
37 But in that land of exile, they might
turn to you in repentance and pray,
'We have sinned, done evil, and acted
wickedly.' 38 If they turn to you with
their whole heart and soul in the land
of their captivity and pray toward the
land you gave to their ancestors—
toward this city you have chosen, and
toward this Temple I have built to
honor your name— 39 then hear their
prayers and their petitions from
heaven where you live, and uphold
their cause. Forgive your people who
have sinned against you.
40 "O my God, may your eyes be
open and your ears attentive to all
the prayers made to you in this place.

41 "And now arise, O LORD God, and
enter your resting place,
along with the Ark, the symbol
of your power.
May your priests, O LORD God, be
clothed with salvation;
may your loyal servants rejoice
in your goodness.
42 O LORD God, do not reject the king
you have anointed.
Remember your unfailing love
for your servant David."

6:13 Hebrew *5 cubits* [2.3 meters] *long, 5 cubits wide, and 3 cubits* [1.4 meters] *high.*

NOTES

6:11 ***the Ark, which contains the covenant.*** Exodus 40:20 recounts how the stone tablets with the terms of the covenant were deposited in the Ark. According to Num 17:10, Aaron's staff was placed "before the Ark of the Covenant" when the Ark and Tabernacle were first built, but the later text of Heb 9:4 states that Aaron's staff, along with a gold jar containing manna, eventually joined the stone tablets. The fate of the Ark in the latter phase of the monarchial period is not known. Jeremiah 3:16 suggests that already in Jeremiah's time it had been removed from the Temple. The Ark is not mentioned in the list of spoil in the account of the exile of Daniel in Dan 1, nor in the description of the destruction of Jerusalem in 2 Kgs 25, nor is it among the spoil that was returned by Cyrus in Ezra 1:7-11. Second Maccabees 2:4-8 claims that Jeremiah hid it in a cave on Mount Nebo. Josephus possibly indicates that it was taken by Shishak (*Antiquities* 8.258), while 2 Esdr 10:20-23 claims it was plundered in the destruction of the Temple in 587 BC. The veracity of these two latter claims is uncertain (see further ABD 1.390). For the Chronicler, the Ark was still in the Temple in the time of Josiah (2 Chr 35:3), even if it appears that during his own time there was no Ark (see Josephus *War* 1.152-153; 5.184-247; *Antiquities* 14.71-72; Tacitus *Historiae* 5.9; *m. Yoma* 5:2; ABD 1.391).

6:12 ***the altar of the LORD.*** This refers to the bronze altar that stood in the courtyard outside the Temple structure (4:1).

6:15 ***your promise to your servant David.*** This is a reference to the dynastic promise of 1 Chr 17.

6:16 ***the additional promise.*** See God's promises in 1 Chr 17:12-14; 22:10; 28:7, 9.

COMMENTARY

Solomon's Acknowledgment of God's Presence (6:1-2). After the cloud's descent, an outward sign of the Lord's "glorious presence" within the Temple, Solomon stepped forward to mark the significance of this event. Addressing the Lord directly, the king identified the "glorious Temple"—or, better, "lofty house"—that he had just built as the dwelling place of the Lord forever. This statement, however, must be read in light of the qualification of 6:18, which reminds the reader that no earthly house can contain the Lord, as well as of the repeated reference to God hearing prayers from heaven in 6:21, 25, 27, 30, 33, 35, 39. This then designates the Temple as the place of God's manifest presence on earth even though he rules from heaven. It is this latter reality that makes possible God's intervention in human affairs no matter where they take place. The Temple must then be viewed as an entranceway into the heavenly throne room of God, rather than the entire throne room itself.

Solomon Addresses the People (6:3-11). Following this declaration to God, Solomon turned to the assembly and blessed them. In this he repeated the action of his father, who blessed the people after transporting the Ark to Jerusalem (1 Chr 16:2). In both cases direct narrative is used without any record of the content of the blessing.[1]

After blessing his people, Solomon offered a speech that set the context for the dedication of the Temple. Although reminiscent of other recitations of this dialogue between God and David (see 1 Chr 17:4-14; 22:7-10; 28:2-7), it does not follow any of them verbatim. Solomon began with an expression of praise to God that serves as an introduction to the speech that begins near the end of 6:4: "For he told my father." The praise keeps the focus on God and emphasizes his faithfulness to the promise made to David. It is this promise that is the focus of Solomon's speech, something made clear near the end of the speech (6:10) when he declares that God has fulfilled the promise he made to David.

It was very important to the Chronicler that he retain this key speech. As noted in the commentary on the dynastic oracle in 1 Chronicles 17, the Chronicler's rendition of the dynastic oracle places much greater emphasis on Solomon's role in confirming and securing the covenant between the Lord and David than is found in the book of Samuel. In this speech Solomon reviews the story of this covenant relationship, citing the interaction between David and the Lord concerning the construction of the Temple (6:4-9).

The first section (6:4-6) highlights God's election of Jerusalem as the place where the Temple would be located and his choice of David as the one who would rule over Israel. The beginning of the story of Israel is clearly traced to the exodus from Egypt, but the climax of that story is reached in the choice of Jerusalem and David, an emphasis made clear by the contrast: "I have never chosen . . . Nor have I chosen . . . But now I have chosen . . . and I have chosen" (6:5-6).[2] Jerusalem's distinction is that it will be the place where God's name will be honored. David's distinction is that he will be "prince" or "ruler" (Heb., *nagid* [TH5057, ZH5592]), a term different from the typical word in Hebrew for royalty (*melek* [TH4428, ZH4889], "king," suggested by the NLT here). This points to David as vice-regent for God on earth (see further the commentary on 1 Chr 11; cf. Boda 2007a). The place and person of God's rule were chosen by God; this double election is a regular component of the Davidic tradition throughout the Old Testament and is reflected in the alternate name of Jerusalem as "the City of David."

In the second section (6:7-9), Solomon explains how God chose him (Solomon) to build the Temple. In contrast to other places where David's role in war is offered as an explanation for why he was not the choice (1 Chr 22:8; 28:3), Solomon here simply reports God's saying to his father, "You are not the one to do it."

The final part of the speech (6:10-11) rehearses the fulfillment of these promises from the Lord to David—beginning with the ascension of Solomon to the throne, moving to the construction of the Temple to honor the Lord, and finally to the deposition of the Ark within the new sanctuary. Thus this speech is a key signal not only of God's faithfulness to David but also of Solomon's confirmation of the covenant between David and the Lord.

Solomon's Prayer of Dedication (6:12-42). The remainder of chapter 6 is filled with Solomon's long prayer to God. The prayer is introduced by a description of Solomon standing in the outer courtyard between the bronze altar and the assembled community of Israel. The Chronicler adds to his source in 1 Kings 8 the description of the bronze platform Solomon had constructed for this occasion (6:13). This verse carefully delineates that although Solomon was standing, he subsequently knelt while lifting his hands toward heaven. The Chronicler's description places Solomon in the posture of humility in this sacred precinct.

The prayer proper (6:14-42) is divided into three parts. The focus of the first section (6:14-17) is on the dynasty of David. The speech accentuates the personal involvement of the Lord in giving and then fulfilling the promise by using the anthropomorphisms of "your own mouth" and "your own hands." Solomon praises God for fulfilling the initial phase of the promise given to David in 1 Chronicles 17 (6:14-15) before asking him to fulfill the second phase of the promise (6:16-17). The initial phase relates to that which was fulfilled "today," which must mean God's raising up Solomon to build the Temple (which was completed on that day and accepted by the Lord). The second phase of the promise relates to God's promise of a perpetual dynasty for David. In the Chronicler's presentation of David and Solomon, this prayer, drawn verbatim from his source in Kings, plays an important role, signaling the confirmation of the covenant between David and the Lord. This prayer reminds the reader that Solomon's obedience to God in the Temple-building project secured an enduring dynasty for David in Israel.

The focus of the second section (6:18-40) is on the role of the Temple as a sanctuary of prayer. The section begins with a general plea for God to listen to the prayers Solomon and his people will direct toward the sanctuary (6:18-21), continues with a list of seven scenarios in which the people would pray toward the Temple for help from the Lord in heaven (6:22-39), and concludes with another general plea for God to listen to prayers made to him in the Temple (6:40).

In the introductory general plea (6:18-21), Solomon admits that although the Temple cannot contain the Creator of the universe, it must remain as a place where God will hear the cry of the people. He speaks of God's watching over the Temple constantly (day and night) and placing his name on the sanctuary. Solomon asks first and foremost that his own prayers may be heard, a prerogative of royal Temple patrons throughout the history of the ancient Near East (see another example in Ezra 6:10).

But clearly the focus of this prayer shifts from the royal patron to his subjects. It is at the end of this introductory plea that the reader is given the first indication that the purpose of prayer is related to the need for forgiveness of the sin of the people (6:21, "and when you hear, forgive"). Although addressed to God, the prayer of Solomon provides guidance to future generations for renewing their relationship with Yahweh. For those responsible for the book of Kings (1 Kgs 8), this was an important prayer because it offered guidance to a generation that lived in the wake of the destruction of Jerusalem.[3] For the Chronicler as well, the instruction regarding repentance had enduring relevance as it placed the Temple as the locus of renewal in his own generation. Up to this point in his account, the Chronicler has accentuated David's role as founder of a new phase of worship in Israel, his role in adding to the Mosaic sacrificial cult, and his role of introducing oral worship through the Levitical guild (1 Chr 15–29). Now in chapter 6, the Chronicler draws on his source in Kings to remind his readers of Solomon's role in the development of oral worship, highlighting the function of the Temple as a place of prayer for the people of God, as well as for the nations caught in a variety of predicaments.

The seven scenarios that follow are not all structured identically, although in each case one can discern the following elements: the description of the scenario, the human action required, and the divine response requested. In two cases (6:28-31, 32-33) an additional element is placed after the divine response, outlining an expected human reaction to the divine response.

The first scenario (6:22-23) is taken from the realm of Israelite jurisprudence, the background for which can be found in Exodus 22:7-14; Leviticus 6:1-7; and Numbers 5:11-31. Details can be found in Leviticus 6:1-7, which concerns the guilt offering, a sacrifice related to acts of deception. The procedure for the discovery of guilt is not provided, but the text does stipulate that the restitution involves the value of the goods plus one-fifth, followed by the sacrifice of a guilt offering. More detail is provided in Exodus 22:7-14, which records the case of goods stolen while in the safekeeping of a neighbor. If no thief can be found, then both parties must appear before God to determine who was responsible. Both parties are to take an oath before the Lord. The assumption is that if a person is willing to take an oath before God, he must be innocent because Exodus 22:11 closes with "the owner must accept the verdict, and no payment will be required." If the accused party is found guilty (which means he or she admits guilt), then that person must pay back double the worth of the stolen goods.

Far more detail is offered in Numbers 5:11-31, which describes the oath procedure used to discern an act of adultery. The procedure is initiated by a husband's suspicion (lit., "spirit of jealousy"). The husband is to bring his wife to the priest at the Tabernacle with a grain offering. The priest has the wife stand before the Lord and prepares holy water mixed with dust from the floor of the Tabernacle and loosens the woman's hair. Priest and woman approach the Lord with the woman carrying the grain offering and the priest the holy water. The priest recites the words of an oath to which the woman responds "amen, amen," signifying her compliance with the oath. The curse is written on a scroll, which is then dipped into the holy water, signifying the transfer of the oath and its attendant curse to the water. The priest takes the grain offering from the woman to the altar and then requires the woman to drink the water. They await the verdict from God in the presence or absence of a swelling of the thigh and abdomen that makes the woman barren.

The scenario in 6:22-23 contains striking points of contact with these descriptions of legal procedure in the Torah. The cases all share in common the fact that they concern offenses between human beings, involve the taking of an oath, and require attendance at a sacred shrine. The reference in 6:22-23 to the location "in front of your altar" suggests that a sacrifice was necessary, as is the case in all three of the legal procedures in the Torah. It is not surprising that the first scenario would

Case #1: 6:22-23	
Scenario	If someone wrongs another person and is required to take an oath of innocence
Human action required	[and he enters into an oath] in front of your altar at this Temple,[4]
Divine response requested	then hear from heaven and judge between your servants—the accuser and the accused. Pay back the guilty as they deserve. Acquit the innocent because of their innocence.
Case #2: 6:24-25	
Scenario	If your people Israel are defeated by their enemies because they have sinned against you,
Human action required	and if they turn back and acknowledge your name and pray to you here in this Temple,
Divine response requested	then hear from heaven and forgive the sin of your people Israel and return them to this land you gave to them and to their ancestors.
Case #3: 6:26-27	
Scenario	If the skies are shut up and there is no rain because your people have sinned against you,
Human action required	and if they pray toward this Temple and acknowledge your name and turn from their sins because you have punished them,
Divine response requested	then hear from heaven and forgive the sins of your servants, your people Israel. Teach them to follow the right path, and send rain on your land that you have given to your people as their special possession.
Case #4: 6:28-31	
Scenario	If there is a famine in the land or a plague or crop disease or attacks of locusts or caterpillars, or if your people's enemies are in the land besieging their towns—whatever disaster or disease there is—
Human action required	and if your people Israel pray about their troubles or sorrow, raising their hands toward this Temple,
Divine response requested	then hear from heaven where you live, and forgive. Give your people what their actions deserve, for you alone know each human heart.
Human reaction expected	Then they will fear you and walk in your ways as long as they live in the land you gave to our ancestors.

concern something in the legal realm since the prayer is associated with Solomon, whose wisdom is linked to jurisprudence in the book of Kings (see 1 Kgs 3). The inclusion of this scenario reveals that the jurisprudence formerly attached to the Tabernacle shrine is now transferred to the Temple. One key role, therefore, for this new sanctuary is the administration of justice for the people of God, justice that is cast as a form of prayer in the Temple that reaches to the heavenly courtroom of the Lord.

The second scenario (6:24-25) assumes that the people have sinned against the Lord and that this sin led not only to their defeat at the hands of their enemies (6:24), but also exile to another land (6:25). The human action required for the divine response is repentance ("turn back"), praise ("acknowledge your name"; better, "give thanks to your name"), and prayer ("pray"; better, "pray and make

Case #5: 6:32-33	
Scenario	In the future, foreigners who do not belong to your people Israel will hear of you.
Human action required	They will come from distant lands when they hear of your great name and your strong hand and your powerful arm. And when they pray toward this Temple,
Divine response requested	then hear from heaven where you live, and grant what they ask of you.
Human reaction expected	In this way, all the people of the earth will come to know and fear you, just as your own people Israel do. They, too, will know that this Temple I have built honors your name.
Case #6: 6:34-35	
Scenario	If your people go out where you send them to fight their enemies,
Human action required	and if they pray to you by turning toward this city you have chosen and toward this Temple I have built to honor your name,
Divine response requested	then hear their prayers from heaven and uphold their cause.
Case #7: 6:36-39	
Scenario	If they sin against you—and who has never sinned?—you might become angry with them and let their enemies conquer them and take them captive to a foreign land far away or near.
Human action required	But in that land of exile, they might turn to you in repentance and pray, "We have sinned, done evil, and acted wickedly." If they turn to you with their whole heart and soul in the land of their captivity and pray toward the land you gave to their ancestors—toward this city you have chosen, and toward this Temple I have built to honor your name—
Divine response requested	then hear their prayers and their petitions from heaven where you live, and uphold their cause. Forgive your people who have sinned against you.

supplication") to the Lord "here in this Temple." This assumes that someone was praying in the Temple itself on behalf of the defeated and exiled warriors. The prayer requests that God hear the prayer, forgive the sin, and return the exiled to the land. This scenario is the first of three that emphasize the precious gift of the land (6:25, 27, 31, 38).

The third scenario (6:26-27), as the second, directly blames the disaster that has befallen the people on their culpability. This time the land is experiencing drought. Although in a different order, the human action required is identical to the previous scenario: prayer (this time "toward" rather than "in" the Temple), praise ("acknowledge your name"; see above), and repentance. The divine response fits the scenario with the same elements of "hear" and "forgive," but now also "teach" and "send rain." God is asked to rectify the situation not just by sending rain but also by instructing the people how to live in holiness so as to avoid such disasters in the future.

The fourth scenario (6:28-31) says nothing at the outset about the sin of the people, but it does assume such by asking God to "forgive" (6:30). While the second and third scenarios were concerned with disasters caused by humans or nature, this fourth scenario encompasses various types of disaster (famine, plague, crop disease, insect invasions, war) before stating the catchall "whatever disaster or disease there is." The human action required, however, is different. No reference is made to repentance or praise, but simply to prayer by raising one's hands toward the Temple. A further difference from the previous scenarios and a similarity to the first scenario is that although the divine response requested is "hear" and "forgive," Solomon also asked that God would "give your people what their actions deserve, for you alone know each human heart." In this case, there is no space for repentance; instead, God's response is based on the level of faithfulness of the human heart. This is the first of two scenarios that ends with a description of the expected human reaction to the divine response: "Then they will fear you and walk in your ways," the first being an internal disposition toward God of awe and respect, recognizing the vast distinction between Creator and created, the second being external evidence of faithfulness to the Lord.

In the fifth scenario (6:32-33) the focus moves outside the community of Israel to encompass foreigners who hear of the Lord; it says nothing about the culpability of the suppliants. If they come to the Temple and direct a prayer toward the Temple, they also will be heard by God, who will grant them their request. Here we see the role of the Temple not only as a sacred space where a penitent and/or needy covenant people are heard by God, but also as a Temple where the prayers of all nations will be heard (cf. Isa 56:7). As with the previous case, the scenario does not end with the divine response, but rather with the human reaction that is expected, this time a "fear" that parallels that of the people of Israel.

The sixth scenario (6:34-35) shifts the focus back on the people of God, but, as with the previous one, it is silent on culpability. This case moves back to a scene of war, this time one in which the people are about to enter into battle. They are instructed that, although they are far away from the Temple, they may turn toward the city and Temple and pray to God. The requested divine response is that he will "hear" and "uphold their cause," that is, give them success in battle.

After a subtle shift away from the focus on culpability in the last three scenarios, the final scenario (6:36-39) emphasizes the guilt of the people. The way it is phrased ("If they sin against you—and who has never sinned?") suggests that sin is an expected reality that must be addressed. This scenario is reminiscent of the second scenario (6:24-25) in which the people are defeated in battle and must be returned to the land, but this seventh scenario is much more extensive and thorough in its description. The scenario makes it very clear that God's anger had been the cause of the disaster, something that is not made clear in any of the other scenarios. Furthermore, while the second scenario mentions exile in the divine response, here the Exile is highlighted from the outset. The human action required in this scenario provides clear evidence that this scenario is the climax of the series. Not only are the human actions of repentance and prayer described twice ("turn to you in repentance and pray . . . turn to you with their whole heart and soul in the land of their captivity and pray toward the land . . . city . . . Temple"), but the actual content of the penitential prayer is offered to the reader: "We have sinned, done evil, and acted wickedly." Here we find the three key words for sinful actions in Hebrew used together to accentuate the depth of the wickedness of the people but at the same time the thoroughness of their confession. There is a play on words in this scenario through the repetition of two Hebrew roots: *shabah/shebi* [TH7617/7628, ZH8647/8660] ("to take captive, exile, captivity"; 6:36, 37, 38) and *shub* [TH7725, ZH8740] ("to turn, repentance"; 6:37, 38; Long 1984:102-103). This play reminds the reader that penitential prayer toward the land, city, and Temple is essential to the resolution of the predicament of the exiled people. It is interesting that the Chronicler abridged his citation of his source in 1 Kings 8:50 at this point, leaving out the climactic reference to the captivity, where Solomon requested compassion from their enemies in exile. In both chapter 6 and 1 Kings 8, God is merely asked to hear their prayers, forgive their sin, and "uphold their cause." He is not asked directly to return them to the land, as was the case in the second scenario.

The conclusion to this second section of the prayer (6:40) forms a bracket with the introduction in 6:19-21, which asked for God to watch and listen to the suppliants at the Temple. This second section of the prayer emphasizes another dimension of the innovation of oral worship at the Temple. Not only will it involve praise to God through Levitical musicians but it will involve prayer and supplication from the people. The various scenarios set the tone for the role of the Temple during times of peace, war, and destruction. Whether the people are near or far, they are encouraged to pray toward the Temple. Retaining this prayer was important to the Chronicler, for whom the support of the Temple and its services was of the highest priority. The list of scenarios encourages support for the Temple by those who had returned to the land in his day, as well as by those who were far away. It also would have discouraged any thought of building a Temple somewhere else because clearly this prayer identifies this land, city, and Temple as the exclusive avenue through which the Lord hears prayer.

One cannot overestimate the impact of this second section of the prayer on the liturgical practices of the exilic and postexilic communities. This prayer provided guidance for the community living in the wake of the greatest disaster they could ever have imagined: the fall of the state and exile of the people. Evidence of this impact can be seen in the use of terminology and concepts from this section in the canonical prayers recorded in Ezra 9; Nehemiah 1, 9; and Daniel 9 (cf. Boda 1999; Werline 1998). For the Chronicler, who placed a premium on repentance, several of these scenarios were very helpful, offering a way ahead for those who had returned to the land, as well as for those who were still in exile.

As already mentioned, the conclusion to this second part of the prayer is changed in the Chronicler's account. Not only did he abridge the final scenario by leaving out half of the divine response requested (cf. 6:39 with 1 Kgs 8:49-50), but he also left off the two causal phrases (1 Kgs 8:51, 53) that locate the foundation for God's attention to his people's supplications in God's rescue of his people from Egypt. As noted in the commentary on 6:4-6 above, this shift of emphasis away from the Exodus is typical of the Chronicler (see endnote 2).

The third section of the prayer (6:41-42) is not found in the Chronicler's source in Kings but rather echoes Psalm 132:1, 8-10. It returns to the themes introduced in the first two sections of the prayer in reverse order. In 6:41a Solomon asks for God to inhabit this dwelling place, an action that would resolve the dilemma introduced at the outset of the second section of the prayer (6:18). In 6:42 he asks for God to remember his unfailing love to David and not reject the anointed king, an action that would resolve the concern introduced at the close of the first section of the prayer (6:16-17). Between these two issues in 6:41b Solomon asks for the priests to be clothed with salvation and the people (loyal servants) to rejoice in God's goodness.

These closing two verses emphasize three key issues for the Chronicler. There was an enduring desire for the manifest presence of God to be experienced in the second Temple of his day and for the restoration of the Davidic line to be the throne of an independent kingdom. Until then, the Chronicler with his Levitical sensibilities asked that both priests and people would experience the grace and goodness of God.

ENDNOTES

1. The NLT's rendering implies that the blessing is in 6:4-11, but the Hebrew text merely says that Solomon blessed the people and then "he said" the speech in 6:4-11. Note Japhet (1993:584), who says, "What follows is not a 'blessing' and is not concerned with the people."
2. Japhet (1993:590) is quick to note that 6:11 replaces the phrase from 1 Kgs 8:21 ("the covenant that the LORD made with our ancestors when he brought them out of Egypt") with "the covenant that the LORD made with the people of Israel." She sees this as another example of the Chronicler playing down "the Exodus as a constitutive act in the history of Israel and the relationship of God and Israel as established by a specific historic 'covenant.'" See also the excision of the Exodus at the end of Solomon's prayer (cf. 6:39-40 with 1 Kgs 8:50-53; see further Japhet 1989:104-105; Williamson 1977b:64-66). It is interesting, however, that the Chronicler allowed the reference to both the Exodus and the covenant to slip through in his replication of Kings in 6:5, 11, a trend seen elsewhere (5:10; 6:5; 7:22; 20:10; 1 Chr 17:21), which leads Dillard (1987:47) to conclude, "The deliverance from Egypt was not unimportant to the Chronicler."

3. The literary history of this part of the prayer of Solomon in 1 Kgs 8:31-51 is quite complex, as indicated by the variety in the style of conditional clauses used in the scenarios. See further Boda 1999:53-54. In any case, it appears to have been preserved in priestly circles prior to its incorporation into the book of Kings. This is not crucial for the study of ch 6, since it follows in the main the form found in 1 Kgs 8.
4. Lit., "If one sins against his neighbor/friend, and he (neighbor/friend) pronounces against him an oath/imposes upon him an oath to require him to swear/to put him under oath, and he enters into an oath before your altar in this house."

◆ F. The Dedication of the Temple and God's Message to Solomon (7:1-22)

When Solomon finished praying, fire
flashed down from heaven and burned up
the burnt offerings and sacrifices, and the
glorious presence of the LORD filled the
Temple. 2The priests could not enter the
Temple of the LORD because the glorious
presence of the LORD filled it. 3When all
the people of Israel saw the fire coming
down and the glorious presence of the
LORD filling the Temple, they fell face
down on the ground and worshiped and
praised the LORD, saying,

"He is good!
His faithful love endures forever!"

4Then the king and all the people of-
fered sacrifices to the LORD. 5King Solo-
mon offered a sacrifice of 22,000 cattle
and 120,000 sheep and goats. And so the
king and all the people dedicated the
Temple of God. 6The priests took their as-
signed positions, and so did the Levites
who were singing, "His faithful love en-
dures forever!" They accompanied the
singing with music from the instruments
King David had made for praising the
LORD. Across from the Levites, the priests
blew the trumpets, while all Israel stood.

7Solomon then consecrated the central
area of the courtyard in front of the LORD's
Temple. He offered burnt offerings and
the fat of peace offerings there, because
the bronze altar he had built could not
hold all the burnt offerings, grain offer-
ings, and sacrificial fat.

8For the next seven days Solomon and all
Israel celebrated the Festival of Shelters.* A
large congregation had gathered from as
far away as Lebo-hamath in the north and
the Brook of Egypt in the south. 9On the
eighth day they had a closing ceremony, for
they had celebrated the dedication of the
altar for seven days and the Festival of
Shelters for seven days. 10Then at the end
of the celebration,* Solomon sent the peo-
ple home. They were all joyful and glad be-
cause the LORD had been so good to David
and to Solomon and to his people Israel.

11So Solomon finished the Temple of
the LORD, as well as the royal palace. He
completed everything he had planned to
do in the construction of the Temple and
the palace. 12Then one night the LORD ap-
peared to Solomon and said,

"I have heard your prayer and have
chosen this Temple as the place for
making sacrifices. 13At times I might
shut up the heavens so that no rain
falls, or command grasshoppers to
devour your crops, or send plagues
among you. 14Then if my people who
are called by my name will humble
themselves and pray and seek my
face and turn from their wicked
ways, I will hear from heaven and
will forgive their sins and restore their
land. 15My eyes will be open and my
ears attentive to every prayer made
in this place. 16For I have chosen this
Temple and set it apart to be holy—a
place where my name will be honored
forever. I will always watch over it, for
it is dear to my heart.

17"As for you, if you faithfully follow
me as David your father did, obeying
all my commands, decrees, and
regulations, 18then I will establish the
throne of your dynasty. For I made this
covenant with your father, David,
when I said, 'One of your descendants
will always rule over Israel.'
19"But if you or your descendants
abandon me and disobey the decrees
and commands I have given you, and
if you serve and worship other gods,
20then I will uproot the people from
this land that I have given them. I
will reject this Temple that I have
made holy to honor my name. I will
make it an object of mockery and
ridicule among the nations. 21And
though this Temple is impressive now,
all who pass by will be appalled. They
will ask, 'Why did the LORD do such
terrible things to this land and to this
Temple?'
22"And the answer will be, 'Because
his people abandoned the LORD, the
God of their ancestors, who brought
them out of Egypt, and they worshiped
other gods instead and bowed down
to them. That is why he has brought
all these disasters on them.'"

7:8 Hebrew *the festival* (also in 7:9); see note on 5:3. **7:10** Hebrew *Then on the twenty-third day of the seventh month.* This day of the ancient Hebrew lunar calendar occurred in October or early November.

NOTES

7:8 ***Festival of Shelters.*** This is traditionally known as the Feast of Tabernacles, which was held from the 15th to the 22nd day of the seventh month.
Lebo-hamath . . . the Brook of Egypt. For these locations as the extent of the land, see Num 13:21; 34:5-8; Josh 13:5; 15:4, 47; Ezek 47:15, 19-20; 48:28.

COMMENTARY

God's Presence Fills the Temple (7:1-3). The events at the outset of chapter 7 are unique to the Chronicler, who has left out from his source in 1 Kings 8:54-61 Solomon's speech wherein he blesses God for fulfilling his promises.[1] Conspicuous is the fact that the abridged section refers to the tradition of Moses, a trend of omission that has been observed elsewhere in the Chronicler's work (see commentary on 6:4-6 above). In its place, the Chronicler has included unique material that helps bring closure to his account by recounting the events of chapter 5 in reverse order (see introduction to chs 5–7).[2]

The final section of Solomon's prayer (6:41-42) invites God to "enter your resting place," a request that is fulfilled immediately at the outset of chapter 7. Just before the glorious presence of the Lord fills the Temple, however, the Chronicler records that God sent down fire from heaven to burn up the sacrifices that had been prepared. This is reminiscent of other incidents in the Old Testament where fire from God consumed a sacrifice as a sign of his approval and acceptance of the offering (Moses and Aaron: Lev 9:23-24; Gideon: Judg 6:20-21; Elijah: 1 Kgs 18; David: 1 Chr 21:26). The link between the action of God here with Solomon and the same one with David in 1 Chronicles 21:26 is clearly intentional since the incident in 1 Chronicles 21:26 is unique to the Chronicler (cf. 2 Sam 24:25). This is another case of the Chronicler linking David and Solomon together, showing how Solomon continues and completes the work of David, who prepared the way (see introduction to chs 1–9).

In addition, there is a connection to the incident in Leviticus 9:23-24, which appears at the end of a long sequence of texts in the Torah: the instructions for and building of the Tabernacle (Exod 25–40), the legislation concerning various sacrifices (Lev 1–7), and the consecration of Aaron and the priests (Lev 8–9). The consecration service lasted for seven days, and on the eighth day there was a sacrifice both for the priests and for the people. The purpose of these events was not merely for the ordination of the priests but also that "the LORD will appear to you . . . so that the glory of the LORD may appear to you" (Lev 9:4, 6). Leviticus 9:22-24 recounts the following events: Aaron blesses the people, Moses and Aaron enter the Tabernacle, Moses and Aaron leave the Tabernacle and bless the people, the glory of the Lord appears to the people, fire comes out from the Lord and consumes the sacrifice, and the people see and fall on their faces. These striking similarities between Leviticus and chapter 7 accentuate further the connections already seen between the Tabernacle and Temple accounts (see introduction to chs 1–9). Here the Chronicler links Solomon to at least Moses and possibly also to Aaron (see further Japhet 1993:609). Unlike 5:13b-14 no mention is made of the "cloud," but once more the manifest presence of God fills the Temple. Again this makes it impossible for the priests to carry out their ministry in the inner sanctuary (see further the commentary on 5:13b-14).

Similar to the incident of God's sending fire from heaven to consume the sacrifice of Aaron (see also Elijah's sacrifice in 1 Kgs 18), the people respond by falling face down on the ground. This is the proper human response to such an amazing miracle of God, as well as an appropriate response of being in close proximity to deity. It is a reminder of humanity's frailty before the holy presence of the creator God. While the first instance of God's presence filling the Temple (5:11-14) was initiated by the Levites' praise, this second instance causes an expression of praise by the people. The content of the praise is identical: "He is good! His faithful love endures forever!" The Levites were depicted as prompters of praise among the people. In this the Chronicler shows that it is "not the priests or king alone, but 'all the children of Israel' who share this moment of worship" (Japhet 1993:610).

Dedicating the Temple Accompanied by Sacrifice at the Festival of Shelters (7:4-10). The Chronicler concludes with a description of the Festival of Shelters (Tabernacles) that is drawn mostly from his source in 1 Kings 8:62-66. The event is described as the dedication of both the Temple (7:5) and the altar (7:9) and involved a great number of sacrifices, paralleling the earlier event of the Ark's transfer during the Festival of Shelters. Not surprisingly, the Chronicler inserts further details on the sacred personnel, noting that the priests took their assigned positions and blew trumpets, while the Levites sang their typical refrain ("His faithful love endures forever!") and played instruments. Prominence is given again to David as the Chronicler notes the source of the instruments. Although not in attendance at the dedication of the house he longed to build, David's presence lived on through his preparations.

Returning to his source, the Chronicler records that so great was the number of animals sacrificed at the dedication ceremonies that the entire courtyard around the bronze altar had to be consecrated and used for the offerings. The people had gathered from the limits of the kingdom: from Lebo-hamath in the far north to the

Brook of Egypt in the far south (cf. Japhet 1979:208-210). Hamath was a district on the northern frontier of Syria to the east of the Orontes River, and "Lebo-hamath" (or "the entrance to Hamath") was probably located on the southern boundary of this district. The Brook of Egypt is known from Neo-Assyrian documents appearing in the inscriptions and annals of Tiglath-pileser I (734–732 BC) and Sargon II (716 BC). It signifies the border between the Negev Desert and the Sinai Peninsula and was located about 50 miles southwest of Gaza (TBD 239). The extent of the land promised to Abraham in Genesis 15:18 is from the Euphrates River to the River of Egypt, the latter probably signifying the easternmost branch of the Nile, which marked Egypt's borders. There are places, however, where the extent given mentions Lebo-hamath and the Brook of Egypt (e.g., Num 13:21; 34:5-8; Josh 13:5; 15:4, 47; Ezek 47:15, 19, 20; 48:28). This notation continues the Chronicler's depiction of the nation's full support of the Temple project. It also reminds the reader that this event is the culmination of the work of Solomon and his father David, who assembled "all Israel, from the Shihor Brook of Egypt . . . all the way to the town of Lebo-hamath" when he set out to bring the Ark into Jerusalem, a detail unique to the Chronicler (cf. 1 Chr 13:5 with 2 Sam 6:1-2; Dillard 1987:57).

This event was but the opening to a grand celebration of the Festival of Shelters, which lasted for the next seven days, ending with great fanfare on the eighth day with the closing ceremony stipulated in Leviticus 23:39 and Numbers 29:35 (see commentary on 5:2-10; cf. 1 Kgs 8:2, 65-66). There is some confusion, however, over the length of the gathering described in chapters 5–7. In 7:8 Solomon is mentioned celebrating the Festival of Shelters for "the next seven days," at the end of which (on the eighth day) there was a closing ceremony (7:9). The Chronicler then makes the following note: "They had celebrated the dedication of the altar for seven days and the Festival of Shelters for seven days" (7:9). The Chronicler appears to have been trying to make sense of an odd note in his source at 1 Kings 8:65, where it reads in Hebrew, "seven days and seven days, fourteen days." It would appear, then, that the two seven-day periods mentioned in 7:9 were observed one after the other, adding up to fourteen. However, the day the people were sent away was the twenty-third of the month, which would indicate that the Festival of Shelters was being celebrated at its normal time: from the fifteenth to the twenty-second of the seventh month. Second Chronicles 5:3, however, recounts that the elders of Israel had gathered together for the Ark transfer and Temple dedication "at the feast which is in the seventh month" (lit., interpreted by the NLT as "at the annual Festival of Shelters"). Counting back fourteen days from the twenty-second of the month would place the beginning of this gathering at the eighth of the month. It is possible that the feast to which they were gathering was actually the Day of Atonement (tenth of the month; Lev 16:29; 23:27; Num 29:7) and that the elders had gathered a couple of days early. Another possibility is that the seven-day celebration for the dedication of the Temple/altar and the seven-day celebration of the Festival of Shelters ran concurrently rather than consecutively and that the note about fourteen days in 1 Kings 8:65 is a scribal gloss reflecting a misunderstanding of the two references to seven days, which may themselves reflect a scribal error (accidental repetition of "seven days").[3] It may be that the Chronicler had this faulty text before him and was seeking to solve the problem. In either case, the Chronicler was careful to note that the festival was kept for the proper length of time, followed by the solemn assembly.

Unlike his source in 1 Kings 8:66, which has Solomon dismissing the people on the eighth day of the festival, the Chronicler carefully notes that the eighth day entailed a solemn assembly, followed by the dismissal of the people on "the twenty-third day of the seventh month" (7:10; see NLT mg). This highlights Solomon's careful attention to the festal legislation (Lev 23:33-44; Num 29:12-35). The people were sent home "joyful and glad," a phrase drawn from the source in 1 Kings 8:66 but which is an important theme for the Chronicler (6:41; 15:15; 20:27; 23:13, 18, 21; 24:10; 29:30, 36; 30:21, 23, 25-26; 1 Chr 12:40; 15:16, 25; 29:9, 17, 22). Proper attention to worship legislation is not seen as dutiful drudgery, but rather joyous celebration. The phrase "and to Solomon" is an addition by the Chronicler to his source, which only speaks of "his servant David." This is an important reminder of the key role that Solomon played in bringing David's dreams for the Temple to reality while also confirming the dynastic promise (see commentary on 6:3-11, 14-17). As Japhet has so aptly written, "The period of 'goodness' in the history of Israel is the combined era of David and Solomon" (1993:613).

Summary Note (7:11). Having depicted the joyous closing to the festival in 7:10, the Chronicler brings the building and dedication account to a close with a summary note in 7:11, a technique that has been a regular feature in the Chronicler's account of Solomon (1:1; 2:1; 3:1-2; 5:1; 7:11; 8:1, 16). This summary note joins with 5:1 to form a bracket around the entire dedication account of 5:1–7:11.[4] A striking difference between this summary note and the one that began the section, however, is the reference to the completion of the Temple, as well as the royal palace, a feature that the Chronicler found in his source in 1 Kings 9:1 but repeated for emphasis in his rendition. Although the Chronicler left out the account of the construction of Solomon's palace from 1 Kings 7:1-12, it is interesting that in his recounting of the communication between Solomon and Hiram of Tyre in chapter 2, he inserted three extra references to the building of a palace not found in his source in 1 Kings 5:1-8, two concerning Solomon's palace (2:1, 12) and one concerning David's palace (2:3b). Although the focus of the Chronicler's attention is clearly on the Temple project, this may suggest that the Chronicler was concerned with the enduring role of the Davidic dynasty, the palace being representative of a minor interest in an enduring role for a royal court. The reference to the palace in 7:11, thus, was important enough to retain from his source, as well as to repeat, because it appears in the transition from the dedication events to the concluding speech of the Lord to Solomon, which will focus on the endurance of both the Temple (7:12-16) and the dynasty (7:17-22).

God's Speech to Solomon (7:12-22). Second Chronicles 7:11 brings closure to Solomon's construction and dedication of the Temple site, but the Lord is given the final word. To this point divine involvement in the dedication has been limited to the physical appearance of the cloud (5:13) and the glorious presence of God (5:14; 7:1), as well as fire from heaven, which consumed the sacrifices (7:1). In 7:12 the Lord responds verbally to Solomon "one night," a temporal designation that links this theophany with the earlier appearance of God to Solomon at the outset of his reign in 1:7-12 but also to the revelation of God to Nathan at night that concerned the building of the Temple (1 Chr 17:3-15). That which was promised in 1 Chronicles 17 and put in motion in chapter 1 at the Tabernacle at Gibeon has now been completed as the Tabernacle at Gibeon is now replaced by the Temple at Jerusalem. The Chronicler did not specify the time of this encounter; he notes only that it occurred after the completion of the Temple (see 1 Kgs 9:1-2).

God's speech is divided into two parts, with the first section focused on God's eternal choice of the Temple as a place of sacrifice and prayer (7:12b-16) and the second section focused on God's eternal choice of the Davidic dynasty and nation (7:17-22). The Chronicler has expanded the first section from one verse in his source (1 Kgs 9:3) to four and a half verses. This part of the speech begins with God's declaration that he has heard Solomon's prayer and that he has indeed chosen the Temple as "the place for making sacrifices" (7:12). Japhet (1993:614-615) notes an important shift in this addition by the Chronicler. Whereas in Solomon's prayer in chapter 6 (//1 Kgs 8), election ("choosing," *bakhar* [TH977, ZH1047]) is associated with Jerusalem and David (6:5-6, 34, 38//1 Kgs 8:16, 44, 48), for the Chronicler election of the "place" is more carefully defined as the Temple. This is a clear signal that the Temple has replaced the Tabernacle as God's chosen sacrificial site. But Solomon's prayer has asked also that the Temple play a role in the oral expression of Israel, that is, as a place for prayer, and this role is given far more emphasis in the Chronicler's version of God's speech.

The Chronicler's expansion expresses the thematic core of the Chronicler's vision for his readers. It is reminiscent of the various scenarios already covered in Solomon's prayer in 6:18-40 with their tripartite structure: Scenario, Human Action, Divine Response. The speech assumes that God will manipulate nature against a sinful people whether that means causing drought, raising up grasshoppers, or sending plagues. In the covenant material so foundational to Old Testament theology, these are never seen as incidents of judgment but rather of discipline because they are intended to draw the people of God back to faithful relationship with their gracious Lord (see Lev 26; Deut 28–30; Amos 4:6-13).

The human components required to move from discipline to forgiveness are fourfold: they must humble themselves, pray, seek God's face, and turn from their wicked ways (7:14a). This vocabulary will appear regularly throughout the Chronicler's ensuing narratives. The first, humility, speaks of an inner disposition, which is the essential starting point for all repentance. The second, prayer, shifts the focus to an external expression, in this case the verbal dimension of repentance, depicted most vividly in the threefold confession of 6:37. The third, seeking God's face, moves back to a key inner disposition, passionate pursuit of God. To seek after the "face of God" is a radical statement in light of God's prohibition of such in Exodus 33:23. The fourth and final element, turn from their wicked ways, shifts the focus again to an external expression, in this case the active dimension of repentance—that is, the practical change of behavior. Exemplary characters are not those who attain perfection but rather who exemplify these characteristics. Dillard (1987:58) has highlighted the importance of 7:12b-15 to the Chronicler's work:

> *It is programmatic for the author's [Chronicler's] presentation of the divided kingdoms (2 Chr 10–36) . . . to specifically enunciate the literary program for his "theology of immediate retribution." In the remainder of his record the author virtually without fail recasts the accounts in his Vorlage to demonstrate his conviction that both obedience and transgression have immediate consequences of blessings and punishment.*

Two reasons are given for why these human responses to God make divine forgiveness possible. The first is expressed at the outset of 7:14, when the community is described as "my people who are called by my name." The title "my people" echoes covenantal language, exemplified most vividly in the regularly appearing covenant formula, "I will be your God and you will be my people" (see Exod 6:7; Lev 26:12; Deut 29:13; Jer 31:33). In this ancient context the "name" is intimately associated with the very essence of the one who bears it; so here to be "called by my name" is to be intricately associated with this deity, that is, to be the people of Yahweh in covenant relationship. Such covenantal language, therefore, assumes the entire foundation of grace that undergirds this relationship. Divine grace thus propels the people of God to respond when he enacts the kind of discipline rehearsed in 7:13. The second reason why the process described in 7:13-14 is possible is given in 7:16: God's attentiveness to his people is linked to his election and passion for the Temple. The Temple, therefore, is now made indispensable to the covenant relationship between God and Israel. For the Chronicler there could be no greater case for the support of the Temple and its services.

The Lord's speech confirms the validity of the scenarios listed by Solomon in 6:18-40 by providing the divine response that can be expected if there is repentance. The Lord promises to hear their prayer, forgive their sin, and restore (traditionally "heal") their land (7:14b). Here God echoes the end of Solomon's prayer (6:40) by promising open eyes and attentive ears to every prayer offered at the Temple (7:15-16). To these external descriptives (eyes, ears), however, he adds his inner passion for the Temple ("it is dear to my heart"). The reason why this Temple receives heightened attention from the Lord is because it is both "chosen" and "sacred" (NLT, "set apart . . . to be holy"). These two characteristics are essential to the Temple's status. It must be a place that God has chosen, but in order for him to dwell there it must be consecrated for his use.

While the first part of the prayer (7:12-16) focuses attention on the Lord's eternal acceptance and choice of the Temple, the second part (7:17-22) of the prayer shifts the attention to the enduring character of the dynasty, introduced by the phrase "As for you" (lit., "But you") at the outset of 7:17. David casts a shadow over this section of the divine speech, as he is identified as the example to which Solomon must aspire ("as David your father did") and the one with whom the covenant was made ("I made this covenant with your father, David"). The terminology of this section is reminiscent of the divine speech in the Lord's appearance to David in 1 Chronicles 17, in particular the phrase "I will establish the throne of your dynasty" (cf. 1 Chr 17:11). For this promise to be fulfilled, however, the Lord places much responsibility on Solomon's shoulders. He must obey all God's "commands, decrees, and regulations," a list that signifies all of the Torah. Failure to do this, described by the Chronicler in his favorite idiom as "forsaking" (*'azab*

[TH5800, ZH6440]; NLT, "abandon"; see commentary on 1 Chr 28:9-10),[5] will result in serious consequences. In the source text in 1 Kings 9:6 reference is made to "you or your descendants" (Solomon and his descendants), and there is a switch from a singular "you" to a plural "you," that is, referring to the potential abandonment of Solomon and his descendants. The Chronicler retains the second-person plural references but eliminates the reference to the descendants (contra NLT's, "you or your descendants," in 7:19). This appears to put greater emphasis on Solomon's role of confirming the dynastic promise (see 1 Chr 28). In addition, while the source in 1 Kings 9:7 speaks of the result of disobedience as being "I will uproot Israel from this land," the Chronicler here writes "I will uproot the people from this land that I have given them." This also has implications for 7:22, where the Hebrew text merely contains the generic "because they abandoned the Lord" (contra NLT, which inserts "his people"). Therefore, in the Chronicler's version, the object of God's discipline is more limited, focusing on God's discipline of the dynasty rather than the nation.

This raises the question of the Chronicler's view of the enduring character of the Davidic dynasty. On the one hand, greater emphasis is placed on Solomon's obedience as crucial for the establishment of the eternal dynasty for David. The Chronicler goes to great pains to eliminate every reference to Solomon's unfaithfulness recorded in his source in 1 Kings, emphasizing that the positive side of this condition at least ("if you faithfully follow me") has been fulfilled by Solomon. On the other hand, the depiction of the consequences of unfaithfulness fits the Chronicler's description of the events at the end of the monarchy of Judah, and the use of plural references when speaking of future disobedience appears to look beyond Solomon to his descendants, whose illicit behavior is well documented in the account of 2 Chronicles. The negative side to this conditional promise actually says nothing that threatens the eternal character of the dynasty. Its focus is on exile of the monarchy and the destruction of the Temple. Thus, according to the Chronicler, the obedience of Solomon has secured an eternal place for the dynasty, but the disobedience of Solomon's descendants explains the ultimate exile of the dynasty and the destruction of the Temple.

The focus on the destruction of the Temple was important for the Chronicler to retain. In his own generation, however, the restoration of the Temple was a sign that reversed the curse of the Exile, which was due to the disobedience of the monarchy, and in turn provided hope for the renewal of the dynasty established by Solomon.

It is striking that the Chronicler retained from his source the reference to the Exodus as the foundational event in the covenant relationship between the Lord and the monarchy. It appears that although the Chronicler shifted the focus to the Davidic-Solomonic kingdom as the crucial era in Israel's redemptive story, in this expected time of crisis, the Exodus remains definitive for this story.

It is in chapters 5–7 that the Chronicler reaches the zenith of his account. It is the Temple's construction that has driven the narrative from the outset in 1 Chronicles; in chapters 5–7 all of David's passions and preparations and Solomon's faithful efforts have come to fulfillment. What is noteworthy about these three key chapters is how much emphasis is placed on the Temple as a means of fostering and renewing covenant relationship with Yahweh. For the Chronicler the Temple was not a place for dead ritual, but rather the place for covenantal encounter with Yahweh. Its loss in the early sixth century BC would signal a serious crisis in the relationship between Yahweh and Israel established at the Exodus; its renewal and restoration signaled for the Chronicler a new day of hope.

ENDNOTES

1. Japhet (1993:613) notes that although some see here the concern of the Chronicler to associate blessing with the priests alone, this cannot be sustained in light of 6:3; 1 Chr 16:2. The reason, however, is more likely linked to a desire to depict God's response to the final request in Solomon's prayer in 6:41-42 (Dillard 1987:57).
2. Dillard (1987:56) sees this as part of the literary presentation of the Chronicler and as referring to the same incident. Japhet (1993:610), drawing on the work of Long (1987:390-392) and Talmon (1978:9-26), sees 7:1-3 as resumptive repetition indicating simultaneity of events with 5:13-14.
3. Japhet (1993:611) distinguishes between an original version and a secondary adaptation, attributing the mention of fourteen days in 1 Kgs 8:65 as a secondary gloss.
4. In this the Chronicler shifts the rhetorical role of this verse from his source in 1 Kgs 9:1, where it is used as an introduction to God's speech to Solomon; cf. Japhet 1993:608.
5. Notice how the Chronicler's source in 1 Kgs 9:6 uses the phrase "do not keep" (*lo' thishmeru*) rather than the Chronicler's *'azab.*

◆ G. Solomon's Achievements (8:1-16)

**It took Solomon twenty years to build the
LORD's Temple and his own royal palace.
At the end of that time, 2Solomon turned
his attention to rebuilding the towns that
King Hiram* had given him, and he settled
Israelites in them.**

**3Solomon also fought against the town
of Hamath-zobah and conquered it. 4He
rebuilt Tadmor in the wilderness and built
towns in the region of Hamath as supply
centers. 5He fortified the towns of Upper
Beth-horon and Lower Beth-horon, re-
building their walls and installing barred
gates. 6He also rebuilt Baalath and other
supply centers and constructed towns
where his chariots and horses* could be
stationed. He built everything he desired
in Jerusalem and Lebanon and throughout
his entire realm.**

**7There were still some people living in
the land who were not Israelites, including
the Hittites, Amorites, Perizzites, Hivites,
and Jebusites. 8These were descendants of
the nations whom the people of Israel had
not destroyed. So Solomon conscripted
them for his labor force, and they serve in
the labor force to this day. 9But Solomon
did not conscript any of the Israelites for
his labor force. Instead, he assigned them
to serve as fighting men, officers in his
army, commanders of his chariots, and
charioteers. 10King Solomon appointed
250 of them to supervise the people.**

**11Solomon moved his wife, Pharaoh's
daughter, from the City of David to the
new palace he had built for her. He said,
"My wife must not live in King David's
palace, for the Ark of the LORD has been
there, and it is holy ground."**

**12Then Solomon presented burnt offer-
ings to the LORD on the altar he had built
for him in front of the entry room of the
Temple. 13He offered the sacrifices for the
Sabbaths, the new moon festivals, and
the three annual festivals—the Passover
celebration, the Festival of Harvest,* and
the Festival of Shelters—as Moses had
commanded.**

[14]In assigning the priests to their duties, Solomon followed the regulations of his father, David. He also assigned the Levites to lead the people in praise and to assist the priests in their daily duties. And he assigned the gatekeepers to their gates by their divisions, following the commands of David, the man of God. [15]Solomon did not deviate in any way from David's commands concerning the priests and Levites and the treasuries.

[16]So Solomon made sure that all the work related to building the Temple of the LORD was carried out, from the day its foundation was laid to the day of its completion.

8:2 Hebrew *Huram,* a variant spelling of Hiram; also in 8:18. **8:6** Or *and charioteers.* **8:13** Or *Festival of Weeks.*

NOTES

8:7 ***Hittites, Amorites, Perizzites, Hivites, and Jebusites.*** This is one of several traditional lists of foreign nations in Canaan before the arrival of Israel (see Gen 15:20; Exod 3:8, 17; 23:23; 33:2; 34:11; Deut 7:1; 20:17; Josh 3:10; 9:1; 11:3; 12:8; 24:11; 1 Kgs 9:20; Ezra 9:1; Neh 9:8; cf. Boda 1999:108-110).

8:11 ***Pharaoh's daughter.*** For this marriage and alliance with Egypt, see 1 Kgs 9:16-17.

City of David. This is the small town that David originally took from the Jebusites (see 1 Chr 11:4-9), which was later renamed Jerusalem. The account of the Ark's transport to David's palace area is found in 1 Chr 15:1.

COMMENTARY

God's speech at the end of chapter 7 nearly brings closure to the Temple-building account of the Chronicler. As is the case in his source in Kings, the focus of the Chronicler's account largely shifts to Solomon's "secular" pursuits, that is, pursuits not directly related to the Temple and its services. For the Chronicler these pursuits are not provided for mere historical interest. Rather, it is essential to his portrayal of Solomon as the ideal royal figure whose obedience and faithfulness were divinely blessed by success: building projects, military prowess, economic achievement, international fame, and border expansion. The account of Solomon ends with the summary notice that is typical of the Chronicler's method.

As mentioned in the introduction to chapters 1–9, this closing section connects with the earlier interaction between Solomon and Hiram in chapter 2. In chapters 8–9 the Queen of Sheba interacts with Solomon, and surrounding this story are two sections highlighting the partnership between Solomon and Hiram. This return to the interaction between Solomon and these Gentiles brings closure to the Chronicler's depiction of Solomon (see further Dillard 1984a:85-93; 1987:5-7, 70-71).

Summary Note: Building of Temple and Palace (8:1). As has been the custom, the Chronicler begins the final phase of his description of Solomon with a summary note drawn from his source in Kings. The dual projects of the Temple and the palace, the latter of which the Chronicler does not describe in detail, consumed the bulk of Solomon's reign, energy, and resources. Nevertheless, Solomon did undertake other activities, and these are recorded in order to show the many ways that God blessed Solomon's reign because of his faithfulness to the Temple project.

Solomon's Construction Projects and Military Resources (8:2–11). The first section focuses attention on Solomon's success in constructing and fortifying cities throughout his kingdom. At the center of the account, largely drawn from his source in Kings, is the summary note of 8:6b: "He built everything he desired in Jerusalem and Lebanon and throughout his entire realm."

For the remainder of his account (chs 8–9), the Chronicler used his source in Kings, following his regular pattern of condensing his account. While not all of his changes can be traced to a historiographic agenda, several are worthy of note, the first of which is found immediately in 8:2. Here, instead of the account of Solomon's payment of 20 Galilean cities to Hiram in payment for the timber and gold the Phoenician king had given Solomon (1 Kgs 9:11-14), the Chronicler records that Solomon rebuilt and resettled cities given to him by Hiram (8:2).[1] This change fits with the agenda of the Chronicler to present Solomon (and to a lesser extent David) as a pristine character who not only followed the Lord faithfully (and thus confirmed the Davidic covenant), but who also was blessed because of this faithfulness. To include the account of Solomon's loss of territory and need to pay a foreign king was not conducive to the Chronicler's account.[2]

At this point the Chronicler also leaves out two accounts from his source in 1 Kings 9:15-17a. The first recounts the forced labor Solomon used for his construction projects in Jerusalem, Hazor, Megiddo, and Gezer. In light of the later note that Israelites were not used for such labor (8:9), the Chronicler may have wanted to avoid any hint of foreign labor in the construction of the Temple. This concern to avoid any stain from foreigners in the internal working of Solomon's kingdom may also lie behind the omission of the account of Pharaoh's gift of daughter and dowry (Gezer) to Solomon: "The Chronicler may have considered it depreciating to Solomon to have a foreigner conquer a city for him. . . . The Chronicler is uniformly opposed to foreign alliances in the remainder of his history" (Dillard 1987:63). The Chronicler in general avoided reference to Solomon's marriage to Pharaoh's daughter, only incorporating it at one place (8:11) from his source (1 Kgs 9:24; cf. 1 Kgs 3:1; 9:16; 11:1) and even then (ironically) using it to accentuate Solomon's concern for purity.

The Chronicler continued his account by recounting Solomon's victory over Hamath-zobah. This is the only time the Chronicler records a military operation led by Solomon, who is considered a man of peace in contrast to his father David (1 Chr 22:9). It is also the only mention of this city in the entire Old Testament. The names Hamath and Zobah are associated with Aramean kingdoms in southern Syria that came into conflict with David during his reign (see 1 Chr 18:3-8; 19:1-19). There are several possible explanations for the mixing of these two terms: (1) The regions of Hamath and Zobah may have been combined by Solomon's time; (2) Zobah may have lain within the boundaries of the province of Hamath during the time of the Chronicler; (3) Hamath-zobah may have been the name of a city in the kingdom of Zobah; (4) Hamath-zobah may have been a scribal error for "Beth-zobah," as major manuscripts of the Septuagint record.[3] All of these options associate this victory with the far northern borders of Israel, showing Solomon's success against the traditional enemy of Aram. In this Solomon preserves the kingdom created by his father David (see 1 Chr 18–19), as Japhet writes, "He is more than the heir of a great conqueror, who first consolidated his father's achievements and eventually began to lose them; rather, he is a man of enterprise in his own right, expanding and fortifying the northern territory of his kingdom" (1993:623).

Solomon's construction at Tadmor and Hamath continues the focus on securing the northern frontier. Tadmor was a key Syrian oasis in the desert halfway between Mari and Damascus—the control of which was key to Solomon's economic success.[4] As already mentioned, Hamath was a traditional Aramean province in southern Syria, although it is not mentioned in the account in 1 Kings 9:17.

The Chronicler's account now shifts from the far north to the south, recounting Solomon's construction at Upper and Lower Beth-horon and Baalath. They also provided access from territories of Benjamin and southern Ephraim to the key ancient Near Eastern trade route known as the Great Trunk Road, one of two routes through the thin land bridge of Israel, which connected Africa, Arabia, Asia, and Europe. In addition, they would have provided protection for the northern approaches to Jerusalem. The precise location of Baalath is uncertain, although it is placed in the traditional tribal region of Dan, which was to the southwest of Gezer in the region between Judah and Ephraim along the Mediterranean coast (Josh 19:40-46; Judg 5:17). Most likely Baalath also controlled another of the valleys of the Shephelah that led to Jerusalem. By adding details on the fortification of these cities ("He fortified the towns . . . rebuilding their walls and installing barred gates," 8:5), the Chronicler ensures that the reader sees the military character of this construction. This martial tone is continued into 8:6 with the sweeping account (drawn from 1 Kgs 9:19) of Solomon's construction of fortified cities serving as supply centers and military outposts.

After his summary note in 8:6b, the Chronicler provides information on the human resources that Solomon exploited to support these construction projects, following his source in Kings. This account is careful to note that Solomon did not use Israelites in his projects, but rather only foreigners.

The final verse in this section (8:11) serves as a segue between the account of Solomon's foreign slaves (8:7-10) and that of his support of the Temple services (8:12-16). Here the Chronicler expands the short reference to Solomon's construction of a house for his Egyptian wife (1 Kgs 9:24) by adding a statement by the king linking the project to his passion for the holiness of a site associated with the Ark (8:11).[5] This is the only time the Chronicler links a foreign marriage to Solomon, a link that is key to the criticism of Solomon in his source in Kings (1 Kgs 3, 11), and ironically the Chronicler uses this link to present Solomon as a king passionate for ritual purity. This addition aids the transition between 8:2-11 and 8:12-16, where Solomon's passion for proper worship ritual will be emphasized further. The account in 1 Kings (1 Kgs 3:1-2; 9:16) reveals that Solomon married the daughter of Pharaoh and was given the town of Gezer as a dowry. This marriage suggests an alliance between Egypt and Israel, a political dimension that is played down in the Chronicler's account.

Solomon's Sacrifice and Praise (8:12-16). In this section, the Chronicler expands the short and generic account of Solomon's offering sacrifices to the Lord in 1 Kings 9:25a by providing details of Solomon's provision for various sacrifices (8:13), as well as provision for regular oral worship (8:14-15). Here the Chronicler parallels the two key figures of authority and innovation in the history of Israel's worship: Moses and David (De Vries 1988:619-639).[6] Interestingly, David is referred to as "the man of God," a term that is associated elsewhere with Moses (Deut 33:1; Josh 14:6) and prophets (1 Sam 9:6-7; 1 Kgs 12:22; 13:1-2), a trend evident throughout Chronicles (11:2; 25:7, 9; 30:16; 1 Chr 23:14). It is possible that David was being compared to a prophet, for through him God revealed his word to Israel (see 1 Chr 28:19),[7] but most likely this is bolstering David's status alongside Moses. Solomon faithfully executes the regulations of these two figures, legitimizing the Temple and its services.

Solomon's attention to sacrifice encompassed the entire worship schedule of Israel including the weekly (Sabbaths; Num 28:9-10), monthly (new moon festivals; Num 28:11-15), and yearly (three annual festivals; Deut 16:16; cf. Lev 23) rhythms. It is possible there is also reference here to daily sacrifices (Num 28:1-8).[8] Solomon not only gave attention to the function of the priests, with their attention to sacrificial cult (8:14a), but also to the function of the Levites, who assisted the priests, led oral worship, and guarded the gates (8:14b). As has been seen throughout this account (especially in 1 Chr 15–16, 23–27), the Chronicler was concerned with the role of Levites in the Temple services.

The Chronicler not only expanded the description of the sacrificial activity of Solomon but also the simple summary statement on the completion of the Temple in 1 Kings 9:25b to read, "So Solomon made sure that all the work related to building the Temple of the LORD was carried out, from the day its foundation was laid to the day of its completion" (8:16). Ancient Near Eastern texts related to Temple building often highlight the day of foundation laying as a key early stage in any Temple-building project, evidence for which can also be discerned in the Old Testament (Ezra 3; Isa 28:16; Hag 2:15-19; Zech 4:6b-10a).[9] This day involved special religious ceremonies, often with the royal figure enacting the laying of the first brick in the new foundation and burying foundation deposits including written texts (with blessings and curses for future royals who rebuild the temple), precious metals, stones, and even fragrant plants. The foundation was seen as key to the endurance of the structure. Prior to the day of foundation laying, there were initial activities on the site, especially the removal of debris from any previous structure. The ceremony that signaled the beginning of the building proper was the day of foundation laying, evidence for which can be discerned in 3:3. The day of completion refers to the ceremonies related to the dedication of the completed Temple. These were the focus of the Chronicler's account in chapters 5–7.

The expansions in 8:12-16 (as with the one in 8:11) are all related to the construction of the Temple and the institution of its services. Thus, even when the Chronicler finally does move out of the realm of the Temple project, as he does in chapters 8–9, he cannot help but mention the Temple and its services. This is a reflection of his agenda not only to highlight their importance in the life of Israel but also to remind his readers that all the success Solomon experienced in the "secular" realm is to be traced to his exhaustive and enduring attention to the "sacred" realm symbolized by the Temple and its services.

ENDNOTES

1. This is described by Japhet (1993:621) as an example of "how Chronicles can transmit the material in a manner diametrically opposed to its original presentation."
2. Some have charged the Chronicler with inventing this account, but there are many ways to explain the divergences between Kings and Chronicles. The cities that were unsatisfactory to Hiram were returned to Solomon, who then developed them, or the two accounts record two sides of an exchange of cities between treaty partners—although see the extensive discussion and review of research by Dillard (1987:62-63). Japhet (1993:621) sees this as an example of the Chronicler's historical work; in light of the Chronicler's view of the Solomon-Hiram relationship as superior-subordinate, the Chronicler must have found the claim of Kings "grossly improbable."
3. For these and the following theories, see ABD 3.37.
4. There is some controversy over this name in the text. In 1 Kgs 9:18 the Kethiv (consonants) read Tamar, while the Qere (vowels) read Tadmor, as here in Chronicles. Tamar was a fortified city in southeast Judah at the border between Israel and Edom (Gen 14:7; Ezek 47:19; 48:28).
5. Dillard (1987:65) claims that the issue may not have been as much that she was a Gentile as that she was female. Similarly Japhet (1993:626) considers this an early example of feared defilement from sexual activity in the holy city, as is found in the sectarian literature ("No man shall lie with a woman in the city of the Sanctuary, to defile the city of the Sanctuary," *Temple Scroll* 65.11-12; cf. 47). However, see also the concern over foreign incursion in 1 Kgs 11 and Ezek 44:9.
6. Cf. Japhet (1993:628), who says, "It is a juxtaposition of 'the command of David' with the 'command of Moses' of v. 13 . . . which embodies the Chronicler's distinct view of the development of cult."
7. See commentary on 1 Chr 25 and also Petersen 1977; Schniedewind 1995; Van Rooy 1994:163-179.
8. The beginning of 8:13 has, lit., "as the duty of each day required"; so also Japhet 1993:627.
9. See Boda 2006c; Boda and Novotny 2009.

◆ H. Solomon's Economic Achievement and International Fame (8:17–9:31)

17 Later Solomon went to Ezion-geber and Elath,* ports along the shore of the Red Sea* in the land of Edom. 18 Hiram sent him ships commanded by his own officers and manned by experienced crews of sailors. These ships sailed to Ophir with Solomon's men and brought back to Solomon almost seventeen tons* of gold.

CHAPTER 9

**When the queen of Sheba heard of Solomon's fame, she came to Jerusalem to test him with hard questions. She arrived with a large group of attendants and a great caravan of camels loaded with spices, large quantities of gold, and precious jewels. When she met with Solomon, she talked with him about everything she had on her mind.
2 Solomon had answers for all her questions; nothing was too hard for him to explain to her.
3 When the queen of Sheba realized how wise Solomon was, and when she saw the palace he had built, 4 she was overwhelmed. She was also amazed at the food on his tables, the organization of his officials and their splendid clothing, the cup-bearers and their robes, and the burnt offerings Solomon made at the Temple of the LORD.**

5She exclaimed to the king, "Everything
I heard in my country about your achieve-
ments* and wisdom is true! 6I didn't be-
lieve what was said until I arrived here
and saw it with my own eyes. In fact, I
had not heard the half of your great wis-
dom! It is far beyond what I was told.
7How happy your people must be! What
a privilege for your officials to stand here
day after day, listening to your wisdom!
8Praise the LORD your God, who delights
in you and has placed you on the throne
as king to rule for him. Because God loves
Israel and desires this kingdom to last
forever, he has made you king over them
so you can rule with justice and righ-
teousness."

9Then she gave the king a gift of 9,000
pounds* of gold, great quantities of spices,
and precious jewels. Never before had there
been spices as fine as those the queen of
Sheba gave to King Solomon.

10(In addition, the crews of Hiram and
Solomon brought gold from Ophir, and they
also brought red sandalwood* and precious
jewels. 11The king used the sandalwood to
make steps* for the Temple of the LORD and
the royal palace, and to construct lyres
and harps for the musicians. Never before
had such beautiful things been seen in
Judah.)

12King Solomon gave the queen of She-
ba whatever she asked for—gifts of great-
er value than the gifts she had given him.
Then she and all her attendants returned
to their own land.

13Each year Solomon received about
25 tons* of gold. 14This did not include
the additional revenue he received from
merchants and traders. All the kings of
Arabia and the governors of the prov-
inces also brought gold and silver to
Solomon.

15King Solomon made 200 large shields
of hammered gold, each weighing more
than 15 pounds.* 16He also made
300 smaller shields of hammered gold,
each weighing more than 7½ pounds.*
The king placed these shields in the Palace
of the Forest of Lebanon.

17Then the king made a huge throne,
decorated with ivory and overlaid with
pure gold. 18The throne had six steps, with
a footstool of gold. There were armrests
on both sides of the seat, and the figure
of a lion stood on each side of the throne.
19There were also twelve other lions, one
standing on each end of the six steps. No
other throne in all the world could be
compared with it!

20All of King Solomon's drinking cups
were solid gold, as were all the utensils
in the Palace of the Forest of Lebanon.
They were not made of silver, for silver
was considered worthless in Solomon's
day!

21The king had a fleet of trading ships*
manned by the sailors sent by Hiram.*
Once every three years the ships returned,
loaded with gold, silver, ivory, apes, and
peacocks.*

22So King Solomon became richer and
wiser than any other king on earth.
23Kings from every nation came to consult
him and to hear the wisdom God had
given him. 24Year after year everyone who
visited brought him gifts of silver and
gold, clothing, weapons, spices, horses,
and mules.

25Solomon had 4,000 stalls for his
horses and chariots, and he had 12,000
horses.* He stationed some of them in the
chariot cities, and some near him in Jeru-
salem. 26He ruled over all the kings from
the Euphrates River* in the north to the
land of the Philistines and the border of
Egypt in the south. 27The king made silver
as plentiful in Jerusalem as stone. And
valuable cedar timber was as common as
the sycamore-fig trees that grow in the
foothills of Judah.* 28Solomon's horses
were imported from Egypt* and many
other countries.

29The rest of the events of Solomon's
reign, from beginning to end, are record-
ed in *The Record of Nathan the Prophet,*
and *The Prophecy of Ahijah from Shiloh,*
and also in *The Visions of Iddo the Seer,*
concerning Jeroboam son of Nebat. 30Sol-
omon ruled in Jerusalem over all Israel for

forty years. [31]When he died, he was buried in the City of David, named for his father. Then his son Rehoboam became the next king.

8:17a As in Greek version (see also 2 Kgs 14:22; 16:6); Hebrew reads *Eloth,* a variant spelling of Elath. **8:17b** As in parallel text at 1 Kgs 9:26; Hebrew reads *the sea.* **8:18** Hebrew *450 talents* [15.3 metric tons]. **9:5** Hebrew *your words.* **9:9** Hebrew *120 talents* [4,000 kilograms]. **9:10** Hebrew *algum wood* (also in 9:11); perhaps a variant spelling of *almug.* Compare parallel text at 1 Kgs 10:11-12. **9:11** Or *gateways.* The meaning of the Hebrew is uncertain. **9:13** Hebrew *666 talents* [23 metric tons]. **9:15** Hebrew *600 [shekels] of hammered gold* [6.8 kilograms]. **9:16** Hebrew *300 [shekels] of gold* [3.4 kilograms]. **9:21a** Hebrew *fleet of ships that could sail to Tarshish.* **9:21b** Hebrew *Huram,* a variant spelling of Hiram. **9:21c** Or *and baboons.* **9:25** Or *12,000 charioteers.* **9:26** Hebrew *the river.* **9:27** Hebrew *the Shephelah.* **9:28** Possibly *Muzur,* a district near Cilicia.

NOTES

9:21 ***trading ships.*** Lit., "ships of Tarshish" (see NLT mg), often identified with a port in the western Mediterranean (see Jonah 1:3), possibly Tartessus in Spain (Dillard 1987:73). These ships probably were not bound for Tarshish but rather were of the type of Phoenician ship known for its trips to Tarshish. Japhet (1993:641) sees this as the Chronicler's expansion of his source to showcase a second fleet of ships in the Mediterranean Sea.

COMMENTARY

Having completed his description of Solomon's sacred activities, the Chronicler now returns to his account of the secular activities of Solomon. The Chronicler interweaves Solomon's economic achievements and international fame, depicting both the centripetal and centrifugal force of these signs of success. That is, Solomon established contacts far beyond his own borders, and other nations began to take an interest in Israel in return. Solomon took the initiative to move beyond his borders (8:17-18; 9:10-11, 21), partnering with Hiram of Tyre to do business with other nations, bringing back precious metal (gold), wood (red sandalwood), stones (jewels), ivory, and exotic animals (apes, peacocks). For Hiram's name to be mentioned at this point is not odd, since the Phoenicians were well-known in the ancient world for their maritime ability and trade. Ezion-geber and Elath were ports in the farthest south of Israel at the head of the Gulf of Aqaba (Red Sea). It is possible that the former was an island just off the coast from Elath (ABD 2.723-726). These trading ships were on a three-year cycle (see 9:21) and, judging by the products mentioned, appear to have visited ports in Africa and Arabia. Ophir (8:18; 9:10) was probably located in the southern Arabian area around present-day Yemen and thus accessible through the Gulf of Aqaba (1 Chr 29:4; see ABD 5.26). Later Jehoshaphat would seek to renew maritime trade through the Red Sea, but the fleet would be destroyed before they set sail (20:35-37).

While Solomon moved out to the nations for trade, "kings from every nation" were coming to Solomon seeking wisdom (9:1-9, 12-14, 23-24), represented for the Chronicler by the Queen of Sheba and the kings of Arabia, depositing into the coffers of Israel precious metal (gold and silver), spices, stones (jewels), clothing, weapons, and animals (horses, mules). Sheba, traditional home of the Sabeans, was located in the southwest corner of the Arabian Peninsula. The Old Testament speaks regularly of Sheba as a source for gold, jewels, incense, and myrrh (Ps 72:15; Isa 60:6; Jer 6:20; Ezek 27:22; 38:13), products all known from this region. In light of the notes about Solomon's economic exploits in the Gulf of Aqaba, it is not surprising to hear of the visit of this woman, who would have been interested in securing trade opportunities for her products carried by Arabian caravans on the routes to Africa, Asia, and Europe, which were controlled by Solomon.

The Chronicler granted the Queen of Sheba an elongated piece of dramatic narrative that draws considerable rhetorical weight (9:5-8). Her words focus not on the material wealth of the kingdom, but rather on the magnitude of Solomon's words and wisdom, noting in one breath that what seemed to be exaggerated reports of his wisdom had spread abroad, while in the next that these reports were clearly inadequate descriptions. She expressed the blessed state not only of those who served in his court but also of this nation over whom Solomon ruled and dispensed wise justice and righteousness. Her speech recognizes the divine source of Solomon's wisdom, blessing Yahweh for delighting in Solomon and setting him on the throne of a nation he had loved and established forever. Solomon's reign is inextricably linked to Israel's covenant relationship with Yahweh. The appearance and speech of this foreign queen is a reminder of Israel's role among the nations, which was already suggested by the introduction to the genealogies in 1 Chronicles 1–9 (see commentary on 1 Chr 1).

With his riches Solomon made gold shields (9:15-16), a gold and ivory throne (9:17-19), and gold drinking cups and utensils (9:20). These items were placed within the "Palace of the Forest of Lebanon," the name given to Solomon's grand palace, which was built with resources from the forests of Hiram (see 2:1, 12; 7:11; 8:1; 9:3, 11; cf. 1 Kgs 7:1-12 for its construction and Isa 22:8 for prophetic criticism). The numerical values as well as the superlatives used throughout this section are intended to showcase Solomon's status among the nations:

> Never before had there been spices as fine as those the queen of Sheba gave to King Solomon (9:9).
> Never before had such beautiful things been seen in Judah (9:11).
> No other throne in all the world could be compared with it (9:19).
> They were not made of silver, for silver was considered worthless in Solomon's day (9:20).
> So King Solomon became richer and wiser than any other king on earth (9:22).
> The king made silver as plentiful in Jerusalem as stone. And valuable cedar timber was as common as the sycamore-fig trees that grow in the foothills of Judah (9:27).

The account highlights not only Solomon's interactions with those outside his borders but also his organization within his borders. Solomon built a strong military presence throughout the land as well as around his royal city, Jerusalem (9:25, 28), and extended the borders of the land from the Euphrates River in the north to the land of the Philistines and the Egyptian border in the south (9:26). Solomon received resources from "governors of the provinces," a sign of the efficient taxation within his kingdom. Furthermore, the account of the queen of Sheba shows that Solomon's successes were to be traced to the advanced character of his royal court (9:4).

Absent from the Chronicler's account at this point, however, is the negative account of Solomon's sin and God's prophetic judgment in 1 Kings 11:1-40. Similar to the elimination of Solomon's payment to Hiram, this change fits with the agenda of the Chronicler to present Solomon as a flawless character who confirmed the Davidic covenant by following the Lord faithfully and was subsequently blessed because of this faithfulness (see introduction to chs 1–9). These descriptions showcase Solomon's reign as one of unparalleled success, evidence of God's blessing on this king who built the Temple and established its services.

Summary Note: Reign of Solomon (9:29–31). Similar to the final summary notation for David's reign (1 Chr 29:29-30), the Chronicler mostly follows his source in Kings (1 Kgs 11:41-43), except that he notes his use of sources traced to prophetic figures, in this case, "*Nathan the Prophet . . . Ahijah from Shiloh . . . Iddo the Seer.*" Both Nathan (2 Sam 7, 12; 1 Kgs 1) and Ahijah (1 Kgs 11) were known as contemporaries of Solomon, while Iddo is mentioned also as a source for Rehoboam's reign in 12:15 (Japhet 1993:644-645). This use of prophetic sources for Solomon (as for David) gives credibility to the Chronicler's account, as well as to Solomon's reign (see commentary on 1 Chr 29:29-30). This notation also reminds the reader that the kingdom has now been transferred to another Davidic scion: Rehoboam, son of Solomon.

With Solomon's death we come to the end of the Chronicler's presentation of the glorious age of David and Solomon, the ideal age that will provide the foundation for evaluating the rest of the Chronicler's story in chapters 10–36, as well as being a foundation for the practices in the Chronicler's own day. But according to Dillard (1987:72-73), the Chronicler has more than the past and present in mind:

> *These features cumulatively are scarcely a simple recalling of fond memories from an idealized past, a mere recitation about the "good old days"—rather they represent an eschatological program and give expression to the fondest hopes of many in the restoration community for the day that a David/Solomon redivivus would again in righteousness lead Israel to glory among the nations, a day when the Gentiles would once again make their pilgrimage to Jerusalem.*

The Chronicler provides insights into the future possibilities and hopes of the community, and he will continue to provide insights into this future throughout the remainder of his story (see introduction to 1 Chr 10–36 and Boda 2009b).

INTRODUCTION TO 2 CHRONICLES 10–36: THE POST-SOLOMONIC ACCOUNT

Second Chronicles 10 shatters the idyllic picture the Chronicler has created in his depiction of the united kingdom to this point (1 Chr 10—2 Chr 9). This negative information represents a significant shift in tone, which will continue for the remainder of the work (chs 10–36). While the Chronicler's narrative has highlighted the glorious foundation of the dynasty by David and Solomon and the positive benefits of obedience to the Lord, the remaining account will supplement this by recounting both the positive benefits of obedience to Yahweh as well as the negative consequences of disobedience. The striking difference can be discerned in terms of both the narrative flow and the theological analysis of the accounts.

Narrative Flow. The Chronicler does not cover up the schism that split the united kingdom in two, but in keeping with his presentation of an ideal Solomon, this schism is not linked to his shortcomings. Instead, the split is considered ordained by God (11:4) and is blamed on a combination of the schemes of Jeroboam and his "whole gang of scoundrels" and the folly of a young, indecisive, and weak Rehoboam (13:6-7; cf. Knoppers 1990:423-440). Even within Rehoboam's reign (11:16-17) and certainly by the reign of his son Abijah (ch 13), conditions were ripe for reunification, but this was rejected by the northern kingdom. Their defeat by the Davidic king Abijah in chapter 13 reveals Yahweh's favor on the southern kingdom of Judah.

Throughout the account, the northern kingdom is largely ignored. By this the Chronicler was not disqualifying the northern tribes from Israel but rather distinguishing between the northern kingdom as a political entity and the population of the north (Williamson 1982:237). As Japhet (1989:324) has written:

> *The northern kingdom was established in sin, its existence constitutes a rebellion against YHWH, and its history is an unbroken chain of transgression leading up to destruction. Yet it is part of Israel, and without the members of the northern tribes, the people of Israel cannot be complete.*

This is confirmed in the reigns of Rehoboam and Asa, who attracted faithful northern defectors to Judah (11:16-17; 15:8-9). In light of this, throughout the post-Solomonic account the Chronicler negatively portrays any treaty made with the northern kingdom, depicting prophetic attacks against kings who make treaties with the north and tracing the devastating effect of such alliances upon the Davidic dynasty. Jehoshaphat's alliance with the northern Omride dynasty (Ahab, Ahaziah) will lead to the corruption of Jehoram (Jehoshaphat's son; 21:6) and Ahaziah (Jehoshaphat's grandson; 22:3, 5) and the near extinction of the Davidic dynasty by Athaliah (22:10-12), a northern Omride princess whose marriage into the Davidic family sealed Jehoshaphat's treaty with the north.

The account of Athaliah is not the only low point in the post-Solomonic account. There are two other major junctures. The first of these is during the reign of Ahaz (ch 28), the first king to reign after the demise of the northern kingdom at the hands of the Assyrians. The great opportunity to reunite the people is lost as Ahaz "brings Judah to its darkest hour" (Lowery 1991:128-129) during what Japhet (1993:897) describes as a "uniformly black" script, "moving toward a climax of evil." Mosis (1973:41-43, 186-188) and Dillard (1987:261) describe this nadir in terms of exile, especially as the doors of the Temple are locked and the Temple vessels are chopped up (cf. De Vries 1989:366). For the Chronicler it is Hezekiah who will foster renewal, not only restoring worship in Jerusalem, but also inviting northerners to join Judah in faithful worship of Yahweh. Throntveit (1987) sees the Chronicler's history divided into three distinct phases: the united kingdom (1 Chr 10—2 Chr 9), the divided kingdom (chs 9–28), and the third, introduced by Hezekiah's reign in chapter 29, the "reunited kingdom."

But there is a fourth phase that Throntveit did not take into account; it is signaled by the final major juncture in the Chronicler's post-Solomonic account, which comes at the end of Josiah's reign (35:20–36:23). After encountering Josiah's great accomplishments in renewing faithful worship in Judah, the reader is surprised to find Josiah's demise at the hand of the Egyptian Neco at the end of chapter 35.

Beginning with Neco, foreign emperors will speak and act in accordance with Yahweh's will, and so with the death of Josiah Judah ceased to exist as an independent kingdom and was led by puppet kings who were appointed and removed at the whim of foreign emperors. Every king but the final one ends up in exile. The story ends with a description of the exilic discipline and the hopeful promise of Cyrus to rebuild the Temple, followed by an invitation to the community to return to the rebuilt Temple.

The post-Solomonic account in Chronicles thus sets up several key models for the Chronicler's audience to follow. In many cases the situations described resonate with their experience. Depictions of normative and ideal royal figures like Hezekiah and even Manasseh display patterns for renewal in their own day (see Boda 2009b). The principles of obedience and blessing established during Solomon's reign (see commentary on ch 7) will be illustrated throughout the reigns of the various Davidic kings.

Theological Analysis. The dominant theological paradigm for the Chronicler's depiction of the failures and successes of the post-Solomonic kings has often been described (negatively) as "Immediate Retribution"—that is, the belief that God's blessing falls immediately upon the individual or generation that obeys and/or turns to the Lord and, conversely, that God's curse falls immediately upon the individual or generation that disobeys or turns away from the Lord. Japhet (1993:44) has described this in the following way: "God's rule of his people is expressed by his constant, direct and immediate intervention in their history." Similarly, Dillard (1987:76) reminds us that "reward and punishment are not deferred, but rather follow immediately on the heels of the precipitating events." Although this paradigm can be discerned at certain points in the Chronicler's source in Samuel—Kings, the authors of the latter work emphasized another theological paradigm often called "Cumulative Guilt." In this paradigm, which helped to explain the severity of God's discipline of the nations, the sin of generations accumulated to the breaking point of the destruction and exile of the kingdom. For the northern kingdom this guilt is traced to the sin of Jeroboam son of Nebat (1 Kgs 14:14-16; 15:30; 2 Kgs 17:21-23; 23:15),[1] while for the southern kingdom it is traced to the sin of Manasseh (2 Kgs 21:9-16; 23:26-27; 24:2-4). Passages like Jeremiah 31:29 and Ezekiel 18:2 (citing the proverb among the people: "The parents have eaten sour grapes, but their children's mouths pucker at the taste") reveal that this latter paradigm had been distorted by the people and used as justification for their lack of repentance. Jeremiah 31:30 and Ezekiel 18 answered this distortion by preaching a theology of immediate retribution—that is, each generation has the opportunity to respond to or reject God. This was never lost in the book of Kings. The theology of cumulative guilt was used to explain the severity of the destruction, even though the generation that faced this destruction was equally guilty of disobedience. The best example for observing the differences between Chronicles and Samuel—Kings is in their portrayal of Manasseh. While in the book of Kings Manasseh was depicted as the worst of all Davidides, in chapter 33 Manasseh is portrayed as an example of an exilic figure whose repentance led to his restoration to the land and kingdom.[2]

This theology of immediate retribution is laid out in several programmatic passages unique to the Chronicler (12:5; 15:2; 20:20; 1 Chr 28:8-9), but there is no better statement than God's speech to Solomon in 7:13-15. There the actions of seeking (*darash* [TH1875, ZH2011], *baqash* [TH1245, ZH1335]), humbling (*kana'* [TH3665, ZH4044]), praying (*palal* [TH6419, ZH7137] in the Hitpael), and turning (*shub* [TH7725, ZH8740]) are signs of a person or generation pursuing covenant relationship with the Lord (cf. Dillard 1984b:164-172; 1987:76-81). This vocabulary reappears regularly throughout chapters 10–36:

Seeking: 11:16; 12:14; 14:4 [3], 7 [6]; 15:2, 4, 12-13, 15; 16:12; 17:4; 18:4; 19:3; 20:4; 22:9; 25:20; 26:5; 30:19; 31:21; 32:31; 34:3 (cf. 1 Chr 10:13-14; 22:19; 28:9)
Humbling: 12:6-7, 12; 28:19; 30:11; 33:12, 19, 23; 34:27; 36:12
Praying: 13:12-15; 14:11 [10]; 18:31; 20:9; 30:18, 27; 32:20, 24; 33:13, 18-19 (cf. 1 Chr 4:10; 5:20; 21:26)
Turning: 15:4; 30:6, 8-9; 36:13

In contrast, the actions of abandoning (*'azab* [TH5800, ZH6440]) and being unfaithful/rebellious (*ma'al* [TH4603, ZH5085]) are signs of a disobedient person or generation.

Abandoning: 12:1, 5; 13:10-11; 15:2; 21:10; 24:18, 20, 24; 28:6; 29:6; 34:25 (cf. 7:19, 22; 1 Chr 28:9, 20)
Being unfaithful/rebellious: 12:2; 26:16, 18; 28:19, 22; 29:6; 30:7; 36:14 (cf. 1 Chr 2:7; 5:25; 10:13)

Signs of God's immediate response to these exemplary human actions are consistent throughout the Chronicler's account. Obedience brings success and prosperity (14:7; 26:5; 31:21; 32:27-30; 1 Chr 22:11, 13; 29:23), exemplified by abundance in the areas of:

Construction: 11:5; 14:6-7; 16:6; 17:12; 24:13; 26:2, 6, 9-10; 27:3-4; 32:3-5, 29-30; 33:14; 34:10-13
Military: 11:1; 13:13-18; 14:8-15; 17:12-19; 20:2-30; 25:5, 14; 26:10-15; 27:5-7; 32:20-22
Progeny: 11:18-22; 13:21; 21:1-3; 1 Chr 3:1-9; 14:2-7; 25:5; 26:4-5
Popularity: 11:13-17; 15:10-15; 17:5; 19:4-11; 20:27-30; 23:1-17; 30:1-26; 34:29-32; 35:24-25
Length of Life/Reign: 9:30; 20:31; 24:1; 25:1

Disobedience brings the lack or opposite of the blessings above:

Military: 12:1-9; 16:1-9; 21:8-11, 16-17; 24:23-24; 25:15-24; 28:4-8, 16-25; 33:10-11; 35:20-24; 36:15-20
Popularity: 16:10; 21:19; 24:25-26; 25:27-28; 28:27; 33:24-25
Length of Life/Reign: 13:1-2; 16:12; 21:5, 16-20; 22:2; 26:16-23

This message was important for the Chronicler's generation, who were seeking to live above and beyond the failures of past generations that had caused the demise of the state and imperial domination. This theological paradigm provided on the one side a warning to the Chronicler's audience that punishment will not be deferred to a future generation as well as an encouragement that they have the opportunity for a new start in their day. This "new start" is made clear in the closing words of the Chronicler's work. Drawing on the theology of Leviticus 25:4; 26:33-35, 2 Chronicles 36:21 conveys that the Exile functioned as a Sabbath rest, cleansing the land from its impurity.

ENDNOTES

1. Fifteen of the northern kings after Jeroboam I are linked with his sin: 1 Kgs 15:25 [Nadab], 34; 16:2, 7 [Baasha], 19 [Zimri], 26 [Omri], 31 [Ahab]; 22:52 [Ahaziah]; 2 Kgs 3:3 [Joram]; 10:29, 31 [Jehu]; 13:2, 6 [Jehoahaz], 11[Jehoash]; 14:24 [Jeroboam II]; 15:9 [Zechariah], 18 [Menahem], 24 [Pekahiah], 28 [Pekah].
2. The description of this theme within Chronicles needs to be carefully explained in light of recent criticism by such people as Kelly and Ben Zvi. Kelly (1996:108) reminds us that the Chronicler employs this theme within the context of the covenant relationship between Yahweh and his people and that the focus is on "Yahweh's mercy and restorative will towards his sinful people." Ben Zvi (2002:263) admits, "There is no doubt whatsoever that the (hi)story of Israel as presented in Chronicles includes numerous instances that exemplify again and again the actual implementation of coherence between human actions and divine responses." However, he goes on to argue that this is not universal because "the same (hi)story contains a very substantial number of instances that unequivocally show a lack of this coherence." First of all, Ben Zvi's descriptives ("numerous instances" versus "very substantial number") are not as precise as one would like. Second, he assumes that events are all considered as "divinely-caused" by the Chronicler. It is clear that the Chronicler's account is dominated by the call to careful obedience and that this was designed to give hope to his Persian-period audience. However, Ben Zvi reminds us that the extension of this theology to a mechanical view of God's grace is not suggested by the Chronicler. The faithful may face difficult, even life-threatening circumstances, whether prophets (e.g., 24:21-22) or kings (ch 32). This, however, does not negate the call to faithfulness of each generation nor God's commitment to discipline those who are unfaithful. Some abuses of the Chronicler's theology can be discerned in Wilkinson 2000; see the critique in Clapp and Wright 2002:29-31.

◆ II. The Account after Solomon (10:1–36:23)
A. Division of the Kingdom (10:1–11:4)

**Rehoboam went to Shechem, where all Is-
rael had gathered to make him king. 2When
Jeroboam son of Nebat heard of this, he
returned from Egypt, for he had fled to
Egypt to escape from King Solomon. 3The
leaders of Israel summoned him, and Jero-
boam and all Israel went to speak with Re-
hoboam. 4"Your father was a hard master,"
they said. "Lighten the harsh labor demands
and heavy taxes that your father imposed
on us. Then we will be your loyal subjects."**

**5Rehoboam replied, "Come back in three
days for my answer." So the people went
away.**

**6Then King Rehoboam discussed the
matter with the older men who had coun-
seled his father, Solomon. "What is your
advice?" he asked. "How should I answer
these people?"**

**7The older counselors replied, "If you
are good to these people and do your best
to please them and give them a favorable**

answer, they will always be your loyal subjects."

8But Rehoboam rejected the advice of the older men and instead asked the opinion of the young men who had grown up with him and were now his advisers. 9"What is your advice?" he asked them. "How should I answer these people who want me to lighten the burdens imposed by my father?"

10The young men replied, "This is what you should tell those complainers who want a lighter burden: 'My little finger is thicker than my father's waist! 11Yes, my father laid heavy burdens on you, but I'm going to make them even heavier! My father beat you with whips, but I will beat you with scorpions!'"

12Three days later Jeroboam and all the people returned to hear Rehoboam's decision, just as the king had ordered. 13But Rehoboam spoke harshly to them, for he rejected the advice of the older counselors 14and followed the counsel of his younger advisers. He told the people, "My father laid* heavy burdens on you, but I'm going to make them even heavier! My father beat you with whips, but I will beat you with scorpions!"

15So the king paid no attention to the people. This turn of events was the will of God, for it fulfilled the LORD's message to Jeroboam son of Nebat through the prophet Ahijah from Shiloh.

16When all Israel realized* that the king had refused to listen to them, they responded,

"Down with the dynasty of David!
We have no interest in the son
of Jesse.
Back to your homes, O Israel!
Look out for your own house,
O David!"

So all the people of Israel returned home. 17But Rehoboam continued to rule over the Israelites who lived in the towns of Judah.

18King Rehoboam sent Adoniram,* who was in charge of the labor force, to restore order, but the people of Israel stoned him to death. When this news reached King Rehoboam, he quickly jumped into his chariot and fled to Jerusalem. 19And to this day the northern tribes of Israel have refused to be ruled by a descendant of David.

CHAPTER 11

When Rehoboam arrived at Jerusalem, he mobilized the men of Judah and Benjamin—180,000 select troops—to fight against Israel and to restore the kingdom to himself.

2But the LORD said to Shemaiah, the man of God, 3"Say to Rehoboam son of Solomon, king of Judah, and to all the Israelites in Judah and Benjamin: 4'This is what the LORD says: Do not fight against your relatives. Go back home, for what has happened is my doing!'" So they obeyed the message of the LORD and did not fight against Jeroboam.

10:14 As in Greek version and many Hebrew manuscripts (see also 1 Kgs 12:14); Masoretic Text reads *I will lay.* **10:16** As in Syriac version, Latin Vulgate, and many Hebrew manuscripts (see also 1 Kgs 12:16); Masoretic Text lacks *realized.* **10:18** Hebrew *Hadoram*, a variant spelling of Adoniram; compare 1 Kgs 4:6; 5:14; 12:18.

NOTES

10:7 *a favorable answer.* Heb., *debarim tobim* [TH1697/2896, ZH1821/3202] (good words). This is probably a reference to an official treaty or pact between king and people, as found in other ancient Near Eastern documents (see 1 Sam 25:30; 2 Sam 7:28; 2 Kgs 25:28-29; cf. Dillard 1987:87; Fox 1973:41-42; Weinfeld 1982:27-53).

10:8 *the older men . . . young men.* These are possibly two different groups of officials in the royal court, the first being for counsel and the other civil servants (see Judg 8:14; 1 Kgs 21:8; 2 Kgs 10:5; cf. Dillard 1987:86; D. Evans 1966:273-279).

10:10 ***My little finger.*** Lit., "my little one." The comparison to Solomon's waist (hips, loins) has suggested to some that this is a euphemism for Rehoboam's genitals, bolstering the folly of this young advice (cf. Dillard 1987:87).

10:18 ***who was in charge of the labor force.*** This title is also known from a seal from the seventh century BC (Avigad 1980:170-173).

COMMENTARY

As noted in the introduction to chapters 10–36, chapter 10 represents a key juncture in the Chronicler's work. Drawn from his source in 1 Kings 12, the account of Rehoboam introduces some new elements: Solomon had faced opposition from a figure named Jeroboam son of Nebat who had fled to safety in Egypt (10:2), the people had struggled under the heavy load of labor and taxes exacted by Solomon (10:4), and God had prophesied disaster for Solomon's son (10:15). It is Solomon's son Rehoboam who must face these serious problems, but it is obvious from the outset that he is not up to the task.

The scene in chapter 10 is not surprising in light of ancient Near Eastern and Israelite history. Times of dynastic succession were often phases of upheaval within ancient kingdoms, especially after a long and successful reign. Furthermore, the history of Israel suggests that there was a natural division between the northern Israelites, led by the Ephraimite tribe of Joseph, and the southern Israelites, led by the tribe of Judah. The first king (Saul) had been chosen from the relatively insignificant tribe of Benjamin, positioned physically in the neutral territory between Judah and Ephraim. After Saul's death the northern tribes rallied around Saul's son Ishbosheth, while the southern tribe rallied around David (2 Sam 2–4). David's transfer of his capital from Hebron in the south to Jerusalem, which lay on the border between Judah and Benjamin, was a geopolitical strategy to keep a firm grip on the northern tribes. Under Solomon's reign, however, the old fissures began to emerge, and a northerner (Ephraimite) named Jeroboam who had served in Solomon's court became a rallying figure for northern disaffection (1 Kgs 11:26). Solomon's death set in motion a series of events that culminated in the crisis faced by Rehoboam.

Upon the death of his father, Rehoboam traveled to Shechem for his coronation. The reason for this is not clear. Shechem served as a key religious center for Israel upon their entrance into the land, and there Joshua led the nation in a renewal of covenant (Josh 24:1). Kingship is linked to Shechem in the failed reign of Abimelech in Judges 9, but beyond that Rehoboam is the only other king who seeks the crown at Shechem. Possibly its location in Ephraimite territory was attractive to a new king who could count on Judahite support or was, as Japhet assesses, "a telling sign either of weakness or of political ineptitude and probably of both" (1993:652).

The contender to the throne (Jeroboam), however, had returned from his exile in Egypt and led a contingent of "all Israel" to address Rehoboam at Shechem. The demand was clear: concessions in the areas of labor and taxes in return for loyalty. Evidence for such expectation at the outset of the reign of a king has been culled from the records of ancient Near Eastern kings.[1] The decision is put off for three days, a move that raises inordinate expectations of a positive answer among the people (see Japhet 1993:653) while suggesting that wisdom does not reside within this new king as it did with his father, Solomon. Rehoboam discussed the matter with both the "older men" as well as the "young men"; the former had counseled his father while the latter "had grown up with him." Although these two groups have been identified with official groups in the royal court (see note on 10:8), the wisdom tone of the terminology and its purpose to contrast Rehoboam and his father should not be missed.[2] The older men counseled the young king to give in to their demands, while the young men counseled a strict reaction. Rehoboam's response is well-known: He foolishly followed the advice of his contemporaries, revealing the stark contrast between himself and his wise father. Not only did the immature king reject their request, but he added insult to injury by promising even more severe conditions.

This prompted the rejection of the Davidic dynasty by "all Israel," here a reference to the northern tribes, since 10:17 reminds the reader that Rehoboam continued to rule over the tribe of Judah. The poem (10:16) that is proclaimed expresses their disgust not only with Rehoboam but with the entire dynasty of David (cf. 1 Sam 25:10; 2 Sam 20:1), a striking contrast to the poem recited by Amasai, leader of the Thirty, in 1 Chronicles 12:18. The contrasting parallelism ("Back to your homes, O Israel! Look out for your own house, O David!") encourages the northern tribes to direct their interests to their own families and tribes, rather than to royal interests, while telling Rehoboam to limit himself to his own tribe. Northern disgust is also expressed in their killing of Rehoboam's taskmaster Adoniram, an action that confirms "that the task is now over, a symbolic act of liberation" (Japhet 1993:658). This rebellion strikes fear in Rehoboam, who flees from Shechem back to his base in Jerusalem. The note in 10:19 reminds the reader of the enduring consequences of this event for the northern tribes, who refused to be ruled by a Davidic king.[3]

Rehoboam's flight to Jerusalem, however, was not the end of the matter. Setting out to restore the northern territories to his kingdom, the young king was encountered by a prophetic figure. Shemaiah, the man of God, prohibited Rehoboam from attacking because "what has happened is [God's] doing" (11:4). Shemaiah's name appears three more times in the Chronicler's account of Rehoboam (12:5, 7, 15), all of these occurrences unique to the Chronicler. This encounter with Shemaiah foreshadows the more positive tone of the Chronicler's presentation of Rehoboam in comparison to his source in Kings (cf. Knoppers 1990:423-440). In 11:2-4, as well as in 11:17; 12:5, 7, he is portrayed as one obedient to God and his prophetic word.

In 11:3 the Chronicler introduces a slight change to his source. Instead of God addressing "all the people of Judah and Benjamin" (1 Kgs 12:23), he addresses "all the Israelites in Judah and Benjamin." This bolsters the identity of the southern tribes (Judah, Benjamin) as the faithful kingdom that preserved the tradition of "all Israel," a trend that will be evident in the rest of the Chronicler's account in which the history of the northern kingdom is largely ignored. This, however, should not be interpreted as an agenda by the Chronicler to reject the northern tribes, who are still considered a legitimate part of the covenant people, even if the idea of a separate kingdom is deemed inappropriate.

Although the later speech of Abijah will lay the blame squarely on the shoulders of Jeroboam and his worthless scoundrels who took advantage of the young, indecisive, and weak Rehoboam (13:6-7), Shemaiah's message to Rehoboam in 11:4 reveals that the schism was still considered God's will. Throntveit (1987:113-120) argues that the north was indeed justified in not following Rehoboam, but that under Abijah's godly rule they should have returned (see ch 13). Even the second phase of Rehoboam's rule (11:5-23) provided conditions ripe for the return of these northerners, and the Chronicler stresses that many faithful priests, Levites, and people did return (11:13-17).

ENDNOTES

1. See Dillard 1987:86. An example from the Persian period can be drawn from the period between the Persian emperors Cambyses and Darius. In March 522 the magus Bardiya/Gaumata (Pseudo-Smerdis) enticed the central part of the Persian Empire to pay homage to him with a promise of relaxed tax policy (cf. Boda 2004).
2. As Japhet (1993:650) notes, the "principal narrative . . . is a wisdom story."
3. The Chronicler omits the invitation by the northern assembly to Jeroboam in 1 Kgs 12:20 from his account, a verse that is often seen in tension with Jeroboam's involvement in the revolt in 1 Kgs 12:2-3. It is possible, however, that this is left out to avoid any evidence of a non-Davidide coronation in Israel.

◆ B. Rehoboam's Period of Success (11:5-23)

[5]Rehoboam remained in Jerusalem and fortified various towns for the defense of Judah. [6]He built up Bethlehem, Etam, Tekoa, [7]Beth-zur, Soco, Adullam, [8]Gath, Mareshah, Ziph, [9]Adoraim, Lachish, Azekah, [10]Zorah, Aijalon, and Hebron. These became the fortified towns of Judah and Benjamin. [11]Rehoboam strengthened their defenses and stationed commanders in them, and he stored supplies of food, olive oil, and wine. [12]He also put shields and spears in these towns as a further safety measure. So only Judah and Benjamin remained under his control.

[13]But all the priests and Levites living among the northern tribes of Israel sided with Rehoboam. [14]The Levites even abandoned their pasturelands and property and moved to Judah and Jerusalem, because Jeroboam and his sons would not allow them to serve the LORD as priests. [15]Jeroboam appointed his own priests to serve at the pagan shrines, where they worshiped the goat and calf idols he had made. [16]From all the tribes of Israel, those who sincerely wanted to worship the LORD, the God of Israel, followed the Levites to Jerusalem, where they could offer sacrifices to the LORD, the God of their ancestors. [17]This strengthened the kingdom of Judah, and for three years they supported Rehoboam son of Solomon, for during those years they faithfully followed in the footsteps of David and Solomon.

[18]Rehoboam married his cousin Mahalath, the daughter of David's son Jerimoth and of Abihail, the daughter of Eliab son of Jesse. [19]Mahalath had three sons—Jeush, Shemariah, and Zaham.

[20]Later Rehoboam married another cousin, Maacah, the daughter of Absalom. Maacah gave birth to Abijah, Attai, Ziza, and Shelomith. [21]Rehoboam loved Maacah more than any of his other wives and concubines. In all, he had eighteen wives and sixty concubines, and they gave birth to twenty-eight sons and sixty daughters.

[22]Rehoboam appointed Maacah's son Abijah as leader among the princes, making it clear that he would be the next king. [23]Rehoboam also wisely gave responsibilities to his other sons and stationed some of them in the fortified towns throughout the land of Judah and Benjamin. He provided them with generous provisions, and he found many wives for them.

NOTES

11:14 ***their pasturelands and property.*** For a review of these, see the extensive lists in 1 Chr 6:54-81. All Israel was responsible to give key towns to the clans of Levi.

COMMENTARY

At this point in his account the Chronicler takes leave of his source. Throughout his account the focus will be on the southern kingdom, and events about the northern kingdom will only be drawn in as they are necessary to explain developments in the south. Thus, Jeroboam's activities in 1 Kings 13:1-34; 14:1-20 are all ignored, and in their place the Chronicler either includes incidents not mentioned in Kings (11:5-12, 18-23) or expands on incidents from Kings (11:13-17; 12:1-12). This contrast between the accounts in Kings and Chronicles is highlighted in the way the Chronicler shapes his new material on Rehoboam in chapter 11 by following the structure of the account of Jeroboam in Kings, a technique that Japhet has called "literary counterpoint" (1993:663):

THEME	JEROBOAM (1 KGS 12–14)	REHOBOAM (2 CHR 11)
Building projects	12:25	11:5-12
Religious reforms	12:26–13:34	11:13-17
Wives and children	14:1-18	11:18-23

In these two chapters the Chronicler's historiography of immediate retribution comes through clearly (see introduction to chs 10–36). The successes of 11:5-23 are linked to the fact that "during those years they faithfully followed in the footsteps of David and Solomon" (11:17), the failure of 12:1-11 to the fact that Rehoboam "abandoned the Law of the LORD, and all Israel followed him in this sin" (12:1), and the renewal of 12:10-13 to the fact that he humbled himself (12:12).

The initial period of success is characterized by Rehoboam's fortification of the defenses of his kingdom (11:5-12), a process that entailed strengthening their defense structures, deploying defense personnel, and providing food reserves and weaponry. The cities mentioned in the list of 11:6-10 suggest a territory restricted to the Judean hill country and the Shephelah (foothills to the west), with only one mention of the Coastal Plain (far west) and no mention of the Negev and Gulf of Aqabah (south). Bethlehem, Etam, and Tekoa formed a power block in the northern part of the Judean hill country and Beth-zur, Hebron, Ziph, and Adoraim in the southern part. These cities either defended the key north–south ridge road that ran to Jerusalem or access to it (Dillard 1987:96). The cities of (north–south) Aijalon, Zorah, Azekah, Socoh, Adullam, Mareshah, and Lachish formed a defense line protecting the five valleys that led from the coastal plain through the Shephelah to the hill country.[1] Gath is the lone city mentioned on the coastal plain, further inland from the lucrative trade route (Great Trunk Road) that ran through Ashdod and Gaza.[2]

The end of the chapter (11:18-23) also depicts a key sign of success: abundant progeny to rule the kingdom and carry on the dynasty. Although Rehoboam had 18 wives and 60 concubines, producing 28 sons and 60 daughters, only two of these wives are mentioned by name: Mahalath and Maacah. Both were his cousins, attesting to the careful attention to bloodlines already developing in the royal house of David. Interestingly, it is not the son of the first wife who is chosen for dynastic succession. Rather, it is the firstborn of the favored second wife, Maacah. There is some debate over the name and lineage of this wife. The dominant tradition names her as the daughter of Absalom (11:20; 1 Kgs 15:2, 10) with a secondary tradition identifying her as the daughter of Uriel of Gibeah (13:2; see the parallel in 1 Kgs 15:2). Complicating matters are the notes that Maacah was the mother of Asa (15:16; 1 Kgs 15:10, 13), that Absalom son of David had only one surviving child (a daughter named Tamar; 2 Sam 14:27; 18:18), and that Abijah (Abijam) was the father of Asa (14:1; 1 Kgs 15:8). Because of the use of the Hebrew terms for father/mother and son/daughter to define relationships between one or more generations (e.g., father, grandfather, great-grandfather), these anomalies can be solved with the theory that Maacah the second wife of Rehoboam was the granddaughter of Absalom through his daughter's marriage to Uriel of Gibeah, the mother of Abijah (Abijam), and the grandmother of Asa. Rehoboam's wisdom is seen in his vigilance to secure a smooth transition to the next generation by "making it clear" who "would be the next king" (11:22),[3] while also caring for the other sons (11:23).

Between these two sections is placed the key to this success (11:13-17). Rather than connecting the success directly to Rehoboam, the Chronicler links it to both the infusion of priests and Levites from the north who had been rejected by Jeroboam's new cult at Bethel and Dan (1 Kgs 12:25-33), as well as to the people from all the northern tribes who "sincerely wanted to worship the LORD, the God of Israel," here using terminology typical of the Chronicler (*baqash* [TH1245, ZH1335], "to seek"; NLT, "to worship"). Not surprisingly, the Chronicler highlights the faithfulness of the sacred personnel, who have played a significant role in his narrative to this point, as well as to the impact that such faithfulness could have on the people as a whole. The standard of faithfulness continues to be David and Solomon, an allusion to the portrait of these kings in 1 Chronicles 10—2 Chronicles 9. The role also that northern Israelites play in this scene is a careful reminder that members of these tribes still had a role to play in the remnant of Israel, even if it suggests a wariness about worship practices in the northern territories, possibly even in the Chronicler's day. In this the Chronicler shows that the values of David and Solomon can endure through the orders they sponsored (priests and Levites) and the community they created, even without the royal house.

At the same time the Chronicler attacks the apostasy of Jeroboam in the north, enhancing his account by citing the use of "goat" idols (cf. Lev 17:7) and noting the rejection of priests. The use of theriomorphic idols in Jeroboam's cult is most likely evidence of Egyptian influence on Jeroboam while in exile.[4] These actions of Jeroboam (more details of which can be found in 1 Kgs 12:25-33) were important for his political survival. Religion and state could not be separated, and the festal rhythms of Israel ensured that the people were constantly returning to Jerusalem both to worship God and also to show loyalty to the king (Ps 122:3-5). Jeroboam's establishment of cult centers in the south (Bethel) and north (Dan) ensured easy access for his people and rendered unnecessary travel to the former capital in Jerusalem. The rejection of the priests and Levites confirms the picture of Davidic sponsorship of these orders in his regime. The connection of these orders to the royal house had a political dimension.

ENDNOTES

1. The cities protected the following valleys (in parentheses): Aijalon (Aijalon); Zorah (Soreq); Azekah, Socoh, and Adullam (Elah); Mareshah (Guvrin); and Lachish (Lachish).
2. Some have suggested that this is a reference to Moresheth-gath near Mareshah (Dillard 1987:97; Japhet 1993:667).
3. For similar preparations by David, see 1 Kgs 1:13, and by Jehoshaphat, see 21:2-4.
4. Interestingly, theriomorphic idolatry is also linked to the period after the exodus from Egypt (Exod 32); Dillard 1987:98; see Oswalt 1973:13-20.

◆ C. Rehoboam's Rebellion and Repentance (12:1-16)

But when Rehoboam was firmly estab-
lished and strong, he abandoned the Law
of the LORD, and all Israel followed him in
this sin. [2]Because they were unfaithful to
the LORD, King Shishak of Egypt came up
and attacked Jerusalem in the fifth year of
King Rehoboam's reign. [3]He came with
1,200 chariots, 60,000 horses,* and a
countless army of foot soldiers, including
Libyans, Sukkites, and Ethiopians.* [4]Shishak
conquered Judah's fortified towns and
then advanced to attack Jerusalem.

[5]The prophet Shemaiah then met with
Rehoboam and Judah's leaders, who had
all fled to Jerusalem because of Shishak.
Shemaiah told them, "This is what the
LORD says: You have abandoned me, so I
am abandoning you to Shishak."

[6]Then the leaders of Israel and the king
humbled themselves and said, "The LORD
is right in doing this to us!"

[7]When the LORD saw their change of
heart, he gave this message to Shemaiah:
"Since the people have humbled themselves,
I will not completely destroy them and will
soon give them some relief. I will not use
Shishak to pour out my anger on Jerusalem.
[8]But they will become his subjects, so they
will know the difference between serving
me and serving earthly rulers."

[9]So King Shishak of Egypt came up and
attacked Jerusalem. He ransacked the
treasuries of the LORD's Temple and the
royal palace; he stole everything, includ-
ing all the gold shields Solomon had
made. [10]King Rehoboam later replaced
them with bronze shields as substitutes,
and he entrusted them to the care of the
commanders of the guard who protected
the entrance to the royal palace. [11]When-
ever the king went to the Temple of the
LORD, the guards would also take the
shields and then return them to the
guardroom. [12]Because Rehoboam hum-
bled himself, the LORD's anger was turned
away, and he did not destroy him com-
pletely. There were still some good things
in the land of Judah.

[13]King Rehoboam firmly established
himself in Jerusalem and continued to
rule. He was forty-one years old when
he became king, and he reigned seven-
teen years in Jerusalem, the city the
LORD had chosen from among all the
tribes of Israel as the place to honor his
name. Rehoboam's mother was Naamah,

a woman from Ammon. 14But he was an
evil king, for he did not seek the LORD
with all his heart.
15The rest of the events of Rehoboam's
reign, from beginning to end, are recorded
in *The Record of Shemaiah the Prophet* and
The Record of Iddo the Seer, which are part
of the genealogical record. Rehoboam and
Jeroboam were continually at war with
each other. 16When Rehoboam died, he
was buried in the City of David. Then his
son Abijah became the next king.

12:3a Or *charioteers*, or *horsemen*. 12:3b Hebrew *and Cushites*.

NOTES

12:2-3 *King Shishak of Egypt . . . Libyans, Sukkites, and Ethiopians.* Shishak, founder of the 22nd Dynasty, was from the Libyan tribe of Meshwesh and rose to power as the commander-in-chief of the Egyptian army. The mention of these other African people groups in the Egyptian political sphere fits the rule of Shishak. The use of the term "Sukkites" here attests to the antiquity of the sources accessed by the Chronicler. This Libyan people group is known from Egyptian records from the thirteenth and twelfth centuries BC (Dillard 1987:100; Japhet 1993:677; Kitchen 1973:295; ABD 5.1221-1222).

COMMENTARY

The Chronicler notes that the faithfulness of the priests, Levites, and people strengthened and supported Rehoboam's kingdom so that he became "firmly established and strong" (12:1).[1] Unfortunately, it is the successes of "strength" (11:11-12, 17; cf. 12:13) that ultimately led to Rehoboam's downfall (cf. Japhet 1993:676). The Chronicler reports that after three years of following the Lord (11:17), the king "abandoned" (*'azab* [TH5800, ZH6440]; 12:1) the law (see also 12:5) and led "all Israel" (12:1) away with him in this act of unfaithfulness (*ma'al* [TH4603, ZH5085]; 12:2). The Chronicler did not reveal the precise nature of their sin, but 1 Kings 14:21-24 lists false worship, which included the installation of high places, pillars, Asherim, and male and female cult prostitutes.

As expected, according to the Chronicler's view of immediate retribution (see introduction to chs 10–36), a mighty Egyptian army arose against Jerusalem. Such an attack is not surprising in light of the recent return of the rival northern king Jeroboam from Egyptian exile, a move that shifted the geopolitics of the region and placed Rehoboam and Judah between two nations (Egypt, Israel) with some form of relationship (whether informal or formal is not known).[2] The Chronicler expanded his source in 1 Kings 14:25-28 considerably, providing details not only on the size and diversity of the force that Shishak king of Egypt raised against Judah (12:3) but also on the progress of the campaign that wiped out Rehoboam's earlier preparations (12:4; see 11:5-12). Evidence for this campaign is recorded on the walls of an Egyptian temple at Karnak. Shishak, who ruled 931–910 BC, lists 150 towns that were taken, with no mention of Jerusalem. This suggests that Rehoboam provided tribute to Shishak to avert the destruction of his capital.[3]

With Shishak's army at the walls of Jerusalem, the prophet Shemaiah delivered a message from God to Rehoboam and his leaders. The inclusion of the "leaders" is key in the Chronicler's account, which consistently emphasizes the community alongside the monarch (Japhet 1993:679). At the beginning of chapter 11, this same prophetic figure had effectively changed the course of Rehoboam's reign, suggesting that he held some credibility with the king. The message of God begins as a simple declaration of

Rehoboam's Reign in Judah, 931–913 BC

judgment in vocabulary that is typical of the Chronicler: "You have abandoned me, so I am abandoning you to Shishak" (12:5). The response of leaders and king is an example of the Chronicler's program laid out in 7:13-15: They humbled themselves (*kana'* [TH3665, ZH4044]) and declared, "The LORD is right in doing this to us!" (12:6). Such a declaration is an admission of one's guilt, typical of the tradition of penitential prayer that came to prominence in the liturgical rhythms of Israel after the fall of Jerusalem (Ezra 9:15; Neh 9:33; Zech 1:6; see Boda 1999; 2003d:49-69). God recognized this humility[4] and offered a message of muted hope: He promised not to destroy them completely ("to pour out my anger on Jerusalem"), but he did say that they will serve Shishak "so they will know the difference between serving me and serving earthly rulers" (12:8). Indeed, Shishak did attack Jerusalem and despoiled the Temple and palace, stealing "everything" (12:9). This statement about the role of foreign kingdoms is programmatic for the Chronicler; it suggests that although his narrative will end with foreign kings used as Yahweh's instruments (see introduction to chs 10–36), these are temporary measures with didactic purposes (see Boda 2009b).

Japhet (1993:678-680) and Lowery (1991:70) have both noted the striking similarities between the Chronicler's accounts of Rehoboam and Hezekiah, a connection prompted by links already established in his source text in Kings (cf. 1 Kgs 14:25 with 2 Kgs 18:13). Both Rehoboam and Hezekiah displayed arrogance followed by humility (12:1, 6-7; 32:24-25); Yahweh's wrath against them was mitigated as treasures were taken but Jerusalem saved. Both of the prophets (Shemaiah, Isaiah) who addressed these kings spoke of repentance.[5] However, the Chronicler accentuated the crisis that Rehoboam faced, adding to his source that the foreign king took the fortified cities (cf. 12:4 with 1 Kgs 14:25), while minimizing the foreign threat to the fortified cities in the case of Hezekiah (cf. 32:1 with 2 Kgs 18:13). Both Rehoboam and Hezekiah are examples of the Chronicler's historical agenda, but Hezekiah is held in higher esteem.

Although considered an "evil king" (12:14) by the Chronicler, even Rehoboam could be used as an example for the Chronicler's historical project. His humility "turned away" the anger of the Lord so that not all was lost, leaving "some good things in the land of Judah" (12:12).

Summary Note: The Reign of Rehoboam (12:13b-16). Drawing from his source in 1 Kings 14:21-22, the Chronicler ended his account of Rehoboam with the citation of the age of the king at coronation, the length of his rule, and the name of his mother. He is evaluated in the end as "an evil king" because he did not exemplify the core values of the Chronicler—that is, seeking (*darash* [TH1875, ZH2011]) the Lord with all his heart, or as the Hebrew reads, "setting his heart to seek the LORD." As with David and Solomon, again the Chronicler makes note of the records of prophetic figures, this time Shemaiah the prophet and Iddo the seer. This use of prophetic sources for Rehoboam (as for David and Solomon) lends increased credibility to the Chronicler's account, as well as to Rehoboam's reign (see commentary on 1 Chr 29:29-30). This notation also reminds the reader that the kingdom has now been transferred to another Davidic scion.

To his Persian-period audience, this story would have had heightened relevance. On the one hand, it encouraged repentance; on the other hand, it explained the purpose behind the despoiling and domination they had experienced by foreign rulers. The prophet's statement revealed that foreign domination was not an eternal condition but has didactic purposes to teach Israel the advantage of serving their gracious God.

ENDNOTES

1. Japhet (1993:676) notes that the first verse uses characteristic Chronistic style, not only the roots *kun* [TH3559, ZH3922] (firmly established) and *khazaq* [TH2388, ZH2616] (strong), but also "the preposition *k-* [TH3509.1, ZH3869] in this specific function, its conjunction with the infinitive to signify an indefinite temporal clause, and the placement of this temporal clause at the beginning of the sentence."
2. Notice how Shishak also harbored the Edomite Hadad in his court (1 Kgs 11:19; cf. ABD 5.1221-1222).
3. See ANET 242-243, 263-264; ANEP 349; see further Dillard 1987:99-100; Kitchen 1973:294-300, 432-477. Japhet (1993:674-675) notes that "the Chronistic version also presents some new historical details (all found in 12:3) which conform to our knowledge of the period, and pass the test of historical probability," suggesting to her that "the Chronicler may have used an additional source." Interestingly, Shishak only mentions Aijalon from the list of Rehoboam's fortifications in 11:5-12, suggesting that Rehoboam's preparations held firm and that he decided to pay tribute rather than lose his fortifications. Because the focus of Shishak's campaign was against the Negev and the northern kingdom, it may be that Jeroboam was the reason for the Egyptian campaign, possibly for not paying his tribute, and that Rehoboam was caught in the fray.
4. The phrase "their change of heart" (12:7a) is a translation for the same term *kana'* [TH3665, ZH4044] (humble themselves) found in 12:6 and 12:7b.
5. The Chronicler has used the description of Sennacherib's invasion from 2 Kgs 18:13, 17 for his description of Shishak's invasion (12:4; "Shishak conquered Judah's fortified towns and then advanced to attack Jerusalem"; cf. 1 Kgs 14:25) and tempered it for Hezekiah (32:1). So Japhet (1993:678-679) concludes, "Thus the Chronicler has formulated the story of Shishak's campaign in analogy to Sennacherib's invasion in II Kings 18–19, even though his own version of the latter takes a much shorter form (cf. II Chron. 32.9-21)."

◆ D. Abijah's Reign (13:1–14:1a)

Abijah began to rule over Judah in the eighteenth year of Jeroboam's reign in Israel. [2]He reigned in Jerusalem three years. His mother was Maacah,* the daughter of Uriel from Gibeah.

Then war broke out between Abijah and Jeroboam. [3]Judah, led by King Abijah, fielded 400,000 select warriors, while Jeroboam mustered 800,000 select troops from Israel.

[4]When the army of Judah arrived in the hill country of Ephraim, Abijah stood on Mount Zemaraim and shouted to Jeroboam and all Israel: "Listen to me! [5]Don't you realize that the LORD, the God of Israel, made a lasting covenant* with David, giving him and his descendants the throne of Israel forever? [6]Yet Jeroboam son of Nebat, a mere servant of David's son Solomon, rebelled against his master. [7]Then a whole gang of scoundrels joined him, defying Solomon's son Rehoboam when he was young and inexperienced and could not stand up to them.

[8]"Do you really think you can stand against the kingdom of the LORD that is led by the descendants of David? You may have a vast army, and you have those gold calves that Jeroboam made as your gods. [9]But you have chased away the priests of the LORD (the descendants of Aaron) and the Levites, and you have appointed your own priests, just like the pagan nations. You let anyone become a priest these days! Whoever comes to be dedicated with a young bull and seven rams can become a priest of these so-called gods of yours!

[10]"But as for us, the LORD is our God, and we have not abandoned him. Only the descendants of Aaron serve the LORD as priests, and the Levites alone may help them in their work. [11]They present burnt offerings and fragrant incense to the LORD every morning and evening. They place the Bread of the Presence on the holy table, and they light the gold lampstand every evening. We are following the instructions of the LORD our God, but you have abandoned him. [12]So you see, God is with us. He is our leader. His priests blow their trumpets and lead us into battle against you. O people of Israel, do not fight against the LORD, the God of your ancestors, for you will not succeed!"

[13]Meanwhile, Jeroboam had secretly sent part of his army around behind the men of Judah to ambush them. [14]When Judah realized that they were being attacked from the front and the rear, they cried out to the LORD for help. Then the priests blew the trumpets, [15]and the men of Judah began to shout. At the sound of their battle cry, God defeated Jeroboam and all Israel and routed them before Abijah and the army of Judah.

[16]The Israelite army fled from Judah, and God handed them over to Judah in defeat. [17]Abijah and his army inflicted heavy losses on them; 500,000 of Israel's select troops were killed that day. [18]So Judah defeated Israel on that occasion because they trusted in the LORD, the God of their ancestors. [19]Abijah and his army pursued Jeroboam's troops and captured some of his towns, including Bethel, Jeshanah, and Ephron, along with their surrounding villages.

[20]So Jeroboam of Israel never regained his power during Abijah's lifetime, and finally the LORD struck him down and he died. [21]Meanwhile, Abijah of Judah grew more and more powerful. He married fourteen wives and had twenty-two sons and sixteen daughters.

[22]The rest of the events of Abijah's reign, including his words and deeds, are recorded in *The Commentary of Iddo the Prophet.*

CHAPTER 14

[1]*When Abijah died, he was buried in the City of David.

13:2 As in most Greek manuscripts and Syriac version (see also 2 Chr 11:20-21; 1 Kgs 15:2); Hebrew reads *Micaiah,* a variant spelling of Maacah. **13:5** Hebrew *a covenant of salt.* **14:1** Verse 14:1 is numbered 13:23 in Hebrew text.

NOTES

13:1 ***Abijah.*** In Kings the name is given as Abijam. Possible reasons for this difference range from orthographic convention, to royal protocol (given name versus throne name), to religious purity (replacement of name of Canaanite god Yam, "Sea," with name of Yahweh), to narrative clarity (avoiding confusion with Abijah son of Jeroboam I in 1 Kgs 14:1). See Dillard 1987:101; Japhet 1993:684.

13:2 ***Maacah, the daughter of Uriel from Gibeah.*** See commentary on 11:5-23.

13:3 ***400,000 . . . 800,000.*** For the interpretation of large numbers such as these, see commentary on 1 Chr 12.

13:5 ***a lasting covenant.*** The NLT mg reads, "a covenant of salt," used also in Num 18:19 (see NLT mg; cf. Lev 2:13), possibly related to the preservative and purifying quality of salt and/or to the role of salt in meals related to covenant agreements (cf. Gen 26:30; 31:54; Ezra 4:14; TBD 327; NBD 1046).

13:8 ***you have those gold. calves.*** This is a reference to the bovine figures placed by Jeroboam at his two new shrines for his new kingdom at Dan in the north and Bethel in the south (1 Kgs 12:25-33). The language here suggests the figures accompanied the army, much like the Ark did in earlier times (cf. 1 Sam 4:1-22).

13:17 ***500,000.*** See commentary on 1 Chr 12.

13:19 ***Bethel, Jeshanah, and Ephron.*** Bethel was just over 10 miles north of Jerusalem and Jeshanah just over 15 miles north of Jerusalem. While Mount Ephron is sometimes placed just over 5 miles west of Jerusalem (cf. Josh 15:9), Ephron here may refer to Ophrah/Ephraim (ABD 2.556), which lay 4 miles northeast of Bethel and 15 miles north-northeast of Jerusalem. This would place all three of these sites in the same region. These sites were in the general area between Mount Zemaraim (2 miles east of Jeshanah) and Jerusalem, which would have fallen into the hands of Abijah with this victory. The loss of Bethel meant the loss of a key worship center of the northern kingdom (1 Kgs 12:25-33). The calf figure was returned at least by the time of Jehu (2 Kgs 10:29; Amos 7:13; cf. 2 Chr 16:1).

COMMENTARY

Summary Note: The Accession of Abijah (13:1-2a). The account of Abijah begins with a summary note drawn from 1 Kings 15:1-2.[1] Interestingly, the Chronicler leaves out 1 Kings 15:3-5 with its negative evaluation of Abijah (Abijam) in 1 Kings 15:3 and its emphasis on the intergenerational grace afforded to the Davidic line due to David's faithfulness in 1 Kings 15:4-5. In its place the Chronicler expands the account of Abijah's war against Jeroboam from one sentence in his source to a full narrative (13:3-21). The Chronicler thus promotes Abijah from a footnote in history in 1 Kings 15 to an exemplar of his theological program. As Japhet (1993:687) has so aptly written:

> *The overall history of Abijah in Chronicles leaves us with the distinct impression that while the reign of Rehoboam was just an unsuccessful digression, it was Abijah who was the true successor of Solomon. The Davidic 'kingship of the Lord', so emphasized in the histories of David and Solomon (1 Chr 17.14; 28.5; 29.11, etc., cf. von Rad, Geschichtsbild, 125-6), is introduced once more in the figure of Abijah (13:5). Even the proper service conducted in the Jerusalem Temple accords with the arrangements made by Solomon (compare 13:10-11 to 2 Chr 8.12ff).*

The Chronicler's expansion of the Abijah account is rather odd in light of Abijah's short tenure (13:2), which is usually a signal of God's curse on an illegitimate leader (see introduction to chs 10–36). This has led many to conclude that the Chronicler must be basing these expansions on a legitimate source that contained evidence of his historical agenda (Deboys 1990:48-62; Dillard 1987:105-106; Japhet 1993:688; Williamson 1982:250).

Battle between Abijah and Jeroboam (13:2b–19). That war broke out at the outset of Abijah's rule is not odd. What is surprising, however, is that Abijah took the initiative, a fact established by the evidence that the battle site was in Ephraimite territory[2] and that it was Abijah who "binds the battle."[3] Possibly this was an attempt to regain the northern kingdom (11:1-4), but in light of the numbers in 13:3, such a move appears to be nothing short of suicide for the new king. Such acts of apparent lunacy, however, are often interpreted as signs of faith in the Old Testament (cf. 1 Sam 17).

With the armies on location, the Chronicler describes a sermon preached by Abijah to the northern army and leader (13:4b-12).[4] It was observed long ago by Noth (1981:5-6, 80-81) and Plöger (1957), who drew on the foundational work of von Rad (1966a:267-280), that the historical books in the Old Testament regularly employ a type of text called the Levitical Sermon (cf. Boda 1999:6-7). Noth and Plöger traced examples of these sermons throughout Deuteronomy—2 Kings and especially the book of Chronicles. In the latter they noted how the Chronicler used every available opportunity to incorporate such speeches into the account and did so not only in the form of sermons, but also in the forms of letters, historical reviews, and even prayers. Throntveit (1987:74-75) provided further reflection, noting the striking similarities between the royal speeches and prayers in Chronicles (6:14-42; 14:11; 1 Chr 17:16-27; 29:10-19). Braun (1986:xxiv-xv) and Mason (1990:133-137, 257) explained the similarities between these various "speeches/prayers" as evidence of reliance on contemporary Persian-period forms, while Mathias (1984:23-49) discounted any reliance on contemporary forms. Von Rad (1966a) originally noted how these speeches often made an appeal to earlier biblical texts and reflected a tripartite structure that included doctrine, application, and exhortation.

Throntveit's work on the rhetorical function of these speeches within the larger work of the Chronicler is very helpful for reading Chronicles. For Throntveit (1987:74-75) these speeches and prayers highlight both the structural framework and the theological message of the Chronicler's work. Through Abijah's speech in chapter 13, the Chronicler offers insight into his view of the northern kingdom and Jeroboam's rule, which provide an opportunity for him to highlight the importance of the Jerusalem Temple, its personnel, and its services.

Abijah's speech begins and ends with an appeal to God's covenant and presence with the southern kingdom ruled by the Davidide (13:4b-5, 10-12). This covenant was made not only with David but also with "his descendants . . . forever," identifying Rehoboam as the only legitimate successor to Solomon and ruler of all Israel (Knoppers 1990). Furthermore, the southern kingdom had remained faithful to the legitimate sacred personnel (13:10a; priests and Levites) and services (13:10b-11; their work includes presenting burnt offerings and fragrant incense, placing the

Bread of the Presence, and lighting the gold lampstand). This is contrasted with the illegitimacy of Jeroboam's rule, which represented rebellion against the legitimate rule of the Davidic dynasty (13:6-8a). The family and social positions of Jeroboam (son of Nebat, servant) and Solomon (son of David, master) emphasize the contrast in legitimacy. Blame for the schism in the nation is laid at the feet of Jeroboam and his henchmen, who rebelled against an immature Rehoboam (see a similar description of Solomon in 1 Chr 22:5; 29:1).[5] The rhetorical question of 13:8a makes it clear that the kingdom is the Lord's (cf. 9:8; 1 Chr 17:14; 28:5; 29:11, 23) while also affirming the key role that the Davidic dynasty plays in leadership. Furthermore, the cult of the northern kingdom is also illegitimate with its use of golden calves, rejection of authorized priests and Levites, and appointment of illicit priests "just like the pagan nations" (13:8b-9).

The interlinking of the Davidic dynasty and Jerusalem Temple services is an important part of the Chronicler's message. Although the revitalization of the Davidic dynasty remained a distant hope in his generation, his generation could at least display faithfulness to the Jerusalem Temple, its services, and its personnel.

Although greater in potential according to human standards, the northern army was no match for the southern army, because its leadership and worship were illegitimate. The divine resources linked to the southern kingdom are articulated clearly in 13:12: God's presence, God's leadership, and thus God's battle.

The truth of Abijah's speech is demonstrated immediately as Jeroboam used clandestine methods to ensure military victory (13:13). As with others in the Old Testament who faced greater military forces, the legitimate force must cast themselves into the hands of a gracious God ("they cried out to the LORD for help," 13:14; "they trusted in the LORD," 13:18), who alone can bring victory ("God defeated . . . and routed them," 13:15; "God handed them over," 13:16). God is notably the active subject of the verbs in 13:15, while Abijah and the army of Judah are depicted in a passive posture observing the rout.[6] Only after the northern army was in flight did Abijah and his troops spring into action, which is depicted as a cleanup operation. Defeat at Mount Zemaraim leads to the fall of the southern region of Ephraim, typified by the capture of the towns of Jeshanah, Bethel, and Ephron.

Fate of Jeroboam and Abijah (13:20-21). The account ends with a note contrasting the fates of Jeroboam and Abijah. This battle signals a downturn in Jeroboam's reign, ending with his death at the hands of God. In contrast, from this point on Abijah's power continued to increase.[7] A sign of God's blessing on him is the number of wives (14) and children (22 sons, 16 daughters) he was given.

Summary Note: The Reign of Abijah (13:22–14:1a). The short summary note at the end of the account of Abijah offers similar information found at the end of the reigns of earlier Davidic kings. Reference is made to a prophetic work that contains other information about his reign, to his death and burial, and finally to the transfer of power to his son Asa. This use of prophetic sources for Abijah (as for David, Solomon, Rehoboam) again lends increased credibility to the Chronicler's account, as well as to Abijah's reign (see commentary on 1 Chr 29:29-30). This notation also reminds the reader that the kingdom had been transferred to another Davidic scion: Asa, son of Abijah. The Chronicler employs subtle rhetoric to minimize the fact that

Jeroboam outlived Abijah. He does not cite the year of Asa's accession to the throne in 14:1-2 (cf. 1 Kgs 15:9) and merely states that Jeroboam did not recover during Abijah's time and that he then died (13:20), not noting that this death was actually after Abijah's, which is recorded in 14:1.

ENDNOTES

1. This is the only time the Chronicler includes a reference to the reign of a northern king in an accession note (Dillard 1987:106).
2. This was Mount Zemaraim, 10 miles north of Jerusalem on the northern border of Benjamin (Josh 18:22), then considered within the hill country of Ephraim (13:4).
3. Heb., *wayye'sor 'abiyyah 'et-hammilkhamah* [TH631/4421, ZH673/4878]; NLT, "Judah, led by King Abijah, fielded."
4. On the sermons that are found throughout Chronicles, see Boda 2005a:806-811 and literature cited there.
5. It is also possible that the antecedent of the "him" in 13:7 is the "master" (that is, Rehoboam) of 13:6; as Williamson thinks (1982:252-253). This would shift some blame onto the young advisers of Rehoboam but still leave Rehoboam and Solomon guiltless.
6. The elements in this battle account are linked by Dillard (1987:119) to the concept of holy war in ancient Israel, which is employed commonly in Chronicles and includes reference to insurmountable odds (13:3; 14:8-9; 20:2; cf. Deut 20:1), a prebattle speech/prayer (13:5-11; 14:11; 20:5-17; cf. Deut 20:2-4), Yahweh as active warrior with Israel's army as passive (13:15-16; 14:12-13; 20:22-24; cf. Deut 20:4), and the fear of Yahweh falling on the enemy (14:14; cf. Exod 23:28; Deut 7:20, 23).
7. See the claim of Asa (16:3; cf. 1 Kgs 15:19) that Abijah made a treaty with Aram, a wise move that would have provided safety from any further attack from Jeroboam (Dillard 1987:109).

◆ E. Asa's Reign (14:1b–16:14)

1. Asa's early years (14:1b-15)

Then his son Asa became the next king. There was peace in the land for ten years.
2*Asa did what was pleasing and good in the sight of the LORD his God. 3He removed the foreign altars and the pagan shrines. He smashed the sacred pillars and cut down the Asherah poles. 4He commanded the people of Judah to seek the LORD, the God of their ancestors, and to obey his law and his commands. 5Asa also removed the pagan shrines, as well as the incense altars from every one of Judah's towns. So Asa's kingdom enjoyed a period of peace. 6During those peaceful years, he was able to build up the fortified towns throughout Judah. No one tried to make war against him at this time, for the LORD was giving him rest from his enemies.

7Asa told the people of Judah, "Let us build towns and fortify them with walls, towers, gates, and bars. The land is still ours because we sought the LORD our God, and he has given us peace on every side." So they went ahead with these projects and brought them to completion.

8King Asa had an army of 300,000 warriors from the tribe of Judah, armed with large shields and spears. He also had an army of 280,000 warriors from the tribe of Benjamin, armed with small shields and bows. Both armies were composed of well-trained fighting men.

9Once an Ethiopian* named Zerah attacked Judah with an army of 1,000,000 men* and 300 chariots. They advanced to the town of Mareshah, 10so Asa deployed his armies for battle in the valley north of Mareshah.* [11]Then Asa cried out to the LORD his God, "O LORD, no one but you can help the powerless against the mighty! Help us, O LORD our God, for we trust in you alone. It is in your name that we have come against this vast horde. O LORD, you are our God; do not let mere men prevail against you!"

[12]So the LORD defeated the Ethiopians* in the presence of Asa and the army of Judah, and the enemy fled. [13]Asa and his army pursued them as far as Gerar, and so many Ethiopians fell that they were unable to rally. They were destroyed by the LORD and his army, and the army of Judah carried off a vast amount of plunder.

[14]While they were at Gerar, they attacked all the towns in that area, and terror from the LORD came upon the people there. As a result, a vast amount of plunder was taken from these towns, too. [15]They also attacked the camps of herdsmen and captured many sheep, goats, and camels before finally returning to Jerusalem.

14:2 Verses 14:2-15 are numbered 14:1-14 in Hebrew text. **14:9a** Hebrew *a Cushite.* **14:9b** Or *an army of thousands and thousands;* Hebrew reads *an army of a thousand thousands.* **14:10** Or *in the Zephathah Valley near Mareshah.* **14:12** Hebrew *Cushites;* also in 14:13.

NOTES

14:3 [2] ***sacred pillars . . . Asherah poles.*** See notes on 17:6 and 31:1.

14:8 [7] ***300,000 warriors . . . 280,000 warriors.*** See commentary on 1 Chr 12:23-40.

14:9 [8] ***an army of 1,000,000 men and 300 chariots.*** On these high numbers, see commentary on 1 Chr 12:23-40.

14:13 [12] ***the LORD and his army.*** The army in view here is most likely that of God's heavenly army, which secured victory for the "army of Judah," enabling them to carry off the plunder.

COMMENTARY

A comparison of the account of Asa in Kings with the account in Chronicles highlights the historiographic purposes of the Chronicler. The book of Kings presents Asa as a king who "did what was pleasing in the LORD's sight, as his ancestor David had done" and who enjoyed a long reign of 41 years (1 Kgs 15:10-11). At the same time, however, the account records that the king constantly faced war against the northern kingdom, entered into an agreement with the Aramean Ben-hadad (1 Kgs 15:6-22), and was afflicted with a foot disease (1 Kgs 15:23). To explain these negative elements, the Chronicler expanded his account and introduced a carefully articulated chronological framework. This framework, which validates the Chronicler's retribution, describes a land at peace for the first decade (14:1), a covenant renewal in the 15th year (15:10-12), and no war until the 35th year (15:19). Only in chapter 16 does the Chronicler finally introduce the negative elements in Asa's reign, a turn precipitated by the conflict with Baasha, which began in Asa's 36th year. As Dillard (1987:123) concludes, "The Chronicler has reshaped the account he found in Kings by elaborating and reinforcing the divine favor enjoyed by an obedient king and by making explicit the nature of the transgressions that led to his disease and death."

Summary Note: The Accession of Asa (14:1b-2). The summary note in 14:1 stands in contrast to most of the other summary notes throughout the accounts of the kings of the divided kingdom in that it provides very little information on the rise of Asa. Missing is a reference to the length of his reign and the name of his queen mother, the latter only missing elsewhere in the Chronicler's narrative for Ahaz at 28:1. These contrasts are not innovations by the Chronicler but were found in his source in Kings. The Chronicler evaluates Asa positively by noting that he did what was "pleasing and good in the sight of the LORD his God" (14:2). However, he left out the allusion to "his ancestor David," which is found in his source at 1 Kings 15:11.

Asa's Early Years of Peace: Religious Reforms (14:3-7). The Chronicler reveals his view of the chronology of Asa's reign in his account of Jehoshaphat, where he speaks of "his father's early years" as a period of religious reform (17:3). The tone of the first phase of the Chronicler's account of Asa is set by the references in 14:1b [13:23] and 14:5-7 [4-6] to "peace" and "rest" (*shaqat* [TH8252, ZH9200] and *nuakh* [TH5117, ZH5663]), conditions that make possible the fortification of the kingdom (*banah* [TH1129, ZH1215]; 14:6-7 [5-6]) and prosperity (*tsalakh* [TH6743A, ZH7503]; NLT, "brought them to completion"). In the Chronicler's work these are signs of God's blessing on the faithful (see introduction to chs 10–36), so it is not surprising that this section also contains many details of Asa's obedience to God.

Vocabulary key to the Chronicler's program is evident throughout this depiction, especially the term "seek" (*darash* [TH1875, ZH2011]), which features in Asa's command to the people in 14:4 [3] and his review of the cause of peace in 14:7 [6]. Seeking God in this context is equated with "doing" (*'asah* [TH6213, ZH6913]; NLT, "obey") his law and commands. The specific actions of Asa's renewal in 14:3-5 (removal of foreign altars, pagan shrines, sacred pillars, Asherah poles, incense altars) are slightly different from those provided in 1 Kings 15:12 (removal of male and female cult prostitutes and idols), but these depictions are not in tension with one another.[1] Nevertheless, the Chronicler's list focuses both on the expulsion of foreign influences, as well as the eradication of worship centers outside of Jerusalem (14:5, "from every one of Judah's towns"). Additionally, the Chronicler removes the references to "idols his ancestors had made" from his source in 1 Kings 15:12 in order to minimize coverage of the disobedience of the Davidic line.

Asa's Early Years of War: Military Accomplishments (14:8-15). Asa's fortification efforts during the time of peace and prosperity foreshadow the challenges he would soon face. The next section begins with a note describing Asa's military resources drawn nearly equally from the two southern tribes: Judah and Benjamin. Judah is given the dominant place with more warriors and larger military equipment. This note prepares the way for the account of a great battle between Asa's army and that of the Ethiopian Zerah. This army not only was 50 percent larger but boasted the more advanced military equipment of chariotry. The battle site of Mareshah, guarding one of the five key valleys (the Guvrin) that linked the coastal plain with the hill country of Judah, is fitting for a force advancing from Africa along the Great Trunk Road (see commentary on 11:5-23).

While the Chronicler depicts Asa's father Abijah as a preacher scolding the northern army in the previous chapter (13:4-12), in this chapter Asa is presented as a mighty prayer warrior, crying to the Lord. This prayer follows the basic structure of "sermon/prayer" common throughout Chronicles: doctrine, application, exhortation (see commentary on 13:2b-19). Fundamental to Asa's prayer is his belief that the Lord God alone is the one who helps the powerless before the mighty. This assumes a belief not only in God's omnipotence but also his grace to assist the powerless. This belief is applied to the present situation in which Asa proclaims the people's trust in God alone as they approach this mighty force in his name. The exhortation is clear: "Help us. . . . Do not let mere men prevail against you!" (14:11).

As soon as the prayer ends, the Chronicler relates God's response. It is strikingly similar to the description of Abijah's victory in the previous chapter, as the army of Judah stands by and observes the Lord's defeat of the enemy (14:12; see 13:15) and only then springs into action in a cleanup operation (14:13-15; see 13:16-19).[2] Gerar was located to the southwest of Mareshah, an appropriate route for an army returning to Africa.

ENDNOTES

1. Dillard (1987:117) notes that the Chronicler omits all references found in Kings to cult prostitution (1 Kgs 14:24; 15:12; 22:46; 2 Kgs 23:7), possibly because it was not relevant to his audience.
2. The elements of this battle account are typical of depictions of holy war in Chronicles. See commentary on the battle of Abijah in 13:2b-19.

◆ 2. Asa's later years (15:1–16:14)

Then the Spirit of God came upon Azariah son of Oded, 2and he went out to meet King Asa as he was returning from the battle. "Listen to me, Asa!" he shouted. "Listen, all you people of Judah and Benjamin! The LORD will stay with you as long as you stay with him! Whenever you seek him, you will find him. But if you abandon him, he will abandon you. 3For a long time Israel was without the true God, without a priest to teach them, and without the Law to instruct them. 4But whenever they were in trouble and turned to the LORD, the God of Israel, and sought him out, they found him.

5"During those dark times, it was not safe to travel. Problems troubled the people of every land. 6Nation fought against nation, and city against city, for God was troubling them with every kind of problem. 7But as for you, be strong and courageous, for your work will be rewarded."

8When Asa heard this message from Azariah the prophet,* he took courage and removed all the detestable idols from the land of Judah and Benjamin and in the towns he had captured in the hill country of Ephraim. And he repaired the altar of the LORD, which stood in front of the entry room of the LORD's Temple.

9Then Asa called together all the people of Judah and Benjamin, along with the people of Ephraim, Manasseh, and Simeon who had settled among them. For many from Israel had moved to Judah during Asa's reign when they saw that the LORD his God was with him. 10The people gathered at Jerusalem in late spring,* during the fifteenth year of Asa's reign.

11On that day they sacrificed to the LORD 700 cattle and 7,000 sheep and goats from the plunder they had taken in the battle. 12Then they entered into a covenant to seek the LORD, the God of their ancestors, with all their heart and soul. 13They agreed that anyone who refused to seek the LORD,

the God of Israel, would be put to death—
whether young or old, man or woman.
14They shouted out their oath of loyalty to
the LORD with trumpets blaring and rams'
horns sounding. 15All in Judah were happy
about this covenant, for they had entered
into it with all their heart. They earnestly
sought after God, and they found him. And
the LORD gave them rest from their enemies on every side.

16King Asa even deposed his grandmother* Maacah from her position as
queen mother because she had made an
obscene Asherah pole. He cut down her
obscene pole, broke it up, and burned it in
the Kidron Valley. 17Although the pagan
shrines were not removed from Israel,
Asa's heart remained completely faithful
throughout his life. 18He brought into the
Temple of God the silver and gold and the
various items that he and his father had
dedicated.

19So there was no more war until the
thirty-fifth year of Asa's reign.

CHAPTER 16

In the thirty-sixth year of Asa's reign,
King Baasha of Israel invaded Judah and
fortified Ramah in order to prevent anyone from entering or leaving King Asa's
territory in Judah.

2Asa responded by removing the silver
and gold from the treasuries of the Temple
of the LORD and the royal palace. He sent it
to King Ben-hadad of Aram, who was ruling in Damascus, along with this message:

> 3"Let there be a treaty* between you
> and me like the one between your
> father and my father. See, I am
> sending you silver and gold. Break
> your treaty with King Baasha of Israel
> so that he will leave me alone."

4Ben-hadad agreed to King Asa's request and sent the commanders of his
army to attack the towns of Israel. They
conquered the towns of Ijon, Dan, Abel-beth-maacah,* and all the store cities in
Naphtali. 5As soon as Baasha of Israel
heard what was happening, he abandoned
his project of fortifying Ramah and
stopped all work on it. 6Then King Asa
called out all the men of Judah to carry
away the building stones and timbers that
Baasha had been using to fortify Ramah.
Asa used these materials to fortify the
towns of Geba and Mizpah.

7At that time Hanani the seer came to
King Asa and told him, "Because you have
put your trust in the king of Aram instead
of in the LORD your God, you missed your
chance to destroy the army of the king of
Aram. 8Don't you remember what happened to the Ethiopians* and Libyans and
their vast army, with all of their chariots
and charioteers?* At that time you relied
on the LORD, and he handed them over to
you. 9The eyes of the LORD search the
whole earth in order to strengthen those
whose hearts are fully committed to him.
What a fool you have been! From now on
you will be at war."

10Asa became so angry with Hanani for
saying this that he threw him into prison
and put him in stocks. At that time Asa also
began to oppress some of his people.

11The rest of the events of Asa's reign,
from beginning to end, are recorded in
The Book of the Kings of Judah and Israel.
12In the thirty-ninth year of his reign, Asa
developed a serious foot disease. Yet even
with the severity of his disease, he did not
seek the LORD's help but turned only to his
physicians. 13So he died in the forty-first
year of his reign. 14He was buried in the
tomb he had carved out for himself in the
City of David. He was laid on a bed perfumed with sweet spices and fragrant
ointments, and the people built a huge
funeral fire in his honor.

15:8 As in Syriac version and Latin Vulgate (see also 15:1); Hebrew reads *from Oded the prophet.* **15:10** Hebrew *in the third month.* This month of the ancient Hebrew lunar calendar usually occurs within the months of May and June. **15:16** Hebrew *his mother.* **16:3** As in Greek version; Hebrew reads *There is a treaty.* **16:4** As in parallel text at 1 Kgs 15:20; Hebrew reads *Abel-maim,* another name for Abel-beth-maacah. **16:8a** Hebrew *Cushites.* **16:8b** Or *and horsemen?*

NOTES

15:16 ***queen mother.*** The queen mother was a position of great prestige and power in the ancient courts, explained by Bathsheba's concern in 1 Kgs 1 and Athaliah's power in chs 22–23. The fortunes of women were tied to the success of their sons (see Ruth 4), since women would usually outlive their older husbands. Several texts indicate that the queen mother held a specific rank in the court. This was true of Solomon (1 Kgs 2:19-20) and the kings of Israel (1 Kgs 11:26; 16:31; 22:52; 2 Kgs 3:2; 9:22), but especially of the kings of Judah (1 Kgs 14:21; 15:2, 10; 22:42; 2 Kgs 8:26; 12:1; 14:2; 15:2, 33; 18:2; 21:1, 19; 22:1; 23:31, 36; 24:8, 18). Asa's need to remove his queen mother from her position (1 Kgs 15:11-13) and Athaliah's ability to order the murder of the Davidic family members (2 Kgs 11:1) reveal not only rank but also considerable power and influence in the court. The precise role is difficult to discern, but it appears to have had at least two aspects: political and religious. Politically, the queen mother was depicted as involved in domestic affairs; she was a key figure at the beginning of her son's rule to ensure transfer of power from her husband to her son (1 Kgs 1–2), and then she wielded influence throughout his reign. However, there also appears to be a religious role for the queen mother, for there are several examples of these figures introducing and supporting rival cults (1 Kgs 18–19). In the present case, Maacah outlived not only her husband Rehoboam but also her son Abijah and was still holding on to her position in the reign of her grandson Asa (see discussion of Maacah in commentary on 11:5-23; cf. Andreasen 1983:179-194; ABD 5.583-586).

Asherah pole. See notes on 17:6 and 31:1.

16:2 ***King Ben-hadad of Aram, who was ruling in Damascus.*** Ben-hadad is the Hebrew form of the Aramaic name Bir-Hadad (son of the god Hadad), linked to kings who ruled the Aramean region around Damascus in the ninth to eighth centuries BC. Evidence for kings with this name can be seen in extrabiblical inscriptions in the early eighth century BC, although there is uncertainty as to which king is in view (ABD 1.663-665; ANET 501; COS 2.152-153).

16:4 ***Ijon, Dan, Abel-beth-maacah.*** The triangle between these three sites has Dan and Abel-beth-maacah at its 4-mile southern base and Ijon at a point 6 miles to the north. See NLT mg on the name Abel-beth-maacah.

COMMENTARY

Asa's Later Years of Peace: Religious Reforms (15:1–19). In the Chronicler's account, military attacks from enemies are often a sign of God's discipline upon the nation. To this point in the account of Asa, no clear indication has been given that there has been a change from the positive reforms described in 14:1-7. However, the encounter between a prophet and Asa at the outset of chapter 15, an incident not found in the Chronicler's source, suggests that more reform was necessary, even though God had just granted the southern kingdom a momentous victory over the Ethiopians. Again, the structure of the typical "sermon/prayer" of Chronicles is evident (doctrine, application, exhortation; cf. Dillard 1987:116). The key doctrine is the reciprocal nature of the covenant relationship between the Lord and Israel: "The LORD will stay with you as long as you stay with him! Whenever you seek him, you will find him. But if you abandon him, he will abandon you" (15:2). This doctrine is applied to Asa's generation, tracing how those who turned to the Lord in dire circumstances found him (15:3-6). The challenging conditions outlined by Azariah in these verses are strikingly similar to the situation depicted elsewhere during the period after the fall of Jerusalem and into the early Persian period (cf. Ezra 8:31; Zech 7:14; Dillard 1987:120). There was a crisis in the wake of the destruction of the Temple and exile of its leadership ("without a priest . . . without the Law") and the destruction of the economic and political infrastructure ("not safe to travel"). This speech would have resonated with the Chronicler's audience; it also suggests that there was a remnant among those who had remained faithful in the land. The speech ends with the exhortation, "Be strong and courageous" (15:7).

This message contains both encouragement to positive behavior and warning against negative behavior, and Asa's response in 15:8-19 contains both kinds of behavior. He took the warning seriously and removed all vestiges of idolatry from the land, an act that meant he would depose his grandmother Maacah as queen mother (15:8, 16). His only failure in this area was his inability to eradicate all the "pagan shrines," or "high places," thus failing to preserve the centrality of Jerusalem as the only place of worship in the southern kingdom.[1]

On the positive side, Asa led the renewal by repairing the altar at the Temple (15:8) and by bringing gifts of gold and silver into the Temple (15:18). Then he summoned the people to Jerusalem in the third month for a covenant renewal, possibly at the annual pilgrimage Festival of Harvest (Exod 23:16; 34:22; Lev 23:15-21; Num 28:26-31; Deut 16:9; Dillard 1987:121). The list of participating tribes includes Judah, Benjamin, Ephraim, Manasseh, and Simeon, a list that reveals membership from the key southern and northern tribes and shows that Asa's renewal was for "all Israel." The seriousness of the covenant is clear: "Anyone who refused to seek the LORD, the God of Israel, would be put to death" (15:13; cf. Deut 13:6-10; 17:2-7; Dillard 1987:122), as is also the universal and enthusiastic response: "All in Judah were happy about this covenant, for they had entered into it with all their heart" (15:15). The Chronicler's depiction reveals the truth of the prophetic words of Azariah: "They earnestly sought after God, and they found him" (15:15). The sign of God's approval is evident at the end of 15:15 with the appearance of the term "rest" (*nuakh* [TH5117, ZH5663]; cf. 14:6).

In the Chronicler's account, the attack of an enemy is usually a sign of God's discipline, awakening the people to their need for renewal. In the Chronicler's pattern the repentance of the people leads to God's miraculous deliverance of his people. In this case, however, God's deliverance was provided without any reference to repentance and was followed by a prophetic call to renewal. Thus, deliverance rather than discipline served as a motivation for renewal. This may be linked in the present case to the absence of a clear link between sin and the attack of the enemy or to the exemplary character of Asa's cry to the Lord in 14:11, which was enough to secure deliverance in the moment of crisis. However, it is possible that the Chronicler's program was multidimensional, in this case providing a model for repentance that followed the gracious intervention of God rather than preceded it. Such a model would have resonated with the Persian-period community, which had experienced the grace of God and was being called to an even deeper level of purity and commitment.

Asa's Later Years of War (16:1-10). The final phase of the Chronicler's account of Asa reverses the positive portrayal that has dominated the report to this point. Nearly all of the account was drawn from the Chronicler's source in 1 Kings 15:16-22, except for the account and speech of the prophet in 16:7-10. In the 36th year of his 41-year reign, Asa faced an intimidating foe: King Baasha of the northern kingdom.[2]

The defeat of Jeroboam I by Asa's father Abijah (13:19) had extended the borders of Judah northward beyond Bethel to Jeshanah. Baasha, however, pushed the borders back to Ramah, hometown of the prophet Samuel (1 Sam 7:16-17). This town lay between Bethel and Jerusalem in the territory of Benjamin (16:1). Unlike his earlier response of faith as he faced Zerah the Ethiopian (14:11), Asa enticed the Syrian king Ben-hadad to abandon his relationship with Baasha in favor of a treaty with Judah. The short note that Asa sent to Ben-hadad reflects language typical of ancient Near Eastern international rhetoric—that is, the tracing of the relationship between the two nations, with focus often on the good past relations enjoyed by the father of one of the covenant partners (see commentary on 2:3-10; cf. Hillers 1964, 1969; Kline 1963; McCarthy 1978). By cutting a deal with the Arameans and mobilizing the Syrian army to attack the northern frontier of Baasha's kingdom, Asa hoped to dilute Baasha's military resources and his threat to the kingdom of Judah. His strategy worked, because Ben-hadad conquered the key northern settlements of Ijon, Dan, and Abel-beth-maacah. As expected, Baasha withdrew from Ramah, abandoning his fortifications, which were promptly carried away by Asa's men to fortify Geba and Mizpah, both towns in Benjamin near Ramah.

The despicable character of Asa's approach to Ben-hadad was that it involved a bribe consisting of the silver and gold from the royal and Temple treasuries, the latter consisting of items Asa had recently contributed to the Temple as an expression of his faithfulness to the Lord (15:18). For the Chronicler, that Asa entered into a foreign alliance was bad enough; using the treasuries protected by the Levites at the Temple (1 Chr 9:26; 26:20, 22) was far worse.

Asa's Reign in Judah, 910–869 BC

It is not surprising that the prophet Hanani confronted Asa with his folly. The prophetic message again contains the elements evident in other speeches in the book of Chronicles (doctrine, application, exhortation; see commentary on 13:2b-19; Dillard 1987:116). In this case, however, the doctrine follows the application. The doctrine is expressed in 16:9a, which highlights the omnipresence of the Lord seeking to strengthen those who are fully committed to him. Asa was told that he had missed the chance to be strengthened by God in order to defeat not only Baasha, but Ben-hadad as well. This is placed immediately in contrast to an earlier application of this doctrine—that is, in Asa's encounter with the Ethiopians and their far greater military power. Finally, 16:9b provides the exhortation in the form of a pronouncement of judgment on Asa, condemning him to war. This prophetic message enraged Asa, who put Hanani in prison and began to oppress the people (16:10).

Asa's alliance with Aram in this passage introduces a dangerous innovation into the southern kingdom's political practices. In this Asa foreshadows the folly of his son Jehoshaphat, whose alliance with the northern kingdom's Omride dynasty (Ahab, Ahaziah) would result in the corruption of Jehoshaphat's son Jehoram (21:6) and grandson Ahaziah (22:3, 5) and nearly led to the extinction of the Davidic line under the bloody reign of Athaliah (22:10-12). This is the first sign that the Chronicler was wary of cooperation with foreign entities, especially the northern kingdom.[3] Knoppers has correctly concluded that "the Chronicler advocates steering a course independent from Judah's neighbors and relying solely upon the deity."[4]

Summary Note: The Reign of Asa (16:11-14). The summary note of Asa includes the usual material, except there is no reference to a prophetic book as a source for the full account of the king, as has been the custom to this point in the Chronicler's history (see chs 9, 12, 13; see also the end of 1 Chr 29). The cause of Asa's death is recounted by the Chronicler as "a serious foot disease," ironic in light of Asa's name, which is probably from a Semitic root related to healing and further evidence of God's discipline of the king (Dillard 1987:126). Tragically, the king who began with such promise and cried out to God for help as he faced the great Ethiopian army, "did not seek (*darash* [TH1875, ZH2011]) the LORD's help but turned only to his physicians."

ENDNOTES

1. Asa's reforms here in 15:8 are those described in the summary statement in 14:3 [2].
2. Three years into the reign of Asa and two years into the reign of Nadab son of Jeroboam I, Baasha son of Ahijah of the tribe of Issachar assassinated the northern king (1 Kgs 15:25-28). Since Baasha only reigned for 24 years, it is difficult to understand why the Chronicler refers to the invasion of Baasha in Asa's 36th year. Possibly Asa had ruled alongside his father Abijah or the number 36 is a scribal mistake (Dillard 1987:124-125). The scribal error may have occurred with the older Hebrew numeral confusion between Yodh (10) and Lamedh (30), thus 15:19 and 16:1 should read 15 and 16, not 35 and 36.
3. See also Ben Zvi (2003:85), who concludes that the ideological implications of the Chronicler's presentation of the secession of the northern kingdom included the fact that the Samarians are Israel, but that their polity is separate from Yehud and should remain that way, because it is Yahweh's will.
4. See Knoppers 1991:524 for a more detailed and nuanced study. See Siedlecki 1999:229-266 for a close study of Judahite identity in relation to foreigners. He concludes that the Chronicler's "view of the relationship between Judah and its neighbors is characterized by a constant mediation of tensions" (1999:265).

◆ F. The Reign of Jehoshaphat (17:1–21:1a)

1. Jehoshaphat rules in Judah (17:1-19)

Then Jehoshaphat, Asa's son, became the
next king. He strengthened Judah to
stand against any attack from Israel. 2He
stationed troops in all the fortified towns
of Judah, and he assigned additional
garrisons to the land of Judah and to the
towns of Ephraim that his father, Asa,
had captured.

3The LORD was with Jehoshaphat be-
cause he followed the example of his

father's early years* and did not worship the images of Baal. [4]He sought his father's God and obeyed his commands instead of following the evil practices of the kingdom of Israel. [5]So the LORD established Jehoshaphat's control over the kingdom of Judah. All the people of Judah brought gifts to Jehoshaphat, so he became very wealthy and highly esteemed. [6]He was deeply committed to* the ways of the LORD. He removed the pagan shrines and Asherah poles from Judah.

[7]In the third year of his reign Jehoshaphat sent his officials to teach in all the towns of Judah. These officials included Ben-hail, Obadiah, Zechariah, Nethanel, and Micaiah. [8]He sent Levites along with them, including Shemaiah, Nethaniah, Zebadiah, Asahel, Shemiramoth, Jehonathan, Adonijah, Tobijah, and Tob-adonijah. He also sent out the priests Elishama and Jehoram. [9]They took copies of the Book of the Law of the LORD and traveled around through all the towns of Judah, teaching the people.

[10]Then the fear of the LORD fell over all the surrounding kingdoms so that none of them wanted to declare war on Jehoshaphat. [11]Some of the Philistines brought him gifts and silver as tribute, and the Arabs brought 7,700 rams and 7,700 male goats.

[12]So Jehoshaphat became more and more powerful and built fortresses and storage cities throughout Judah. [13]He stored numerous supplies in Judah's towns and stationed an army of seasoned troops at Jerusalem. [14]His army was enrolled according to ancestral clans.

From Judah there were 300,000 troops
organized in units of 1,000, under
the command of Adnah. [15]Next in
command was Jehohanan, who
commanded 280,000 troops. [16]Next
was Amasiah son of Zicri, who
volunteered for the LORD's service, with
200,000 troops under his command.

[17]From Benjamin there were 200,000
troops equipped with bows and
shields. They were under the command
of Eliada, a veteran soldier. [18]Next in
command was Jehozabad, who
commanded 180,000 armed men.

[19]These were the troops stationed in Jerusalem to serve the king, besides those Jehoshaphat stationed in the fortified towns throughout Judah.

17:3 Some Hebrew manuscripts read *the example of his father, David.* 17:6 Hebrew *His heart was courageous in.*

NOTES

17:3 *the images of Baal.* As is well-known from the stories of Elijah, the Baal religion dominated the northern kingdom during this period. The wife of the northern king Ahab, Jezebel, was the daughter of Ethbaal, king of the Phoenician city-state of Sidon. Baal was the storm- and fertility-god of Canaan referred to regularly in Ugaritic and Phoenician sources; cf. ABD 1.546; Smith 2002:43-46, 65-107; Day 2000:68-127.

17:5 *highly esteemed.* The second word here in Hebrew is *kabod* [TH3519, ZH3883], often translated as "glory" or "honor." However, it is also used in a few places in the OT for wealth/riches (Gen 31:1; Isa 10:3; 61:6; 66:12), which is probably the connotation here.

17:6 *Asherah poles.* These were manufactured wooden objects, possibly in the form of stylized trees, which symbolized the goddess Asherah. This goddess is well attested in the Old Testament. In the Ugaritic texts, Athirat (= Asherah) was the consort of the chief god El and mother of the gods. Inscriptions from Kuntillet 'Ajrud in northeast Sinai and Khirbet el-Qom near Hebron refer to Yahweh and "his Asherah" (ABD 1.483-486). See further note on 31:1.

17:7 *In the third year of his reign.* Many consider this to be actually the first year of Jehoshaphat's sole reign, since he probably reigned alongside his father Asa in the final three years of Asa's reign (Dillard 1987:132; Williamson 1982:282).

COMMENTARY

With the close of his account of Asa, the Chronicler skips over a considerable portion of his source (1 Kgs 15:25–21:29), an excision attributed to the Chronicler's lack of interest in the northern kingdom. In the process not only were the stories of Elijah eliminated but also the early history of the Omride dynasty (Omri, Ahab, Ahaziah, Jehoram), ironic in light of the fact that Israel became known to the Mesopotamians as the "land of Omri."[1] The Chronicler, however, had a different agenda, one dominated by different political and theological interests.

While excising large amounts of the northern history, the Chronicler expanded his account of Jehoshaphat, doubling its size in comparison to the space given to him in the book of Kings (Japhet 1993:743). In this way the account of Jehoshaphat's reign is second in size only to Hezekiah's reign (chs 29–32), the zenith of the Chronicler's post-Solomonic history.

Although the Chronicler devoted considerable space to Jehoshaphat and evaluated him positively, he admitted his faults (20:33; 22:9). Dillard (1986:17-22; 1987:129-130) argues that the account of Jehoshaphat is styled after his work on Asa, a view he says is suggested by the Chronicler himself, who compares the two in 17:3; 20:32; and 21:12 (cf. Japhet 1993:743). Many of the connections highlighted by Dillard are common to other post-Solomonic kings, but a couple are key and highlight the development of negative patterns in the Davidic line that threatened the endurance of the line. First, both kings entered into foreign alliances. Asa's foreign alliance with Ben-hadad, king of Aram, was prompted by a threat from the northern king Baasha. Asa convinced Ben-hadad to join him and break his alliance with Baasha (ch 16). Jehoshaphat's alliance was with the northern kingdom (which his father opposed), symbolized in the marriage of his son Jehoram to Ahab's daughter Athaliah (ch 18), whose murderous reign nearly extinguished the line of David (chs 22–23). Second, both kings are confronted by prophets who were, ironically, father (Hanani, 16:7-9) and son (Jehu, 19:1-3). In both cases they confronted the respective king over their foreign alliances. In the case of Hanani, Asa threw the prophet into prison, while in the case of Jehu, Jehoshaphat responded by establishing his judicial system. These comparisons highlight the more positive tone of Jehoshaphat's reign in comparison to his father. Although Jehoshaphat failed, his development of systems of teaching and judging throughout the land appear to have outweighed the evil of his alliance with the northern kingdom.

Summary Note: The Accession of Jehoshaphat (17:1a). This summary note completes the transitional summary note at the end of his father's Asa's reign (16:11-14). Fuller information (including the evaluation, length of reign, queen mother's name) is provided in Jehoshaphat's case at the end of his reign (20:31-33).

Jehoshaphat's Early Years of Prosperity (17:1b-19). As with his father, Asa, the first phase of Jehoshaphat's reign was marked by successes in the areas of the military, religion, politics, and wealth. It appears that his initial concern was the northern kingdom (17:1),[2] understandable in light of Baasha's attack against his father in the previous chapter. According to the Chronicler, Jehoshaphat followed the military strategy of his father, refortifying the key cities of Judah (14:6) as well as the towns he captured in the southern region of Ephraim (15:8; cf. 13:19). Although such preparations are a typical sign of God's blessing on a monarch in the Chronicler's work, they paled in significance to the divine protection secured through Jehoshaphat's faithful attention to religious purity. Second Chronicles 17:10-19 reveals that Jehoshaphat was protected from an advance by the northern kingdom as well as from "all the surrounding kingdoms" (17:10), a protection linked not to Jehoshaphat's preparations but rather to "the fear of the LORD."[3] According to 17:11, these nations not only refrained from attacking Jehoshaphat but took the extraordinary step of bringing tribute to the king in precious metals (Philistines) and animals (Arabs). This, in turn, provided the peaceful space for Jehoshaphat to increase in power, building fortresses throughout the land stocked with the supplies and personnel necessary to protect his kingdom (Japhet 1993:751).

An interesting parallel between Jehoshaphat's internal and external affairs can be discerned in this account. As already noted, 17:10-11 links the fear the Lord placed on the surrounding nations to the external security of Jehoshaphat's kingdom; this fear leads to generous gifts of tribute from surrounding nations to the king. Similarly, 17:5 identifies the Lord as the one who established the internal security of his kingdom, an establishment that leads to generous gifts of tribute to the king from his subjects.

All these marks of success flow from the religious reforms that Jehoshaphat initiated in his early years (17:3-9). The link between Jehoshaphat and Asa is clear from the outset, although the Chronicler was careful to associate Jehoshaphat only with the early phase of Asa's reign (ch 14). In a fashion typical of the Chronicler, Jehoshaphat "sought" (Heb., *darash* [TH1875, ZH2011]) God and "obeyed his commands" (lit., "walked in his commands")—generic terms that describe the engagement of the entire being, both in terms of affection as well as action. These terms are made concrete in the actions described: refusal to worship idols (17:3) and removal of illicit worship sites and objects from Judah (17:6). In an ironic twist the Chronicler uses a phrase linked in his history to the inappropriate pride of later kings (*gabah leb* [TH1361/3820, ZH1467/4213]; 26:16; 32:25) to describe Jehoshaphat's passion for the "ways of the LORD" (17:6; NLT, "he was deeply committed to"; cf. NASB, "he took great pride in").

The Chronicler, however, was not satisfied with this list of concrete reforms, which were merely corrective in character (that is, they involved the removal of false worship). In addition, he recorded that Jehoshaphat took the positive step of commissioning his officials to teach the law to the people in the towns of Judah (17:7-9), an act that portrays him as fulfilling the ideals laid out in Deuteronomy 17:18-20. The Chronicler stresses two things in this positive reform. First, he identified three groups of leaders who were authorized to do this kind of teaching: officials, Levites, and priests. His emphasis was placed on the Levites (nine names given), followed by the officials (five given), and finally the priests (only two given). To this point, the Chronicler has already linked several key functions to the Levitical orders: carrying the Ark, assisting the priests, providing music for worship, and guarding the Temple and storerooms. In this account the Levites (and lay officials) were also commissioned to teach the people, even though such a role was usually associated with "priests" (Lev 10:11; Deut 33:10; Jer 18:18; Hos 4:6; Mal 2:7; cf. 2 Chr 15:3; cf. Dillard 1987:134). Here the Chronicler may be providing the historical foundation for the broadening of the teaching role to Levites and laity in the Second Temple period (see also Neh 8:7; Japhet 1993:748-749).

Second, the Chronicler emphasized the written character of the authoritative source of this teaching. The "Book of the Law of the LORD" (Heb., *seper torath yhwh* [TH8451, ZH9368], 17:9) was "with them" (Heb., *'immahem* [TH5973, ZH6640]; NLT, "They took copies of"). Third, the Chronicler noted the decentralized character of this teaching from this book, which took place as they "traveled around through all the towns of Judah." This stands out in the Chronicler's account, which places great stress on the centralization of worship at Jerusalem. These features suggest that such a ministry of teaching must have been important to the Chronicler and to his community. This approach to teaching the Torah must have become essential to the preservation of Jewish identity after the loss of Temple, land, and monarchy and may offer some of the earliest evidence for the development of the synagogue in Judaism.

ENDNOTES

1. See, for instance, the Black Obelisk of Shalmaneser III, which depicts Jehu kneeling before the Assyrian king and identified as "the man of Bit-Humri (Omri)" (mid-ninth century BC; cf. ANET 280-281; COS 2.269-270). (This identification is ironic, since it was Jehu who brought the Omride dynasty to an end.) See also references to Omri and Ahab on the Kurkh Monolith of Shalmaneser III (mid-ninth century BC; ANET 278-279; COS 2.261-264), the Moabite Stone (late ninth century BC; ANET 320-321; ANEP 274; COS 2.137-138), and the Assyrian accounts of the fall of Samaria (late eighth century BC; COS 2.298).
2. The verb used here (*khazaq* [TH2388, ZH2616] Hitpael) is usually employed by the Chronicler to signal a king's consolidation of power of his own kingdom (1:1; 12:13; 13:21; 21:4; 27:6; cf. 32:5). Second Chronicles 1:1 and 17:1 are the only instances in Chronicles where this verb is followed by the preposition *'al*. In 1:1 the Hebrew text reads, lit., "Solomon, son of David, strengthened himself over (preposition *'al*) his kingdom," while 17:1 reads, "and he strengthened himself 'over/against' (preposition *'al* [TH5921, ZH6584]) Israel." In 1:1 the noun after the preposition is clearly the entity over which the king's power was exerted. However, this may be the case in 17:1 in the Chronicler's account, where Jehoshaphat's kingdom is consistently identified as Judah (17:2, 5, 6, 7, 9, etc.) and the northern kingdom as "Israel" (17:4). There is an instance elsewhere in the Hebrew Bible where the preposition *'al* after the verb *khazaq* Hitpael introduces the opponent of the subject of the verb (Dan 10:21). For an opposing view, however, see Japhet (1993:745), who interprets Israel "in its general connotation as 'the people', or 'the kingdom,'" a view that may be bolstered by the reference to Jehoshaphat as the king "of Israel" in the Hebrew text of 21:2 (see NLT mg note on "of Judah").
3. Elsewhere in his account the Chronicler uses the phrases "all the surrounding kingdoms" (12:8; 20:29; 1 Chr 29:30) and the "fear of the LORD" (14:14; 19:7).

◆ 2. Jehoshaphat's inappropriate alliance with Ahab of Israel (18:1-34)

Jehoshaphat enjoyed great riches and high esteem, and he made an alliance with Ahab of Israel by having his son marry Ahab's daughter. [2]A few years later he went to Samaria to visit Ahab, who prepared a great banquet for him and his officials. They butchered great numbers of sheep, goats, and cattle for the feast. Then Ahab enticed Jehoshaphat to join forces with him to recover Ramoth-gilead.

3 "Will you go with me to Ramoth-gilead?" King Ahab of Israel asked King Jehoshaphat of Judah.

Jehoshaphat replied, "Why, of course! You and I are as one, and my troops are your troops. We will certainly join you in battle." 4 Then Jehoshaphat added, "But first let's find out what the LORD says."

5 So the king of Israel summoned the prophets, 400 of them, and asked them, "Should we go to war against Ramoth-gilead, or should I hold back?"

They all replied, "Yes, go right ahead! God will give the king victory."

6 But Jehoshaphat asked, "Is there not also a prophet of the LORD here? We should ask him the same question."

7 The king of Israel replied to Jehoshaphat, "There is one more man who could consult the LORD for us, but I hate him. He never prophesies anything but trouble for me! His name is Micaiah son of Imlah."

Jehoshaphat replied, "That's not the way a king should talk! Let's hear what he has to say."

8 So the king of Israel called one of his officials and said, "Quick! Bring Micaiah son of Imlah."

9 King Ahab of Israel and King Jehoshaphat of Judah, dressed in their royal robes, were sitting on thrones at the threshing floor near the gate of Samaria. All of Ahab's prophets were prophesying there in front of them. 10 One of them, Zedekiah son of Kenaanah, made some iron horns and proclaimed, "This is what the LORD says: With these horns you will gore the Arameans to death!"

11 All the other prophets agreed. "Yes," they said, "go up to Ramoth-gilead and be victorious, for the LORD will give the king victory!"

12 Meanwhile, the messenger who went to get Micaiah said to him, "Look, all the prophets are promising victory for the king. Be sure that you agree with them and promise success."

13 But Micaiah replied, "As surely as the LORD lives, I will say only what my God says."

14 When Micaiah arrived before the king, Ahab asked him, "Micaiah, should we go to war against Ramoth-gilead, or should I hold back?"

Micaiah replied sarcastically, "Yes, go up and be victorious, for you will have victory over them!"

15 But the king replied sharply, "How many times must I demand that you speak only the truth to me when you speak for the LORD?"

16 Then Micaiah told him, "In a vision I saw all Israel scattered on the mountains, like sheep without a shepherd. And the LORD said, 'Their master has been killed.* Send them home in peace.'"

17 "Didn't I tell you?" the king of Israel exclaimed to Jehoshaphat. "He never prophesies anything but trouble for me."

18 Then Micaiah continued, "Listen to what the LORD says! I saw the LORD sitting on his throne with all the armies of heaven around him, on his right and on his left. 19 And the LORD said, 'Who can entice King Ahab of Israel to go into battle against Ramoth-gilead so he can be killed?'

"There were many suggestions, 20 and finally a spirit approached the LORD and said, 'I can do it!'

" 'How will you do this?' the LORD asked.

21 "And the spirit replied, 'I will go out and inspire all of Ahab's prophets to speak lies.'

" 'You will succeed,' said the LORD. 'Go ahead and do it.'

22 "So you see, the LORD has put a lying spirit in the mouths of your prophets. For the LORD has pronounced your doom."

23 Then Zedekiah son of Kenaanah walked up to Micaiah and slapped him across the face. "Since when did the Spirit of the LORD leave me to speak to you?" he demanded.

24 And Micaiah replied, "You will find out soon enough when you are trying to hide in some secret room!"

[25]"Arrest him!" the king of Israel or-
dered. "Take him back to Amon, the gov-
ernor of the city, and to my son Joash.
[26]Give them this order from the king: 'Put
this man in prison, and feed him nothing
but bread and water until I return safely
from the battle!'"
[27]But Micaiah replied, "If you return
safely, it will mean that the LORD has not
spoken through me!" Then he added to
those standing around, "Everyone mark
my words!"

[28]So King Ahab of Israel and King Jeho-
shaphat of Judah led their armies against
Ramoth-gilead. [29]The king of Israel said to
Jehoshaphat, "As we go into battle, I will
disguise myself so no one will recognize
me, but you wear your royal robes." So the
king of Israel disguised himself, and they
went into battle.
[30]Meanwhile, the king of Aram had is-
sued these orders to his chariot com-
manders: "Attack only the king of Israel!
Don't bother with anyone else." [31]So when
the Aramean chariot commanders saw Je-
hoshaphat in his royal robes, they went
after him. "There is the king of Israel!"
they shouted. But Jehoshaphat called out,
and the LORD saved him. God helped him
by turning the attackers away from him.
[32]As soon as the chariot commanders re-
alized he was not the king of Israel, they
stopped chasing him.
[33]An Aramean soldier, however, random-
ly shot an arrow at the Israelite troops and
hit the king of Israel between the joints of
his armor. "Turn the horses* and get me out
of here!" Ahab groaned to the driver of the
chariot. "I'm badly wounded!"
[34]The battle raged all that day, and the
king of Israel propped himself up in his
chariot facing the Arameans. In the eve-
ning, just as the sun was setting, he
died.

18:16 Hebrew *These people have no master.* **18:33** Hebrew *Turn your hand.*

NOTES

18:1 ***high esteem.*** See note on 17:5.

18:2 ***Samaria.*** This city in the northern kingdom was founded by Ahab's father Omri as his capital in the early ninth century BC (1 Kgs 16:23-24), continuing as such until its destruction by the Assyrians in the late eighth century BC (2 Kgs 17:1-6). See Assyrian texts in ANET 284-285; COS 2.295, 298.

18:14 ***sarcastically.*** This is not found in the Hebrew text, which merely records "Micaiah said."

18:18 ***all the armies of heaven.*** This is traditionally translated as the "hosts of heaven," which may have its roots in a military context, possibly related to the dominance of the military role for ancient kings and their courts. In other contexts, however, the membership of the council is not always linked to military terminology (Job 1–2; Isa 6; Zech 3). Here in 18:18 the military nuance does not appear to be in view.

COMMENTARY

As is often the case in the Deuteronomic History (Judges—Kings) as well as Chronicles, a blessing from the Lord can easily lead to the downfall of a leader or people. The same terms used in 18:1 ("great riches and high esteem"; better, "great riches and wealth"—see note on 17:5) were also used in 17:5 to indicate God's favor upon Jehoshaphat. In this case, these terms immediately precede the king's downfall, signified by the alliance he made with King Ahab of Israel, an act that is regularly denounced in the Chronicler's history (16:1-3; 20:35-37; 25:6-8; 28:16-23; Dillard 1987:139; Knoppers 1991). The depiction of such an alliance bolsters the parallels the Chronicler was seeking to establish between Jehoshaphat and his father, Asa. Even worse is the fact that this alliance is sealed by a marriage between Jehoshaphat's son Jehoram and Ahab's daughter Athaliah (2 Kgs 8:18, 27), a marriage that will lead to the corruption of Jehoram (21:6) and Jehoram's son Ahaziah (22:3, 5) and the near extinction of the Davidic line (22:10-12).

The folly of this move is readily seen by highlighting key references to Israel in the early verses of the Chronicler's account of Jehoshaphat. The new southern king had carefully fortified his kingdom from any military threat from the northern Israelite kingdom and rejected all deviant religious practices of that neighboring state. Yet Jehoshaphat became a victim of this success. In his carelessness he invited the enemy into his own royal court through alliance and marriage.

The relationship between Jehoshaphat and Ahab was clearly based upon the mutual need for military resources, whether that meant a nonaggression pact, which would free up military resources to pursue an enemy, as appears to be the case in the treaty between Asa and Ben-hadad (16:2-3), or a coalition pact that would increase the military resources available to face superior forces, as appears to be the case in the treaty here between Jehoshaphat and Ahab. Ahab's marriage to Jezebel suggests that the northern kingdom was already in an alliance with the Phoenicians to the north. Jehoshaphat, thus, was joining a potent coalition of states in the Levant.

Jehoshaphat traveled to Samaria to visit Ahab, probably an indication of his inferior status in the relationship, understandable in light of the power of the Omride dynasty that ruled Israel during this time (Omri, Ahab, Ahaziah, Joram). Ahab impressed Jehoshaphat through a grand banquet with the hidden agenda of enticing[1] Jehoshaphat to join him in battle to recover Ramoth-gilead. This was a fortress city of the northern kingdom on the Transjordanian plateau, south of the Golan at the eastern edge of northern Gilead. Possibly this fortress had been lost in the military campaign of Ben-hadad against Israel (described in 1 Kgs 20).

Upon Ahab's invitation to join him in battle, Jehoshaphat expressed his commitment to the alliance (18:3). But the southern king revealed his spiritual sensitivity by encouraging Ahab to discover the Lord's will on this matter. Ahab invited his 400 prophets to provide this information (a positive answer as expected), but this was not adequate for Jehoshaphat, who recognized that there was something amiss. The southern king requested "a prophet of the LORD" (18:6), and Ahab admitted that there was one prophet in the land who was out of favor with the royal court because he "never prophesies anything but trouble for me!" Jehoshaphat rebuked Ahab for such sacrilege and insisted that this prophet, Micaiah son of Imlah, be brought to the court.

This motif of the many prophets versus the one prophet is common in the Ahab tradition in the Chronicler's source in Kings, echoing the challenges of Elijah, who faced 450 prophets of Baal and 400 prophets of Asherah (1 Kgs 18:19; Japhet 1993:759). In that case, Obadiah had hidden 100 true prophets (1 Kgs 18:4, 13). Of course, in Chronicles these earlier incidents are not included, but the motif endures in the present incident and invites the reader to consider the nature of true prophecy, here identified as the lone voice that stands against the many voices—in this passage the voices of other prophets but often of the people as a whole.

With 18:9, the account, drawn from the Chronicler's source in 1 Kings 22, either returns to an earlier point of the story (offering more details than those given in 18:5) or else depicts an elongated process of prophetic revelation from Ahab's prophets that had continued while the kings deliberated in 18:6-8. The kings are seated on thrones at the threshing floor near the gate of Samaria (18:9). The gate of Samaria was the location of the grain market during Joram's reign (2 Kgs 7:1), and thus this threshing floor would have provided an open space for the court to meet. A structure unearthed in the gate of Dan has been identified by many as the base for a throne (see Biran 1974), probably revealing the desire of royal authorities to be close to the place of civic decision making in that city and associated region (see Ruth 4; cf. 2 Sam 19:8). The account notes that they were "dressed in their royal robes," foreshadowing the role that these "royal robes" will play in the battle narrative (18:29, 31; Japhet 1993:760-761).

This section isolates one particular prophet among the group (18:10): Zedekiah son of Kenaanah. The Chronicler depicts his use of a form of prophetic revelation called a "sign-act," which utilized some visual aid or act to express revelation.[2] His prophetic utterance is then cited: "With these horns you will gore the Arameans to death!" The role of prophets in the northern court is made clear in the mouth of the messenger who fetches Micaiah for Ahab: They were to promise victory and success (18:12). Micaiah, however, revealed that he was different from Ahab's prophets, seen in his reply to the messenger that he would "say only what my God says" (18:13). As Japhet so aptly describes, "The issue is not whether 'good' or 'evil' tidings are given to the king, but whether the word of the Lord is faithfully transmitted" (1993:761).

The surprise of 18:14 is that Micaiah appeared to follow the messenger's advice, as Micaiah used the same verbs as Ahab's prophets: "Go up . . . be victorious . . . have victory" (18:11, 14; see note on 18:14). However, there is a slight change between the two messages in the Chronicler's account (1 Kgs 22:15). While Ahab's prophets identify "the LORD" as the subject of the final active verb (18:11), Micaiah cast it in the passive, lit., "they will be given into your hand" and makes the enemy the subject (18:14), thus not specifically promising the Lord's intervention. Additionally, while Ahab's prophets refer to Ahab alone (singular imperatives and "the king"; 18:11), in the Chronicler's account Micaiah refers to Ahab and Jehoshaphat (plural imperatives and pronouns).[3] These changes subtly distance Micaiah from Ahab's prophets while also reminding the reader that Jehoshaphat would entangle himself in the coming disaster and barely escape with his life.

Ahab was wary of this speech of Micaiah, possibly due to its uncharacteristic agreement with his own court prophets or possibly also because of a tone in his voice on the oral level, now lost in written expression (so NLT). The northern king demanded that he speak the truth. This prompted Micaiah to reveal the full picture: He was actually encouraging the king to engage in battle because it would bring the deserved judgment of God upon him. But even then, Micaiah was not done. He revealed still more, explaining that the message of Ahab's prophets and of Micaiah's initial word found their source in the Lord's divine court as a spirit was sent to cause the prophets to deceive Ahab.

With his credibility and that of his companions on the line, the leader of Ahab's prophetic corps, Zedekiah son of Kenaanah, flew into a rage, slapping Micaiah as an act of "insolence and insult" (Japhet 1993:765)[4] and then challenging the authority of Micaiah, questioning whether Micaiah possessed the Spirit of the Lord. Ahab reached the limit of his patience (18:25-26) and ordered Micaiah imprisoned, an act that echoes Asa's earlier confinement of Hanani in 16:10. Micaiah reminded the reader of the divine source of his prophetic message as he was led off to detention.

The concept of a divine council is well attested in the Old Testament (Job 1:6-12; 2:1-7; Pss 82; 89:5-8; Isa 6:1-3; 40:1-8; Jer 23:16-22; Zech 3:1-10), as well as throughout the ancient Near East and, in particular, the Canaanite religious context.[5] The leader of council in the Old Testament is God/the Lord, although in Zechariah 3 he is represented by the "messenger (angel) of the LORD." The membership of the council comprises heavenly beings identified by various names, including: the armies of heaven (1 Kgs 22:19; Ps 89:8), spirits (1 Kgs 22:21-22), seraphim (Isa 6:2, 6), gods (Ps 82:6), sons of the Most High/God (Job 1:6; 2:1; Pss 82:6; 89:6), holy ones (literal rendering of Ps 89:7), and the Satan (Job 1–2; Zech 3). While most likely some of these terms are merely different ways of referring to spiritual beings subservient to Yahweh in the heavenly realms (armies of heaven, spirits, gods, sons of the Most High/God, holy ones), others appear to indicate specific roles played by heavenly beings (seraphim, the Satan). However, the one human participant allowed into the council was the prophet (Isa 6, 40; Jer 23:16-22; Zech 3), a role articulated clearly in chapter 18. His participation here means that he was included in the divine council and could hear its deliberations. In a royal council, participation may be done very passively (indeed, it had better be) until a question was asked and there was opportunity for response.

According to the Old Testament texts available, the function of the council was twofold: "to exercise judgment and to provide revelation" (McGinn 2005:174). Exercising judgment involved a three-stage process: deliberation, decision/decree, and commission—a process that is evident in the court scene in chapter 18. The court also provided revelation: "The divine council makes decrees about fateful events for both individuals and groups in both the heavenly and earthly realms and commissions a messenger to report these decrees" (McGinn 2005:174). These two functions are not mutually exclusive, as can be seen in the report of Micaiah here in chapter 18.

What is interesting about this story in chapter 18 is the insight it offers into the role of the divine council and prophecy in ancient Israel. First, it shows that God can send council members to do harm as well as good, something that echoes the Lord's commission of a "spirit" to torment Saul (1 Sam 16:14). In chapter 18 (//1 Kgs 22) the spirit is sent to "deceive" the king, which is identified as the will of the Lord. Second, it shows that the Lord also influenced the prophets in Ahab's court, even though they were most likely prophets of Baal and/or Asherah (see 1 Kgs 18:19).[6] This may echo the Lord's use of a prophet like Balaam son of Beor (Num 22–24).

The narrative section in 18:9-27 parallels two royal courts, first the human court of Ahab (18:9-17) and second the divine court of Yahweh (18:18-22). Thrones signify royal authority in both scenes, and in both, deliberations are under way among the royal council over a potential battle at Ramoth-gilead. The deliberations involve a series of questions voiced by the royal figure to the royal council. Both royal councils are comprised of multiple members. In Ahab's council there are officials (18:2) and prophets (18:5), while in the Lord's there are "all the armies (hosts) of heaven" (18:18). In both scenes one member of the council is isolated to carry out the will of the council. In the human court it is the messenger who is commissioned to retrieve Micaiah, and in the divine court it is the spirit who places deceit in the mouths of Ahab's prophets. In both, a particular prophetic figure emerges (notice that for both we are given their father's name: Zedekiah son of Kenaanah, Micaiah son of Imlah). It is the confrontation between these two prophetic figures that highlights the competing values of the two courts.

One should not miss the passive role that Jehoshaphat plays in 18:9-27, contrasting his earlier active posture in 18:1-8. Jehoshaphat recedes into the background of the story, merely sitting on his throne next to Ahab in the council.[7] Nevertheless, his physical position in the story reveals the compromise he made. He was in the illegitimate human royal council of Ahab, which stood in opposition to the divine royal council of Yahweh.

Following Micaiah's imprisonment in 18:27, the account describes the ensuing battle led by Ahab and Jehoshaphat, again emphasizing their partnership by changing the verb "went into battle" at the end of 18:29 from the singular to the plural (cf. 1 Kgs 22:30). Ahab's folly is seen in his attempt to thwart the will of the Lord by disguising himself in the battle (see similarly 35:22; cf. Gen 38:14; 1 Sam 28:8; 1 Kgs 14:2; Dillard 1987:142). As expected, the Aramean enemy sends its most advanced weaponry after the one royal figure on the battlefield (see similarly 2 Kgs 3:26), Jehoshaphat, hoping to break the unity and will of the Israelite army. But the king of Judah cried to God, and God spared his life (see similarly 13:14-15; 14:11-12; 20:9; 32:20; 1 Chr 5:20). Instead, it was a random arrow from the least advanced unit (an Aramean soldier) that mortally wounded Ahab, who died by the end of the battle at sunset, just as the prophet Micaiah had promised.

ENDNOTES

1. A term that Dillard (1987:141) and Japhet (1993:756) note often connotes prompting to do something evil (32:11, 15; 1 Chr 21:1), although Dillard admits not always (cf. 18:31).
2. See further Fohrer 1952:101-120; 1968; Friebel 1999; 2001:25-45.
3. So also Japhet 1993:761; see also the Chronicler's change from singular to plural imperative ("Listen") in the second phase of his message in 18:18 (see 1 Kgs 22:19), again broadening the address to both kings.
4. Cf. Job 16:10; Isa 50:6; Lam 3:30.
5. For this I am thankful for the superb research of McGinn (2005), from which I have drawn this review of the divine council, as well as the key elements of parallel between the divine and human royal councils.
6. This question is much debated. The text actually never doubts their status as prophets of the Lord, although Jehoshaphat's second request for "a prophet of the LORD" after the appearance of the 400 court prophets introduces some concern over their status. The revelation of Micaiah, however, shows that they were actually inspired by a spirit from the divine council and thus were indeed fulfilling the will of God; even if

this message is "false," it is "authentic" in that it was commissioned by the Lord. As Japhet (1993:764) writes, "On the one hand, we find here a very strong emphasis on the understanding of the prophet as an unresisting channel for God's own purposes. On the other hand, by this same obedience a prophet may be an instrument of false action, and the credibility of the prophetic vocation on the human plane greatly shaken." Notice also the prophetic word of Elisha to Hazael in 2 Kgs 8:9-10, which instructs Hazael to tell his master that he will certainly recover, even though in the next phrase he admits that the Lord has shown him that he will certainly die.

7. This characterization, along with the fact that he travels to Ahab's court, offers all his resources to Ahab, and agrees to go into the battle in full regalia while Ahab disguises himself, are all factors contributing to the conclusion that the Omride dynasty controlled the southern kingdom (Dillard 1987:143). Although Japhet (1993:756) is correct that the Chronicler does transform this story from its source in Kings from a narrative deeply rooted in the Ahab tradition to one that serves the Jehoshaphat tradition, the spotlight remains on Ahab in 18:19-27. Japhet (1993:757) also claims that in contrast to the Deuteronomic source (1 Kgs 22), where Ahab is clearly the superior, the Chronicler presents the story differently—"as an expression of the Chronicler's systematic effort to describe the kings as equals." This claim appears true for the initial verses (18:1-8), where the Chronicler introduces a key additional text into his account, bolstering Jehoshaphat's successes (18:1; cf. 1 Kgs 22:1-2), highlighting Ahab's special treatment of Jehoshaphat (18:2b; cf. 1 Kgs 22:2), eliminating Ahab's initial address to his servants (18:2-3; cf. 1 Kgs 22:3), emphasizing their mutual status as "King . . . of Israel . . . King . . . of Judah" (18:3; cf. 1 Kgs 22:4), and having Ahab describe the battle as joint rather than individual effort (18:5; cf. 1 Kgs 22:6). I am not convinced, however, that the Chronicler continued this strategy beyond 18:8. By remaining faithful to his source in 18:9-27, Jehoshaphat disappears into the background, a dimension that strengthens the negative critique of alliances.

◆ 3. Jehoshaphat appoints judges (19:1-11)

When King Jehoshaphat of Judah arrived safely home in Jerusalem, [2]Jehu son of Hanani the seer went out to meet him. "Why should you help the wicked and love those who hate the LORD?" he asked the king. "Because of what you have done, the LORD is very angry with you. [3]Even so, there is some good in you, for you have removed the Asherah poles throughout the land, and you have committed yourself to seeking God."

[4]Jehoshaphat lived in Jerusalem, but he went out among the people, traveling from Beersheba to the hill country of Ephraim, encouraging the people to return to the LORD, the God of their ancestors. [5]He appointed judges throughout the nation in all the fortified towns, [6]and he said to them, "Always think carefully before pronouncing judgment. Remember that you do not judge to please people but to please the LORD. He will be with you when you render the verdict in each case. [7]Fear the LORD and judge with integrity, for the LORD our God does not tolerate perverted justice, partiality, or the taking of bribes."

[8]In Jerusalem, Jehoshaphat appointed some of the Levites and priests and clan leaders in Israel to serve as judges for cases involving the LORD's regulations and for civil disputes. [9]These were his instructions to them: "You must always act in the fear of the LORD, with faithfulness and an undivided heart. [10]Whenever a case comes to you from fellow citizens in an outlying town, whether a murder case or some other violation of God's laws, commands,

decrees, or regulations, you must warn them not to sin against the LORD, so that he will not be angry with you and them. Do this and you will not be guilty.

11"Amariah the high priest will have final say in all cases involving the LORD. Zebadiah son of Ishmael, a leader from the tribe of Judah, will have final say in all civil cases. The Levites will assist you in making sure that justice is served. Take courage as you fulfill your duties, and may the LORD be with those who do what is right."

NOTES

19:3 ***Asherah poles.*** See notes on 17:6 and 31:1.

19:8 ***In Jerusalem . . . for civil disputes.*** The Hebrew text can be rendered "and Jerusalem repented," thereby providing a record of a penitential response by the people of Jerusalem, which matches the earlier response of those outside of Jerusalem in 19:4.

COMMENTARY

Jehoshaphat's alliance with Ahab and the resulting battle is not explicitly condemned, but, as previously noted, they contain all the signs of God's displeasure, especially the prophetic condemnation of the proposed battle and the near death of Jehoshaphat. Furthermore, alliances with foreign powers are regularly condemned in the Chronicler's work (16:2-9; 19:1-3; 22:3-9; 25:7-13; 28:16-21; 32:31). In spite of his misbehavior, the Lord miraculously saved the southern king in the midst of the battle (18:31). This experience of Jehoshaphat parallels that of his father Asa, who faced the military crisis presented by Zerah the Ethiopian (14:9-15), cried to God for help (14:11), and was rescued. Similarly, just as Asa was confronted by a prophet as he returned from his battle (15:2; *yatsa'* [TH3318, ZH3655] *lipne;* NLT, "went out to meet"), so Jehoshaphat was confronted by a prophet as he returned from battle (19:2; *yatsa' 'el-paneh* [TH6440, ZH7156]; NLT, "went out to meet"). Additionally, just as Asa was confronted by the prophet Hanani for an alliance with a foreign power (16:7-10), so Jehoshaphat was confronted by Hanani's son Jehu for the same misdeed (19:2). From this point on the Chronicler's material regarding Jehoshaphat (except for the summary notation on his reign, 20:31-37) is unique. The material expresses some of the main emphases of the Chronicler's theology.

The prophet's message in this case, however, was more explicitly negative than it was for Asa. Jehu son of Hanani scolded Jehoshaphat for entering into an alliance with the northern kingdom (19:2a). Such an alliance is defined as "helping" and "loving." The first term ("help"; Heb., *'azar* [TH5826, ZH6468]) is a favorite of the Chronicler; it describes the external, pragmatic quality of inappropriate alliances.[1] The second ("love"; Heb., *'ahab* [TH157, ZH170]) is related to covenant fidelity in ancient Near Eastern treaty materials and describes the internal, affective quality that in this case threatens the covenant between God and his people (Dillard 1987:144; cf. Moran 1963:77-87). The northern kingdom is blatantly designated as "the wicked" and "those who hate the LORD," making clear the spiritual distinction between the two kingdoms. As a result of this alliance, God's judgment is clear: "The LORD is very angry with you" (19:2b). However, the prophet revealed that God saw goodness in Jehoshaphat because of the king's earlier reforms (see ch 17).

Although no specific link is made between the narrative that follows in 19:4-11 and the prophetic announcement in 19:1-3, it appears that the ensuing narrative is seen as a response to the confrontation, especially in light of the parallel structure of the account of his father Asa (15:8). First of all, the Chronicler, with his favorite vocabulary (*shub* [TH7725, ZH8740]; see introduction to chs 10–36, "Theological Analysis"), presents Jehoshaphat as a popular preacher of repentance. Although based at the central place of worship in Jerusalem, the king traveled among his people from the deepest south (Beersheba) to the farthest north (the hill country of Ephraim) to cause the people "to return to the LORD, the God of their ancestors" (19:4).

Second, in keeping with his name ("Yahweh judges"), Jehoshaphat is depicted as a judicial reformer, creating a legal infrastructure that would encourage faithfulness to the law to which his people were turning. Deuteronomy 16:18–17:13 may lie behind these reforms, although there are some points of contrast (Dillard 1987:147; Japhet 1993:775). The impact of such reforms on the sociology of Israel was probably immense, even though it is not certain that Jehoshaphat was an innovator in his initiatives (Dillard 1987:148). Justice was administered in the earliest eras of Israel by the patriarchal clan leader (Gen 38:24-26) and later by village elders (Ruth 4). Under the monarchy there would have been a move toward centralization of justice, which would ultimately challenge and overrule the authority of the clan systems.

The Chronicler distinguished the infrastructure Jehoshaphat established "in all the fortified towns" (19:5) from that established "in Jerusalem" (19:8). This probably reflects a distinction between the lower courts of Deuteronomy 16:18-20 and the higher court of appeal, which, according to Deuteronomy 17:8-13, was to be located at "the place the LORD your God will choose" (Deut 17:8), that is, Jerusalem (Japhet 1993:777). While he appointed judges in both areas (19:5, 8), the identities of those appointed in the fortified cities are not given, while for Jerusalem the Chronicler states explicitly that this judiciary was drawn from among the Levites, priests, and clan leaders (19:8). More detail is also offered for the types of law under the purview of this infrastructure in Jerusalem; they were commissioned to judge "cases involving the LORD's regulations and . . . disputes," most likely distinguishing between sacral and civil law (19:8). Verse 11 suggests that the priests were assigned to sacral cases, thus making the high priest the final authority on such litigation (*kol debar-yhwh* [TH3068, ZH3378]; "all matters of the LORD"), and the clan leaders were assigned to civil cases, thus making the tribal leader from Judah (Zebadiah son of Ishmael) the final authority on civil law (*kol debar-hammelek* [TH4428, ZH4889]; "all matters of the king"). The Levites also had a role to play as assistants to these two groups to ensure the proper administration of justice.

The Chronicler provided the record of an important speech by Jehoshaphat to each of the groups of judicial appointees (19:6-7, 9-10). Great concern is expressed in these two speeches over any threat to the impartiality of the justice system. The judicial system will be protected by remembering the divine dimension of the judiciary, a dimension highlighted by reference to the approval, fear, and presence of the Lord (19:7, 9, 11) who "does not tolerate perverted justice, partiality, or the taking of bribes" (19:7; cf. the same list in Deut 16:19). Japhet writes, "The Lord is both the source and authority of the law; it is to him that the human magistrate is responsible, as human deputy of the supreme judge of the universe" (1993:775).

While there are consequences for those who violate the law, there are also risks for those who administer justice, who can raise the ire of God ("angry with you") and incur guilt ("be guilty," 19:10). The standard that is to be followed in the administration of justice is clearly outlined in 19:10: "God's laws, commands, decrees, or regulations." Nevertheless, it also demands careful investigation by the judge ("always think carefully," 19:6) and courage ("Take courage as you fulfill your duties," 19:11). The closing exhortation reminds the judges that it is the presence of God that accompanies "those who do what is right" (19:11b).

Japhet (1993:778) identifies three terms in 19:10 that typify the Chronicler's view of the role of the justice system: guilt, wrath, and warning. This terminology emphasizes "the clear distinction between willful and inadvertent transgression . . . Culpability is incurred only for willful transgression, and the distinction is made through the provision of 'warning.'" Warning is to lead to repentance if the party desists in the behavior or to a state of guilt and wrath if they persist.

While in the early years of his reign Jehoshaphat had appointed teachers to go throughout the land, now the king himself not only went throughout his land to encourage repentance but also appointed judges throughout the land who could administer justice according to the law. Therefore, Jehoshaphat's reforms provide two institutions key to the development of Torah faithfulness both inside and outside of Jerusalem. Since the Chronicler provides these stories, it appears these institutions were important in his generation. While there was to be considerable focus and support of the central Temple in Jerusalem, this did not preclude the development of religious education and justice in the outlying areas. In both education and justice, the Chronicler encouraged participation by priest, Levite, and laity.

ENDNOTES

1. "Helping" (Heb., *'azar* [TH5826, ZH6468]) is a favorite term for the Chronicler, both for God's help of the king (14:11; 25:8; 26:7, 15; 32:8; 1 Chr 5:20; 12:18) and for seeking help from or giving help to the ungodly (28:16, 23; Dillard 1987:143).

◆ 4. Jehoshaphat's victories and inappropriate alliance with Ahaziah of Israel (20:1–21:1a)

After this, the armies of the Moabites, Ammonites, and some of the Meunites* declared war on Jehoshaphat. [2]Messengers came and told Jehoshaphat, "A vast army from Edom* is marching against you from beyond the Dead Sea.* They are already at Hazazon-tamar." (This was another name for En-gedi.)

[3]Jehoshaphat was terrified by this news and begged the LORD for guidance. He also ordered everyone in Judah to begin fasting. [4]So people from all the towns of Judah came to Jerusalem to seek the LORD's help.

[5]Jehoshaphat stood before the community of Judah and Jerusalem in front of the new courtyard at the Temple of the LORD. [6]He prayed, "O LORD, God of our ancestors, you alone are the God who is in heaven. You are ruler of all the kingdoms of the earth. You are powerful and mighty; no one can stand against you! [7]O our God, did you not drive out those who lived in this land when your people Israel arrived? And did you not give this land forever to the descendants of your friend Abraham? [8]Your people settled here and built this

Temple to honor your name. 9They said,
'Whenever we are faced with any calam-
ity such as war,* plague, or famine, we can
come to stand in your presence before
this Temple where your name is honored.
We can cry out to you to save us, and you
will hear us and rescue us.'
10"And now see what the armies of Am-
mon, Moab, and Mount Seir are doing.
You would not let our ancestors invade
those nations when Israel left Egypt, so
they went around them and did not de-
stroy them. 11Now see how they reward
us! For they have come to throw us out of
your land, which you gave us as an in-
heritance. 12O our God, won't you stop
them? We are powerless against this
mighty army that is about to attack us.
We do not know what to do, but we are
looking to you for help."
13As all the men of Judah stood before
the LORD with their little ones, wives, and
children, 14the Spirit of the LORD came
upon one of the men standing there. His
name was Jahaziel son of Zechariah, son
of Benaiah, son of Jeiel, son of Mattaniah,
a Levite who was a descendant of Asaph.
15He said, "Listen, all you people of Ju-
dah and Jerusalem! Listen, King Jeho-
shaphat! This is what the LORD says: Do
not be afraid! Don't be discouraged by
this mighty army, for the battle is not
yours, but God's. 16Tomorrow, march out
against them. You will find them coming
up through the ascent of Ziz at the end of
the valley that opens into the wilderness
of Jeruel. 17But you will not even need to
fight. Take your positions; then stand still
and watch the LORD's victory. He is with
you, O people of Judah and Jerusalem. Do
not be afraid or discouraged. Go out
against them tomorrow, for the LORD is
with you!"
18Then King Jehoshaphat bowed low
with his face to the ground. And all the
people of Judah and Jerusalem did the
same, worshiping the LORD. 19Then the Le-
vites from the clans of Kohath and Korah
stood to praise the LORD, the God of Israel,
with a very loud shout.
20Early the next morning the army of
Judah went out into the wilderness of
Tekoa. On the way Jehoshaphat stopped
and said, "Listen to me, all you people of
Judah and Jerusalem! Believe in the LORD
your God, and you will be able to stand
firm. Believe in his prophets, and you will
succeed."
21After consulting the people, the king
appointed singers to walk ahead of the
army, singing to the LORD and praising
him for his holy splendor. This is what
they sang:

"Give thanks to the LORD;
his faithful love endures forever!"

22At the very moment they began to
sing and give praise, the LORD caused the
armies of Ammon, Moab, and Mount Seir
to start fighting among themselves. 23The
armies of Moab and Ammon turned
against their allies from Mount Seir and
killed every one of them. After they had
destroyed the army of Seir, they began at-
tacking each other. 24So when the army of
Judah arrived at the lookout point in the
wilderness, all they saw were dead bodies
lying on the ground as far as they could
see. Not a single one of the enemy had
escaped.
25King Jehoshaphat and his men went
out to gather the plunder. They found vast
amounts of equipment, clothing,* and
other valuables—more than they could
carry. There was so much plunder that it
took them three days just to collect it all!
26On the fourth day they gathered in the
Valley of Blessing,* which got its name
that day because the people praised and
thanked the LORD there. It is still called
the Valley of Blessing today.
27Then all the men returned to Jerusa-
lem, with Jehoshaphat leading them,
overjoyed that the LORD had given them
victory over their enemies. 28They marched
into Jerusalem to the music of harps,
lyres, and trumpets, and they proceeded
to the Temple of the LORD.
29When all the surrounding kingdoms
heard that the LORD himself had fought

against the enemies of Israel, the fear of
God came over them. [30]So Jehoshaphat's
kingdom was at peace, for his God had
given him rest on every side.

[31]So Jehoshaphat ruled over the land of
Judah. He was thirty-five years old when
he became king, and he reigned in Jeru-
salem twenty-five years. His mother was
Azubah, the daughter of Shilhi.

[32]Jehoshaphat was a good king, follow-
ing the ways of his father, Asa. He did
what was pleasing in the LORD's sight.
[33]During his reign, however, he failed to
remove all the pagan shrines, and the
people never fully committed themselves
to follow the God of their ancestors.

[34]The rest of the events of Jehoshaphat's
reign, from beginning to end, are recorded
in *The Record of Jehu Son of Hanani*,
which is included in *The Book of the Kings
of Israel*.

[35]Some time later King Jehoshaphat of
Judah made an alliance with King Ahaziah
of Israel, who was very wicked.* [36]Togeth-
er they built a fleet of trading ships* at
the port of Ezion-geber. [37]Then Eliezer son
of Dodavahu from Mareshah prophesied
against Jehoshaphat. He said, "Because
you have allied yourself with King Aha-
ziah, the LORD will destroy your work." So
the ships met with disaster and never put
out to sea.*

CHAPTER 21

When Jehoshaphat died, he was buried
with his ancestors in the City of David.

20:1 As in some Greek manuscripts (see also 26:7); Hebrew repeats *Ammonites*. **20:2a** As in one Hebrew manuscript; most Hebrew manuscripts and ancient versions read *Aram*. **20:2b** Hebrew *the sea*. **20:9** Or *sword of judgment;* or *sword, judgment*. **20:25** As in some Hebrew manuscripts and Latin Vulgate; most Hebrew manuscripts read *corpses*. **20:26** Hebrew *valley of Beracah*. **20:35** Or *who made him do what was wicked*. **20:36** Hebrew *fleet of ships that could go to Tarshish*. **20:37** Hebrew *never set sail for Tarshish*.

NOTES

20:2 ***Messengers came and told.*** In the Hebrew text no subject is specified; it simply reads, "They came and told."

Edom. Most Hebrew manuscripts read "Aram" (NLT mg), but many scholars consider this an early scribal error for "Edom," the reading in one Hebrew manuscript and the Old Latin (Dillard 1987:153).

Hazazon-tamar. Genesis 14:7 cites this as a location conquered by the Elamite King Kedorlaomer and his allies. It is also identified as En-gedi, which is located in the Dead Sea region.

20:16 ***the ascent of Ziz at the end of the valley that opens into the wilderness of Jeruel.*** The ascent of Ziz is often associated with the Wadi Hasasa just north of En-gedi but recently has been linked to a military road that climbed the hills above En-gedi. See ABD 6.1105.

20:22 ***the LORD caused the armies of Ammon, Moab, and Mount Seir to start fighting among themselves.*** Lit., "The Lord set ambushes against the sons of Ammon, Moab, and Mount Seir, who had come against Judah; so they were struck down." The exact nature of these ambushes is unclear (see same verb in Judg 9:25), but probably refers to the heavenly armies.

COMMENTARY

Jehoshaphat's Victorious War against Moab, Ammon, and Edom (20:1-30). Like the previous chapter, the final narrative of the Chronicler's account of Jehoshaphat in chapter 20 is also not found in his source in the book of Kings. The account is divided into four basic sections: the declaration of war (20:1-2), the assembly of fasting (20:3-19), the battle (20:20-24), and the aftermath (20:25-30).

The opening section (20:1-2) provides details on the crisis that Jehoshaphat faced. The precise composition of the military force that declared war on the kingdom of Judah is difficult to ascertain. The Hebrew text of 20:1 lists Moabites, Ammonites, and "some from among the Ammonites," the final group appearing superfluous. The Septuagint reads here "Meunites" (see NLT mg), a people group referred to in 26:7 and 1 Chronicles 4:41 and linked often to the town of Ma'an, an Arabian settlement in the region traditionally associated with Edom (19 miles southeast of Petra; Dillard 1987:155) or to Beth-baal-meon, a Moabite settlement near Medeba (Num 32:38; Jer 48:23). The report of the messengers refers to an army from "Aram" in the Hebrew tradition and, similarly, "Syria" in the Greek tradition. This region is to the north of the kingdom of Israel, whereas the regions of the list in 20:1, 10 are to the east of the kingdom of Judah. In Jehoshaphat's speech in 20:10, the list of armies includes "Ammon, Moab, and Mount Seir," the latter a synonym for the country of Edom (see Gen 33:14, 16; 36:8-9; Deut 2:4-5; Josh 24:4).

At least two of these people groups had reason to attack Jehoshaphat's Judah. First, Edom was under Judean domination at the time (see 1 Kgs 22:47-48; 2 Kgs 3:9; 8:20-22) and would have desired freedom from Jehoshaphat's hegemony.[1] They were certainly willing to revolt against Judah under the reign of Jehoshaphat's son Jehoram (21:8-10). Second, 2 Kings 3 reveals that there was heightened tension between the Moabites and the northern kingdom of Israel during the period of the Omride dynasty (Omri, Ahab, Ahaziah, Jehoram) and that this tension led to a serious Moabite revolt from Israel's domination after the death of Ahab. This tension and the record of the successful Moabite revolt from Israelite control is recorded on an inscription discovered in the Transjordanian Plateau (Moabite/Mesha Stone; ANEP 274; ANET 320-321; COS 2.137-138). Considering Jehoshaphat's close relationship with the Omride dynasty and the northern kingdom, Jehoshaphat was a natural target for Moabite hatred.

These three kingdoms were located in the order listed here (Ammon, Moab, Edom) from north to south on the Transjordanian Plateau, with Ammon lying roughly between the Jabbok and Arnon valleys, Moab between the Arnon and Zered valleys, and Edom south of the Zered Valley. Key to the development of these kingdoms was the King's Highway, a major ancient trade route that ran the length of the Transjordanian Plateau connecting the Red Sea port of Ezion-geber and routes from Arabia and the Sinai in the south with Damascus in the north. On this route the kings of these people groups could tax much of the lucrative trade moving between Asia, Europe, Africa, and Arabia.

By the time Jehoshaphat was informed, this "vast" army had already reached En-gedi. This means that the route of their march ran around the southern tip of the Dead Sea (or across the Dead Sea at the Lisan Peninsula by ferry; cf. Aharoni 2002:98) and up the western Judean side, stopping for rest and water at the oasis of En-gedi halfway up the Dead Sea. From there they would ascend the valley and enter the wilderness of Judah before moving north to attack Jerusalem.

Although a military attack on Judah is usually a sign of God's displeasure with his people in the Chronicler's work (as in ch 18), there is no reason to suspect unfaithfulness by Jehoshaphat or his people in this case. In contrast, the previous chapter detailed the policies instigated by Jehoshaphat that were to ensure faithfulness among the people. Therefore, this may be a case in Chronicles where war was used not to signal disobedience, but rather to showcase the faith of a righteous generation and the faithfulness of the Lord their God.

With an imposing force just over 40 miles away, the Chronicler describes Jehoshaphat's action as he "set his face to seek the LORD" (*wayyitten . . . 'et-panayw lidrosh layhwh;* NLT, "begged the LORD for guidance"), employing one of his favorite terms, "seek" (*darash* [TH1875, ZH2011]). The king, however, also involved the entire kingdom in this seeking by proclaiming a fast. Such a proclamation was declared at times of emergency (cf. Jer 36:6, 9; Joel 1:14; 2:15; Jonah 3:5) and required the gathering of the people in Jerusalem. After the fall of Jerusalem a cycle of fasting appears to have arisen among the Israelites (see Zech 8:19) at which first lamentation (see Lam 1–2, 4–5) and ultimately penitential prayer (Ezra 9; Neh 1, 9; Lam 3; Dan 9) would become the dominant prayer forms (Boda 1999, 2003a, 2003b, 2003d). The Chronicler describes the purpose of this fast with his typical vocabulary: "to seek (*baqash* [TH1245, ZH1335], Piel) the LORD's help" (20:4).

The assembly, composed of people from both Jerusalem and Judah (20:5), including men, women, children, and infants (20:13), gathered in the Temple courtyard, and there Jehoshaphat led the community in a mighty prayer. The form of prayer used is not that of penitential prayer but rather a prayer of confidence based on the agenda for prayer outlined by Solomon in chapter 6. The prayer follows the sermon/prayer structure so common in the Chronicler's work: doctrine, application, exhortation (see commentary on 13:2b-19). The first part of the prayer (20:6-9) rehearses the doctrine foundational to this cry for help. Jehoshaphat's hope is based on the covenant relationship ("LORD, God of our ancestors") that his nation enjoyed with the only true God ("you alone") who rules the kingdoms of the earth from his exalted place in heaven ("the God who is in heaven . . . ruler of all the kingdoms of the earth"). This ruling God is omnipotent, a characteristic proven in the Conquest when God drove out the Canaanites and gave the land to "the descendants of your friend Abraham" (20:7; cf. Isa 41:8). This focus on Abraham is not typical of the Chronicler (Japhet 1989:497; Williamson 1977a:62-63).[2] The doctrinal section ends climactically with a summary of Solomon's agenda that the Temple be a sanctuary for prayer (ch 6; 1 Kgs 8). Interestingly, this prayer shifts away from the individual accomplishments and actions of Solomon and the Davidic dynasty to the corporate acts of the people who "settled here and built this Temple" (20:8) and "said, 'Whenever we are faced with any calamity . . . we can cry out to you'" (20:9). Here we see the Chronicler's agenda of democratization at its apex. This rich doctrinal section is then applied to the present crisis that Jehoshaphat faced (20:10-11) before the prayer exhorts God to stop their advance (20:12). The initial question of 20:12, "Won't you stop them?" is more precisely in Hebrew "Won't you judge them?" a further play on Jehoshaphat's name, which means "The LORD has judged." On the basis of the revealed character and action of God, in light of the gift of the land to his people, and because of the role of the Temple as a place where prayer will be heard, Jehoshaphat implored the Lord to save his people in the present emergency.

No sooner did this prayer leave the lips of the king, with the people of Judah standing before the Lord (20:13), than one of the Levites from the family of Asaph, Jahaziel son of Zechariah, son of Benaiah, son of Jeiel, son of Mattaniah, began to preach a sermon inspired by the Spirit of the Lord (20:14). His name, which means "He sees God," and the descent of "the Spirit of the Lord" are two features that link this Levite to the prophetic tradition in Israel. This is another example of the Chronicler's expansion of both the prophetic as well as the Levitical office in his work (see further commentary on 1 Chr 25).

The Levitical prophet Jahaziel addressed both the people and king, interestingly in an order that places emphasis on the people (further evidence of his corporate theme). Prophets had a role to play in response to communal laments, providing God's answer to the cry of the people (cf. Boda 2001:186-197; Ogden 1982:89-97; 1983:97-106). The address here is what is often called "Encouragement to a Task," calling the people to avoid fear and discouragement, trust in God's presence (20:17, "He is with you. . . . The LORD is with you"), and follow carefully God's instructions. This is based on the theology of holy war that is a regular feature of the Chronicler's work (see commentary on chs 13 and 14)—that is, that the battle will be fought by the Lord alone and that human effort is irrelevant to the victory (20:15, "for the battle is not yours, but God's").[3] The only actions required of the Judean army are merely to "go out against them"— that is, to march to the battle site, take positions, and "stand still and watch the LORD's victory" (20:17), actions that are an echo of those commanded by Moses at the crossing of the Red Sea in Exodus 14:13-14 (Japhet 1993:795).

To this point, the day of fasting involved a prayer of confidence to God by the king (20:5-12) and a prophetic message of encouragement and instruction from a Levite (20:13-17). It concluded with worship first by the king, then by the people of Judah and Jerusalem, and finally by the Levites of the clans of Kohath and Korah (20:18-19). The king and people worshiped with heads bowed on the ground, while the Levites worshiped with a very loud shout in a standing position.

The third part of this account in chapter 20 focuses on the depiction of the battle in 20:20-24. "Early the next morning" the army arose to confront their foe, heading south out of Jerusalem to the wilderness of Tekoa. The town of Tekoa lay 10 miles south of Jerusalem on the edge of the wilderness of Judah, which spread out to the east. With the Transjordanian army taking the route from En-gedi to Jerusalem through the wilderness via the ascent of Ziz, Jehoshaphat planned to encounter them before they arrived at the walls of Jerusalem. While they marched, Jehoshaphat delivered a message of hope and confidence to his troops calling them to believe in both the Lord and the prophets he sent (cf. Isa 7:9). This message represents a strong affirmation of the Levitical prophecy uttered on the day of fasting.

As another sign of the democratic character of Jehoshaphat's kingdom, the Chronicler has the king consult the people before appointing singers to lead the army. Since the only singers the Chronicler highlights throughout his work are the Levitical singers, it is most likely that this is another example of the Chronicler commending the work of the Levites. The Levitical service of music not only accompanies the sacrifices and secures the presence of God in the constructed Temple, but now it also leads the military into battle (cf. Josh 6:4-20; Judg 7:18-20; Dillard 1987:158). The Chronicler's favorite praise refrain is cited verbatim: "Give thanks to the LORD; his faithful love endures forever!" (20:21). The Chronicler makes it clear in 20:22 that it is this praise that initiates the holy war: "At the very moment they began to sing and give praise, the LORD caused the armies . . . to start fighting." The armies of Ammon, Moab, and Mount Seir were surprised by ambushes set by the Lord's army (see note on 20:22), leading to confusion so that the armies slaughtered each other as they marched toward Jerusalem, first the Moabites and Ammonites turning on the Edomites (or Arabians), then the Moabites and Ammonites on each other (cf. Judg 7:22; 1 Sam 14:20). As has been the case in previous battles in Chronicles, the Israelites were passive observers of the war, this time after it was over.

The only role to be played by the Judean army was to simply pick up the plunder from the fallen enemy, a task that took three days to complete (20:25). The Chronicler made sure to include an assembly of praise on site in the wilderness on the fourth day (20:26). This praise continued as the army returned to Jerusalem, and their march into the city was accompanied by the Levitical musical instruments and ended at the Temple site, the location where Jehoshaphat's initial cry was uttered. The impact of this great victory had massive implications for Jehoshaphat's kingdom. The "surrounding kingdoms" were filled with the "fear of God" (20:29), returning Jehoshaphat's kingdom to the state it enjoyed at the outset of his reign (17:10).

First Summary Note: The Reign of Jehoshaphat (20:31-34). The summary note on Jehoshaphat returns to the pattern of citing the mother of the king, a pattern that was not followed for Asa, most likely because his grandmother Maacah functioned as the queen mother during his reign after the death of Asa's mother (see 15:16). The Chronicler evaluated Jehoshaphat positively, linking him to the faithfulness of his father, Asa (20:32). Like his father, however, Jehoshaphat did not remove the pagan shrines (high places).

This short summary includes information similar to that found at the end of the reign of earlier Davidic kings. All the summary notes for kings to this point have included references to prophetic works, except the previous one (Asa's), which refers only to "*The Book of the Kings of Judah and Israel*" (16:11). For Jehoshaphat, the Chronicler refers to a prophetic work ("*The Record of Jehu Son of Hanani*"), which formed part of "*The Book of the Kings of Israel.*" The Chronicler sees this work as providing more information about Jehoshaphat's reign, but it is likely that the allusion to prophetic sources lends increased credibility to the Chronicler's account, as well as to Jehoshaphat's reign (see commentary on 1 Chr 29:29-30).

Jehoshaphat's Inappropriate Alliance with Ahaziah of Israel (20:35-37). Following the structure of his source in 1 Kings 22:48-50, the Chronicler included one additional account—in the space between the source citation in the summary note and the expected death and accession notice (see 21:1). In details, however, the two accounts are different: The Chronicler highlighted an alliance with Ahaziah to build the ships before they were destroyed in port, while the Deuteronomist highlighted only an advance by Ahaziah after the destruction. Furthermore, the Chronicler included a prophetic speech that presages the destruction of the fleet.

This account spoils the idyllic ending to the portrait of Jehoshaphat in 20:1-30; it depicts his proclivity to enter into alliances with the northern kingdom, this time with Ahab's son Ahaziah, who reigned for just over one year (1 Kgs 22:40, 49, 51-53; 2 Kgs 1:1-18) and was evaluated negatively by the Chronicler (20:35; cf. 1 Kgs 22:52-53). Such alliances were always a problem, according to the Chronicler (16:2-9; 19:1-3; 22:3-9; 25:7-13; 28:16-21; 32:31). The alliance between these two kings was not military in nature but rather economic, as they sought together to resurrect the maritime fleet that garnered Solomon and Hiram so much wealth (see 8:17-18; 9:10-11). The enterprise ended in failure as the ships were destroyed before even putting out to sea. The Chronicler makes explicit the reason for the failure of this enterprise, introducing into the account a prophetic word delivered by "Eliezer son of Dodavahu from Mareshah," who declared that the alliance with the wicked Ahaziah would lead to the destruction of the ships (20:37). Nothing else is known about this prophet, only that he came from Mareshah, which lay in the western foothills of Judah.

Second Summary Note: The Death of Jehoshaphat (21:1a). After the insertion of the additional account in 20:35-37, the summary note was completed with the notice of Jehoshaphat's death and burial in the City of David, followed by the accession of his son Jehoram. This is a reminder of the fulfillment of the dynastic promise to David.

ENDNOTES

1. The fact that Edom was under Judean domination certainly would not discourage but rather encourage their participation in the force, contra Japhet (1993:786).
2. See also the importance of Abraham to the hope of Israel in the Persian period in Neh 9 (Holmgren 1992; Boda 1999).
3. Japhet (1993:783) distinguishes between holy war as a form-critical term, implying both sociological setting and literary genre (noting Dillard 1987:154-161; von Rad 1990; Williamson 1982:291-301) and broader theological presuppositions—that is, the "tenet that human wars and their outcome are in fact determined by divine intervention," which "is common to all literary strata in the Bible, whether or not a war is presented within the genre-framework of a 'holy war.'"

◆ G. Jehoram's Reign (21:1b-20)

Then his son Jehoram became the next king.

**[2]Jehoram's brothers—the other sons of
Jehoshaphat—were Azariah, Jehiel, Zecha-
riah, Azariahu, Michael, and Shephatiah; all
these were the sons of Jehoshaphat king of
Judah.* [3]Their father had given each of
them valuable gifts of silver, gold, and cost-
ly items, and also some of Judah's fortified
towns. However, he designated Jehoram as
the next king because he was the oldest.
[4]But when Jehoram had become solidly es-
tablished as king, he killed all his brothers
and some of the other leaders of Judah.**

**[5]Jehoram was thirty-two years old
when he became king, and he reigned in
Jerusalem eight years. [6]But Jehoram fol-
lowed the example of the kings of Israel
and was as wicked as King Ahab, for he
had married one of Ahab's daughters. So
Jehoram did what was evil in the LORD's
sight. [7]But the LORD did not want to de-
stroy David's dynasty, for he had made a
covenant with David and promised that**

his descendants would continue to rule, shining like a lamp forever.

[8]During Jehoram's reign, the Edomites revolted against Judah and crowned their own king. [9]So Jehoram went out with his full army and all his chariots. The Edomites surrounded him and his chariot commanders, but he went out at night and attacked them* under cover of darkness. [10]Even so, Edom has been independent from Judah to this day. The town of Libnah also revolted about that same time. All this happened because Jehoram had abandoned the LORD, the God of his ancestors. [11]He had built pagan shrines in the hill country of Judah and had led the people of Jerusalem and Judah to give themselves to pagan gods and to go astray.

[12]Then Elijah the prophet wrote Jehoram this letter:

> "This is what the LORD, the God of your ancestor David, says: You have not followed the good example of your father, Jehoshaphat, or your grandfather King Asa of Judah. [13]Instead, you have been as evil as the kings of Israel. You have led the people of Jerusalem and Judah to worship idols, just as King Ahab did in Israel. And you have even killed your own brothers, men who were better than you. [14]So now the LORD is about to strike you, your people, your children, your wives, and all that is yours with a heavy blow. [15]You yourself will suffer with a severe intestinal disease that will get worse each day until your bowels come out."

[16]Then the LORD stirred up the Philistines and the Arabs, who lived near the Ethiopians,* to attack Jehoram. [17]They marched against Judah, broke down its defenses, and carried away everything of value in the royal palace, including the king's sons and his wives. Only his youngest son, Ahaziah,* was spared.

[18]After all this, the LORD struck Jehoram with the severe intestinal disease. [19]The disease grew worse and worse, and at the end of two years it caused his bowels to come out, and he died in agony. His people did not build a great funeral fire to honor him as they had done for his ancestors.

[20]Jehoram was thirty-two years old when he became king, and he reigned in Jerusalem eight years. No one was sorry when he died. They buried him in the City of David, but not in the royal cemetery.

21:2 Masoretic Text reads *of Israel;* also in 21:4. The author of Chronicles sees Judah as representative of the true Israel. (Some Hebrew manuscripts, Greek and Syriac versions, and Latin Vulgate read *of Judah.*) 21:9 Or *he went out and escaped.* The meaning of the Hebrew is uncertain. 21:16 Hebrew *the Cushites.* 21:17 Hebrew *Jehoahaz,* a variant spelling of Ahaziah; compare 22:1.

NOTES

21:3 ***he designated Jehoram as the next king because he was the oldest.*** This reflects a sociological framework of royal succession with all sons receiving inheritance, but the firstborn receiving authority—kingship in this case. Interestingly, this was not true for Solomon (1 Chr 3:5) or Abijah (11:21-22); thus, the procedure must have been established at a later point (Japhet 1993:808).

21:4 ***But when Jehoram had become solidly established as king.*** The Hebrew phrase here (*wayyaqom . . . 'al mamlekath 'abiw* [TH6965, ZH7756]) elsewhere denotes "to rise against" and here means "But Jehoram rose against the kingdom of his father" (Deut 19:11; Judg 9:18; 1 Sam 17:35; Amos 7:9), rather than NLT's "had become solidly established as king." This is unique for a king to rise against his own kingdom and sets in motion motifs repeated by his wife Athaliah in 22:10.

21:6 ***one of Ahab's daughters.*** This is a reference to Athaliah, probably the daughter of Ahab and Jezebel (18:1; 2 Kgs 8:18). See note on 22:2 below.

21:7 ***shining like a lamp forever.*** On the image of a lamp, see 1 Kgs 11:36.

21:12 ***letter.*** On such a medium for prophecy, see evidence from Mari cited by Williamson (1982:307).

21:14 ***your people.*** Japhet (1993:814) argues that here "your people" refers only to Jehoram's family, ignoring the fact that the king's actions in Chronicles often affect the people and that 21:17 refers to an attack on Judah.

21:16 ***Ethiopians.*** See NLT mg, which identifies these as the Cushites. This may be a reference to Egypt as Ethiopia (because of Ethiopian hegemony in the late eighth and early seventh centuries BC; ABD 2.666). It may reflect close associations between Ethiopians and Sabeans or Arabs or migrations of Ethiopians to the Arabian Peninsula, the Negev, or Edom (ABD 2.666). It may also be a reference not to the Ethiopians but to a Bedouin tribe to the south of Judah (Williamson 1982:308). Note the reference to the Cushites in relation to southwest Judah in 2 Chr 14:13 (Japhet 1993:814).

COMMENTARY

It was noted at the outset of the account of Jehoshaphat that the Chronicler skipped over a large portion of his source (1 Kgs 15:25–21:29) when moving from his account of Asa to his account of Jehoshaphat. This happened again when he moved from the account of Jehoshaphat to that of his son Jehoram, excising in the process 1 Kings 22:51—2 Kings 8:16 and with it the record of (1) the ministry of the prophet Elisha and his contemporaries, (2) the northern kings Ahaziah and Joram (Jehoram), (3) the two sons of Ahab, and (4) the final members of the Omride dynasty. In this the Chronicler revealed his agenda to focus on the southern kingdom with its Davidic dynasty.

According to Japhet (1993:806), the narrative sequence found in chapter 21 is typical of the Chronicler, who writes of sin, punishment, further sin, warning, realization of sin, warning, and conclusion. With the death of Jehoshaphat, the southern kingdom moves into its first extended period of crisis, a period that continues for the next two chapters through the accounts of Jehoram, Ahaziah, and Athaliah. The final account takes Judah to the nadir of despair, threatening the survival of the dynasty itself.

Although Jehoshaphat's faith will be celebrated throughout these accounts (21:12; 22:9), the stimulus for the decline of the kingdom can be traced to Jehoshaphat's penchant for alliances with the northern kingdom (18:1–19:3; 20:35-37). Such alliances brought Jehoshaphat under the political domination of the more powerful Omride dynasty, which ruled the north, not only through military and economic partnerships and enterprises (chs 18, 20) but ultimately and more precariously through intermarriage with the Omrides. The power of intermarriage to enable the Omrides to influence the internal affairs of the southern kingdom is evident in the similarity of royal names in this period—northern kingdom: Omri, Ahab, *Ahaziah, Jehoram;* southern kingdom: Asa, Jehoshaphat, *Jehoram, Ahaziah.* The marriage of Jehoshaphat's son Jehoram to Ahab's daughter Athaliah (2 Kgs 8:18, 27) ensured northern meddling in southern political and religious affairs (21:6; 22:4-5) and nearly led to the extinction of the Davidic dynasty by the Omride princess Athaliah (22:10). Japhet (1993:807) argues that this event is "the most severe crisis in the history of the Judean monarchy—excepting only the destruction itself."[1]

This concern of dynastic extinction serves as a consistent leitmotif in the Chronicler's account throughout these two chapters; it sets the tone for and contributes significantly to the darkness of the narrative. This leitmotif, which De Vries (1989:335) calls "the schema of Dynastic Endangerment," is introduced in the description of the early phase of Jehoram's reign, as the new king purges the royal house of all his brothers (21:4), an act that prompts divine judgment in the letter from Elijah (21:13). The motif is reintroduced in the following: (1) the attack of the Philistine-Arab coalition, who carried away all of Jehoram's sons except one (21:17); (2) the reminder of this event in the accession note of Ahaziah (22:1); (3) Jehu's assassination of Ahaziah and the sons of his brothers (22:8-9); and (4) Athaliah's purge of the rest of the Judean royal family save one (22:10-12). In an ironic twist, this trend of purging proves positive for the Davidic line since it leads to the removal from the Davidic dynasty of the stain and influence of the Omrides introduced by Athaliah.

Summary Note: The Accession of Jehoram (21:1b). The account of Jehoram begins in typical fashion with the announcement of the beginning of his reign. The note on his father's burial with the other kings is a sign of a peaceful end to Jehoshaphat's life and the burial site in Jerusalem of the respect with which he was honored. Information on Jehoram's age at accession and length of reign is left off until 21:5.

Jehoshaphat's Preparations for Succession and Jehoram's Assassinations (21:2-4). At this point the Chronicler inserts an extended note describing Jehoram's purge of the royal house after his father's death. There were potential successors to the throne of Jehoshaphat, a sign of God's blessing of the dynasty in general and Jehoram's father in particular. In case of the premature death of the crown prince, there were others who could be called upon to rule. Jehoshaphat appears to have followed the wise policy of his great-grandfather Rehoboam by appointing one of his sons as crown prince and providing economic and political resources for the others (11:22-23), a move that was designed to sustain a stable and faithful court. Unfortunately, Jehoram found this intimidating; upon the death of his father, and with a strong hold on the royal throne, he proceeded to purge the royal court of any potential threats both inside and outside his family. This kind of move at the outset of a reign was not atypical in the ancient Near East (Judg 9:5-6; 1 Kgs 2; 2 Kgs 10:11; 11:1; Dillard 1987:165; Williamson 1982:304),[2] but it is certainly not celebrated by the Chronicler. De Vries (1989:335) highlights the way in which Jehoram's evil returns on his own head: "Just as Jehoram, the *bekor* [TH1060, ZH1147], firstborn, has disposed of sibling rivals, he is in the end punished by having all but the very youngest of his sons, Ahaziah, murdered by the Arabs."

Length of Reign (21:5). Returning to his source in Kings, the Chronicler provides information on the age of Jehoram at accession (32) and the length of his reign (8 years). In light of the assassinations of 21:2-4, the reader would have understood the reason for such a short reign.

Evaluation of Jehoram's Reign (21:6-7). Continuing with this source, the Chronicler includes the typical material on the evaluation of the king's reign, here noting that "Jehoram did what was evil in the LORD's sight." This evil is defined in the previous sentence as following the example of the northern kings, singling out the wickedness of King Ahab. The conduit for this wickedness is clearly identified as the daughter of Ahab, named as Athaliah in 2 Kings 8:26. This note is very important because it reveals that the kingdom of David, which had divided after the reign of Solomon, was now reuniting, but now around a common agenda of evil and a common dynasty without Davidic credentials. In spite of this the text notes God's enduring commitment to the Davidic dynasty because of the covenant he had made. The Chronicler had changed the form of this link to the Davidic line: Second Kings 8:19 speaks of the Lord's unwillingness to destroy "Judah" for the sake of David, but the Chronicler speaks of the Lord's unwillingness to destroy "David's dynasty" because of his covenant with David, a change that Williamson (1982:305) sees as strengthening "the allusion to the unconditional promise to the Davidic dynasty" (cf. 6:42; 13:5; 1 Chr 17).[3] This greater emphasis on the dynastic promise reveals the Chronicler's hope for the reinstitution of the line (cf. Williamson 1977a:148-149).[4] As Dillard (1987:169) has so aptly written:

> *It is precisely at this nadir of religious fidelity that the Chronicler reiterates and elaborates on God's promises to David (21:7). The Chronicler's treatment of the validity of the Davidic covenant in the past no doubt spoke also to the dynastic aspirations of his post-exilic audience; it is hard to believe that the author would invoke God's fidelity to this promise to David for the past unless hope of a dynastic restoration was also a feature of his own faith.*

Selman (1994b:433-434) compares this emphasis on the Davidic covenant to the earlier one at 13:5 (Abijah), where the Davidic house was also under severe threat (there also from the northern kingdom). Both there and here reference is made to 1 Chronicles 17:4-14, where provision is made for discipline of the Davidic house (7:19-22; 1 Chr 28:9).

Some see the image of the "lamp," so important to the Davidic tradition (see 1 Kgs 11:36), as signifying the life of the line (Hanson 1968), but Selman (1994b:434) argues convincingly that it signifies permanence (cf. the impermanent lamp of the wicked: Job 18:5; Prov 13:9; 24:20). In this way the passage emphasizes the fragility of the dynasty apart from God's providential care. The reference to this promise in the midst of chapters 21–22 is very important, since these chapters reveal one of the greatest threats to the dynasty in the nation's history, seen especially in the recurring motif of the purging of the royal family. As noted earlier, this endangerment of the line would ultimately lead to its cleansing from the influence of the northern Omrides.

Revolts of Edom and Libnah from Jehoram's Rule (21:8-11). The short account of Jehoram stands in stark contrast to the account of his father in chapters 17–20, not only in length but in tone. In his source in Kings, the Chronicler found two short stories describing revolts that took place during his reign, the first by Edom, who crowned their own king (21:8-9), and the second by Libnah (21:10). Edom lay in the territory to the southeast of the Dead Sea, Libnah in the southwestern territory of Judah, most likely in the Shephelah.[5]

The reason for these revolts is expressed in an addition by the Chronicler, who reflects his favorite language and historiographic agenda: "because Jehoram had abandoned (*'azab* [TH5800, ZH6440]) the LORD, the God of his ancestors" (21:10b). This abandonment is specified in 21:11 as the building of "pagan shrines" (high places) in the hill country of Judah and leading the people into idolatry. Japhet (1993:811) highlights the dreadful character of Jehoram's reign when she writes, "Jehoram's special guilt was in his willful and malicious incitement of the people to the wrong way. More than any other king—even Manasseh (cf. 2 Chr 33.9)—Jehoram is presented as intentionally leading the people astray."

Elijah's Letter of Judgment (21:12-15). As has been the custom in the account of the divided kingdom, the Chronicler now introduces a proclamation of the prophetic word, this time by Elijah the prophet, whose tradition has been entirely ignored in the Chronicler's use of the book of Kings. Using a prophet known for his attack on a northern king in the book of Kings to speak to a southern king is a motif that appears not only here; just as Elijah is known in the book of Kings for his rebuke of Ahab, Jehu son of Hanani is known for his rebuke of Baasha in 1 Kings 16:1, 7, yet he also addresses King Jehoshaphat of Judah (19:1-3). The appearance of this motif in the accounts of both Jehoshaphat and Jehoram highlights even further the dangerous liaison between the legitimate southern kingdom and the illegitimate northern kingdom.

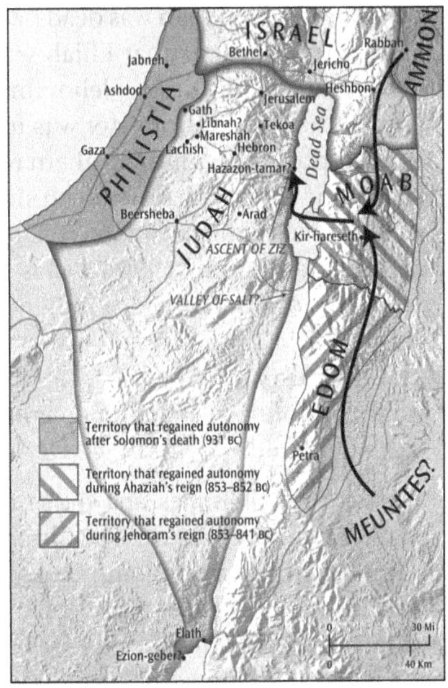

Judah from Jehoshaphat to Ahaziah, 872–841 BC

Here the prophetic message comes in the form of a letter, which accurately reviews the wickedness of Jehoram, contrasting him with his father, Jehoshaphat, and his grandfather Asa, and comparing him to Ahab, his father-in-law. This connection to Ahab is what Mason (1990:78) calls "a fearful warning against 'Israel-like' behavior." Dillard (1987:164) wisely notes that Jehoram's reign is presented by the Chronicler as the unraveling of the accomplishments of his grandfather (Asa) and father (Jehoshaphat): losing the regions captured by them in the east and south (21:8-10; cf. 14:9-15; ch 20), facing attacks from Philistines and Arabs (21:16), and fostering worship at the high places (21:11). Jehoram was also attacked for the murder of his brothers.

One of the main emphases of the prophetic attack is what Japhet (1993:814) calls the "emphatic familial context of Jehoram's transgressions." He not only betrayed the ideals of his predecessors David, Jehoshaphat, and Asa, but threatened the dynasty through his murderous rampage. As Japhet (1993:814) concludes: "The most elementary of a man's obligations, loyalty to his own kindred, his 'father's house', has been abandoned."

The pronouncement of judgment was not limited to Jehoram alone, for it says that the Lord will strike the king, his people, his children, his wives, and all his possessions with a "plague" (NLT, "a heavy blow"), the same term used in

1 Chronicles 21:17, 22 for the punishment of God on Jerusalem because of the sin of David. While increase in progeny and possessions is a sign of God's blessing in Chronicles, loss is seen as a sign of God's judgment (cf. Mason 1990:77; see introduction to chs 10–36). The one who would suffer the most is Jehoram himself, who would experience a "severe intestinal disease" that would ultimately lead to his bowels coming out. Lack of health has been cited before as a form of God's judgment, in particular in the case of Jehoram's grandfather Asa (16:12).

There have been many questions as to the authenticity of this letter from Elijah (see De Vries 1989:333; Mason 1990:75, note 113; Williamson 1982:306-307). First, the letter reflects the vocabulary and agenda of the Chronicler, and second, the letter form used here does not reflect the examples of correspondence that have been uncovered by archaeologists in Israel (Pardee and Sperling 1982). While some have claimed that Elijah was dead before the reign of Jehoram (cf. Japhet 1993:812), 2 Kings 1:17 suggests that Elijah was alive for at least the first couple of years of Jehoram's reign, the time of Jehoram's bloody purge of the royal family. Others have claimed that Elijah's ministry was focused on the northern kingdom, but 1 Kings 19:3, 8 reports forays into southern regions: Beersheba and Sinai. Although the final form of the letter has clearly been shaped by the Chronicler, a historical link to Elijah is not out of the question (cf. Dillard 1987:167-168; Selman 1994b:435-436).[6] Furthermore, Mason (1990:74) has shown how the letter follows the structure of a prophetic announcement of judgment with the typical elements of the messenger formula (21:12), the basis for accusation introduced by a Hebrew causal particle (21:12-13; usually *ki* [TH3588, ZH3954], but here *takhat 'asher* [TH8478/834A, ZH9393/889]), and the announcement of judgment introduced by the Hebrew word *hinneh* [TH2009, ZH2180] ("behold," 21:14-15; cf. De Vries 1989:333).

An Attack of Philistines and Arabs against Jehoram (21:16-17). The judgment of Jehoram was not complete. The Chronicler also included an attack that came from the southwest, from a group comprised of Philistines and Arabs living near the Ethiopians (described as "marauding bands of Arabs" in 22:1 mg). The defeat this time was severe, with the army breaking the defenses of the nation and taking the palace in Jerusalem, which was then looted of everything of value including (and especially) the king's children and wives. This loss of the royal family, except the crown prince Ahaziah, is ironic in light of Jehoram's purge of his own family at the outset of the account.

The phrase used here for the attack of the Philistine and Arabs is literally, "the LORD stirred up the spirit of" (NLT, "the LORD stirred up"). This makes it clear that this was divine discipline on Jehoram. But more importantly, this phrase is the same one used in connection with the exile of the Transjordanian northern tribes in 1 Chronicles 5:26.[7] This is ironic in light of the fact that Jehoram had married the northern princess Athaliah. The attack by the Philistine-Arab coalition nearly extinguished the Davidic line. Jehoram's reign placed the Davidic line in a situation as precarious as the ultimate exile of Judah.

Jehoram's Health Crisis (21:18-19). The Chronicler includes, finally, the account of the fulfillment of Elijah's prophetic judgment from 21:12-15. Though nothing is said about a plague upon the nation as a whole, the Chronicler was careful to catalogue Jehoram's health crisis. As promised, the disease "caused his bowels to come out," possibly a reference to a fatal bout of diarrhea or to ulcers causing rectal collapse (see further Williamson 1982:308; though note the caution of Japhet 1993:816). The Chronicler notes that the great funeral fire that had burned for Jehoram's grandfather Asa did not burn for Jehoram because of the lack of honor he suffered among the people.

Summary Note: The Reign of Jehoram (21:20). This verse represents a repeat of 21:5, with the added comment of the peoples' lack of regret over his death. While popularity is a sign of blessing in Chronicles, the lack of it is a sign of curse. Further dishonor is highlighted by the fact that although Jehoram's body was buried in the City of David, it was not placed in the cemetery of the kings as was his father, Jehoshaphat, who was buried "with his ancestors" (21:1).

The Chronicler's account of Jehoram reveals the discipline that awaits the king who disobeys Yahweh. Jehoram's paranoid eradication of the royal house at the outset of his reign came back on his own head; by the end of this story his own court was left with only one heir to the throne. Elijah's prophetic letter reveals that Jehoram was really a northern king within the Davidic dynasty, and the sickness he experienced revealed God's deep displeasure with him. Yet, in spite of this, the Chronicler does not abandon the promise of an enduring dynasty for David, citing the promise of a lamp to burn forever (21:7). It is important that the Chronicler notes this during the reign of Jehoram, for the following chapters will describe the descent of the dynasty into its greatest crisis yet.

ENDNOTES

1. Japhet (1993:806-807) notes that concern for succession is found in Samuel—Kings at the time of Solomon (1 Kgs 1-2) and Athaliah (2 Kgs 11). Since the Chronicler removes any question of succession at the time of Solomon's accession, even greater emphasis is placed on the period of Athaliah.
2. In the Persian period Cyrus's son Cambyses eliminated his brother before leaving for his Egyptian campaign, a move intended to secure his hold on the central part of the kingdom during his extended military campaign; see Briant 2002. However, this strategy was a complete failure for Cambyses, as the central part of the empire rebelled anyway, leading to the accession of Darius to the throne.
3. Japhet (1993:809) suspects 2 Kgs 8:19 is corrupt and originally read as Chronicles does, but the evidence is insufficient.
4. Contra Mason (1990:76), who speaks of the theocratic community "which we have seen to be the true manifestation of the Davidic line."
5. Some say Libnah should be identified as Tel es-Safi at the western end of the Elah Valley (Dillard 1987:166), but this is almost certainly not the case, since Tel es-Safi is now linked to Gath (Negev 1990:s.vv. "Gath"); see also Selman 1994b:435, note 431. It was regained by Hezekiah.
6. Mason (1990:78-79) argues that the letter form reflects the Chronicler's sense of a canonical corpus of prophecy that speaks to all time. In his opinion Elijah cannot personally confront Jehoram except through written form. This echoes the use of earlier prophecy in passages like Zech 1:4-6 (cf. Ackroyd 1973:154).
7. It is true that this phrase is usually used more positively to refer to God's arousing people to do his will (36:22-23; Hag 1:14); however, another negative example appears in Jer 51:11.

◆ H. Ahaziah's Reign (22:1-9)

Then the people of Jerusalem made Aha-
ziah, Jehoram's youngest son, their next
king, since the marauding bands who
came with the Arabs* had killed all the
older sons. So Ahaziah son of Jehoram
reigned as king of Judah.
2Ahaziah was twenty-two* years old
when he became king, and he reigned in
Jerusalem one year. His mother was Ath-
aliah, a granddaughter of King Omri.
3Ahaziah also followed the evil example of
King Ahab's family, for his mother en-
couraged him in doing wrong. 4He did
what was evil in the LORD's sight, just as
Ahab's family had done. They even be-
came his advisers after the death of his
father, and they led him to ruin.
5Following their evil advice, Ahaziah
joined King Joram,* the son of King Ahab
of Israel, in his war against King Hazael of
Aram at Ramoth-gilead. When the
Arameans wounded Joram in the battle,
6he returned to Jezreel to recover from the
wounds he had received at Ramoth.* Be-
cause Joram was wounded, King Ahaziah*
of Judah went to Jezreel to visit him.
7But God had decided that this visit
would be Ahaziah's downfall. While he
was there, Ahaziah went out with Joram
to meet Jehu grandson of Nimshi,* whom
the LORD had appointed to destroy the dy-
nasty of Ahab.
8While Jehu was executing judgment
against the family of Ahab, he happened to
meet some of Judah's officials and Aha-
ziah's relatives* who were traveling with
Ahaziah. So Jehu killed them all. 9Then
Jehu's men searched for Ahaziah, and they
found him hiding in the city of Samaria.
They brought him to Jehu, who killed him.
Ahaziah was given a decent burial because
the people said, "He was the grandson of
Jehoshaphat—a man who sought the LORD
with all his heart." But none of the surviv-
ing members of Ahaziah's family was ca-
pable of ruling the kingdom.

22:1 Or *marauding bands of Arabs.* **22:2** As in some Greek manuscripts and Syriac version (see also 2 Kgs 8:26); Hebrew reads *forty-two.* **22:5** Hebrew *Jehoram,* a variant spelling of Joram; also in 22:6, 7. **22:6a** Hebrew *Ramah,* a variant spelling of Ramoth. **22:6b** As in some Hebrew manuscripts, Greek and Syriac versions, and Latin Vulgate (see also 2 Kgs 8:29); most Hebrew manuscripts read *Azariah.* **22:7** Hebrew *descendant of Nimshi;* compare 2 Kgs 9:2, 14. **22:8** As in Greek version (see also 2 Kgs 10:13); Hebrew reads *and sons of the brothers of Ahaziah.*

NOTES

22:1 ***Then the people of Jerusalem made Ahaziah . . . their next king.*** Participation of citizenry in the accession process always follows a violent death in Chronicles (23:1-3; 26:1; 33:25; 36:1; cf. De Vries 1989:334; Japhet 1993:818).

22:2 ***twenty-two years old.*** See NLT mg. The age 42 (in the Hebrew text) is impossible if Ahaziah's father Jehoram died at 40 (21:5, 20).

granddaughter of King Omri. Second Kings 8:26 refers to Athaliah as "daughter of Omri," but the NLT is justified in translating the Hebrew word *bath* [TH1323, ZH1426] as granddaughter since, like the Hebrew word *ben* [TH1121, ZH1201] (which often means "son"), it signifies "descendant of." Japhet (1993:809) sees this as a generic term for "Omride" (that is, someone from the house or dynasty of the northern king Omri, father of Ahab).

22:3 ***for his mother encouraged him in doing wrong.*** For the expected role of the queen mother, see note on 15:16 above; cf. 1 Kgs 1:11-31; 2:13-21; 15:13; 21:5-7; 2 Kgs 10:13; 24:12, 15; Jer 13:18. See Andreasen 1983:179-194; Dillard 1987:174; ABD 5.583-586.

22:5 ***King Hazael of Aram.*** Hazael is known from biblical and Assyrian sources in the latter half of the ninth century BC as a ruler in Damascus who faced serious challenges from Assyria at times but who was able to lead the Aramean kingdom of Damascus to dominance in the Levant (see 2 Kgs 10:32-33; 12:17-18; 13:22).

Ramoth-gilead. This was the chief city of the tribe of Gad, about 70 miles south of Damascus and about 50 miles east-northeast of Samaria in the northern Transjordan region. It is regularly cited in conflicts between Israel and Damascus (e.g., 1 Kgs 22:3; cf. 1 Kgs 15:20), most likely due to its strategic position on the key international trade route (the King's Highway) that ran along the Transjordanian plateau.

COMMENTARY

With the end of Jehoram's reign, signaled by his burial (21:20b), the Chronicler moves with his source to the reign of Jehoram's youngest son, Ahaziah, the only survivor of the attack of the Philistine-Arab coalition in 21:17. Although there is a change in royal figures, the enduring presence of Athaliah and the threat to the Davidic dynasty suggest to Williamson (1982:309) that 22:1-9 is but a "close continuation of Jehoram's reign" (see list of common expressions in Selman 1994b:431-432).

Ahaziah, whose name is also given as Jehoahaz (see 21:17; 25:23) and Azariah (22:6),[1] was the only surviving son of Athaliah, daughter of the northern king Ahab (22:10). This lineage means that Ahaziah was the first ruler of the southern kingdom with genealogical connections to the northern kingdom, a fact that explains the close relationship he shared with his uncle Joram on the northern throne, a relationship that would lead to his untimely death (22:7-10).

Summary Note: The Accession of Ahaziah (22:1-4). Ahaziah's reign began when he was 22 years old, raising expectations that this royal child who was the lone hope for the Davidic line had the potential to bring stability to the southern kingdom through a long tenure. However, this hope was immediately dashed—he reigned for only one year. The Chronicler attributes his short tenure to the fact that he "did what was evil in the LORD's sight."

The account of this evil is dominated by references to the intrusion of the northern kingdom, an intrusion emphasized by the Chronicler's threefold use of the Hebrew root *y-'-ts* [TH3289, ZH3619] (counsel), appearing in 22:3 ("his mother *encouraged* him in doing wrong"), 22:4 ("they even became his *advisers* . . . and they led him to ruin"), and 22:5 ("following their evil *advice*").[2] This evaluation, drawn predominantly from the Chronicler's source in 2 Kings 8:25-29, cites the example and advice of "King Ahab's family," mediated and encouraged by his mother, "Athaliah, a granddaughter of King Omri" (22:2-4). The Chronicler's account thus casts Ahaziah "as a victim rather than as an instigator" (Japhet 1993:821). The seeds planted when Jehoshaphat made alliances with the Omride dynasty had now germinated and grown as weeds about to choke out the dynastic promise given to David.

Ahaziah's Alliance with Joram and Execution by Jehu (22:5-9a). Following the advice of advisers from the northern kingdom, which showed that for all intents and purposes the northern kingdom had staged a coup over their southern neighbors, Ahaziah mobilized his army to join the northern army of Joram against the Arameans led by Hazael. Second Kings 8:7-15 describes Elisha's role in affirming Hazael's successful coup against his master Ben-hadad, who ruled the Arameans in the area around Damascus. The site of conflict between Israel and the Arameans was Ramoth-gilead (see note on 22:5).

While Jehoshaphat barely escaped with his life in his involvement in Ahab's war at Ramoth-gilead (18:30-32), his grandson Ahaziah would not be so blessed when he joined Ahab's son Joram at the same location. During the battle Joram was wounded and was taken for convalescence to Jezreel, the winter capital of the Omride dynasty located at the foot of Mount Gilboa in the Jezreel Valley (1 Kgs 18:45-46; 21:1; 2 Kgs 9:30). Ahaziah paid his respects to his ailing uncle by visiting him and there met his death at the hand of Jehu. Since the Chronicler left out the narratives about Elijah and Elisha, the background to Jehu's rampage is only available in 2 Kings 9. There Jehu is identified as a military leader in the northern army who was anointed by Elisha's servant to bring an end to the Omride dynasty by assassinating the wounded Joram and his family. The full account of Jehu's plot is provided in the Chronicler's source in Kings, but the Chronicler truncated it substantially, choosing to focus on the movements of the southern king. The Chronicler affirmed that God's will was the cause behind the death of Ahaziah on that fateful day (22:7). Although Ahaziah escaped the initial attack at Jezreel that claimed Joram's life, the Chronicler records that he was finally captured in Samaria and brought to Jehu for execution.[3] The Chronicler's source in Kings gives more detail on the pursuit, capture, and execution in the region of Samaria. Second Kings 9:27 records that Jehu pursued Ahaziah in the direction of Beth-haggan and that his men shot the southern king while he was fleeing in his chariot at the ascent of Gur near Ibleam and he died at Megiddo. Ibleam and Beth-haggan are approximately 7 miles south of Jezreel on the southern side of the Jezreel Valley; Megiddo is on the same southern side about 11 miles northwest of Ibleam. These locations show that Ahaziah was trying to escape south to safety in Jerusalem through the major passes. Chariots could be used in the Jezreel Valley but probably would have been abandoned as the king moved into the hill country. Not only did the southern king Ahaziah die on that day, but also a substantial group of his officials and relatives who were in his entourage.

Selman (1994b:437) probably goes too far in saying that the "real subject of chapter 22 is the *house of Ahab.*" Rather, it is better to see that chapter 22 relates the first stage in the eradication of the house of Ahab (Omride dynasty) from the Davidic line. De Vries (1989:337) expresses this well when he notes that the Chronicler "makes sure to repeat from Kings that this includes such Judahite royalty as have descended from Ahab and have been under his influence." After Athaliah's bloody purge at the end of chapter 22, only the infant Joash will remain, one who could be shaped in new ways by the faithful priest Jehoiada (ch 23). The concern expressed over inappropriate northern religious practices may be a reminder to the Chronicler's audience that although members of the northern tribes are truly part of "all Israel," there will be no compromises in religious purity.

Summary Note: The Reign of Ahaziah (22:9b). The final summary note typical at the close of royal accounts is truncated in the Chronicler's source (2 Kgs 9:28), providing information only on his burial in the tomb of his fathers in the City of David. From this summary note, the Chronicler retains only the words "they buried him" (NLT, "Ahaziah was given a decent burial") but then adds an extended note that justifies burial for this wicked king by appealing to the righteousness of his grandfather Jehoshaphat, "who sought (*darash* [TH1875, ZH2011]) the LORD with all his heart" (22:9), an action celebrated throughout the book of Chronicles. The lack of reference to burial in the royal cemetery is a trend throughout chapters 21–23 and suggests to Japhet (1993:824) that for "Chronicles, then, none of the Judaean rulers affiliated with the Ahab line was buried in a manner proper to descendants of the house of David" (cf. 21:20; 22:9; 23:14-15, 21).

In the account in Kings, Ahaziah's death is followed by an odd repetition of the year of Ahaziah's accession to the throne, then by an extended account on Jehu's campaign against Ahab's family, noting the execution of Jezebel and Ahab's sons and the elimination of Baal worship (2 Kgs 9:30–10:28), and concludes with the downfall of Jehu himself (2 Kgs 10:29-36). This is all eliminated by the Chronicler, who keeps his focus on the southern kingdom. Instead of the note on Ahaziah's accession to the throne, the Chronicler accentuates the lack of a capable heir to ascend to the throne (22:9b). Whereas at the end of the reign of each of the previous kings of the southern kingdom there has been an heir waiting in the wings, this time there is none, a reality that deepens the crisis in Judah, creating a parallel to the crisis at the end of the reign of Saul (see 1 Chr 10:6, 13-14)[4] and providing a segue to Athaliah's reign of terror (22:10-12).

Such a note of despair as this must have resonated with the Chronicler's audience and suggests that part of the Chronicler's agenda is to encourage hope in a future royal rule, as Dillard (1987:175) has written: "Surely the lesson was not lost on his post-exilic audience: even in adversity the royal line was preserved and would eventually regain the kingdom. Davidic hopes did not die at the time of Ahaziah, Athaliah, and Joash; they should not die in the post-exilic period." This "close call" for the Davidic line has a redemptive purpose, something suggested by Mosis (1973:179) when he identifies Ahaziah's death with his "exile" motif and Joash with "restoration." Connections forged between the death of Ahaziah and that of Saul at the outset of the Chronicler's story in 1 Chronicles 10 (cf. Mitchell 2006; Williamson 1982:109-110) suggest that Joash was being presented as a new David.[5]

ENDNOTES

1. Jehoahaz is simply a reversal of the elements of the name of Ahaziah (*'ahaz* + *yah*), placing Yahweh's name first (*yah*) and *'ahaz* second. Azariah appears to be a scribal error.
2. Japhet 1993:820-821. Compare the Chronicler's source text in 2 Kgs 8:27. De Vries (1989:336) notes that a prophet should have functioned in this role of counsel (cf. 25:16).
3. See Dillard 1987:172-173 for a detailed discussion of contrasts between Kings and Chronicles on the account of Ahaziah. What is often missed in these discussions is that the term "Samaria" was the provincial name of the northern region during the period of the Persian Empire. It is plausible that the Chronicler was warning his audience about the danger of close associations with the administration in the province of Samaria by using this term.
4. For this see Williamson (1982:309-310), who follows Mosis (1973:179) in seeing the end of Saul's reign as resulting in conditions akin to the Exile. Additionally, this serves to link Ahaziah to Saul, whose dynasty came to an end.
5. Although see Selman (1994b:441-442), who attacks this and claims it is better to see here the fate of the Davidic house (rather than Saulide house) in exile (see Jer 22:29-30).

◆ I. Athaliah's Reign until Overthrown by Jehoiada (22:10–23:21)

10When Athaliah, the mother of King
Ahaziah of Judah, learned that her son
was dead, she began to destroy the rest of
Judah's royal family. 11But Ahaziah's sister
Jehosheba,* the daughter of King Je-
horam, took Ahaziah's infant son, Joash,
and stole him away from among the rest
of the king's children, who were about to
be killed. She put Joash and his nurse in a
bedroom. In this way, Jehosheba, wife of
Jehoiada the priest and sister of Ahaziah,
hid the child so that Athaliah could not
murder him. 12Joash remained hidden in
the Temple of God for six years while Ath-
aliah ruled over the land.

CHAPTER 23

In the seventh year of Athaliah's reign,
Jehoiada the priest decided to act. He
summoned his courage and made a pact
with five army commanders: Azariah son
of Jeroham, Ishmael son of Jehohanan,
Azariah son of Obed, Maaseiah son of
Adaiah, and Elishaphat son of Zicri. 2 These
men traveled secretly throughout Judah
and summoned the Levites and clan lead-
ers in all the towns to come to Jerusalem.
3They all gathered at the Temple of God,
where they made a solemn pact with
Joash, the young king.

Jehoiada said to them, "Here is the
king's son! The time has come for him to
reign! The LORD has promised that a de-
scendant of David will be our king. 4This
is what you must do. When you priests
and Levites come on duty on the Sabbath,
a third of you will serve as gatekeepers.
5Another third will go over to the royal
palace, and the final third will be at the
Foundation Gate. Everyone else should
stay in the courtyards of the LORD's Tem-
ple. 6Remember, only the priests and Le-
vites on duty may enter the Temple of the
LORD, for they are set apart as holy. The
rest of the people must obey the LORD's
instructions and stay outside. 7You Le-
vites, form a bodyguard around the king
and keep your weapons in hand. Kill any-
one who tries to enter the Temple. Stay
with the king wherever he goes."

8So the Levites and all the people of
Judah did everything as Jehoiada the
priest ordered. The commanders took
charge of the men reporting for duty that
Sabbath, as well as those who were going
off duty. Jehoiada the priest did not let
anyone go home after their shift ended.
9Then Jehoiada supplied the commanders
with the spears and the large and small
shields that had once belonged to King
David and were stored in the Temple of
God. 10He stationed all the people around
the king, with their weapons ready. They
formed a line from the south side of the
Temple around to the north side and all
around the altar.

11Then Jehoiada and his sons brought
out Joash, the king's son, placed the crown
on his head, and presented him with a
copy of God's laws.* They anointed him
and proclaimed him king, and everyone
shouted, "Long live the king!"

12When Athaliah heard the noise of the
people running and the shouts of praise
to the king, she hurried to the LORD's
Temple to see what was happening.
13When she arrived, she saw the newly
crowned king standing in his place of
authority by the pillar at the Temple en-
trance. The commanders and trumpeters
were surrounding him, and people from
all over the land were rejoicing and blow-
ing trumpets. Singers with musical instru-
ments were leading the people in a great
celebration. When Athaliah saw all this,
she tore her clothes in despair and shout-
ed, "Treason! Treason!"

14Then Jehoiada the priest ordered the
commanders who were in charge of the
troops, "Take her to the soldiers in front of
the Temple,* and kill anyone who tries to
rescue her." For the priest had said, "She
must not be killed in the Temple of the
LORD." 15So they seized her and led her out
to the entrance of the Horse Gate on the
palace grounds, and they killed her there.

16Then Jehoiada made a covenant be-
tween himself and the king and the peo-
ple that they would be the LORD's people.
17And all the people went over to the
temple of Baal and tore it down. They de-
molished the altars and smashed the idols,
and they killed Mattan the priest of Baal
in front of the altars.

18Jehoiada now put the priests and Le-
vites in charge of the Temple of the LORD,
following all the directions given by Da-
vid. He also commanded them to present
burnt offerings to the LORD, as prescribed
by the Law of Moses, and to sing and re-
joice as David had instructed. 19He also
stationed gatekeepers at the gates of the
LORD's Temple to keep out those who for
any reason were ceremonially unclean.

20Then the commanders, nobles, rulers,
and all the people of the land escorted
the king from the Temple of the LORD.
They went through the upper gate and
into the palace, and they seated the king
on the royal throne. 21So all the people of
the land rejoiced, and the city was peace-
ful because Athaliah had been killed.

22:11 As in parallel text at 2 Kgs 11:2; Hebrew lacks *Ahaziah's sister* and reads *Jehoshabeath* [a variant spelling of Jehosheba]. 23:11 Or *a copy of the covenant.* 23:14 Or *Bring her out from between the ranks;* or *Take her out of the Temple precincts.* The meaning of the Hebrew is uncertain.

NOTES

23:1 ***five army commanders.*** The Hebrew text reads "captains of hundreds" (*sare hamme'oth* [TH8269, ZH8569]). In 2 Kgs 11:4 these are identified as "Carites" and "guards," while in Chronicles five names of individuals are given.

23:2 ***traveled secretly.*** Although one can imagine that these men would have had to be discreet in their travels, the word "secretly" is not found in the Hebrew text.

23:3 ***king.*** Although not officially crowned, the Chronicler considered Joash the legitimate monarch during the reign of Athaliah (Williamson 1982:315).

Here is the king's son! The time has come for him to reign! Lit., "The son of the king shall be king" (JPS).

23:13 ***the pillar.*** This is a reference to one of two massive pillars in the Temple vestibule, the southern one called Jakin and the northern one Boaz (see 3:17; 1 Kgs 7:21). The Hebrew text calls this "his pillar," referring to the king, and 2 Kgs 11:14 says there was a royal custom associated with the pillar. Possibly this means that it had become customary for royal pronouncements or coronations to be announced there. See also how Josiah made his proclamation of a renewed covenant by the pillar in 34:31.

she tore her clothes. This action is used in the OT as a symbol of mourning, submission, repentance, fear, and/or despair (cf. Num 14:6; 2 Kgs 5:7-8; 19:1). Japhet (1993:834) sees this as a sign of Athaliah's powerlessness.

23:11 ***a copy of God's laws.*** What accompanied the crown is not clear; some have suggested it was jewelry or an insignia corresponding to the crown (reading *'adi* [TH5716, ZH6344] instead of *'eduth* [TH5715, ZH6343]) or some kind of document (see Selman 1994b:447). The latter is more likely and could refer to the Torah (as NLT; cf. Deut 17:14-20) or the covenant made with the people in 23:3.

23:14 ***to the soldiers in front of the Temple.*** Note here the two marginal readings in NLT: "Bring her out from between the ranks" and "Take her out of the Temple precincts." These readings are based on the ambiguity of the term *sederah* [TH7713, ZH8444], which is often traced to a root that means "arrange, order" but may be related either to the arrangement of soldiers or the arrangement of a building structure (see parallel in 2 Kgs 11:8, 15, as well as the use in 1 Kgs 6:9).

precincts, his military forces killed her in "the entrance of the Horse Gate on the palace grounds" (23:15). There may be some ironic play here as the hated Jezebel, from whose court Athaliah had come and whose religion she shared, had been trampled to death by horses (see 2 Kgs 9:33; cf. Dillard 1987:183). The lack of a death notice at this point and also lack of succession note at the outset shows that the Chronicler (and his source in Kings) refused to give Athaliah legitimacy as a royal ruler in Judah. The lack of reference to burial in the royal cemetery is something Athaliah shared with all the other "rulers" affiliated with the Ahab line (cf. 21:20; 22:9; 23:14-15, 21; Japhet 1993:824).

With the evil queen dead, Jehoiada is depicted as making a covenant between himself, the people, and the king (23:16). Selman (1994b:449) notes wisely that the climax of the account is not the coronation but rather the covenant that restores the "twin pillars of the Davidic covenant": worship at the Temple (23:17-19) and the king on the throne (23:20-21). Such a covenant is not left in the abstract, however, but results in a series of actions in 23:17-19. These included not only the destruction of the cult of Baal,[4] which had been imported from the northern kingdom through Athaliah, but also the implementation of proper Yahwistic worship. Japhet (1993:836) wisely notes that "for the Chronicler both Israel's worship and idolatry are exclusive; 'evil' rulers introduced 'other gods' not as optional additions to, but as active replacements of God's worship." Such pure worship demanded the functioning of priests and Levites in their proper roles of sacrifice according to the instructions of Moses and of song according to the instructions of David. This is another example of how the Chronicler emphasized David alongside Moses as worship founders in Israel (De Vries 1988:619-639).

Jehoiada's final action is to orchestrate the procession of the people as they transport the new king from the Temple to his royal throne at the palace. The Chronicler emphasizes popular support for this kingship by having the people seat him on the throne (23:20) instead of having the king seat himself on the throne (2 Kgs 11:19). The sign that a new day was dawning for Judah is evident in the Chronicler's description of the joy and peace of the people (23:21), recurring leitmotifs throughout Chronicles. Peace (or quiet) represents lack of struggle and division in the land, while joy represents passionate engagement and support (for joy, see 15:15; 24:10; 30:25; 1 Chr 29:9; for peace, see 14:1; 14:4-6; 20:30).

The Chronicler's source (2 Kgs 11:1-4) depicts how the young Joash remained with Jehosheba, daughter of Jehoram ("with her . . . hid in the house of the LORD"; contrast NLT at 2 Kgs 11:3), followed by the initiative of Jehoiada, the priest, to overthrow Athaliah and place Joash on the throne. The Chronicler explains the connection between Jehosheba and Jehoiada as one of marriage and thus speaks of Joash remaining "with *them* . . . in the house of God" (22:12, lit.). The Chronicler was concerned for proper maintenance of the sacred precincts, and this confirms the legitimacy of Jehosheba's preservation of Joash in the Temple.

This clarification of his source in 22:10-12 explains some of the changes that the Chronicler introduced into his depiction of the overthrow of Athaliah. There is elucidation throughout that the priests and Levites were involved in the overthrow, coronation, and renewal.[5] The captains[6] are sent throughout Judah to gather Levites

(23:2), and "priests and Levites" are mentioned in 23:4, 7, 8, 18-19. The Chronicler makes it clear that Levitical musicians led the coronation trumpets (23:13), that the watchmen placed over the house of Yahweh (23:18) were under the direction of priests and Levites, that the priests and Levites followed the instructions David laid down, and that proper gatekeepers were commissioned.

The Chronicler added a strong directive from Jehoiada in 23:6 that makes it clear that the "house of the LORD" was only accessible to the priests and Levites, who may enter "for they are set apart as holy" (cf. Num 1:51; 3:10; 18:7; Japhet 1993:832). This concern for the sanctity of the house is also emphasized in 23:5, where the people are said to be in the courts, in 23:7 as the Chronicler makes clear that the phrase "tries to break through" (2 Kgs 11:8) means "enter the Temple," and in 23:19, where gatekeepers were placed at the gates of the Temple "to keep out those who for any reason were ceremonially unclean."[7] Furthermore, the king is depicted by the Chronicler as standing "by the pillar at the Temple entrance" (2 Kgs 11:14, "by the pillar, as was the custom"), showing that the king had not breached the sacred precincts.

At the same time, however, the Chronicler expanded this rebellion beyond the loyal guard in Jerusalem to include not only Levites "in all the towns" (lit., "Levites from all the towns of Judah"), but also "the heads of the fathers' houses of Israel" (NLT, "clan leaders"). This emphasis on the larger community is also seen in the Chronicler's addition of references to "all the assembly" in 23:3 (NLT, "they all gathered"), to "all the people" in 23:5 (NLT, "everyone else"), to "all the people of Judah" in 23:8 who obeyed Jehoiada's commission, to "all the people" in 23:10 who participate in guarding the king, and to the inclusion of "nobles" and "rulers" in the royal procession of 23:20.

Although emphasizing the role of the Levites, the Chronicler sought to clarify the relationship between the priestly and royal houses. Jehoiada is given greater voice by the Chronicler, who depicts him introducing Joash and legitimizing the royal line in 23:3: "Here is the king's son! The time has come for him to reign! The LORD has promised that a descendant of David will be our king," in contrast to 2 Kgs 11:4, which merely states, "Then he showed them the king's son." In the coronation proper, the Chronicler makes explicit that the "they" who anointed Joash were "Jehoiada and his sons" (23:11; cf. 2 Kgs 11:12); thus, the priests are depicted as having the responsibility of anointing as well as of legitimizing the royal house. In the account in 2 Kings 11, a covenant was made first between Yahweh, the king, and the people and then between the king and the people (2 Kgs 11:17). In contrast, in the Chronicler's account the covenant between the people and the king is cited in 23:3 as sealing the people's commitment to support Joash against Athaliah (contrast 2 Kgs 11:4, where Jehoiada puts the guards under oath) and later speaks only of a covenant to be "the LORD's people" that was made between Jehoiada, all the people, and the king (23:16). This change certainly raises the level of the priestly caste, involving them in the covenant but also deemphasizing any enduring "secular" covenant between the people and the royal house. Jehoiada's involvement, and thus by extension priestly involvement, in the leadership of the community is deemed important. The truth of this will be confirmed in the Chronicler's depiction of Joash's rule that follows in chapter 24. As long as Jehoiada was alive, Joash and the people obeyed, but the moment he died, they fell away. At the same time the royal house was not expendable, retaining its rightful role of leadership.[8]

This account emphasizes the key role the priests must play in the preservation of true religion in Judah. Furthermore, the contrasts between chapters 23 and 24 suggest that the Chronicler was providing an appropriate model for a future renewal of the royal line, one in which the royal house is guided by the wise and godly counsel of the priestly line. This appears to match the vision provided by Zechariah in the early restoration period (Zech 3; 6:9-15).[9]

ENDNOTES

1. As compared to Chronicles, there is a more powerful literary play between three women in the account in 2 Kings: Jezebel, Athaliah, and Jehosheba. The Chronicler retains only the play between the latter two. The Chronicler only refers to Jehosheba as "the daughter of King Jehoram."
2. Japhet (1993:833) suggests that these were placed in the Temple as votive gifts (5:1; 15:18; 1 Chr 26:26), which could not be used (Lev 27:28), but there is no reason to assume this—the necessity of weapons for the defense of the Temple is not odd.
3. It is uncertain whether this refers to the Sinai covenant, a copy of which was to be given to the king (Deut 17:18), or the covenant ("solemn pact") made between the captains/Levites/clan leaders and Joash mentioned in 23:3.
4. Notice how the Baal priest is slain in that temple's sacred precincts, creating a clear contrast to the sacred precincts of the Yahwistic sanctuary. The Chronicler's source in 2 Kgs 11:18 focuses only on the eradication of the Baal cult, while the Chronicler also includes the positive implementation of Yahwistic worship according to the pattern set out by David.
5. See Dillard 1987:180-182 for the "quasi-military role" of the Levites.
6. Williamson (1982:315) notes that all the captains listed in 23:1, except for Elishaphat, can be found in various lists of priests and Levites elsewhere in Chronicles. Japhet (1993:829) argues that the text does not present them as Levites because the title and organizational structure is never used in Chronicles of Levites. Dillard (1987:180-181) presents evidence on both sides of the issue.
7. Japhet (1993:832) contrasts the Chronicler's account with that found in Kings, noting that whereas in Kings trespassers are slain for political reasons, in Chronicles they are slain for religious reasons: "to prevent the desecration of the Temple."
8. See further Williamson (1982:314), who argues against those who would see here the Chronicler promoting royal prerogatives for the priests when he writes, "The work of Jehoiada, the Chronicler's ideal high priest (cf. 24:15-16), is not at any point that of substitute for the king, but rather of preserver of the dynastic household, of king-maker and of faithful adviser to the crown." Here he sees "a mild polemic against the tendency of the post-exilic high priest to usurp all authority in Jerusalem and an encouragement rather for them to maintain a vision for, and where possible to work towards the realisation of, what the Chronicler always regarded as the ideal for the theocracy of a balance between royal and religious leadership."
9. See Boda 2006d. De Vries (1989:345, 347) emphasizes the subordination of Joash to Jehoiada in these accounts; however, the same elements could be seen as openness to wise counsel.

◆ J. Joash's Reign (24:1-27)

Joash was seven years old when he became king, and he reigned in Jerusalem forty years. His mother was Zibiah from Beersheba. [2]Joash did what was pleasing in the LORD's sight throughout the lifetime of Jehoiada the priest. [3]Jehoiada chose two wives for Joash, and he had sons and daughters.

[4]At one point Joash decided to repair and restore the Temple of the LORD. [5]He summoned the priests and Levites and gave them these instructions: "Go to all the towns of Judah and collect the required annual offerings, so that we can repair the Temple of your God. Do not delay!" But the Levites did not act immediately.

[6]So the king called for Jehoiada the high priest and asked him, "Why haven't you demanded that the Levites go out and collect the Temple taxes from the towns of Judah and from Jerusalem? Moses, the servant of the LORD, levied this tax on the community of Israel in order to maintain the Tabernacle of the Covenant.*"

[7]Over the years the followers of wicked Athaliah had broken into the Temple of God, and they had used all the dedicated things from the Temple of the LORD to worship the images of Baal.

[8]So now the king ordered a chest to be made and set outside the gate leading to the Temple of the LORD. [9]Then a proclamation was sent throughout Judah and Jerusalem, telling the people to bring to the LORD the tax that Moses, the servant of God, had required of the Israelites in the wilderness. [10]This pleased all the leaders and the people, and they gladly brought their money and filled the chest with it.

[11]Whenever the chest became full, the Levites would carry it to the king's officials. Then the court secretary and an officer of the high priest would come and empty the chest and take it back to the Temple again. This went on day after day, and a large amount of money was collected. [12]The king and Jehoiada gave the money to the construction supervisors, who hired masons and carpenters to restore the Temple of the LORD. They also hired metalworkers, who made articles of iron and bronze for the LORD's Temple.

[13]The men in charge of the renovation worked hard and made steady progress. They restored the Temple of God according to its original design and strengthened it. [14]When all the repairs were finished, they brought the remaining money to the king and Jehoiada. It was used to make various articles for the Temple of the LORD—articles for worship services and for burnt offerings, including ladles and other articles made of gold and silver. And the burnt offerings were sacrificed continually in the Temple of the LORD during the lifetime of Jehoiada the priest.

[15]Jehoiada lived to a very old age, finally dying at 130. [16]He was buried among the kings in the City of David, because he had done so much good in Israel for God and his Temple.

[17]But after Jehoiada's death, the leaders of Judah came and bowed before King Joash and persuaded him to listen to their advice. [18]They decided to abandon the Temple of the LORD, the God of their ancestors, and they worshiped Asherah poles and idols instead! Because of this sin, divine anger fell on Judah and Jerusalem. [19]Yet the LORD sent prophets to bring them back to him. The prophets warned them, but still the people would not listen.

[20]Then the Spirit of God came upon Zechariah son of Jehoiada the priest. He stood before the people and said, "This is what God says: Why do you disobey the LORD's commands and keep yourselves from prospering? You have abandoned the LORD, and now he has abandoned you!"

[21]Then the leaders plotted to kill Zechariah, and King Joash ordered that they stone him to death in the courtyard of the LORD's Temple. [22]That was how King Joash repaid Jehoiada for his loyalty—by killing

his son. Zechariah's last words as he died
were, "May the LORD see what they are
doing and avenge my death!"
23 In the spring of the year* the Aramean
army marched against Joash. They invaded
Judah and Jerusalem and killed all the
leaders of the nation. Then they sent all the
plunder back to their king in Damascus.
24 Although the Arameans attacked with
only a small army, the LORD helped them
conquer the much larger army of Judah.
The people of Judah had abandoned the
LORD, the God of their ancestors, so judg-
ment was carried out against Joash.
25 The Arameans withdrew, leaving Joash
severely wounded. But his own officials
plotted to kill him for murdering the son*
of Jehoiada the priest. They assassinated
him as he lay in bed. Then he was buried
in the City of David, but not in the royal
cemetery. 26 The assassins were Jozacar,*
the son of an Ammonite woman named
Shimeath, and Jehozabad, the son of a
Moabite woman named Shomer.*
27 The account of the sons of Joash, the
prophecies about him, and the record of
his restoration of the Temple of God are
written in *The Commentary on the Book of
the Kings.* His son Amaziah became the
next king.

24:6 Hebrew *Tent of the Testimony.* **24:23** Hebrew *At the turn of the year.* The first day of the year in the ancient Hebrew lunar calendar occurred in March or April. **24:25** As in Greek version and Latin Vulgate; Hebrew reads *sons.* **24:26a** As in parallel text at 2 Kgs 12:21; Hebrew reads *Zabad.* **24:26b** As in parallel text at 2 Kgs 12:21; Hebrew reads *Shimrith,* a variant spelling of Shomer.

NOTES

24:6 ***Moses, the servant of the LORD, levied this tax.*** See the census tax in Exod 30:12-16.

Tabernacle of the Covenant. Lit., "tent of the testimony," a term unique to the Chronicler describing the Tabernacle in which the Ark of the Covenant was kept during the wilderness wanderings.

24:7 ***Baal.*** See note on 17:3.

24:11 ***the Levites would carry it to the king's officials.*** Dillard (1987:191) points out that Mesopotamian temples had a royal official who protected the financial interests of the crown.

24:15 ***Jehoiada lived to a very old age.*** Lit., "Jehoiada grew old and was full of days," a phrase also used of David by the Chronicler in 1 Chr 23:1.

24:18 ***Asherah poles.*** See notes on 17:6 and 31:1.

24:20 ***the Spirit of God came upon.*** Lit., "the Spirit of God clothed," the same expression used of Amasai in 1 Chr 12:18 [19] (but not of Azariah in 15:1).

24:23 ***In the spring of the year.*** Lit., "at the turn of the year" (see NLT mg), which occurred in March/April. It was the time when kings would venture off for war in a period after harvest when supplies, tribute, and taxes were readily available (see 1 Chr 20:1; cf. 2 Sam 11:1; 1 Kgs 20:26).

the Aramean army. The parallel account in 2 Kgs 12:17 gives more details, identifying the Syrian king as Hazael and showing that this followed an initial victory at Gath. Hazael, whose reign was prophesied by Elisha (2 Kgs 8:7-15), was able to create an empire in the mid to lower Levant, making Israel and Judah his vassals (2 Kgs 8:28-29; 9; 10:32-33; 12:17-18) and possibly also the Transjordanian kingdoms of Ammon, Moab, and Edom (ABD 3.83).

COMMENTARY

Summary Note: The Reign of Joash (24:1-3). After the hiatus of chapter 23, the Chronicler was finally able to provide an accession note for the Davidic king. From his source in Kings he left out the reference to Jehu (2 Kgs 12:1) but also clarified the evaluation of Joash. The writer of Kings claimed that "all his life Joash did what was pleasing in the LORD's sight because Jehoiada the priest instructed him" (2 Kgs 12:2), but then admitted immediately that Joash "did not destroy the pagan shrines, and the people still offered sacrifices and burned incense there" (2 Kgs 12:3). The Chronicler understood this to mean that Joash's righteous actions were related to the counsel he received from Jehoiada, but not his unrighteous actions. The Chronicler's account of Joash is divided into two phases: a righteous phase during the lifetime of Jehoiada (24:4-16) and an unrighteous phase after his death (24:17-22). This unrighteous phase also demonstrates the Chronicler's principle that those who do not follow Yahweh will receive retribution. This arrangement of the narrative into positive and negative phases will be used by the Chronicler for his accounts of Joash (ch 24), Amaziah (ch 25), and Uzziah (ch 26).

The Chronicler also added into his account in 24:3 that Jehoiada was responsible for Joash's marriages and that Joash was blessed with children. On one hand, this is the Chronicler's way of signaling God's blessing for a king (see elsewhere 11:18-23; 13:21; 1 Chr 14:3-7; cf. Williamson 1982:319); on the other hand, it is a sign of a new start for the Davidic line. Japhet (1993:841) states, "the 'sons and daughters' born of these unions give concrete expression to both the physical renewal and the moral blessing of the Davidic line." Greater care had to be taken in this area after the debacle caused by the inappropriate marriage of Jehoram to the northern Omride princess Athaliah that nearly resulted in the annihilation of the Davidic line (chs 18–22).

Joash's Reforms during the Lifetime of Jehoiada (24:4-14). After arranging proper marriages for Joash, Jehoiada begins to fade into the background, and Joash's character comes to the fore. The new king embarked on the most notable work of his tenure, the restoration of the house of Yahweh, a restoration needed not only due to inattention during Athaliah's rule but, according to the Chronicler, because of Athaliah's plundering of the Temple's articles for her Baal temple (24:7). For the Chronicler this account would be as important to his generation as the account of Solomon's construction of the Temple because it showcased the actions and structures essential for the proper maintenance of the Temple and its worship. In addition, the involvement of the entire nation reflects "the Chronicler's predilection for decentralization and democratization" (Japhet 1993:843), as he called his own community to support the second Temple.

The Chronicler described how Joash gathered the priests and Levites and ordered them to go out to the cities of Judah to collect money for the restoration of the Temple (24:5). Here the Chronicler used a play on the Hebrew root *qabats* [TH6908, ZH7695] (gather, collect) to link the actions of Joash and the priests (De Vries 1989:345). When this was not done immediately, he called Jehoiada and commanded that a chest be created and a proclamation made throughout the land to collect the money (24:6-9).[1]

These orders, however, were not immediately carried out; consequently, the king was forced to confront his mentor Jehoiada on the issue (24:6). His speech alludes to the tax levied by Moses. Such an allusion links together the Tabernacle and Temple, a regular feature of the Chronicler's account, which legitimizes the Temple as the true heir of the Tabernacle traditions of Moses. Furthermore, Japhet

(1993:844) notes that "the point being made in the present text is that Joash is not issuing an arbitrary command; he was simply enforcing an old statute" (see Exod 30:11-16; cf. De Vries 1989:345).

The collection of the taxes reveals some tension between king and priests, possibly because a portion of the revenues that would have gone to priestly support was to be used for the construction project.[2] Some kind of compromise is evident in the description of the king's action after his meeting with Jehoiada. There was a creation of a new chest to which the people would bring their donations, a proclamation was sent out to inform people to bring their contributions to Jerusalem, and there was shared supervision of the revenues by priestly and royal officials (24:8-9).

The response of the people is described as comprehensive ("all the leaders and the people," 24:10), celebratory ("gladly," 24:10), consistent ("day after day," 24:11), and abundant ("a large amount," 24:11). Together king and priest distributed the money for the restoration of the Temple (24:12), and the Temple was restored (24:13). So much money was donated that the king and priest were able to allot resources for the restoration of the utensils that had been pilfered by Athaliah for the temple of Baal (24:14; cf. 24:7). The Chronicler ended this section of the account by showing that the restoration fostered the renewal of sacrifice at the Temple (24:14). The closing phrase ("during the lifetime of Jehoiada the priest") signals that the first and positive phase of Joash's reign was coming to an end (cf. 24:2).[3]

A regular feature of the Chronicler's account is his emphasis on the role the Levites played alongside the priests in caring for the worship at the Temple, so it is not surprising that the first action of Joash was to assemble these two groups (24:5). It is clear that Jehoiada as chief priest was responsible for the Levites (24:6). While the writer of Kings began the account at the point where money had already been given for work (2 Kgs 12:4-5), the Chronicler began with the command to the priests and Levites to go out to the "towns of Judah" to gather the money to repair the house (24:5). The initial crisis in Kings was the lack of repair on the house, while the initial crisis in Chronicles was the lack of funds to finance the repairs. The Chronicler appears to be concerned about the financing of the Temple of his day and highlights the responsibility of Levites to collect these funds. The Chronicler had focused on the Levites' involvement in many aspects of the worship at the Temple, but here he reminds his own generation of their role in raising funds for the Temple, not just for special crises but on an annual basis (24:5). Twice in the passage this role is legitimized by appeal to the authority of "Moses, the servant of the LORD" and the practice of the congregation in the wilderness (24:6, 9).[4]

The shift of emphasis in the account from crisis over lack of building to crisis over lack of giving highlights the key role that the people did and could play. Therefore, throughout his account the Chronicler regularly introduces references to the participation of the entire kingdom, that is, Judah and Jerusalem (24:5, 6, 9-10). Their response is described by the Chronicler as one of joy (24:10) as they provided all the funds needed to repair the Temple.

As already mentioned, the king comes into greater prominence. The Chronicler says Joash decided to restore the Temple (24:4) and that he needed even to summon Jehoiada to ensure the Levites fulfilled their responsibility according to the instructions of Moses (24:6). In 24:8 the Chronicler reveals that it was the king who commanded the chest for donations to be made (2 Kgs 12:9 depicts only Jehoiada making it). However, as the money comes in, it is interesting that the Chronicler has the king's secretary and the officer of the chief priest empty the chest (24:11), in contrast to Kings, which has the king's secretary and the high priest count the money (2 Kgs 12:10). Then in 24:12 it is the king and Jehoiada who give it together to those who had charge of the work, while in 2 Kings 12:11 it was "they" (the king's secretary and the high priest) who do this. Again in 24:14 both king and Jehoiada distribute the extra money for the creation of utensils for the Temple. Although at the outset the king took the initiative for the restoration work, royal and priestly figures worked alongside one another to ensure its completion.[5]

Summary Note: The Death of Jehoiada (24:15-16). At this point the Chronicler left his source, to which he would not return until 24:23, where he begins the description of Joash's military defeat and assassination. He first honored Jehoiada with a full death and burial notice, with years lived, age at death, burial place, and evaluation ("he had done so much good in Israel"). The Chronicler was revealing that Jehoiada (not Joash) was his "hero" (De Vries 1989:345) by providing such detail for Jehoiada and so little for Joash at his death (24:25-27), by describing Jehoiada's death of great old age in contrast to Joash's premature death after battle and palace intrigue (24:25), and by noting that Jehoiada was buried "among the kings in the City of David," while Joash was buried "in the City of David, but not in the royal cemetery" (24:25). In this he emphasized the key role that a priest must play alongside a royal ruler. This must have had implications for the Chronicler's community. While Jehoiada never usurped or disparaged the royal line, his character highlighted the importance of the priestly office alongside the royal leadership for the proper maintenance of worship in Israel.

Joash's Reversal of Reforms after Jehoiada's Death (24:17-22). Once Jehoiada was dead, Joash began to "listen" to the advice of the "leaders of Judah," who filled the vacuum left by the loss of the priest. This listening to the wrong advice is reminiscent of the earlier tragic story of Rehoboam in chapter 10, which had major repercussions for the history of the southern kingdom and the Davidic monarchy (De Vries 1989:348).

The leaders of Judah were able to convince Joash to reverse all the reforms that were accomplished under Jehoiada. While Athaliah instituted Baal worship, Joash introduced the worship of the Asherim, a cult in honor of the goddess Asherah, female consort of the chief Canaanite god, El, and mother of the pantheon (known in Ugaritic as Athirat). There is evidence that Asherah was appropriated by Israelites at times as the consort of Yahweh.[6] The most common cult object associated with Asherah was a wooden pole; the reference to the plural here (lit., "Asherim"; NLT, "Asherah poles") probably indicates a collection of these objects (33:19; 34:3-4, 7; Deut 7:5; 12:3; Mic 5:13-14).

The terms used in this section highlight again the complete distinction in the Chronicler's mind between worshiping Yahweh and worshiping other gods. Here the switch of allegiance is signaled by the terms "abandon" (Heb., *'azab* [TH5800, ZH6440]) and "worship" (Heb., *'abad* [TH5647, ZH6268], which can also be rendered "serve"). The Temple was so important to Judah's worship that this act of idolatry is seen not as abandoning Yahweh but as abandoning "the Temple of the LORD, the God of their ancestors" (24:18).[7] These acts invited God's wrath upon "Judah and Jerusalem" (24:18), a reference most likely to the military defeat described in 24:23-26. But before this is described, the Chronicler highlights God's grace in sending his prophets to turn them to Yahweh (24:19), a trend seen elsewhere in this work (e.g., 12:1-12 with Rehoboam; ch 16 with Asa; chs 17–20 with Jehoshaphat; 36:15-16 with the Exile; cf. Williamson 1982:323). While the people would merely ignore the first prophets who were sent, by the time the prophet Zechariah delivered his message, the people turned on him and killed God's messenger.

As we have seen at earlier points in the Chronicler's history, the Lord raised up a prophetic witness from the ranks of the sacred personnel connected to the Temple (see comments on 1 Chr 25; cf. 2 Chr 20; 29; 34:30; and 35:15). While in other episodes these prophetic figures are related to the Levitical orders, here an individual from the priestly caste is named. Zechariah's prophetic word reflects the key vocabulary of the Chronicler, emphasizing the core principles that transgression of the commandments of God disqualifies one from prosperity and that abandonment of God results in abandonment by God (24:20). Although it was the leaders of Judah who conspired against Zechariah, the Chronicler makes it clear that this was done "at the command of the king" (NLT, "King Joash ordered").

There is tragic irony at work here, for this priestly figure is none other than the son of Jehoiada, who had not only preserved Joash's life and the Davidic line in the previous chapters (acts the Chronicler defines as "loyalty," using the term *khesed* [TH2617, ZH2876], which denotes covenant faithfulness) but also preserved the kingdom morally.[8] Irony is also seen in the contrast between Jehoiada's concern that a murder not defile this holy space in the death of Athaliah and Joash's order to murder Jehoiada's son in the same space (cf. Dillard 1987:183). Even the name of Jehoiada's son suggests tragic irony. According to De Vries (1989:346), the Chronicler played on the name of Jehoiada's son Zechariah, which is based on the Hebrew root *zakar* [TH2142, ZH2349] (to remember). The first phrase of 24:22 reads literally, "Joash the king did not remember [*zakar*] the loyalty that his father Jehoiada had shown him." By not remembering Jehoiada's loyalty, Joash killed his son named "Yahweh has remembered." Additionally, Zechariah's dying words ("May the LORD see what they are doing and avenge my death!") may also play on his name. The dying words of the prophet set in motion a curse that will come to fruition in the next section.

At the end of his account (36:15), the Chronicler will remind his readers of events such as this in which Yahweh sent prophets to warn the people: "The LORD, the God of their ancestors, repeatedly sent his prophets to warn them, for he had compassion on his people and his Temple." Such warnings in the Chronicler's perspective were expressions of Yahweh's grace to his people, but they were met with derision: "But the people mocked these messengers of God and despised their words. They scoffed at the prophets until the LORD's anger could no longer be restrained and nothing could be done" (36:16).

This theme of the abuse of prophets in Chronicles was not lost on Jesus, who, in his woes against the religious leaders of his day, used the violent death depicted in this chapter as an example of his people's treatment of the prophets (Matt 23:35; Luke 11:51).[9]

Joash's Military Defeat and Assassination (24:23-25a). It was expected that a king who abandoned God would be judged in his generation, but added to this in the case of Joash is the prophetic curse of the dying Zechariah. Retribution came from outside and inside his kingdom, a sequence of events not uncommon in the history of the ancient Near East (see 32:21). The army that defeated and severely wounded Joash appears to be related to the abandonment of God by Joash and the leaders of Judah (notice how the Chronicler mentions that the Aramean army "killed all the leaders of the nation," 24:23, and "judgment was carried out against Joash," 24:24). His actual death at the hands of his own officials, however, was related to the killing of the prophet Zechariah ("for murdering the son of Jehoiada the priest," 24:25). Second Kings 12:20 reveals that this court conspiracy took place at "Beth-millo on the road to Silla," most likely a house in the "Millo," an area of fill on the eastern slope of the City of David (2 Sam 5:9; 1 Kgs 9:15, 24; 11:27; ABD 1.690; see further note on 27:3). There is irony in Joash's death as a result of a treasonous act (Heb., *qashar* [TH7194, ZH8003]; NLT, "plotted," 24:25), reminiscent of Athaliah's cry at her death: "Treason! Treason!" (*qesher* [TH7195, ZH8004]; 23:13; Dillard 1987:193). The Chronicler repeats the names of the officials involved in the assassination of Joash found in his source in 2 Kgs 12:21 but adds to this that each was born to a foreign woman. The fact that this was followed immediately by a reference to the "account of the sons of Joash" in 24:27 implies that these two officials were of royal blood but were born to foreign wives. This may be an attempt by the Chronicler to show the danger of foreign marriages and show that Joash planted the seeds of his own assassination not only in his wicked behavior related to the care for the Temple and treatment of prophets but also in his royal marriages.

Summary Note: The Reign of Joash (24:25b-27). As already noted above, the sparseness of the succession note stands in stark contrast to the death notice of Jehoiada in 24:15-16. Jehoiada, a priest who had rescued Joash from death at the hands of the queen mother Athaliah, was honored with burial among the kings of Judah, while Joash, a king who had killed Jehoiada's son, was denied burial among the kings. The Chronicler emphasizes the quantity of prophetic oracles that were delivered against Joash in this closing note but does credit Joash with undertaking the great task of rebuilding the Temple.

ENDNOTES

1. According to 24:8, the chest was placed "outside the gate leading to the Temple of the LORD" in contrast to 2 Kgs 12:9, where it was set "on the right-hand side of the altar at the entrance of the Temple of the LORD." This continues the trend in Chronicles that the sacred precincts only be entered by sacred personnel.
2. Williamson (1982:320-321) argues that 24:5b-6 is a late addition, but this is refuted by Dillard (1987:190) and Japhet (1993:843-844).
3. The differences between 24:14 and 2 Kgs 12:13-16 can be explained from the fact that the items created in 24:14 were made once the reconstruction was complete. One, however, should not miss the allusion in Chronicles to the Tabernacle construction in Exod 25; 31:1-10, in which the offerings were also used for the furnishings of the Tabernacle (Dillard 1987:191).
4. Such appeals to the authority of Moses are evident elsewhere in Chronicles, especially in the construction of the Temple (see introduction to chs 1–9).

5. This is contra Japhet (1993:842), who sees in Joash's initiative "the king's intervention in the Temple's financial administration—a realm initially seen as a priestly prerogative—and the establishment of the royal responsibility for the restoration of the Temple."
6. See ABD 1.484 and inscriptions at Kuntillet 'Ajrud in northeast Sinai and Khirbet el-Qom near Hebron. Cf. Smith 2002:xxx-xxxvi, 47-53, 108-147; Day 2000:42-67; Hess 2007:283-289, 308-311; see notes on 17:6 and 31:1.
7. To have the Temple as an object rather than Yahweh, though "unusual," is "fully intelligible," according to Williamson (1982:324), who points to 12:1, which has "Law of the LORD" as the object of this verb.
8. Japhet (1993:850) notices that the focus of the Chronicler's attack on Joash is on his ingratitude, not his shedding innocent blood.
9. The account in Luke only refers to a certain "Zechariah," but in Matthew to a "Zechariah son of Barachiah," the latter suggesting a link between the Zechariah in ch 24 and the prophet in the book of Zechariah (cf. Ezra 5–6). See further Gundry 1967:86-88; Davies and Allison 1988:318-319; Luz 1989:154-155; and Blomberg 2007:84-85 for various theories on the relationship between these New Testament passages and the figures of Zechariah in 2 Chr 24 and the prophet Zechariah in Ezra and the book of Zechariah. Note especially the evidence of *Targum Lamentations* 2:20 and *Midrash Ecclesiastes* 3:16, which witness to later rabbinic tradition of the death of the prophet Zechariah son of Berekiah at the Temple (cf. Blomberg 2007:85).

◆ K. The Reign of Amaziah (25:1-28)

Amaziah was twenty-five years old when
he became king, and he reigned in Jeru-
salem twenty-nine years. His mother was
Jehoaddin* from Jerusalem. 2Amaziah did
what was pleasing in the LORD's sight, but
not wholeheartedly.

3When Amaziah was well established as
king, he executed the officials who had
assassinated his father. 4However, he did
not kill the children of the assassins, for
he obeyed the command of the LORD as
written by Moses in the Book of the Law:
"Parents must not be put to death for the sins of their children, nor children for the sins of their parents. Those deserving to die must be put to death for their own crimes."*

5Then Amaziah organized the army, as-
signing generals and captains* for all Ju-
dah and Benjamin. He took a census and found that he had an army of 300,000 select troops, twenty years old and older, all trained in the use of spear and shield.
6He also paid about 7,500 pounds* of sil-
ver to hire 100,000 experienced fighting men from Israel.

7But a man of God came to him and
said, "Your Majesty, do not hire troops from Israel, for the LORD is not with Israel. He will not help those people of Ephraim!
8If you let them go with your troops into
battle, you will be defeated by the enemy no matter how well you fight. God will overthrow you, for he has the power to help you or to trip you up."

9Amaziah asked the man of God, "But
what about all that silver I paid to hire the army of Israel?"

The man of God replied, "The LORD is able to give you much more than this!"
10So Amaziah discharged the hired troops
and sent them back to Ephraim. This made them very angry with Judah, and they returned home in a great rage.

11Then Amaziah summoned his courage
and led his army to the Valley of Salt, where they killed 10,000 Edomite troops from Seir.
12They captured another 10,000
and took them to the top of a cliff and threw them off, dashing them to pieces on the rocks below.

13Meanwhile, the hired troops that

Amaziah had sent home raided several of
the towns of Judah between Samaria and
Beth-horon. They killed 3,000 people and
carried off great quantities of plunder.
14 When King Amaziah returned from
slaughtering the Edomites, he brought
with him idols taken from the people of
Seir. He set them up as his own gods,
bowed down in front of them, and offered
sacrifices to them! 15 This made the LORD
very angry, and he sent a prophet to ask,
"Why do you turn to gods who could not
even save their own people from you?"
16 But the king interrupted him and
said, "Since when have I made you the
king's counselor? Be quiet now before I
have you killed!"
So the prophet stopped with this warn-
ing: "I know that God has determined to
destroy you because you have done this
and have refused to accept my counsel."
17 After consulting with his advisers,
King Amaziah of Judah sent this chal-
lenge to Israel's king Jehoash,* the son of
Jehoahaz and grandson of Jehu: "Come
and meet me in battle!"*
18 But King Jehoash of Israel replied to
King Amaziah of Judah with this story:
"Out in the Lebanon mountains, a thistle
sent a message to a mighty cedar tree:
'Give your daughter in marriage to my
son.' But just then a wild animal of Leba-
non came by and stepped on the thistle,
crushing it!
19 "You are saying, 'I have defeated
Edom,' and you are very proud of it. But
my advice is to stay at home. Why stir up
trouble that will only bring disaster on
you and the people of Judah?"
20 But Amaziah refused to listen, for God
was determined to destroy him for turn-
ing to the gods of Edom. 21 So King Je-
hoash of Israel mobilized his army against
King Amaziah of Judah. The two armies
drew up their battle lines at Beth-shemesh
in Judah. 22 Judah was routed by the army
of Israel, and its army scattered and fled
for home. 23 King Jehoash of Israel cap-
tured Judah's king, Amaziah son of Joash
and grandson of Ahaziah, at Beth-
shemesh. Then he brought him to Jerusa-
lem, where he demolished 600 feet* of
Jerusalem's wall, from the Ephraim Gate
to the Corner Gate. 24 He carried off all the
gold and silver and all the articles from
the Temple of God that had been in the
care of Obed-edom. He also seized the
treasures of the royal palace, along with
hostages, and then returned to Samaria.
25 King Amaziah of Judah lived on for
fifteen years after the death of King Je-
hoash of Israel. 26 The rest of the events in
Amaziah's reign, from beginning to end,
are recorded in *The Book of the Kings of
Judah and Israel.*
27 After Amaziah turned away from the
LORD, there was a conspiracy against his life
in Jerusalem, and he fled to Lachish. But his
enemies sent assassins after him, and they
killed him there. 28 They brought his body
back on a horse, and he was buried with his
ancestors in the City of David.*

25:1 As in parallel text at 2 Kgs 14:2; Hebrew reads *Jehoaddan*, a variant spelling of Jehoaddin. **25:4** Deut 24:16. **25:5** Hebrew *commanders of thousands and commanders of hundreds.* **25:6** Hebrew *100 talents* [3,400 kilograms]. **25:17a** Hebrew *Joash*, a variant spelling of Jehoash; also in 25:18, 21, 23, 25. **25:17b** Hebrew *Come, let us look one another in the face.* **25:23** Hebrew *400 cubits* [180 meters]. **25:28** As in some Hebrew manuscripts and other ancient versions (see also 2 Kgs 14:20); most Hebrew manuscripts read *the city of Judah.*

NOTES

25:1 ***he reigned in Jerusalem twenty-nine years.*** It appears that Amaziah's son Uzziah became co-regent with his father in Amaziah's fifth year, probably related to Amaziah's capture by King Jehoash of Israel (25:23) and his release only when Jehoash had died in Amaziah's fifteenth year (25:25).

25:5 ***generals and captains.*** Lit., "commanders of thousands and commanders of hundreds" (see NLT mg). The Hebrew text also has here the phrase "by house of fathers" (left untranslated in the NLT), which suggests that the military organization was according to clan.

He took a census. Although this verb can be used for mustering or reviewing a group of people or an army, it is related to numbering people and troops at several points in the OT (see Exod 30:13-14; 38:25-26; Num 1–4, 26; 1 Sam 11:8; 13:15; 15:4).

all trained in the use of spear and shield. Spear and shield designate one offensive and one defensive weapon (11:12; 14:8; 2 Kgs 11:10; 1 Chr 12:8). The phrase here describes a standing infantry army that involved a group set apart, supported, and trained for military action, rather than a "people's militia" (as per the book of Judges). The spear was "standard equipment for heavy-armed infantry," which enabled the army to face "chariot and infantry charges" (TBD 112). Nevertheless, it is still a rudimentary force in that no reference was made to cavalry, chariotry, or archers (TBD 1295).

25:5-6 ***300,000 . . . 100,000.*** On these high numbers, see commentary on 1 Chr 12:23-40.

experienced fighting men. Lit., "mighty men of valor," a phrase used of warriors elsewhere (13:3; 17:16, 17; 32:21; 1 Chr 12:28; 28:1; cf. Judg 6:12; 11:1; 1 Sam 9:1; 16:18).

25:7 ***a man of God.*** This is a term regularly used for someone able to relate a divine message or perform a miracle (1 Sam 2:27; 9:6-10; 1 Kgs 12:22; 13:1-31; 1 Kgs 17:18, 24; 2 Kgs 1:10-13). Extrabiblical texts also identify prophetic figures in similar ways; for example, the Hittite texts as early as the mid-second millennium BC speak of a man of God who might come and declare the cause of someone's suffering (ABD 5.477).

25:13 ***the towns of Judah between Samaria and Beth-horon.*** Upper Beth-horon lay on the border between Ephraim and Benjamin (Josh 16:5; 18:13-14), but in this account the southern section of Israel (northern kingdom) appears to lie within the kingdom of Judah (see commentary).

25:21 ***Beth-shemesh.*** Although not the location where one would expect the conflict to take place (such as the northern border of Judah), this suggests to Dillard (1987:201) that Jehoash may have been interested in controlling trade routes, either the lucrative north–south Great Trunk Road or the east–west highway between the Great Trunk Road and the King's Highway in the Transjordan.

25:23 ***from the Ephraim Gate to the Corner Gate.*** The Ephraim Gate was located immediately west of the Temple Mount on the northern side of the city. The Corner Gate was most likely the most northwestern corner of the wall surrounding the city. This would have left the city vulnerable to the advance of troops from the north, that is, from the northern kingdom.

25:27 ***Lachish.*** A Judean fortified city protecting one of the key valleys of the Shephelah that led from the Coastal Plain into the Judean mountains and Jerusalem. It was fortified by Rehoboam (11:9) and later would be commemorated in history by Sennacherib, whose successful siege against Hezekiah would be carved into his throne room in Nineveh (32:9).

COMMENTARY

As was the pattern in his narrative of Joash (ch 24) and will be his pattern for Uzziah (ch 26), the Chronicler organizes his account of Amaziah into two phases, one highlighting positive aspects of his reign (25:5-12) and the other negative (25:13-24). This kind of structuring explains the Chronicler's consistent excision of verses like 2 Kings 14:4 (see commentary on 24:1-4), which emphasize the king's negative actions too early in the account for his historiographic restructuring (so also 2 Kgs 12:3; 15:4; 15:35). Each phase is structured according to this pattern: (1) The action of Amaziah that arouses God's anger (25:5-6, 14-15a); (2) the prophetic voice that confronts Amaziah (25:7-8, 15b); (3) the question of Amaziah (25:9a, 16a); (4) the response of the prophetic voice (25:9b, 16b); (5) the obedience/disobedience of Amaziah (25:10, 17-20); (6) success/failure in battle (25:11-12, 21-24).

To achieve this structure, the Chronicler expanded his account of Amaziah considerably from the one he found in 2 Kings 14, which only referred to his success against the Edomites (2 Kgs 14:7). In this expansion (25:5-10, 12-16) the Chronicler depicts two prophetic figures confronting Amaziah. Some have questioned the authenticity of the material in this section, but the fact that 25:13 does not fit neatly into the Chronicler's theological program or literary structure suggests that he had been constrained by a source.[1]

Summary Note: The Accession of Amaziah (25:1-4). Because of his focus on the southern kingdom and disregard of the northern kingdom as a political entity, the Chronicler excised date references to the kings of Israel that were found in his source at 2 Kings 14:1, 15-16 (see comments on 25:25 below). Unlike his father Joash, Amaziah took over the reins of power as an adult (25 years old), signaling a return to normalcy after the unsettledness of the Athaliah-Jehoiada-Joash period (see 22:10–24:27). The Chronicler carried over the positive evaluation of his source in Kings ("did what was pleasing in the LORD's sight"); then he summarized the qualification in Kings ("but not like his ancestor David. Instead, he followed the example of his father, Joash. Amaziah did not destroy the pagan shrines, and the people still offered sacrifices and burned incense there," 2 Kgs 14:3b-4) with the simple statement "but not wholeheartedly" (so similarly 15:17; 16:9; 19:9). This may be an attempt to distance Amaziah from both David (called "his ancestor" in Kings) and Joash. David's image should not be tarnished by this descendant, but neither should Joash be judged by his son's reputation. This elimination of references to dynastic founder (David) and father (Joash) was probably shaped by the retribution theology that the Chronicler found in his source in the two verses that follow (25:3-4//2 Kgs 14:5-6).

The sign of Amaziah's firm grasp on the reins of power in Judah was his ability to deal with his "servants" (NLT, "officials") who had killed his father, Joash. These servants were most likely his brothers, born to two foreign wives of his father (see commentary on 24:23-25a). His lack of retribution toward the children of these conspirators is explained by reference to the theology of retribution found in Deuteronomy 24:16 (and filled out in later passages like Ezek 18).[2] This has significance in the account of the southern kingdom at this point, for whom intergenerational fratricide had nearly led to the extinction of the Davidic line in the previous chapters. Often the historiography of Joshua—Kings is contrasted with the historiography found in Chronicles on the basis of competing views of retribution. In this view Joshua—Kings expounds a cumulative retribution theory (God's wrath is compounded over several generations and finally falls upon a later generation because of the sins of the past), while Chronicles expounds an immediate retribution theory (God's wrath falls upon each generation according to their own deeds). Here we see that the historiography of Joshua—Kings is more complex and that the Chronicler found precedents for his theology of immediate retribution in his source in Kings.[3]

Amaziah, the Man of God, and Edom (25:5-12). The positive account begins with the king mustering an army for war, presumably against the Edomites, although this does not become apparent until 25:11. Although reference is made to military leaders (NLT, "generals and captains"; see NLT mg), the Hebrew text also makes reference to the "house of the fathers" (lit., "Amaziah assembled Judah, and he appointed them by house of the fathers under commanders of thousands and commanders of hundreds"). These clan groups underlying the military organization would have highlighted the antiquity of similar clan groups within Judah and Benjamin in the Persian period.

This mustering included careful attention to the enumeration of the forces, which revealed that the army was comprised of 300,000 warriors. In this Amaziah followed earlier precedents by David (1 Chr 27:23-24), Solomon (2:17), Asa (14:8), and Jehoshaphat (17:14-19). To this Amaziah added 100,000 mercenaries from Israel, hired for one hundred talents of silver. This focus on numbering the troops and especially the hiring of the mercenaries highlights Amaziah's reliance on human military strength for victory rather than on the Divine Warrior, Yahweh. David's numbering of his troops (in 1 Chr 21) had dire consequences for the nation. It is not surprising, then, that a man of God confronted the king (25:7).

This prophetic man of God (see note on 25:7) focused his warning on Amaziah's inclusion of Israelite mercenaries in his army, declaring that God's presence was not with the northern kingdom (cf. Abijah's sermon in 13:4-12). Such repudiation of foreign alliances is typical of the Chronicler in general (16:2-9; 19:1-3; 20:15-17, 35-37; 32:7-8; Dillard 1987:199). But the case of Israel is special in that in the preceding chapters the Chronicler has shown the devastation that came upon Judah when they entered into alliance with the northern kingdom through marriage, which nearly led to the extinction of the Davidic dynasty. In this new phase, liaisons with the northern kingdom's (Israel's) royal administration would not be tolerated. This does not mean, however, that the Chronicler was against the northern tribes, especially in light of his broader theology of "all Israel."

Through this man of God, the Chronicler reminds his readers that the decisive factor in any military operation is not the human resources but rather Yahweh's presence: "For he has the power to help you or to trip you up" (25:8). To intermingle with a force that does not have the presence of God is to strip the entire army of that presence.

Amaziah's immediate concern was over the money he had just spent to hire the mercenaries, but the man of God reminded him of the much greater resources of Yahweh to replace these lost resources. Amaziah obeyed the man of God, discharging the mercenaries (25:10). Although it appears they retained the money with which they were hired, this dismissed group was angry. This is probably related to the fact that the money was only the base pay for these warriors. Greater benefits could be gained following a successful battle when the plunder was divided.

In light of the Chronicler's theology, one is not surprised at the success that Amaziah experienced against the Edomites, a success that the Chronicler enhances with the addition of 25:12. Those who obey the word of Yahweh experience success in battle.

Amaziah, the Prophet, and Israel (25:13-24). While Amaziah was off defeating the Edomites near the southern end of the Dead Sea (25:11-12), the Israelite mercenaries attacked the towns of Judah between Beth-horon and Samaria in order to gain their lost opportunity for plunder (25:13). The fact that the region between Beth-horon and Samaria was considered part of Judah may reflect the Chronicler's view of an expanded province of Yehud in the Persian period, although it is possible that the word "Samaria" represents an early copyist error for a city within the territory of Benjamin.[4]

At first sight the violent reaction of the northern mercenaries on the way home seems to go against the Chronicler's theology, but it is 25:14 that explains this violent reaction. Amaziah had taken idols from the spoil of Edom and instituted worship of them.[5] This explains why the Chronicler delayed his description of the northern violence until after Amaziah's defeat of the Edomites (25:11-12).

As in the earlier case of relying on mercenaries, Amaziah was confronted by a prophet. This time, however, the king rejected the prophet's counsel, threatening execution. This precipitated the prophet's curse: "I know that God has determined to destroy you because you have done this and have refused to accept my counsel" (25:16). These last words of the prophet to the king are eerily reminiscent of the final words of the priestly-prophet Zechariah to Amaziah's father Joash (24:22). This foreshadows their common destiny (24:25; 25:27). The Chronicler returned to his source in Kings at 25:17 and inserted the phrase "after consulting with his advisers" (lit., "Amaziah took counsel"). By using the same Hebrew root (*ya'ats* [TH3289, ZH3619]) as the final word of the prophet's message in 25:16, the Chronicler emphasized Amaziah's rejection of Yahweh's counsel.

Amaziah's move against the northern kingdom appears to be an act of revenge for the violent actions of the northern mercenaries (25:13). Amaziah challenged the northern king Jehoash (son of Jehoahaz, son of Jehu), but his challenge was met with a message that carried the tone of a prophetic word, employing an allegory and accusing Amaziah of acting out of pride. Adding to his source in Kings, the Chronicler picked up on the prophetic edge and normative status of this message by commenting, "But Amaziah refused to listen, for God was determined to destroy him for turning to the gods of Edom" (25:20). Interestingly, the prophet of God (25:16) had already pointed out Amaziah's inability to listen (using the same Hebrew phrase). In similar fashion Josiah would refuse to listen to God's word through a foreign king (the Egyptian Neco; 35:22).[6] In this the Chronicler continued to expand the sources for God's word. For the Chronicler, God's voice may come through the traditional avenues of the prophets but also through Levites and even foreign kings.

The battle took place at the traditional border of Judahite tribal territory, at Beth-shemesh, which guarded the Sorek Valley, one of the key western valley accesses into Jerusalem. Following his source, the Chronicler related that Judah was soundly defeated, resulting in the capture of Amaziah, the looting of Jerusalem's Temple[7] and royal treasures, the destruction of the northern section of the capital city's wall defenses (see note on 25:23), and the taking of hostages.

Summary Note: The Reign of Amaziah (25:25-28). The Chronicler's excision of the summary, source, and death notice of the northern king Jehoash son of Jehoahaz, which is found in his source at 2 Kings 14:15-16, makes the reference to the northern king Jehoash son of Jehoahaz in 25:25 (= 2 Kgs 14:17) somewhat awkward. This may be the Chronicler's way of reminding the reader of God's continued blessing on the Davidic line, which here outlived the tenure of a northern king even though that northern king had defeated the army of Judah.

Notwithstanding this possible allusion to the endurance of the Davidic dynasty, the Chronicler explicitly traces the origins of the conspiracy against Amaziah to the time he turned away from Yahweh. This emphasizes the surety of the prophetic word against Amaziah in 25:19-20. The conspiracy broke out within the court in Jerusalem, the center of his power, so he was forced to flee to one of his fortified cities guarding one of the key valleys between the coastal plain and Jerusalem. But there would be no fleeing the prophetic word, for he was killed there. The reference to his return to the city upon "a horse" (25:28//2 Kgs 14:20) may continue a motif connected with Jezebel (2 Kgs 9:33) and Athaliah (2 Kgs 11:16) in the Chronicler's source of Kings.

ENDNOTES

1. For this, see Dillard (1987:197) and Williamson (1982:327-329), who note especially the tension between 25:9 and 25:13.
2. In 25:4 the Chronicler changes the passive Hophal of *mwt* in his source in Kings (2 Kgs 14:6; lit., "fathers shall not be put to death on account of sons"), to the active Qal: lit., "fathers shall not die on account of sons."
3. For this, see further Boda 2006a; Kaminsky 1995; 1997:319-332.
4. If the mercenaries were returning from the kingdom of Judah to Israel, the path of their attack would not be from Samaria to Beth-horon but rather Beth-horon to Samaria.
5. It is not extraordinary for the conqueror to honor or worship the gods of the conquered in the ancient Near East, especially if the conqueror attributed his success to the will of these gods. See Dillard 1987:201, contra Williamson 1982.
6. See also how Rehoboam refused to listen to his people (10:15) and how this also led to the fulfillment of a prophecy against the king.
7. Concerned for ritual precision, the Chronicler adds here the reference to Obed-edom's care for the articles in the Temple (25:24). The Hebrew text does not indicate that he was taken into captivity, although the Septuagint and Vulgate do.

◆ L. The Reign of Uzziah (26:1-23)

All the people of Judah had crowned Amaziah's sixteen-year-old son, Uzziah, as king in place of his father. [2]After his father's death, Uzziah rebuilt the town of Elath* and restored it to Judah.

[3]Uzziah was sixteen years old when he became king, and he reigned in Jerusalem fifty-two years. His mother was Jecoliah from Jerusalem. [4]He did what was pleasing in the LORD's sight, just as his father, Amaziah, had done. [5]Uzziah sought God during the days of Zechariah, who taught him to fear God.* And as long as the king sought guidance from the LORD, God gave him success.

[6]Uzziah declared war on the Philistines and broke down the walls of Gath, Jabneh, and Ashdod. Then he built new towns in the Ashdod area and in other parts of Philistia. [7]God helped him in his

wars against the Philistines, his battles with the Arabs of Gur,* and his wars with the Meunites. [8]The Meunites* paid annual tribute to him, and his fame spread even to Egypt, for he had become very powerful.

[9]Uzziah built fortified towers in Jerusalem at the Corner Gate, at the Valley Gate, and at the angle in the wall. [10]He also constructed forts in the wilderness and dug many water cisterns, because he kept great herds of livestock in the foothills of Judah* and on the plains. He was also a man who loved the soil. He had many workers who cared for his farms and vineyards, both on the hillsides and in the fertile valleys.

[11]Uzziah had an army of well-trained warriors, ready to march into battle, unit by unit. This army had been mustered and organized by Jeiel, the secretary of the army, and his assistant, Maaseiah. They were under the direction of Hananiah, one of the king's officials. [12] These regiments of mighty warriors were commanded by 2,600 clan leaders. [13]The army consisted of 307,500 men, all elite troops. They were prepared to assist the king against any enemy.

[14]Uzziah provided the entire army with shields, spears, helmets, coats of mail, bows, and sling stones. [15]And he built structures on the walls of Jerusalem, designed by experts to protect those who shot arrows and hurled large stones* from the towers and the corners of the wall. His fame spread far and wide, for the LORD gave him marvelous help, and he became very powerful.

[16]But when he had become powerful, he also became proud, which led to his downfall. He sinned against the LORD his God by entering the sanctuary of the LORD's Temple and personally burning incense on the incense altar. [17]Azariah the high priest went in after him with eighty other priests of the LORD, all brave men. [18]They confronted King Uzziah and said, "It is not for you, Uzziah, to burn incense to the LORD. That is the work of the priests alone, the descendants of Aaron who are set apart for this work. Get out of the sanctuary, for you have sinned. The LORD God will not honor you for this!"

[19]Uzziah, who was holding an incense burner, became furious. But as he was standing there raging at the priests before the incense altar in the LORD's Temple, leprosy* suddenly broke out on his forehead. [20]When Azariah the high priest and all the other priests saw the leprosy, they rushed him out. And the king himself was eager to get out because the LORD had struck him. [21]So King Uzziah had leprosy until the day he died. He lived in isolation in a separate house, for he was excluded from the Temple of the LORD. His son Jotham was put in charge of the royal palace, and he governed the people of the land.

[22]The rest of the events of Uzziah's reign, from beginning to end, are recorded by the prophet Isaiah son of Amoz. [23]When Uzziah died, he was buried with his ancestors; his grave was in a nearby burial field belonging to the kings, for the people said, "He had leprosy." And his son Jotham became the next king.

26:2 As in Greek version (see also 2 Kgs 14:22; 16:6); Hebrew reads *Eloth,* a variant spelling of Elath. **26:5** As in Syriac and Greek versions; Hebrew reads *who instructed him in divine visions.* **26:7** As in Greek version; Hebrew reads *Gur-baal.* **26:8** As in Greek version; Hebrew reads *Ammonites.* Compare 26:7. **26:10** Hebrew *the Shephelah.* **26:15** Or *to shoot arrows and hurl large stones.* **26:19** Or *a contagious skin disease.* The Hebrew word used here and throughout this passage can describe various skin diseases.

NOTES

26:1 ***All the people of Judah had crowned Amaziah's sixteen-year-old son, Uzziah, as king.*** Uzziah's succession note in 26:1 is unlike other succession notes because it speaks of an action by the people to crown him. A similar phrase is used at the accession of young Josiah after the assassination of his father, Amon (33:25). See also note on 22:1.

Uzziah. Uzziah is called Azariah in 2 Kgs 14–15 (see 2 Kgs 14:21, NLT mg). Most likely Uzziah was the king's throne name (Isa 1:1; 6:1; 7:1; Hos 1:1; Amos 1:1; Zech 14:5), while Azariah was his personal name (ABD 6.777). The Chronicler probably favors the name Uzziah so as not to confuse the reader with Azariah the priest, who confronted the king (26:16-20).

26:2 *the town of Elath.* This was the southernmost extent of Judahite control, a port on the Gulf of Aqaba that allowed Judean kings to trade with Africa, India, and Asia (8:17). Traditionally associated with Edom, this port may have become available to Judah again after Amaziah's defeat of Edom (25:11-12), but according to this account it was not incorporated into the southern kingdom until Uzziah's reign.

26:3 *fifty-two years.* Uzziah's co-regency with his father, Amaziah, as well as his co-regency with his son Jotham (26:21), explains the extraordinary length of Uzziah's reign.

26:6 *Gath, Jabneh, and Ashdod.* Originally Philistine, Gath and Ashdod were two of the five cities on the coastal plain to the west of the traditional lands of Judah. Jabneh was a town along the northern border of Judah (Josh 15:11), but it was held by the Philistines at the time of Uzziah.

26:7 *the Arabs of Gur . . . Meunites.* Heb., *gur-ba'al* [TH1485, ZH1597], while the LXX and Codex Amiatinus of the Vulgate respectively translate "rock" and "Tur(baal)," suggesting an original *tsur-ba'al* [TH6697/1168, ZH7446/1252] (ABD 2.1100). The Meunites are sometimes identified as a Transjordanian or Arabian people (ABD 4.801). Possibly these groups lived east of Judah.

26:9 *Corner Gate . . . Valley Gate . . . angle in the wall.* The Corner Gate was most likely at the northwest corner of the city of Jerusalem, the Valley Gate on the western side of the City of David opening into the Tyropoeon Valley (ABD 6.784). The "angle in the wall" is simply called "the angle" in the Hebrew text. This term is used for the corner of a building (Exod 26:24) or corner post of an altar (Ezek 41:22), but is mentioned here and in Nehemiah's reconstruction of the wall of Jerusalem in Neh 3:19-20, 24-25. This section of the wall appears to have run alongside the eastern side of Jerusalem (ABD 1.255).

26:10 *wilderness . . . foothills of Judah . . . on the plains.* The wilderness here may refer to the dry region that lay to the south of Judah (Negev) or to the arid region between Jerusalem and the Dead Sea (Josh 15:61; Judg 1:16; Ps 63:1). "The foothills of Judah" (Heb., *shepelah* [TH8219, ZH9169]) refers to the region that lay to the west between the Judean hill country and the Coastal Plain. The plains here may be a reference to the Coastal Plain but more likely the high plateau between the Arnon and Heshbon rivers in the central Transjordan (Deut 3:10; 4:43; Josh 13:9, 16-17, 21; 20:8; Jer 48:21).

26:13 *307,500.* On these high numbers, see commentary on 1 Chr 12:23-40.

26:14 *shields, spears, helmets, coats of mail, bows, and sling stones.* Here we are given one of the most detailed descriptions of ancient Judean soldiers. Their equipment was both for defensive (shields, helmets, coats of mail) and offensive (spears, bows, sling stones) purposes. These shields were probably smaller shields to be carried by the individual soldier, rather than the larger shields that required a shield bearer (1 Sam 17). Although Goliath and Saul were depicted as wearing helmets (1 Sam 17), the helmet does not appear as a standard piece of equipment in Israel until the time of Uzziah. Coats of mail were developed in the Late Bronze Age, comprised of hundreds of small metal pieces sewn to cloth or leather. Early bows were constructed from wood, later of combinations of materials to create the composite bow; bow strings were made from natural cord or animal parts. Sling stones could be hurled as far as 600 feet and were readily available. The sling itself was cheap and simple to construct from two leather thongs on either side of a pocket that held the projectile (TBD 111-113).

26:15 ***structures.*** Here we see further innovations by Uzziah; they were possibly stationary devices or, at the least, structural innovations at key points along the wall to protect or facilitate those hurling arrows and dropping large stones on the heads of attacking troops. Such innovations were important to successful offense or defense.

26:16 ***incense altar.*** The altar within the Holy Place in the Temple was placed in front of the veil outside the Most Holy Place; it was composed of gold-coated cedar (see 4:19; 1 Chr 28:18). Incense was burned to provide a nice smell in the place where the priests met with Yahweh, which, along with the soft light of the lampstand and the Bread of the Presence, symbolized the place of fellowship between Yahweh and his people.

26:19 ***incense burner.*** This was a gold vessel held in the hand to carry coals (cf. Ezek 8:11; TWOT 2011g).

leprosy. This skin disease was probably not the disease called "leprosy" today, because it could be cured in ancient times (see Lev 13); for further disconnections with "leprosy," see ABD 4.278. The term is also related to growths on clothing and fabric (e.g., Lev 13:47), leather (Lev 13:48), or a wall (Lev 14:34). In reference to human beings, it is described as "several types of skin lesions which exhibit exfoliation or scaling of the skin and which persist and do not exhibit a course of healing with the prescribing quarantine periods" (ABD 4.279). In relation to inanimate objects, it probably referred to some kind of deadly mold (see ABD 4.279). The resulting condition is one of uncleanness, for which the sufferer must be isolated "outside the camp" (Lev 13–14; Num 5).

26:21 ***His son Jotham was put in charge.*** Due to the divine judgment on Uzziah, Jotham would be pushed onto the throne at an early stage and would share a co-regency with his father.

the people of the land. See note on 23:20.

COMMENTARY

The Chronicler's depiction of Uzziah is strikingly similar to his depiction of another young king, Joash (ch 24), evaluating his reign positively ("he did what was pleasing in the LORD's sight") but qualifying that by linking this behavior to the influence of a mentor figure. For Joash it was the priest Jehoiada; for Uzziah it is a man named Zechariah, whose status or role is left ambiguous but who is credited with instructing Uzziah in the fear of God. The account of Uzziah is thus divided (as Joash's) into two phases: one in which he sought God (*darash* [TH1875, ZH2011], 26:5) and as a result prospered (*tsalakh* [TH6743A, ZH7503], 26:5) and a second in which he "became proud" (*gabah* [TH1361, ZH1467], 26:16) and "unfaithful" (*ma'al* [TH4603, ZH5085], 26:16)—consequently he was dishonored, struck with poor health, and disqualified from rule. This kind of structuring explains the Chronicler's consistent excision of verses like 2 Kings 15:4, which emphasize the king's negative actions too early in the account (so also 2 Kgs 12:3; 14:4; 15:35).

The depiction of Uzziah's reign in the book of Kings comprises only seven verses. The Chronicler expands this considerably to 23 verses, with unique material in the positive phase of his reign (26:6-15) and expanded material in the negative phase (26:16-23). This arrangement of the narrative into positive and negative phases was also used by the Chronicler for his accounts of Joash (ch 24) and Amaziah (ch 25), but following Uzziah, the pattern will change to an exclusively positive or negative account (Jotham, positive, ch 27; Ahaz, negative, ch 28; Hezekiah, positive, chs 29–32).

In light of his theology of retribution, the Chronicler makes sense of the long reign of Uzziah (usually a sign of blessing) by revealing that the first part of his reign was marked by considerable blessing due to the instruction of the godly Zechariah and that the latter part of his long rule was spent suffering with a disease that resulted in him reigning in name only. Uzziah provided another opportunity for the Chronicler to teach about the sanctity of the sacred space and the exclusivity of the priestly vocation to his readership.

Summary Note: The Accession of Uzziah (26:1-5). With the premature death of his father, who was assassinated in a palace coup, Uzziah was placed on the throne at the age of 16. Uzziah's restoration of Elath (see note on 26:2) to Judean control signaled an initial return to Solomonic glory (1 Kgs 9:26). The excision of the account of Jeroboam in 2 Kings 14:23-29 from the Chronicler's account explains the repetitious character of Uzziah's accession note (twice he becomes king at 16 years old).

Although it is impossible that the Zechariah of 26:5 is the same Zechariah son of Jehoiada who was killed by Uzziah's grandfather Joash (24:20-22), the name of the later mentor does recall the earlier individual and his cry to follow God and experience prosperity (*tsalakh* [TH6743A, ZH7503]; 24:20; 26:5). Here the Chronicler emphasizes the importance of instruction in the fear of God as the core of what it means to "seek" (*darash* [TH1875, ZH2011]) Yahweh, a key motif throughout the book of Chronicles.

The fear of God is an important motif in the Old Testament and represents the human covenantal response to the awesome presence of the holy God. The initial reaction of the people to the presence of God on Sinai is one of abject fear (Deut 5:5), a reaction that leads to the people's commissioning Moses as their mediator (Deut 5:22-27). God's response is his desire that they would indeed "fear" him, which means to keep all his commands (Deut 5:29). Such a "fear" is listed alongside instructions to keep his statutes, to listen, to obey, and even to love the Lord with one's whole being and keep God's commands on one's heart (Deut 6:1-6). The fear of the Lord is, thus, the human covenantal response to Yahweh's gracious initiative and will be considered as foundational to a life of wisdom (Prov 1:7).

Uzziah's Actions during the Lifetime of Zechariah (26:6-15). In the first phase of the Chronicler's depiction of Uzziah's reign, apparently the period during the lifetime of his mentor Zechariah, the Chronicler portrays Uzziah's prosperity mainly in terms of military successes on all sides of his kingdom: the western territories near the Philistines (26:6-7), the southern and eastern territories near the Arabs (26:7), the eastern territories in the Transjordan (26:8), and the southern territories in the Negev (26:8). It may be suggested that Uzziah's strategy was related to the capture of the lucrative trade routes of the Great Trunk Road (Coastal Plain) and the King's Highway (Transjordanian Plateau). These offensive successes were balanced with defensive fortifications in Jerusalem and the wilderness (26:9-10, 15). This was all made possible by a large, well-trained, and supplied army (26:11-14).[1] The only nonmilitary reference is found in 26:10, which refers to cisterns dug and agriculture maintained, but this may provide insight into how he was able to support this large and effective military force.

Uzziah's Corruption (26:16-21). In his source in 2 Kings 15 the Chronicler found only a reference to Yahweh striking Uzziah with a disease that incapacitated him from ruling. The Chronicler provided details that explain this severe judgment upon Uzziah. Twice in his unique account of Uzziah's success, the Chronicler speaks of the king's fame (lit., "his name") spreading far because of his military strength (Heb., *khazaq* [TH2388, ZH2616]; 26:8, 15). It is this strength (*khazaq*) that is identified as the source of his pride (*gabah* [TH1361, ZH1467]) and ultimately his destruction at the outset of the account of his downfall (26:16). It was his pride that led to his downfall or, better, to his "corruption" (Heb., *shakhath* [TH7843, ZH8845]).

Uzziah's pride prompted him to commit what was for the Chronicler one of the worst violations imaginable, infringement of the sacred precincts, where only the priests were allowed to enter (see his deep concern for this in the overthrow of Athaliah in 23:6-7, 14-15). His action is described as *ma'al* [TH4603, ZH5085] (NLT, "sinned"), a term that occurs regularly in priestly literature in the Old Testament and is defined by Milgrom (1976) as "a sin against God," in contrast to a sin against humanity. This sin is categorized in two ways: the Sancta Trespass, referring to inappropriate contact with that which is holy (Lev 5:14-19; 14:10-14, 21-25; 22:14-16; Num 6:12; Ezra 10:19; Jer 2:3) and Oath Violation, that is, the violation of God's name that was sworn in the oath (Lev 6:1-7; Num 5:6-8). Milgrom concludes that "*ma'al*, then, means trespassing upon the divine realm either by poaching on his sancta or breaking his covenant oath; it is a lethal sin which can destroy both the offender and his community" (1976:21; cf. Boda 2006c).

Uzziah invaded the Holy Place, where the altar of incense was located, in order to burn his own incense (26:16). The Chronicler lauded the courage of Azariah and his priestly attendants, citing the challenge Azariah gave to the proud king (26:17-18). This speech lays out the Chronicler's view on the function of the Aaronide priesthood for whom alone was reserved the privilege of entering the sanctuary and burning the incense.

No sooner was Uzziah filled with a rage that may have resulted in the priest's death than a skin disease broke out on his forehead in full view of everyone (26:19). Such a condition was simultaneously a sign of Yahweh's judgment and a mark of uncleanness (Lev 13–14), complicating further the king's disqualification from being in the Holy Place. Because Uzziah's transgression was cultic in nature, judgment was immediate (Dillard 1987:210).[2]

Various priestly categories are indicated in Leviticus 10:10-11 as "sacred–common, clean–unclean" with common/clean as the two unmarked (normal) categories of the created order and sacred/unclean as the two marked categories within creation (Nelson 1993). Yahweh is "holy," a term that simply means "the divine."[3] That which is common is not allowed in God's presence but must be "sanctified," that is, made holy or separated for use by the divine. It is assumed that the common object or person who is to be made holy will be clean rather than unclean. The unclean and holy are never to come into contact with one another. As "common," King Uzziah was not qualified to be in the place of the divine (holy); God's judgment upon him that made him unclean compounded the situation and led to the reaction of the priests, who, once they saw the skin condition, "rushed him out," an action welcomed by the stricken king, who feared for his life (26:20).

The Chronicler ended his account by revealing that this condition was not only chronic ("until the day he died") but also devastating for his reign because he was confined to a house separate from the court, so his son Jotham took the reins of the government. Sickness as a sign of God's retribution for sin is also evident in the Chronicler's portrayal of Asa and Jehoram (16:11-14; 21:18-20).

Summary Note: The Reign of Uzziah (26:22-23). As has been the custom at several points in his account, the Chronicler reveals that the sources for his account are linked to the prophets, specifically Isaiah (see commentary on 1 Chr 29:29-30). This source is most likely not the book of Isaiah, which mentions Uzziah only in Isaiah 6—a prophecy that is dated in the year of the king's death. Whereas the Chronicler's source in 2 Kings 15:7 records that Uzziah was buried with his fathers in the City of David, the Chronicler qualifies this by noting that he was buried in a burial field belonging to the kings because of his chronic skin disease, which rendered him unclean. According to the Chronicler, any king who would threaten the holiness of the sanctuary would not only be rendered unclean in life and separated from the royal house but would be so also in death. He would bear forever the stigma of being placed "outside the camp" because of his folly. Ever the careful historian of priestly situations, the Chronicler provided a warning to any secular leader who would dare invade sacred space or assume priestly prerogatives.

ENDNOTES

1. Large armies depicting divine blessing can be found in 13:3-4, 17; 14:7; 17:12-19; 25:5-6; 28:6-8; 1 Chr 12:23-40; 21:1-30; 27:1-34; see introduction to chs 10–36 and Dillard 1987:209. Some see a reference to Uzziah (Azariah) in the Calah Annals attributed by some to Tiglath-pileser III, which mentions a figure named Azriyahu (see COS 2.284-285 for text and short review of debate).
2. Whereas at times Yahweh would send a prophet to warn the king, the nature of Uzziah's offense was so grave that punishment was immediate.
3. Levine (1989:257) notes, "When speaking of God, it is recognized that holiness is inextricable from His being; it is a constant, divine attribute." Jenson (1992:48) defines the holy as "that which belongs to the sphere of God's being or activity." Brueggemann (1997:288) calls holiness "the radical otherness of Yahweh," and Goldingay (2006:23), "Yhwh's metaphysical distinctiveness over against humanity." Of course, "holy" in reference to the created refers to the setting apart of elements within the creation in order to make it possible for the created to come in contact with the Creator. Thus, Nelson (1993:26) states, "To be holy was to be in the realm of the divine, in close conceptual proximity to whatever pertains to divinity. The conventional notion that the so-called 'basic meaning' of the verbal root is 'to separate' has little to commend it, although separation could be the consequence of holiness (Lev 20:24, 26; Num 6:5)."

◆ M. The Reign of Jotham (27:1-9)

Jotham was twenty-five years old when
he became king, and he reigned in Jeru-
salem sixteen years. His mother was Je-
rusha, the daughter of Zadok.
[2]Jotham did what was pleasing in the
LORD's sight. He did everything his father,
Uzziah, had done, except that Jotham did
not sin by entering the Temple of the
LORD. But the people continued in their
corrupt ways.
[3]Jotham rebuilt the upper gate of the
Temple of the LORD. He also did extensive
rebuilding on the wall at the hill of Ophel.
[4]He built towns in the hill country of Ju-
dah and constructed fortresses and tow-
ers in the wooded areas. [5]Jotham went to
war against the Ammonites and con-
quered them. Over the next three years he
received from them an annual tribute of
7,500 pounds* of silver, 50,000 bushels of
wheat, and 50,000 bushels of barley.*
[6]King Jotham became powerful because
he was careful to live in obedience to the
LORD his God.
[7]The rest of the events of Jotham's reign,
including all his wars and other activities,
are recorded in *The Book of the Kings of
Israel and Judah.* [8]He was twenty-five years
old when he became king, and he reigned
in Jerusalem sixteen years. [9]When Jotham
died, he was buried in the City of David.
And his son Ahaz became the next king.

27:5a Hebrew *100 talents* [3,400 kilograms]. **27:5b** Hebrew *10,000 cors* [1,820 kiloliters] *of wheat, and 10,000 cors of barley.*

NOTES

27:1 ***sixteen years.*** This figure includes the ten years of co-regency between Jotham and his sickly father, Uzziah (see 26:21) but does not include four years of co-regency between Jotham and his son Ahaz (see 2 Kgs 15:30; cf. Dillard 1987:214).

27:3 ***the upper gate of the Temple of the LORD.*** The location is uncertain, but if the upper gate in 23:20 is the same gate, it suggests that this was on the south side of the Temple courts, giving access to the royal palace. It may be better translated "the upper gate to the Temple of the LORD" (cf. Ezek 9:2). Ezekiel 9:2 speaks of an upper gate that "faces north." This would apply to a gate on the south side of the Temple courts, which would be the north side of the city proper.

the wall at the hill of Ophel. Ophel was a fortified mound or hill within the city of Jerusalem between the Temple Mount and the lower City of David (cf. Isa 32:14, NLT mg). The Millo divided the Temple Mount from the Ophel (2 Sam 5:9; 1 Kgs 9:15); for this and other views see ABD 4.834.

27:4 ***wooded areas.*** Although parts of Judah were once covered with scrub forests (Achtemeier 1996:1094), this may be a proper noun referring to a specific location, Horesh (NBD 381).

27:5 ***Ammonites.*** The Ammonite kingdom was founded at the end of the fourteenth century BC (along with Moab and Edom) and reached its height in the period of the divided kingdom in Israel. Even under Assyrian hegemony in the seventh century BC, Ammon would flourish (NBD 30). After the fall of Jerusalem, the Ammonite kingdom harbored some members of the Judean royal family (Ishmael; Jer 41:10, 15). This may explain the appearance of an Ammonite official with a Jewish name (Tobiah, meaning "Yahweh is my good") in the Persian period who opposed Nehemiah (Neh 4:7-8 [1-2]).

7,500 . . . 50,000 . . . 50,000. On these high numbers, see the commentary on 1 Chr 12:23-40.

COMMENTARY

The Chronicler's accounts of Joash (ch 24), Amaziah (ch 25), and Uzziah (ch 26) were arranged into positive and negative phases. Beginning now with Jotham and continuing for the next two reigns (Ahaz, Hezekiah), the Chronicler provides an exclusively positive or negative account (Jotham, positive, ch 27; Ahaz, negative, ch 28; Hezekiah, positive, chs 29–32).

Summary Note: The Accession of Jotham (27:1-2). Jotham is an enigma in that he reigned for so short a time in comparison to his father and yet was given a positive evaluation by the Chronicler. The Chronicler drew in extra material to bolster his positive description of Jotham, even though the amount of material is still limited compared to other kings. In past accounts the Chronicler excised references to enduring activity at the high places (2 Kgs 14:4; 15:4), but there it was argued that this was due to his desire to structure his presentation into obedient and disobedient phases of activity. Here, however, the Chronicler has only good to say about Jotham but still excises the reference to the high places, probably not to introduce any defamation of Jotham's leadership. He put the blame for any inappropriate activity on the people.

While the Chronicler connected Jotham to the good that Uzziah accomplished in his lifetime, he distanced the son from his father by noting that he "did not sin by entering the Temple of the LORD." Here we see the Chronicler's concern again over this sacral offense against the sanctuary. The Chronicler traced the enduring impact of Uzziah's unfaithfulness, described in 2 Chronicles 26:16 using the root *shakhath* [TH7843, ZH8845] (NLT, "his downfall"; lit., "corruption"); the same root is used to describe the people in 2 Chronicles 27:2 (NLT, "their corrupt ways"). The Chronicler's description of the activities of Jotham in the following verses (27:3-6) may be a deliberate attempt to show Jotham's activities as a match for those of his father, Uzziah (26:8-10), who rebuilt gates in Jerusalem, built towers in the outlying areas, and received tribute from the Ammonites (Dillard 1987:215). Interestingly, if the "upper gate" referred to here was that gate that linked the royal palace to the Temple courts (cf. 23:20), Jotham's reconstruction work may signal a desire to protect the Temple courts from royal intrusion (ABD 6.765).

Activities of Jotham (27:3-6). The Chronicler expanded his description of Jotham considerably beyond his source in Kings (2 Kgs 15:32-38) in order to highlight the result of the faithfulness of Jotham, a common motif in the Chronicler's presentation (cf. 11:5-12; 14:6-7; 17:12-13; 26:9-10; 33:14; Dillard 1987:215). Jotham was credited with building activities, but these were probably used to highlight his military success both in terms of defense and offense. For defensive purposes he strengthened the fortifications of Jerusalem (27:3) and built a network of fortifications throughout the Judean hill country (27:4). This lays the foundation for his foray into the Transjordan area, where he was able to exact tribute from the Ammonites for a period of three years (27:5). The Ammonite kingdom lay on the lucrative King's Highway, along which goods between Asia, Arabia, and Africa would flow and could be taxed.

The Chronicler ends this description by using the same verb he had used for Jotham's father, Uzziah, at the end of his first phase of reign: "became [very] powerful" (Heb., *khazaq* [TH2388, ZH2616]; 27:6; cf. 26:15). In the case of Uzziah, such "power" led to his pride and corruption (26:16), but such was not the case for Jotham, who "was careful to live in obedience to the LORD his God" (27:6). Here the Hebrew is, literally, "He made firm his ways before Yahweh his God," an expression that refers to doing something without flinching or wavering (see Prov 21:29 for the same phrase).

So focused is the Chronicler on emphasizing the positive results of Jotham's obedience that he left out the reference to Yahweh's sending the Syrians and Israelites against Judah (2 Kgs 15:37). Jotham did face challenges due to the actions of his people, but the Chronicler wanted to accentuate the results for those who will follow Yahweh wholeheartedly.

Summary Note: The Reign of Jotham (27:7-9). By being buried in the City of David, Jotham also stands in contrast to his father Uzziah, the unclean king whom the Chronicler describes in 26:23 as being buried in a royal burial field (with no reference to the City of David). Jotham's son Ahaz took over the reins of power from his father.

◆ N. The Reign of Ahaz (28:1-27)

Ahaz was twenty years old when he became king, and he reigned in Jerusalem sixteen years. He did not do what was pleasing in the sight of the LORD, as his ancestor David had done. [2]Instead, he followed the example of the kings of Israel. He cast metal images for the worship of Baal. [3]He offered sacrifices in the valley of Ben-Hinnom, even sacrificing his own sons in the fire.* In this way, he followed the detestable practices of the pagan nations the LORD had driven from the land ahead of the Israelites. [4]He offered sacrifices and burned incense at the pagan shrines and on the hills and under every green tree.

[5]Because of all this, the LORD his God allowed the king of Aram to defeat Ahaz and to exile large numbers of his people to Damascus. The armies of the king of Israel also defeated Ahaz and inflicted many casualties on his army. [6]In a single day Pekah son of Remaliah, Israel's king, killed 120,000 of Judah's troops, all of them experienced warriors, because they had abandoned the LORD, the God of their ancestors. [7]Then Zicri, a warrior from Ephraim, killed Maaseiah, the king's son; Azrikam, the king's palace commander; and Elkanah, the king's second-in-command. [8]The armies of Israel captured 200,000 women and children from Judah and seized tremendous amounts of plunder, which they took back to Samaria.

[9]But a prophet of the LORD named Oded was there in Samaria when the army of Israel returned home. He went out to meet them and said, "The LORD, the God of your ancestors, was angry with Judah and let you defeat them. But you have gone too far, killing them without mercy, and all heaven is disturbed. [10]And now you are planning to make slaves of these people from Judah and Jerusalem. What about your own sins against the LORD your God? [11]Listen to me and return these prisoners you have taken, for they are your own relatives. Watch out, because now the LORD's fierce anger has been turned against you!"

[12]Then some of the leaders of Israel*—Azariah son of Jehohanan, Berekiah son of Meshillemoth, Jehizkiah son of Shallum, and Amasa son of Hadlai—agreed with this and confronted the men returning from battle. [13]"You must not bring the prisoners here!" they declared. "We cannot afford to add to our sins and guilt. Our guilt is

already great, and the LORD's fierce anger is already turned against Israel."

[14]So the warriors released the prisoners and handed over the plunder in the sight of the leaders and all the people. [15]Then the four men just mentioned by name came forward and distributed clothes from the plunder to the prisoners who were naked. They provided clothing and sandals to wear, gave them enough food and drink, and dressed their wounds with olive oil. They put those who were weak on donkeys and took all the prisoners back to their own people in Jericho, the city of palms. Then they returned to Samaria.

[16]At that time King Ahaz of Judah asked the king of Assyria for help. [17]The armies of Edom had again invaded Judah and taken captives. [18]And the Philistines had raided towns located in the foothills of Judah* and in the Negev of Judah. They had already captured and occupied Beth-shemesh, Aijalon, Gederoth, Soco with its villages, Timnah with its villages, and Gimzo with its villages. [19]The LORD was humbling Judah because of King Ahaz of Judah,* for he had encouraged his people to sin and had been utterly unfaithful to the LORD.

[20]So when King Tiglath-pileser* of Assyria arrived, he attacked Ahaz instead of helping him. [21]Ahaz took valuable items from the LORD's Temple, the royal palace, and from the homes of his officials and gave them to the king of Assyria as tribute. But this did not help him.

[22]Even during this time of trouble, King Ahaz continued to reject the LORD. [23]He offered sacrifices to the gods of Damascus who had defeated him, for he said, "Since these gods helped the kings of Aram, they will help me, too, if I sacrifice to them." But instead, they led to his ruin and the ruin of all Judah.

[24]The king took the various articles from the Temple of God and broke them into pieces. He shut the doors of the LORD's Temple so that no one could worship there, and he set up altars to pagan gods in every corner of Jerusalem. [25]He made pagan shrines in all the towns of Judah for offering sacrifices to other gods. In this way, he aroused the anger of the LORD, the God of his ancestors.

[26]The rest of the events of Ahaz's reign and everything he did, from beginning to end, are recorded in *The Book of the Kings of Judah and Israel.* [27]When Ahaz died, he was buried in Jerusalem but not in the royal cemetery of the kings of Judah. Then his son Hezekiah became the next king.

28:3 Or *even making his sons pass through the fire.* **28:12** Hebrew *Ephraim,* referring to the northern kingdom of Israel. **28:18** Hebrew *the Shephelah.* **28:19** Masoretic Text reads *of Israel;* also in 28:23, 27. The author of Chronicles sees Judah as representative of the true Israel. (Some Hebrew manuscripts and Greek version read *of Judah.*) **28:20** Hebrew *Tilgath-pilneser,* a variant spelling of Tiglath-pileser.

NOTES

28:2 *he followed the example of the kings of Israel.* This is a reference to the idolatrous pattern in the northern kingdom typified by Jeroboam I, their first king, to set up gold calves at Dan in the far north and Bethel in the far south. It is the "sin of Jeroboam" that is identified regularly throughout the account of Kings in the negative evaluation of the northern kingdom (1 Kgs 16:31; 2 Kgs 3:3; 10:29, 31; 13:2, 11; 14:24; 15:9, 18, 24, 28) and is linked to the fall of this wicked kingdom (2 Kgs 17:22).

Baal. See note on 17:3.

28:3 *the valley of Ben-Hinnom.* This valley winds along the southern side of Jerusalem. While the western side of the small City of David was originally bounded by the Tyropoeon Valley, the city expanded in later years to reach a northern leg of the valley of Ben-Hinnom, which formed the new western boundary. It is called the valley (e.g., 26:9; Neh 2:13), the valley of Hinnom (e.g., Neh 11:30) and, as here, the valley of the son of Hinnom (Heb., *ben-hinnom* [TH2011A, ZH1208]; e.g., 33:6).

sacrificing his own sons in the fire. Lit., "making his sons pass through the fire" (see NLT mg). Some have seen this as some ritual ordeal, but most see this now as a sacrificial act (ABD 1.106).

the detestable practices of the pagan nations the Lord had driven from the land ahead of the Israelites. The term "detestable practices" (often translated as "abomination") is used in the OT to refer to sexual perversity (Lev 18; 20), consumption of unclean meat (Deut 14:3), remarriage of a divorced woman to a previous husband (Deut 24:4), improper sacrifice (Deut 17:1), and dishonest measures (Deut 25:16), but especially the worship of foreign gods (Deut 13:13; 17:3; 32:16; Isa 44:19). Both Lev 18:21 and Deut 12:31 refer to the sacrifice of children to foreign gods. These last two references explain why in the Chronicler's source in 2 Kgs 16:3 it is the child sacrifice that is directly related to abominable practices of the nations and why the phrase above is used also in relation to Manasseh (33:2), who also practiced child sacrifice (33:6).

28:4 ***pagan shrines.*** Lit., "high places." This is a reference to elevated locations that were used for worship practice, especially sacrifice. When occurring in the plural, it is always associated with illicit worship (11:15; 14:3, 5; 15:17; 17:6; 20:33; 21:11; 28:25; 31:1; 32:12; 33:3, 17, 19; 34:3), but when occurring in the singular is related to the site of the Tabernacle (1:3, 13; 1 Chr 16:39; 21:29).

28:5 ***the king of Aram . . . Damascus.*** The account in 2 Kgs 16:5 identifies this king as Rezin. Damascus was the capital of a key Aramean (Syrian) kingdom to the north of Israel. Rezin joined forces with King Pekah of Israel to oppose the rising power of Assyria and sought to bully Ahaz and Judah into joining this coalition (see further Isa 7–8). Rezin would be the final king of this Aramean kingdom before it was conquered by the Assyrians in 732 BC. By 722 BC the other partner in that coalition, Israel, would be part of the Assyrian Empire as well.

28:16 ***the king of Assyria.*** In the book of Kings this king is identified as Tiglath-pileser III (2 Kgs 16:7), as he is later in this chapter (28:20). Tiglath-pileser, sometimes called Pul in the OT (a nickname attested in the cuneiform records as Pulu), ruled Assyria from 744 to 727 BC (ABD 6.552; COS 2.284-287).

28:18 ***the foothills of Judah . . . the Negev of Judah . . . Beth-shemesh, Aijalon, Gederoth, Soco with its villages, Timnah with its villages, and Gimzo with its villages.*** The foothills of Judah were called the Shephelah or "lowland," a name reflecting the perspective of the Judeans living in the hills. This region lay between the hill country of Judah and the Coastal Plain and was the area of conflict between the Judeans and the Philistines, typified by stories like David-Goliath and Samson-Delilah. The Negev of Judah was the region to the south of the hill country of Judah, an area that would not sustain agricultural enterprise. All the towns listed here were located in the Shephelah.

28:20 ***he attacked Ahaz.*** Better, "he harassed Ahaz," as per HALOT 1058 (cf. Deut 28:52; 1 Kgs 8:37; 2 Chr 6:28; 28:22; 33:12; Neh 9:27; Jer 10:18; Zeph 1:17). What is in view in these various texts is not always a military attack of an enemy, but oppression in some form. See especially the Chronicler's use of this verb in 33:12 to refer to Manasseh's distress in bondage in Babylon (where he was clearly not being attacked militarily).

28:22 ***trouble.*** See note on 28:20, where this term refers to harassment.

COMMENTARY

While in his accounts of Joash (ch 24), Amaziah (ch 25), and Uzziah (ch 26) the Chronicler arranged his description into positive and negative phases, for Jotham (ch 27, positive), Ahaz (ch 28, negative), and Hezekiah (chs 29–32, positive) the

Chronicler provided an exclusively positive or negative account. From the heights of the exclusively positive evaluation of Jotham, the Chronicler presents an exclusively negative evaluation of Ahaz.

Many have noticed how the account of Ahaz plays a significant role in the book of Chronicles, signaling a transition between eras (Ben Zvi 1993:218; Lowery 1991:128-129; Raney 2003:144-148). With the fall of the northern kingdom to Assyria during his reign, Ahaz had the greatest opportunity since the time of Solomon to unite the two kingdoms under a Davidic royal figure. Yet, as Lowery (1991:129) notes, Ahaz and his kingdom "stand as the photographic negative of the Chronicler's Davidic-Solomonic ideal."[1] While in the book of Kings, Manasseh represents the lowest point in the history, in the book of Chronicles Ahaz plays this role (Smelik 1992:182-183; 1998:164, 181). Hezekiah will soon appear on the scene and usher in a new ideal period of renewal for Judah, inviting faithful northerners to join him in worship at Jerusalem. But before Hezekiah arrives, it is Ahaz who creates the conditions of nothing short of "exile" as he first desecrates the land with inappropriate worship practices, sees a foreign emperor take control of his kingdom, then closes the Temple (cf. Dillard 1987:261; Mosis 1973:41-43, 186-188).

Summary Note: The Accession of Ahaz (28:1-2a). As in his source in 2 Kings 16, the Chronicler provides Ahaz's age at accession (20), length of reign (16 years), place of reign (Jerusalem), and evaluation of reign ("did not do what was pleasing in the sight of the LORD, as his ancestor David had done"). However, his mother's name is not recorded. The reason for this may be related to his evaluation (in both 28:2 and 2 Kgs 16:3) as following "the example of the kings of Israel" (lit., "walked in the ways of the kings of Israel"). Throughout the book of Kings the succession notes of the kings of Judah contain the names of the queen mother, while those for the kings of Israel do not (cf. 2 Kgs 15:27 with 15:32-33).[2] The writer of Kings may have been subtly strengthening the link between Ahaz and the northern kings (see also 33:1-2).

Ahaz and the Northern Kingdom: Idolatry and Defeat (28:2b-7). The Chronicler immediately defines what it means to follow the ways of the northern kings of Israel: participating in idolatry, here identified as creating images of Baals, burning incense, and sacrificing sons throughout the land both at high places and under sacred trees. These "molten images" were made of metal poured in a cast and differentiated from graven or carved images (often cited alongside one another: Deut 27:15; Judg 17:3-4; 18:14; Nah 1:14). Burning incense in ancient religion was related to offering a sweet smell to the gods (see ABD 3.406), similar to the sweet smell of burnt offerings. If the reference to "causing his sons to be burned in the fire" (NLT, "sacrificing his own sons in the fire") is the same as the illicit act of, literally, "making his son or daughter pass through the fire" in Deuteronomy 18:10-11, it may be related to divination or magical practice, since these kinds of acts are what follow in Deuteronomy 18 (and in 33:6; ABD 4.468). However, the verb used in chapter 28 is different, and even the Deuteronomy 18 reference may be simply child sacrifice as a propitiatory act. This abhorrent act is also attested in Jeremiah 7:31; 19:5; 32:35 (cf. Ezek 16:20). Child sacrifice is mentioned also in the reign of Manasseh (2 Kgs 21:6) and in the northern kingdom after the fall of Samaria (2 Kgs 17:17; see ABD 2.767).

The comparison of Ahaz's action to "the detestable practices of the pagan nations the LORD had driven from the land ahead of the Israelites" is repeated also at the outset of the account of Manasseh's reign (33:2) and in a shortened version at the end of the history of the kingdom (36:14; cf. 34:33; 36:8). It is child sacrifice that is most likely the reason for this comparison to the Canaanites who preceded Israel, since the same phrase is also used of Manasseh (33:2), who also sacrificed his children in the Hinnom valley on the edge of Jerusalem (33:6). The wickedness was not only evident in Jerusalem, however, but throughout the entire land (high places, hills, every green tree).

Following the report of illicit worship in his source, the Chronicler found only a simple report of an unsuccessful attack by a coalition Aramean-Israelite army (2 Kgs 16:5). The Chronicler's account goes in a radically different direction in 28:5, making an explicit causal link ("because of all this") between Ahaz's idolatrous activity and the advance of the Aramean (Syrian) and Israelite armies, identifying Yahweh as the one ultimately responsible for this attack ("the LORD his God allowed"), and reporting separate and devastating defeats by Aram and Israel. The first defeat results in many captives and the second in a great slaughter that included key members in the royal court. The kind of detail offered in the Chronicler's account suggests that he was drawing his information from another source.

The key in this account is that the Chronicler used Ahaz as an exemplar for his theology of retribution: If you are unfaithful to God, he will abandon you to your enemies, and you will suffer military defeat. One should not miss the irony that no sooner had Ahaz followed in the ways of the northern kingdom than he was attacked by that same kingdom.

Prophet Oded Confronts the Northern Kingdom (28:8-15). While the Chronicler usually ignores the history of the northern kingdom, at this point the focus of the narrative shifts to the north. One can discern the hand of the Chronicler at work in the design since the narrative showcases the prophetic word. The devastating defeat of Ahaz led to a significant number of Judeans not only slaughtered in the fight, but an even greater number being taken captive to Samaria (28:8). At this point, however, a prophet named Oded confronted the men, telling them that by intending to make these captives their slaves (28:9-11) they had overstepped their limited role in bringing the wrath of God upon an unfaithful Judah. While the prophet admitted that Yahweh "was angry with Judah" (28:9), he revealed that "now the LORD's fierce anger has been turned against you" (28:11). He commanded them to send back the captives to Judah. The word of the Ephraimite leaders listed in 28:12 (Azariah, Berekiah, Jehizkiah, and Amasa) supports the prophet's words but also admits the guilt the northern kingdom possessed even before this act. At this the army released the captives. The account relates how these four Ephraimite chiefs clothed, fed, and anointed the captives and transported them safely back to Jericho (called the city of palm trees) on donkeys.

Through this account the Chronicler continued to showcase the usefulness and effectiveness of the prophetic word within the community of God. It is possible, however, that the Chronicler also had in view some abuse that had been directed by Jews in the province of Samaria toward those in the province of Yehud in his own time period. One does not have to look far for evidence of tension (Ezra 3–6;

Neh 1–7) between these two political entities in the Persian period, but the nature or time period of the tension cannot be identified with precision.

Ahaz and the Foreign Nations: Appeal and Defeat (28:16-21). In the midst of this crisis at the hands at Aram and Israel from the north, attacks also came from the east (Edom's invasion and defeat of Judah)[3] and the west (Philistine raids on cities throughout the Shephelah). The Chronicler reiterated his theological belief in 28:19 that these invasions were evidence of Yahweh's direct retribution (using his favorite vocabulary of "humbling," *kana'* [TH3665, ZH4044]) and were directly related to Ahaz, who had "encouraged his people to sin" or better, had "removed restraint" or "let unbridled freedom have its way" (*para'* [TH6544, ZH7277], Hiphil; HALOT 970). He also had been "utterly unfaithful" to Yahweh, noted here by a double use of that Hebrew root *ma'al* [TH4603, ZH5085], which had typified Uzziah's act of sacrilege in the Temple and which the Chronicler regularly used to refer to acts of unfaithfulness (12:2; 26:16, 18; 28:22; 29:6, 19; 30:7; 33:19; 36:14; 1 Chr 2:7; 5:25; 9:1; 10:13; see comment on 1 Chr 10:13).

In dire straits, Ahaz turned to mighty Assyria for help (see Isa 7–8).[4] Tuell (2001:210) concluded that the Chronicler's "unstinting condemnation of Ahaz" was related to the fact "that he was the first king to succumb to a foreign power, and he did so willingly, without resistance."[5] While David and Solomon had received tribute from the nations, "Ahaz frantically stripped the Temple and handed over Jerusalem's cultic and royal treasuries in a disastrous attempt to enlist Assyria's assistance (28:16-21)" (Lowery 1991:130). According to 2 Kings 16:6-9, Ahaz had to pay off the Assyrians with silver and gold from the Temple and palace, payment that motivated the Assyrians to attack and capture Damascus. The Chronicler was not interested in portraying any relief for the wicked Ahaz, so he left out Tiglath-pileser's defeat of Aram and instead interpreted the transfer of funds as evidence that the Assyrians turned against Ahaz and "harassed" (NLT, "attacked"; see notes above) Ahaz (28:20-21).

Ahaz's Reign in Judah, 732–716 BC

Ahaz, Idolatry, and the Temple (28:22-25). Such deep crisis, however, did not lead this Judean king to depend on Yahweh, as will be the case with his son Hezekiah in chapters 29–32. Instead, the Chronicler relates that he "continued to reject the LORD," again employing the root *ma'al* [TH4603, ZH5085] (see above, 28:16-21). This summary statement is then backed up with the evidence of 28:23-25, which describes his capitulation to the gods of the Arameans in a fashion typical of a defeated people in the ancient world; the defeated ones would have assumed that since they had been defeated by a foreign people, the god of that foreign people was more powerful than their god. This is precisely the logic of his statement: "Since these gods helped the kings of Aram, they will help me, too, if I sacrifice to them" (28:23). Instead, they only contributed to his ruin and the ruin of Israel.

Ahaz's illicit worship of the Aramean gods was just the beginning. Eventually, Ahaz would damage utensils within the Temple and even shut down its worship. In its place, he instituted altars throughout Jerusalem and all the towns of Judah. This reverses the instruction of Moses in Deuteronomy 12 that Israel would choose one place of worship, an instruction that was facilitated by the Davidic dynasty in the development of Jerusalem as a worship center (see the results of violation of this principle in Judg 17–21, especially 17:6; 18:1; 19:1; 21:25; and see the ideal Davidic solution in Ps 122:1-5). The closing words of the section again remind the readers that Ahaz's activity "aroused the anger of the LORD, the God of his ancestors" (28:25).

The Chronicler excised a large portion of his source in Kings (2 Kgs 16:10-18). This portion depicts the role that Uriah the priest played in facilitating Ahaz's innovations and activities at the Temple. By ignoring this section, the Chronicler probably did not want to highlight priestly involvement in the affair, nor could he stomach reproducing such sacrilege taking place in the Temple structure and courts.

Summary Note: The Reign of Ahaz (28:26-27). After reviewing his source for his account, the Chronicler followed the account in Kings that Ahaz was buried in the city of Jerusalem (though leaving out the qualifier "in the City of David") but quickly added an extra note, "but not in the royal cemetery of the kings of Judah." Such a despicable character as Ahaz would be dishonored in death like his wicked grandfather Uzziah in 26:23. The crown would then pass to Ahaz's son Hezekiah.

ENDNOTES

1. Williamson (1982:343-344) highlights deep contrasts between Abijah and Ahaz, noting how Abijah was the Davidic king who was called to unite the kingdoms immediately after the schism.
2. The only other place the mother's name is left out is with Jehoram (2 Kgs 8:16-17). The Chronicler follows his source in leaving out the mother of Jehoram and Ahaz, but then after Hezekiah, he stops recording the name of the queen mother from his source. This may indicate his view toward the history after Hezekiah.
3. According to his source in 2 Kgs 16:6 Edom recovered Elath.
4. The theme of trusting in Yahweh rather than the nations is the major theme of Isa 7–39 and the juxtaposition in that book between the figures of Ahaz (Isa 7–12) and Hezekiah (Isa 36–38). Notice how Isa 13–35 is focused on the nations and their fragility before Yahweh (Boda 2009b).
5. Note Mitchell (2001:266), who contrasts Ahaz with "previous kings who had called for help from Yhwh (like Abijah)"; cf. Ben Zvi 1993:227.

◆ O. The Reign of Hezekiah (29:1–32:33)

1. Hezekiah takes the throne and reopens the Temple (29:1–36)

Hezekiah was twenty-five years old when he became the king of Judah, and he reigned in Jerusalem twenty-nine years. His mother was Abijah, the daughter of Zechariah. [2]He did what was pleasing in the LORD's sight, just as his ancestor David had done.

3 In the very first month of the first year
of his reign, Hezekiah reopened the doors
of the Temple of the LORD and repaired
them. 4 He summoned the priests and Le-
vites to meet him at the courtyard east of
the Temple. 5 He said to them, "Listen to
me, you Levites! Purify yourselves, and
purify the Temple of the LORD, the God of
your ancestors. Remove all the defiled
things from the sanctuary. 6 Our ancestors
were unfaithful and did what was evil in
the sight of the LORD our God. They aban-
doned the LORD and his dwelling place;
they turned their backs on him. 7 They also
shut the doors to the Temple's entry room,
and they snuffed out the lamps. They
stopped burning incense and presenting
burnt offerings at the sanctuary of the
God of Israel.

8 "That is why the LORD's anger has fall-
en upon Judah and Jerusalem. He has
made them an object of dread, horror, and
ridicule, as you can see with your own
eyes. 9 Because of this, our fathers have
been killed in battle, and our sons and
daughters and wives have been captured.
10 But now I will make a covenant with the
LORD, the God of Israel, so that his fierce
anger will turn away from us. 11 My sons,
do not neglect your duties any longer! The
LORD has chosen you to stand in his pres-
ence, to minister to him, and to lead the
people in worship and present offerings
to him."

12 Then these Levites got right to work:

From the clan of Kohath: Mahath son
of Amasai and Joel son of Azariah.
From the clan of Merari: Kish son of
Abdi and Azariah son of Jehallelel.
From the clan of Gershon: Joah son of
Zimmah and Eden son of Joah.
13 From the family of Elizaphan: Shimri
and Jeiel.
From the family of Asaph: Zechariah
and Mattaniah.
14 From the family of Heman: Jehiel and
Shimei.
From the family of Jeduthun:
Shemaiah and Uzziel.

15 These men called together their fellow
Levites, and they all purified themselves.
Then they began to cleanse the Temple of
the LORD, just as the king had commanded.
They were careful to follow all the LORD's
instructions in their work. 16 The priests
went into the sanctuary of the Temple of
the LORD to cleanse it, and they took out to
the Temple courtyard all the defiled things
they found. From there the Levites carted
it all out to the Kidron Valley.

17 They began the work in early spring,
on the first day of the new year,* and in
eight days they had reached the entry
room of the LORD's Temple. Then they pu-
rified the Temple of the LORD itself, which
took another eight days. So the entire task
was completed in sixteen days.

18 Then the Levites went to King Heze-
kiah and gave him this report: "We have
cleansed the entire Temple of the LORD,
the altar of burnt offering with all its
utensils, and the table of the Bread of the
Presence with all its utensils. 19 We have
also recovered all the items discarded by
King Ahaz when he was unfaithful and
closed the Temple. They are now in front
of the altar of the LORD, purified and
ready for use."

20 Early the next morning King Hezekiah
gathered the city officials and went to the
Temple of the LORD. 21 They brought seven
bulls, seven rams, and seven male lambs
as a burnt offering, together with seven
male goats as a sin offering for the king-
dom, for the Temple, and for Judah. The
king commanded the priests, who were
descendants of Aaron, to sacrifice the
animals on the altar of the LORD.

22 So they killed the bulls, and the priests
took the blood and sprinkled it on the al-
tar. Next they killed the rams and sprin-
kled their blood on the altar. And finally,
they did the same with the male lambs.
23 The male goats for the sin offering were
then brought before the king and the as-
sembly of people, who laid their hands on
them. 24 The priests then killed the goats
as a sin offering and sprinkled their blood
on the altar to make atonement for the

sins of all Israel. The king had specifically commanded that this burnt offering and sin offering should be made for all Israel.
25King Hezekiah then stationed the Levites at the Temple of the LORD with cymbals, lyres, and harps. He obeyed all the commands that the LORD had given to King David through Gad, the king's seer, and the
prophet Nathan. 26The Levites then took their positions around the Temple with the instruments of David, and the priests took their positions with the trumpets.
27Then Hezekiah ordered that the burnt offering be placed on the altar. As the burnt offering was presented, songs of praise to the LORD were begun, accompanied by the trumpets and other instruments of David, the former king of Israel.
28The entire assembly worshiped the LORD as the singers sang and the trumpets blew, until all the burnt offerings were
finished. 29Then the king and everyone
with him bowed down in worship. 30King
Hezekiah and the officials ordered the Levites to praise the LORD with the psalms written by David and by Asaph the seer. So they offered joyous praise and bowed down in worship.

31Then Hezekiah declared, "Now that you have consecrated yourselves to the LORD, bring your sacrifices and thanksgiving offerings to the Temple of the LORD." So the people brought their sacrifices and thanksgiving offerings, and all whose hearts were willing brought burnt offer-
ings, too. 32The people brought to the LORD 70 bulls, 100 rams, and 200 male
lambs for burnt offerings. 33They also brought 600 cattle and 3,000 sheep and goats as sacred offerings.
34But there were too few priests to prepare all the burnt offerings. So their relatives the Levites helped them until the work was finished and more priests had been purified, for the Levites had been more conscientious about purifying them-
selves than the priests had been. 35There
was an abundance of burnt offerings, along with the usual liquid offerings, and a great deal of fat from the many peace offerings.

So the Temple of the LORD was restored
to service. 36And Hezekiah and all the
people rejoiced because of what God had done for the people, for everything had been accomplished so quickly.

29:17 Hebrew *on the first day of the first month.* This day in the ancient Hebrew lunar calendar occurred in March or early April, 715 B.C.

NOTES

29:1 ***twenty-nine years.*** This number includes the 15 years added to his life (2 Kgs 20:6).

29:4 ***the courtyard east of the Temple.*** Precision is difficult on this location, but it is possibly the same "square just inside the Water Gate" mentioned in Neh 8:1, 3 (Dillard 1987:34).

29:11 ***present offerings to him.*** This action (lit., "burning") could refer to sacrificing (e.g., Exod 29:18) or burning incense (Exod 30:7-8).

29:16 ***the sanctuary of the Temple of the LORD.*** The Hebrew term for sanctuary here is *penimah* [TH6441, ZH7163], which can refer to either the sanctuary in general or to the Most Holy Place (4:22; 1 Kgs 6:27; 7:12, 50; 1 Chr 28:11; Dillard 1987:235).

Kidron Valley. This is the valley on the eastern side of the city of Jerusalem, across from which rises the Mount of Olives.

29:18 ***the altar of burnt offering . . . the table of the Bread of the Presence.*** The altar was located in the courtyard outside the sanctuary. The table was located within the Holy Place upon which twelve pieces of bread were placed to represent the twelve tribes of Israel before Yahweh's presence (Lev 24:5-9).

29:21 ***burnt offering . . . sin offering.*** For the burnt offering legislation, see Lev 1; for the sin offering, see Lev 4–5; also see Ezek 43:18-27; 44:27; 45:18-20, 21-25, where sin offerings are used to purify the altar, sanctuary, and priests in preparation for Passover (Dillard 1987:236; Williamson 1982:356).

29:22 ***So they killed the bulls, and the priests took the blood and sprinkled it on the altar.*** The subject of the first verb must be Hezekiah and the city officials of 29:20, since in Lev 1:4-5 the person who brings the sacrifice also slaughtered the animal (Williamson 1982:357).

29:23 ***laid their hands on them.*** In the legislation for the sin offering in Lev 4:4, the hand of the offerer was laid on the head of the animal (Lev 16:21).

29:31 ***consecrated yourselves.*** Lit., "filled your hand," an idiom usually employed to speak of consecrating someone as priest (13:9; Exod 28:41; 29:9, 29, 33, 35; Lev 8:33; 16:32; 21:10; Num 3:3; 1 Kgs 13:33) but which can be used of laity who consecrate themselves for the purpose of worship (Exod 32:29; 1 Chr 29:5).

29:34 ***to prepare all the burnt offerings.*** The verb used here (*pashat* [TH6584, ZH7320], Hiphil) means to remove the skin of the animal to be sacrificed. In Lev 1:6 it is the offerer who is required to do this action, but here the priests were clearly responsible. This may reflect a different priestly tradition, but more likely it was due to the inexperience of a generation that had not been involved in sacrifice.

29:35 ***liquid offerings . . . peace offerings.*** The former are sometimes translated as drink offerings, which in Num 15:1-10 accompanied burnt and peace offerings and consisted of wine (Exod 29:40) or "alcoholic drink" (Num 28:7). Among other uses, they also accompanied the daily sacrifice (Exod 29:40-41; Num 28:7) and the Sabbath offering (Num 28:9). For peace offerings, see note on 30:22.

COMMENTARY

The Chronicler used the account of Hezekiah as an opportunity to insert a considerable amount of new material into his history. The restoration of the Temple in 29:3-36, the renewal of Passover in 30:1-27, the reform of worship practices in 31:2-21, and a short piece in the description of Sennacherib's invasion (32:2-8) are all unique to the Chronicler. Dillard (1987:227-229) has described how the writer of Kings identified the reign of Josiah as the "zenith" of the history of the divided kingdom, while the Chronicler identified this zenith with the reign of Hezekiah (Japhet 1993:936; Mitchell 2006:429; Raney 2003:159). This height is discerned in three key emphases of Hezekiah's reign: (1) Hezekiah's actions to reunify Israel after the fall of the northern kingdom to Assyrian aggression, (2) Hezekiah's affinity with the values and actions of David and Solomon (union of the kingdoms, reforms of worship, accumulation of great wealth, attention by Gentiles, royal practice of prayer), and (3) Hezekiah's demonstration of the validity of the Chronicler's theology of retribution.

While the account of Hezekiah in the book of Kings (2 Kgs 18–20) and Isaiah (Isa 36–39) is dominated by Sennacherib's attack, the Chronicler's account is dominated by Hezekiah's attention to worship reforms and the restoration of the physical infrastructure, but more so by attention to the renewal of the worship rhythms and practices of the Temple. The account is not entirely positive, since the Chronicler revealed the stories of Hezekiah's sickness, which he linked to Hezekiah's arrogance. But in the end Hezekiah is also used as a positive example for renewal because he repented and enjoyed success, according to the account's closing verses (see Boda 2009b).

Summary Note: The Accession of Hezekiah (29:1-2). The Chronicler introduced Hezekiah by removing the reference to his father Ahaz that he saw in his source in 2 Kings 18:1. This removal may be merely stylistic, appearing repetitious to the Chronicler once he had excised (as was his practice) the dating of Hezekiah's accession to the reign of the northern king Hoshea in 2 Kings 18:1. It is possible, however, that the Chronicler wanted to play down any connection between his positive exemplar Hezekiah and his negative predecessor Ahaz. The Chronicler retained his source's connection, however, between Hezekiah and David, a connection that will be strengthened throughout his account of Hezekiah (29:25, 27, 30; 30:26; 32:5, 30, 33). As son of David, Hezekiah is presented as a second Solomon (30:26).[1]

The Cleansing and Rededication of the Temple (29:3-36). The Chronicler emphasized that at the outset of his reign ("In the very first month of the first year of his reign"), Hezekiah reversed the key negative legacy of his father Ahaz—that is, the closing of the Temple and abandonment of its worship services (28:24). The date given here refers to the beginning of the first full year of Hezekiah's reign after his father's death (called his "regnal year"). The Temple project may have been chosen to commemorate this special day, setting the tone for Hezekiah's reign.[2] This restoration project must begin with the reopening and repair of the doors of the Temple (29:3), but anything beyond this would require the assistance of the priests and Levites.

Hezekiah's speech to the priests and Levites is presented in 29:4-11, where he commissions them to cleanse the Temple so that a new phase of worship could begin.[3] This speech expresses some of the key values of the Chronicler within his own community living in a period when restoring and maintaining the Temple and return from captivity were recent and enduring priorities.[4] Hezekiah's speech isolates the priests and Levites as the legitimate groups for this restoration and maintenance, calling them first to sanctify themselves so that they might sanctify the Temple. The Chronicler (29:6) explains that the sorry state of affairs is related to the "unfaithful" (*ma'al* [TH4603, ZH5085]) actions of "our ancestors" described as "abandoning" (*'azab* [TH5800, ZH6440]) Yahweh, vocabulary prominent throughout the Chronicler's account, related immediately (29:7) to the absence of legitimate worship practices in the Temple. It is this that brought the "LORD's anger" upon them and resulted in the exile of the people (29:8-9). The anger of God was brought on by Ahaz, who followed the patterns of the northern kingdom, which also was under God's anger.

Hezekiah signaled a new era of relationship with Yahweh by declaring his intention to "make a covenant with the LORD" (29:10)[5] with the hope that this would bring an end to the anger of God that was aroused by his father (28:25). This language echoes the earlier speech of Solomon when the Temple was dedicated (6:14-16). Hezekiah ended the speech by calling the Levites to fulfill their responsibilities, reminding them of Yahweh's election of them to "stand in his presence, to minister to him, and to lead the people in worship and present offerings to him" (29:11). The Levites were set apart to worship Yahweh on behalf of the nation.

The particulars of this speech can be related to the actions of Ahaz and his generation (28:17, 24-25; cf. 28:8, 13), who would be considered "our ancestors" (29:6). But one should not miss how this speech would have been heard by the Chronicler's audience, who would also have associated the abuse of the Temple and the exile of the people with the exilic experience that endured throughout the sixth century BC, first under Babylonian rule but continuing for many years throughout the Persian period and beyond (see Esther and Daniel and the elongation of the exile in Daniel 9).[6] The Chronicler was using the conditions in Hezekiah's day to encourage and challenge the people of his generation to value the maintenance of the Temple and its services. The tone of the message to the priests and Levites suggests either a need to legitimize the duties of both priests and Levites in this period or possibly to challenge certain sectors among these sacred personnel to fulfill their responsibilities.

In 29:12 the Chronicler highlights the immediate response of the Levites (lit., "they arose") and provides an extensive list of the leaders from each of the key Levitical families, who then motivated and organized the members of their clans to undertake the work.[7] Emphasis is placed in 29:15 on their detailed attention to the specific commands of King Hezekiah ("just as the king had commanded"), as well as Yahweh's ("they were careful to follow all the LORD's instructions in their work"). The subsequent account of the Chronicler and the report of the priests reveal that the process of cleansing involved the removal of unclean objects (29:16), as well as the recovery and sanctifying of the building and its many sacred objects (29:18-19).

The Chronicler continued his trend of normative characters following proper protocol. According to 29:16, it was the "priests" who entered the sanctuary proper as they removed the "defiled things." Although the term here is more generic ("uncleanness") and usually refers to a condition (Lev 5:3; 7:20-21; 15:25-26, 30), at times it is associated with inanimate things like food (Judg 13:7, 14) and objects (Ezek 24:11). Here it clearly refers to objects that were then transferred to the non-priestly Levites for transport out of the city on the eastern side toward the Kidron Valley (see the cleansing of Asa in 15:16 and Josiah in 30:14). The precise day on which the restoration began is identified in 29:17—the "first day of the new year." This appears to be connected to the date given in 29:3 and refers to the first month of the first full year of Hezekiah's reign after his father's death (Dillard 1987:234).[8] This shows that the priests and Levites began their work on the same day they received their commission. The Chronicler also provides the precise length of the project, dividing the project into two phases. The first phase took eight days and was focused on the restoration of the sacred courts, while the second took another eight days and was focused on the restoration of the sanctuary proper. The shortness of time shows that the damage was not extensive and that the focus was on removal of impure objects, the restoration of pure utensils, and ritual cleansing of the sacral area. Although quick (29:36), the project was not completed in time for the celebration of Passover, which would have been scheduled for the 14th day of the month, explaining why the Passover was delayed until the next month (30:1-3).

The remainder of the account (29:20-36) provides an extensive description of the rededication ceremonies for the restored Temple. In 29:20-21, Hezekiah and the city officials go to the Temple with animals (bulls, rams, male lambs, and male goats) for burnt and sin offerings. These were for the kingdom, the Temple, and Judah. This tripartite structure suggests the importance of royal, priestly, and popular interests for the proper maintenance of this community. The Chronicler was probably reminding his later audience of the enduring need for balance between these three groups in his own era. By commanding the priests to offer these sacrifices, Hezekiah showed he was in control of the situation. This affirms an enduring role for the royal line in the maintenance of worship.

Next (29:22-24), Hezekiah and the city officials killed the animals (bulls, rams, and male lambs), the priests sprinkled their blood on the altar (29:22), and the king and the assembly (the latter probably consisting of city officials who represented the people as a whole) laid hands on male goats, which were then sacrificed as sin offerings and their blood sprinkled on the altar "to make atonement for the sins of all Israel" (29:23-24). The Chronicler again emphasizes (end of 29:24) that all had been done at the command of Hezekiah, who was ultimately responsible for these actions. The reference to "all Israel" at the end of the verse highlights the Chronicler's passion for a united Israel around the Davidic king. The fall of the northern kingdom and thus the removal of the rival political entity to the north provided Hezekiah the first opportunity since Solomon for a Davidic king to unite the people in one kingdom.

Hezekiah then stationed the Levites with their worship instruments (29:25-26), following the instructions of David through the prophets Gad and Nathan (see 1 Chr 16, 25) and even using the very instruments of David. Priests with trumpets were also placed in position. With all preparations complete, the sacred precincts and utensils sanctified, the people sanctified and the musicians in place, it was time to sacrifice the burnt offering on the altar (29:27-30). This was done to the accompaniment of the musicians, citing again David as the one who established these personnel and the worship of the entire assembly. The sacrifice was followed by the response of the king and the people in bowed worship, followed by the singing of psalms of David and Asaph by the Levites. As is evident elsewhere in the Chronicler's work, the Levites were depicted as taking on prophetic roles (20; 34:30; 35:15; 1 Chr 25:5; see Petersen 1977:57-87). So here Asaph is called "the seer," a term often associated with a traditional prophet (9:29; 12:15; 19:2; 29:25; 33:18; 1 Chr 21:9; 29:29).

According to 29:31-33, Hezekiah invited the newly consecrated people (through the sprinkled blood of the goats and the burnt offering sacrificed for the entire community) to bring sacrifices and thanksgiving offerings to the Temple. Those who did so are described as "all whose hearts were willing." The response of the people was so great that the priests were unable to handle the multitude of offerings. Thus, in 29:34-35a the Chronicler described Levitical participation alongside the priests for these offerings. This note seems to cast a slightly negative light on the priests, praising the Levites for being "more upright of heart" (NLT, "more conscientious") than the priests by consecrating themselves and setting a precedent for Levitical involvement in the preparation of the burnt offerings (and possibly also the liquid and peace offerings of 29:35a). This may reflect a desire on the Chronicler's part for flexibility in the use of Levites in the sacrificial worship of his own day.

The account ends with a key summarizing statement in 29:35b, noting that the worship at the Temple was established; this echoes a similar statement at the end of the Temple-building account (8:16; cf. Williamson 1982:360). A response typical of the Chronicler's accounts and signaling the end of the first phase of the Chronicler's account is recorded in 29:36: "Hezekiah and all the people rejoiced" (see also 30:25-26). Here we see king and people unified in joy around the common task of worship at the Temple, echoing the joy at the original dedication of this Temple in Solomon's day (7:10).

Through the picture of the people gathered around the Davidic king in chapter 29, the Chronicler speaks to his own generation in the Persian period. First, the people were encouraged to rally around worship at the Temple, as the people did of old. Second, the function of Hezekiah as the key initiator in this passage suggests that the Chronicler retains his vision for the return of the Davidic line as patron of Temple worship in Jerusalem (see Boda 2009b).

ENDNOTES

1. See Throntveit 1987:121-125 for a superb review of the various views on the Chronicler's connection of Hezekiah to an earlier dynastic figure, with Mosis (1973) seeing him as a "second David," Williamson (1977b:119-125) as a "second Solomon," and Ackroyd (1973:179-189) as a combination of both (second David-Solomon).
2. The Temple restoration accounts of ancient kings often speak about an "auspicious day" in connection with the restoration of Temple structures (see Boda 2006c; Boda and Novotny 2009).
3. The generic vocative "Levites" in 29:5 must include both priestly and Levitical orders.
4. Von Rad (1966b:275) identified this speech as a Levitical Sermon; see further Mason 1990; Throntveit 1987; Williamson 1982:355.
5. The NLT does not translate the opening part of this verse in Hebrew, "[It is] in my heart," a phrase that is used elsewhere in Chronicles of David and Solomon's desire to build the Temple (6:7; 1 Chr 22:7; 28:2), so Williamson (1982:353).
6. Many confirm this by noting a close relationship between Hezekiah's speech in 29:8 and Jer 29:18 (Dillard 1987:234). Williamson (1982:353) notes also Jer 15:4; 25:9, 18; 34:17; Ezek 23:46. In his letter to the exiles (Jer 29:4-23), Jeremiah warns the exiles not to listen to their prophets in exile but rather to listen to God's word through him. Jeremiah prophesies that the Exile will last seventy years, after which God will bring them back to the land. As for "the king who sits on David's throne and all those still living here in Jerusalem—your relatives who were not exiled to Babylon," that is, those who would experience the final fall of Jerusalem in 587 under King Zedekiah, here was Jeremiah's message to them:

    > I will send war, famine, and disease upon them and make them like bad figs, too rotten to eat. Yes, I will pursue them with war, famine, and disease, and I will scatter them around the world. In every nation where I send them, I will make them an object of damnation (*ze'awah* [TH2189, ZH2400]), horror (*shammah* [TH8047, ZH9014]), contempt (*shereqah* [TH8322, ZH9240]), and mockery (*kherpah* [TH2781, ZH3075]). For they refuse to listen to me, though I have spoken to them repeatedly through the prophets I sent. And you who are in exile have not listened either.

Hezekiah states, "He has made them an object of dread (*ze'awah* [TH2189, ZH2400], horror (*shammah* [TH8047, ZH9014]), and ridicule (*shereqah* [TH8322, ZH9240])" (29:8). The two passages share two words in common, and they are listed in the same order. The possibility of literary dependence cannot be confirmed, although a common tradition of speaking about exile is probable (see also Mic 6:16).

7. This list contains representatives from the three key Levitical families (Kohath, Merari, Gershon) and from the three Levitical musician families (Asaph, Heman, Jeduthun). The clan of Elizaphan was actually a family within Kohath but must have gained significant size or status to take on the role of a fourth Levitical family (Dillard 1987:234-235). Dillard notes that the Levitical singers here have replaced the Levitical families of Hebron and Uzziel, who were listed in 1 Chr 15:5-10 under David's leadership.
8. The first year in the postdating method is the first full year during the reign of Hezekiah, as opposed to the first month of his reign after the death of his father (antedating). It appears that the postdating method was used here for this "first month," which is connected to the first month of the calendar year (cf. 30:1-2).

2. Renewal of the Passover and Festival of Unleavened Bread (30:1–31:1)

King Hezekiah now sent word to all Israel
and Judah, and he wrote letters of invita-
tion to the people of Ephraim and Ma-
nasseh. He asked everyone to come to the
Temple of the LORD at Jerusalem to cele-
brate the Passover of the LORD, the God of
Israel. 2The king, his officials, and all the
community of Jerusalem decided to cele-
brate Passover a month later than usual.*
3They were unable to celebrate it at the
prescribed time because not enough priests
could be purified by then, and the people
had not yet assembled at Jerusalem.

4This plan for keeping the Passover
seemed right to the king and all the peo-
ple. 5So they sent a proclamation through-
out all Israel, from Beersheba in the south
to Dan in the north, inviting everyone to
come to Jerusalem to celebrate the Pass-
over of the LORD, the God of Israel. The
people had not been celebrating it in
great numbers as required in the Law.

6At the king's command, runners were
sent throughout Israel and Judah. They
carried letters that said:

"O people of Israel, return to the LORD,
the God of Abraham, Isaac, and Israel,*
so that he will return to the few of us
who have survived the conquest of
the Assyrian kings. 7Do not be like
your ancestors and relatives who
abandoned the LORD, the God of their
ancestors, and became an object of
derision, as you yourselves can see.
8Do not be stubborn, as they were, but
submit yourselves to the LORD. Come
to his Temple, which he has set apart
as holy forever. Worship the LORD your
God so that his fierce anger will turn
away from you.

9"For if you return to the LORD,
your relatives and your children will
be treated mercifully by their captors,
and they will be able to return to
this land. For the LORD your God is
gracious and merciful. If you return
to him, he will not continue to turn
his face from you."

10The runners went from town to town
throughout Ephraim and Manasseh and
as far as the territory of Zebulun. But
most of the people just laughed at the
runners and made fun of them. 11How-
ever, some people from Asher, Manasseh,
and Zebulun humbled themselves and
went to Jerusalem.

12 At the same time, God's hand was on the people in the land of Judah, giving them all one heart to obey the orders of the king and his officials, who were following the word of the LORD. 13 So a huge crowd assembled at Jerusalem in midspring* to celebrate the Festival of Unleavened Bread. 14 They set to work and removed the pagan altars from Jerusalem. They took away all the incense altars and threw them into the Kidron Valley.

15 On the fourteenth day of the second month, one month later than usual,* the people slaughtered the Passover lamb. This shamed the priests and Levites, so they purified themselves and brought burnt offerings to the Temple of the LORD. 16 Then they took their places at the Temple as prescribed in the Law of Moses, the man of God. The Levites brought the sacrificial blood to the priests, who then sprinkled it on the altar.

17 Since many of the people had not purified themselves, the Levites had to slaughter their Passover lamb for them, to set them apart for the LORD. 18 Most of those who came from Ephraim, Manasseh, Issachar, and Zebulun had not purified themselves. But King Hezekiah prayed for them, and they were allowed to eat the Passover meal anyway, even though this was contrary to the requirements of the Law. For Hezekiah said, "May the LORD, who is good, pardon those 19 who decide to follow the LORD, the God of their ancestors, even though they are not properly cleansed for the ceremony." 20 And the LORD listened to Hezekiah's prayer and healed the people.

21 So the people of Israel who were present in Jerusalem joyously celebrated the Festival of Unleavened Bread for seven days. Each day the Levites and priests sang to the LORD, accompanied by loud instruments.* 22 Hezekiah encouraged all the Levites regarding the skill they displayed as they served the LORD. The celebration continued for seven days. Peace offerings were sacrificed, and the people gave thanks to the LORD, the God of their ancestors.

23 The entire assembly then decided to continue the festival another seven days, so they celebrated joyfully for another week. 24 King Hezekiah gave the people 1,000 bulls and 7,000 sheep and goats for offerings, and the officials donated 1,000 bulls and 10,000 sheep and goats. Meanwhile, many more priests purified themselves.

25 The entire assembly of Judah rejoiced, including the priests, the Levites, all who came from the land of Israel, the foreigners who came to the festival, and all those who lived in Judah. 26 There was great joy in the city, for Jerusalem had not seen a celebration like this one since the days of Solomon, King David's son. 27 Then the priests and Levites stood and blessed the people, and God heard their prayer from his holy dwelling in heaven.

CHAPTER 31

When the festival ended, the Israelites who attended went to all the towns of Judah, Benjamin, Ephraim, and Manasseh, and they smashed all the sacred pillars, cut down the Asherah poles, and removed the pagan shrines and altars. After this, the Israelites returned to their own towns and homes.

30:2 Hebrew *in the second month.* Passover was normally observed in the first month (of the ancient Hebrew lunar calendar). **30:6** *Israel* is the name that God gave to Jacob. **30:13** Hebrew *in the second month.* The second month of the ancient Hebrew lunar calendar usually occurs within the months of April and May. **30:15** Hebrew *On the fourteenth day of the second month.* Passover normally began on the fourteenth day of the first month (see Lev 23:5). **30:21** Or *sang to the LORD with all their strength.*

NOTES

30:2 *a month later than usual.* Lit., "in the second month." Traditionally Passover is celebrated in the first month (Abib, March/April), with the Passover lamb chosen on the 10th of the month, slain on the 14th of the month, and eaten in a meal as the evening gives way to the 15th (Exod 12:1-14; Lev 23:5; Num 9:1-14; 28:16; Deut 16:1-7). This then becomes the first day of the Festival of Unleavened Bread, which lasts until the 21st of the month. The Festival of Unleavened Bread was one of the three required festivals during the year to which Israelites were to bring their tithes and offerings (Exod 12:15-20; 13:3-10; Lev 23:6-8; Num 28:17-25; Deut 16:3-4, 8). It coincided with the barley harvest in the spring.

30:5 ***from Beersheba . . . to Dan.*** This is a typical merism (the use of two extremes or poles to signify the entire expanse, whether spatial or temporal, between them) for "all Israel," identifying two settlements considered the farthest south and north, respectively (Judg 20:1; 1 Sam 3:20; 2 Sam 3:10; 17:11; 24:2, 15; 1 Kgs 4:25; 1 Chr 21:2; cf. Amos 8:14).

30:6 ***the God of Abraham, Isaac, and Israel.*** The dominant version of this formula is "Abraham, Isaac, and Jacob." This form is used elsewhere in the Hebrew text only in Exod 32:13; 1 Kgs 18:36 (see NLT mg); 1 Chr 29:18. It may be that the Chronicler was forging a connection here between Hezekiah and David. This would also have facilitated his "all Israel" theme in the Hezekiah narrative. Elsewhere in his work he always used "Israel" in place of "Jacob" (Williamson 1977b:62-63).

the conquest of the Assyrian kings. Incursions by the Assyrians into the northern kingdom began in earnest under Tiglath-pileser III and continued under Shalmaneser V and Sargon II (2 Kgs 16–17; Isa 7–8).

30:14 ***Kidron Valley.*** This valley lay to the east of Jerusalem.

30:22 ***Peace offerings . . . gave thanks.*** For peace offerings, see Lev 3; 7:11-36 (cf. Amos 5:22). They were not related to sin but rather were voluntary and used for thanksgiving to God or fulfillment of a vow.

30:25 ***foreigners.*** Heb., *ger* [TH1616, ZH1731], either temporary or permanent dwellers with no inheritance rights (Gen 15:13; 23:4; Exod 20:10; 23:9; Deut 5:14).

30:26 ***since the days of Solomon, King David's son.*** See this celebration in ch 7.

31:1 ***sacred pillars . . . Asherah poles . . . pagan shrines.*** Sacred pillars (Heb., *matsebah* [TH4676, ZH5167]) were associated with orthodox worship (Gen 28:18, 22; 31:13; Exod 24:4; Isa 19:19) but also condemned in Deuteronomic literature due to association with foreign gods (14:3; Lev 26:1; Deut 16:22; 1 Kgs 14:23; 2 Kgs 17:10; 18:4; 23:14; Mic 5:13). Asherah can refer to the Canaanite goddess, consort of the high god El and mother of the gods, but also to the wooden cult objects associated with her worship. Here the latter is the case. These objects could be living trees (see Deut 16:21) but more often were wooden poles (1 Kgs 14:15; 16:33). Archaeological evidence shows that in popular religion Asherah was associated with Yahweh as his consort. See further on Asherah and her relationship to Yahweh in Smith 2002:xxx-xxxvi, 47-53, 108-147; Day 2000:42-67; Hess 2007:283-289, 308-311; see also note on 2 Chr 17:6. "Pagan shrines" is a translation of the term *bamoth* [TH1116, ZH1195] (lit., "high places"), denoting shrines originally placed on hills and mountains (due to association between mountains and the domain of the gods), but later the term was attached to places of worship. In limited cases the term could be used in relation to orthodox worship (1:3, 13; 1 Chr 16:39; 21:29), but the term is often connected with illicit worship practices (11:15; 14:3, 5; 15:17; 20:33; 34:3; cf. Num 22:41; Isa 15:2; 16:12; Jer 19:5; 32:35).

COMMENTARY

The king continues to drive the narrative as we move into the next episode in the Chronicler's account of Hezekiah. The Chronicler begins his new section with a summary statement in 30:1 that provides an overview of the first half of the chapter

(30:2-11).[1] The statement begins by noting generally that Hezekiah invited "all Israel and Judah," but then specifically describes "letters of invitation" that he wrote to "the people of Ephraim and Manasseh," representative of the northern kingdom. This is an important theme in the Chronicler's account of Hezekiah, foreshadowed already in 29:24, which spoke about the sin offering "made for all Israel." Hezekiah, as the first king of Judah after the fall of the northern kingdom, is portrayed as the first king to unite the tribes since Solomon.[2]

According to the summary statement, this unity will be accomplished through the celebration of a common Passover festival. As the description proceeds, it will become obvious that the Passover is understood merely as the introduction to the subsequent Festival of Unleavened Bread, which ran for the following seven days (see Exod 12–13; 23:14-17; 34:18-23; Lev 23; Deut 16:1-17). In Torah legislation the Passover lamb is chosen on the 10th day of the first month, sacrificed on the 14th day, and eaten in an evening meal as the 15th day of the month began. The Festival of Unleavened Bread then ran from the 15th to the 21st day of the first month.[3]

Before revealing the process for the proclamation of the festival (30:5-10a), the Chronicler describes the process that led to the reinstitution of the festival (30:2-4). The decision was reached between Hezekiah, his officials, and "all the community of Jerusalem." The latter evidences not only the democratizing tone of the Chronicler's account but also his emphasis on Jerusalem's leadership role in the worship of Judah. The reason a decision had to be made, according to the Chronicler, was because the first month—the time when the festivals were required to be celebrated—had already passed. The Chronicler explained this anomaly by appealing to the lack of qualified priests to carry on the services (29:34) and the lack of people to form an assembly. It was decided to celebrate Passover one month later than usual, in the second month, a provision that appears dependent on the legislation in Numbers 9:1-14. Second Chronicles 30:4 again emphasizes the unanimity of both king and "all the people" on this issue.

With this settled by the faithful worshiping community in Jerusalem, Hezekiah is depicted as sending a proclamation "throughout all Israel," from Beersheba, the traditional southern inhabited boundary of Israel, to Dan, the traditional northern inhabited boundary of Israel (30:5). The extent of the land to which this proclamation is targeted highlights Hezekiah's reign over "all Israel." This proclamation was delivered through "runners," that is, couriers who went "throughout Israel and Judah" (30:6).

The content of the letter (30:6-9) the couriers carried with them was designed by the Chronicler for his Persian-period audience. The letter has in view a community (both north and south; see "us" in 30:6) that "survived the conquest of the Assyrian kings" and remained under "their captors." The cause of the challenges these communities faced is linked to their abandonment of the Lord (*ma'al* [TH4603, ZH5085]; 30:7). The call to both communities is to "return to the LORD" (30:6, 9), a return that is defined by the key directive in 30:8: "Come to his Temple, which he has set apart as holy forever. Worship the LORD your God so that his fierce anger will turn away from you." For the community that has "survived the conquest," the hope is that the Lord "will return to the few of us" (30:6). For the community in captivity, the hope is that "they will be able to return to this land" (30:9). This hope is based solely on the character of the Lord as "gracious and merciful" (30:9). The community in Hezekiah's time is thus depicted in ways that would have resonated with the community in the time of the Chronicler, a community with people both in exilic lands as well as in Judah. The Chronicler identifies repentance in worship practice as essential to the experience of the presence of Yahweh, as well as to the safe return of more exiles from captivity. This raises the profile of the Temple and its worship in the Chronicler's day, placing the lives of the exiles at stake.

The couriers are depicted as running through Ephraim and Manasseh, even into Zebulun, which along with Issachar had traditional clan lands immediately north of Manasseh. The Chronicler reports that "most of the people just laughed at the runners and made fun of them," a statement that reflects badly on the northern kingdom and is possibly directed at the spiritual condition of Jews in the province of Samaria during the time of the Chronicler. There was some reason for hope, however, because there was response from "some people from Asher, Manasseh, and Zebulun" who "humbled themselves" (*kana'* [TH3665, ZH4044]), one of the responses regularly affirmed as normative by the Chronicler in his work. According to 30:18, the number also included members of other tribes, so that the final list of northern tribes represented included Ephraim, Manasseh, Issachar, Zebulun, and Asher. This shows a focus on the tribal territories in the Cisjordan with no mention of Transjordanian tribes. This may provide the Chronicler's view of the extent of the Promised Land but also may reflect the reality that the Transjordan region had been subjugated and its peoples deported in an earlier phase under Tiglath-pileser III (cf. 2 Kgs 15:29; 1 Chr 5:26).[4]

While there was limited (but some) response from members of the northern tribes, there were divinely motivated unanimous and passionate responses from members of the tribe of Judah (30:12). It was "all the community of Jerusalem" that had joined wholeheartedly with Hezekiah and his officials to set the festivals in 30:2, and it was "the people in the land of Judah" who now with "all one heart" followed the leadership of Hezekiah and his officials. The Chronicler held out realistic hope for participation by non-Judahite Israelites in the worship at the Temple in Jerusalem, but he had high expectations for the participation of inhabitants of Jerusalem and the province of Yehud.

These three streams of people converge in 30:13, as "a huge crowd" assembled in Jerusalem in what is called only "the second month." Before they could begin the celebration, however, the Chronicler depicted them cleaning out the pagan altars from Jerusalem and throwing them into the Kidron Valley. In chapter 29 the priests and Levites joined forces to clean out the Temple defiled by Ahaz (28:22-24), and then the laity gathered together to clean out the city streets on whose corners Ahaz had set up altars to pagan gods (28:24).

Having cleansed the city, the people were able to slaughter the Passover lamb on the 14th day. Again it is noted that this was the "second month" (NLT mg; NLT, "one month later than usual"), emphasizing the oddity of this celebration. This popular slaughter is seen as shaming the priests and Levites, who must purify themselves and bring burnt offerings to the Temple. The Chronicler states that they assumed their proper roles in the Temple "as prescribed in the Law of Moses, the man of God" (30:16). These roles are then illustrated in the second half of 30:16, as "the Levites brought the sacrificial blood to the priests, who then sprinkled it on the altar." The reference to the shaming of the priests and Levites may suggest some criticism of both orders for not fulfilling their responsibilities on behalf of the people in the Chronicler's day.

An odd twist in the Chronicler's history is introduced in 30:17-20. To this point the Chronicler has carefully regarded and consistently affirmed proper worship protocol. In 30:17-20, however, the account describes a group of northern Israelites (from Ephraim, Manasseh, Issachar, and Zebulun) who had not properly purified themselves prior to the festival, thus disqualifying them from participation. The Chronicler, however, portrays the Levites as slaughtering their lambs and Hezekiah praying for them that they may participate in the Passover meal without ramifications. This "stretching" of the legal requirements is one of the strongest indications in the books of Chronicles of an agenda to include members from the northern tribes in the worship at Jerusalem. It is also another indication of the importance of prayer within the Chronicler's work—that is, prayer here takes the place of sacrificial purification rites.

As the account nears its conclusion (30:21-26) the Chronicler depicts "the people of Israel" joyously celebrating the Festival of Unleavened Bread. This reference to joy signals the end of the second major phase of Hezekiah's reign (cf. 29:36). The Chronicler drew attention to the musical tone of the events throughout the festival ("each day," 30:21) and noted how Hezekiah "spoke on the heart" (NLT, "encouraged"; 30:22) to all the Levites for their practical wisdom in relation to the sacrifices. It is uncertain whether this is a reference to both priests and Levites (as in 29:5), but in either case the Chronicler was encouraging careful attention to the protocols for worship.

The festival of this reunified Israel lasted not only for the prescribed seven days but for an additional seven days. In 30:25 this "assembly of Judah" is enumerated by the following categories: "the priests, the Levites, all who came from the land of Israel, the foreigners who came to the festival, and all those who lived in Judah." Here we see one of the clearest pictures of the Chronicler's vision for "all Israel," one that would include both Israel and Judah. What should not be missed is that there is room in the Chronicler's theology for "foreigners" to participate in the worship of Israel.

The comparison in 30:26 to Solomon's reign makes explicit what has been implicit throughout chapters 29–30—that is, that Hezekiah is the second Solomon, uniting the tribes both north and south around the Temple in Jerusalem. Dillard (1987:242-243) argues that in this chapter not only is Hezekiah linked to Solomon by being the first king to reunite the nation at the Temple since his forefather (ch 7), by holding an extended two-week celebration (ch 7), and by praying before the assembly (ch 6), but also throughout chapter 30 the vocabulary of God's speech to Solomon in 7:14 is used, a speech that identified for the Chronicler the normative vocabulary of response by Israel and Yahweh:

> *Then if my people who are called by my name will humble themselves [30:11] and pray [30:18] and seek [30:19, "follow"] my face and turn [30:9, "return"] from their wicked ways, I will hear [30:20, "listen"] from heaven and will forgive their sins and restore [30:20, "heal"] their land.*

The Chronicler presented Hezekiah and his generation as an example of the kind of community that fulfills Yahweh's agenda.

In 30:27 the priests and Levites bless the people, and the Chronicler reveals that God heard their prayer from his holy dwelling. Here one can discern a link to 6:14-42 and Solomon's hope that the Temple would be a place where prayer is heard (6:20-21). This role for prayer in the Temple is apparent twice in this account of the Passover/Festival of Unleavened Bread and must have been important to the Chronicler. This verse also is included to remind the people that God's blessing comes to the community through a functioning and supported Temple.

While his source in 2 Kings 18:4-8 focused on Hezekiah's removal of idolatrous objects, the Chronicler depicted how this renewal of worship in Jerusalem resulted in a popular response ("the Israelites who attended") that eradicated these objects from the land. In the Hebrew text, mention is made at first only of "all the towns of Judah," most likely to emphasize Hezekiah's removal of the last of Ahaz's idolatrous initiatives (28:24-25 [Temple, Jerusalem, all the towns of Judah]; 29:15-19 [Temple]; 30:14 [Jerusalem]; 31:1 [all the towns of Judah]). But the text expands this to include then all of "Judah, Benjamin, Ephraim, and Manasseh." Hezekiah's influence is thus expanded to include eradication of idolatry throughout "all Israel." The Chronicler effectively displayed a strategy for defeating idolatry in the land, namely, the positive institution of proper worship.

Through this chapter and the next, the Chronicler continues to stress his key themes to his Persian-period audience. He continues to encourage celebration of the festivals at the second Temple in Jerusalem and here shows how the negative eradication of idolatry must be followed by the positive inauguration of proper worship of Yahweh. The emphasis on broad and passionate communal participation continues in this chapter, here highlighting the way in which the example of the people shamed even the priestly leadership. So passionate is this community about worship that they continue the celebration of the festival a second week. The chapter also reaches out to faithful Israelites from the former northern kingdom, even as it recognizes that there are some within that group that continue to reject the invitation to Jerusalem. Through Hezekiah's letter, the Chronicler reveals a way in which the community's (both north and south) response in repentance and adherence to the worship at Jerusalem will have an impact even on those who are still scattered in exile. This is interesting in that the closing invitation in the book of Chronicles (36:22-23) is for this exilic community to return to the land and Temple; it has vocabulary strikingly similar to that found in the account of Hezekiah in chapters 29–30.[5] Both chapter 36 and chapter 30 intertwine the themes of captivity, escape, and attention to the Temple. In the case of chapter 30, however, a Davidic figure rallies the people around the Temple after severe punishment by a Mesopotamian power (Assyria) with the hope of the return of still more from exile. These connections to the closing chapter of Chronicles suggest potential for a Davidic king to reassume the role that had been taken over by Mesopotamian powers.

ENDNOTES

1. So Rudolph 1955; cf. Williamson 1982:365.
2. At this point in history, however, the northern kingdom had not yet technically fallen, although it had suffered serious setbacks at the hands of the Assyrians (2 Kgs 17) and for all intents and purposes was under Assyrian rule (2 Kgs 17:1-6). Hezekiah is depicted as one who had influence in the northern region before the fall of Samaria.
3. For debate over the relationship between these two festivals, see Dillard 1987:241-242 and McConville 1984b:99-123.
4. For the latter, see Dillard 1987:244.
5. See further Boda 2009b: *'lh* ("go up," 29:20//36:23), *'br* with *qol* ("sent a proclamation," 30:5//36:22), *sh'r* ("who have survived," 30:6//36:20).

◆ 3. Reform of worship practices (31:2-21)

[2]Hezekiah then organized the priests and Levites into divisions to offer the burnt offerings and peace offerings, and to worship and give thanks and praise to the LORD at the gates of the Temple. [3]The king also made a personal contribution of animals for the daily morning and evening burnt offerings, the weekly Sabbath festivals, the monthly new moon festivals, and the annual festivals as prescribed in the Law of the LORD. [4]In addition, he required the people in Jerusalem to bring a portion of their goods to the priests and Levites, so they could devote themselves fully to the Law of the LORD.

[5]When the people of Israel heard these requirements, they responded generously by bringing the first share of their grain, new wine, olive oil, honey, and all the produce of their fields. They brought a large quantity—a tithe of all they produced. [6]The people who had moved to Judah from Israel, and the people of Judah themselves, brought in the tithes of their cattle, sheep, and goats and a tithe of the things that had been dedicated to the LORD their God, and they piled them up in great heaps. [7]They began piling them up in late spring, and the heaps continued to grow until early autumn.* [8]When Hezekiah and his officials came and saw these huge piles, they thanked the LORD and his people Israel!

[9]"Where did all this come from?" Hezekiah asked the priests and Levites.

[10]And Azariah the high priest, from the family of Zadok, replied, "Since the people began bringing their gifts to the LORD's Temple, we have had enough to eat and plenty to spare. The LORD has blessed his people, and all this is left over."

[11]Hezekiah ordered that storerooms be prepared in the Temple of the LORD. When this was done, [12]the people faithfully brought all the tithes and gifts to the Temple. Conaniah the Levite was put in charge, assisted by his brother Shimei. [13]The supervisors under them were Jehiel, Azaziah, Nahath, Asahel, Jerimoth, Jozabad, Eliel, Ismakiah, Mahath, and Benaiah. These appointments were made by King Hezekiah and Azariah, the chief official in the Temple of God.

[14]Kore son of Imnah the Levite, who was the gatekeeper at the East Gate, was put in charge of distributing the voluntary offerings given to God, the gifts, and the things that had been dedicated to the LORD. [15]His faithful assistants were Eden, Miniamin, Jeshua, Shemaiah, Amariah, and Shecaniah. They distributed the gifts among the families of priests in their towns by their divisions, dividing the gifts fairly among old and young alike. [16]They distributed the gifts to all males three years old or older, regardless of their place in the genealogical records. The distribution went to all who would come to the LORD's Temple to perform their daily duties according to their divisions. [17]They

distributed gifts to the priests who were listed by their families in the genealogical records, and to the Levites twenty years old or older who were listed according to their jobs and their divisions. [18]Food allotments were also given to the families of all those listed in the genealogical records, including their little babies, wives, sons, and daughters. For they had all been faithful in purifying themselves.

[19]As for the priests, the descendants of Aaron, who were living in the open villages around the towns, men were appointed by name to distribute portions to every male among the priests and to all the Levites listed in the genealogical records.

[20]In this way, King Hezekiah handled the distribution throughout all Judah, doing what was pleasing and good in the sight of the LORD his God. [21]In all that he did in the service of the Temple of God and in his efforts to follow God's laws and commands, Hezekiah sought his God wholeheartedly. As a result, he was very successful.

31:7 Hebrew *in the third month . . . until the seventh month.* The third month of the ancient Hebrew lunar calendar usually occurs within the months of May and June; the seventh month usually occurs within September and October.

NOTES

31:3 *morning and evening burnt offerings . . . Sabbath festivals . . . new moon festivals . . . annual festivals.* For the sacrificial requirements of these various events, see Num 28–29.

31:7 *in late spring . . . until early autumn.* Lit., "in the third month . . . until the seventh month" (see NLT mg). The Festival of Weeks (also called Festival of Harvest) took place on the sixth day of the third month (Sivan) at the time of the wheat harvest (May/June; Exod 23:16; 34:22; Lev 23:15-21; Num 28:26-31; Deut 16:9-12), while the Festival of Shelters (Tabernacles, also called Booths or Ingathering) is from the 15th until the 22nd of the seventh month (Tishri) at the time of the grape, fig, and olive harvests (September/October; Exod 23:16; 34:22; Lev 23:33-36, 39-43; Num 29:12-38; Deut 16:13-15). These were the other two required festivals besides that of Unleavened Bread, which had already passed (and coincided with the barley harvest). The people were to bring their tithes and offerings to these festivals.

COMMENTARY

With the Temple dedicated, the festal calendar set in motion, and idolatry removed from the land, the Chronicler describes the steps taken for continual worship at the Temple. This section is again unique to the Chronicler. The presentation in chs 29–31 suggests that the reforms happened all in Hezekiah's regnal year: cleansing and dedication of the Temple (29:3—first month), Passover and Festival of Unleavened Bread (30:15, 21—second month), and provision for worship (31:4-7—third to seventh months; Dillard 1987:249).

At the beginning of the account (31:2), Hezekiah is depicted as organizing priests and Levites into divisions to carry on the service of God. The character of this service reflects David's innovations with a balance of material sacrifice ("to offer the burnt offerings and peace offerings") and verbal worship ("give thanks and praise"). The following verse (31:3) lists the many worship services that needed to be supported. Although not explicit in the Hebrew text, the list is organized by frequency of practice from daily (morning and evening burnt offerings), to weekly (Sabbath festivals), to monthly (new moon festivals), to annual (festivals) events. This list provides insight into the complex and demanding character of worship in Judah and is an essential foundation for understanding why priestly and Levitical orders needed to "devote themselves fully to the Law of the LORD" (31:4).

According to 31:3, Hezekiah made personal contributions and required the people of Jerusalem to bring their portion (31:4-8), a pattern that echoes the earlier example of David, Solomon, and their communities (9:10-11; 1 Chr 29:1-9; Dillard 1987:249). The account relates the immediate response of the people "of Israel," a response that is linked in the Hebrew text to the spread of the word ("as soon as the word spread"; NLT, "When the people . . . heard"). The people who brought their tithes are identified as both northerners who had moved to Judah as well as the people of Judah, again emphasizing the unity of "all Israel" around the Temple and its services. The allusion to those of the northern kingdom who had moved to Judah may be an encouragement to those Jews living in the province of Samaria in the Chronicler's time that they were welcome to join the Jews in the province of Judah and to participate in worship. Reference to the continual bringing of offerings from "the third month" until the "seventh month" (31:7, see NLT note) reflects the cycle of harvests in Israel.

By depicting the royal house's surprise at the size of the contributions (31:8-9), the Chronicler was accentuating the popular and willing response to the example and request of Hezekiah. The king thanked Yahweh, whose blessing lay behind these contributions (see also 31:10b). This example was designed to show the community in the Chronicler's day that the care of the Temple was not merely a royal responsibility but should be the duty of the community as a whole.

The interchange between Hezekiah and Azariah in 31:9-10 repeats the Chronicler's concern for the support of the priests and Levites (see 31:4). For the Chronicler the priestly and Levitical orders should be fully released from raising their own living so as to facilitate worship at the Temple. By noting Azariah's genealogy as "from the family of Zadok," the Chronicler linked Hezekiah to David and Solomon under whose reign Zadok served.[1] Additionally, the Chronicler affirmed the leadership of the Zadokite priesthood of his own day.

While the account so far has focused on the "contribution," the remainder is focused on what the concluding summary statement in 31:20 calls the "distribution" (31:11-20). Hezekiah ordered storerooms built to stockpile all these contributions (31:11), even as the people continued to faithfully bring their contributions (31:12). Creating storerooms also links Hezekiah to David (1 Chr 9:26; 23:28; 26:22; 28:12; Dillard 1987:251). A system of distribution was organized, and people were appointed (under the authority of the royal and priestly offices; see 31:13-14b) to distribute these contributions to the priests and Levites throughout the land. Although the distribution would be fair ("old and young alike," 31:15; "regardless of their place in the genealogical records," 31:16) and supportive of the entire family unit (31:16-18), it was given only to those who had purified themselves (31:18), who were listed in the genealogical records (31:16-19), and who performed their duties (31:16-17). The section ends with a summary statement for the preceding section, noting that the distribution was within "all Judah" and that Hezekiah did this in a way that "was pleasing and good in the sight of the LORD."

Using his characteristic vocabulary, the Chronicler brings closure to his section (in 31:21) on Hezekiah's worship reforms and initiatives. He notes that in these reforms and initiatives Hezekiah was an example of what it meant to seek (*darash* [TH1875, ZH2011]) God wholeheartedly and because of this enjoyed success (*tsalakh* [TH6743A, ZH7502]; cf. 7:11; 13:12; 14:6; 18:11, 14; 20:20; 24:20; 32:30; 1 Chr 22:11, 13; 29:23; Dillard 1987:251).

For his community, this part of the Chronicler's account of Hezekiah would have served two purposes. First, it would have challenged them to give generously to the service of the Temple, especially focusing on tithing their harvests. Such gifts, according to the Chronicler, are essential so that the priests and Levites "could devote themselves fully to the Law of the LORD," that is, the stipulations for worship contained in the Torah. The ideal scenario is described by Azariah, the Zadokite high priest, in 31:10: "We have had enough to eat and plenty to spare." This is explicitly tied to the generosity of the people ("Since the people began bringing their gifts to the LORD's Temple"), which is a reflection of the blessing of the Lord upon them ("The LORD has blessed his people, and all this is left over"). The people of Jerusalem appear to have a role to play as examples to the rest of the community for this generosity (31:4), but the responsibility for the Temple and its personnel could not be borne by them alone. This was a task for all those living in the province of Judah.

Second, the account would have provided an administrative system for distributing the resources of the Temple to priestly and Levitical personnel throughout the province. This may suggest some conflict over this issue in the Chronicler's time, but it may also simply be an affirmation of a system that was working well.

ENDNOTES

1. The name Azariah appears three times in the high priestly genealogy in 1 Chr 6:1-15, once in the period of David-Solomon (1 Chr 6:9), once in the generation of Solomon (1 Chr 6:10; cf. 1 Kgs 4:2), and then again just before the Exile, following the reign of Josiah (6:14). The Azariah in 1 Chr 31, however, is not mentioned in the Chronicler's genealogy in 1 Chr 6:1-15, which appears to skip generations. Neither is the Azariah mentioned in 26:17 in Uzziah's reign included in the Chronicler's genealogy in 1 Chr 6.

◆ 4. Rescue from Assyrian attack (32:1-23)

After Hezekiah had faithfully carried out this work, King Sennacherib of Assyria invaded Judah. He laid siege to the fortified towns, giving orders for his army to break through their walls. 2When Hezekiah realized that Sennacherib also intended to attack Jerusalem, 3he consulted with his officials and military advisers, and they decided to stop the flow of the springs outside the city. 4They organized a huge work crew to stop the flow of the springs, cutting off the brook that ran through the fields. For they said, "Why should the kings of Assyria come here and find plenty of water?"

5Then Hezekiah worked hard at repairing all the broken sections of the wall, erecting towers, and constructing a second wall outside the first. He also reinforced the supporting terraces* in the City of David

and manufactured large numbers of weapons and shields. 6He appointed military officers over the people and assembled them before him in the square at the city gate. Then Hezekiah encouraged them by saying: 7"Be strong and courageous! Don't be afraid or discouraged because of the king of Assyria or his mighty army, for there is a power far greater on our side! 8He may have a great army, but they are merely men. We have the LORD our God to help us and to fight our battles for us!" Hezekiah's words greatly encouraged the people.

9While King Sennacherib of Assyria was still besieging the town of Lachish, he sent his officers to Jerusalem with this message for Hezekiah and all the people in the city:

> 10"This is what King Sennacherib of Assyria says: What are you trusting in that makes you think you can survive my siege of Jerusalem? 11Hezekiah has said, 'The LORD our God will rescue us from the king of Assyria.' Surely Hezekiah is misleading you, sentencing you to death by famine and thirst! 12Don't you realize that Hezekiah is the very person who destroyed all the LORD's shrines and altars? He commanded Judah and Jerusalem to worship only at the altar at the Temple and to offer sacrifices on it alone.
>
> 13"Surely you must realize what I and the other kings of Assyria before me have done to all the people of the earth! Were any of the gods of those nations able to rescue their people from my power? 14Which of their gods was able to rescue its people from the destructive power of my predecessors? What makes you think your God can rescue you from me? 15Don't let Hezekiah deceive you! Don't let him fool you like this! I say it again—no god of any nation or kingdom has ever yet been able to rescue his people from me or my ancestors. How much less will your God rescue you from my power!"

16And Sennacherib's officers further mocked the LORD God and his servant Hezekiah, heaping insult upon insult. 17The king also sent letters scorning the LORD, the God of Israel. He wrote, "Just as the gods of all the other nations failed to rescue their people from my power, so the God of Hezekiah will also fail." 18The Assyrian officials who brought the letters shouted this in Hebrew* to the people gathered on the walls of the city, trying to terrify them so it would be easier to capture the city. 19These officers talked about the God of Jerusalem as though he were one of the pagan gods, made by human hands.

20Then King Hezekiah and the prophet Isaiah son of Amoz cried out in prayer to God in heaven. 21And the LORD sent an angel who destroyed the Assyrian army with all its commanders and officers. So Sennacherib was forced to return home in disgrace to his own land. And when he entered the temple of his god, some of his own sons killed him there with a sword.

22That is how the LORD rescued Hezekiah and the people of Jerusalem from King Sennacherib of Assyria and from all the others who threatened them. So there was peace throughout the land. 23From then on King Hezekiah became highly respected among all the surrounding nations, and many gifts for the LORD arrived at Jerusalem, with valuable presents for King Hezekiah, too.

32:5 Hebrew *the millo.* The meaning of the Hebrew is uncertain. **32:18** Hebrew *in the dialect of Judah.*

NOTES

32:1 ***laid siege to the fortified towns, giving orders for his army to break through their walls.*** In Sennacherib's annals the great king reports, "As for Hezekiah, the Judean, I besieged forty-six of his fortified walled cities and surrounding smaller towns, which were without number. Using packed-down ramps and applying battering rams, infantry attacks by mines, breeches, and siege machines, I conquered (them)" (COS 2.303).

32:6 ***He appointed military officers over the people.*** Sennacherib's annals speak about Hezekiah's "elite troops (and) his best soldiers, which he had brought in as reinforcements to strengthen Jerusalem" (COS 2.303).

32:18 ***in Hebrew.*** Lit., "in the dialect of Judah" (see NLT mg). The account in 2 Kgs 18:26 provides more detail on this, citing the request of Hezekiah's officials to the Assyrian officers: "Please speak to us in Aramaic, for we understand it well. Don't speak in Hebrew, for the people on the wall will hear." Aramaic was the diplomatic language of the ancient Near East and was thus preferred by Hezekiah's officials to keep the negotiations secret from the populace. The Assyrians, well-known for their psychological warfare in the ancient world, wanted the people to hear their taunts in hopes that the populace would overthrow Hezekiah.

32:21 ***So Sennacherib was forced to return home in disgrace to his own land.*** In his annals, Sennacherib only speaks of Hezekiah "locked up within Jerusalem, his royal city, like a bird in a cage," but never speaks of taking the city (COS 2.303). The lack of capture is confirmed by the fact that the walls of Sennacherib's throne room were etched with a depiction of his siege of Lachish during this campaign. Lachish was one of the last of the 46 fortified cities to fall (2 Kgs 18:14; 19:8) and the place from which he sent his officers to taunt Hezekiah (32:9).

when he entered the temple of his god, some of his own sons killed him there with a sword. A letter by Esarhaddon (Sennacherib's heir) and another "letter from gods" confirm the intrigue within the royal court that led to the murder of Sennacherib by his sons (COS 3.244). This event happened in 681 BC.

32:22 ***there was peace.*** The Hebrew text reads here "he guided them," but the NLT is based on evidence from the LXX and Latin Vulgate. The phrase presupposed by the LXX and Vulgate is very common in Chronicles (14:7; 15:15; 20:30; 1 Chr 22:9, 18).

COMMENTARY

Hezekiah's major accomplishment in the book of 2 Kings is his faith in the face of the great Assyrian king Sennacherib's attack on the small Judean kingdom. The Chronicler shifted the focus considerably, introducing three chapters (chs 29–31) that describe Hezekiah's reformation of the worship of all Israel at the Temple. The Chronicler did not completely ignore Sennacherib's invasion but presented it in chapter 32 in a considerably abridged form. This has the effect of keeping the focus on Hezekiah's worship reforms but also of showcasing the military success that accompanies proper care of the Temple and its worship.

The account begins in 32:1 with Sennacherib invading Judah, laying siege to the fortified towns with the intention to breach the walls. The Aramean kingdom with its capital at Damascus and the Israelite kingdom with its capital of Samaria had already been incorporated into the Assyrian Empire by Sennacherib's predecessors, and he would seek to make his name in western Asia by subjugating the southern regions. Sennacherib ascended the throne after the assassination of his father, Sargon, in 705 BC. He relates his invasion on the Rassam Cylinder, which reports that he moved down the Mediterranean coast in 701 BC, subjugating the Phoenician and Philistine regions before moving inland to attack Hezekiah's Judean kingdom (COS 2.302).

By replacing the reference to the fourth year of Hezekiah in his source (2 Kgs 18:9) with a vague Hebrew phrase that literally reads "after these things and this faithfulness," the Chronicler created a closer sense of cause and effect between the actions of chapters 29–31 and those of chapter 32. At first sight this may appear at odds with the Chronicler's agenda to depict blessings for those who are faithful and curses to those who are unfaithful. But one must not caricature the Chronicler's agenda to mean that those who seek God are above problems and challenges. In the end Hezekiah will be rescued by God's miraculous angel when he and Isaiah pray to God (32:20-22), affirming the Chronicler's principle that those who seek Yahweh will enjoy military success, even against the greatest empire of its day.

Although abridging his source considerably, at this point the Chronicler introduces an expansion in 32:2-8. This expansion catalogues Hezekiah's leadership over extensive preparations for the approaching Assyrians: stopping up sources of water, strengthening the fortifications (wall, towers, and the Millo), stockpiling weapons, and organizing the army. Although not emphasized in the books of Kings or Isaiah, these activities fit the context of Hezekiah's crisis and are corroborated by several archaeological discoveries. First, archaeologists have uncovered in Jerusalem a 190-foot portion of a wall, called the "Broad Wall," that was built during this time and encircled the "suburbs" that had developed on the western side of the city in an area called the "Second Quarter" (*mishneh* [TH4932A, ZH5467]; 2 Kgs 22:14; Zeph 1:10-11; cf. also Zeph 1:11, *maktesh* [TH4389, ZH4847], "market area"). Second, the water supply for Jerusalem was increased and secured during this time by the creation of a tunnel that ran from the Gihon Spring (the only underground source of water for Jerusalem) in the Kidron Valley to the Pool of Siloam in the Tyropoeon Valley, which lay inside the city walls. This tunnel replaced a channel that had run from the Gihon Spring along the Kidron Valley and had been used for irrigation of fields in the Kidron (see Isa 8:6) but was not secure enough for a siege. The elimination of the channel may be what is in view in 32:4 when it speaks of "a huge work crew to stop the flow of the springs, cutting off the brook that ran through the fields." Third, in his annals relating his attack on Judah, Sennacherib talks about Hezekiah bringing elite troops into Jerusalem to strengthen the city (see note on 32:6). Fourth, the preparations listed here suggest an expectation of an elongated siege of the city and land. The character of this siege is vividly described in Sennacherib's annals (see note on 32:1).

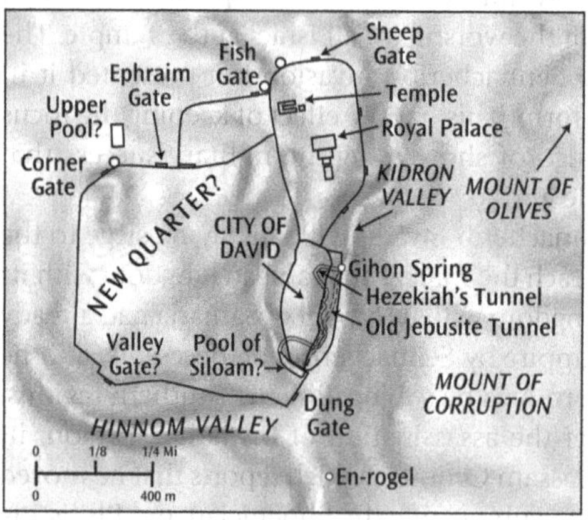

Jerusalem, 705–621 BC

To the newly appointed military officers, Hezekiah gave a short speech (32:7-8a), an "Encouragement to a Task," which is a form of speech used regularly by normative figures throughout Chronicles as a catalyst for faith in Yahweh instead of fear of an opposing force (Mason 1990:110-111). Sennacherib's resources are not underestimated ("his mighty army . . . a great army") but rather put in proper perspective. They are but mortal forces ("they are merely men"), but Israel had "a power far greater on our side," that is, Yahweh, who would "fight our battles for us." The impact of these words is noted immediately as they "greatly encouraged the people." In this the reader again sees the Chronicler's theocentric approach. For a community that lacked a national army and identity in his own day, the Chronicler consistently placed the focus on Yahweh as the only source of hope.

These preparations are followed by the account of Sennacherib's verbal threats directed toward "Hezekiah and all the people in the city" (32:9). To avoid detracting from his focus on the faith of Hezekiah, the Chronicler left out 2 Kings 18:14-22, which depicts Hezekiah's partial capitulation to Sennacherib while the emperor was at Lachish. In Kings, Hezekiah pays Sennacherib from silver and gold in the Temple, a strategy that did not work. This would have connected Hezekiah too closely with his father's foolish Assyrian policy related in 28:16, 20-21.[1]

In 32:10-15 the Chronicler provides, in light of this account, a significant speech delivered by Sennacherib's officers to Hezekiah. A comparison of this speech with the Chronicler's source in 2 Kings 18 reveals that the Chronicler significantly shortened and summarized this speech, a point admitted readily in 32:16. Kings contains two elongated and separate approaches to Hezekiah by Sennacherib's agents, a strategy reminiscent of the siege in 1 Kings 20 and thus possibly reflective of ancient military strategy.[2] In Chronicles the second approach by Sennacherib is collapsed into a few verses (32:17-19).[3]

The Chronicler finished his description of the taunt of Sennacherib's officers by describing how they had "talked about the God of Jerusalem as though he were one of the pagan gods, made by human hands" (32:19). In the Chronicler's worldview such blasphemy was the worst of sins.

In the account of Kings, there is a phase of intercession by Isaiah (2 Kgs 19:1-7) and later one by Hezekiah (2 Kgs 19:14-19), but in the streamlined version in Chronicles, these are collapsed into one that immediately precedes the divine response.[4] The Chronicler thus intertwines royal and prophetic intercession, which accentuates further the positive depiction of Hezekiah in this book. Elsewhere the Chronicler depicts the tumultuous relationship between prophets and kings (24:17-22; 36:15-16). The description of this intercession as "prayer to God in heaven" is reminiscent of Solomon's prayer in chapter 6, which asked that God hear prayers "from heaven" (6:21).

As promised in 2 Chronicles 6, Yahweh answered the prayers of the prophet and king, sending his destroying angel against the Assyrian army. The account in Kings speaks of the death of 185,000 in the camp and notes, as did the Chronicler, that this was the entire camp (2 Kgs 19:35). The Chronicler communicates the total devastation by referring to three levels in the military: mighty warrior, commander, and officer (32:21, literal rendering). Herodotus, writing in the fifth century BC, claims Sennacherib experienced defeat in his campaign against Egypt at Pelusium (*Histories* 2.141) because field mice consumed the quivers, bows, and shield handles in the Assyrian camp.[5] The much-later Josephus, writing in the first century AD, also speaks of a siege at Pelusium, Sennacherib receiving news of the approach of the Ethiopian Tirhaka, and of the death of 185,000 (*Antiquities* 10.1-23; *War* 5.386-388, 404-408). The Chronicler emphasized the divine cause of Assyria's defeat.

The account ends in 32:22 with a summarizing statement showing, with its reference to "all the others who threatened them," that this event was being used as an example of God's protection over Hezekiah and Jerusalem from all foes. The phrase "so there was peace throughout the land" is typical of the Chronicler's depiction of blessing that follows faithfulness (14:6, 7; 15:15; 20:30; 1 Chr 22:9, 18; 23:25). Through the notation of international fame and gifts in 32:23, the Chronicler forged another link between Hezekiah and Solomon (9:23-24).

ENDNOTES

1. Dillard (1987:255) writes, "For the Chronicler, trust in foreign alliances was always wrong since it implied a distrust in Yahweh, and it would be out of accord with his portrayal of Hezekiah to suggest such dependence."
2. Some scholars see these two approaches in 2 Kgs 18–20 as evidence of two competing sources underlying the account. However, such is at least a narrative strategy in the ancient world, if not a military strategy. With thanks to Paul Evans (2008, 2009).
3. Dillard (1987:255) makes the claim that the Chronicler's "narrative supports only one invasion and combines the two parallel accounts of Sennacherib's efforts at intimidation (2 Kgs 18:17–19:35) into a single narrative recast in accord with his own intentions. Accounts B-1 and B-2 were not read by him as successive events, but as varying versions of a single event which he has reintegrated." However, the Chronicler's account distinguishes between two communiqués between Sennacherib and Hezekiah, the first in a message through his officials (32:9) and the other in letter form (32:17).
4. The result is that the Chronicler significantly plays down the role of Isaiah in this story. Dillard (1987:255-256) notes that the Chronicler's account "eliminates the mediatorial role played by Isaiah in receiving the oracle of deliverance; for the Chronicler, Hezekiah is unafraid and is himself the recipient of direct revelation."
5. Pelusium was located 13 miles east of the present-day Suez Canal, just south of the Mediterranean coast (Ezek 30:15-16; ABD 5.221).

◆ 5. Hezekiah's sickness, pride, repentance, and later accomplishments (32:24-33)

24 About that time Hezekiah became deathly ill. He prayed to the LORD, who healed him and gave him a miraculous sign. 25 But Hezekiah did not respond appropriately to the kindness shown him, and he became proud. So the LORD's anger came against him and against Judah and Jerusalem. 26 Then Hezekiah humbled himself and repented of his pride, as did the people of Jerusalem. So the LORD's anger did not fall on them during Hezekiah's lifetime.

27 Hezekiah was very wealthy and highly honored. He built special treasury buildings for his silver, gold, precious stones, and spices, and for his shields and other valuable items. 28 He also constructed many storehouses for his grain, new wine, and olive oil; and he made many stalls for his cattle and pens for his flocks of sheep and goats. 29 He built many towns and acquired vast flocks and herds, for God had given him great wealth. 30 He blocked up the upper spring of Gihon and brought the water down through a tunnel to the west side of the City of David. And so he succeeded in everything he did.

31 However, when ambassadors arrived from Babylon to ask about the remarkable events that had taken place in the land, God withdrew from Hezekiah in order to test him and to see what was really in his heart.

32 The rest of the events in Hezekiah's reign and his acts of devotion are recorded in *The Vision of the Prophet Isaiah Son of Amoz*, which is included in *The Book of the Kings of Judah and Israel*. 33 When Hezekiah died, he was buried in the upper area of the royal cemetery, and all Judah and Jerusalem honored him at his death. And his son Manasseh became the next king.

NOTES

32:30 *blocked up the upper spring of Gihon and brought the water down through a tunnel to the west side of the City of David.* This tunnel has been discovered and indeed runs from the Kidron Valley on the east side of the city to the Tyropoeon Valley on the west side, the latter being slightly lower at the point where the tunnel ends than the Gihon is in the Kidron Valley.

COMMENTARY

In 32:24 the Chronicler summarizes 2 Kings 20:1-11 (see also Isa 38:1-8, 21-22) into one sentence. While sickness is often portrayed as punishment for unfaithfulness in Chronicles (16:7-12; 21:18-19; 26:19-21), this is always made explicit by the Chronicler. Here no explanation is given for the illness. Therefore, as with the attack of Sennacherib, the Chronicler does not portray a life secure from difficulty, but does show that Yahweh will rescue his people from crises, especially (as evident here again) when his people pray for deliverance.

For the Chronicler, the accounts of Sennacherib's attack on Hezekiah and Hezekiah's sickness become accounts confirming his principle that God's blessing accompanies the king and community who place their priorities on the Temple and worship. While in Kings the narrator draws the reader into these accounts to experience the tension and challenge of faith for Hezekiah, in Chronicles the accounts are collapsed considerably because they serve to confirm God's blessing on faithful Hezekiah.

Hezekiah's Sickness, Pride, Repentance, and Later Accomplishments (32:25-31). Surprisingly, in the closing paragraph of his depiction of Hezekiah's reign, the Chronicler provides the first negative evaluation of the king, as he highlights Hezekiah's pride in 32:25. Such pride is seen as an inappropriate response to the "kindness" (or "benefits"; cf. Ps 103:2) Yahweh had given him, portrayed in the rescue from his enemies and death. The Chronicler merely speaks of God's "anger" against him, Judah, and Jerusalem. As the entire community was united with Hezekiah in his faithfulness, so they joined him in his faithlessness and received the brunt of God's discipline. The Chronicler then relates that Hezekiah and his community "humbled" (*kana'* [TH3665, ZH4044]; 32:26) themselves, a normative action encouraged throughout Chronicles and essential to receiving God's blessing.

For the Chronicler, Hezekiah, even in his moment of unfaithfulness, continues to function as a normative character within this book. Hezekiah's response to God's discipline opens the way for the blessing described in 32:27-30, blessing that included great wealth and many building projects (see note on 32:30), and is summarized at the end of 32:30 in the typical phraseology of the Chronicler: "And so he succeeded (*tsalakh* [TH6743A, ZH7503]) in everything he did" (7:11; 13:12; 14:7; 18:11, 14; 20:20; 24:20; 26:5; 31:21; 32:30; 1 Chr 22:11, 13; 29:23).

The final verse of the section (32:31) either represents an additional act of testing by God, or fills out further Hezekiah's act of pride (32:25-26), reminding the reader that God brings testing into the lives of his people through which they have the opportunity to demonstrate covenant faithfulness. The emphasis in this final verse is on the purpose of such testing, rather than on Hezekiah's response. For the Chronicler the reception of foreign envoys is inappropriate (see commentary on 19:1-11).

Summary Note: The Reign of Hezekiah (32:32-33). This summary note brings to an end the longest account of a king during the period of the divided kingdom, the length serving as another link between Hezekiah and the founders of the dynasty. The reader is referred to a work related to a prophetic figure as well as a work related to royal figures. The special character of Hezekiah's reign is displayed in the reference by the Chronicler not only to "the events" of his reign, but also "his acts of devotion" (*khesed* [TH2617, ZH2876]; 32:32) that display his covenant faithfulness to Yahweh. Again the Chronicler reveals his affection for prophetic sources in composing his history. Unlike his father, Ahaz (28:27), Hezekiah is buried in the royal cemetery. The Chronicler takes special effort to note that "all Judah and Jerusalem honored him at his death" (32:33), heightening his portrayal of Hezekiah even in his death.

◆ P. The Reigns of Manasseh and Amon (33:1-25)

Manasseh was twelve years old when he
became king, and he reigned in Jerusalem
fifty-five years. 2He did what was evil in
the LORD's sight, following the detestable
practices of the pagan nations that the
LORD had driven from the land ahead of
the Israelites. 3He rebuilt the pagan
shrines his father, Hezekiah, had broken
down. He constructed altars for the images of Baal and set up Asherah poles. He
also bowed before all the powers of the
heavens and worshiped them.

4He built pagan altars in the Temple of
the LORD, the place where the LORD had
said, "My name will remain in Jerusalem
forever." 5He built these altars for all the
powers of the heavens in both courtyards
of the LORD's Temple. 6Manasseh also sacrificed his own sons in the fire* in the valley of Ben-Hinnom. He practiced sorcery,
divination, and witchcraft, and he consulted with mediums and psychics. He did
much that was evil in the LORD's sight,
arousing his anger.

7Manasseh even took a carved idol he
had made and set it up in God's Temple,
the very place where God had told David
and his son Solomon: "My name will be
honored forever in this Temple and in
Jerusalem—the city I have chosen from
among all the tribes of Israel. 8If the Israelites will be careful to obey my commands—all the laws, decrees, and
regulations given through Moses—I will
not send them into exile from this land
that I set aside for your ancestors." 9But
Manasseh led the people of Judah and
Jerusalem to do even more evil than the
pagan nations that the LORD had destroyed when the people of Israel entered
the land.

10The LORD spoke to Manasseh and his
people, but they ignored all his warnings.
11So the LORD sent the commanders of the
Assyrian armies, and they took Manasseh
prisoner. They put a ring through his nose,
bound him in bronze chains, and led him
away to Babylon. 12But while in deep distress, Manasseh sought the LORD his God
and sincerely humbled himself before the
God of his ancestors. 13And when he
prayed, the LORD listened to him and was
moved by his request. So the LORD brought
Manasseh back to Jerusalem and to his
kingdom. Then Manasseh finally realized
that the LORD alone is God!

14After this Manasseh rebuilt the outer
wall of the City of David, from west of the
Gihon Spring in the Kidron Valley to the
Fish Gate, and continuing around the hill
of Ophel. He built the wall very high. And
he stationed his military officers in all of
the fortified towns of Judah. 15Manasseh
also removed the foreign gods and the
idol from the LORD's Temple. He tore down
all the altars he had built on the hill where

the Temple stood and all the altars that
were in Jerusalem, and he dumped them
outside the city. 16 Then he restored the
altar of the LORD and sacrificed peace of-
ferings and thanksgiving offerings on it.
He also encouraged the people of Judah
to worship the LORD, the God of Israel.
17 However, the people still sacrificed at
the pagan shrines, though only to the
LORD their God.
18 The rest of the events of Manasseh's
reign, his prayer to God, and the words
the seers spoke to him in the name of the
LORD, the God of Israel, are recorded in
The Book of the Kings of Israel. 19 Ma-
nasseh's prayer, the account of the way
God answered him, and an account of all
his sins and unfaithfulness are recorded
in *The Record of the Seers.** It includes a
list of the locations where he built pagan
shrines and set up Asherah poles and idols
before he humbled himself and repented.
20 When Manasseh died, he was buried in
his palace. Then his son Amon became the
next king.
21 Amon was twenty-two years old when
he became king, and he reigned in Jeru-
salem two years. 22 He did what was evil
in the LORD's sight, just as his father,
Manasseh, had done. He worshiped and
sacrificed to all the idols his father had
made. 23 But unlike his father, he did not
humble himself before the LORD. Instead,
Amon sinned even more.
24 Then Amon's own officials conspired
against him and assassinated him in his
palace. 25 But the people of the land killed
all those who had conspired against King
Amon, and they made his son Josiah the
next king.

33:6 Or *also made his sons pass through the fire.* 33:19 Or *The Record of Hozai.*

NOTES

33:3 ***images of Baal . . . Asherah poles . . . all the powers of the heavens.*** For Baal, see note on 17:3. For Asherah poles, see notes on 17:6 and 31:1 and commentary on 24:17-22. "All the powers of heavens" reads in the Hebrew text as "all the host of heaven," elsewhere referring to the sun, moon, and stars, including the worship of these celestial bodies (Deut 4:19; 17:3; 2 Kgs 17:16; 23:4-5; Jer 8:2; 19:13; Zeph 1:5).

33:11 ***a ring through his nose, bound him in bronze chains.*** Assyrian monuments reveal such treatment of their captives (NBD 479; ANEP 447).

led him away to Babylon. This may be using Babylon figuratively for "Mesopotamia" to create a link with the Chronicler's audience. It may suggest that Babylon was responsible for Judah or may indicate that Manasseh had joined a rebellion with Babylonian officials against the Assyrian court (see commentary below).

33:12 ***deep distress.*** See notes on 28:20, 22.

33:14 ***outer wall.*** This may be a reference to a second wall structure outside the present wall or work on the outside sections of the wall. Many fortified cities in Israel display a two-wall structure, for instance Lachish (stratum III, Assyrian period), which had an inner wall 18 feet thick and then an outer wall 17 feet high.

from west of the Gihon Spring in the Kidron Valley to the Fish Gate, and continuing around the hill of Ophel. This reconstruction would have begun on the eastern side of the city and continued north around the Temple Mount.

fortified towns of Judah. Sennacherib claims there were 46 fortified cities in Judah (see note on 32:1; cf. 2 Kgs 18:13; 19:25).

33:16 ***peace offerings and thanksgiving offerings.*** In Lev 3 and 7:11-18 these are associated with fulfilling a vow to the Lord or giving thanks for a blessing received. Both types of offerings would be appropriate in the case for Manasseh.

33:19 ***pagan shrines . . . Asherah poles.*** See notes on 17:6 and 31:1 and commentary on 24:17-22.

33:25 ***the people of the land.*** See note on 23:20.

COMMENTARY

The Chronicler's source in Kings presented Manasseh's reign as the nadir of the southern kingdom, identifying the "sin of Manasseh" as the cause of the defeat, destruction, and exile of Judah and Jerusalem (2 Kgs 21:11-15; 23:26-27; 24:3-4; cf. 2 Kgs 24:20).[1] Even the faithful deeds of Manasseh's grandson Josiah, the figure who symbolizes the zenith of the history of the divided kingdom for the writer of Kings, could only delay God's judgment on Judah rather than reverse it (2 Kgs 23:25-27).

The Chronicler agrees with his source that Manasseh's reign is among the lowest points in the history of the divided kingdom (33:2). However, the Chronicler appears to try to explain why Manasseh enjoyed the longest reign in the Chronicler's history (the closest rival being Uzziah, who reigned 52 years according to 26:3).[2] The Chronicler accomplished this by introducing a section that traces God's discipline of Manasseh, Manasseh's repentance and restoration, and his subsequent success and faithfulness. Also, since the Chronicler placed emphasis in his history on the theological stream in the book of Kings that considers each generation on its own terms before Yahweh (see commentary on 25:4), he ignored Yahweh's long speech that has Manasseh's sin sealing Judah's fate in 2 Kings 21:11-16 (and all related statements in 2 Kgs 23:26-27; 24:3-4). The resulting account renovates Manasseh as an example of the effect the Chronicler's agenda for renewal can have even within a generation that has been so despicably unfaithful. As Williamson (1982:389) has written: "Manasseh furnishes the most explicit and dramatic example of the efficacy of repentance in the whole of the Chronicler's work."

In this section the Chronicler accentuates the opportunity Yahweh offers to any generation to turn from their wicked ways, thus justifying God's discipline that eventually falls. Manasseh's experience parallels the eventual experience of Judah, who was taken into exile in Babylon. Some have questioned the validity of this account, especially considering the fact that Assyria was the aggressor (33:11a) and yet Babylon was the destination of Manasseh's exile (33:11b). Interestingly, however, Isaiah's prophetic message against Hezekiah in 2 Kings 20:16-19 suggests that a significant despoiling and exile to Babylon was expected to occur immediately following Hezekiah's reign:

> *Then Isaiah said to Hezekiah, "Listen to this message from the* LORD*: The time is coming when everything in your palace—all the treasures stored up by your ancestors until now—will be carried off to Babylon. Nothing will be left, says the* LORD*. Some of your very own sons will be taken away into exile. They will become eunuchs who will serve in the palace of Babylon's king." Then Hezekiah said to Isaiah, "This message you have given me from the* LORD *is good." For the king was thinking, "At least there will be peace and security during my lifetime."*

It is possible that Manasseh's internment in Babylon is related to the relationship fostered by Hezekiah with Merodach-baladan (also known as Marduk-apla-iddina), king of Babylon, a figure who consistently led revolts against the Assyrians during Hezekiah's period (ABD 4.704-705; COS 2.299-302, 305). Assyrian annals show clearly that Manasseh was forced into submission, his name appearing in a text during the reign of the Assyrian emperor Esarhaddon that lists those who gave tribute for building projects in Nineveh and among a list of kings who supported Esharaddon's son Ashurbanipal against Egypt (see ANET 291, 294; cf. Dillard 1987:264-265). During Manasseh's reign, several revolts were launched against the Assyrians, most notably by Ashurbanipal's twin brother, Shamash-shum-ukin, in Babylon (652–648 BC), but possibly also by leaders in the Levant region.[3] It may be that Manasseh was implicated or participated in one of these. If it was the former, this would explain his exile in Babylon.

In the end, however, one should not miss the relevance of this story of Manasseh to the community living in the wake of the Babylonian exile and Persian restoration. With its depiction of Manasseh's exile to Babylon, his subsequent humble prayer and restoration to his kingdom, 33:11-13 reflects a regular typology used by the Chronicler, that of exile and restoration.[4] On one level the story is related to the agenda of the Chronicler to encourage continuing returns of people from Mesopotamian exile (cf. 30:6-9; 36:20-23) and to identify the true ideals of the restoration, especially repentance. On another level, however, its single focus on a Davidic royal figure (without any mention of people accompanying him) suggests that Manasseh was to serve as a role model for the return of the Davidic house (see Boda 2009b).

Summary Note: The Accession of Manasseh (33:1-2). Manasseh assumed the throne at the young age of twelve, which partly, though not entirely, helps to explain the significant length of his 55-year reign. Most suggest that he shared the throne in a co-regency with his father Hezekiah for about 10 years (Dillard 1987:266). Interestingly, the queen mother's name is ignored by the Chronicler from his source text. To this point the queen mother's name was not given for Jehoram and Ahaz, but this was because it was absent in the source in Kings, the reason for which is not clear but possibly relates to the close association between Jehoram, Ahaz, and the northern kings (see commentary on ch 28). The Chronicler does not provide the name of the queen mother after the account of Hezekiah, even though it was available in his source in Kings. This may have been intended to accentuate Hezekiah's reign as the zenith of the history of the divided kingdom.[5]

Manasseh is evaluated in the strongest negative terms found in the Chronicles, linking him to the "detestable practices of the pagan nations that the LORD had driven from the land ahead of the Israelites," an evaluation used elsewhere only of the wicked Ahaz (28:1-3). This creates a bracket of two wicked kings around the central account of the faithful Hezekiah. What this does is accentuate the glory of his reign that will reveal the theology of generational responsibility expressed in 25:3-4, and it illustrates the tenuous character of reforms within any generation. Besides considerable idolatry, Ahaz and Manasseh shared in common the abomination of child sacrifice (33:6; see note on 28:3).

Manasseh's Evil (33:3-9). Borrowing from his source in 2 Kings 21, the Chronicler makes clear that Manasseh reversed the reforms instituted by his father Hezekiah, reintroducing the worship of Canaanite deities (Baal, Asherah) with their cultic symbols (altars, poles), as well as the worship of celestial bodies (see note on 33:3). The Chronicler and his audience must have been revolted by the reference to his construction of altars to these celestial bodies in the Temple structure (for incense) and in the courtyards (for sacrifice). An association between child sacrifice and divination (see comment on 28:3) may be suggested in 33:6. The list contained in this verse is reminiscent of Deuteronomy 18:9-14, which lists the sins of the nations that were driven out of Canaan by the Israelites and whose behavior was to be rejected. The depth of Manasseh's evil is reached in 33:7, which informs us that he placed an idol in the Temple, after which the Chronicler cites God's warning of exile. The Chronicler's evaluation in 33:9 is that Manasseh had not only replicated the patterns of the nations that preceded Judah's entrance into the land (33:2) but had exceeded these patterns.

Prophetic Warning, Divine Discipline, Manasseh's Repentance, Divine Rescue (33:10-13). One regular pattern in the Chronicler's work is the prophetic word of warning that follows disobedience and precedes God's disciplinary action (11:2-4; 15:1-8; 16:7-10; 18:9-27; 21:12-15; 24:20-22; 25:7-10, 15-16; 28:9-15). This is presented as a sign of God's patience, providing an opportunity for repentance. In some cases the kings heed the message. Typical of the Chronicler's democratizing tone, in the case of Manasseh the message is directed to the king and his people (33:10). By not heeding the message, they invited Yahweh's discipline, which came in the form of an attack by the Assyrian army, who captured Manasseh and took him captive to Babylon (33:11). In Babylon he exemplified the normative values of the Chronicler: He entreated God's favor by humbling himself (*kana'* [TH3665, ZH4044]) "greatly" (NLT, "sincerely") and praying (*palal* [TH6419, ZH7137]). Hearing his prayer, God granted his request and returned him to his throne. This highlights God's grace for any generation who will humbly pray to him. Even if that generation has sinned greatly (and one could not imagine any generation worse than Manasseh's), they would get a hearing before Yahweh.

There are signs, however, that Manasseh provided for the Chronicler not just a role model for the community—what Schniedewind (1991:450) calls a "paradigm of a contrite sinner"—but he serves as a model for a penitent royal house.[6]

First of all, Manasseh's repentance echoes the earlier ideal royal penitent, David himself, in 1 Chronicles 21 (Abadie 2003:102). Thus, in the closing phase of his narrative the Chronicler reminds his audience of the kind of royal penitence that can preserve the kingdom and the royal house. Second, the Chronicler's account of Manasseh displays considerable links to the chosen royal line which went into exile in chapter 36. The Chronicler's description of Manasseh's exile to Babylon in 33:11 is identical to the one used for the exile of Jehoiakim in 36:6. Similarly, the vocabulary used to describe Jehoiachin's exile in 36:9-10 and Ezekiel 19:9-11 is identical to that used for Manasseh in 33:11 (Abadie 2003:102). These links to the key chosen line in exile (see commentary on ch 36) show that Manasseh provides a model for the renewal of the royal line, one that promotes humility and repentance (see Boda 2009b).

Manasseh's Success and Faithfulness (33:14-17). The Chronicler completed his account of the reign of Manasseh with a description of his life after his restoration. The account is designed to showcase the fact that he followed through on his repentance with righteous actions related to the reformation of worship practices in Judah (33:15-16). Even though he was not able to completely eradicate worship outside the central shrine in Jerusalem, at least the unorthodox "high places" (NLT, "pagan shrines") were devoted to Yahweh alone (33:17). The account also highlights God's blessing by describing his building and refortification projects in Jerusalem and his militarization of the fortified cities of Judah (33:14).

Summary Note: The Reign of Manasseh (33:18-20). A comparison of the concluding summary note of Manasseh in 2 Kings 21:17-18 with the one in 33:18-20 reveals the differing nuances of each account.[7] The book of Kings emphasizes "the sins he committed" while Chronicles highlights "his prayer to God." The Chronicler mentions two sources for his account of Manasseh, one *The Book of the Kings of Israel,* and the other *The Record of the Seers.* The role of the prophetic voice is emphasized in this closing note ("the words the seers spoke to him in the name of the LORD, the God of Israel"), and this record of the seers is said to contain details on locations of idolatrous sites. Although penitent in life, Manasseh was denied the honor of burial with the kings of Judah in death.

The Reign of Amon (33:21-25). The Chronicler offers an even shorter account of Amon than the abbreviated account he found in Kings (2 Kgs 21:19-26). As is true of all kings after Hezekiah, the Chronicler ignores the reference to the queen mother, suggesting that the zenith had been reached with Hezekiah's rule (see commentary on 33:1-2). Manasseh's son came to the throne at age 22 and reigned for only two years. He followed the early idolatrous patterns of his father, Manasseh. The difference, however, is introduced with the unique statement of the Chronicler in 33:23. Amon failed to humble himself (*kana'* [TH3665, ZH4044]) before Yahweh, as his father had done; as a result, he was assassinated by his servants in the royal court. The usual summary note on the king's reign is not included by the Chronicler, who moved quickly to the reign of Amon's son, Josiah.

ENDNOTES

1. One should not miss a minor witness in Kings that places the blame for this defeat, destruction, and exile at the feet of Hezekiah (2 Kgs 20:12-21). It may be that this message to Hezekiah reflects a defeat and exile that occurred in the reign of Manasseh, evidence for which is now found only in the Chronicler's account of Manasseh.
2. Dillard (1987:267) argues that "the Chronicler does show awareness of length of reign as an indicator of divine blessing in one context (1 Chr 29:28; 2 Chr 24:15-16); length of life is simply an extension of the health/illness motif of which the Chronicler does make repeated use."
3. For Shamash-shum-ukin's rebellion, see ABD 4.1041; ANET 298. For the rebellions of leaders in the Levant, see ANET 290-292; cf. Dillard 1987:264-265.
4. See Dillard 1987:271; Mosis 1973:192-194; Raney 2003:165; Schniedewind 1991:450; Smelik 1992:188; Williamson 1982:389.
5. Williamson (1982:390) affirms the conclusion of McKay (1973) that this is related to the Arabian origins of the mothers of Manasseh, Amon, and Josiah. Dillard (1987:267) remains unconvinced and suggests that it was done "for reasons no longer apparent to us." He does note that other aspects of the death formula would also disappear after Hezekiah including "with his fathers" and "in the City of David." Dillard cites Macy 1975 and McKenzie 1985:174-176 as finding here evidence for a change in the Chronicler's sources.

6. Mitchell (2001:272) observes how Manasseh is "the only king who is depicted as starting out evil and ending up as a good ruler." In this way Manasseh stands out among the Davidides as a unique model that would provide a model for moving from the final depiction of the royal house in Chronicles to the ideal of Hezekiah-David-Solomon.
7. Dillard (1987:264) sees the repetitious character of this concluding note as suggesting textual corruption at some point.

Q. The Reign of Josiah (34:1–35:27)

1. Josiah's accession and reform of worship (34:1-33)

Josiah was eight years old when he became king, and he reigned in Jerusalem thirty-one years. [2]He did what was pleasing in the LORD's sight and followed the example of his ancestor David. He did not turn away from doing what was right.

[3]During the eighth year of his reign, while he was still young, Josiah began to seek the God of his ancestor David. Then in the twelfth year he began to purify Judah and Jerusalem, destroying all the pagan shrines, the Asherah poles, and the carved idols and cast images. [4]He ordered that the altars of Baal be demolished and that the incense altars which stood above them be broken down. He also made sure that the Asherah poles, the carved idols, and the cast images were smashed and scattered over the graves of those who had sacrificed to them. [5]He burned the bones of the pagan priests on their own altars, and so he purified Judah and Jerusalem.

[6]He did the same thing in the towns of Manasseh, Ephraim, and Simeon, even as far as Naphtali, and in the regions* all around them. [7]He destroyed the pagan altars and the Asherah poles, and he crushed the idols into dust. He cut down all the incense altars throughout the land of Israel. Finally, he returned to Jerusalem.

[8]In the eighteenth year of his reign, after he had purified the land and the Temple, Josiah appointed Shaphan son of Azaliah, Maaseiah the governor of Jerusalem, and Joah son of Joahaz, the royal historian, to repair the Temple of the LORD his God. [9]They gave Hilkiah the high priest the money that had been collected by the Levites who served as gatekeepers at the Temple of God. The gifts were brought by people from Manasseh, Ephraim, and from all the remnant of Israel, as well as from all Judah, Benjamin, and the people of Jerusalem.

[10]He entrusted the money to the men assigned to supervise the restoration of the LORD's Temple. Then they paid the workers who did the repairs and renovation of the Temple. [11]They hired carpenters and builders, who purchased finished stone for the walls and timber for the rafters and beams. They restored what earlier kings of Judah had allowed to fall into ruin.

[12]The workers served faithfully under the leadership of Jahath and Obadiah, Levites of the Merarite clan, and Zechariah and Meshullam, Levites of the Kohathite clan. Other Levites, all of whom were skilled musicians, [13]were put in charge of the laborers of the various trades. Still others assisted as secretaries, officials, and gatekeepers.

[14]While they were bringing out the money collected at the LORD's Temple, Hilkiah the priest found the Book of the Law of the LORD that was written by Moses. [15]Hilkiah said to Shaphan the court secretary, "I have found the Book of the Law in the LORD's Temple!" Then Hilkiah gave the scroll to Shaphan.

[16]Shaphan took the scroll to the king and reported, "Your officials are doing everything they were assigned to do. [17]The money that was collected at the Temple of the

LORD has been turned over to the supervisors and workmen." 18 Shaphan also told the king, "Hilkiah the priest has given me a scroll." So Shaphan read it to the king.

19 When the king heard what was written in the Law, he tore his clothes in despair. 20 Then he gave these orders to Hilkiah, Ahikam son of Shaphan, Acbor son of Micaiah,* Shaphan the court secretary, and Asaiah the king's personal adviser: 21 "Go to the Temple and speak to the LORD for me and for all the remnant of Israel and Judah. Inquire about the words written in the scroll that has been found. For the LORD's great anger has been poured out on us because our ancestors have not obeyed the word of the LORD. We have not been doing everything this scroll says we must do."

22 So Hilkiah and the other men went to the New Quarter* of Jerusalem to consult with the prophet Huldah. She was the wife of Shallum son of Tikvah, son of Harhas,* the keeper of the Temple wardrobe.

23 She said to them, "The LORD, the God of Israel, has spoken! Go back and tell the man who sent you, 24 'This is what the LORD says: I am going to bring disaster on this city* and its people. All the curses written in the scroll that was read to the king of Judah will come true. 25 For my people have abandoned me and offered sacrifices to pagan gods, and I am very angry with them for everything they have done. My anger will be poured out on this place, and it will not be quenched.'

26 "But go to the king of Judah who sent you to seek the LORD and tell him: 'This is what the LORD, the God of Israel, says concerning the message you have just heard: 27 You were sorry and humbled yourself before God when you heard his words against this city and its people. You humbled yourself and tore your clothing in despair and wept before me in repentance. And I have indeed heard you, says the LORD. 28 So I will not send the promised disaster until after you have died and been buried in peace. You yourself will not see the disaster I am going to bring on this city and its people.'"

So they took her message back to the king.

29 Then the king summoned all the elders of Judah and Jerusalem. 30 And the king went up to the Temple of the LORD with all the people of Judah and Jerusalem, along with the priests and the Levites—all the people from the greatest to the least. There the king read to them the entire Book of the Covenant that had been found in the LORD's Temple. 31 The king took his place of authority beside the pillar and renewed the covenant in the LORD's presence. He pledged to obey the LORD by keeping all his commands, laws, and decrees with all his heart and soul. He promised to obey all the terms of the covenant that were written in the scroll. 32 And he required everyone in Jerusalem and the people of Benjamin to make a similar pledge. The people of Jerusalem did so, renewing their covenant with God, the God of their ancestors.

33 So Josiah removed all detestable idols from the entire land of Israel and required everyone to worship the LORD their God. And throughout the rest of his lifetime, they did not turn away from the LORD, the God of their ancestors.

34:6 As in Syriac version. Hebrew reads *in their temples*, or *in their ruins*. The meaning of the Hebrew is uncertain. **34:20** As in parallel text at 2 Kgs 22:12; Hebrew reads *Abdon son of Micah*. **34:22a** Or *the Second Quarter*, a newer section of Jerusalem. Hebrew reads *the Mishneh*. **34:22b** As in parallel text at 2 Kgs 22:14; Hebrew reads *son of Tokhath, son of Hasrah*. **34:24** Hebrew *this place*; also in 34:27, 28.

NOTES

34:3-4 ***Asherah poles . . . carved idols and cast images . . . altars of Baal.*** For Asherah poles, see notes on 17:6 and 31:1 and commentary on 24:17-22. Molten images were made of metal poured in a cast and thereby differentiated from graven (i.e., carved) images. These are often cited alongside one another (Deut 27:15; Judg 17:3-4; 18:14; Nah 1:14).

34:24 *the curses written in the scroll.* If this book was Deuteronomy, these are found in Deut 27–28. Such curses for disobedience were typical at the end of covenant documents (see Lev 26).

34:31 *his place of authority beside the pillar.* See note on 23:13.

COMMENTARY

The Chronicler appears to compare and contrast Josiah to two earlier kings in his history by highlighting common activities and evaluations. First, Josiah shares some key things in common with Joash (Dillard 1987:277-282). Both come to the throne at an early age (24:1; 34:1) and lead a restoration of the Temple that relies on offerings from the people (24:4-14; 34:8-13), both stand at some point "in the king's place" (NLT, "his place of authority by/beside the pillar," 23:13; 34:31), and both lead the nation in covenant renewal at the Temple (23:16-17; 34:29-32). However, there is a clear difference in that Joash's faithfulness lasted only during the lifetime of Jehoiada (24:2), while Josiah would lead a faithful nation throughout his lifetime (34:33).

The second king is Hezekiah. Only Josiah and Hezekiah are given the distinction in the Chronicler's account of being compared positively to David (29:2; 34:2). Other links between these two leaders can be discerned in the Chronicler's account. Both accounts are focused on the renovation of the Temple (chs 29, 34), which opens the way for a celebration of Passover (chs 30, 35). Both recount the eradication of idolatry in the southern and northern kingdoms (31:1; 34:3-8), and both kings make a covenant (29:10; 34:30-32). Both kings have Levites with similar names (31:12-13; 35:9). Hezekiah and Josiah are the only two kings besides David (1 Chr 22:2) and Solomon (2:17) whose domain is called the "land of Israel" (see 30:25 for Hezekiah and 34:7 for Josiah; Dillard 1987:279). Josiah is clearly placed among great company. Both accounts have similar characterization, with the kings portrayed as normative characters for most of the account but with both ultimately displaying flaws in character and action near the end of their otherwise glorious reigns.

However, the Chronicler elevated his account of Hezekiah's reign (chs 29–32) considerably from his source in Kings with the effect that Josiah (who is the hero in the latter part of 2 Kings) takes second place to Hezekiah (whose failure at the end of his reign in 2 Kings identifies him as the one who began the slide toward—or worse, inaugurated—the Exile). The sheer size of the Hezekiah account (chs 29–32) compared to that of the Josiah account (chs 34–35) is evidence of the heightened status of Hezekiah, especially considering that three-quarters of the Chronicler's account consists of accounts not found in 2 Kings. It is true that the Chronicler compared Hezekiah's Passover to the celebration during the time of Solomon, while Josiah's Passover is compared to the time of Samuel, and that furthermore the Chronicler said of Josiah that "none of the kings of Israel had ever kept a Passover as Josiah did" (35:18). However, a look at his source in 2 Kings 23:22 reveals that the Chronicler had excised the term "or of the kings of Judah," probably to protect the image of Hezekiah's Passover.[1] Although both accounts end with a final phase in which the king's flaws are revealed, in the end Josiah fared far worse than Hezekiah in the Chronicler's account, with Hezekiah being used even in his failure as an example of penitential sensitivity, while Josiah was judged for failing to listen to God. Nevertheless, Josiah confirmed the values the Chronicler had already affirmed through Hezekiah, for he "did not turn away from doing what was right."

Josiah's reign, however, ended in tragedy; many have noted the striking similarities between Josiah's death in battle and the deaths of at least Saul and Ahab, if not also Amaziah and Ahaziah.[2] Through these connections, the Chronicler villainizes Josiah and shows how with Josiah, for all intents and purposes, "the story of Israel now passes from monarchy to exile" (Johnstone 1997:2.260). From this point on foreign emperors will speak and act for Yahweh rather than Davidic kings. Riley (1993:142-143) sees in this the end of the Davidic monarchy as an institution. However, the Chronicler's earlier accounts of positive royal models as well as earlier allusions to the endurance of the Davidic line should not be ignored (see Boda 2009b).

The account of Josiah is divided into three major phases divided by narrative summary statements at the end of each section (34:33; 35:18-19; 35:25).

Summary Note: The Accession of Josiah (34:1-2). With the reign of Amon cut short by an assassination, it is not surprising that the "people of the land" (most likely the landed gentry; see note on 23:20) needed to crown Josiah king when he was merely eight years old (640 BC). He was evaluated very positively by the Chronicler, who declared that he "followed the example of his ancestor David," a comparison only bestowed on one other king in the post-Solomonic kingdom of Judah,[3] that is, Hezekiah (29:2).

Josiah's Reform of Worship (34:3-33). The first phase of the Chronicler's account of Josiah focuses on his reformation of worship, not only reversing the practices his father had instituted during his two-year reign, but also leading a renewal that had an impact on territories in the northern kingdom. This phase is described in three stages using chronological notes as structural markers that highlight his eighth (633 BC), twelfth (628 BC), and eighteenth years (623 BC).[4] Josiah's successful reign makes sense within the broader ancient Near Eastern political environment in which he ruled. The latter third of the seventh century BC witnessed the slow demise of the once-mighty Assyrian Empire, especially after the death of Ashurbanipal in 627 BC. Babylonian and Median power were on the rise, and Assyria's days were numbered.

Josiah's eighth year (at 16 years old) marks the first stage when he "began to seek the God of his ancestor David" (34:3a). The use of the term "seek" (*darash* [TH1875, ZH2011]) is a signal from the Chronicler of the normativeness of this character. The second stage occurs in his twelfth year (at 20 years old). The Chronicler now depicts him as an adult (see 25:5; Num 1:3; 26:2; 1 Chr 27:23),[5] able to purify both Judah and Jerusalem (34:3b-5) and then towns in the former northern kingdom (34:6-7; Manasseh, Ephraim, Simeon, Naphtali). These forays into the former northern kingdom (even into northern Galilee) are not surprising in light of the weak condition of the Assyrian Empire in the latter third of the seventh century BC.

The identification of these first two stages is unique to the Chronicler,[6] who then picks up with his source in Kings for the third stage (34:8-13), which occurred in Josiah's eighteenth year,[7] with the Chronicler's explicit notation that this occurred only "after he had purified the land and the Temple" (34:8). This order is important to the Chronicler as is evident in his depiction of Hezekiah in chapters 29–31.

The activities of the eighteenth year began with Josiah's appointment of a triumvirate (Shaphan, Maaseiah, Joah) to coordinate renovations on the Temple. As in the account of Joash (ch 24), the Chronicler provides details on the collection and distribution of funds for the project, but this time the high priest Hilkiah was given sole control over the funds collected by the Levites at the gate.[8] The Chronicler expanded the generic reference in Kings to "the people" from whom the money was raised (2 Kgs 22:4) to "Manasseh, Ephraim, and . . . all the remnant of Israel, as well as . . . all Judah, Benjamin, and the people of Jerusalem" (34:9). The Levites are explicitly cited in Chronicles as being responsible for collecting the funds.[9] The Chronicler's expansions here reflect not only his desire to see "all Israel" in his day participating in the Temple worship and support but also to empower the Levites to collect these funds.

The Chronicler provided considerably more details on the renovation project than those found in his source in Kings, citing specific names and clans of those involved (34:12-13). It is not surprising that Levites and even Levitical musicians were deeply involved and that they filled a diversity of roles ranging from supervisors to scribes, officials, and gatekeepers.[10]

These extensive renovations led to the discovery of the law with its subsequent covenant renewal (34:14-32). For this event the Chronicler was largely dependent on his source in 2 Kings 22:8–23:3. It is the priest Hilkiah who is presented as discovering a law book in the Temple, which is then delivered to Josiah through his court secretary (scribe), Shaphan. Shaphan delivered the scroll amidst a progress report on the project. He subsequently read the scroll to the king.

The identity of this book has been the object of much discussion throughout the history of scholarship. Most would agree that it was a form of the book that today is called Deuteronomy, because Josiah's reforms as depicted in the book of Kings involved: centralized worship (2 Kgs 23:4-20; cf. Deut 12), Passover as a national event (2 Kgs 23:21-22; cf. Deut 16), the removal of mediums and spiritists (2 Kgs 23:24; cf. Deut 18:14-22), a law book with curses (2 Kgs 22:13, 19; cf. Deut 28), a king who reads the law (2 Kgs 22:11; 23:2-3; cf. Deut 17:18-19), a "Book of the Covenant" (2 Kgs 23:2; Deuteronomy is a covenant document), concern for the name of Yahweh (2 Kgs 23:27; cf. Deut 12:5, 11), stress on the inevitability of judgment (2 Kgs 22:16-20; 23:26-27; cf. Deut 31:24-29), and a citation from the book of Deuteronomy (2 Kgs 23:25; cf. Deut 6:5). Some see a political agenda behind this "discovery," suggesting that the book was created by Josiah to justify and lend authority to his initiatives (ABD 3.1016-1017; cf. Noth 1981; Römer and de Pury 2000:24-141). For the Chronicler, however, this book is nothing short of "the word of the LORD" (34:21). This identity means that this book carries immeasurable authority; his audience's respect and response to this word must be in line with that of King Josiah.

The response in 34:19 is immediate ("When the king heard") and passionate ("he tore his clothes in despair"), displaying a response typical of lament and penitence. He immediately sprang into action, giving orders to inquire at the Temple for a word from Yahweh "for me and for all the remnant of Israel and Judah" (34:21). The words "all the remnant" are an expansion in the Chronicler's account; for a community living in the period after the Babylonian exile these words would have helped them apply this story to their own situation as "the remnant." The command to inquire at the Temple assumes the operation of a corps of Temple prophets who were stationed at the sanctuary and responsible for providing a relevant word from God on a specific matter (Boda 2001:192; A. Johnson 1962; Tournay 1991). It is interesting that the inscripturated tradition was not seen as adequate, but rather a prophetic word was needed to clarify the response of the king to the Word.

The royal officials knew an appropriate prophet, a woman named Huldah, who was found and consulted (34:22). Her response confirmed Josiah's greatest fears: The curses written in the scroll would fall upon the city and could not be averted (34:23-25). However, she offered some hope. Because of his humble penitential response to the message of the scroll, Yahweh would suspend the disaster to a later era (34:26-28).

In 34:29-32 Josiah is shown following through on his initial penitential response by renewing the covenant. This renewal involved the elders and all the people of Judah and Jerusalem ("from the greatest to the least"), the priests, and the Levites. The replacement of "Levites" in this list for "prophets" in 2 Kings 23:2 reflects the Chronicler's penchant for associating prophetic functions with the Levites (see 20:14; 29:25, 30; 35:15; 1 Chr 25:1-8; see commentary on 1 Chr 25; Dillard 1987:282). The renewal took place at the Temple with the king positioned, literally, "in his place" (i.e., "his place of authority beside the pillar," as in NLT), which according to the account in Kings was "beside the pillar" (2 Kgs 23:3). The order of the ceremony was as follows: (1) The king read the entire Book of the Covenant; (2) the king stood at his place to renew the covenant in God's presence, pledging to obey Yahweh by keeping the commandments and to obey all the terms of the covenant; and (3) the people made the same pledge.[11] This last element is unique to the Chronicler and is consistent with his pattern of highlighting the people's response alongside royal or leadership figures. Emphasis was placed on the participation of those present in Jerusalem, another trend seen in the Chronicler's account, suggesting that the people of Jerusalem were held to a higher standard than any other group for the support of the Temple and Torah.

The summary statement in 34:33 signals the end of the account and highlights Josiah's work at removing idolatry from "the entire land of Israel" as well as restoring the worship of Yahweh. The people's covenant renewal is pictured as being sincere because it lasted "throughout the rest of his lifetime."

ENDNOTES

1. It is possible that the reference here is to the amount of animals and celebrants involved; see Dillard 1987:291 and compare 35:7-9 with 30:23-24.
2. Dillard 1987:292; Japhet 1993:1043; Kalimi 2005b:23; Ristau 2004:75-77; Tuell 2001:241; but especially the work of Mitchell (2006:421-435).

3. Although the people during the first three years of Rehoboam's reign "faithfully followed in the footsteps of David and Solomon" (11:17), Ahaz did not do "as his ancestor David had done" (28:1).
4. See Dillard (1980:215), who says this is typical of the Chronicler.
5. What Dillard (1987:278) calls "the age of majority" in Israel.
6. The description of the cleansing of the northern territories appears to be drawn from 2 Kgs 23:6.
7. The activities of this eighteenth year continue until 35:19, which with its notation "in the eighteenth year of Josiah's reign" forms a bracket around the positive worship renewal of Josiah.
8. In ch 24 the Chronicler emphasizes balance between royal and priestly authority in the collection and distribution of funds (see especially 24:11-14).
9. Notice how the Chronicler leaves out the sentence, "But don't require the construction supervisors to keep account of the money they receive, for they are honest and trustworthy men" (2 Kgs 22:7), just like he did at 2 Kgs 12:15 in the collection taken by Joash: "No accounting of this money was required from the construction supervisors, because they were honest and trustworthy men." Possibly this reflects the Chronicler's concern for proper protocol, which may have been extended into accounting practices of his own day.
10. Dillard (1987:280) notes that musicians were used on ancient construction sites, setting "the pace for the various tasks much as the ubiquitous radios on a contemporary construction site."
11. Many have noted a distinction between covenant ceremonies in the preexilic and postexilic periods, with the latter being more democratized and delineating specific commitments. See Baltzer 1971:45, 50, 92; Eskenazi 1988:103-104, 111; Japhet 1988; McCarthy 1982a, 1982b; Sperling 1989. The account here follows the preexilic pattern.

◆ 2. Josiah's celebration of the Passover and Festival of Unleavened Bread (35:1-19)

Then Josiah announced that the Passover of the LORD would be celebrated in Jerusalem, and so the Passover lamb was slaughtered on the fourteenth day of the first month.* 2Josiah also assigned the priests to their duties and encouraged them in their work at the Temple of the LORD. 3He issued this order to the Levites, who were to teach all Israel and who had been set apart to serve the LORD: "Put the holy Ark in the Temple that was built by Solomon son of David, the king of Israel. You no longer need to carry it back and forth on your shoulders. Now spend your time serving the LORD your God and his people Israel. 4Report for duty according to the family divisions of your ancestors, following the directions of King David of Israel and the directions of his son Solomon.

5"Then stand in the sanctuary at the place appointed for your family division and help the families assigned to you as they bring their offerings to the Temple. 6Slaughter the Passover lambs, purify yourselves, and prepare to help those who come. Follow all the directions that the LORD gave through Moses."

7Then Josiah provided 30,000 lambs and young goats for the people's Passover offerings, along with 3,000 cattle, all from the king's own flocks and herds. 8The king's officials also made willing contributions to the people, priests, and Levites. Hilkiah, Zechariah, and Jehiel, the administrators of God's Temple, gave the priests 2,600 lambs and young goats and 300 cattle as Passover offerings. 9The Levite leaders—Conaniah and his brothers

Shemaiah and Nethanel, as well as Hashabiah, Jeiel, and Jozabad—gave 5,000 lambs and young goats and 500 cattle to the Levites for their Passover offerings.

10When everything was ready for the Passover celebration, the priests and the Levites took their places, organized by their divisions, as the king had commanded. 11The Levites then slaughtered the Passover lambs and presented the blood to the priests, who sprinkled the blood on the altar while the Levites prepared the animals. 12They divided the burnt offerings among the people by their family groups, so they could offer them to the LORD as prescribed in the Book of Moses. They did the same with the cattle. 13Then they roasted the Passover lambs as prescribed; and they boiled the holy offerings in pots, kettles, and pans, and brought them out quickly so the people could eat them.

14Afterward the Levites prepared Passover offerings for themselves and for the priests—the descendants of Aaron—because the priests had been busy from morning till night offering the burnt offerings and the fat portions. The Levites took responsibility for all these preparations.

15The musicians, descendants of Asaph, were in their assigned places, following the commands that had been given by David, Asaph, Heman, and Jeduthun, the king's seer. The gatekeepers guarded the gates and did not need to leave their posts of duty, for their Passover offerings were prepared for them by their fellow Levites.

16The entire ceremony for the LORD's Passover was completed that day. All the burnt offerings were sacrificed on the altar of the LORD, as King Josiah had commanded. 17All the Israelites present in Jerusalem celebrated Passover and the Festival of Unleavened Bread for seven days. 18Never since the time of the prophet Samuel had there been such a Passover. None of the kings of Israel had ever kept a Passover as Josiah did, involving all the priests and Levites, all the people of Jerusalem, and people from all over Judah and Israel. 19This Passover celebration took place in the eighteenth year of Josiah's reign.

35:1 This day in the ancient Hebrew lunar calendar was April 5, 622 B.C.

NOTES

35:1 ***fourteenth day of the first month.*** See note on 30:2.

35:3 ***holy Ark.*** See note on the fate of the Ark at 6:11.

who had been set apart to serve the LORD. Lit., "holy to the LORD." Similar phrases are used of the Sabbath (Exod 16:23; 31:15), the high priest (Exod 28:36; 39:30), priests (Ezra 8:28), contributions to God including tithes (Lev 27:14, 21-23, 30, 32; Deut 15:19), the people of Israel (Deut 26:19), spoil (Isa 23:18), a battlefield (Jer 31:40), Levitical territory (Ezek 48:14), and, in the future Jerusalem, formerly common items like bells of horses and cooking pots (Zech 14:20-21).

35:17 ***Passover and the Festival of Unleavened Bread.*** See note on 30:2.

COMMENTARY

As was the case with Hezekiah, the restoration of the Temple paves the way for a celebration of the Passover followed by the Festival of Unleavened Bread. The Chronicler expanded this account considerably from his source in 2 Kings, which covers it in three verses (2 Kgs 23:21-23). This once again reveals the Chronicler's interest in the proper protocol and faithful practice of worship.

Second Chronicles 35:1 functions as a summary statement for the entire account, citing the precise day on which the Passover lamb was slaughtered, in keeping with Torah legislation (Exod 12:1-14; Lev 23:5; Num 9:1-14; 28:16; Deut 16:1-7). The lamb was slain on the 14th day and eaten in the evening of the 15th as the Festival of Unleavened Bread began (see 35:17; cf. Exod 12:15-20; 13:3-10; Lev 23:6-8; Num 28:17-25; Deut 16:3-4, 8).

The account proper begins in 35:2-6, which tells the reader that Josiah assigned the priests and Levites to their duties. The Chronicler mentions the priests at the outset, noting that Josiah not only assigned them their duties but also encouraged them in their service (35:2). The main focus of this section is on the assignment of duties for the Levites, employing a speech by Josiah that brings considerable narrative attention to the issue. The fact that Josiah mentions that the Levites' original assignment of carrying the Ark was no longer needed ("You no longer need to carry it back and forth on your shoulders," 35:3) suggests that the Chronicler was using this opportunity to delineate the tasks of the Levites in the Temple.

The Chronicler assumed that the Levites ("who were holy to the LORD," 35:3, lit.; NLT, "who had been set apart to serve the LORD") functioned in the role of teaching the people. Teaching was a key responsibility of the priestly orders. Although the Torah was extremely detailed, there was a constant need for what are called "Torah rulings" by the priests, rulings that would provide decisions on matters of law, especially ritual law (cf. Lev 10:10-11; Deut 17:8-13; Ezek 44:23-31; Hag 2:11-13; Mal 2:5-8).[1] Here this responsibility is extended to the Levites, suggesting that they were to play a role within the broader region ("all Israel").

By noting the Levites were "holy to the LORD" (35:3, see note) and giving special attention to their sacred duties, the Chronicler appears to be creating space for the Levitical orders, granting them the status of the priestly orders. The Chronicler has employed similar language in his account of Hezekiah—in 30:17 of the act of consecrating oneself in order to participate in a festival and in 31:6 of the tithe that is dedicated to Yahweh.

The speech proper commissions the Levites to assist families in the other tribes with their offerings at the Temple, a service that is considered mediatorial, for it is related both to Yahweh and to Israel. The Levites would need to give careful attention to purification rites as they slaughtered the Passover lambs. The speech emphasizes proper protocol ("Report for duty according to the family divisions of your ancestors"), established on the authority of David and Solomon (35:4), as well as Moses (35:6). Such weighty figures could not be ignored.

As in Hezekiah's Passover celebration (30:24), the king and his officials contributed animals from their own resources for the sacrifices (35:7-8). In Josiah's time Levitical leaders also contributed (35:9). With the personnel and resources in place, it was possible for them to celebrate the Passover, a detailed description of which is provided by the Chronicler in 35:10-17. As with Hezekiah's Passover, this festival included both sacrificial (35:10-14) and musical (35:15) aspects. The identification of Jeduthun as "the king's seer" is typical of the Chronicler's portrayal of Levites as prophets (see 2 Chr 20:14; 29:25, 30; 1 Chr 25:1-8; see commentary on 1 Chr 25 and 2 Chr 34:29-32). The Chronicler once again notes the authority of Moses (35:12) and David (35:15).

This Passover introduces a seven-day celebration of the Festival of Unleavened Bread, but unlike those under Hezekiah (and Solomon), the festival lasted only for seven days. The closing summary note in 35:18-19 claims this Passover was unparalleled in the history of Israel—"never since the time of the prophet Samuel had there been such a Passover." The Chronicler transformed his source slightly at this point (2 Kgs 23:22), replacing the reference to the period of the judges with the reference to Samuel the prophet, probably to highlight a Levitical prophet in his story (1 Chr 6:28; cf. 1 Sam 1–7, where Samuel is presented as both priest and prophet) as was his custom (see commentary on 1 Chr 25). The fact that the Chronicler retained this summary note balances slightly his greater emphasis on Hezekiah. The Chronicler added a list of those who were involved in this Passover: "Josiah . . . all the priests and Levites, all the people of Jerusalem, and people from all over Judah and Israel." This accentuates the need for full participation by all in the community for this royal initiative. With the mention of "the eighteenth year of Josiah's reign" (622 BC) in 35:19, the Chronicler brings to an end the worship reforms of Josiah begun in 34:8.

ENDNOTE

1. Prophets indicted the priests for abusing this duty (Jer 18:18; Ezek 7:26; 22:26; Zeph 3:4) and linked it to the profanation of God's name.

◆ 3. Josiah's death with a summary of his reign (35:20-27)

20After Josiah had finished restoring the Temple, King Neco of Egypt led his army up from Egypt to do battle at Carchemish on the Euphrates River, and Josiah and his army marched out to fight him.* **21**But King Neco sent messengers to Josiah with this message:

> "What do you want with me, king of Judah? I have no quarrel with you today! I am on my way to fight another nation, and God has told me to hurry! Do not interfere with God, who is with me, or he will destroy you."

22But Josiah refused to listen to Neco, to whom God had indeed spoken, and he would not turn back. Instead, he disguised himself and led his army into battle on the plain of Megiddo. **23**But the enemy archers hit King Josiah with their arrows and wounded him. He cried out to his men, "Take me from the battle, for I am badly wounded!"

24So they lifted Josiah out of his chariot and placed him in another chariot. Then they brought him back to Jerusalem, where he died. He was buried there in the royal cemetery. And all Judah and Jerusalem mourned for him. **25**The prophet Jeremiah composed funeral songs for Josiah, and to this day choirs still sing these sad songs about his death. These songs of sorrow have become a tradition and are recorded in *The Book of Laments.*

26The rest of the events of Josiah's reign and his acts of devotion (carried out according to what was written in the Law of the LORD), **27**from beginning to end—all are recorded in *The Book of the Kings of Israel and Judah.*

35:20 Or *Josiah went out to meet him.*

NOTES

35:20 *Carchemish.* This was about 56 miles west of Haran, on the Euphrates River, which formed a natural boundary separating Mesopotamia from western Asia.

35:25 The Book of Laments. This is not a reference to the biblical book of Lamentations, which mourns the destruction of Jerusalem, not Josiah's death.

COMMENTARY

Josiah's Death (35:20-25). With such high praise heaped upon Josiah at the close of the Chronicler's account of the Passover (35:18), it is quite surprising that he presented this final tragic chapter of Josiah's reign (609 BC). The Chronicler expanded his account of Josiah's death from what he found in his source in 2 Kings 23:28-30 by incorporating direct speeches by Neco (35:21) and the dying Josiah (35:23), as well as commentary in 35:22, 25. The description of Josiah's death in Chronicles bears close resemblance to the death of a significant negative character in his source text in Samuel—Kings: Ahab (1 Kgs 22:29-40).[1] Like Ahab, Josiah defied a prophetic warning by going to war, disguised himself in vain, was mortally wounded by enemy archers, cried out similar words when wounded, and was carried in and out of battle in a chariot. In the words of Tuell (2001:241), "Perhaps the most tragic aspect of Josiah's sad story is that this righteous, reforming king should end up just like the wicked apostate Ahab." By associating Josiah in his death with this king, the Chronicler accentuated Josiah's loss of divine favor (see Boda 2009b:252).

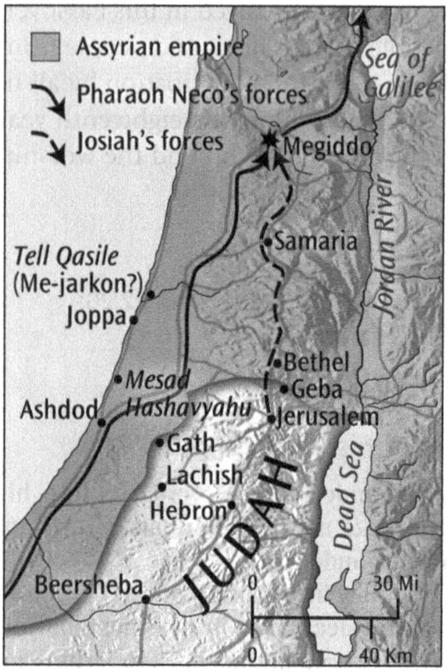

The Land of Israel during Josiah's Reign, 621–609 BC

Pharaoh Neco II (609–594 BC) continued his father's policy of supporting the Assyrians against the rising tide of the Babylonian-Median coalition; as a result, he marched through Judah on his way to Carchemish at the Euphrates (ABD 3.1017). This battle appears to have taken place in 610–609 BC during Josiah's reign and four years before the final battle at Carchemish (605 BC; Jer 46:2), which would prove decisive in that it marked the end of any hopes for a renewal of the Assyrian Empire (Nineveh had fallen in 612, but a rump empire continued in the northwestern part of its territory).[2]

Neco asked for safe passage of his army through the land because he was on his way to battle "another nation" (Babylon). Since the battle took place on the "plain of Megiddo" (Valley of Jezreel), it is most likely that control over the pass at Megiddo was in dispute. This pass would be important for Neco to control because it was essential to secure his communication lines and escape route back to Egypt, especially in case a retreat was necessary (ABD 3.1017). Even though the battle was indecisive, Neco claimed Palestine. In the coming era, Egypt and Babylon would vie for control over the region of Judah—Egypt needing it as a buffer zone from Babylon and Babylon desiring it as a launching point for a conquest of Egypt (see commentary on ch 36).

The Chronicler's presentation is typical of his accounts, especially in the provision of a message. Here we see a further development in the Chronicler's view of prophecy as Pharaoh Neco's message is subtly given the status of a word from God: "to whom God had indeed spoken" (35:22). Such a speech is not improbable in the ancient context, because kings (especially in the Egyptian context) considered themselves closely related to the nation's deities (cf. the Assyrian rhetoric in 2 Kgs 18:25). Josiah is presented as one who "refused to listen" to God's word; as a result, his life was cut short.

Neco's speech signals a key shift in the Chronicler's account. After this point, foreign emperors would control the political agenda of Judah, and various foreign emperors (the Egyptian Neco, the Babylonian Nebuchadnezzar, and the Persian Cyrus) will be identified as agents of Yahweh, either performing actions for Yahweh or speaking in his name. Josiah's death signals the death of the independent kingdom and the beginning of exile among the nations (Johnstone 1997:2.260).

The Chronicler is careful to protect the veracity of Huldah's prophetic word in 34:28, where she promised that Josiah would be "buried in peace," by clarifying that Josiah remained alive until he was safe in Jerusalem (the city of peace) where he died (cf. 2 Kgs 23:29-30). The Chronicler's words masterfully draw readers into the account, not only with the speech of Neco, but also with the dying words of Josiah (35:23). Special honor is given to the king as he is buried in the royal cemetery and "all Judah and Jerusalem" mourn for him, and even a prophetic figure (Jeremiah) composed poetic dirges for him, commemorating his death. These songs of sorrow were still being sung during the time of the Chronicler. Although foolish in his death, Josiah was still praised because of his great accomplishments for the Temple and worship in Israel.

Summary Note: The Reign of Josiah (35:26-27). The summary statement of Josiah cites only *The Book of the Kings of Israel and Judah.* A link is created with Hezekiah's reign with the mention not only of "the rest of the events" of his reign but also of "his acts of devotion" (*khesed* [TH2617, ZH2876]; cf. 32:32)—that is, acts of "covenant faithfulness." Hezekiah and Josiah were the only two kings in Chronicles who were given this evaluation in sections that are unique to the Chronicler.

ENDNOTES

1. See Dillard 1987:292; Japhet 1993:1043; Tuell 2001:241; Kalimi 2005b:23; Mitchell 2006.
2. There is no mention of an Assyrian army at Carchemish, so it may have only been Egypt that remained.

◆ R. The Reigns of Jehoahaz, Jehoiakim, Jehoiachin, Zedekiah, and the Fall of Jerusalem (36:1-23)

Then the people of the land took Josiah's son Jehoahaz and made him the next king in Jerusalem.

2 Jehoahaz* was twenty-three years old when he became king, and he reigned in Jerusalem three months.

3 Then he was deposed by the king of Egypt, who demanded that Judah pay 7,500 pounds of silver and 75 pounds of gold* as tribute.

4 The king of Egypt then installed Eliakim, the brother of Jehoahaz, as the next king of Judah and Jerusalem, and he changed Eliakim's name to Jehoiakim. Then Neco took Jehoahaz to Egypt as a prisoner.

5 Jehoiakim was twenty-five years old when he became king, and he reigned in Jerusalem eleven years. He did what was evil in the sight of the LORD his God.

6 Then King Nebuchadnezzar of Babylon came to Jerusalem and captured it, and he bound Jehoiakim in bronze chains and led him away to Babylon. 7 Nebuchadnezzar also took some of the treasures from the Temple of the LORD, and he placed them in his palace* in Babylon.

8 The rest of the events in Jehoiakim's reign, including all the evil things he did and everything found against him, are recorded in *The Book of the Kings of Israel and Judah.* Then his son Jehoiachin became the next king.

9 Jehoiachin was eighteen* years old when he became king, and he reigned in Jerusalem three months and ten days. Jehoiachin did what was evil in the LORD's sight.

10 In the spring of the year* King Nebuchadnezzar took Jehoiachin to Babylon. Many treasures from the Temple of the LORD were also taken to Babylon at that time. And Nebuchadnezzar installed Jehoiachin's uncle,* Zedekiah, as the next king in Judah and Jerusalem.

11 Zedekiah was twenty-one years old when he became king, and he reigned in Jerusalem eleven years. 12 He did what was evil in the sight of the LORD his God, and he refused to humble himself when the prophet Jeremiah spoke to him directly from the LORD. 13 He also rebelled against King Nebuchadnezzar, even though he had taken an oath of loyalty in God's name. Zedekiah was a hard and stubborn man, refusing to turn to the LORD, the God of Israel.

14 Likewise, all the leaders of the priests and the people became more and more unfaithful. They followed all the pagan practices of the surrounding nations, desecrating the Temple of the LORD that had been consecrated in Jerusalem.

15 The LORD, the God of their ancestors, repeatedly sent his prophets to warn them, for he had compassion on his people and his Temple. 16 But the people mocked these messengers of God and despised their words. They scoffed at the prophets until the LORD's anger could no longer be restrained and nothing could be done.

17 So the LORD brought the king of Babylon against them. The Babylonians* killed Judah's young men, even chasing after them into the Temple. They had no pity on the people, killing both young men and young women, the old and the infirm. God handed all of them over to Nebuchadnezzar. 18 The king took home to Babylon all the articles, large and small, used in the Temple of God, and the treasures from both the LORD's Temple and from the palace of the king and his officials. 19 Then his army burned the Temple of God, tore down the walls of Jerusalem, burned all the palaces, and completely destroyed everything of value.* 20 The few who survived were taken as exiles to Babylon, and they became servants to the king and his sons until the kingdom of Persia came to power.

21 So the message of the LORD spoken through Jeremiah was fulfilled. The land finally enjoyed its Sabbath rest, lying desolate until the seventy years were fulfilled, just as the prophet had said.

22 In the first year of King Cyrus of Persia,* the LORD fulfilled the prophecy he had given through Jeremiah.* He stirred the heart of Cyrus to put this proclamation in writing and to send it throughout his kingdom:

23 "This is what King Cyrus of Persia says:
"The LORD, the God of heaven, has given

me all the kingdoms of the earth. He has appointed me to build him a Temple at Jerusalem, which is in Judah. Any of you who are the LORD's people may go there for this task. And may the LORD your God be with you!"

36:2 Hebrew *Joahaz,* a variant spelling of Jehoahaz; also in 36:4. **36:3** Hebrew *100 talents* [3,400 kilograms] *of silver and 1 talent* [34 kilograms] *of gold.* **36:7** Or *temple.* **36:9** As in one Hebrew manuscript, some Greek manuscripts, and Syriac version (see also 2 Kgs 24:8); most Hebrew manuscripts read *eight.* **36:10a** Hebrew *At the turn of the year.* The first day of this year in the ancient Hebrew lunar calendar was April 13, 597 B.C. **36:10b** As in parallel text at 2 Kgs 24:17; Hebrew reads *brother,* or *relative.* **36:17** Or *Chaldeans.* **36:19** Or *destroyed all the valuable articles from the Temple.* **36:22a** The first year of Cyrus's reign over Babylon was 538 B.C. **36:22b** See Jer 25:11-12; 29:10.

NOTES

36:1 ***the people of the land.*** See note on 23:20.

36:6 ***and he bound Jehoiakim in bronze chains and led him away to Babylon.*** More precisely, the Hebrew here indicates that Jehoiakim was bound in chains "in order to transport him to Babylon" (see commentary below).

36:10 ***Jehoiachin's uncle, Zedekiah.*** Heb., *'akhiw* [TH251, ZH278]. This usually means "his brother," which would be consistent with his genealogy in 1 Chr 3:16 (see NLT mg). There is some confusion over Zedekiah's place in Josiah's family. The genealogy in 1 Chr 3:15-16 lists two men called Zedekiah, one the son of Josiah and the other the grandson of Josiah (son of Jehoiakim and brother of Jehoiachin). In 36:10 the Hebrew calls Zedekiah Jehoiachin's brother; 2 Kgs 24:17 in LXX calls Zedekiah a son of Jehoiachin; 36:10 in LXX and 2 Kgs 24:17 in Hebrew calls Zedekiah Jehoiachin's uncle. It is possible that the Zedekiah who ruled was actually Jehoiachin's brother, but most have taken the term "brother" in 36:10 in its broadest sense of "blood relation," as appears to be the case in the uncle-nephew relationship of Abraham and Lot (Gen 13:8; 14:16; 29:15; cf. 2 Sam 1:26 for its use for a close friend). See note on 1 Chr 3:16 and commentary on 1 Chr 3:1-24.

COMMENTARY

For the Chronicler, Josiah's death signaled the end of the independent kingdom of Judah. From this point on in the Chronicler's account, foreign emperors (Neco, Nebuchadnezzar, Cyrus) will act and speak for Yahweh, often closely linked with prophetic figures (36:12-13, 15-21, 22-23). The fact that three of his sons (as well as a grandson) are able to sit on the throne of Judah and do so for such short periods of time is evidence that the kingdom lived at the whim of imperial interests far greater than it. This final section of Chronicles contains short accounts of the last four kings of Judah: Jehoahaz (36:1-3), Jehoiakim (36:4-8), Jehoiachin (36:9-10), and Zedekiah (36:11-20), all of whom experienced exile to a foreign land. After a quick reference to how the Exile fulfilled the prophetic word and gave Sabbath rest to the land (36:21), the Chronicler recounts the invitation Cyrus gave for the people to return to the land in 539 BC.

The Chronicler shaped his account to accentuate parallels between the last four kings of Judah. None of the deaths of these kings are recorded by the Chronicler, even though the information was available for two of them in his source. Three of the four experienced exile in a foreign land: Jehoahaz to Egypt and Jehoiakim and Jehoiachin to Babylon (Zedekiah's exile is not specifically mentioned). The two kings who are exiled to Babylon were taken together with the treasures of the Temple, suggesting a link between their fates. This evidence suggests that the Chronicler was seeking to highlight (1) the enduring character of the royal line, (2) the line of Josiah-Jehoiakim-Jehoiachin as the legitimate royal line for Judah (see also 1 Chr 3:15-24), and (3) the inseparable link between the renewal of the Temple and the renewal of the royal house (Boda 2009b).

Reign of Jehoahaz (36:1-3). As noted in the commentary on chapter 35, the fall of Nineveh in 612 BC to Babylonian and Median forces was evidence of the advanced progress of a major political transition in the ancient Near East. The Assyrian royal family retreated to Haran, crowning Asshur-uballit as their new king. By 610–609 BC the Babylonians attacked Haran, forcing the Assyrians to flee to Carchemish to regroup and to await Egyptian reinforcements. They would never retake Haran (see 35:20-25).

Neco II killed Josiah on his way to assist the Assyrians against the Babylonians at Carchemish but was far too preoccupied with the Babylonian threat to venture an assault on insignificant Jerusalem after the defeat of Josiah's army. While Neco was engaging the Babylonians in support of the Assyrians, the "people of the land" (see note on 23:20) installed Josiah's son Jehoahaz as king, repeating the pattern already seen at the outset of the reign of Joash (23:13, 20-21) and of Josiah (33:25). Josiah's long reign meant that Jehoahaz was of sufficient age to reign (23 years old), but his reign (cf. Jer 22:11-17) would be cut short by Pharaoh Neco, who, having inherited the Levant with the demise of Assyria, had set up his headquarters at Riblah (2 Kgs 23:33). This city was in Aramean territory about midway between Carchemish and Israel; it is the same location that would host Nebuchadnezzar's military headquarters at the fall of Jerusalem (2 Kgs 25:6). According to 2 Kings 23:33-34, Jehoahaz was summoned to Riblah, deposed, put in chains, and ultimately sent into exile in Egypt, where he died (Jer 22:11-12). The sign of Egyptian hegemony over Judah is the imposition of the tribute demands described in 36:3. For some unexplained reason, the Chronicler ignored the evaluation of Jehoahaz in his source in 2 Kings 23:32, which identified him as one who was evil in the sight of the Lord.

Reign of Jehoiakim (36:4-8). Neco II made it clear from the outset that Eliakim was to rule as his puppet by changing his name to Jehoiakim. This brother of Jehoahaz and son of Josiah and ultimately father of Jehoiachin inherited the heavy tribute demands imposed by Neco (cf. Jer 22:18-23; 25:1–26:24; 36:1-32). Jehoiakim's age at accession was 25 years old, which shows that he was actually older than his brother Jehoahaz (1 Chr 3:15). This technicality may have provided an excuse for Neco to make an example of his brother and to install a candidate who would owe his throne to Egypt rather than Judah, a strategy that seemed to work as long as Egypt controlled the Levant and Jehoiakim reigned.

However, in 605 BC the Babylonians would set their sights on western Asia and defeat the Egyptians (and any Assyrian forces still in existence), first at Carchemish (Jer 46:2) and then at Hamath. Poised to conquer Egypt, Nebuchadnezzar, who was leading the Babylonian army, received word that his father Nabopolassar had died. This forced him to return to Babylon to assume the throne, sparing Egypt an invasion. From this point on, however, Babylon would control the Levant, as 2 Kings 24:7 notes: "The king of Egypt did not venture out of his country after that, for the king of Babylon captured the entire area formerly claimed by Egypt—from the Brook of Egypt to the Euphrates River."[1] This shift meant that Jehoiakim would need to submit to a new master, Babylon (36:6; 2 Kgs 24:1; see Dan 1:1-3 for the deportation at this time).

The Chronicler's account of Jehoiakim differs slightly from his source in 2 Kings 23:36–24:7. In both accounts this king is evaluated as "evil in the sight of the LORD," and in both accounts Nebuchadnezzar invades the land. In 2 Kings, however, a rebellion against Nebuchadnezzar after three years leads to an invasion of Jehoiakim's kingdom by a mixed force of peoples under Babylonian hegemony (Babylonians, Syrians, Moabites, Ammonites), which is seen as the fulfillment of God's judgment of the sins of Manasseh. Jehoiakim dies and is buried with his fathers, and his son Jehoiachin is enthroned. In contrast, the Chronicler ignores the description of Jehoiakim's rebellion against Nebuchadnezzar, creating an account where Babylonian aggression arises in direct relation to the Chronicler's evaluation of Jehoiakim in 36:5: "He did what was evil in the sight of the LORD his God," this evil being clarified by the Chronicler in 36:8 as "evil things" (*to'ebah* [TH8441, ZH9359]), the term used of the despicable acts of Ahaz (see 28:3 and note) and Manasseh (33:2; cf. 34:33). Jehoiakim was bound in chains and exiled to Babylon along with the treasures of the Temple.[2] The description of Jehoiakim in 36:6 is identical to the Chronicler's description of Manasseh in 33:11; through this the Chronicler provides Manasseh as a model for the reemergence of this disgraced yet chosen line of David (Boda 2009b). Hope for this renewal can be discerned in the absence of a death notice for Jehoiakim, a feature he shared with the other three kings who reigned after the death of Josiah, three of whom the Chronicler links explicitly to exile in a foreign land.

Reign of Jehoiachin (36:9-10). As did his uncle Jehoahaz, Jehoiachin survived a short time (three months and ten days) on the throne of Judah, but unlike his uncle, Jehoiachin's negative evaluation is carried over by the Chronicler from his source in 2 Kings. The Chronicler shortened this account significantly, transforming an account of a successful siege against Jerusalem, despoliation of Temple and palace, and deportation of the elite by Nebuchadnezzar, which covers seven verses in 2 Kings, into less than one verse that focuses entirely on Jehoiachin's exile to Babylon along with the treasures of the Temple.[3] One reason for this may be to focus his account on the exile of each of the kings to foreign lands and the fate of the Temple treasures for each of the last three kings. Another reason may be that the Chronicler was seeking to make the Babylonian attack under Zedekiah the most devastating of all, possibly because he traced the line of David through Jehoiachin and not Zedekiah (see commentary on 1 Chr 3:15-24). The vocabulary used to describe Jehoiachin's exile in 36:10 and Ezekiel 19:9 is identical to that used for Manasseh in 33:11 (Abadie 2003:102). As he did in the account of Jehoiakim, once again the Chronicler provides Manasseh as a model of repentance for the exiled Davidic line (Boda 2009b).

Nebuchadnezzar's attack on Jerusalem and replacement of Jehoiachin with Zedekiah is recorded in a Babylonian source and dated to 597 BC. It claims that in the seventh year of his reign Nebuchadnezzar marched to "the city of Judah"

(*Ya-a-hu-du;* i.e., Jerusalem), and on the second of Adar, he captured the city and its king, appointed "a king of his choosing," and received heavy tribute (COS 1.468).

The Reign of Zedekiah and Fall of Jerusalem (36:11-20). As was true with Jehoiakim, the one who was placed on the throne by a foreign power had an opportunity to elongate his reign as long as he was satisfied with his submissive posture. Zedekiah matched Jehoiakim's longevity, reigning for 11 years (cf. Jer 27:1–28:17; 34:1-22; 37:1–38:28). As with his two predecessors, Zedekiah was evaluated negatively, although the comparison to Jehoiakim found in his source in 2 Kings 24:19b is not mentioned. In its place, the Chronicler describes Zedekiah's defiance of the prophetic voice of Jeremiah, not surprising in light of the Chronicler's penchant for portrayals of the prophets in his work as a whole.

As with Neco in the account of Josiah's death, so now the Chronicler intertwines a foreign king (here Nebuchadnezzar) with Yahweh, narrating that Zedekiah had sworn loyalty by God and then had rebelled. The terms that follow—"he stiffened his neck and hardened his heart" (NLT, "was a hard and stubborn man")—are associated with the refusal to listen to God's prophets who called the people to repent. Zedekiah's rebellion against Nebuchadnezzar became an expression of rebellion against Yahweh.[4]

Zedekiah is joined by the "leaders of the priests and the people" (36:14), who committed sins that are portrayed as abhorrent throughout the Chronicler's account; thus, they are characterized as being "unfaithful" (*ma'al* [TH4603, ZH5085]), doing "pagan practices" (*to'ebah* [TH8441, ZH9359]) that are "desecrating" (*tame'* [TH2930, ZH3237]). By mentioning the priests and not the Levites, the Chronicler lays blame at the feet of the priestly orders, justifying his special emphasis on the Levites throughout.

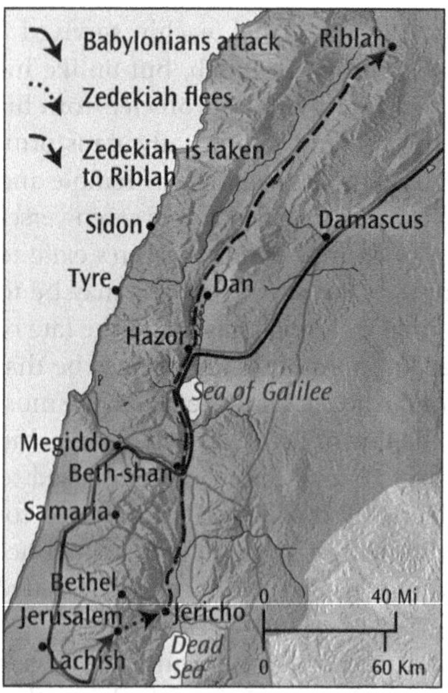

The Babylonian Invasions of Judah, 605–586 BC

As has been the case often throughout the Chronicler's work, the Chronicler presents the repeated appeal of Yahweh through his prophets. This is identified by the Chronicler in 36:15 as an expression of his compassion (*khamal* [TH2550, ZH2798]) toward his people, as well as (not surprisingly for the Chronicler) his Temple. But the people rejected these prophets, mocking, despising, and scoffing at them, actions that left Yahweh with no choice but to bring judgment upon Jerusalem.

The fall of Jerusalem (587/586) is summarized briefly in the Chronicler's account compared to his source in 2 Kings. His descriptions usually begin with the Temple and then move out to the city as a whole. Thus, he begins the description of the massacre of the people who had sought sanctuary in the Temple (36:17), then moves out to the rest of the populace. He begins the description of the despoliation of the treasures (36:18) with those in the Temple and then moves out to those within the palace. Finally, he begins the account of the destruction of the city (36:19) with the conflagration of the Temple and then moves out to the rest of the city. As for the exile of the people (36:20), the Chronicler made no such distinction, but rather concluded with the general statement about "the few who survived."

Sabbath Rest of the Land (36:21). In line with the Chronicler's emphasis on the prophetic role throughout his account, the exile of the people is interpreted as a fulfillment of the word of Jeremiah that the Exile would last 70 years (Jer 25:12; 29:10; cf. Dan 9:2; Zech 1:12; 7:5). The fall of Zedekiah's kingdom to the Babylonians in 36:11-21 is dated to the year 587/586 BC, and the first year of Cyrus's reign over the former Babylonian Empire can be dated to 539 BC. The period of exile, then, according to the events in chapter 36 was not even 50 years, far short of the 70 that the Chronicler notes on two occasions (36:21, 22). It must be noted that "seventy years" probably functions as a round figure in ancient literature. This figure is often linked to the length of a king's reign (Isa 23:15-18) or length of a human life (Ps 90:10); it is connected with the length of the destruction of a city in the ancient world.[5]

Johnstone (1997:2.260), however, has argued that the Chronicler probably has a precise 70 years in mind. The Chronicler identifies the death of Josiah as the key transition in the late history of Judah, an event that marks a permanent loss of independence, thus movement from kingdom to exilic status (see commentary on ch 34 and 35:20-25). Using the death of Josiah (in 609 BC) as the beginning of exile, Johnstone argues that the Chronicler's 70 years end precisely in 539 BC in the first year of Cyrus, king of Persia.

The Chronicler also links the 70 years to priestly legislation (see Lev 25; cf. Exod 23:11; Deut 15:2-18; Neh 10:31; Jer 34:14-22). The exile of the people from the land allowed the land to remain fallow and finally enjoy the Sabbaths that had been commanded through Moses. In this way the Exile cleansed the land through careful observance of Sabbath practice and prepared it for the new day of restoration in which the Chronicler's audience presently lived.

Invitation from Cyrus to Return (36:22-23). The book of Chronicles ends by quoting the first few verses of the book of Ezra (Ezra 1:1-3): the account of Cyrus's proclamation inviting the exiles to return to Judah.[6] Cyrus is the third foreign emperor to act or speak as an agent of Yahweh (who "stirred the heart of Cyrus") in the final phase of Judah's history (cf. Neco in 35:21-22; Nebuchadnezzar in 36:12-13). Cyrus spoke to a community that had lived in the wake of the fall of their state. Immediately after the fall of Jerusalem (587/586), the Babylonians organized Judah as a province of the empire, appointing a Jewish governor named Gedaliah over them (Jer 39–43). His tenure was short-lived because he was soon assassinated; this resulted in a further deportation of people from the land (581 BC; Jer 52:30). Whether in exile or in their own land, the people of Judah would live under Babylonian hegemony until 539 BC, when Cyrus II would cross the Zagros mountains, ford the Tigris at Opis, conquer Babylon, and dethrone its emperor Nabonidus and his son Belshazzar (see Dan 5;

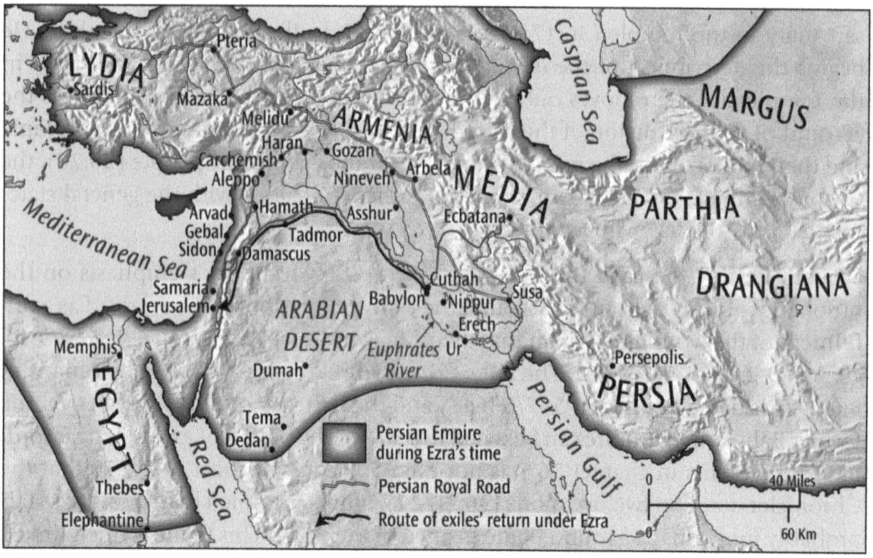

The Persian Empire of Cyrus II, 539–530 BC, with the Path of Ezra's Return

Boda 2004:23-29). At that moment the land of Judah and its exiles spread throughout Mesopotamia; the peoples of western Asia would become subjects of the Persians.

There is little need to doubt the veracity of this proclamation, especially in light of ancient documents like the Cyrus Cylinder, a clay barrel found in Mesopotamia in which Cyrus describes the initial phase of his inclusion of the Babylonian kingdom into his empire. In it he describes how he restored gods to their sanctuaries, rebuilt their temples, and returned their people. For the worship of Yahweh only the latter two actions were appropriate, although we do see in Ezra 1 that Cyrus also restored the Temple vessels to the land, possibly seen as the closest equivalent to the gods of the other peoples. This proclamation in chapter 36 and Ezra 1 is the message declared to the Jewish exiles in Mesopotamia. Ezra 6:1-5 contains the official Aramaic document that was the basis for this proclamation (cf. Williamson 1985:6-7; 1999:236-265).

Kalimi (2005a:148-155) offers several reasons for the placement of the proclamation in the final place in the book. First, it shows the fulfillment of God's word in history. The prophetic word related to priestly law was used to give meaning to the Exile in 36:21, and it is the prophetic word that assured the new era of restoration. Second, the full account of this proclamation can be read in Ezra 1, where it is apparent that the Chronicler borrowed the first half of the proclamation from that book, especially because the final line of the Chronicler's version cuts off half way through a sentence. In the Hebrew text the final words of the book are "and let him go up," which is completed in Ezra as "to Jerusalem in Judah to rebuild this Temple of the LORD, the God of Israel" (Ezra 1:3). This technique of stopping midsentence "could be seen as a practical 'Zionistic' encouragement of the Chronicler for immigration. . . . This mission was desirable in the time of the Chronicler as in early post-exilic time" (Kalimi 2005a:153). It also suggests that rebuilding was no longer the issue in the Chronicler's day; the focus was on continued return from exile and support for the Temple and its services. Third, it stresses at the book's conclusion that "the destruction and exile are not the end of history but merely necessary steps to achieve purification of the land in order to create a new hopeful beginning for the nation" (Kalimi 2005a:154). The Chronicler began his history with Adam (1 Chr 1:1); then in his first chapter he traced how Israel emerged from the nations. In his concluding chapter, he shows how Israel, assimilated among the nations through disciplinary exile, reemerged at the command of Yahweh prophesied by Jeremiah and proclaimed by Cyrus.

ENDNOTES

1. This did not mean that Egypt ceased being a player in western Asia. Ezekiel 17:11-18 suggests that Zedekiah was tempted to turn to Egypt for help against Babylon.
2. The Hebrew text does not actually say that Jehoiakim went into exile but rather that Nebuchadnezzar "bound him with bronze chains to transport him to Babylon." It may be that he died before even leaving Jerusalem, as the text in 2 Kings may indicate.
3. See the Babylonian Chronicle, which describes actions by Babylonian leaders from the mid-eighth century BC until the second century BC and records in Nebuchadnezzar's seventh year (598–597 BC) that he "called out his army and marched to Hattu. He set his camp against the city of Judah [Ya-a-hu-du], and on 2nd Adar he took the city and captured the king. He appointed a king of his choosing there, took heavy tribute and returned to Babylon" (COS 1.468). The Weidner Tablets (ANET 308) represent administrative documents that record the daily rations of Jehoiachin and his sons during the reign of Nebuchadnezzar (see commentary on 1 Chr 3:1-24 for the text of these tablets). See also the report of Jehoiachin's release and support under Nebuchadnezzar's son Amel-Marduk (Heb., Evil-merodach) in 2 Kgs 25:27-30.
4. Ezekiel 17:11-18 claims that Zedekiah sought help from Egypt, an act that may have prompted Nebuchadnezzar's response.
5. On the Black Stone of Esarhaddon the 70 years refers to the length of desolation for the city of Babylon, which was later reduced to only 11 years by turning the tablet upside down (see Borger 1967:12-19; cf. Boda 2004:198-199; Leuchter 2004).
6. Williamson (1982:419) considers that the "Chronicler's own work finished at 36:21" so that the final two verses "have been added subsequently from Ezra 1:1-3." In his opinion, this addition was probably motivated by liturgical reasons and provided a less pessimistic ending to the book. It also directs the reader to the continuation of the story in Ezra. A slight change can be discerned in the citation from Ezra 1:1-3 ("through [the mouth of] Jeremiah" in Ezra 1:1 is *mippi* [TH4480/6310, ZH4946/7023], whereas in 36:22 it is *bepi* [TH871.2/6310, ZH928/7023]), and this change is identical to the phrase used in 36:21 ("through Jeremiah," *bepi*). Williamson (1977b:9) concludes that "the form in Chr. might well have been influenced by the preceding verse." In response it may be said that the reason for this change is because the same person responsible for 36:21 is the one who completed the book and copied the concluding piece from Ezra 1:1-3.

BIBLIOGRAPHY

Abadie, Philippe

2003 From the Impious Manasseh (2 Kings 21) to the Convert Manasseh (2 Chronicles 33): Theological Rewriting by the Chronicler. Pp. 89-104 in *The Chronicler as Theologian: Essays in Honour of Ralph W. Klein.* Editors, M. Patrick Graham, Steven L. McKenzie, and Gary N. Knoppers. Journal for the Study of the Old Testament Supplement 371. Sheffield: Sheffield Academic.

Achtemeier, Paul J., editor

1996 *The HarperCollins Bible Dictionary.* San Francisco: HarperSanFrancisco.

Ackroyd, Peter R.

1973 *I & II Chronicles, Ezra, Nehemiah.* Torch Bible Commentaries. London: SCM.

1977 The Chronicler as Exegete. *Journal for the Study of the Old Testament* 2:2-32.

Aharoni, Yohanan, et al.

2002 *The Carta Bible Atlas.* Jerusalem: Carta.

Allen, Leslie C.

1974 *The Greek Chronicles: The Relation of the Septuagint of I and II Chronicles to the Massoretic Text.* Vetus Testamentum Supplement 25, 27. Leiden: Brill.

1999 *The First and Second Book of Chronicles.* New Interpreter's Bible 3. Nashville: Abingdon.

Anbar, M.

1988 La "Reprise." *Vetus Testamentum* 38:385-398.

Andreasen, N. A.

1983 The Role of the Queen Mother in Israelite Society. *Catholic Biblical Quarterly* 45:179-194.

Aufrecht, Walter E.

1988 Genealogy and History in Ancient Israel. Pp. 205-235 in *Ascribe to the Lord: Biblical and Other Studies in Memory of Peter C. Craigie.* Editors, L. Eslinger and G. Taylor. Journal for the Study of the Old Testament Supplement 67. Sheffield: Journal for the Study of the Old Testament Press.

Auld, A. Graeme

2000a Joshua and 1 Chronicles. Pp. 132-140 in *Studies in Historical Geography and Biblical Historiography: Presented to Zecharia Kallai.* Editors, Gershon Galil and Moshe Weinfeld. Vetus Testamentum Supplement. Leiden: E. J. Brill.

2000b What If the Chronicler Did Use the Deuteronomistic History? *Biblical Interpretation* 8:137-150.

Avigad, N.

1976 *Bullae and Seals from a Post-exilic Judean Archive.* Qedem 4. Jerusalem: Hebrew University.

1980 The Chief of the Corvée. *Israel Exploration Journal* 30:170-173.

Bailey, Noel

1994 David's Innocence: A Response to J. Wright. *Journal for the Study of the Old Testament* 64:83-90.

1999 David and God in 1 Chronicles 21: Edged with Mist. Pp. 337-359 in *The Chronicler as Author: Studies in Text and Texture.* Editors, M. Patrick Graham and Steven L. McKenzie. Journal for the Study of the Old Testament Supplement 263. Sheffield: Sheffield Academic.

Baltzer, Klaus

1971 *The Covenant Formulary in Old Testament, Jewish and Early Christian Writings.* Oxford: Blackwell.

Beitzel, Barry J.

1985 *The Moody Atlas of Bible Lands.* Chicago: Moody.

Bendor, S.

1996 *The Social Structure of Ancient Israel: The Institution of the Family (Beit 'Ab) from the Settlement to the End of the Monarchy.* Jerusalem Biblical Studies 7. Jerusalem: Simor.

Ben Zvi, Ehud

1993 A Gateway to the Chronicler's Teaching: The Account of the Reign of Ahaz in 2 Chr 28,1-27. *Scandinavian Journal of the Old Testament* 7:216-249.

2002 The Book of Chronicles: Another Look. *Studies in Religion/Sciences Religieuses* 31:261-281.

2003 The Secession of the Northern Kingdom in Chronicles: Accepted "Facts" and New Meanings. Pp. 61-88 in *The Chronicler as Theologian: Essays in Honour of Ralph W. Klein.* Editors, M. Patrick Graham, Steven L. McKenzie, and Gary N. Knoppers. Journal for the Study of the Old Testament Supplement 371. Sheffield: Sheffield Academic.

Biran, Avraham

1974 Tel Dan. *Biblical Archaeologist* 37:26-51.

Blenkinsopp, Joseph

1972 *Gibeon and Israel: The Role of Gibeon and the Gibeonites in the Political and Religious History of Early Israel.* Cambridge: Cambridge University Press.

Blomberg, Craig

2007 Matthew. Pp. 1-109 in *Commentary on the New Testament Use of the Old Testament.* Editors, G. K. Beale and D. A. Carson. Grand Rapids / Nottingham: Baker Academic / Apollos.

Boda, Mark J.

1996 Chiasmus in Ubiquity: Symmetrical Mirages in Nehemiah 9. *Journal for the Study of the Old Testament* 71:55-70.

1999 *Praying the Tradition: The Origin and Use of Tradition in Nehemiah 9.* Beihefte zur Zeitschrift für die alttestamentliche Wissenschaft 277. Berlin: Walter de Gruyter.

2001 From Complaint to Contrition: Peering through the Liturgical Window of Jer 14,1–15,4. *Zeitschrift für die alttestamentliche Wissenschaft* 113:186-197.

2003a From Fasts to Feasts: The Literary Function of Zechariah 7–8. *Catholic Biblical Quarterly* 65:390-407.

2003b The Priceless Gain of Penitence: From Communal Lament to Penitential Prayer in the "Exilic" Liturgy of Israel. *Horizons in Biblical Theology* 25:51-75.

2003c Reading Between the Lines: Zechariah 11:4-16 in Its Literary Contexts. Pp. 277-291 in *Bringing Out the Treasure: Inner Biblical Allusion and Zechariah 9–14.* Editors, Mark J. Boda and Michael H. Floyd. Journal for the Study of the Old Testament Supplement 304. Sheffield: Sheffield Academic.

2003d Zechariah: Master Mason or Penitential Prophet? Pp. 49-69 in *Yahwism after the Exile: Perspectives on Israelite Religion in the Persian Era.* Editors, Bob Becking and Rainer Albertz. Studies in Theology and Religion 5. Assen: Royal Van Gorcum.

2004 *Haggai/Zechariah.* Grand Rapids: Zondervan.

2005a Prayer. Pp. 806-811 in *Dictionary of the Old Testament: Historical Books.* Editors, Bill T. Arnold, H. G. M. Williamson, and Daniel G. Reid. Downers Grove, IL: InterVarsity.

2005b Terrifying the Horns: Persia and Babylon in Zechariah 1:7–6:15. *Catholic Biblical Quarterly* 67:22-41.

2006a Confession as Theological Expression: Ideological Origins of Penitential Prayer. Pp. 21-50 in *Seeking the Favor of God: Volume 1—The Origin of Penitential Prayer in Second Temple Judaism.* Editors, Mark J. Boda, Daniel K. Falk, and Rodney A. Werline. Early Judaism and Its Literature 21. Atlanta: Society of Biblical Literature.

2006b Form Criticism in Transition: Penitential Prayer and Lament, *Sitz im Leben* and Form. Pp. 181-192 in *Seeking the Favor of God: Volume 1—The Origin of Penitential Prayer in Second Temple Judaism.* Editors, Mark J. Boda, Daniel K. Falk, and Rodney A. Werline. Early Judaism and Its Literature 21. Atlanta: Society of Biblical Literature.

2006c From Dystopia to Myopia: Utopian (re)visions in Haggai and Zechariah 1–8. Pp. 211-249 in *Utopia and Dystopia in Prophetic Literature.* Editor, Ehud Ben Zvi. Publications of the Finnish Exegetical Society 92. Helsinki / Göttingen: Finnish Exegetical Society / Vandenhoeck & Ruprecht.

2006d Oil, Crowns and Thrones: Prophet, Priest and King in Zechariah 1:7–6:15. Pp. 379-404 in *Perspectives on Hebrew Scriptures.* Editor, Ehud Ben Zvi. Piscataway, NJ: Gorgias Press.

2007a *After God's Own Heart: The Gospel according to David.* Gospel according to the Old Testament. Phillipsburg, NJ: Presbyterian & Reformed.

2007b Haggai, Book of. Pp. 715-718 in *The New Interpreter's Dictionary of the Bible.* Editor, K. D. Sakenfield. Nashville: Abingdon.

2008 Redaction in the Book of Nehemiah: A Fresh Proposal. Pp. 25-54 in *Unity and Disunity of Ezra-Nehemiah: Redaction, Rhetoric, Reader.* Editors, Mark J. Boda and Paul Redditt. Hebrew Bible Monographs. Sheffield: Sheffield Phoenix.

2009a Declare His Glory among the Nations: The Psalter as Missional Collection in *Christian Mission: Old Testament Foundations and New Testament Developments.* Editors, Stanley E. Porter and Cynthia Long Westfall. Grand Rapids: Eerdmans.

2009b Identity and Empire, Reality and Hope in the Chronicler's Perspective. Pp. 249-272 in *Community Identity in Judean Historiography: Biblical and Comparative Perspectives.* Editors, Gary Knoppers and Ken Ristau. Winona Lake, IN: Eisenbrauns.

2009c Legitimizing the Temple: The Chronicler's Temple Building Account. Forthcoming in *From the Foundations to the Crenellations: Essays on Temple Building in the Ancient Near East and Hebrew Bible.* Editors, Mark J. Boda and Jamie R. Novotny. Alter Orient und Altes Testament. Münster: Ugarit-Forschungen Verlag.

2009d *A Severe Mercy: Sin and Its Remedy in the Old Testament.* Siphrut: Literature and Theology of the Hebrew Scriptures. Winona Lake, IN: Eisenbrauns.

Forthcoming-a Judges in *Expositors Bible Commentary, Volume 2: Numbers—Ruth.* Editors, Tremper Longman III and David E. Garland. Grand Rapids: Zondervan.

Forthcoming-b Walking in the Light of Yahweh: Zion and the Empires in the Book of Isaiah. Forthcoming in *Empire in the New Testament.* Editors, Stanley E. Porter and Cynthia Long Westfall. McMaster New Testament Studies. Grand Rapids: Eerdmans.

Boda, Mark J., and Jamie R. Novotny, editors

2009 *From the Foundations to the Crenellations: Essays on Temple Building in the Ancient Near East and Hebrew Bible.* Alter Orient und Altes Testament. Münster: Ugarit-Forschungen Verlag.

Boda, Mark J., and Paul Redditt, editors

2008 *Unity and Disunity of Ezra-Nehemiah: Redaction, Rhetoric, Reader.* Hebrew Bible Monographs. Sheffield: Sheffield Phoenix Press.

Borger, Riekele

1967 *Die Inschriften Asarhaddons, Königs von Assyrien.* Archiv für Orientforschung 9. Osnabrèuck: Biblio-Verlag.

Braun, Roddy L.

1971 Message of Chronicles: Rally 'round the Temple. *Concordia Theological Monthly* 42:502-514.

1973 Solomonic Apologetic in Chronicles. *Journal of Biblical Literature* 92:503-516.

1976 Solomon, the Chosen Temple Builder: The Significance of 1 Chronicles 22, 28, and 29 for the Theology of Chronicles. *Journal of Biblical Literature* 95:581-590.

1979 Chronicles, Ezra and Nehemiah: Theology and Literary History. Pp. 52-64 in *Studies in the Historical Books of the Old Testament.* Editor, J. A. Emerton. Vetus Testamentum Supplement 30. Leiden: E. J. Brill.

1986 *1 Chronicles.* Word Biblical Commentary 14. Waco: Word Books.

Briant, Pierre

2002 *From Cyrus to Alexander: A History of the Persian Empire.* Translator, Peter T. Daniels. Winona Lake, IN: Eisenbrauns.

Brueggemann, Walter

1984 *The Message of the Psalms: A Theological Commentary.* Augsburg Old Testament Studies. Minneapolis: Augsburg.

1997 *Theology of the Old Testament: Testimony, Dispute, Advocacy.* Minneapolis: Fortress.

Brueggemann, Walter, and Patrick D. Miller

1995 *The Psalms and the Life of Faith.* Minneapolis: Fortress.

Clapp, Rodney, and John Wright

2002 God as Santa. *Christian Century* 119:29-31.

Cogan, Mordechai

1979 The Men of Nebo—Repatriated Reubenites. *Israel Exploration Journal* 29:37-39.

Cross, F. M.

1975 A Reconstruction of the Judean Restoration. *Journal of Biblical Literature* 94:4-18.

Curtis, Edward Lewis, and Albert Alonzo Madsen

1910 *A Critical and Exegetical Commentary on the Books of Chronicles.* Edinburgh: Scribner.

Davies, W. D., and Dale C. Allison

1988 *A Critical and Exegetical Commentary on the Gospel According to Matthew.* International Critical Commentary. Edinburgh: T&T Clark.

Day, John

2000 *Yahweh and the Gods and Goddesses of Canaan.* Journal for the Study of the Old Testament Supplement 265. Sheffield: Sheffield Academic.

De Vries, Simon J.
1988 Moses and David as Cult Founders in Chronicles. *Journal of Biblical Literature* 107:619-639.

1989 *1 and 2 Chronicles*. Forms of Old Testament Literature 11. Grand Rapids: Eerdmans.

Deboys, David G.
1990 History and Theology in the Chronicler's Portrayal of Abijah. *Biblica* 71:48-62.

Demsky, Aaron
1982 The Genealogies of Manasseh and the Location of the Territory of Milcah Daughter of Zelophehad. *Eretz Israel* 16:70-75.

Dillard, Raymond B.
1980 The Reign of Asa (2 Chr 14-16): An Example of the Chronicler's Theological Method. *Journal of the Evangelical Theological Society* 23:207-218.

1981 The Chronicler's Solomon. *Westminster Theological Journal* 43:289-300.

1984a The Literary Structure of the Chronicler's Solomon Narrative. *Journal for the Study of the Old Testament* 30:85-93.

1984b Reward and Punishment in Chronicles: The Theology of Immediate Retribution. *Westminster Theological Journal* 46:164-172.

1986 The Chronicler's Jehoshaphat. *Trinity Journal* New Series 7:17-22.

1987 *2 Chronicles*. Word Biblical Commentary 15. Waco: Word Books.

Dragga, Sam
1987 In the Shadow of the Judges: The Failure of Saul. *Journal for the Study of the Old Testament* 38:39-46.

Duke, Rodney K.
1990 *The Persuasive Appeal of the Chronicler: A Rhetorical Analysis*. Journal for the Study of the Old Testament Supplement 88. Sheffield: Almond.

Edelman, Diana
1991 The Manassite Genealogy of 1 Chronicles 7:14-19: Form and Source. *Catholic Biblical Quarterly* 53:179-201.

Ellis, Richard S.
1968 *Foundation Deposits in Ancient Mesopotamia*. Yale Near Eastern Researches. New Haven, CT: Yale.

Elmslie, William Alexander Leslie
1916 *The Books of Chronicles, with Maps, Notes, and Introduction*. 2nd ed. The Cambridge Bible for Schools and Colleges 12a. Cambridge: Cambridge University Press.

Eskenazi, Tamara Cohn
1988 *In an Age of Prose: A Literary Approach to Ezra-Nehemiah*. Atlanta: Scholars Press.

Evans, D. G.
1966 Rehoboam's Advisers at Shechem and Political Institutions in Israel and Sumer. *Journal of Near Eastern Studies* 25:273-279.

Evans, Paul
2005 Divine Intermediaries in 1 Chronicles 21: An Overlooked Aspect of the Chronicler's Theology. *Biblica* 85:545-558.

2008 Sennacherib's 701 Invasion into Judah: What Saith the Scriptures? Pp. 57-77 in *The Function of Ancient Historiography in Biblical and Cognate Studies*. Editors, Patricia G. Kirkpatrick and Timothy Goltz. Library of Hebrew Bible/Old Testament Studies 489. London: T&T Clark.

2009 *Sennacherib's Invasion in the Book of Kings: A Source-critical and Rhetorical Study of 2 Kings 18–19*. Vetus Testamentum Supplement. Leiden: E. J. Brill.

Flanagan, James W.
1979 The Relocation of the Davidic Capital. *Journal of the American Academy of Religion* 47:223-244.

1982 Genealogy and Dynasty in the Early Monarchy of Israel and Judah. Pp. 23-28 in *Proceedings of the Eighth World Congress of Jewish Studies. Division A: The Period of the Bible*. Jerusalem: World Union of Jewish Studies.

Fohrer, G.
1952 Die Gattung der Berichte über symbolische Handlungen der Propheten. *Zeitschrift für die alttestamentliche Wissenschaft* 64:101-120.

1968 *Die symbolische Handlungen der Propheten*. 2nd ed. Abhandlungen zur Theologie des Alten und Neuen Testaments 54. Zurich: Zwingli Verlag.

Fox, M.
1973 Tôb as Covenant Terminology. *Bulletin of the American Schools of Oriental Research* 209:41-42.

Freedman, David Noel
1961 The Chronicler's Purpose. *Catholic Biblical Quarterly* 23:436-442.

Friebel, Kelvin G.
1999 *Jeremiah's and Ezekiel's Sign-acts.* Journal for the Study of the Old Testament Supplement 283. Sheffield: Sheffield Academic.

2001 A Hermeneutical Paradigm for Interpreting Prophetic Sign-actions. *Didaskalia* 12.2:25-45.

Glatt-Gilad, David
2001 Regnal Formulae as a Historiographic Device in the Book of Chronicles. *Revue Biblique* 108:184-209.

Goldingay, John
2006 *Israel's Faith.* Downers Grove, IL: InterVarsity Press.

Gundry, Robert H.
1967 *The Use of the Old Testament in St. Matthew's Gospel: With Special Reference to the Messianic Hope.* Supplements to Novum Testamentum 18. Leiden: Brill.

Gurney, O. R.
1957 The Sultantepe Tablets (continued), VI. A Letter of Gilgamesh. *Anatolian Studies* 7:127-136.

Halpern, Baruch
1981 Sacred History and Ideology: Chronicles' Thematic Structure: Indications of an Earlier Source. Pp. 35-54 in *The Creation of Sacred Literature: Composition and Redaction of the Biblical Text.* Editor, Richard E. Friedman. Berkeley: University of California Press.

Hanson, Paul D.
1968 Song of Heshbon and David's Nir. *Harvard Theological Review* 61:297-320.

Harper, Robert F.
1904 *Assyrian and Babylonian Literature: Selected Translations.* New York: D. Appleton & Co.

Hess, Richard S.
2007 *Israelite Religions: An Archaeological and Biblical Survey.* Grand Rapids / Nottingham: Baker Academic / Apollos.

Hess, Richard S., and Gordon J. Wenham, editors
1999 *Zion, City of Our God.* Grand Rapids: Eerdmans.

Hill, Andrew E.
2003 *1 & 2 Chronicles.* The NIV Application Commentary. Grand Rapids, MI: Zondervan.

Hillers, Delbert R.
1964 *Treaty Curses and the Old Testament Prophets.* Biblical et Orientalia 16. Rome: Pontifical Biblical Institute.

1969 *Covenant: The History of a Biblical Idea.* Baltimore: Johns Hopkins.

Holmgren, Fredrick C.
1992 Faithful Abraham and the 'amanâ Covenant: Nehemiah 9,6-10,1. *Zeitschrift für die alttestamentliche Wissenschaft* 104:249-254.

Hoppe, Leslie J.
2000 *The Holy City: Jerusalem in the Theology of the Old Testament.* Collegeville, MN: Liturgical Press.

Hurowitz, Victor Avigdor
1985 The Priestly Account of Building the Tabernacle. *Journal of the American Oriental Society* 105:21-30.

1992 *I Have Built You an Exalted House: Temple Building in the Bible in Light of Mesopotamian and North-West Semitic Writings.* Journal for the Study of the Old Testament Supplement 115. Sheffield: Sheffield Academic.

1993 Temporary Temples. Pp. 37-50 in *Raphael Kutscher Memorial Volume.* Editor, Anson F. Rainey. Tel Aviv: Tel Aviv University.

Hurvitz, Avi
1982 A Linguistic Study of the Relationship between the Priestly Source and the Book of Ezekiel: A New Approach to an Old Problem. *Cahiers de la Revue biblique* 20. Paris: J. Gabalda.

Japhet, Sara
1968 The Supposed Common Authorship of Chronicles and Ezra-Nehemiah Investigated Anew. *Vetus Testamentum* 18:330-371.

1979 Conquest and Settlement in Chronicles. *Journal of Biblical Literature* 98:205-218.

1985 Historical Reliability of Chronicles: History of the Problem and Its Place in Biblical Research. *Journal for the Study of the Old Testament* 33:83-107.

1988 Law and "the Law" in Ezra-Nehemiah. Pp. 99-115 in *Proceedings of the Ninth World Congress of Jewish Studies*. Editor, Moshe H. Goshen-Gottstein. Jerusalem: Magnes.

1989 *The Ideology of the Book of Chronicles and Its Place in Biblical Thought*. Beiträge zur Erforschung des Alten Testaments und des antiken Judentums 9. Frankfurt am Main: Peter Lang.

1993 *I & II Chronicles: A Commentary*. Old Testament Library. Louisville: Westminster/John Knox.

2006 The Wall of Jerusalem from a Double Perspective: Kings versus Chronicles. Pp. 205-219 in *Essays on Ancient Israel in Its Near Eastern Context: A tribute to Nadav Na'aman*. Editors, Yaira Amit, Ehud Ben Zvi, Israel Finkelstein, and Oded Lipschits. Winona Lake, IN: Eisenbrauns.

Jenson, Philip P.

1992 *Graded Holiness: A Key to the Priestly Conception of the World*. Journal for the Study of the Old Testament Supplement 106. Sheffield: Journal for the Study of the Old Testament Press.

Johnson, Aubrey Rodway

1962 *The Cultic Prophet in Ancient Israel*. Cardiff: University of Wales.

1979 *The Cultic Prophet and Israel's Psalmody*. Cardiff: University of Wales.

Johnson, Marshall D.

1988 *The Purpose of the Biblical Genealogies: With Special Reference to the Setting of the Genealogies of Jesus*. 2nd ed. Cambridge: Cambridge University Press.

Johnstone, William

1997 *1 and 2 Chronicles*. Journal for the Study of the Old Testament Supplement 253-254. Sheffield: Sheffield Academic.

1998 *Chronicles and Exodus: An Analogy and Its Application*. Journal for the Study of the Old Testament Supplement 275. Sheffield: Sheffield Academic.

Kalimi, Isaac

2002 The View of Jerusalem in the Ethnographical Introduction of Chronicles (1 Chr 1–9). *Biblica* 83:556-562.

2005a An Ancient Israelite Historian: Studies in the Chronicler, His Time, Place and Writing. *Studia Semitica Neerlandica* 46. Assen: Royal Van Gorcum.

2005b *The Reshaping of Ancient Israelite History in Chronicles*. Winona Lake, IN: Eisenbrauns.

Kaminsky, Joel S.

1995 *Corporate Responsibility in the Hebrew Bible*. Journal for the Study of the Old Testament Supplement 196. Sheffield: Sheffield Academic.

1997 The Sins of the Fathers: A Theological Investigation of the Biblical Tension between Corporate and Individualized Retribution. *Judaism* 46:319-332.

Kang, S-M.

1989 *Divine War in the Old Testament and in the Ancient Near East*. Beihefte zur Zeitschrift für die alttestamentliche Wissenschaft 177. Berlin: de Gruyter.

Kapelrud, A.

1963 Temple Building: A Task for Gods and Kings. *Orientalia* 32:56-62.

Kartveit, M.

1989 *Motive und Schichten der Landtheologie in I Chronik 1 9*. Coniectanea Biblica Old Testament Series 28. Stockholm: Almqvist & Wiksell.

Katzenstein, H. Jacob

1973 *The History of Tyre, from the Beginning of the Second Millennium B.C.E. until the Fall of the Neo-Babylonian Empire in 538 B.C.E.* Jerusalem: Schocken Institute for Jewish Research of the Jewish Theological Seminary of America.

Kelly, Brian E.

1996 *Retribution and Eschatology in Chronicles*. Journal for the Study of the Old Testament Supplement 211. Sheffield: Sheffield Academic.

Kitchen, K. A.

1973 *The Third Intermediate Period in Egypt*. Warminster: Aris & Phillips.

Klein, Ralph W.

1997 How Many in a Thousand? Pp. 150-177 in *Chronicler as Historian*. Editors, M. Patrick Graham, Kenneth G. Hoglund, and Steven L. McKenzie. Journal for the Study of the Old Testament Supplement 238. Sheffield: Sheffield Academic.

2006 *1 Chronicles: A Commentary*. Hermeneia. Minneapolis: Fortress Press.

Kleinig, John W.

1993 *The Lord's Song: The Basis, Function, and Significance of Choral Music in Chronicles*. Journal for the Study of the Old Testament Supplement 156. Sheffield: Journal for the Study of the Old Testament Press.

1994 Recent Research in Chronicles. *Currents in Research: Biblical Studies* 2:43-76.

Kline, Meredith G.

1963 *Treaty of the Great King: The Covenant Structure of Deuteronomy: Studies and Commentary*. Grand Rapids: Eerdmans.

Knoppers, Gary N.

1990 Rehoboam in Chronicles: Villain or Victim? *Journal of Biblical Literature* 109:423-440.

1991 Reform and Regression: The Chronicler's Presentation of Jehoshaphat. *Biblica* 72:500-524.

1995 Images of David in Early Judaism. *Biblica* 76:449-470.

1997 History and Historiography: The Royal Reforms. Pp. 178-203 in *Chronicler as Historian*. Editors, M. Patrick Graham, Kenneth G. Hoglund, and Steven L. McKenzie. Journal for the Study of the Old Testament Supplement 238. Sheffield: Sheffield Academic.

2001 The Davidic Genealogy: Some Contextual Considerations from the Ancient Mediterranean World. *Transeuphrates* 22:35-50.

2003 Shem, Ham and Japheth: The Universal and the Particular in the Genealogy of Nations. Pp. 13-31 in *Chronicler as Theologian*. Editors, Gary Knoppers, M. P. Graham, and S. L. McKenzie. Journal for the Study of the Old Testament Supplement 371. London: T&T Clark.

2004 *I Chronicles: A New Translation with Introduction and Commentary*. Anchor Bible 12. New York: Doubleday.

Knoppers, Gary N., and Paul B. Harvey

2002 Omitted and Remaining Matters: On the Names Given to the Book of Chronicles in Antiquity. *Journal of Biblical Literature* 121:227-243.

Kraft, Charles H.

1979 *Christianity in Culture: A Study in Dynamic Biblical Theologizing in Cross-cultural Perspective*. Maryknoll, NY: Orbis Books.

Kraus, F. R.

1980 Der Brief des Gilgameš. *Anatolian Studies* 30:109-121.

Leuchter, Mark

2004 Jeremiah's 70-year Prophecy and the ששך/לב קמי *Atbash* Codes. *Biblica* 85:503-522.

Levine, Baruch A.

1989 *Leviticus*. JPS Torah Commentary. Philadelphia: Jewish Publication Society.

Levy, T. E., R. B. Adams, M. Najjar, A. Hauptmann, J. D. Anderson, B. Brandl, et al.

2004 Reassessing the Chronology of Biblical Edom: New Excavations and ^{14}C Dates from Khirbat en Nahas (Jordan). *Antiquity* 78:863-876.

Lipschits, Oded

2005 *The Fall and Rise of Jerusalem: Judah under Babylonian Rule*. Winona Lake, IN: Eisenbrauns.

Long, Burke O.

1984 *1 Kings: With an Introduction to Historical Literature*. The Forms of the Old Testament Literature 9. Grand Rapids: Eerdmans.

1987 Framing Repetitions in Biblical Historiography. *Journal of Biblical Literature* 106:390-392.

Longman, Tremper, III, and Raymond B. Dillard

2006 *An Introduction to the Old Testament*. 2nd ed. Grand Rapids: Zondervan.

Longman, Tremper, III, and Daniel G. Reid

1995 *God Is a Warrior*. Studies in Old Testament Biblical Theology. Grand Rapids: Zondervan.

Lowery, R. H.

1991 *The Reforming Kings: Cult and Society in First Temple Judah*. Journal for the Study of the Old Testament Supplement 120. Sheffield: Journal for the Study of the Old Testament Press.

Luz, Ulrich

1989 *Matthew: A Commentary.* Hermeneia. Minneapolis: Augsburg.

Macy, Howard R.

1975 The Sources of the Books of Chronicles: A Reassessment. Ph.D. diss., Harvard University.

Mason, Rex A.

1990 *Preaching the Tradition: Homily and Hermeneutics after the Exile.* Cambridge: Cambridge University Press.

Mathias, Dietmar

1984 "Levitische Predigt" und Deuteronomismus. *Zeitschrift für die alttestamentliche Wissenschaft* 96:23-49.

Mazar, Amihai

2006 Jerusalem in the 10th Century B.C.E.: The Glass Half Full. Pp. 255-272 in *Essays on Ancient Israel in Its Near Eastern Context: A Tribute to Nadav Na'aman.* Editors, Yaira Amit, Ehud Ben Zvi, Israel Finkelstein, and Oded Lipschits. Winona Lake, IN: Eisenbrauns.

McCann, J. Clinton

1993 *The Shape and Shaping of the Psalter.* Journal for the Study of the Old Testament Supplement 159. Sheffield: Journal of the Study of the Old Testament Press.

McCarter, P. Kyle

1984 *II Samuel: A New Translation with Introduction, Notes and Commentary.* Anchor Bible 9. Garden City, NY: Doubleday.

McCarthy, Dennis J.

1978 *Treaty and Covenant: A Study in Form in the Ancient Oriental Documents and in the Old Testament.* 2nd ed. Analecta Biblica 21a. Rome: Pontifical Biblical Institute.

1982a Covenant and Law in Chronicles—Nehemiah. *Catholic Biblical Quarterly* 44:25-44.

1982b Covenant in Narratives from Late OT Times. Pp. 77-94 in *The Quest for the Kingdom of God, Studies in Honor of George E. Mendenhall.* Editors, Herbert B. Huffmon, Frank A. Spina, and Alberto R. W. Green. Winona Lake, IN: Eisenbrauns.

McConville, J. G.

1984a *I & II Chronicles.* Daily Study Bible Series. Philadelphia: Westminster.

1984b *Law and Theology in Deuteronomy.* Journal for the Study of the Old Testament Supplement. Sheffield: Journal for the Study of the Old Testament Press.

McGinn, Andrew

2005 The Divine Council and Israelite Monotheism. Th.M. diss., McMaster Divinity College, McMaster University.

McKay, John W.

1973 *Religion in Judah under the Assyrians, 732–609 BC.* Studies in Biblical Theology New Series 26. Naperville, IL: A. R. Allenson.

McKenzie, Steven L.

1985 *The Chronicler's Use of the Deuteronomistic History.* Harvard Semitic Monographs 33. Atlanta: Scholars Press.

Mettinger, T. N. D.

1976 *King and Messiah: The Civil and the Sacral Legitimation of the Israelite Kings.* Coniectanea Biblica Old Testament Series 8. Lund: Gleerup.

Meyers, E. M.

1985 The Shelomith Seal and Aspects of the Judean Restoration: Some Additional Reconsiderations. *Eretz Israel* 18:33*-38*.

Milgrom, Jacob

1976 *Cult and Conscience: The Asham and the Priestly Doctrine of Repentance.* Studies in Judaism in Late Antiquity 18. Leiden: E. J. Brill.

Mitchell, Christine

2001 The Ideal Ruler as Intertext in 1–2 Chronicles and the Cyropaedia. Ph.D. diss., Carleton University.

2006 The Ironic Death of Josiah in 2 Chronicles. *Catholic Biblical Quarterly* 68:421-435.

Moran, W. L.

1963 The Ancient Near Eastern Background of the Love of God in Deuteronomy. *Catholic Biblical Quarterly* 25:77-87.

Mosis, Rudolf

1973 *Untersuchungen zur Theologie des Chronistischen Geschichtswerkes.* Freiburger Theologische Studien 92. Freiburg: Herder.

Myers, Jacob M.

1965 *I Chronicles.* Anchor Bible 12. Garden City, NY: Doubleday.

Negev, Avraham

1990 *The Archaeological Encyclopedia of the Holy Land.* 3rd ed. New York: Prentice Hall Press.

Nelson, Richard D.

1993 *Raising Up a Faithful Priest: Community and Priesthood in Biblical Theology.* Louisville: Westminster/ John Knox.

Newsome, James D.

1975 Toward a New Understanding of the Chronicler and His Purposes. *Journal of Biblical Literature* 94:201-217.

Noth, Martin

1981 *The Deuteronomistic History.* Journal for the Study of the Old Testament Supplement 15. Sheffield: Journal for the Study of the Old Testament Press.

Novotny, Jamie Robert

2003 Ehulhul, Egipar, Emelamana, and Sîn's Akitu-house: A Study of Assyrian Building Activities at Harran. Ph.D. diss., Near and Middle Eastern Civilizations, University of Toronto.

O'Connell, Robert H.

1996 *The Rhetoric of the Book of Judges.* Vetus Testamentum Supplement 63. Leiden: E. J. Brill.

Oded, B.

1997 The Inscriptions of Tiglath-Pileser III: Review Article. *Israel Exploration Journal* 47:104-110.

Oeming, M.

1990 *Das Wahre Israel. Die "Genealogische Vorhalle" 1 Chronik 1–9.* Beiträge zur Wissenschaft vom Alten und Neuen Testament 128. Stuttgart: Kohlhammer.

Ogden, G.

1982 Prophetic Oracles against Foreign Nations and Psalms of Communal Lament. *Journal for the Study of the Old Testament* 24:89-97.

1983 Joel 4 and Prophetic Responses to National Laments. *Journal for the Study of the Old Testament* 26:97-106.

Ollenburger, Ben C.

1987 *Zion, the City of the Great King: A Theological Symbol of the Jerusalem Cult.* Journal for the Study of the Old Testament Supplement 41. Sheffield: Journal for the Study of the Old Testament Press.

Oswalt, John

1973 The Golden Calves and the Egyptian Concept of Deity. *Evangelical Quarterly* 45:13-20.

Pardee, Dennis, and S. David Sperling

1982 *Handbook of Ancient Hebrew Letters.* Chico, CA: Scholars Press.

Payne, J. B.

1979 The Validity of Numbers in Chronicles. *Bibliotheca Sacra* 136:109-128, 206-220.

Peltonen, Kai

1996 *History Debated: The Historical Reliability of Chronicles in Pre-critical and Critical Research.* Helsinki / Göttingen: Finnish Exegetical Society / Vandenhoeck & Ruprecht.

Perdue, Leo G., editor

1997 *Families in Ancient Israel.* The Family, Religion, and Culture. Louisville: Westminster John Knox.

Petersen, David L.

1977 *Late Israelite Prophecy: Studies in Deutero-prophetic Literature and in Chronicles.* Society of Biblical Literature Monograph Series 23. Missoula, MT: Scholars Press.

Pitard, Wayne Thomas

1987 *Ancient Damascus: A Historical Study of the Syrian City-state from Earliest Times until Its Fall to the Assyrians in 732 B.C.E.* Winona Lake, IN: Eisenbrauns.

Pleins, J. David

2001 *The Social Visions of the Hebrew Bible: A Theological Introduction.* Louisville: Westminster/John Knox.

Plöger, Otto

1957 Reden und Gebete im deuteronomistischen und chronistischen Geschichtswerk. Pp. 35-49 in *Festschrift für Günther Dehn zum 75 Geburstag.* Editor, W. Schneemelcher. Neukirchen-Vluyn: Neukirchener.

Polzin, Robert

1976 *Late Biblical Hebrew: Toward an Historical Typology of Biblical Hebrew Prose.* Missoula, MT: Scholars Press.

Rad, Gerhard von

1966a The Levitical Sermon in the Books of Chronicles. Translator, E. W. Trueman Dicken. Pp. 267-280 in *The Problem of the Hexateuch and Other Essays.* London: Oliver & Boyd.

1966b *The Problem of the Hexateuch and Other Essays.* London: Oliver & Boyd.

1990 *Holy War in Ancient Israel.* Translator, Marva J. Dawn. Grand Rapids: Eerdmans.

Raney, Donald C.

2003 *History as Narrative in the Deuteronomistic History and Chronicles.* Studies in the Bible and Early Christianity 56. Lewiston, NY: Mellen Press.

Rendsburg, Gary A.

1987 Gen 10:13-14: An Authentic Hebrew Tradition Concerning the Origin of the Philistines. *Journal of Northwest Semitic Languages* 13:89-96.

Riley, William

1993 *King and Cultus in Chronicles: Worship and the Reinterpretation of History.* Journal for the Study of the Old Testament Supplement 160. Sheffield: Sheffield Academic.

Ristau, Ken

2004 Reading and Re-reading Josiah: A Critical Study of Josiah in Chronicles. M.A. thesis, University of Alberta.

Römer, Thomas, and Albert de Pury

2000 Deuteronomistic Historiography: History of Research and Debated Issues. Pp. 24-141 in *Israel Constructs Its History: Deuteronomist Historiography in Recent Research.* Editors, Albert de Pury, Thomas Römer, and Jean Macchi. Journal for the Study of the Old Testament Supplement 306. Sheffield: Sheffield Academic.

Rooke, D. W.

2000 *Zadok's Heirs: The Role and Development of the High Priesthood in Ancient Israel.* Oxford Theological Monographs. Oxford: Oxford University.

Rudolph, W.

1955 *Chronikbücher.* Handbuch zum Alten Testament 21. Tübingen: J. C. B. Mohr.

Sacchi, Paolo

2000 *The History of the Second Temple Period.* Translator, Thomas Kirk. Journal for the Study of the Old Testament Supplement 285. Sheffield: Sheffield Academic.

Sasson, J. M.

1978 Genealogical "Convention" in Biblical Chronography. *Zeitschrift für die alttestamentliche Wissenschaft* 90:171-185.

Schniedewind, William M.

1991 The Source Citations of Manasseh: King Manasseh in History and Homily. *Vetus Testamentum* 41:450-461.

1995 *The Word of God in Transition: From Prophet to Exegete in the Second Temple Period.* Journal for the Study of the Old Testament Supplement 197. Sheffield: Journal for the Study of the Old Testament Press.

1999 *Society and the Promise of David: The Reception History of 2 Samuel 7:1-17.* Oxford: Oxford University Press.

Selman, Martin J.

1994a *1 Chronicles: An Introduction and Commentary.* The Tyndale Old Testament Commentaries. Downers Grove, IL: InterVarsity.

1994b *2 Chronicles: A Commentary.* The Tyndale Old Testament Commentaries. Downers Grove, IL: InterVarsity.

Sherlock, Charles

1993 *The God Who Fights: The War Tradition in the Holy Scripture.* Rutherford Studies in Contemporary Theology 6. Lewiston: Mellen.

Siedlecki, Armin

1999 Foreigners, Warfare and Judahite Identity in Chronicles. Pp. 229-266 in *The Chronicler as Author: Studies in Text and Texture.* Editors, M. Patrick Graham and Steven L. McKenzie. Journal for the Study of the Old Testament Supplement 263. Sheffield: Sheffield Academic.

Sklar, Jay

2005 *Sin, Impurity, Sacrifice, Atonement: The Priestly Conceptions.* Hebrew Bible Monographs 2. Sheffield: Sheffield Phoenix Press.

Smelik, Klaas A. D.

1992 *Converting the Past: Studies in Ancient Israelite and Moabite Historiography.* Oudtestamentische Studiën 28. Leiden: E. J. Brill.

1998 The Representation of King Ahaz in 2 Kings 16 and 2 Chronicles 28. Pp. 143-185 in *Intertextuality in Ugarit and Israel: Papers Read at the Tenth Joint Meeting of the Society for Old Testament Study and het Oudtestamentisch Werkgezelschap in Nederland en Belgie held at Oxford, 1997.* Editor, Johannes Cornelis de Moor. Oudtestamentische Studiën 40. Leiden: E. J. Brill.

Smith, Mark S.

2002 *The Early History of God: Yahweh and the Other Deities in Ancient Israel.* 2nd ed. The Biblical Resource Series. Grand Rapids: Eerdmans.

Snyman, Gerrie F.

2003 A Possible World of Text Production for the Genealogy in 1 Chronicles 2.3–4.23. Pp. 32-60 in *Chronicler as Theologian.* Editors, Gary Knoppers, M. P. Graham, and S. L. McKenzie. Journal for the Study of the Old Testament Supplement 371. London: T&T Clark.

Sperling, S. David

1989 Rethinking Covenant in Late Biblical Books. *Biblica* 70:50-73.

Spinoza, Benedictus de, and Martin D. Yaffe

2004 *Theologico-political Treatise: Containing some dissertations by which it is shown not only that the freedom of philosophizing can be granted in keeping with piety and the peace of the republic, but that it cannot be removed unless along with that very piety and the peace of the republic.* Focus Philosophical Library. Newburyport, MA: Focus Pub., R. Pullins & Co.

Talmon, S.

1978 The Presentation of Synchroneity and Simultaneity in Biblical Narrative. *Scripta Hierosolymitana* 27:9-26.

Talshir, David

1988 A Reinvestigation of the Linguistic Relationship between Chronicles and Ezra-Nehemiah. *Vetus Testamentum* 38:165-193.

Thompson, J. A.

1994 *1, 2 Chronicles.* The New American Commentary. Nashville: Broadman & Holman.

Throntveit, Mark A.

1982 Linguistic Analysis and the Question of Authorship in Chronicles, Ezra and Nehemiah. *Vetus Testamentum* 32:201-216.

1987 *When Kings Speak: Royal Speech and Royal Prayer in Chronicles.* Society of Biblical Literature Dissertation Series 93. Atlanta: Scholars Press.

Tournay, Raymond J.

1991 *Seeing and Hearing God with the Psalms: The Prophetic Liturgy of the Second Temple in Jerusalem.* Journal for the Study of the Old Testament Supplement 118. Sheffield: Journal for the Study of the Old Testament Press.

Tuell, Steven S.

2001 *First and Second Chronicles.* Interpretation. Louisville: John Knox Press.

Van Rooy, Harry V.

1994 Prophet and Society in the Persian Period according to Chronicles. Pp. 163-179 in *Second Temple Studies: 2. Temple and Community in the Persian Period.* Editors, T. C. Eskenazi and K. H. Richards. Journal for the Study of the Old Testament Supplement 175. Sheffield: Journal for the Study of the Old Testament Press.

VanderKam, James C.

1998 *Calendars in the Dead Sea Scrolls: Measuring Time.* The Literature of the Dead Sea Scrolls. London: Routledge.

Vaughn, Andrew G.
1999 *Theology, History, and Archaeology in the Chronicler's Account of Hezekiah.* Archaeology and Biblical Studies 4. Atlanta: Scholars Press.

Walters, Stanley D.
1991 Saul of Gibeon. *Journal for the Study of the Old Testament* 52:61-76.

Waltke, Bruce K.
1991 The Literary Genre of Genesis, Chapter One. *Crux* 27:2-10.

Waltke, Bruce K., and Cathi J. Fredricks
2001 *Genesis: A Commentary.* Grand Rapids: Zondervan.

Walton, John H.
2001 *Genesis: From Biblical Text to Contemporary Life.* The NIV Application Commentary. Grand Rapids: Zondervan.

Waters, M.M.
1996 Darius and the Achaemenid Line. *Ancient History Bulletin* 10:11-18.

Weinberg, Joel P.
1992 *The Citizen-temple Community.* Translator, Daniel L. Smith-Christopher. Journal for the Study of the Old Testament Supplement 151. Sheffield: Sheffield Academic.

Weinfeld, Moshe
1982 The Counsel of the "Elders" to Rehoboam and Its Implications. *Maarav* 3:27-53.

1995 *Social Justice in Ancient Israel and in the Ancient Near East.* Minneapolis / Jerusalem: Fortress / Magnes.

Wenham, Gordon J.
1987 *Genesis 1–15.* Word Biblical Commentary 1. Waco: Word Books.

Wenham, John
1993 The Large Numbers in the Bible. *Jewish Bible Quarterly* 21:116-120.

Werline, Rodney A.
1998 *Penitential Prayer in Second Temple Judaism: The Development of a Religious Institution.* Society of Biblical Literature Early Judaism and Its Literature 13. Atlanta: Scholars Press.

Westermann, Claus
1981 *Praise and Lament in the Psalms.* Atlanta: John Knox.

1984 *Genesis 1–11: A Commentary.* Continental Commentaries. Minneapolis: Augsburg.

Wilkinson, Bruce
2000 *The Prayer of Jabez: Breaking through to the Blessed Life.* Sisters, OR: Multnomah.

Williamson, H. G. M.
1976 The Accession of Solomon in the Book of Chronicles. *Vetus Testamentum* 26:351-361.

1977a Eschatology in Chronicles. *Tyndale Bulletin* 28:115-154.

1977b *Israel in the Books of Chronicles.* Cambridge: Cambridge University Press.

1979a The Origins of the Twenty-four Priestly Courses: A Study of 1 Chronicles 23–27. Pp. 251-268 in *Studies in the Historical Books of the Old Testament.* Editor, John A. Emerton. Vetus Testamentum Supplement 30. Leiden: E. J. Brill.

1979b Sources and Redaction in the Chronicler's Genealogy of Judah. *Journal of Biblical Literature* 98:351-359.

1982 *1 and 2 Chronicles.* New Century Bible. Grand Rapids: Eerdmans.

1983 The Dynastic Oracle in the Books of Chronicles. Pp. 305-318 in *Isaac Leo Seeligmann Volume: Essays on the Bible and Ancient World.* Editors, A. Rofé and Y. Zakovitch III. Jerusalem: Rubinstein.

1985 *Ezra, Nehemiah.* Word Biblical Commentary 16. Waco: Word Books.

1999 Exile and After. Historical Study. Pp. 236-265 in *The Face of Old Testament Studies. A Survey of Contemporary Approaches.* Editors, David W. Baker and Bill T. Arnold. Grand Rapids: Baker Books.

Wilson, Gerald Henry
1985 *The Editing of the Hebrew Psalter.* Chico, CA: Scholars Press.

Wilson, Robert R.
1975 The Old Testament Genealogies in Recent Research. *Journal of Biblical Literature* 1975:169-189.

1977 *Genealogy and History in the Biblical World.* Yale Near Eastern Researches 7. New Haven, CT: Yale University Press.

Wright, John W.

1990 Guarding the Gates: 1 Chronicles 26:1-19 and the Roles of Gatekeepers in Chronicles. *Journal for the Study of the Old Testament* 48:69-81.

1991 The Legacy of David in Chronicles: The Narrative Function of 1 Chronicles 23-27. *Journal of Biblical Literature* 110:229-242.

1993 The Innocence of David in 1 Chronicles 21. *Journal for the Study of the Old Testament* 60:87-105.

1999 The Fabula of the Book of Chronicles. Pp. 136-155 in *The Chronicler as Author: Studies in Text and Texture*. Editors, M. Patrick Graham and Steven L. McKenzie. Journal for the Study of the Old Testament Supplement 263. Sheffield: Sheffield Academic.

Zalewski, S.

1989 The Purpose of the Story of the Death of Saul in 1 Chronicles X. *Vetus Testamentum* 39:449-467.